MATH, SCIENCE, AND
UNIX UNDERPANTS

Other *FoxTrot* Books by Bill Amend

FoxTrot • Pass the Loot • Black Bart Says Draw • Eight Yards, Down and Out
Bury My Heart at Fun-Fun Mountain • Say Hello to Cactus Flats • May the Force Be with Us, Please
Take Us to Your Mall • The Return of the Lone Iguana • At Least This Place Sells T-Shirts
Come Closer, Roger, There's a Mosquito on Your Nose • Welcome to Jasorassic Park
I'm Flying, Jack . . . I Mean, Roger • Think iFruity • Death by Field Trip
Encyclopedias Brown and White • His Code Name Was The Fox
Your Momma Thinks Square Roots Are Vegetables • Who's Up for Some Bonding?
Am I a Mutant or What! • Orlando Bloom Has Ruined Everything
My Hot Dog Went Out, Can I Have Another? • How Come I'm Always Luigi?
Houston, You Have a Problem • And When She Opened the Closet, All the Clothes Were Polyester

Anthologies

FoxTrot: The Works • FoxTrot *en masse* • Enormously FoxTrot • Wildly FoxTrot
FoxTrot Beyond a Doubt • Camp FoxTrot • Assorted FoxTrot • FoxTrot: Assembled with Care
FoxTrotius Maximus • Jam-Packed FoxTrot • Wrapped-Up FoxTrot

MATH, SCIENCE, AND UNIX UNDERPANTS

A Themed *FoxTrot* Collection by Bill Amend

Andrews McMeel
Publishing, LLC
Kansas City • Sydney • London

FoxTrot is distributed internationally by Universal Press Syndicate.

 For information, write Andrews McMeel Publishing, LLC, an Andrews McMeel Universal company, 1130 Walnut Street, Kansas City, Missouri 64106.

09 10 11 12 13 BBG 10 9 8 7 6 5 4 3 2 1

ISBN-13: 978-0-7407-9140-6
ISBN-10: 0-7407-9140-0

Library of Congress Control Number: 2009934089

www.andrewsmcmeel.com
www.foxtrot.com

INTRODUCTION

I realize that not everyone enjoys seeing math and science and computer terminology in their comics. I realize that a lot of people would prefer jokes about normal things such as golf and shopping to jokes about calculus and Ohm's law. Which is why I've put together this book.

If you don't care much for math and science, this book is my gift to you. Think of this as a handy guide to all of the *FoxTrot* strips to skip when reading my regular, chronological collections. Sure, it might take some extra effort to cross-check whether the particular strip you're about to read is included in this book, but at least for the first time you now have that option.

Picking out which strips to include in this book proved to be more difficult than I expected. When I made a list of all the *FoxTrot* strips most likely to irritate math/science/computerphobes, it turned out that after the twenty-plus years of my strip, I had way more than this book could fit. Unfortunately, this meant I had to make tough choices to pare things down to just those strips that nonmathy, nonsciency readers should avoid at all costs. Strips that were only superficially about these topics have been left out, as were some computer strips that are so dated that they no longer make sense.

So, to my math-fearing, science-loathing, computer-squeamish readers, I say enjoy.

To the rest of you, the people who *do* like math and science in your comics, I beg your patience until I can put together a book with all of the nonmathy, nonsciency strips that *you* should avoid. In the meantime, I guess you can read this book.

Bill Amend
August 2009

NOTE TO TEACHERS: My syndicate and I are generally pretty thrilled and flattered when you reproduce *FoxTrot* strips for classroom use. We just ask that you follow the guidelines at http://www.amuniversal.com/ups/permissions/reprints_edu.html.

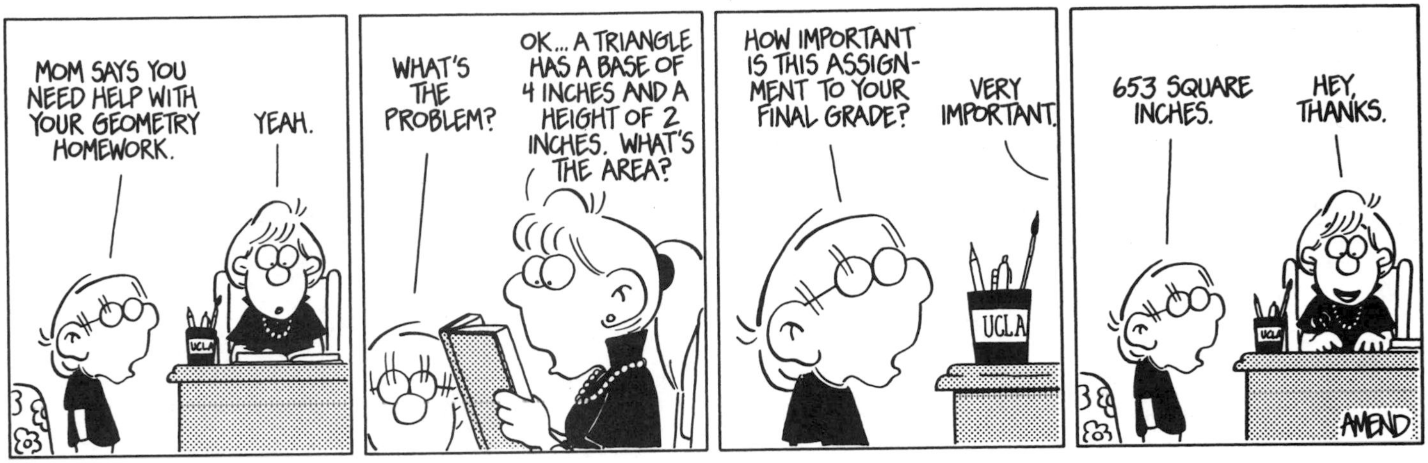
MOM SAYS YOU NEED HELP WITH YOUR GEOMETRY HOMEWORK.
YEAH.
WHAT'S THE PROBLEM?
OK... A TRIANGLE HAS A BASE OF 4 INCHES AND A HEIGHT OF 2 INCHES. WHAT'S THE AREA?
HOW IMPORTANT IS THIS ASSIGNMENT TO YOUR FINAL GRADE?
VERY IMPORTANT.
UCLA
653 SQUARE INCHES.
HEY, THANKS.
AMEND

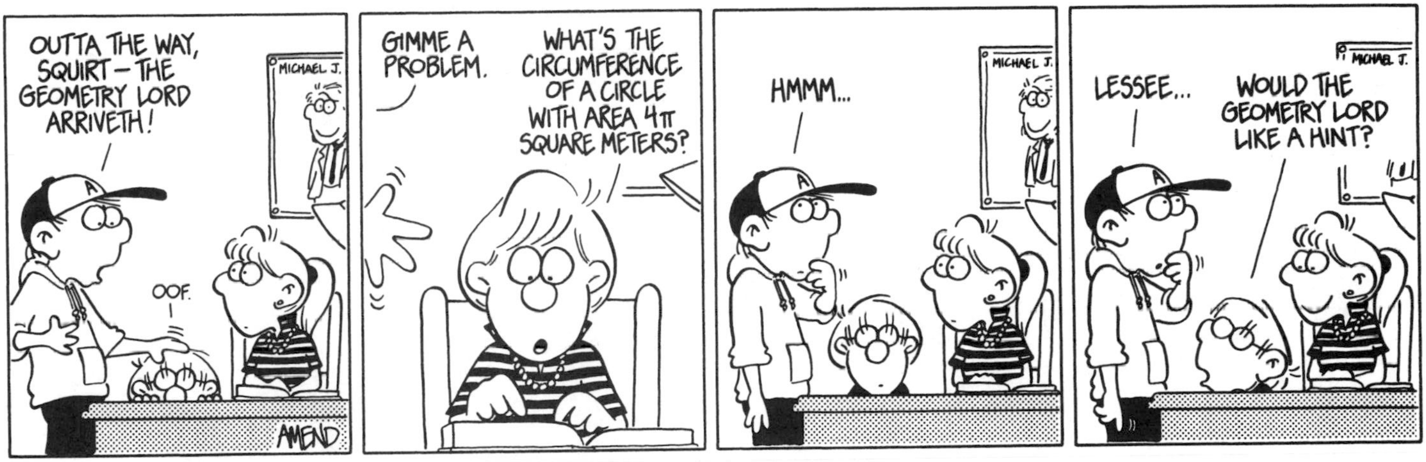
OUTTA THE WAY, SQUIRT – THE GEOMETRY LORD ARRIVETH!
MICHAEL J.
OOF.
AMEND
GIMME A PROBLEM.
WHAT'S THE CIRCUMFERENCE OF A CIRCLE WITH AREA 4π SQUARE METERS?
HMMM...
MICHAEL J.
LESSEE...
WOULD THE GEOMETRY LORD LIKE A HINT?
MICHAEL J.

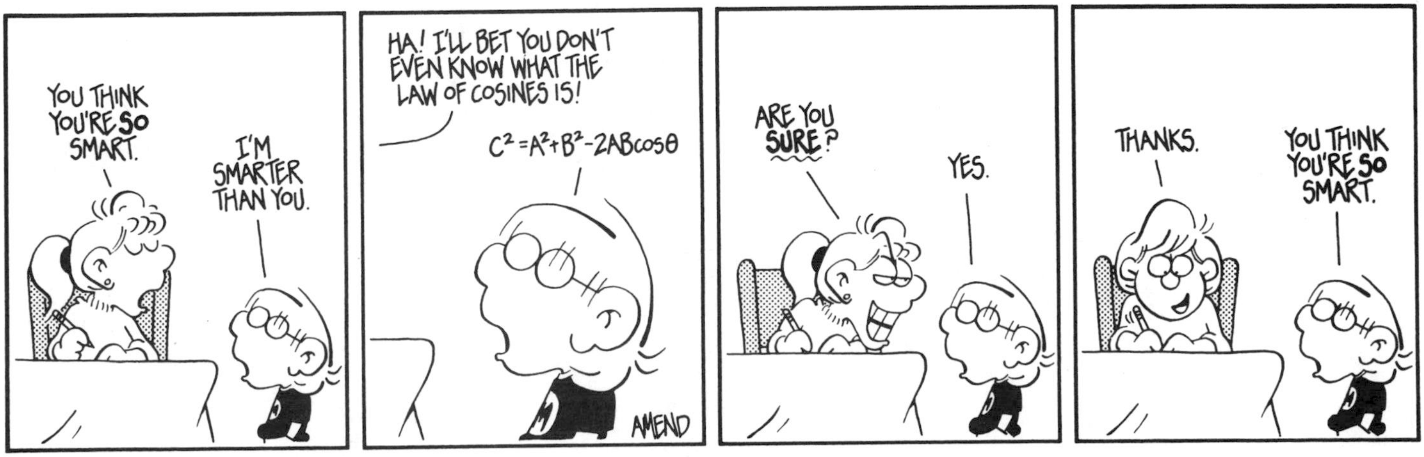
YOU THINK YOU'RE **SO** SMART.
I'M SMARTER THAN YOU.
HA! I'LL BET YOU DON'T EVEN KNOW WHAT THE LAW OF COSINES IS!
$C^2 = A^2 + B^2 - 2AB\cos\theta$
AMEND
ARE YOU **SURE**?
YES.
THANKS.
YOU THINK YOU'RE **SO** SMART.

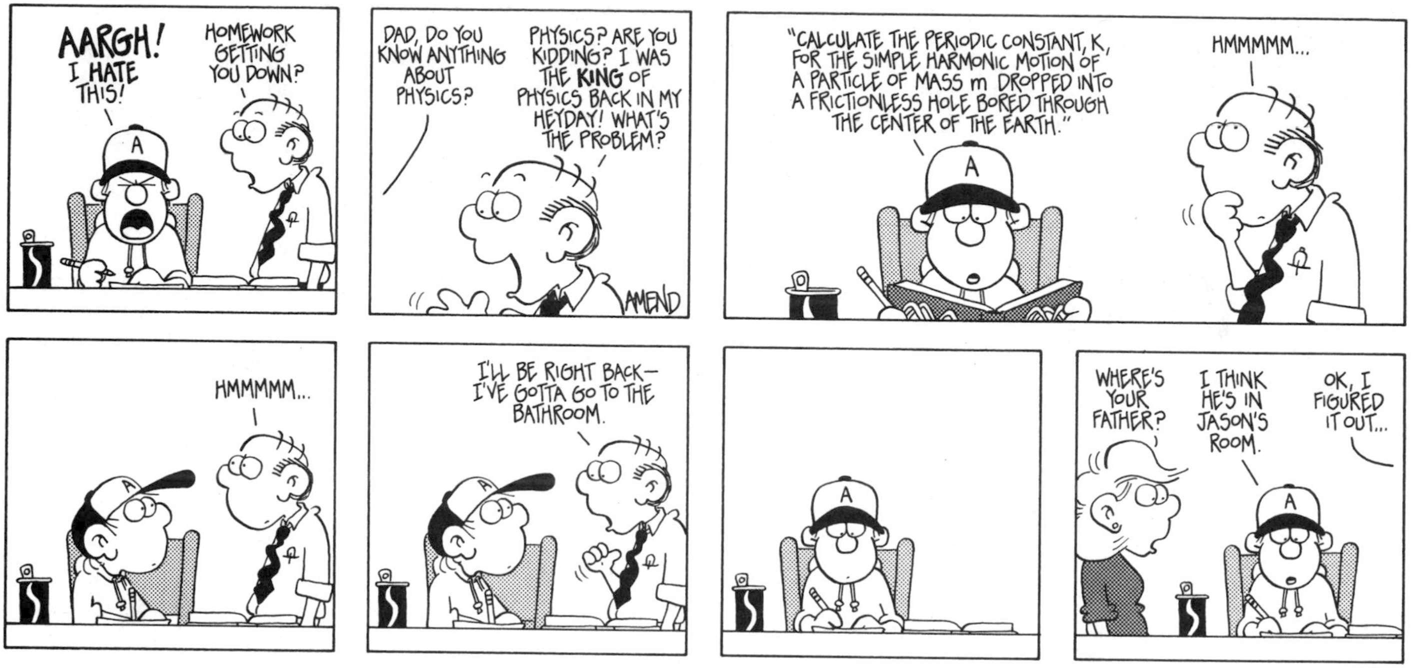
AARGH! I HATE THIS!
HOMEWORK GETTING YOU DOWN?
DAD, DO YOU KNOW ANYTHING ABOUT PHYSICS?
PHYSICS? ARE YOU KIDDING? I WAS THE KING OF PHYSICS BACK IN MY HEYDAY! WHAT'S THE PROBLEM?
AMEND
"CALCULATE THE PERIODIC CONSTANT, K, FOR THE SIMPLE HARMONIC MOTION OF A PARTICLE OF MASS m DROPPED INTO A FRICTIONLESS HOLE BORED THROUGH THE CENTER OF THE EARTH."
HMMMMM...
HMMMMM...
I'LL BE RIGHT BACK— I'VE GOTTA GO TO THE BATHROOM.
WHERE'S YOUR FATHER?
I THINK HE'S IN JASON'S ROOM.
OK, I FIGURED IT OUT...

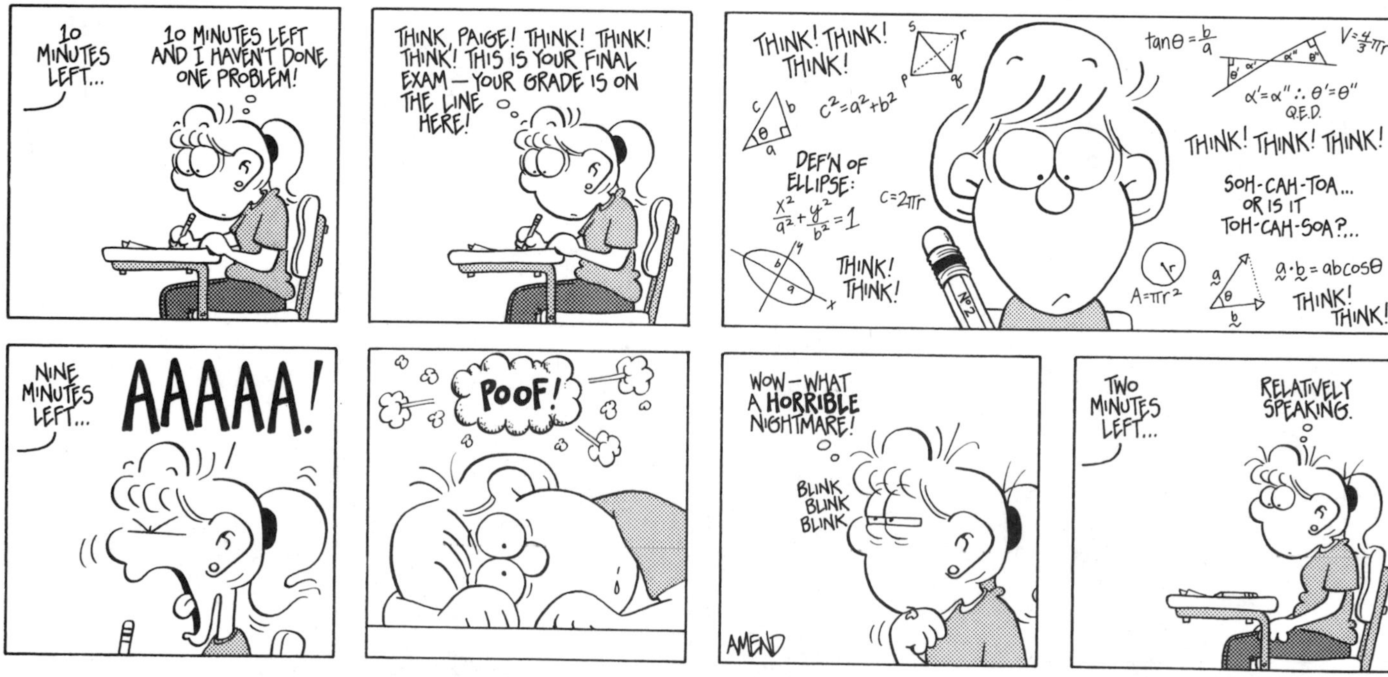
10 MINUTES LEFT...
10 MINUTES LEFT AND I HAVEN'T DONE ONE PROBLEM!
THINK, PAIGE! THINK! THINK! THINK! THIS IS YOUR FINAL EXAM — YOUR GRADE IS ON THE LINE HERE!
THINK! THINK! THINK!
$c^2=a^2+b^2$
$\tan\theta = \frac{b}{a}$
$V=\frac{4}{3}\pi r^3$
$\alpha'=\alpha'' \therefore \theta'=\theta''$
Q.E.D.
THINK! THINK! THINK!
DEF'N OF ELLIPSE: $\frac{x^2}{a^2}+\frac{y^2}{b^2}=1$
$c=2\pi r$
SOH-CAH-TOA... OR IS IT TOH-CAH-SOA?...
THINK! THINK!
$A=\pi r^2$
$a \cdot b = ab\cos\theta$
THINK! THINK!
NINE MINUTES LEFT...
AAAAA!
POOF!
WOW—WHAT A HORRIBLE NIGHTMARE!
BLINK BLINK BLINK
AMEND
TWO MINUTES LEFT...
RELATIVELY SPEAKING.

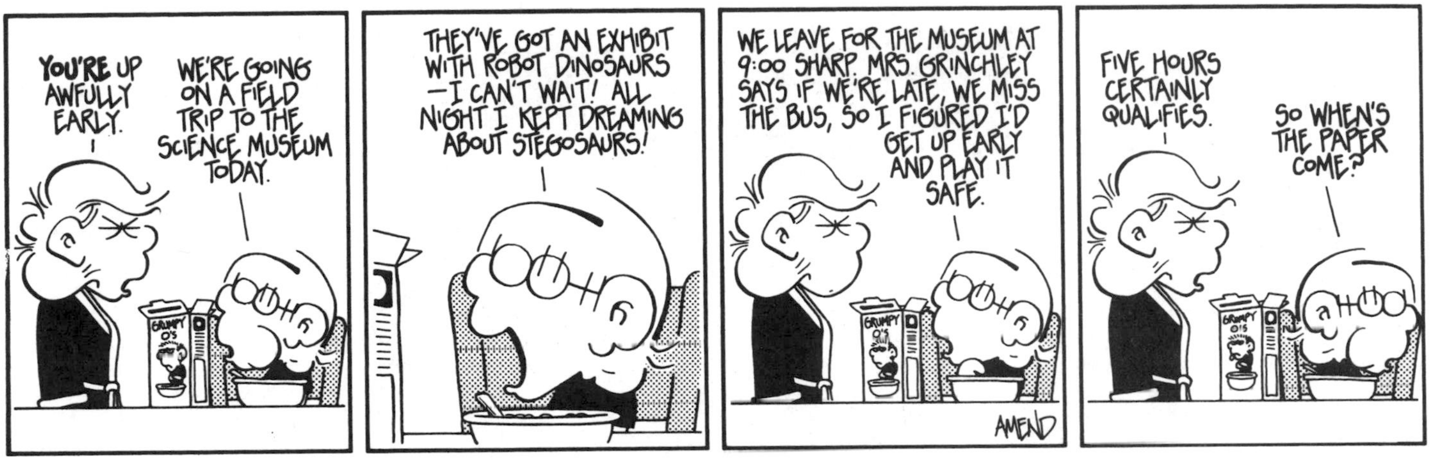
YOU'RE UP AWFULLY EARLY.
WE'RE GOING ON A FIELD TRIP TO THE SCIENCE MUSEUM TODAY.
THEY'VE GOT AN EXHIBIT WITH ROBOT DINOSAURS — I CAN'T WAIT! ALL NIGHT I KEPT DREAMING ABOUT STEGOSAURS!
WE LEAVE FOR THE MUSEUM AT 9:00 SHARP. MRS. GRINCHLEY SAYS IF WE'RE LATE, WE MISS THE BUS, SO I FIGURED I'D GET UP EARLY AND PLAY IT SAFE.
AMEND
FIVE HOURS CERTAINLY QUALIFIES.
SO WHEN'S THE PAPER COME?
GRUMPY O'S

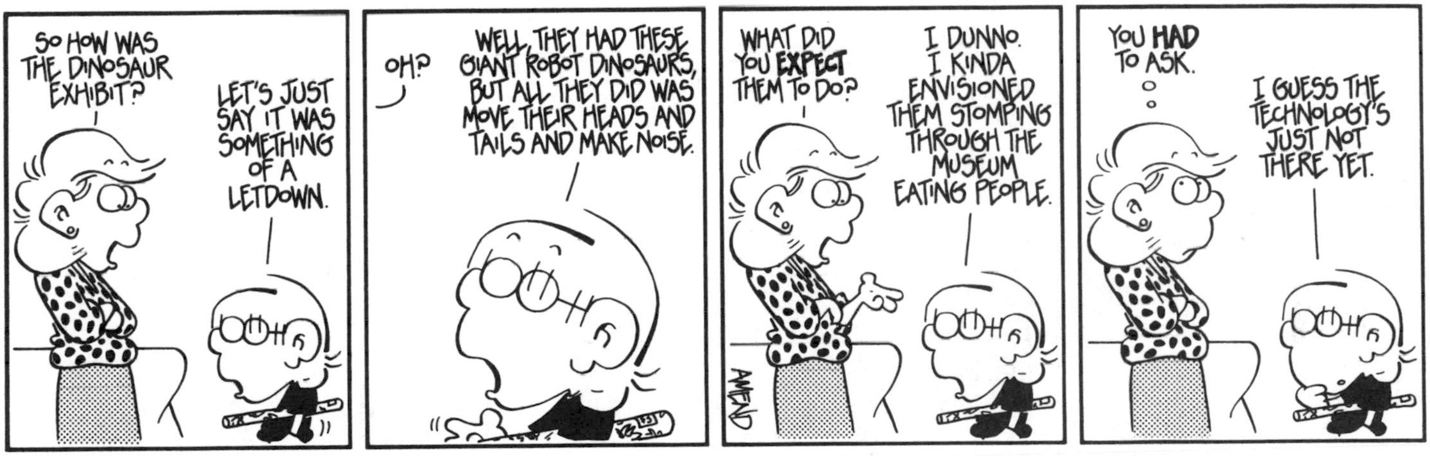
SO HOW WAS THE DINOSAUR EXHIBIT?
LET'S JUST SAY IT WAS SOMETHING OF A LETDOWN.
OH?
WELL, THEY HAD THESE GIANT ROBOT DINOSAURS, BUT ALL THEY DID WAS MOVE THEIR HEADS AND TAILS AND MAKE NOISE.
WHAT DID YOU EXPECT THEM TO DO?
I DUNNO. I KINDA ENVISIONED THEM STOMPING THROUGH THE MUSEUM EATING PEOPLE.
AMEND
YOU HAD TO ASK.
I GUESS THE TECHNOLOGY'S JUST NOT THERE YET.

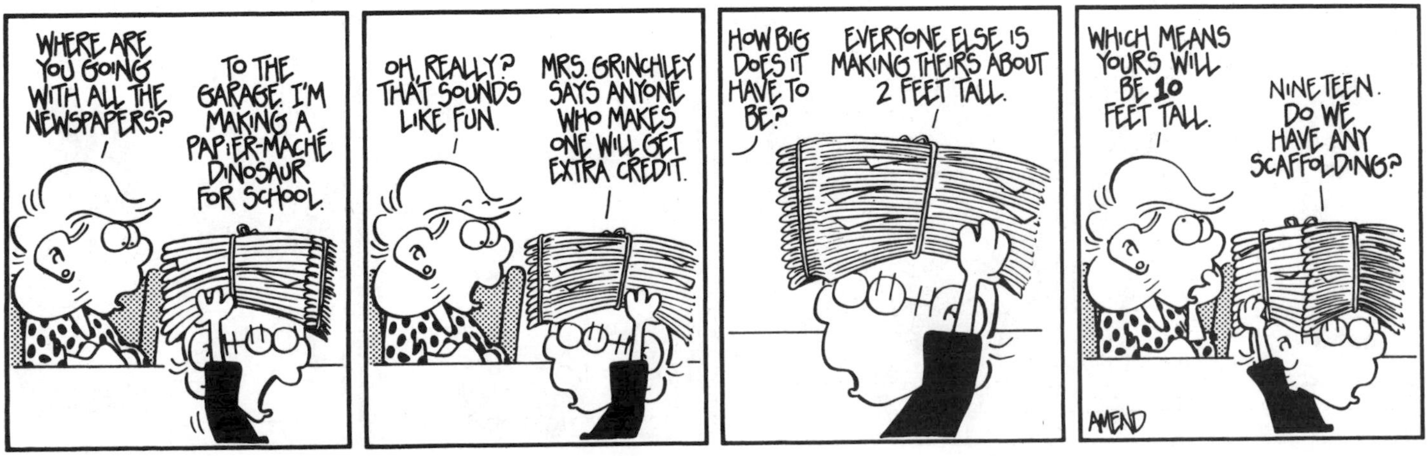
WHERE ARE YOU GOING WITH ALL THE NEWSPAPERS?
TO THE GARAGE. I'M MAKING A PAPIER-MACHE DINOSAUR FOR SCHOOL.
OH, REALLY? THAT SOUNDS LIKE FUN.
MRS. GRINCHLEY SAYS ANYONE WHO MAKES ONE WILL GET EXTRA CREDIT.
HOW BIG DOES IT HAVE TO BE?
EVERYONE ELSE IS MAKING THEIRS ABOUT 2 FEET TALL.
WHICH MEANS YOURS WILL BE 10 FEET TALL.
NINETEEN. DO WE HAVE ANY SCAFFOLDING?
AMEND

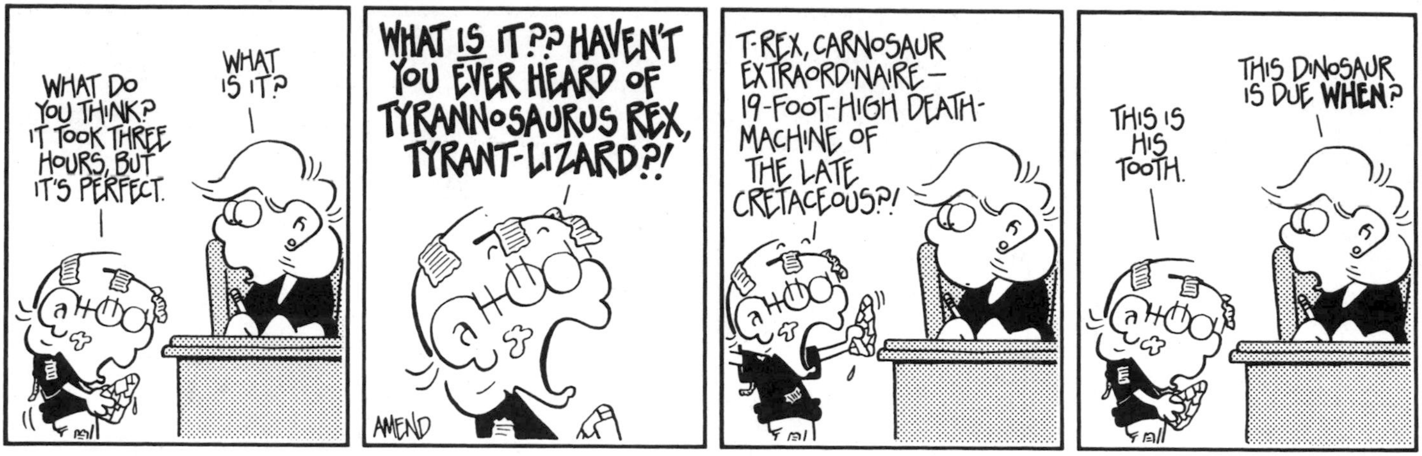
WHAT IS IT?
WHAT DO YOU THINK? IT TOOK THREE HOURS, BUT IT'S PERFECT.
WHAT IS IT?? HAVEN'T YOU EVER HEARD OF TYRANNOSAURUS REX, TYRANT-LIZARD?!
AMEND
T-REX, CARNOSAUR EXTRAORDINAIRE— 19-FOOT-HIGH DEATH-MACHINE OF THE LATE CRETACEOUS?!
THIS DINOSAUR IS DUE WHEN?
THIS IS HIS TOOTH.

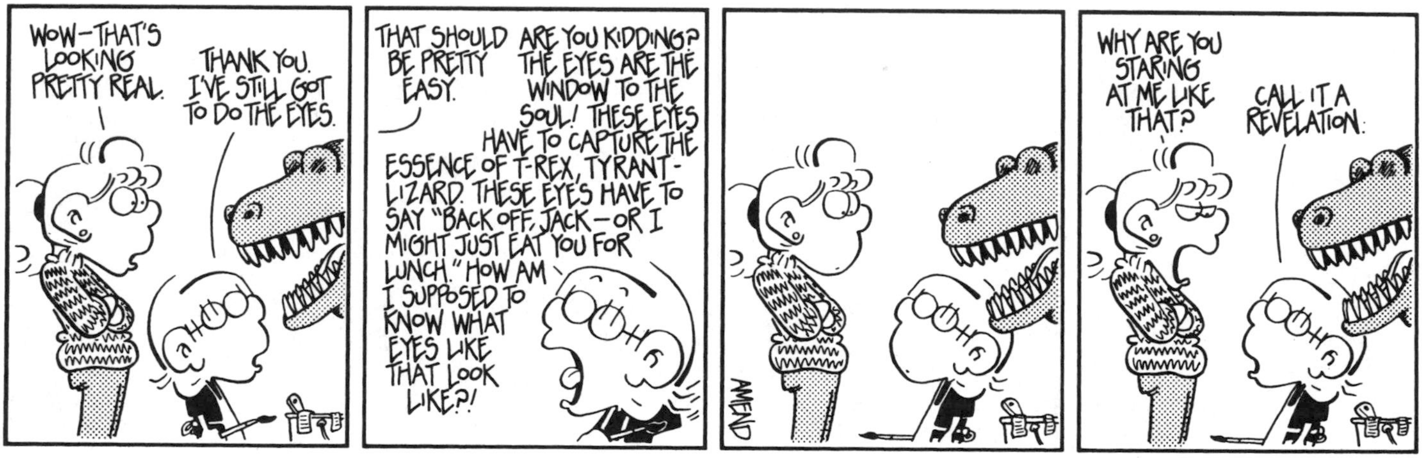
WOW—THAT'S LOOKING PRETTY REAL.
THANK YOU. I'VE STILL GOT TO DO THE EYES.
THAT SHOULD BE PRETTY EASY.
ARE YOU KIDDING? THE EYES ARE THE WINDOW TO THE SOUL! THESE EYES HAVE TO CAPTURE THE ESSENCE OF T-REX, TYRANT-LIZARD. THESE EYES HAVE TO SAY "BACK OFF, JACK—OR I MIGHT JUST EAT YOU FOR LUNCH." HOW AM I SUPPOSED TO KNOW WHAT EYES LIKE THAT LOOK LIKE?!
AMEND
WHY ARE YOU STARING AT ME LIKE THAT?
CALL IT A REVELATION.

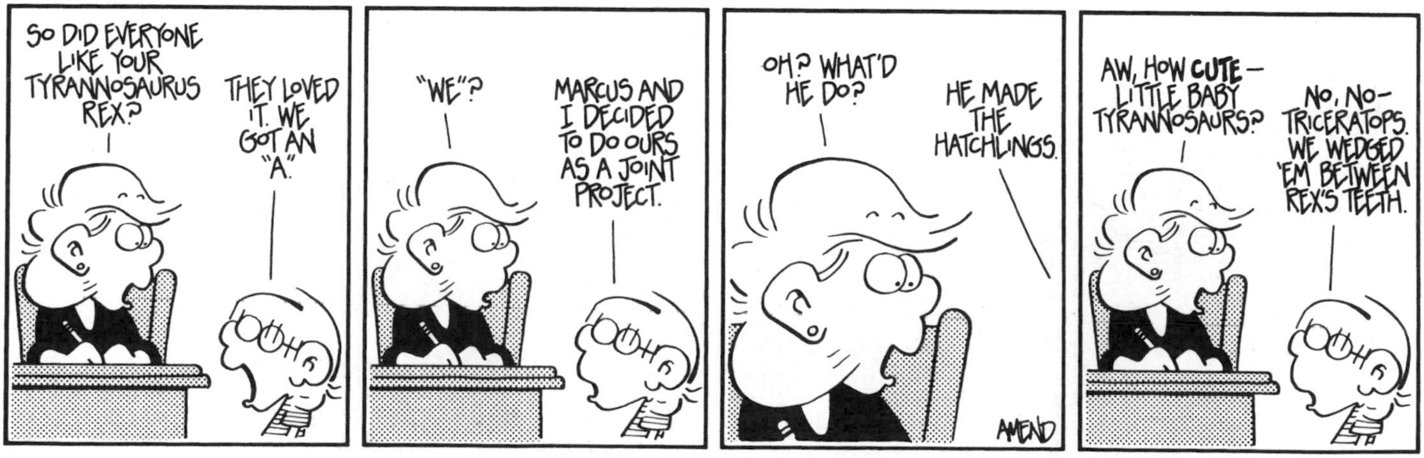
SO DID EVERYONE LIKE YOUR TYRANNOSAURUS REX?
THEY LOVED IT. WE GOT AN "A."
"WE"?
MARCUS AND I DECIDED TO DO OURS AS A JOINT PROJECT.
OH? WHAT'D HE DO?
HE MADE THE HATCHLINGS.
AMEND
AW, HOW CUTE—LITTLE BABY TYRANNOSAURS?
NO, NO—TRICERATOPS. WE WEDGED 'EM BETWEEN REX'S TEETH.

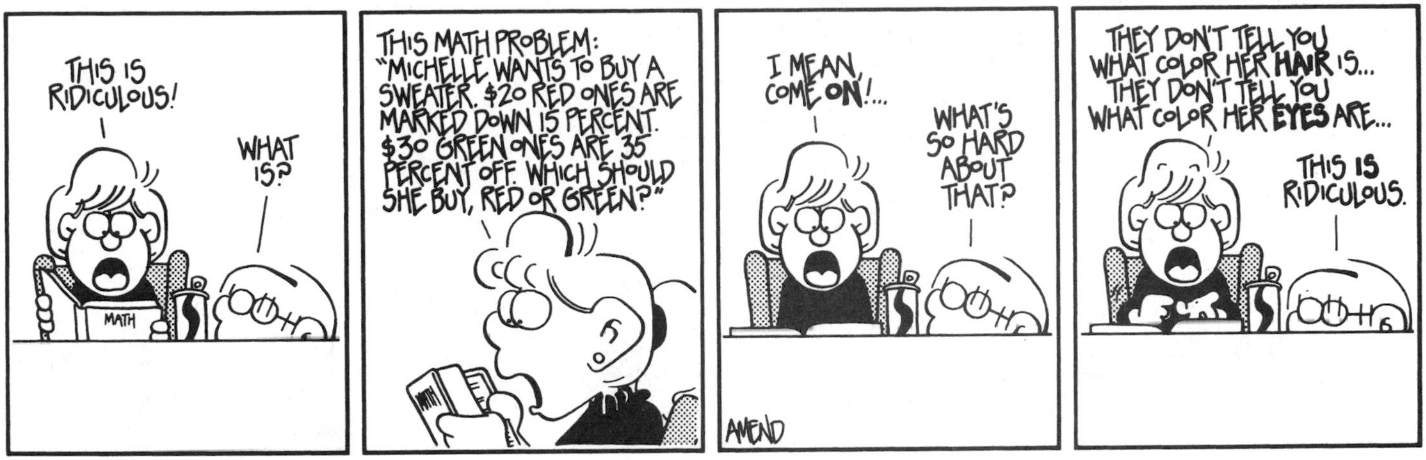
THIS IS RIDICULOUS!
WHAT IS?
MATH
THIS MATH PROBLEM: "MICHELLE WANTS TO BUY A SWEATER. $20 RED ONES ARE MARKED DOWN 15 PERCENT. $30 GREEN ONES ARE 35 PERCENT OFF. WHICH SHOULD SHE BUY, RED OR GREEN?"
MATH
I MEAN, COME ON!...
WHAT'S SO HARD ABOUT THAT?
AMEND
THEY DON'T TELL YOU WHAT COLOR HER HAIR IS... THEY DON'T TELL YOU WHAT COLOR HER EYES ARE...
THIS IS RIDICULOUS.

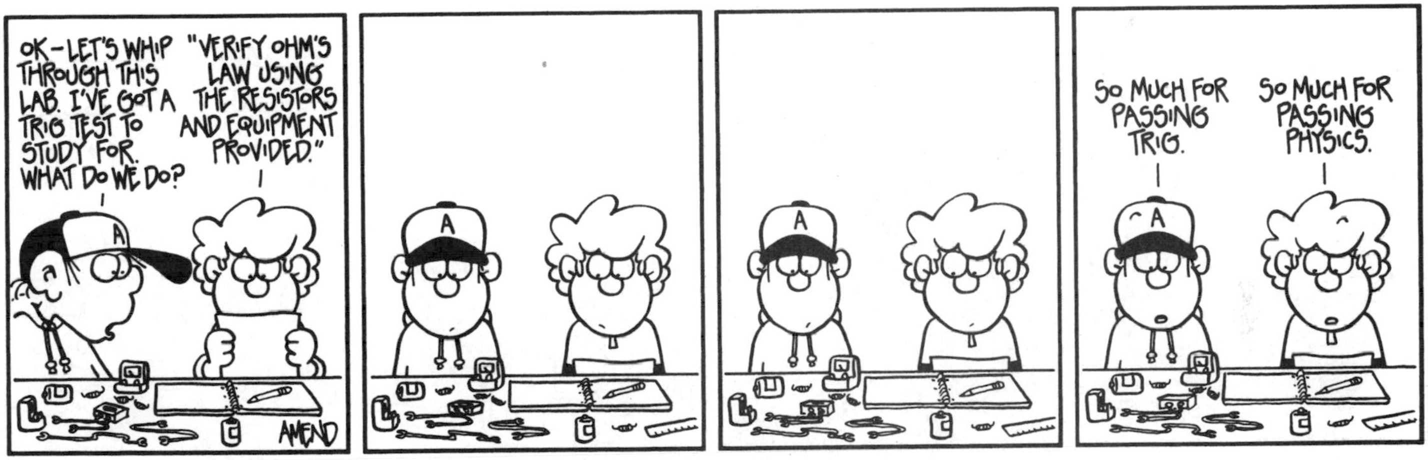
OK-LET'S WHIP THROUGH THIS LAB. I'VE GOT A TRIG TEST TO STUDY FOR. WHAT DO WE DO?
"VERIFY OHM'S LAW USING THE RESISTORS AND EQUIPMENT PROVIDED."
A
AMEND
SO MUCH FOR PASSING TRIG.
SO MUCH FOR PASSING PHYSICS.

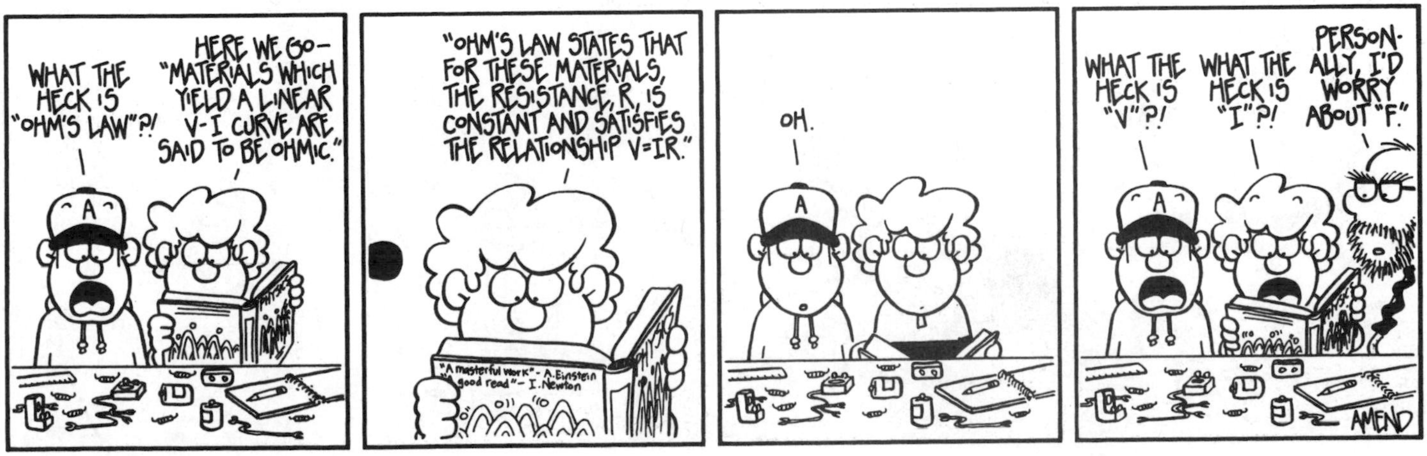
WHAT THE HECK IS "OHM'S LAW"?!
HERE WE GO- "MATERIALS WHICH YIELD A LINEAR V-I CURVE ARE SAID TO BE OHMIC."
"OHM'S LAW STATES THAT FOR THESE MATERIALS, THE RESISTANCE, R, IS CONSTANT AND SATISFIES THE RELATIONSHIP V=IR."
"A masterful work" - A.Einstein
"A good read" - I.Newton
OH.
WHAT THE HECK IS "V"?!
WHAT THE HECK IS "I"?!
PERSON-ALLY, I'D WORRY ABOUT "F."
AMEND

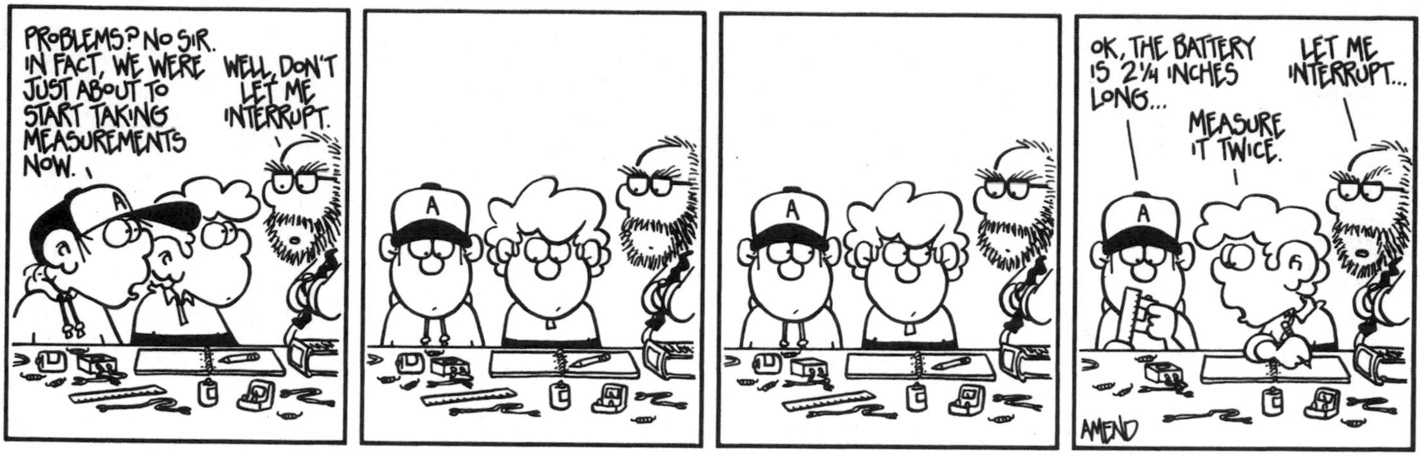
PROBLEMS? NO SIR. IN FACT, WE WERE JUST ABOUT TO START TAKING MEASUREMENTS NOW.
WELL, DON'T LET ME INTERRUPT.
OK, THE BATTERY IS 2¼ INCHES LONG...
MEASURE IT TWICE.
LET ME INTERRUPT...
AMEND

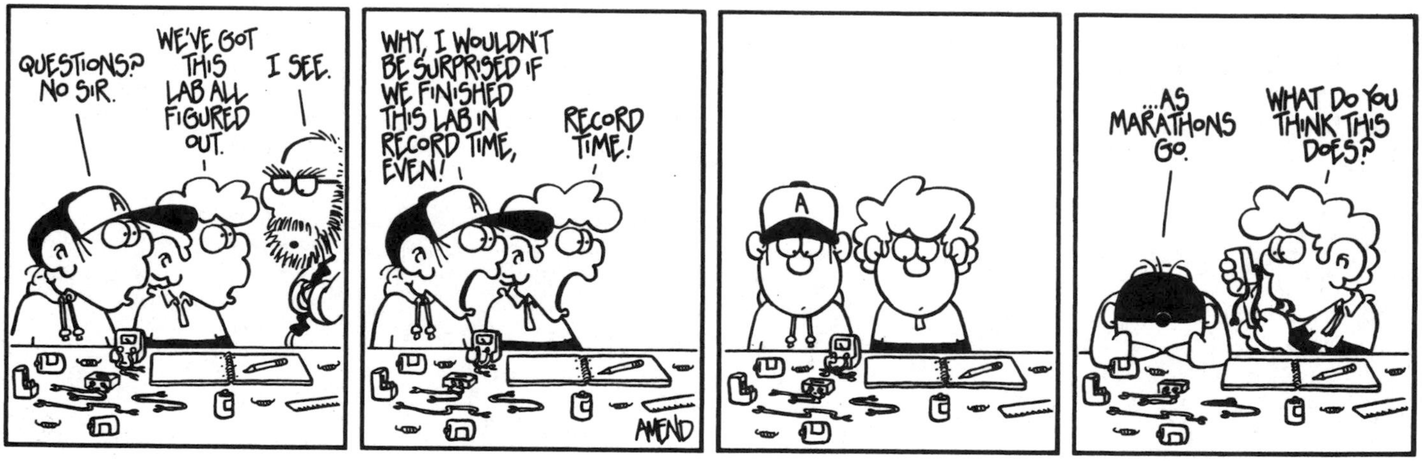
QUESTIONS? NO SIR.
WE'VE GOT THIS LAB ALL FIGURED OUT.
I SEE.
WHY, I WOULDN'T BE SURPRISED IF WE FINISHED THIS LAB IN RECORD TIME, EVEN!
RECORD TIME!
AMEND
...AS MARATHONS GO.
WHAT DO YOU THINK THIS DOES?

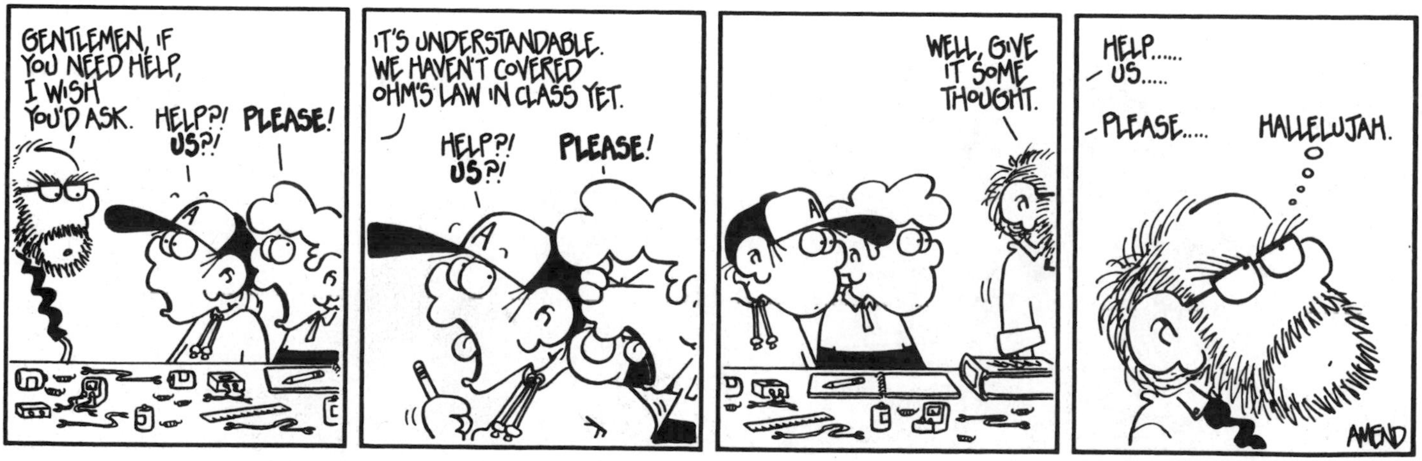
GENTLEMEN, IF YOU NEED HELP, I WISH YOU'D ASK.
HELP?! US?!
PLEASE!
IT'S UNDERSTANDABLE. WE HAVEN'T COVERED OHM'S LAW IN CLASS YET.
HELP?! US?!
PLEASE!
WELL, GIVE IT SOME THOUGHT.
HELP...... US.....
PLEASE.....
HALLELUJAH.
AMEND

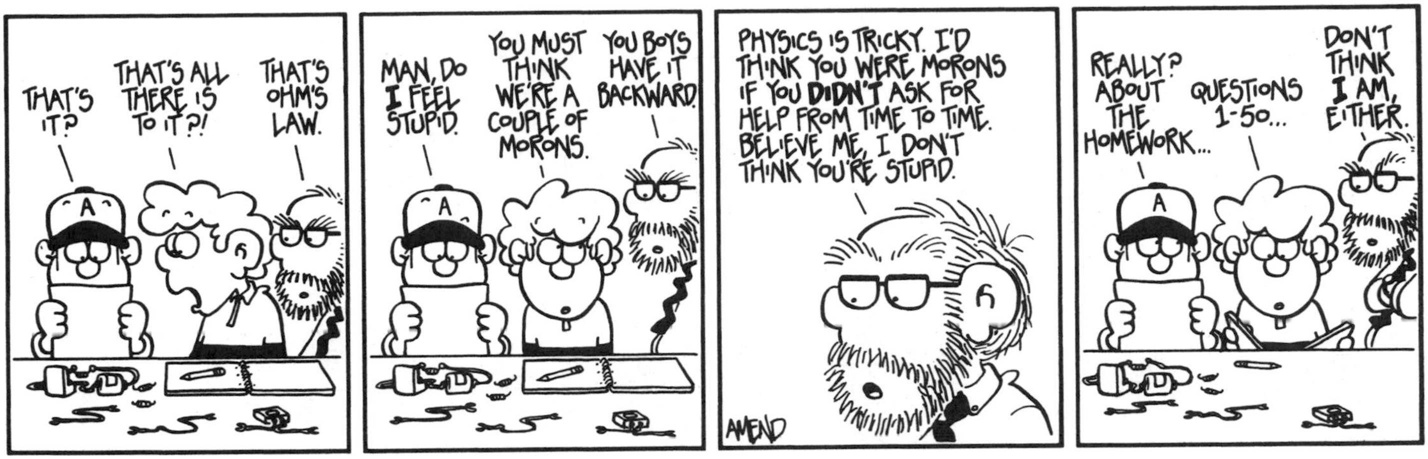
THAT'S IT?
THAT'S ALL THERE IS TO IT?!
THAT'S OHM'S LAW.
MAN, DO **I** FEEL STUPID.
YOU MUST THINK WE'RE A COUPLE OF MORONS.
YOU BOYS HAVE IT BACKWARD.
PHYSICS IS TRICKY. I'D THINK YOU WERE MORONS IF YOU **DIDN'T** ASK FOR HELP FROM TIME TO TIME. BELIEVE ME, I DON'T THINK YOU'RE STUPID.
AMEND
REALLY? ABOUT THE HOMEWORK...
QUESTIONS 1-50...
DON'T THINK **I** AM, EITHER.

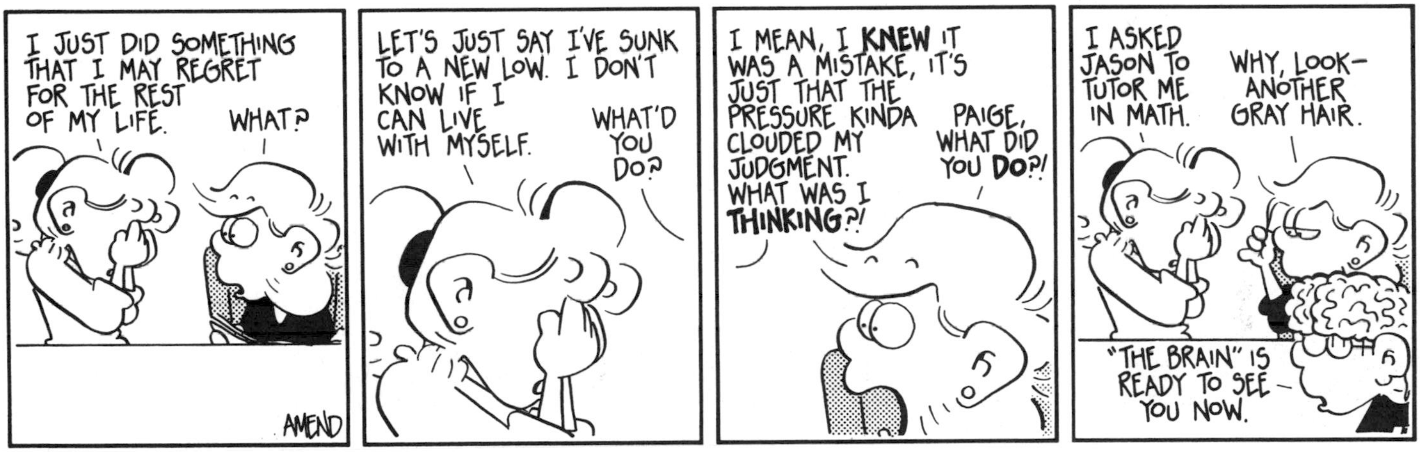
I JUST DID SOMETHING THAT I MAY REGRET FOR THE REST OF MY LIFE.
WHAT?
AMEND
LET'S JUST SAY I'VE SUNK TO A NEW LOW. I DON'T KNOW IF I CAN LIVE WITH MYSELF.
WHAT'D YOU DO?
I MEAN, I **KNEW** IT WAS A MISTAKE, IT'S JUST THAT THE PRESSURE KINDA CLOUDED MY JUDGMENT. WHAT WAS I **THINKING**?!
PAIGE, WHAT DID YOU **DO**?!
I ASKED JASON TO TUTOR ME IN MATH.
WHY, LOOK– ANOTHER GRAY HAIR.
"THE BRAIN" IS READY TO SEE YOU NOW.

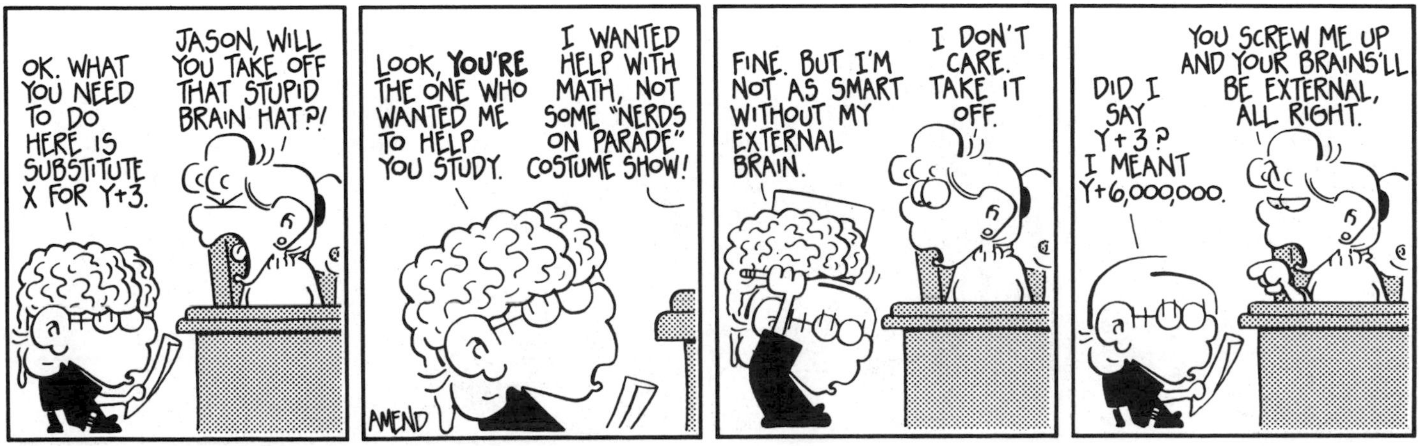
OK. WHAT YOU NEED TO DO HERE IS SUBSTITUTE X FOR Y+3.
JASON, WILL YOU TAKE OFF THAT STUPID BRAIN HAT?!
LOOK, **YOU'RE** THE ONE WHO WANTED ME TO HELP YOU STUDY.
I WANTED HELP WITH MATH, NOT SOME "NERDS ON PARADE" COSTUME SHOW!
AMEND
FINE. BUT I'M NOT AS SMART WITHOUT MY EXTERNAL BRAIN.
I DON'T CARE. TAKE IT OFF.
DID I SAY Y+3? I MEANT Y+6,000,000.
YOU SCREW ME UP AND YOUR BRAINS'LL BE EXTERNAL, ALL RIGHT.

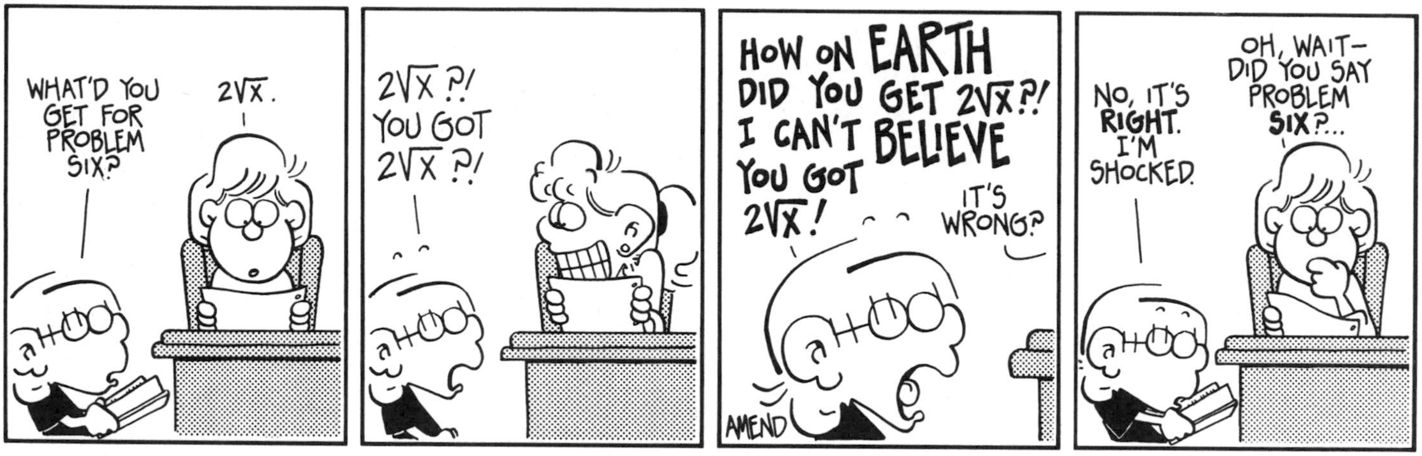
WHAT'D YOU GET FOR PROBLEM SIX?
$2\sqrt{X}$.
$2\sqrt{X}$?! YOU GOT $2\sqrt{X}$?!
HOW ON EARTH DID YOU GET $2\sqrt{X}$?! I CAN'T BELIEVE YOU GOT $2\sqrt{X}$!
IT'S WRONG?
AMEND
NO, IT'S RIGHT. I'M SHOCKED.
OH, WAIT– DID YOU SAY PROBLEM SIX?...

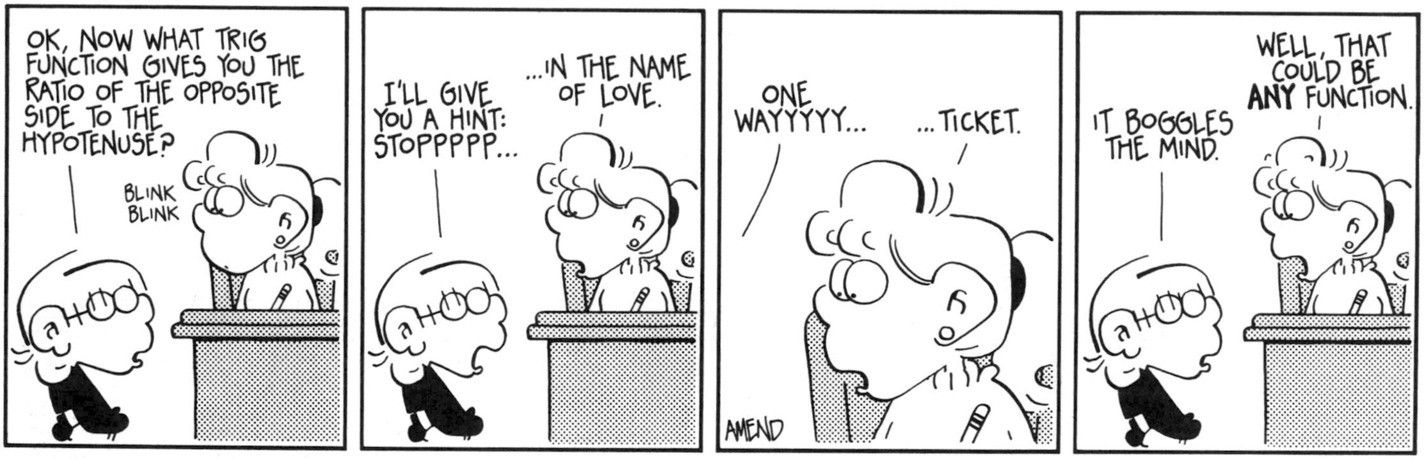
OK, NOW WHAT TRIG FUNCTION GIVES YOU THE RATIO OF THE OPPOSITE SIDE TO THE HYPOTENUSE?
BLINK BLINK
I'LL GIVE YOU A HINT: STOPPPPP...
...IN THE NAME OF LOVE.
ONE WAYYYYY...
...TICKET.
AMEND
IT BOGGLES THE MIND.
WELL, THAT COULD BE ANY FUNCTION.

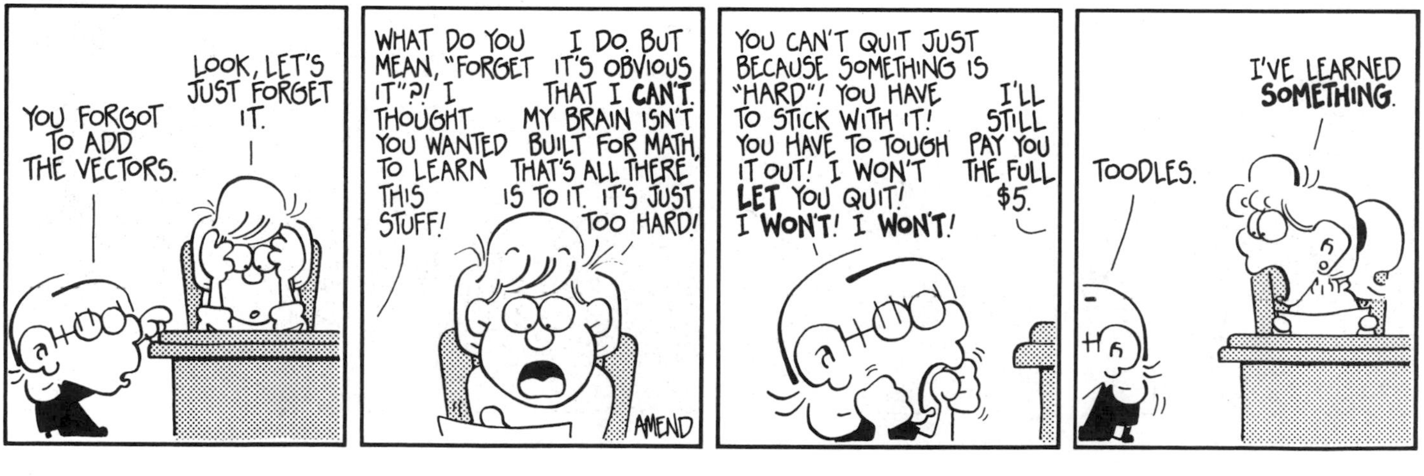
YOU FORGOT TO ADD THE VECTORS.
LOOK, LET'S JUST FORGET IT.
WHAT DO YOU MEAN, "FORGET IT"?! I THOUGHT YOU WANTED TO LEARN THIS STUFF!
I DO. BUT IT'S OBVIOUS THAT I CAN'T. MY BRAIN ISN'T BUILT FOR MATH. THAT'S ALL THERE IS TO IT. IT'S JUST TOO HARD!
AMEND
YOU CAN'T QUIT JUST BECAUSE SOMETHING IS "HARD"! YOU HAVE TO STICK WITH IT! YOU HAVE TO TOUGH IT OUT! I WON'T LET YOU QUIT! I WON'T! I WON'T!
I'LL STILL PAY YOU THE FULL $5.
TOODLES.
I'VE LEARNED SOMETHING.

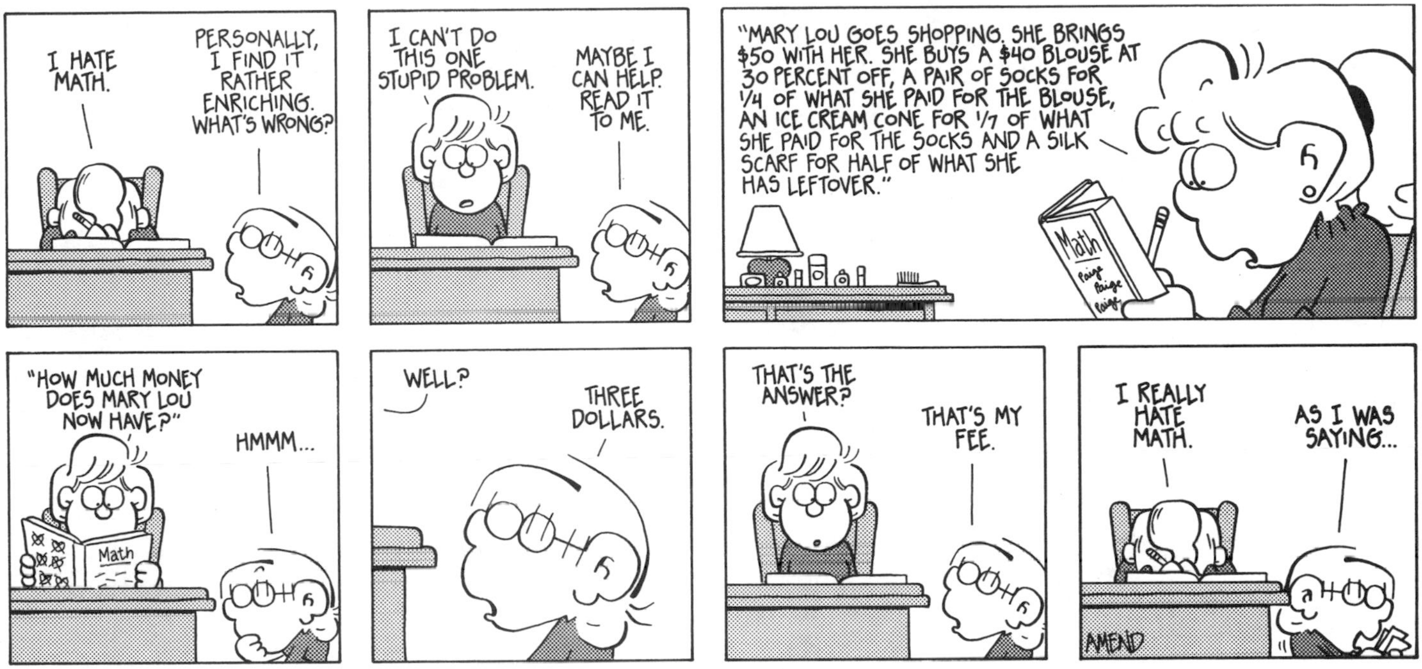
I HATE MATH.
PERSONALLY, I FIND IT RATHER ENRICHING. WHAT'S WRONG?
I CAN'T DO THIS ONE STUPID PROBLEM.
MAYBE I CAN HELP. READ IT TO ME.
"MARY LOU GOES SHOPPING. SHE BRINGS $50 WITH HER. SHE BUYS A $40 BLOUSE AT 30 PERCENT OFF, A PAIR OF SOCKS FOR 1/4 OF WHAT SHE PAID FOR THE BLOUSE, AN ICE CREAM CONE FOR 1/7 OF WHAT SHE PAID FOR THE SOCKS AND A SILK SCARF FOR HALF OF WHAT SHE HAS LEFTOVER."
Math
Paige
Paige
Paige
"HOW MUCH MONEY DOES MARY LOU NOW HAVE?"
HMMM...
Math
WELL?
THREE DOLLARS.
THAT'S THE ANSWER?
THAT'S MY FEE.
I REALLY HATE MATH.
AS I WAS SAYING...
AMEND

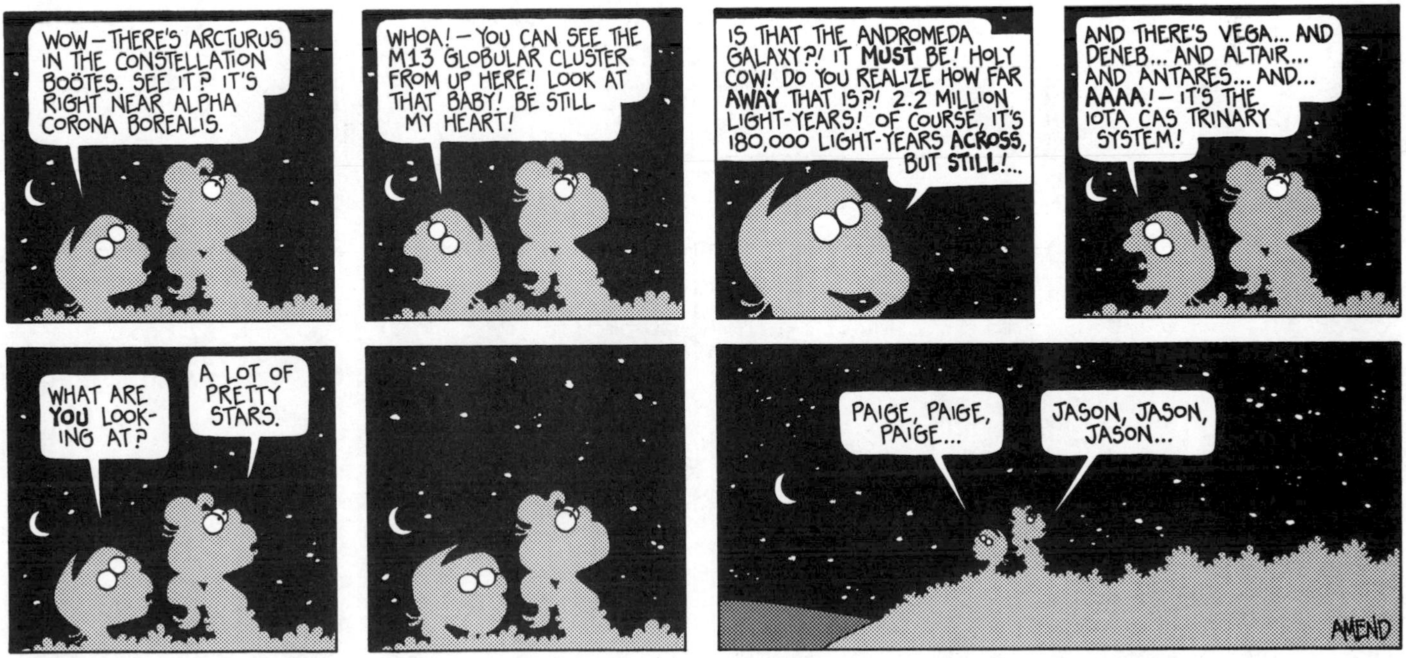
WOW—THERE'S ARCTURUS IN THE CONSTELLATION BOÖTES. SEE IT? IT'S RIGHT NEAR ALPHA CORONA BOREALIS.
WHOA!—YOU CAN SEE THE M13 GLOBULAR CLUSTER FROM UP HERE! LOOK AT THAT BABY! BE STILL MY HEART!
IS THAT THE ANDROMEDA GALAXY?! IT **MUST** BE! HOLY COW! DO YOU REALIZE HOW FAR **AWAY** THAT IS?! 2.2 MILLION LIGHT-YEARS! OF COURSE, IT'S 180,000 LIGHT-YEARS **ACROSS**, BUT **STILL**!...
AND THERE'S VEGA... AND DENEB... AND ALTAIR... AND ANTARES... AND... **AAAA**!—IT'S THE IOTA CAS TRINARY SYSTEM!
WHAT ARE **YOU** LOOKING AT?
A LOT OF PRETTY STARS.
PAIGE, PAIGE, PAIGE...
JASON, JASON, JASON...
AMEND

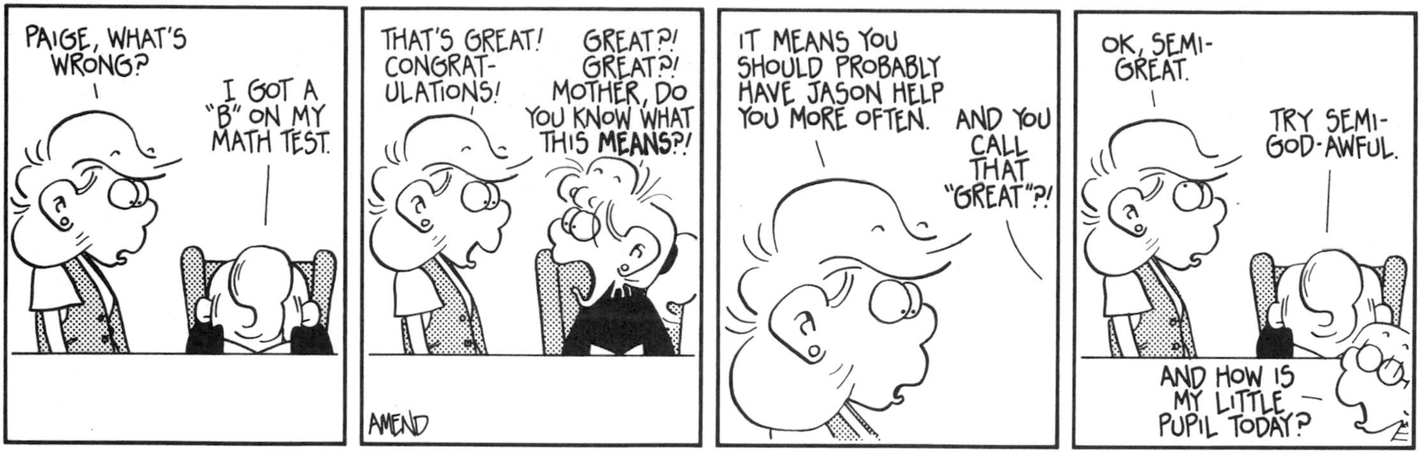
PAIGE, WHAT'S WRONG?
I GOT A "B" ON MY MATH TEST.
THAT'S GREAT! CONGRAT-ULATIONS!
GREAT?! GREAT?! MOTHER, DO YOU KNOW WHAT THIS **MEANS**?!
AMEND
IT MEANS YOU SHOULD PROBABLY HAVE JASON HELP YOU MORE OFTEN.
AND YOU CALL THAT "GREAT"?!
OK, SEMI-GREAT.
TRY SEMI-GOD-AWFUL.
AND HOW IS MY LITTLE PUPIL TODAY?

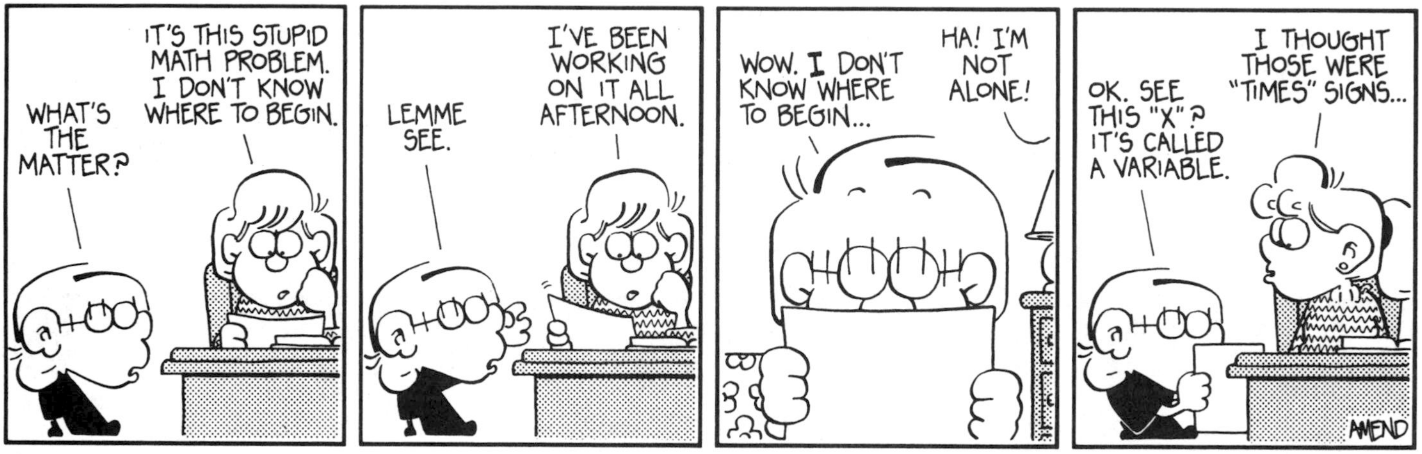
WHAT'S THE MATTER?
IT'S THIS STUPID MATH PROBLEM. I DON'T KNOW WHERE TO BEGIN.
LEMME SEE.
I'VE BEEN WORKING ON IT ALL AFTERNOON.
WOW. **I** DON'T KNOW WHERE TO BEGIN...
HA! I'M NOT ALONE!
OK. SEE THIS "X"? IT'S CALLED A VARIABLE.
I THOUGHT THOSE WERE "TIMES" SIGNS...
AMEND

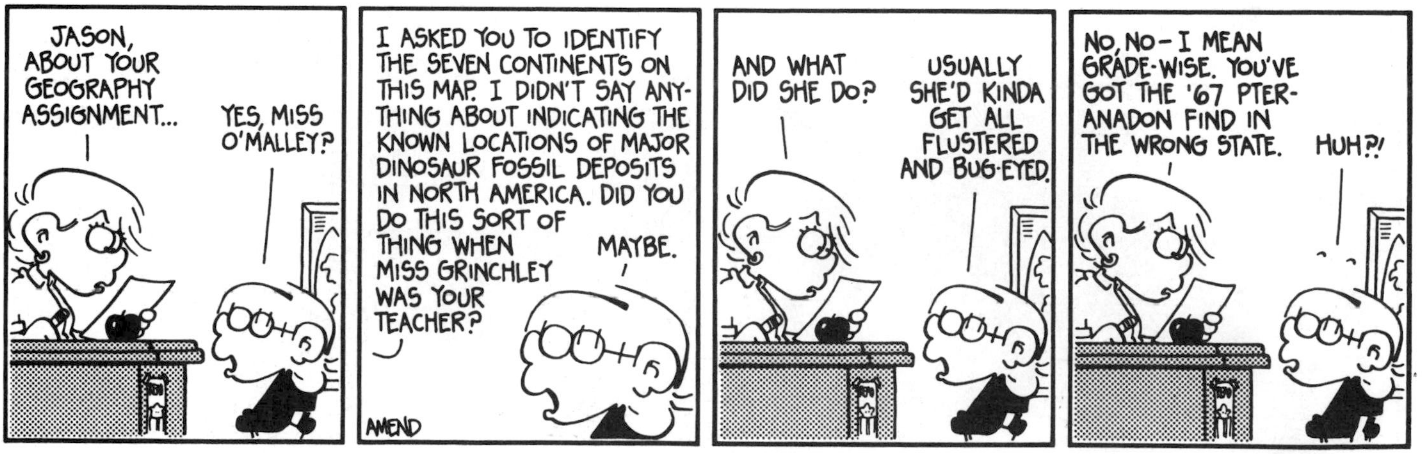
JASON, ABOUT YOUR GEOGRAPHY ASSIGNMENT...
YES, MISS O'MALLEY?
I ASKED YOU TO IDENTIFY THE SEVEN CONTINENTS ON THIS MAP. I DIDN'T SAY ANY-THING ABOUT INDICATING THE KNOWN LOCATIONS OF MAJOR DINOSAUR FOSSIL DEPOSITS IN NORTH AMERICA. DID YOU DO THIS SORT OF THING WHEN MISS GRINCHLEY WAS YOUR TEACHER?
MAYBE.
AMEND
AND WHAT DID SHE DO?
USUALLY SHE'D KINDA GET ALL FLUSTERED AND BUG-EYED.
NO, NO–I MEAN GRADE-WISE. YOU'VE GOT THE '67 PTER-ANADON FIND IN THE WRONG STATE.
HUH?!

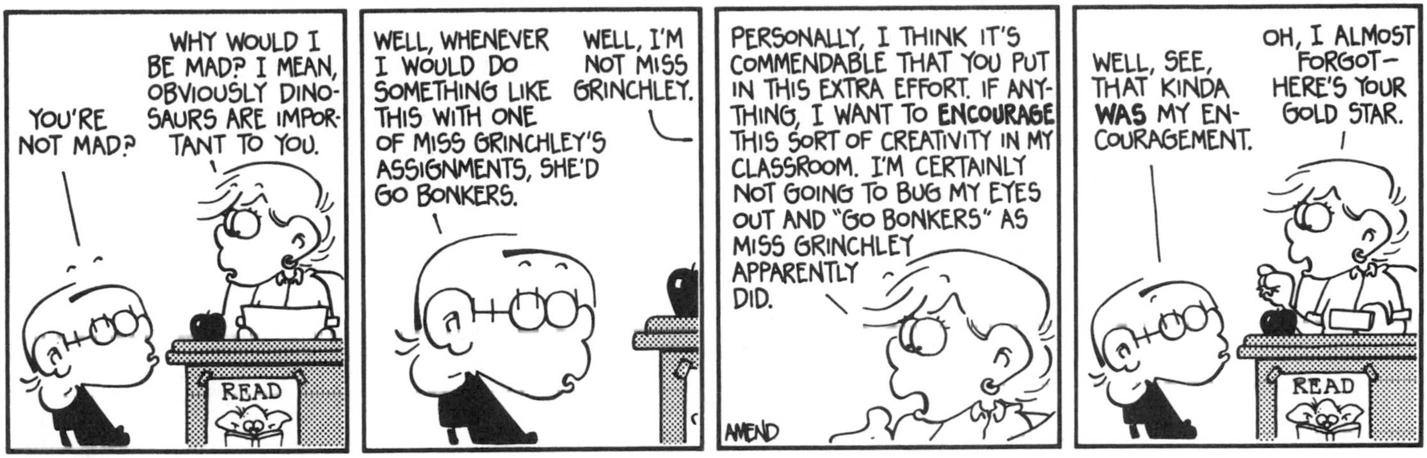
YOU'RE NOT MAD?
WHY WOULD I BE MAD? I MEAN, OBVIOUSLY DINOSAURS ARE IMPORTANT TO YOU.
WELL, WHENEVER I WOULD DO SOMETHING LIKE THIS WITH ONE OF MISS GRINCHLEY'S ASSIGNMENTS, SHE'D GO BONKERS.
WELL, I'M NOT MISS GRINCHLEY.
PERSONALLY, I THINK IT'S COMMENDABLE THAT YOU PUT IN THIS EXTRA EFFORT. IF ANYTHING, I WANT TO **ENCOURAGE** THIS SORT OF CREATIVITY IN MY CLASSROOM. I'M CERTAINLY NOT GOING TO BUG MY EYES OUT AND "GO BONKERS" AS MISS GRINCHLEY APPARENTLY DID.
AMEND
WELL, SEE, THAT KINDA **WAS** MY ENCOURAGEMENT.
OH, I ALMOST FORGOT— HERE'S YOUR GOLD STAR.
READ

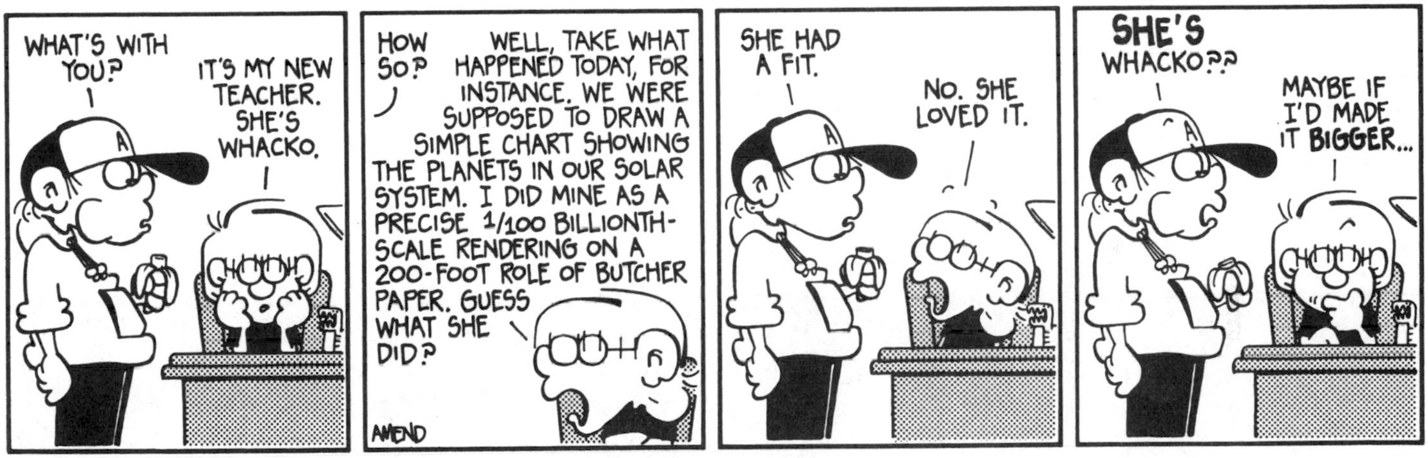
WHAT'S WITH YOU?
IT'S MY NEW TEACHER. SHE'S WHACKO.
HOW SO?
WELL, TAKE WHAT HAPPENED TODAY, FOR INSTANCE. WE WERE SUPPOSED TO DRAW A SIMPLE CHART SHOWING THE PLANETS IN OUR SOLAR SYSTEM. I DID MINE AS A PRECISE 1/100 BILLIONTH-SCALE RENDERING ON A 200-FOOT ROLE OF BUTCHER PAPER. GUESS WHAT SHE DID?
AMEND
SHE HAD A FIT.
NO. SHE LOVED IT.
SHE'S WHACKO?!?
MAYBE IF I'D MADE IT **BIGGER**...

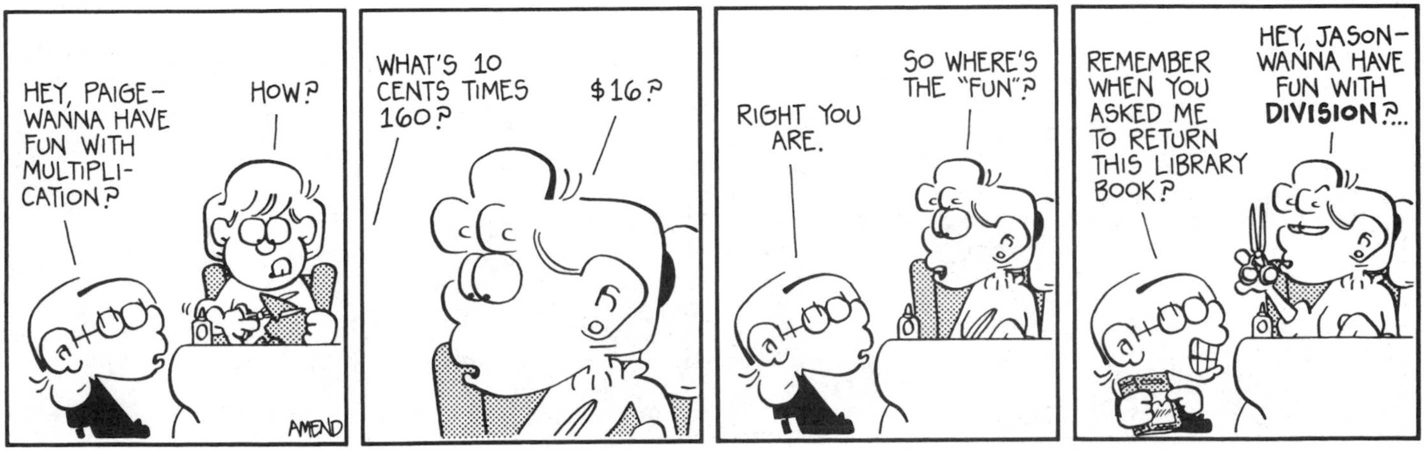
HEY, PAIGE— WANNA HAVE FUN WITH MULTIPLICATION?
HOW?
AMEND
WHAT'S 10 CENTS TIMES 160?
$16?
RIGHT YOU ARE.
SO WHERE'S THE "FUN"?
REMEMBER WHEN YOU ASKED ME TO RETURN THIS LIBRARY BOOK?
HEY, JASON— WANNA HAVE FUN WITH **DIVISION**?...

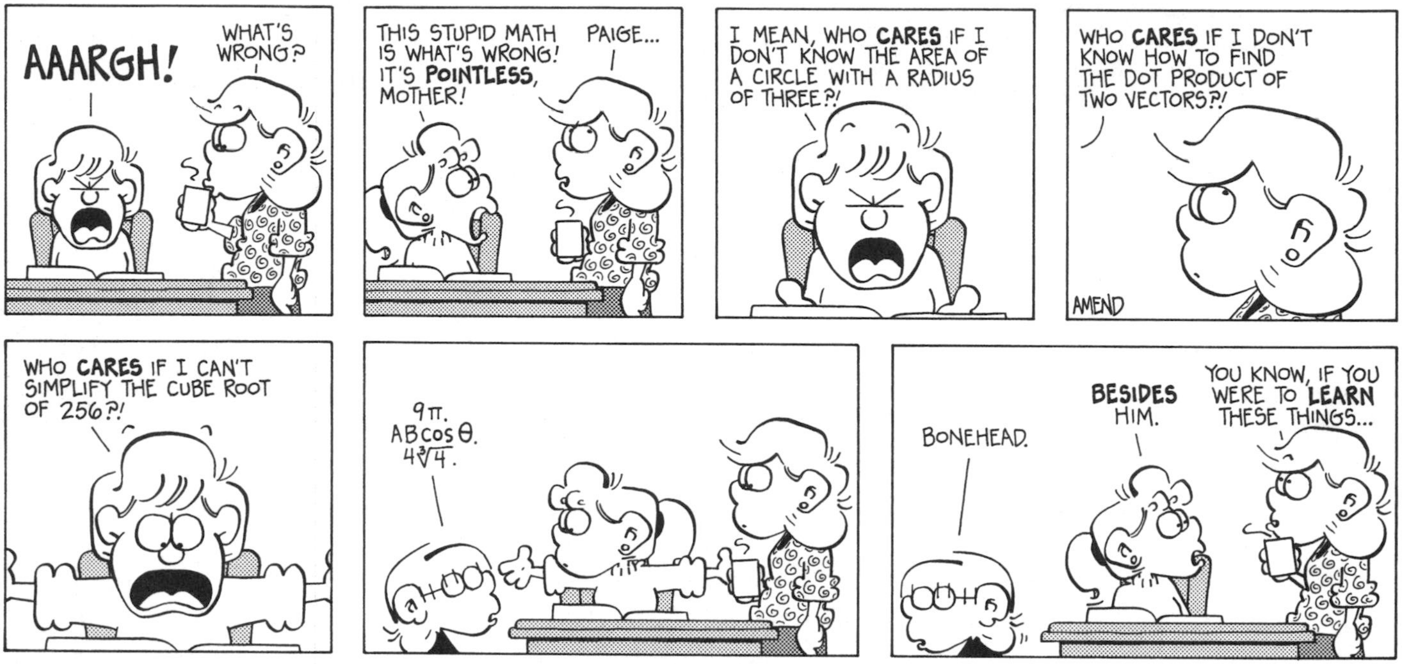
AAARGH!
WHAT'S WRONG?
THIS STUPID MATH IS WHAT'S WRONG! IT'S **POINTLESS**, MOTHER!
PAIGE...
I MEAN, WHO **CARES** IF I DON'T KNOW THE AREA OF A CIRCLE WITH A RADIUS OF THREE?!
WHO **CARES** IF I DON'T KNOW HOW TO FIND THE DOT PRODUCT OF TWO VECTORS?!
AMEND
WHO **CARES** IF I CAN'T SIMPLIFY THE CUBE ROOT OF 256?!
9π. $AB\cos\theta$. $4\sqrt[3]{4}$.
BONEHEAD.
BESIDES HIM.
YOU KNOW, IF YOU WERE TO **LEARN** THESE THINGS...

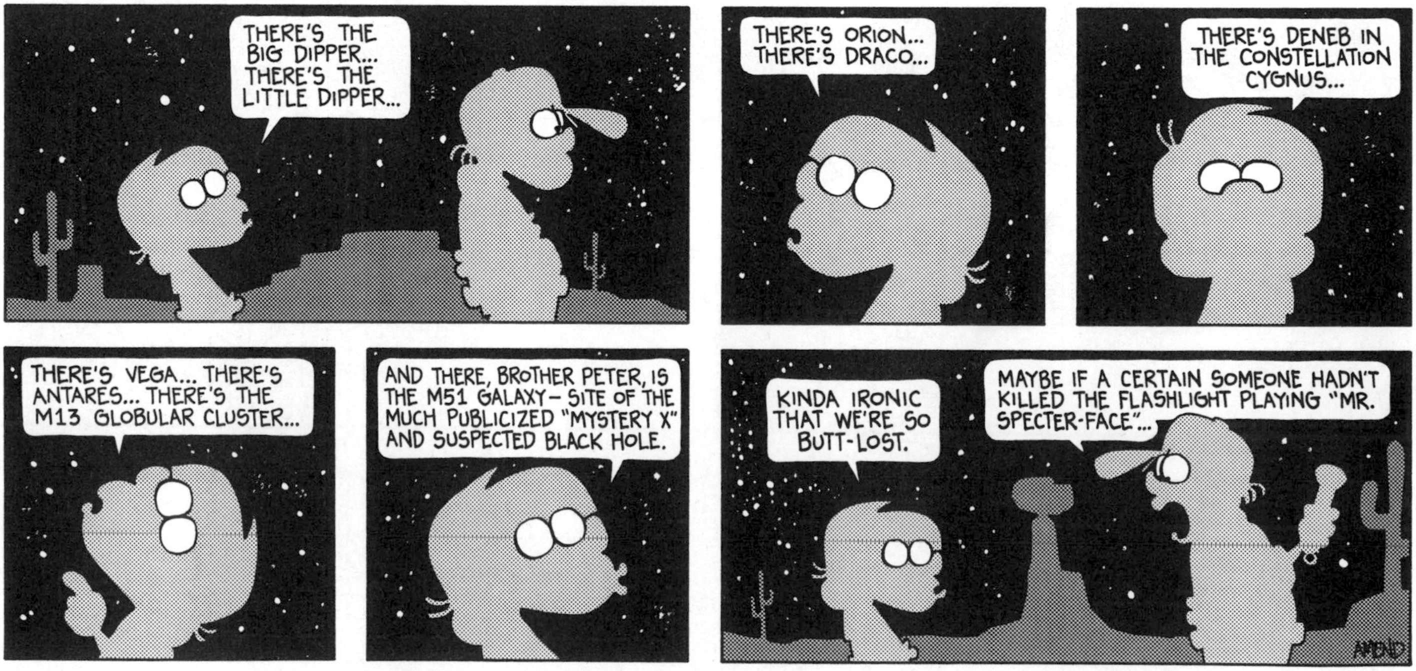
THERE'S THE BIG DIPPER... THERE'S THE LITTLE DIPPER...
THERE'S ORION... THERE'S DRACO...
THERE'S DENEB IN THE CONSTELLATION CYGNUS...
THERE'S VEGA... THERE'S ANTARES... THERE'S THE M13 GLOBULAR CLUSTER...
AND THERE, BROTHER PETER, IS THE M51 GALAXY– SITE OF THE MUCH PUBLICIZED "MYSTERY X" AND SUSPECTED BLACK HOLE.
KINDA IRONIC THAT WE'RE SO BUTT-LOST.
MAYBE IF A CERTAIN SOMEONE HADN'T KILLED THE FLASHLIGHT PLAYING "MR. SPECTER-FACE"...
AMEND

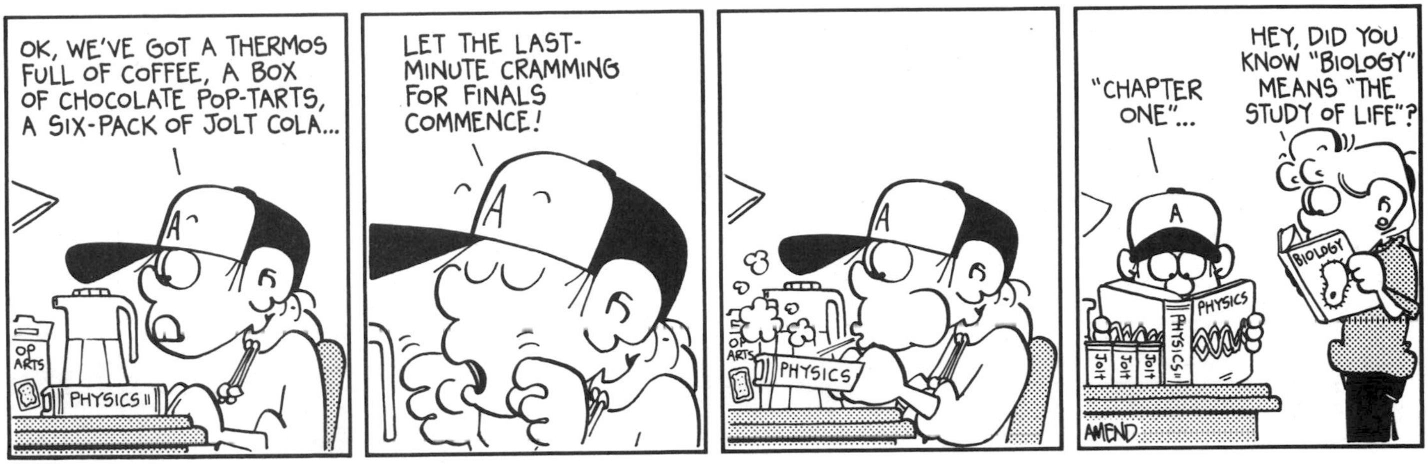
OK, WE'VE GOT A THERMOS FULL OF COFFEE, A BOX OF CHOCOLATE POP-TARTS, A SIX-PACK OF JOLT COLA...
OP ARTS
PHYSICS II
LET THE LAST-MINUTE CRAMMING FOR FINALS COMMENCE!
PHYSICS
"CHAPTER ONE"...
HEY, DID YOU KNOW "BIOLOGY" MEANS "THE STUDY OF LIFE"?
PHYSICS
PHYSICS II
BIOLOGY
Jolt
AMEND

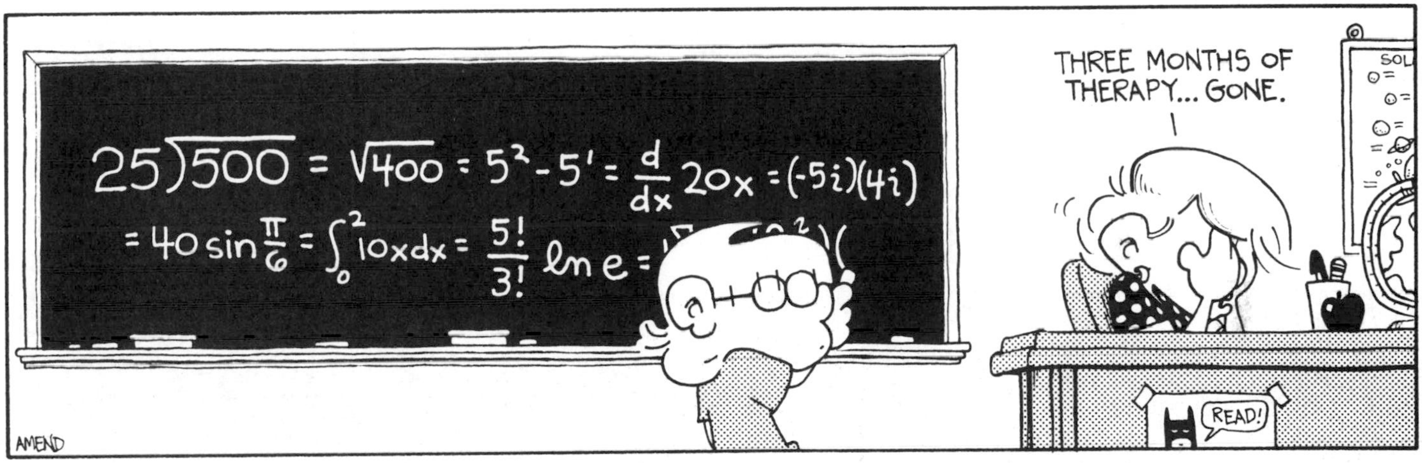
$25\overline{)500} = \sqrt{400} = 5^2 - 5^1 = \frac{d}{dx}20x = (-5i)(4i)$
$= 40\sin\frac{\pi}{6} = \int_0^2 10x\,dx = \frac{5!}{3!}\ln e =$
THREE MONTHS OF THERAPY... GONE.
READ!
AMEND

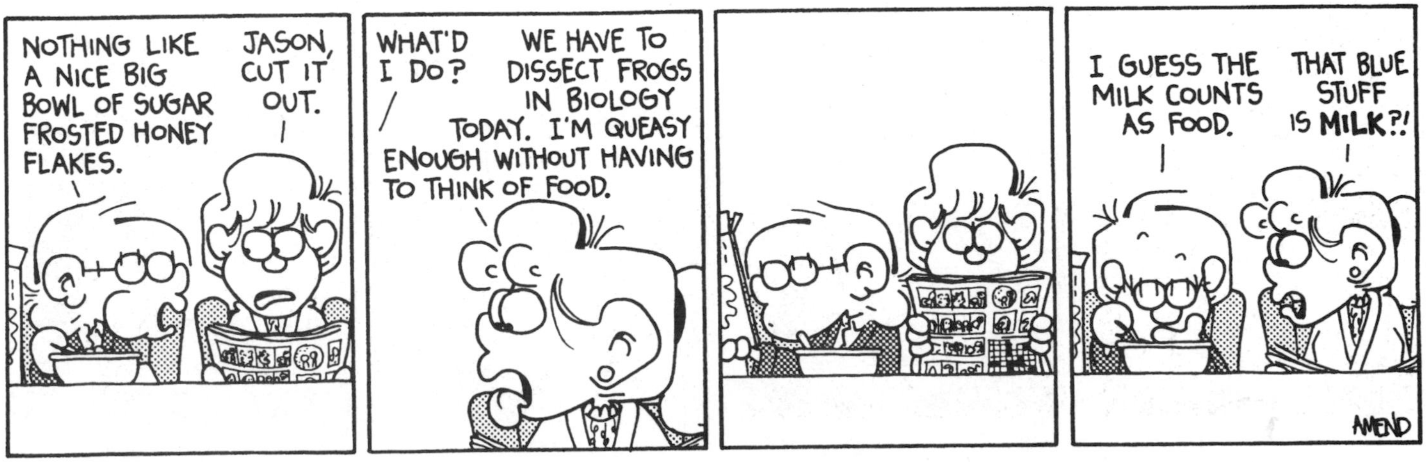
NOTHING LIKE A NICE BIG BOWL OF SUGAR FROSTED HONEY FLAKES.
JASON, CUT IT OUT.
WHAT'D I DO?
WE HAVE TO DISSECT FROGS IN BIOLOGY TODAY. I'M QUEASY ENOUGH WITHOUT HAVING TO THINK OF FOOD.
I GUESS THE MILK COUNTS AS FOOD.
THAT BLUE STUFF IS **MILK**?!
AMEND

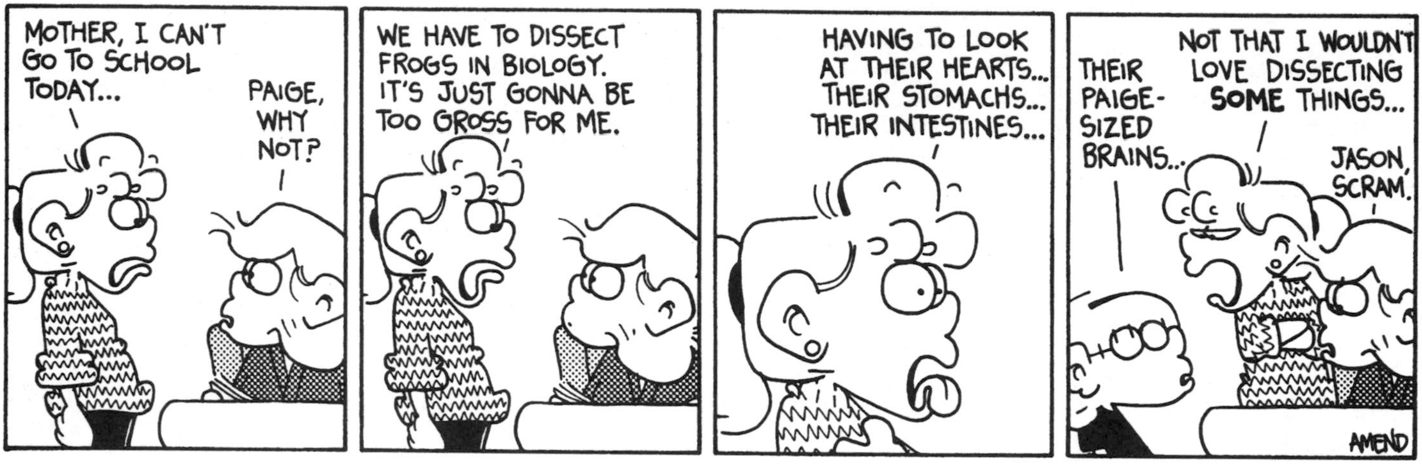
MOTHER, I CAN'T GO TO SCHOOL TODAY...
PAIGE, WHY NOT?
WE HAVE TO DISSECT FROGS IN BIOLOGY. IT'S JUST GONNA BE TOO GROSS FOR ME.
HAVING TO LOOK AT THEIR HEARTS... THEIR STOMACHS... THEIR INTESTINES...
THEIR PAIGE-SIZED BRAINS...
NOT THAT I WOULDN'T LOVE DISSECTING **SOME** THINGS...
JASON, SCRAM.
AMEND

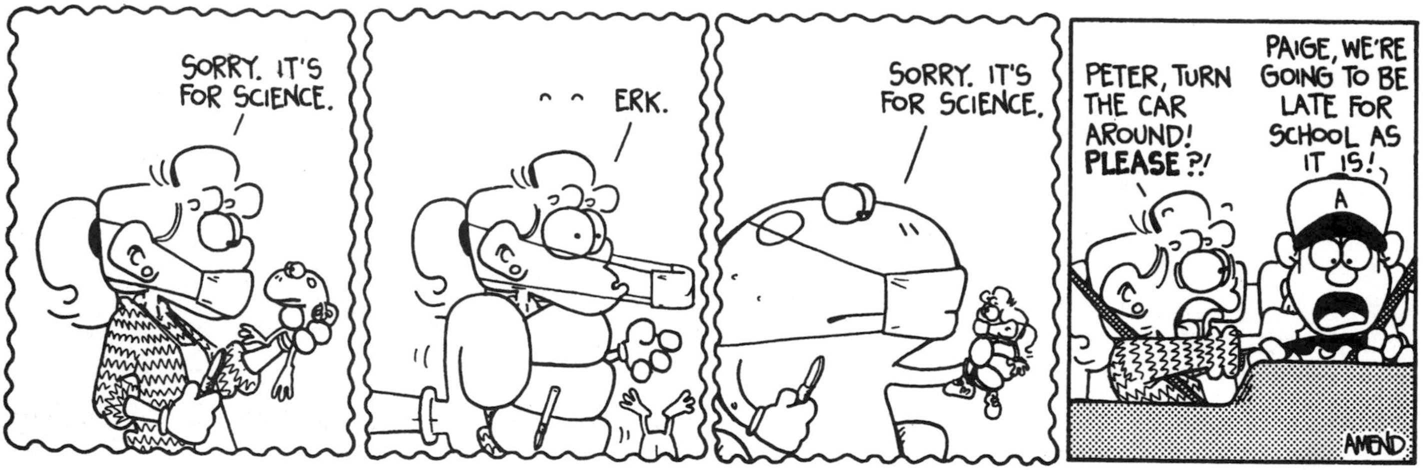
SORRY. IT'S FOR SCIENCE.
ERK.
SORRY. IT'S FOR SCIENCE.
PETER, TURN THE CAR AROUND! **PLEASE**?!
PAIGE, WE'RE GOING TO BE LATE FOR SCHOOL AS IT IS!
A
AMEND

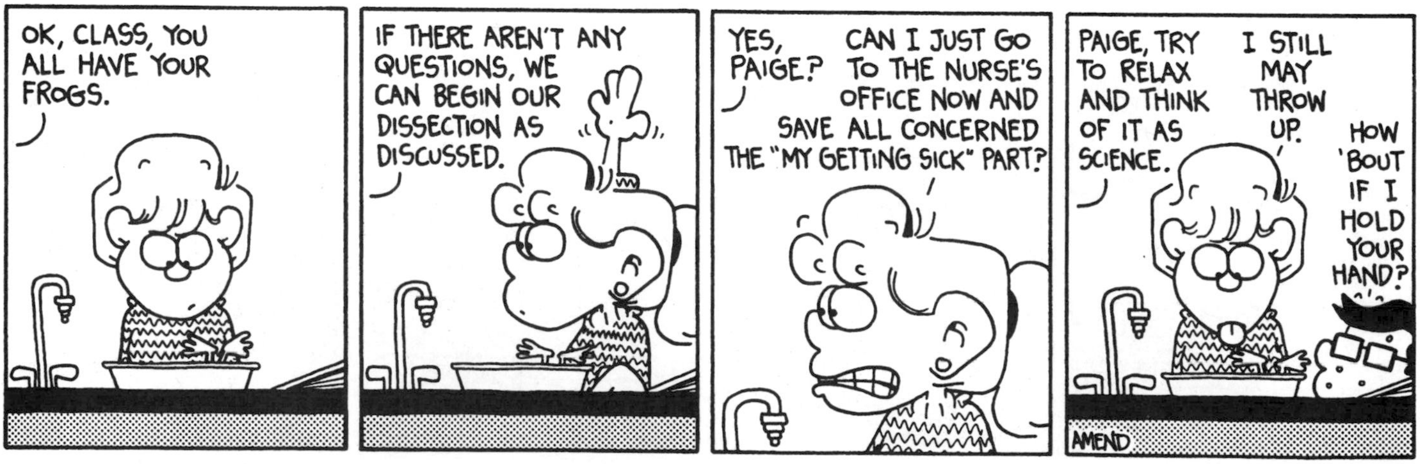
OK, CLASS, YOU ALL HAVE YOUR FROGS.
IF THERE AREN'T ANY QUESTIONS, WE CAN BEGIN OUR DISSECTION AS DISCUSSED.
YES, PAIGE?
CAN I JUST GO TO THE NURSE'S OFFICE NOW AND SAVE ALL CONCERNED THE "MY GETTING SICK" PART?
PAIGE, TRY TO RELAX AND THINK OF IT AS SCIENCE.
I STILL MAY THROW UP.
HOW 'BOUT IF I HOLD YOUR HAND?
AMEND

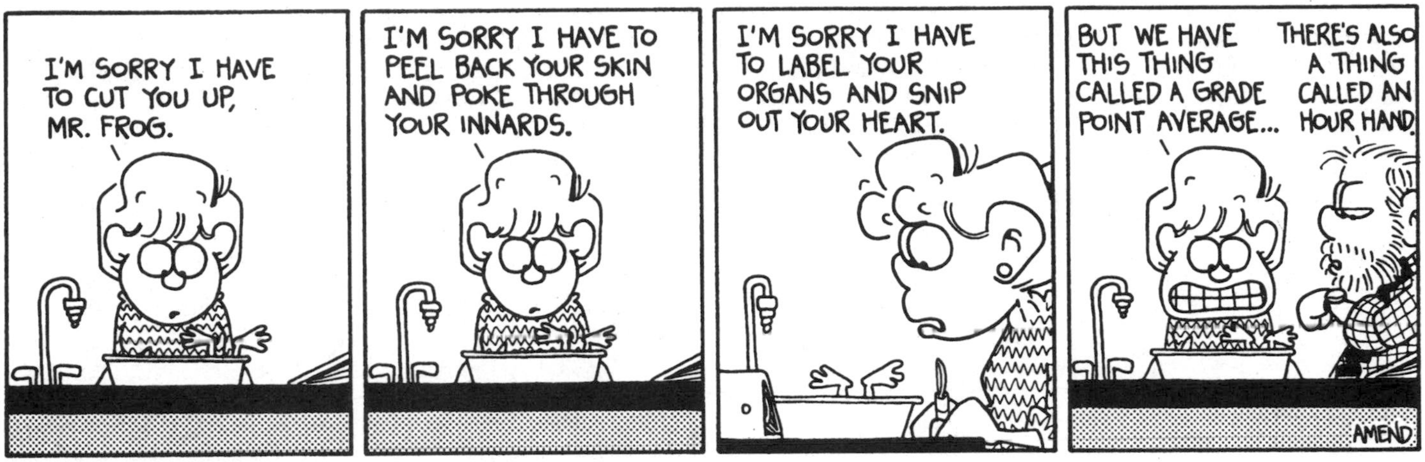
I'M SORRY I HAVE TO CUT YOU UP, MR. FROG.
I'M SORRY I HAVE TO PEEL BACK YOUR SKIN AND POKE THROUGH YOUR INNARDS.
I'M SORRY I HAVE TO LABEL YOUR ORGANS AND SNIP OUT YOUR HEART.
BUT WE HAVE THIS THING CALLED A GRADE POINT AVERAGE...
THERE'S ALSO A THING CALLED AN HOUR HAND.
AMEND

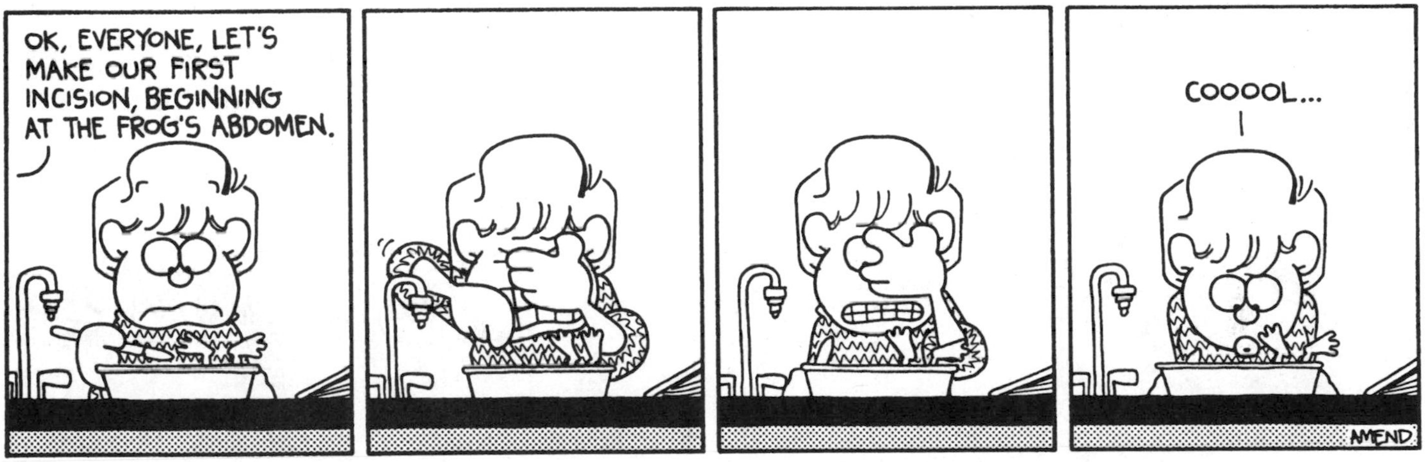
OK, EVERYONE, LET'S MAKE OUR FIRST INCISION, BEGINNING AT THE FROG'S ABDOMEN.
COOOOL...
AMEND

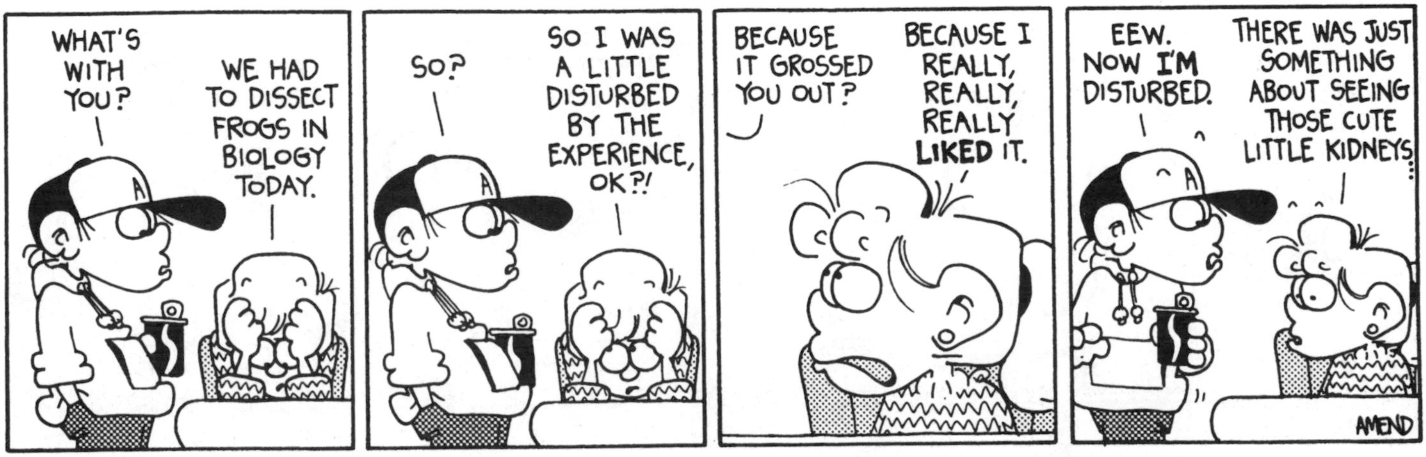
WHAT'S WITH YOU?
WE HAD TO DISSECT FROGS IN BIOLOGY TODAY.
SO?
SO I WAS A LITTLE DISTURBED BY THE EXPERIENCE, OK?!
BECAUSE IT GROSSED YOU OUT?
BECAUSE I REALLY, REALLY, REALLY **LIKED** IT.
EEW. NOW **I'M** DISTURBED.
THERE WAS JUST SOMETHING ABOUT SEEING THOSE CUTE LITTLE KIDNEYS...
AMEND

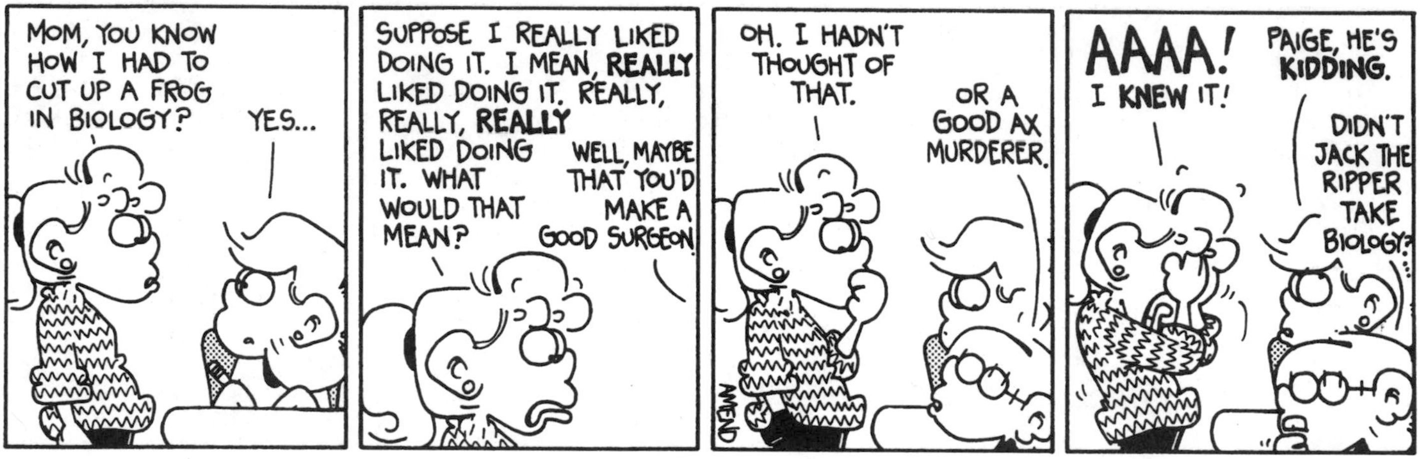
MOM, YOU KNOW HOW I HAD TO CUT UP A FROG IN BIOLOGY?
YES...
SUPPOSE I REALLY LIKED DOING IT. I MEAN, REALLY LIKED DOING IT. REALLY, REALLY, REALLY LIKED DOING IT. WHAT WOULD THAT MEAN?
WELL, MAYBE THAT YOU'D MAKE A GOOD SURGEON.
OH. I HADN'T THOUGHT OF THAT.
OR A GOOD AX MURDERER.
AMEND
AAAA! I KNEW IT!
PAIGE, HE'S KIDDING.
DIDN'T JACK THE RIPPER TAKE BIOLOGY?

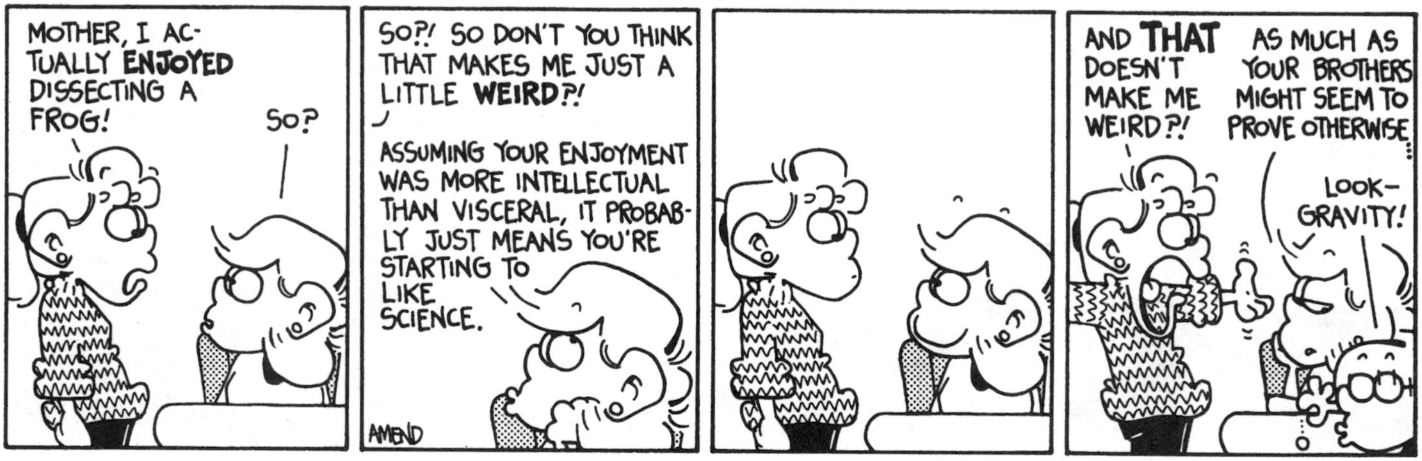
MOTHER, I ACTUALLY ENJOYED DISSECTING A FROG!
SO?
SO?! SO DON'T YOU THINK THAT MAKES ME JUST A LITTLE WEIRD?!
ASSUMING YOUR ENJOYMENT WAS MORE INTELLECTUAL THAN VISCERAL, IT PROBABLY JUST MEANS YOU'RE STARTING TO LIKE SCIENCE.
AMEND
AND THAT DOESN'T MAKE ME WEIRD?!
AS MUCH AS YOUR BROTHERS MIGHT SEEM TO PROVE OTHERWISE...
LOOK- GRAVITY!

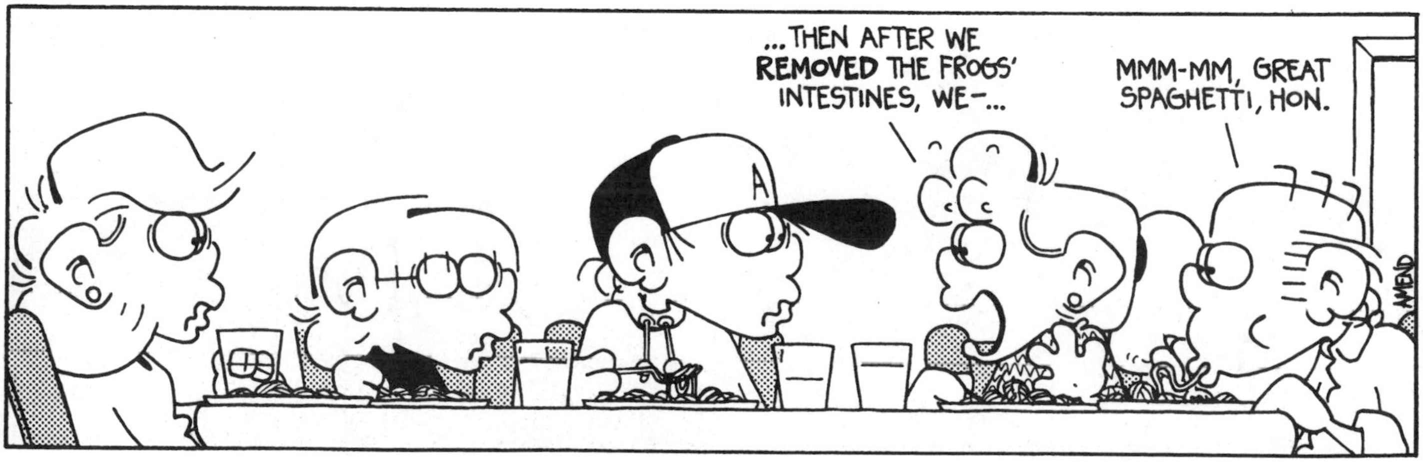
...THEN AFTER WE REMOVED THE FROGS' INTESTINES, WE-...
MMM-MM, GREAT SPAGHETTI, HON.
AMEND

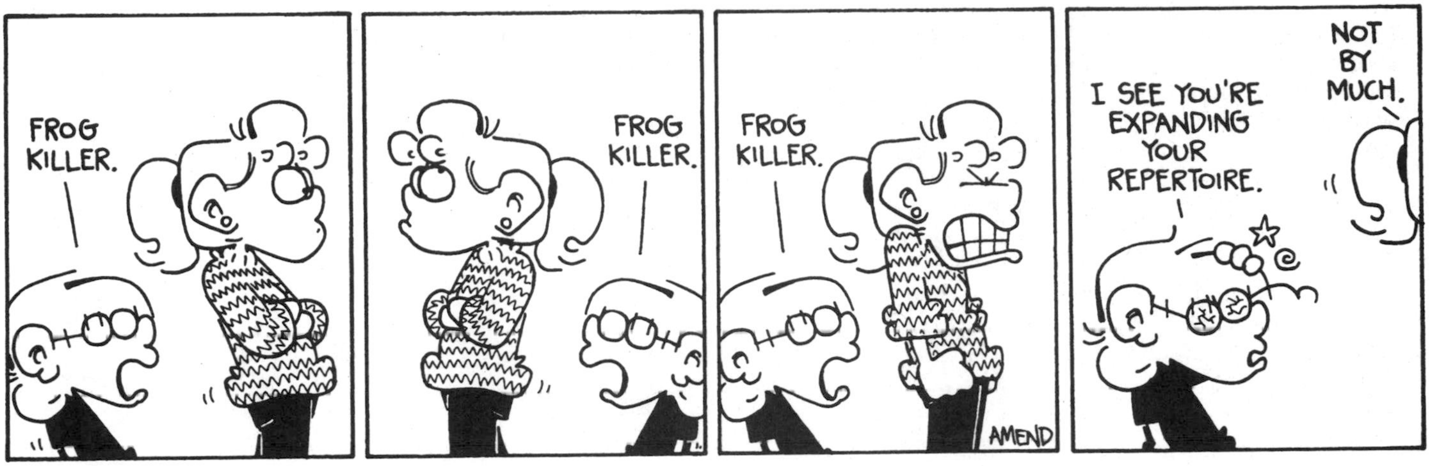
FROG KILLER.
FROG KILLER.
FROG KILLER.
AMEND
I SEE YOU'RE EXPANDING YOUR REPERTOIRE.
NOT BY MUCH.

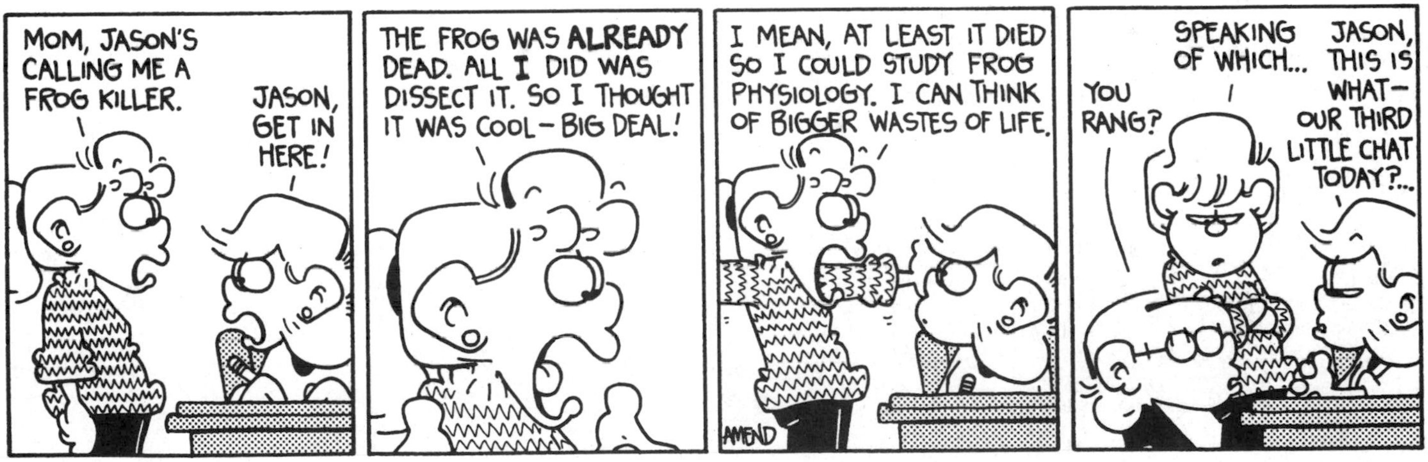
MOM, JASON'S CALLING ME A FROG KILLER.
JASON, GET IN HERE!
THE FROG WAS **ALREADY** DEAD. ALL **I** DID WAS DISSECT IT. SO I THOUGHT IT WAS COOL – BIG DEAL!
I MEAN, AT LEAST IT DIED SO I COULD STUDY FROG PHYSIOLOGY. I CAN THINK OF BIGGER WASTES OF LIFE.
AMEND
YOU RANG?
SPEAKING OF WHICH...
JASON, THIS IS WHAT– OUR THIRD LITTLE CHAT TODAY?...

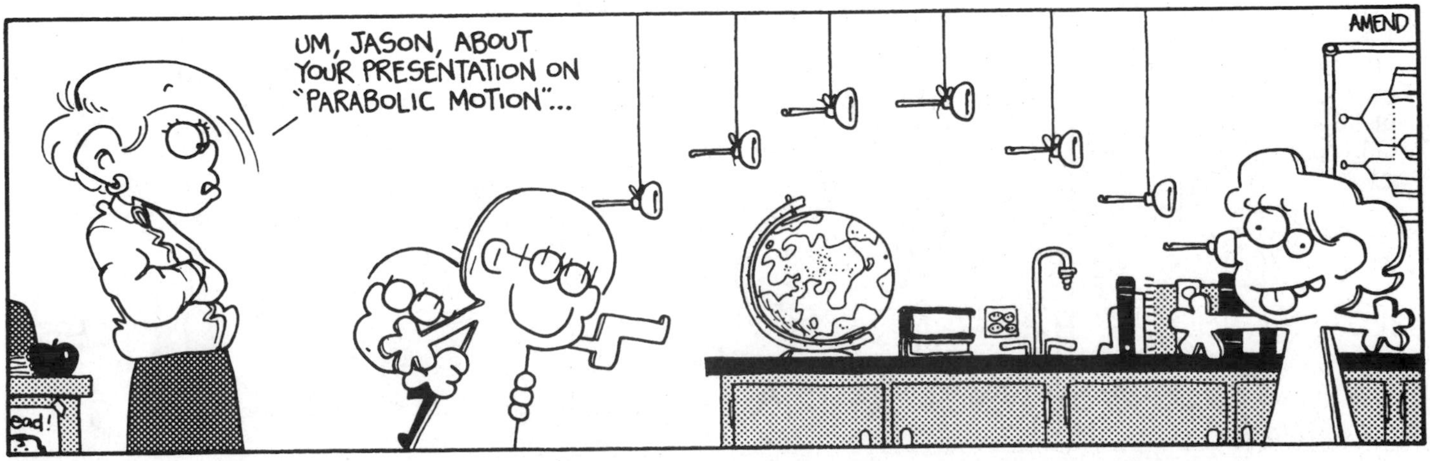
AMEND
UM, JASON, ABOUT YOUR PRESENTATION ON "PARABOLIC MOTION"...

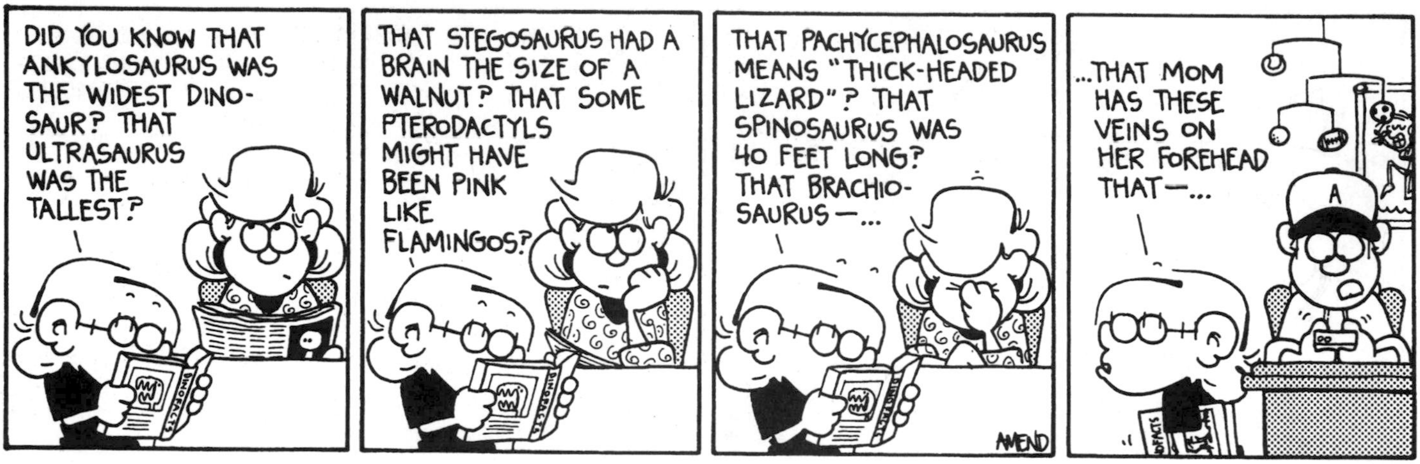
DID YOU KNOW THAT ANKYLOSAURUS WAS THE WIDEST DINO-SAUR? THAT ULTRASAURUS WAS THE TALLEST?
THAT STEGOSAURUS HAD A BRAIN THE SIZE OF A WALNUT? THAT SOME PTERODACTYLS MIGHT HAVE BEEN PINK LIKE FLAMINGOS?
THAT PACHYCEPHALOSAURUS MEANS "THICK-HEADED LIZARD"? THAT SPINOSAURUS WAS 40 FEET LONG? THAT BRACHIO-SAURUS —...
AMEND
...THAT MOM HAS THESE VEINS ON HER FOREHEAD THAT —...

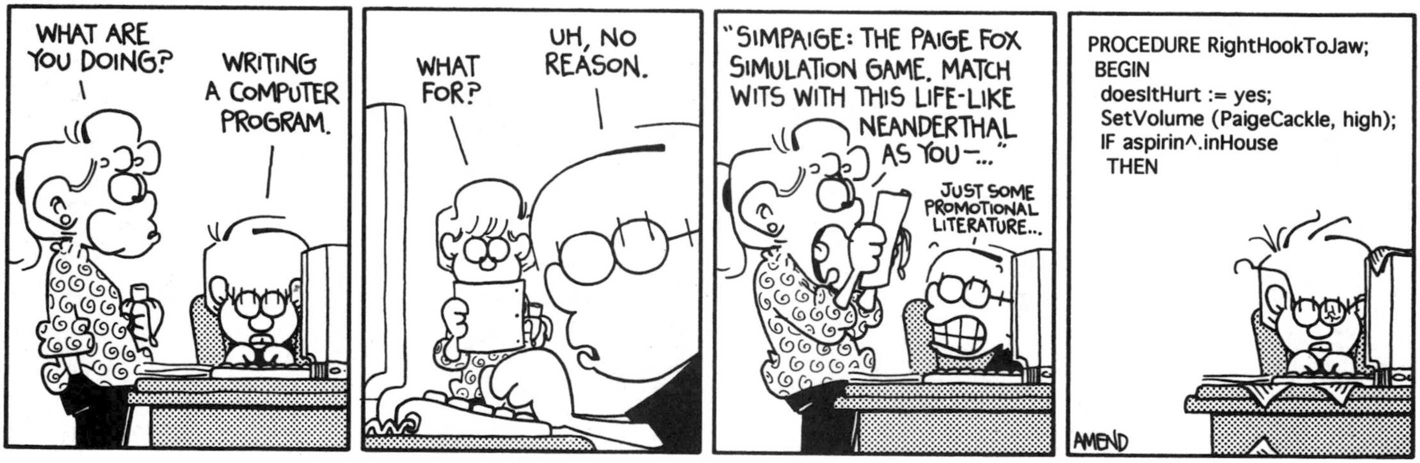
WHAT ARE YOU DOING?
WRITING A COMPUTER PROGRAM.
WHAT FOR?
UH, NO REASON.
"SIMPAIGE: THE PAIGE FOX SIMULATION GAME. MATCH WITS WITH THIS LIFE-LIKE NEANDERTHAL AS YOU —..."
JUST SOME PROMOTIONAL LITERATURE...
PROCEDURE RightHookToJaw;
BEGIN
doesItHurt := yes;
SetVolume (PaigeCackle, high);
IF aspirin^.inHouse
THEN
AMEND

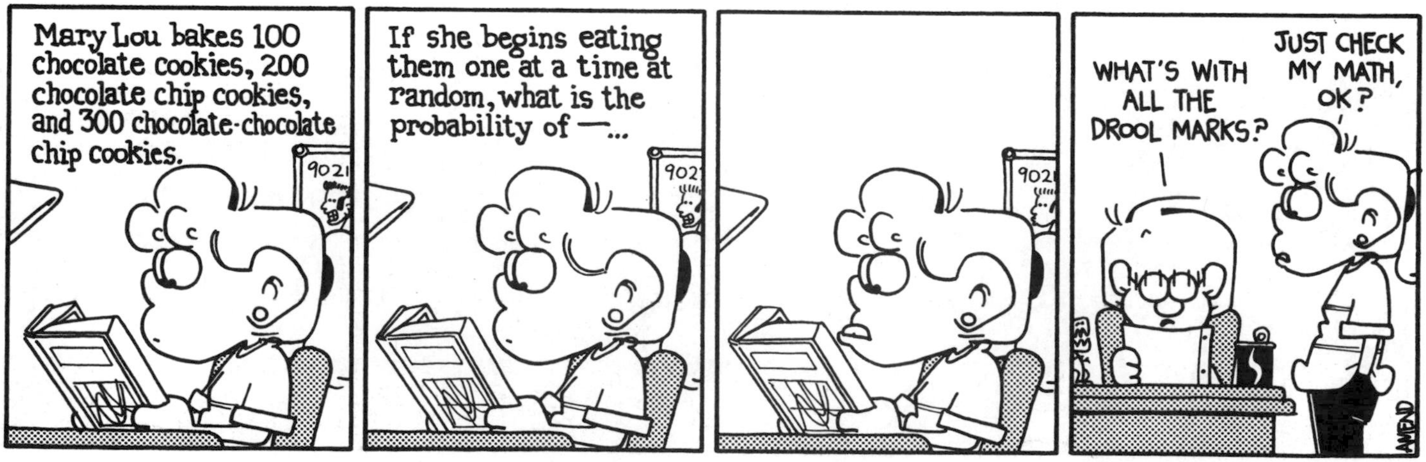
Mary Lou bakes 100 chocolate cookies, 200 chocolate chip cookies, and 300 chocolate-chocolate chip cookies.
If she begins eating them one at a time at random, what is the probability of —...
WHAT'S WITH ALL THE DROOL MARKS?
JUST CHECK MY MATH, OK?
AMEND

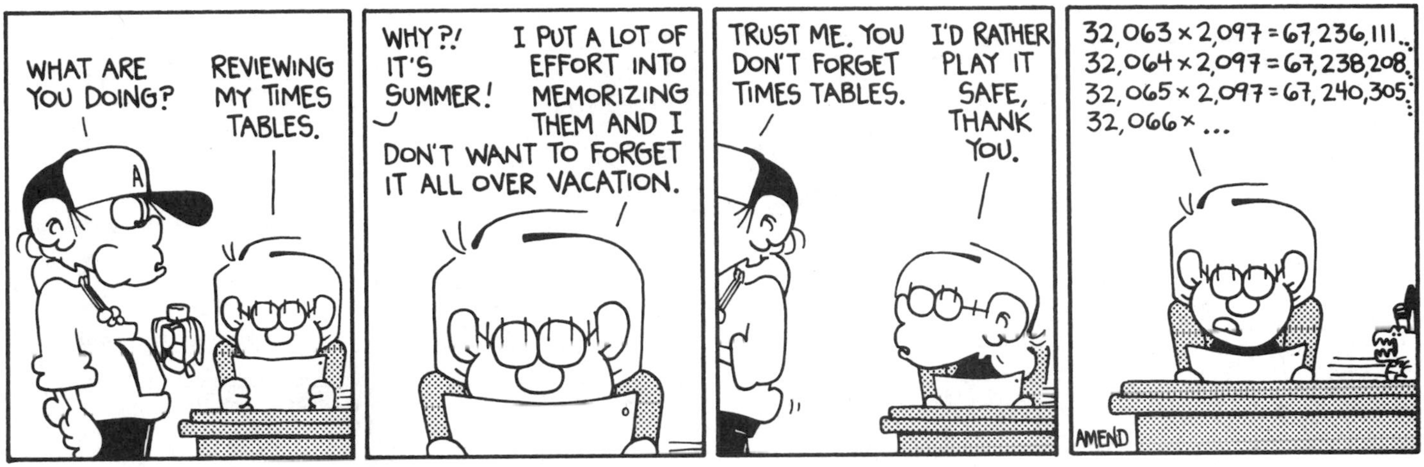
WHAT ARE YOU DOING?
REVIEWING MY TIMES TABLES.
WHY?! IT'S SUMMER!
I PUT A LOT OF EFFORT INTO MEMORIZING THEM AND I DON'T WANT TO FORGET IT ALL OVER VACATION.
TRUST ME. YOU DON'T FORGET TIMES TABLES.
I'D RATHER PLAY IT SAFE, THANK YOU.
32,063 × 2,097 = 67,236,111
32,064 × 2,097 = 67,238,208
32,065 × 2,097 = 67,240,305
32,066 × ...
AMEND

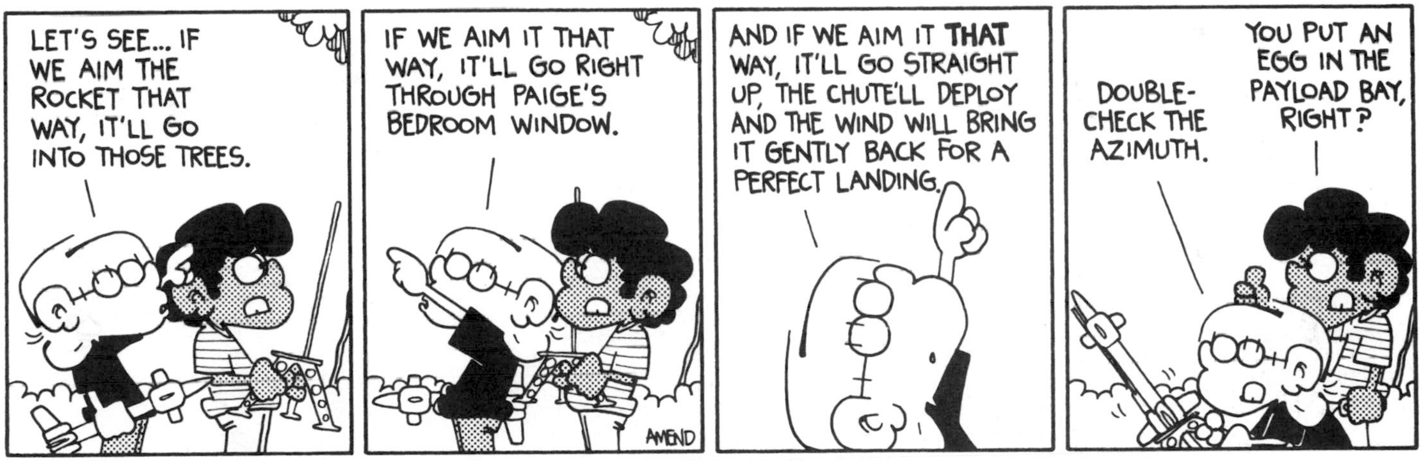
LET'S SEE... IF WE AIM THE ROCKET THAT WAY, IT'LL GO INTO THOSE TREES.
IF WE AIM IT THAT WAY, IT'LL GO RIGHT THROUGH PAIGE'S BEDROOM WINDOW.
AMEND
AND IF WE AIM IT **THAT** WAY, IT'LL GO STRAIGHT UP, THE CHUTE'LL DEPLOY AND THE WIND WILL BRING IT GENTLY BACK FOR A PERFECT LANDING.
DOUBLE-CHECK THE AZIMUTH.
YOU PUT AN EGG IN THE PAYLOAD BAY, RIGHT?

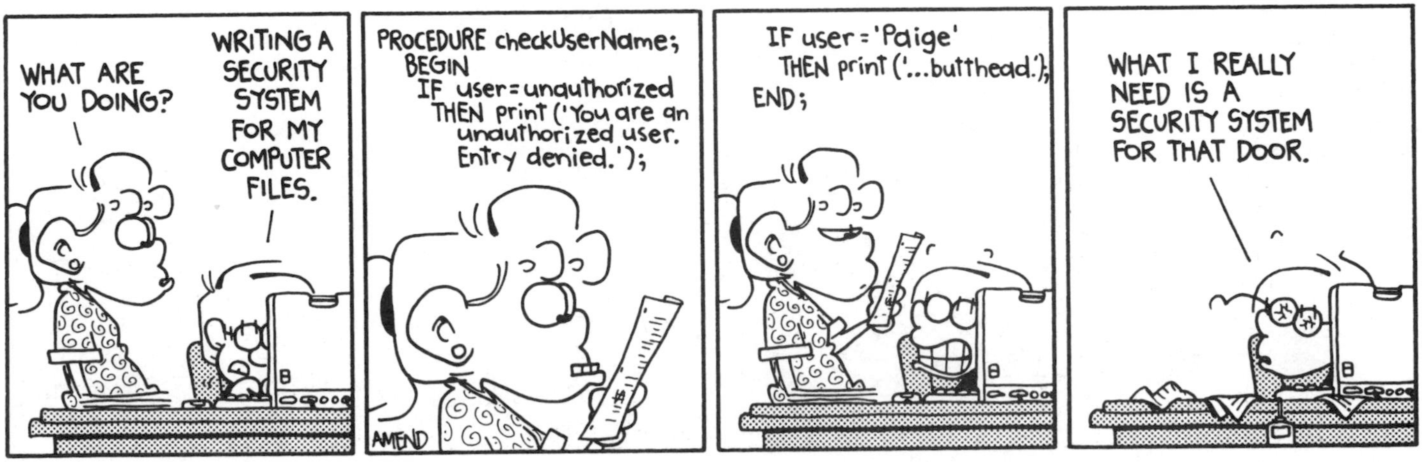
WHAT ARE YOU DOING?
WRITING A SECURITY SYSTEM FOR MY COMPUTER FILES.
PROCEDURE checkUserName;
BEGIN
IF user=unauthorized
THEN print ('You are an unauthorized user. Entry denied.');
AMEND
IF user='Paige'
THEN print ('...butthead.');
END;
WHAT I REALLY NEED IS A SECURITY SYSTEM FOR THAT DOOR.

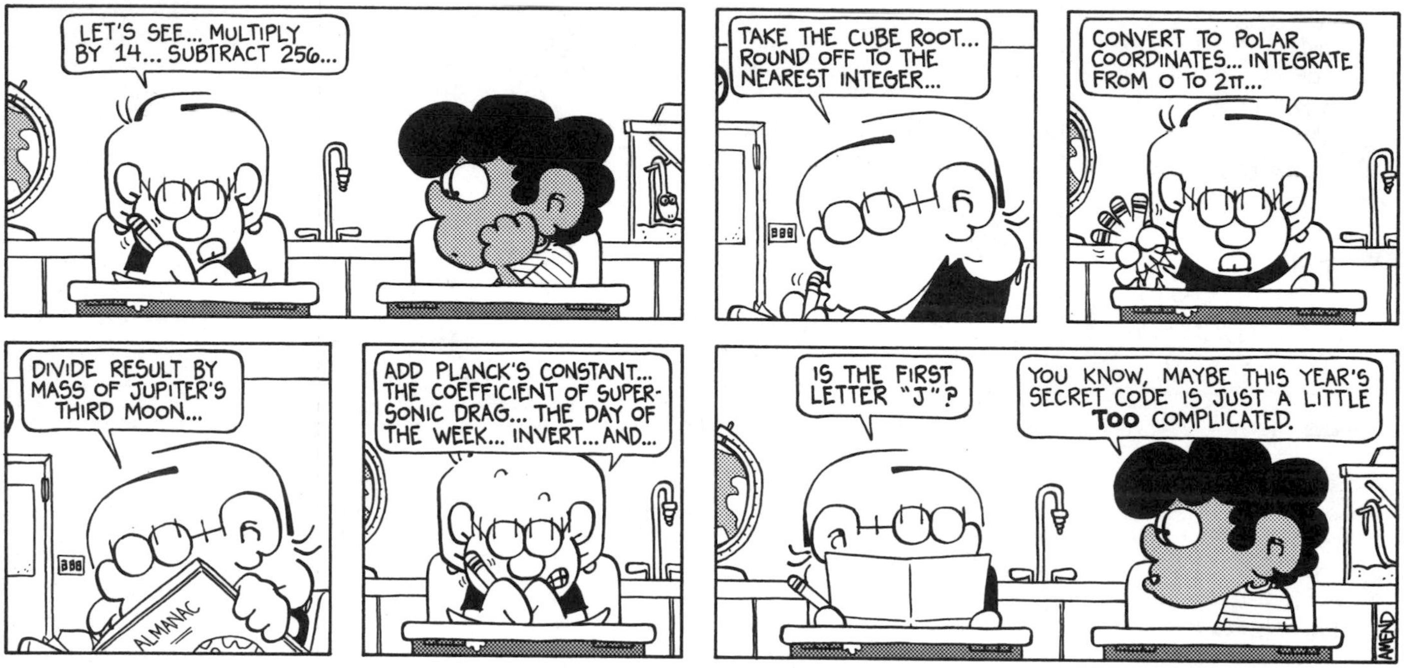
LET'S SEE... MULTIPLY BY 14... SUBTRACT 256...
TAKE THE CUBE ROOT... ROUND OFF TO THE NEAREST INTEGER...
CONVERT TO POLAR COORDINATES... INTEGRATE FROM 0 TO 2π...
DIVIDE RESULT BY MASS OF JUPITER'S THIRD MOON...
ALMANAC
ADD PLANCK'S CONSTANT... THE COEFFICIENT OF SUPER-SONIC DRAG... THE DAY OF THE WEEK... INVERT... AND...
IS THE FIRST LETTER "J"?
YOU KNOW, MAYBE THIS YEAR'S SECRET CODE IS JUST A LITTLE **TOO** COMPLICATED.
AMEND

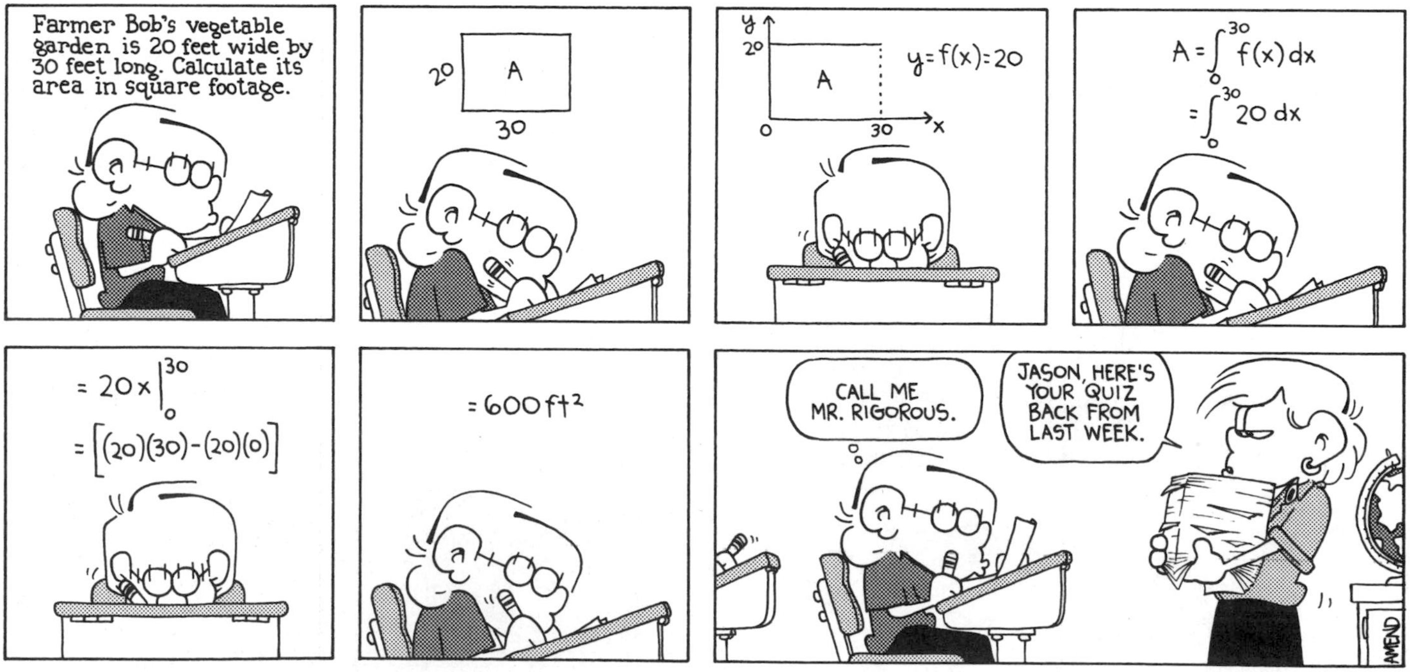
Farmer Bob's vegetable garden is 20 feet wide by 30 feet long. Calculate its area in square footage.
20 A 30
y 20 A 0 30 x
y=f(x)=20
A = ∫ from 0 to 30 f(x) dx
= ∫ from 0 to 30 20 dx
= 20x | from 0 to 30
= [(20)(30)-(20)(0)]
= 600 ft²
CALL ME MR. RIGOROUS.
JASON, HERE'S YOUR QUIZ BACK FROM LAST WEEK.
AMEND

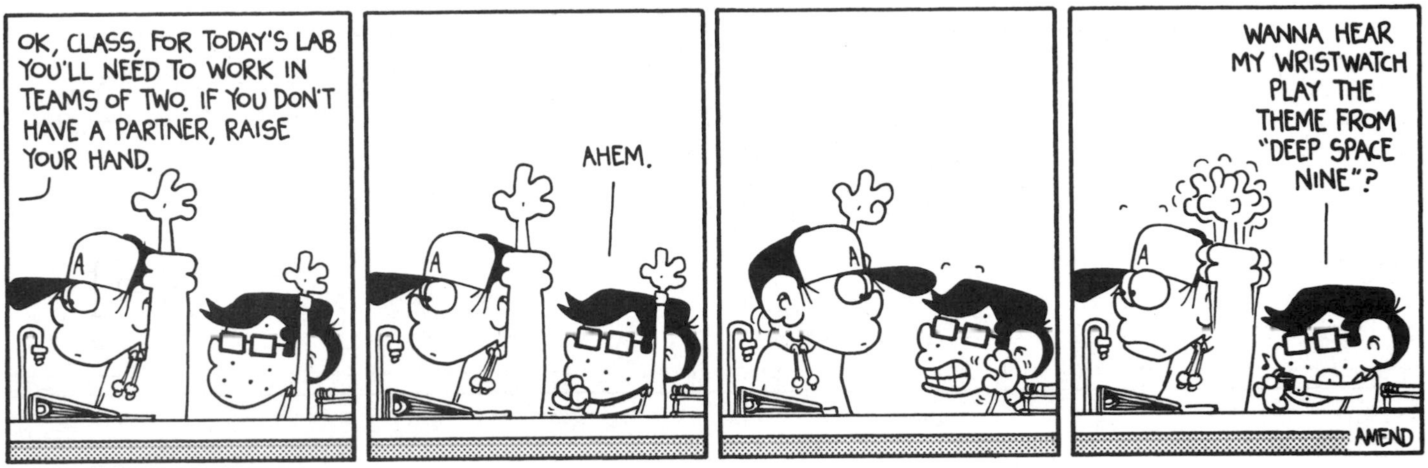
OK, CLASS, FOR TODAY'S LAB YOU'LL NEED TO WORK IN TEAMS OF TWO. IF YOU DON'T HAVE A PARTNER, RAISE YOUR HAND.
AHEM.
WANNA HEAR MY WRISTWATCH PLAY THE THEME FROM "DEEP SPACE NINE"?
AMEND

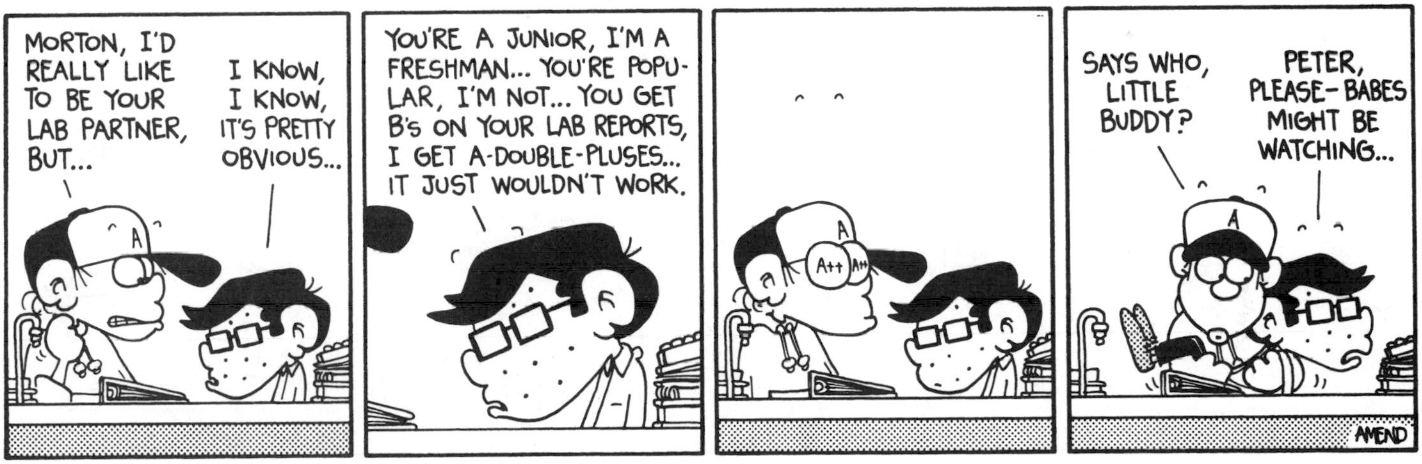
MORTON, I'D REALLY LIKE TO BE YOUR LAB PARTNER, BUT...
I KNOW, I KNOW, IT'S PRETTY OBVIOUS...
YOU'RE A JUNIOR, I'M A FRESHMAN... YOU'RE POPULAR, I'M NOT... YOU GET B'S ON YOUR LAB REPORTS, I GET A-DOUBLE-PLUSES... IT JUST WOULDN'T WORK.
A++
SAYS WHO, LITTLE BUDDY?
PETER, PLEASE- BABES MIGHT BE WATCHING...
AMEND

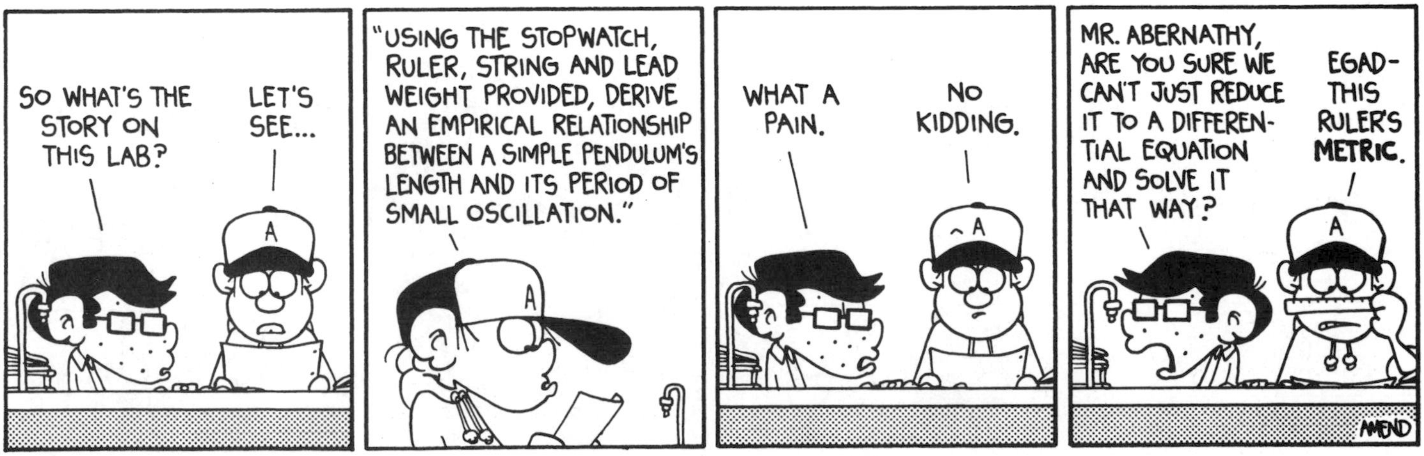
SO WHAT'S THE STORY ON THIS LAB?
LET'S SEE...
"USING THE STOPWATCH, RULER, STRING AND LEAD WEIGHT PROVIDED, DERIVE AN EMPIRICAL RELATIONSHIP BETWEEN A SIMPLE PENDULUM'S LENGTH AND ITS PERIOD OF SMALL OSCILLATION."
WHAT A PAIN.
NO KIDDING.
MR. ABERNATHY, ARE YOU SURE WE CAN'T JUST REDUCE IT TO A DIFFERENTIAL EQUATION AND SOLVE IT THAT WAY?
EGAD- THIS RULER'S METRIC.
AMEND

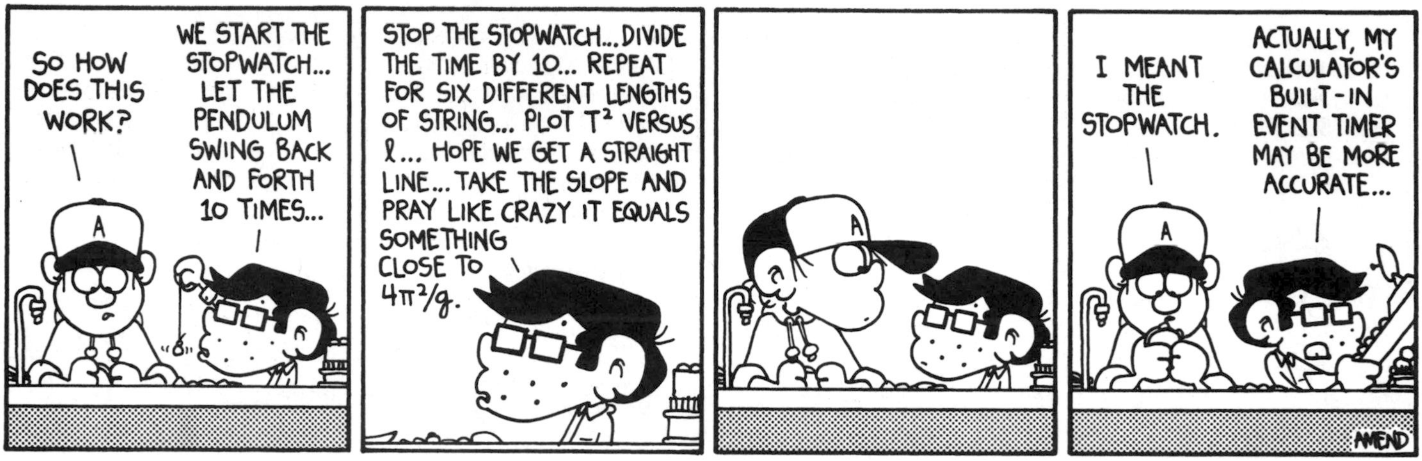
SO HOW DOES THIS WORK?
WE START THE STOPWATCH... LET THE PENDULUM SWING BACK AND FORTH 10 TIMES...
STOP THE STOPWATCH... DIVIDE THE TIME BY 10... REPEAT FOR SIX DIFFERENT LENGTHS OF STRING... PLOT T² VERSUS ℓ... HOPE WE GET A STRAIGHT LINE... TAKE THE SLOPE AND PRAY LIKE CRAZY IT EQUALS SOMETHING CLOSE TO 4π²/g.
I MEANT THE STOPWATCH.
ACTUALLY, MY CALCULATOR'S BUILT-IN EVENT TIMER MAY BE MORE ACCURATE...
AMEND

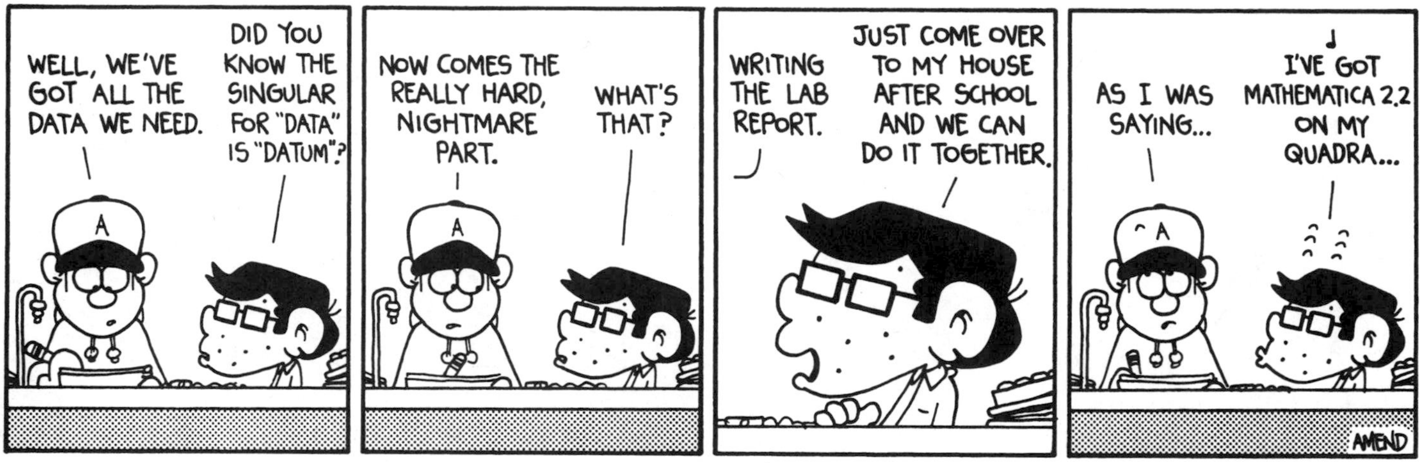
WELL, WE'VE GOT ALL THE DATA WE NEED.
DID YOU KNOW THE SINGULAR FOR "DATA" IS "DATUM"?
NOW COMES THE REALLY HARD, NIGHTMARE PART.
WHAT'S THAT?
WRITING THE LAB REPORT.
JUST COME OVER TO MY HOUSE AFTER SCHOOL AND WE CAN DO IT TOGETHER.
AS I WAS SAYING...
I'VE GOT MATHEMATICA 2.2 ON MY QUADRA...
AMEND

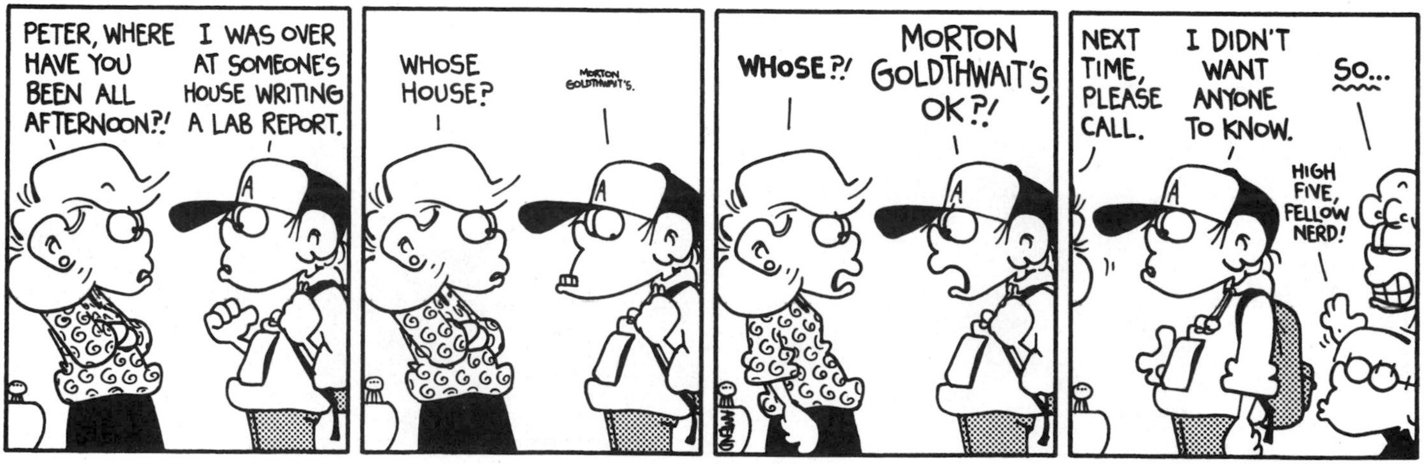
PETER, WHERE HAVE YOU BEEN ALL AFTERNOON?!
I WAS OVER AT SOMEONE'S HOUSE WRITING A LAB REPORT.
WHOSE HOUSE?
MORTON GOLDTHWAIT'S.
WHOSE?!
MORTON GOLDTHWAIT'S, OK?!
AMEND
NEXT TIME, PLEASE CALL.
I DIDN'T WANT ANYONE TO KNOW.
SO...
HIGH FIVE, FELLOW NERD!

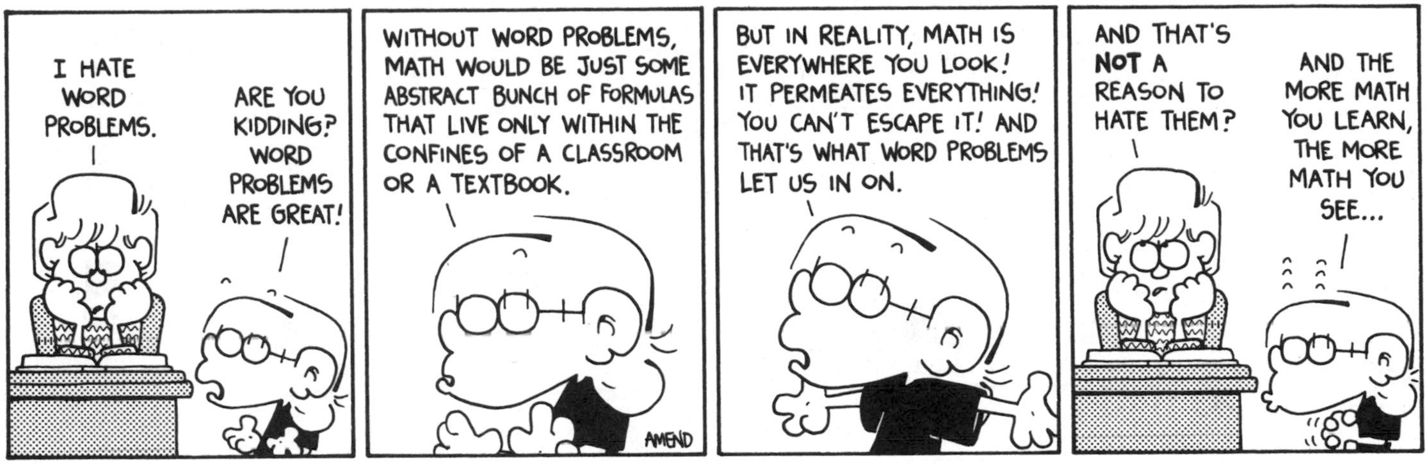
I HATE WORD PROBLEMS.
ARE YOU KIDDING? WORD PROBLEMS ARE GREAT!
WITHOUT WORD PROBLEMS, MATH WOULD BE JUST SOME ABSTRACT BUNCH OF FORMULAS THAT LIVE ONLY WITHIN THE CONFINES OF A CLASSROOM OR A TEXTBOOK.
AMEND
BUT IN REALITY, MATH IS EVERYWHERE YOU LOOK! IT PERMEATES EVERYTHING! YOU CAN'T ESCAPE IT! AND THAT'S WHAT WORD PROBLEMS LET US IN ON.
AND THAT'S **NOT** A REASON TO HATE THEM?
AND THE MORE MATH YOU LEARN, THE MORE MATH YOU SEE...

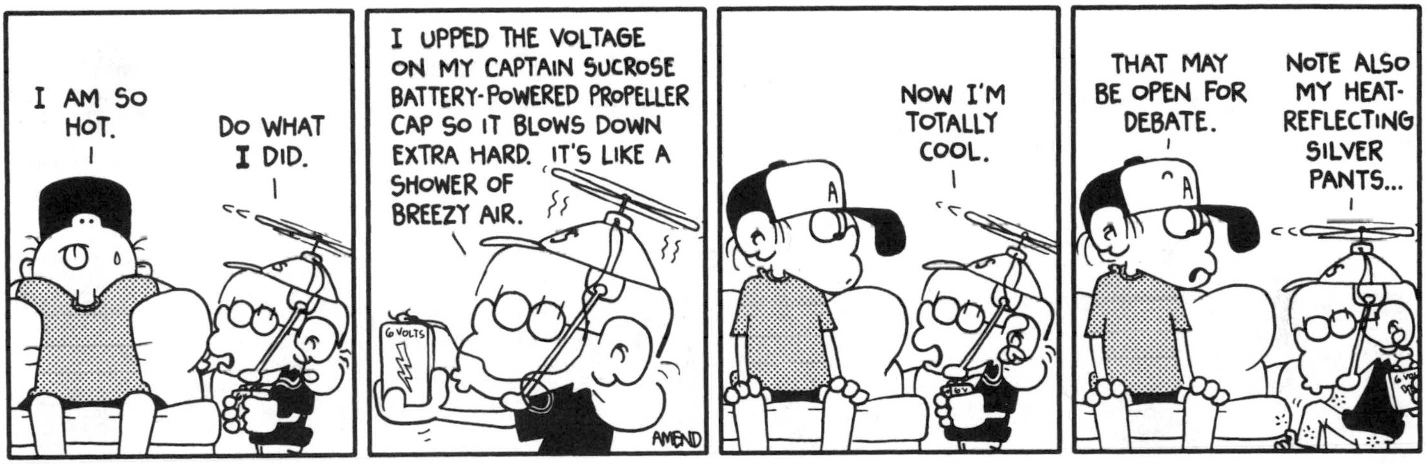
I AM SO HOT.
DO WHAT **I** DID.
I UPPED THE VOLTAGE ON MY CAPTAIN SUCROSE BATTERY-POWERED PROPELLER CAP SO IT BLOWS DOWN EXTRA HARD. IT'S LIKE A SHOWER OF BREEZY AIR.
6 VOLTS
AMEND
NOW I'M TOTALLY COOL.
THAT MAY BE OPEN FOR DEBATE.
NOTE ALSO MY HEAT-REFLECTING SILVER PANTS...

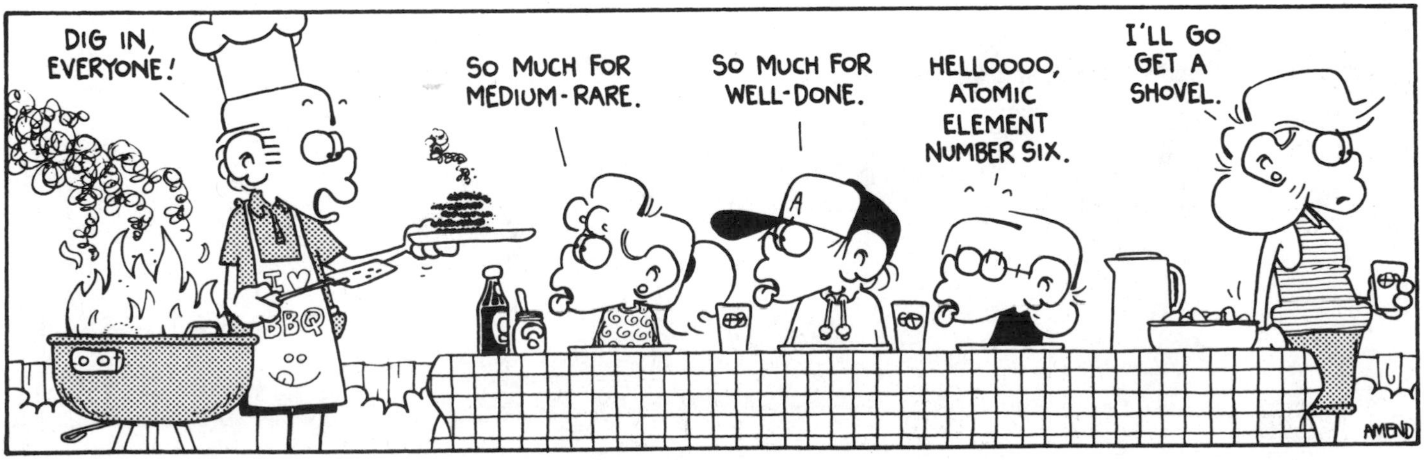
DIG IN, EVERYONE!
SO MUCH FOR MEDIUM-RARE.
SO MUCH FOR WELL-DONE.
HELLOOOO, ATOMIC ELEMENT NUMBER SIX.
I'LL GO GET A SHOVEL.
AMEND

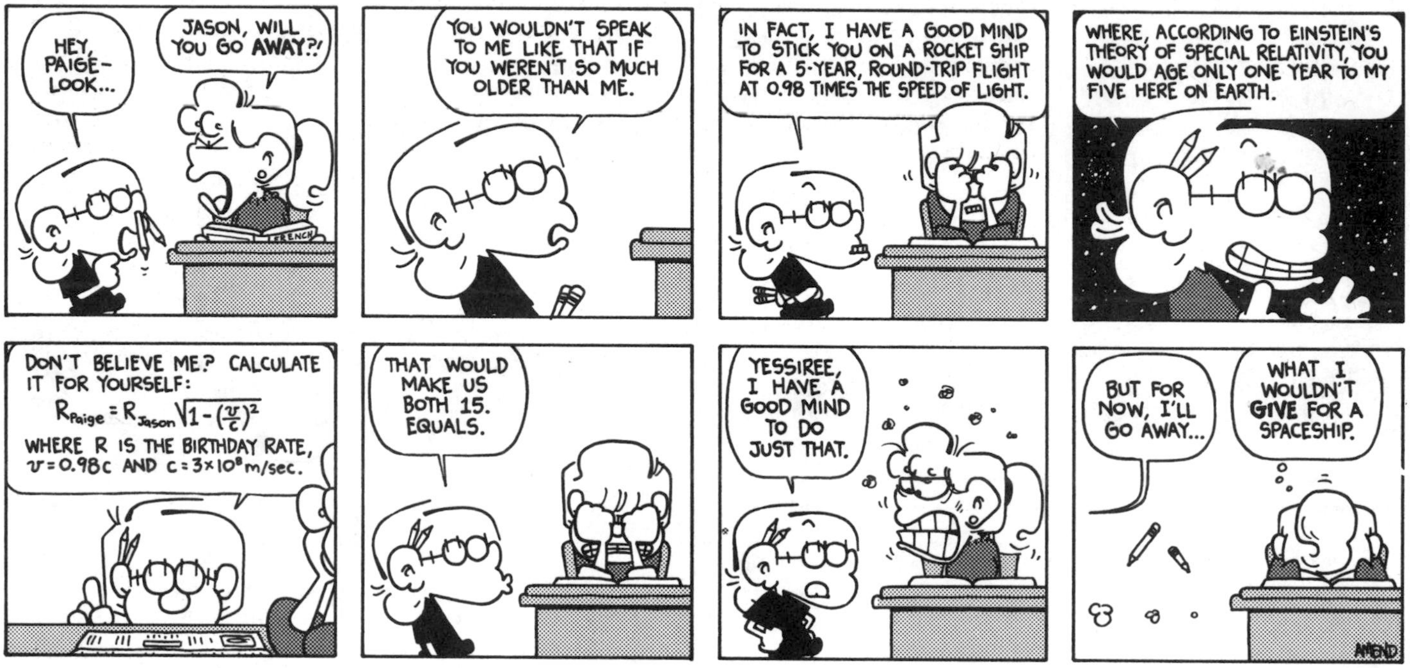
HEY, PAIGE-LOOK...
JASON, WILL YOU GO **AWAY**?!
FRENCH
YOU WOULDN'T SPEAK TO ME LIKE THAT IF YOU WEREN'T SO MUCH OLDER THAN ME.
IN FACT, I HAVE A GOOD MIND TO STICK YOU ON A ROCKET SHIP FOR A 5-YEAR, ROUND-TRIP FLIGHT AT 0.98 TIMES THE SPEED OF LIGHT.
WHERE, ACCORDING TO EINSTEIN'S THEORY OF SPECIAL RELATIVITY, YOU WOULD AGE ONLY ONE YEAR TO MY FIVE HERE ON EARTH.
DON'T BELIEVE ME? CALCULATE IT FOR YOURSELF:
$R_{Paige} = R_{Jason}\sqrt{1-(\frac{v}{c})^2}$
WHERE R IS THE BIRTHDAY RATE, $v = 0.98c$ AND $c = 3\times10^8$ m/sec.
THAT WOULD MAKE US BOTH 15. EQUALS.
YESSIREE, I HAVE A GOOD MIND TO DO JUST THAT.
BUT FOR NOW, I'LL GO AWAY...
WHAT I WOULDN'T **GIVE** FOR A SPACESHIP.
AMEND

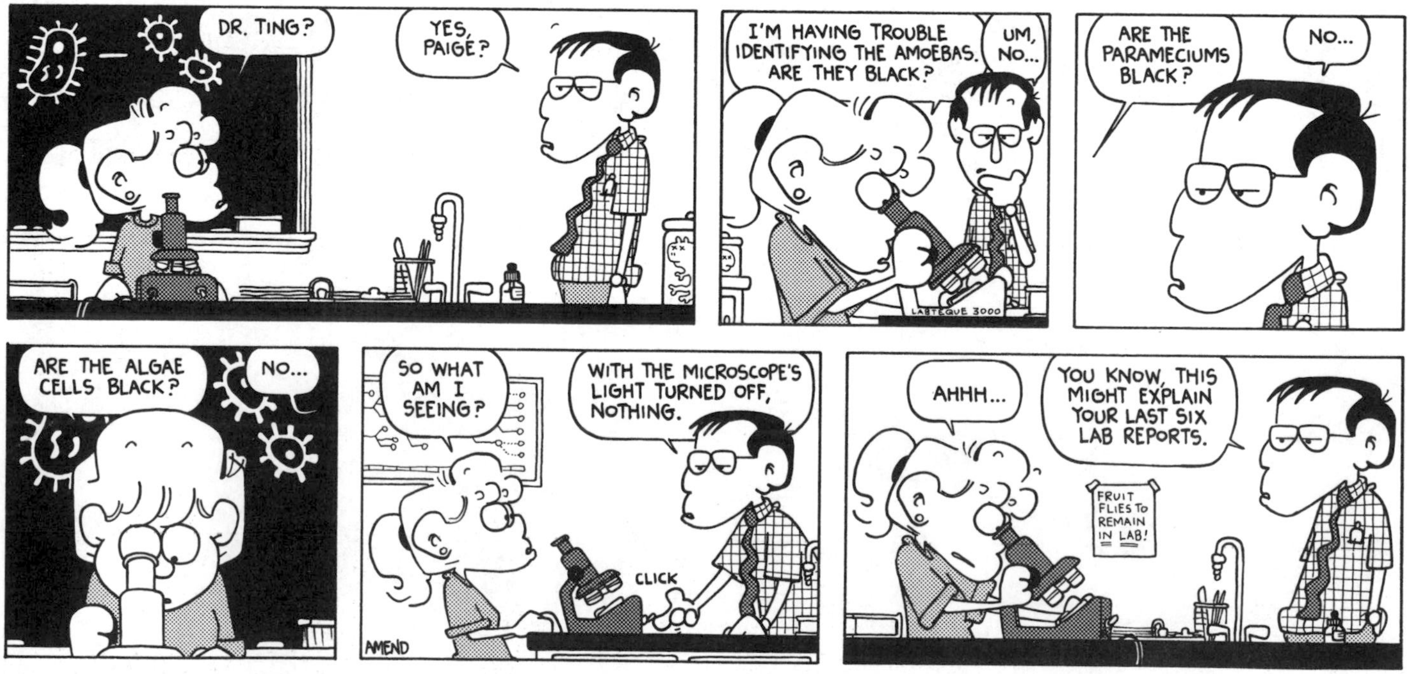
DR. TING?
YES, PAIGE?
I'M HAVING TROUBLE IDENTIFYING THE AMOEBAS. ARE THEY BLACK?
UM, NO...
LABTEQUE 3000
ARE THE PARAMECIUMS BLACK?
NO...
ARE THE ALGAE CELLS BLACK?
NO...
SO WHAT AM I SEEING?
WITH THE MICROSCOPE'S LIGHT TURNED OFF, NOTHING.
CLICK
AMEND
AHHH...
YOU KNOW, THIS MIGHT EXPLAIN YOUR LAST SIX LAB REPORTS.
FRUIT FLIES TO REMAIN IN LAB!

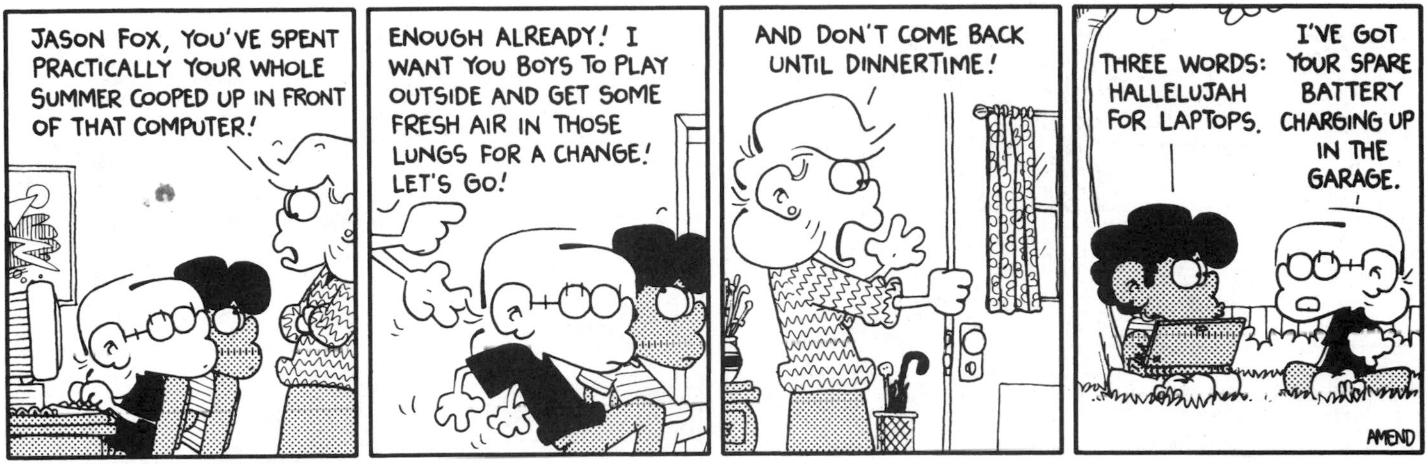
JASON FOX, YOU'VE SPENT PRACTICALLY YOUR WHOLE SUMMER COOPED UP IN FRONT OF THAT COMPUTER!
ENOUGH ALREADY! I WANT YOU BOYS TO PLAY OUTSIDE AND GET SOME FRESH AIR IN THOSE LUNGS FOR A CHANGE! LET'S GO!
AND DON'T COME BACK UNTIL DINNERTIME!
THREE WORDS: HALLELUJAH FOR LAPTOPS.
I'VE GOT YOUR SPARE BATTERY CHARGING UP IN THE GARAGE.
AMEND

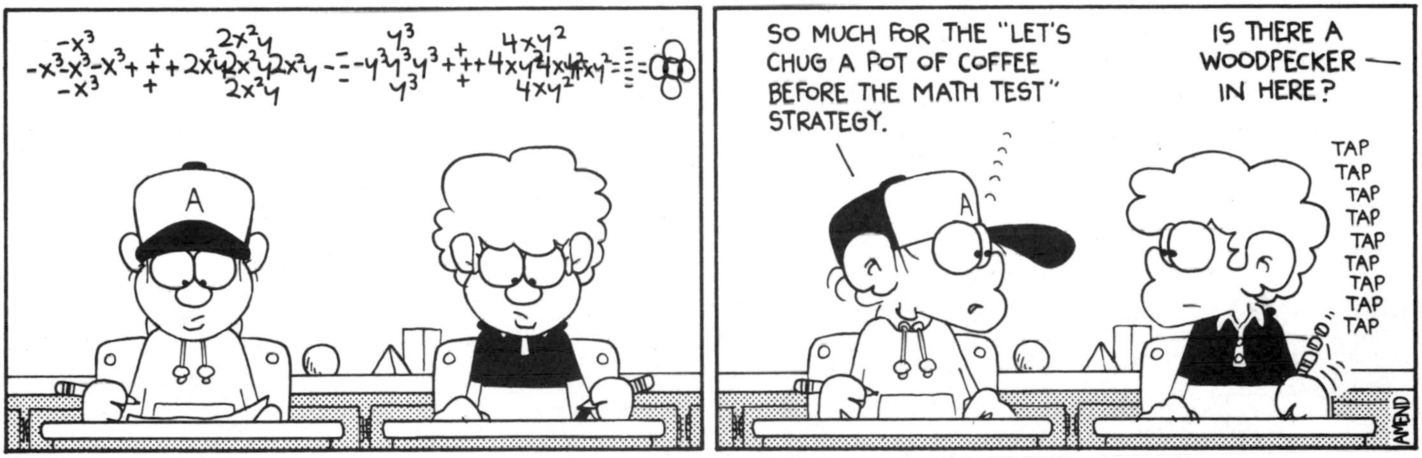
SO MUCH FOR THE "LET'S CHUG A POT OF COFFEE BEFORE THE MATH TEST" STRATEGY.
IS THERE A WOODPECKER IN HERE?
TAP TAP TAP TAP TAP TAP TAP TAP TAP
AMEND

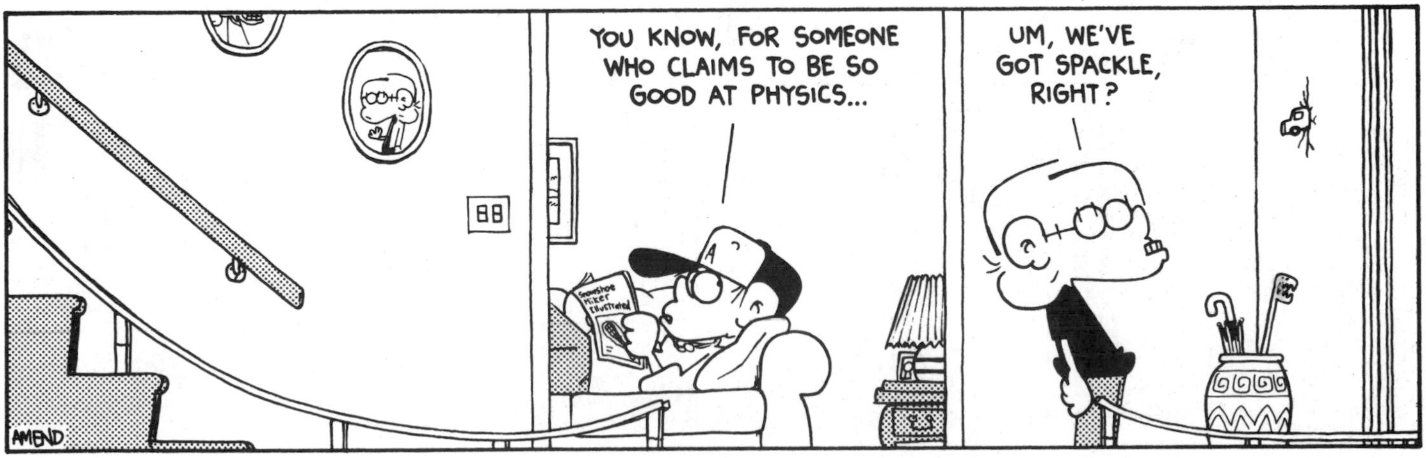
AMEND
YOU KNOW, FOR SOMEONE WHO CLAIMS TO BE SO GOOD AT PHYSICS...
UM, WE'VE GOT SPACKLE, RIGHT?

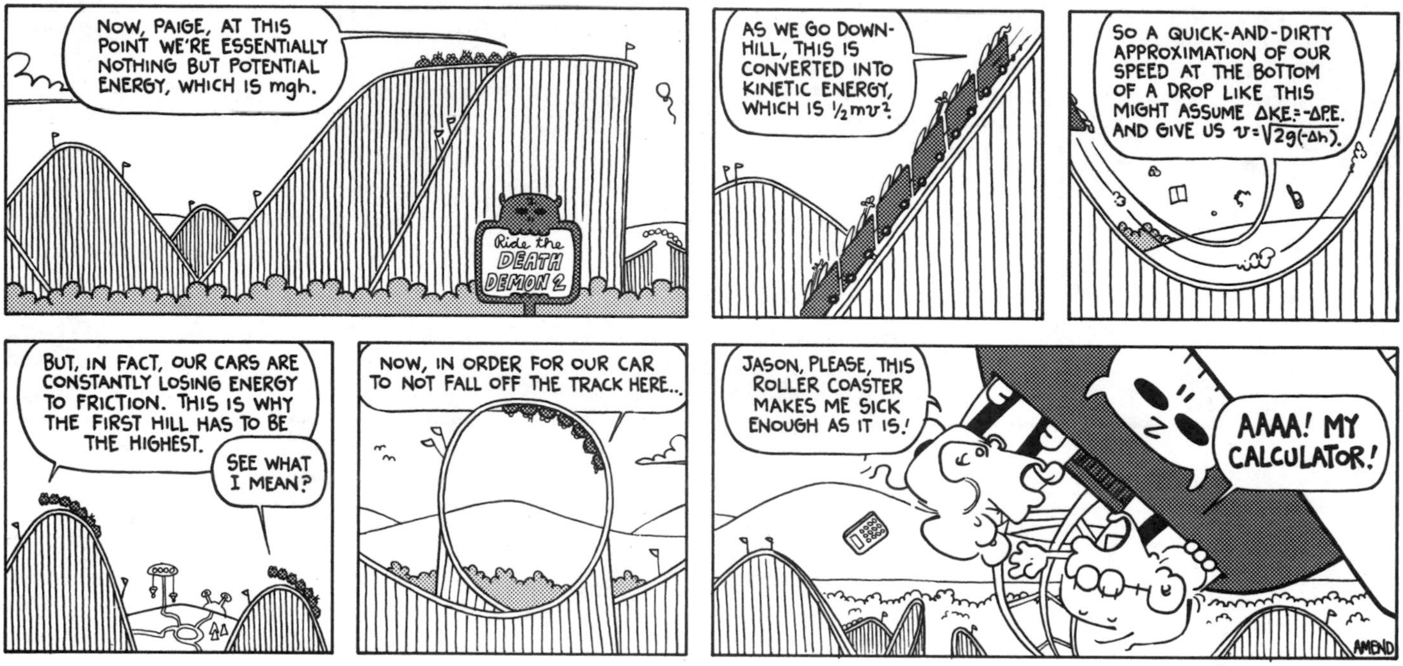
NOW, PAIGE, AT THIS POINT WE'RE ESSENTIALLY NOTHING BUT POTENTIAL ENERGY, WHICH IS mgh.
Ride the DEATH DEMON 2
AS WE GO DOWNHILL, THIS IS CONVERTED INTO KINETIC ENERGY, WHICH IS $\frac{1}{2}mv^2$.
SO A QUICK-AND-DIRTY APPROXIMATION OF OUR SPEED AT THE BOTTOM OF A DROP LIKE THIS MIGHT ASSUME $\Delta KE = -\Delta PE$. AND GIVE US $v = \sqrt{2g(-\Delta h)}$.
BUT, IN FACT, OUR CARS ARE CONSTANTLY LOSING ENERGY TO FRICTION. THIS IS WHY THE FIRST HILL HAS TO BE THE HIGHEST.
SEE WHAT I MEAN?
NOW, IN ORDER FOR OUR CAR TO NOT FALL OFF THE TRACK HERE...
JASON, PLEASE, THIS ROLLER COASTER MAKES ME SICK ENOUGH AS IT IS!
AAAA! MY CALCULATOR!
AMEND

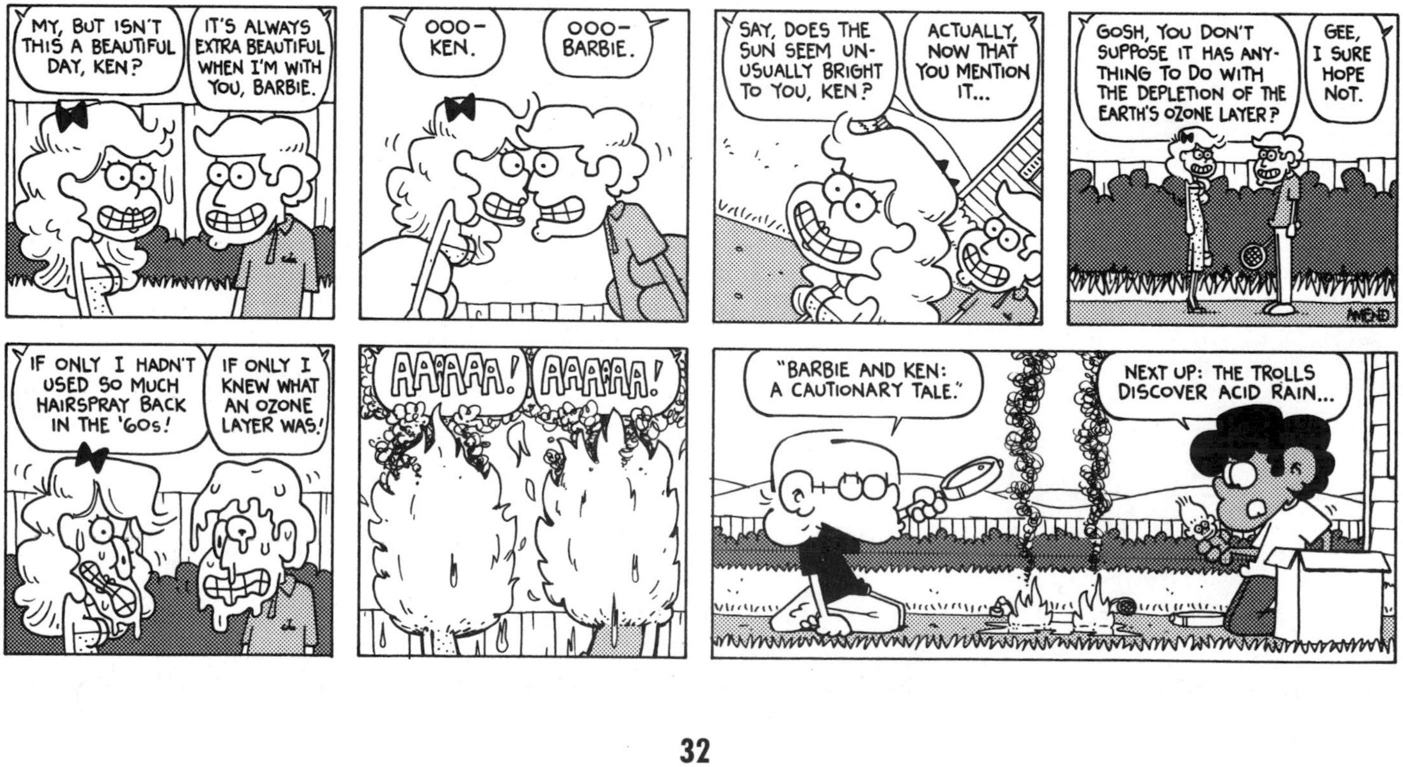
MY, BUT ISN'T THIS A BEAUTIFUL DAY, KEN?
IT'S ALWAYS EXTRA BEAUTIFUL WHEN I'M WITH YOU, BARBIE.
OOO-KEN.
OOO-BARBIE.
SAY, DOES THE SUN SEEM UNUSUALLY BRIGHT TO YOU, KEN?
ACTUALLY, NOW THAT YOU MENTION IT...
GOSH, YOU DON'T SUPPOSE IT HAS ANYTHING TO DO WITH THE DEPLETION OF THE EARTH'S OZONE LAYER?
GEE, I SURE HOPE NOT.
AMEND
IF ONLY I HADN'T USED SO MUCH HAIRSPRAY BACK IN THE '60s!
IF ONLY I KNEW WHAT AN OZONE LAYER WAS!
AAAAAA!
AAAAAA!
"BARBIE AND KEN: A CAUTIONARY TALE."
NEXT UP: THE TROLLS DISCOVER ACID RAIN...

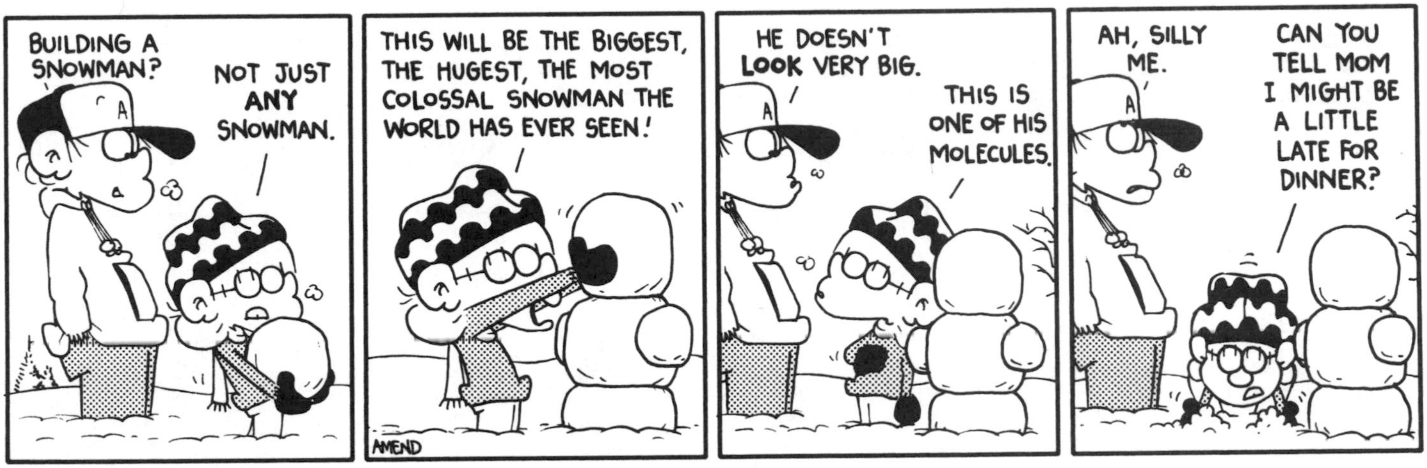
BUILDING A SNOWMAN?
NOT JUST ANY SNOWMAN.
THIS WILL BE THE BIGGEST, THE HUGEST, THE MOST COLOSSAL SNOWMAN THE WORLD HAS EVER SEEN!
AMEND
HE DOESN'T LOOK VERY BIG.
THIS IS ONE OF HIS MOLECULES.
AH, SILLY ME.
CAN YOU TELL MOM I MIGHT BE A LITTLE LATE FOR DINNER?

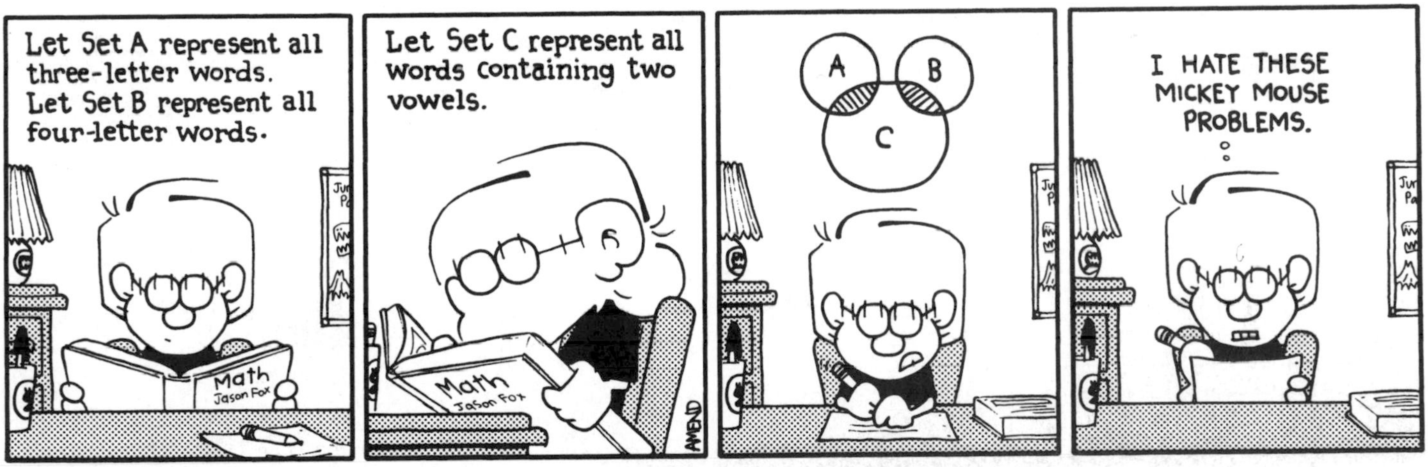
Let Set A represent all three-letter words.
Let Set B represent all four-letter words.
Math
Jason Fox
Let Set C represent all words containing two vowels.
Math
Jason Fox
AMEND
A
B
C
I HATE THESE MICKEY MOUSE PROBLEMS.

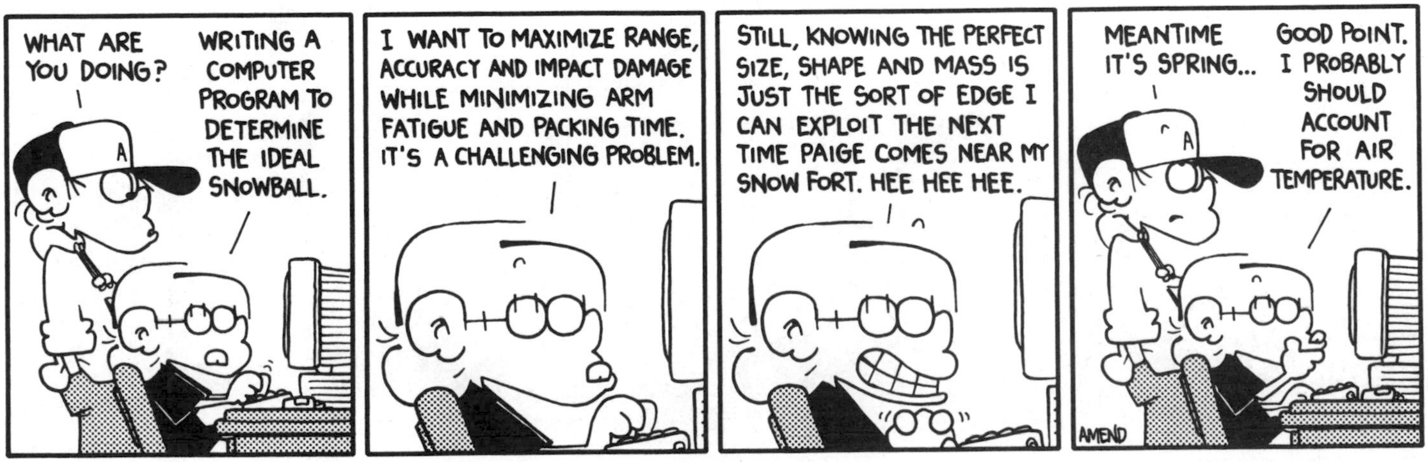
WHAT ARE YOU DOING?
WRITING A COMPUTER PROGRAM TO DETERMINE THE IDEAL SNOWBALL.
I WANT TO MAXIMIZE RANGE, ACCURACY AND IMPACT DAMAGE WHILE MINIMIZING ARM FATIGUE AND PACKING TIME. IT'S A CHALLENGING PROBLEM.
STILL, KNOWING THE PERFECT SIZE, SHAPE AND MASS IS JUST THE SORT OF EDGE I CAN EXPLOIT THE NEXT TIME PAIGE COMES NEAR MY SNOW FORT. HEE HEE HEE.
MEANTIME IT'S SPRING...
GOOD POINT. I PROBABLY SHOULD ACCOUNT FOR AIR TEMPERATURE.
AMEND

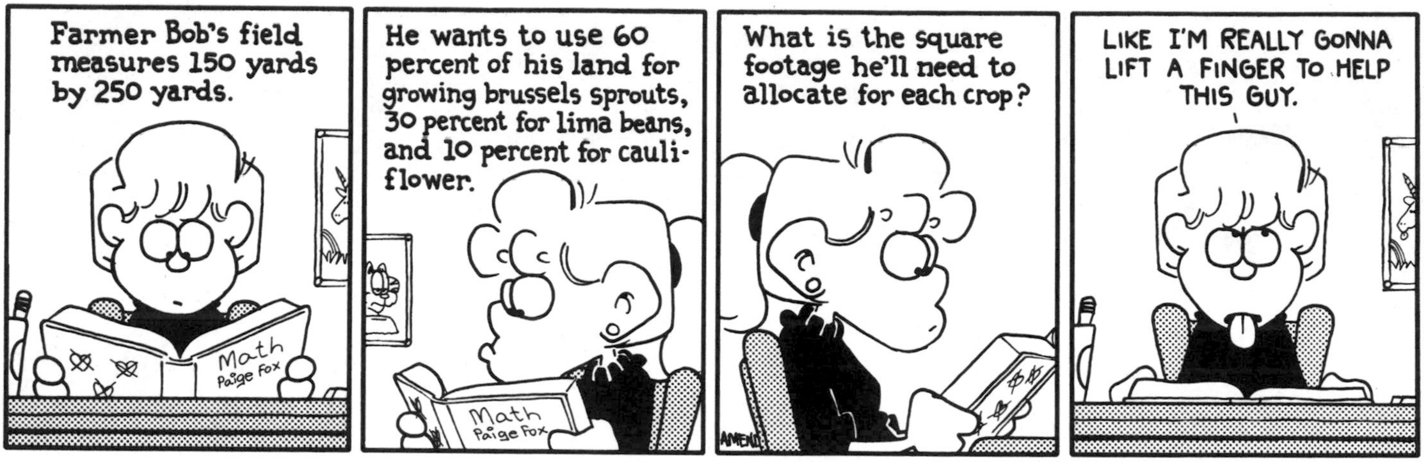
Farmer Bob's field measures 150 yards by 250 yards.
He wants to use 60 percent of his land for growing brussels sprouts, 30 percent for lima beans, and 10 percent for cauli-flower.
What is the square footage he'll need to allocate for each crop?
LIKE I'M REALLY GONNA LIFT A FINGER TO HELP THIS GUY.
Math
Paige Fox
AMEND

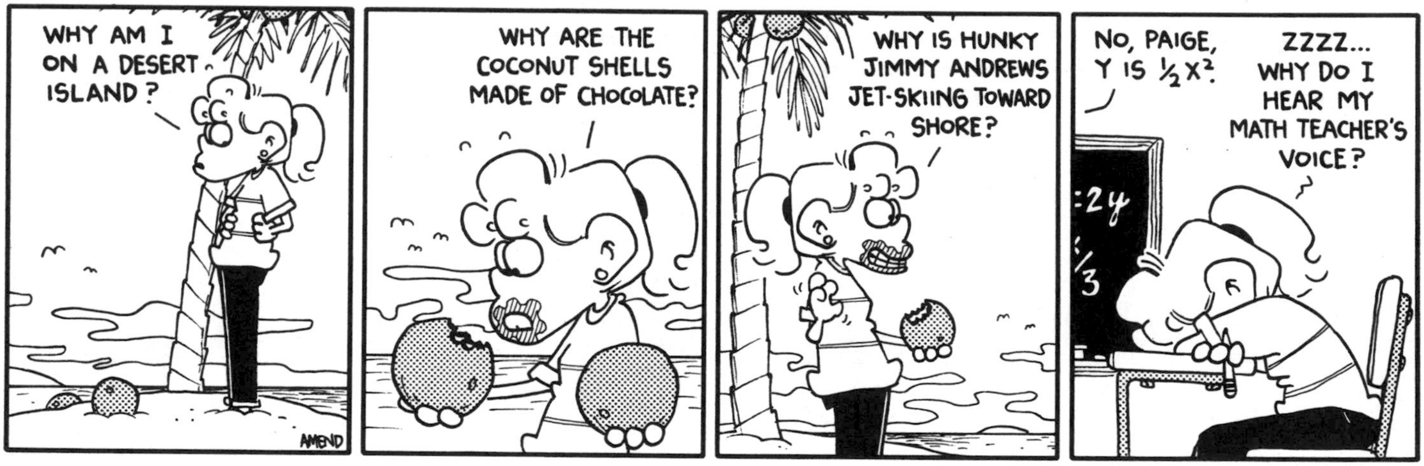
WHY AM I ON A DESERT ISLAND?
WHY ARE THE COCONUT SHELLS MADE OF CHOCOLATE?
WHY IS HUNKY JIMMY ANDREWS JET-SKIING TOWARD SHORE?
NO, PAIGE, Y IS $\frac{1}{2}X^2$.
ZZZZ... WHY DO I HEAR MY MATH TEACHER'S VOICE?
AMEND

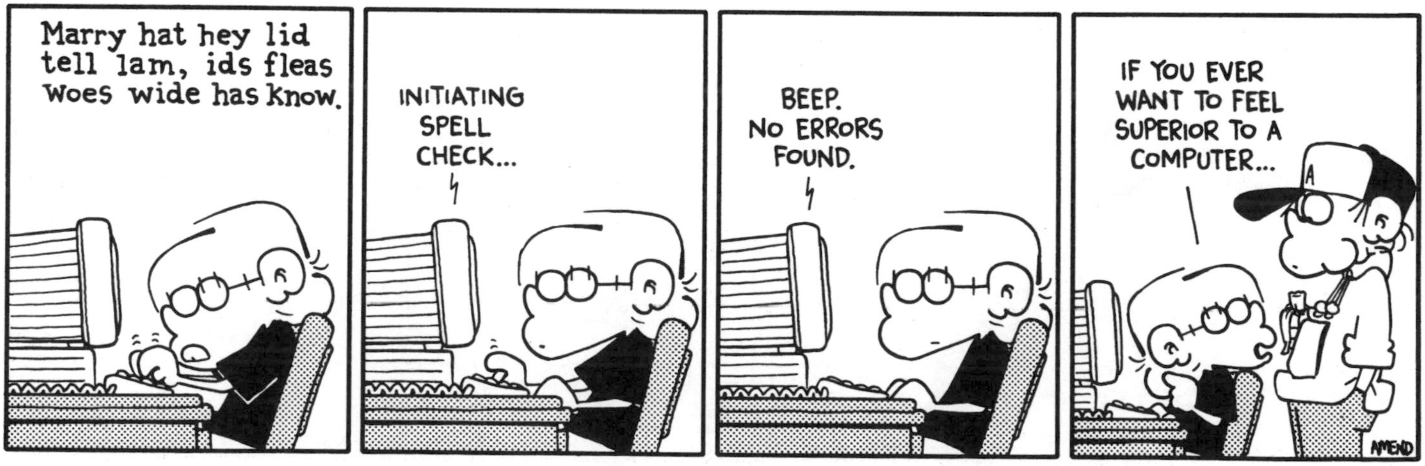
Marry hat hey lid tell lam, ids fleas woes wide has know.
INITIATING SPELL CHECK...
BEEP. NO ERRORS FOUND.
IF YOU EVER WANT TO FEEL SUPERIOR TO A COMPUTER...
AMEND

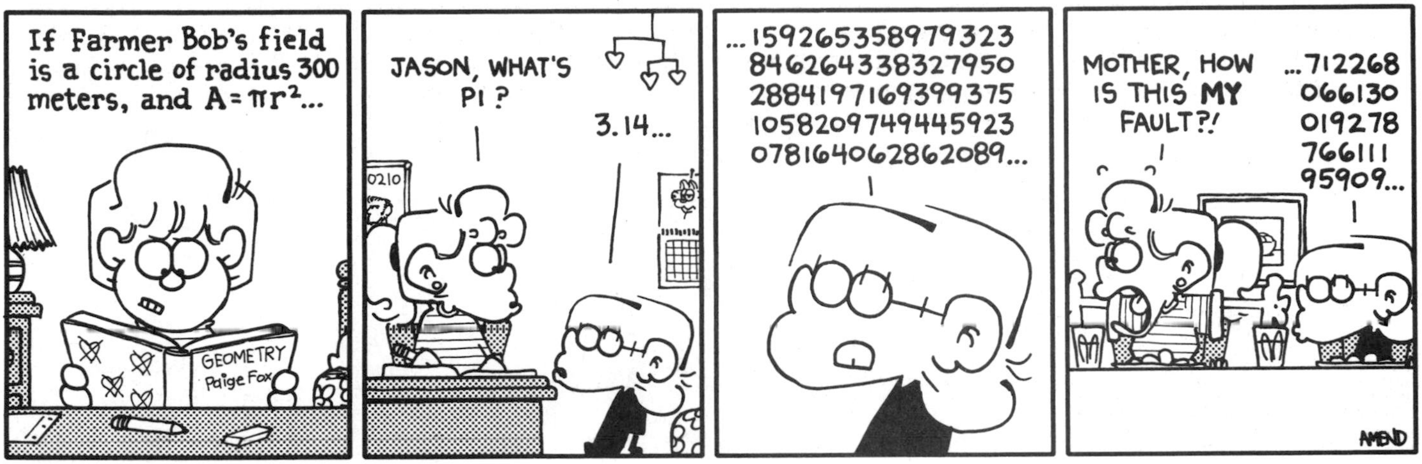
If Farmer Bob's field is a circle of radius 300 meters, and A=πr²...
GEOMETRY Paige Fox
JASON, WHAT'S PI?
3.14...
...159265358979323
846264338327950
2884197169399375
1058209749445923
078164062862089...
MOTHER, HOW IS THIS **MY** FAULT?!
...712268
066130
019278
766111
95909...
AMEND

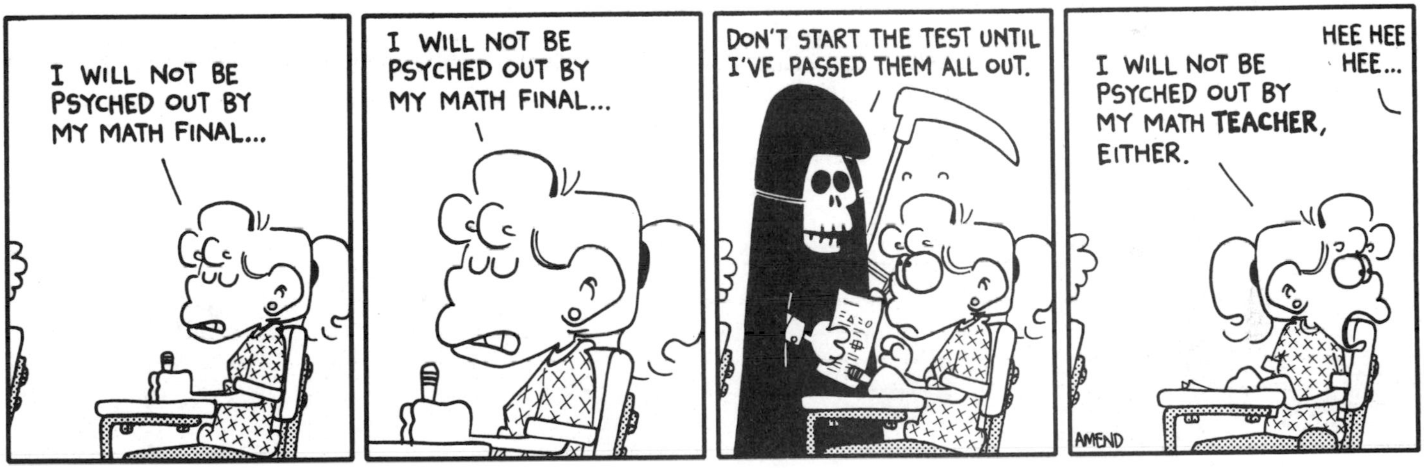
I WILL NOT BE PSYCHED OUT BY MY MATH FINAL...
I WILL NOT BE PSYCHED OUT BY MY MATH FINAL...
DON'T START THE TEST UNTIL I'VE PASSED THEM ALL OUT.
I WILL NOT BE PSYCHED OUT BY MY MATH **TEACHER**, EITHER.
HEE HEE HEE...
AMEND

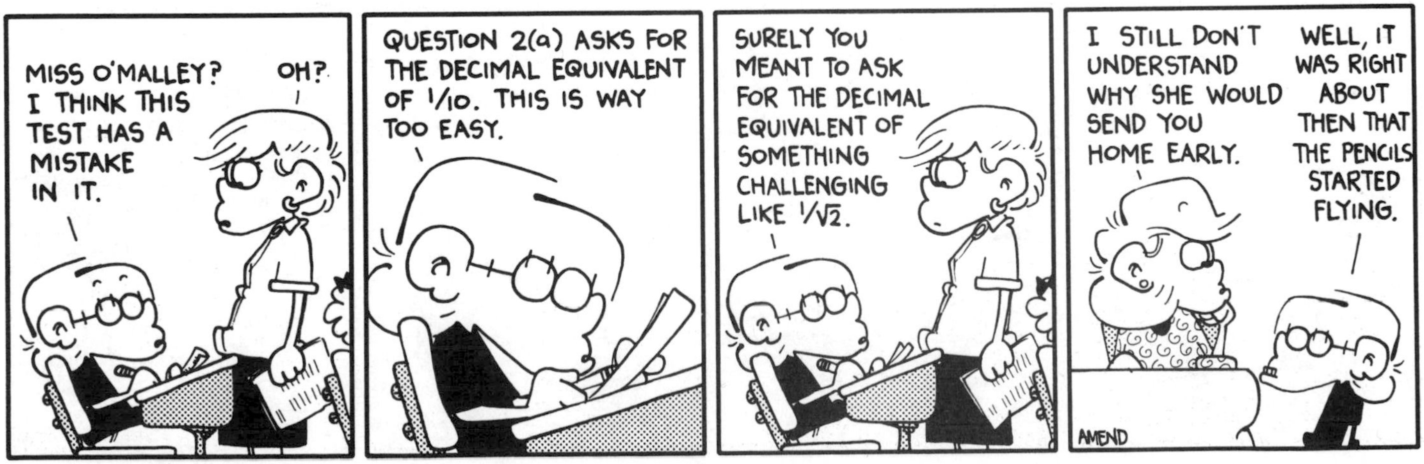
MISS O'MALLEY? I THINK THIS TEST HAS A MISTAKE IN IT.
OH?
QUESTION 2(a) ASKS FOR THE DECIMAL EQUIVALENT OF 1/10. THIS IS WAY TOO EASY.
SURELY YOU MEANT TO ASK FOR THE DECIMAL EQUIVALENT OF SOMETHING CHALLENGING LIKE 1/√2.
I STILL DON'T UNDERSTAND WHY SHE WOULD SEND YOU HOME EARLY.
WELL, IT WAS RIGHT ABOUT THEN THAT THE PENCILS STARTED FLYING.
AMEND

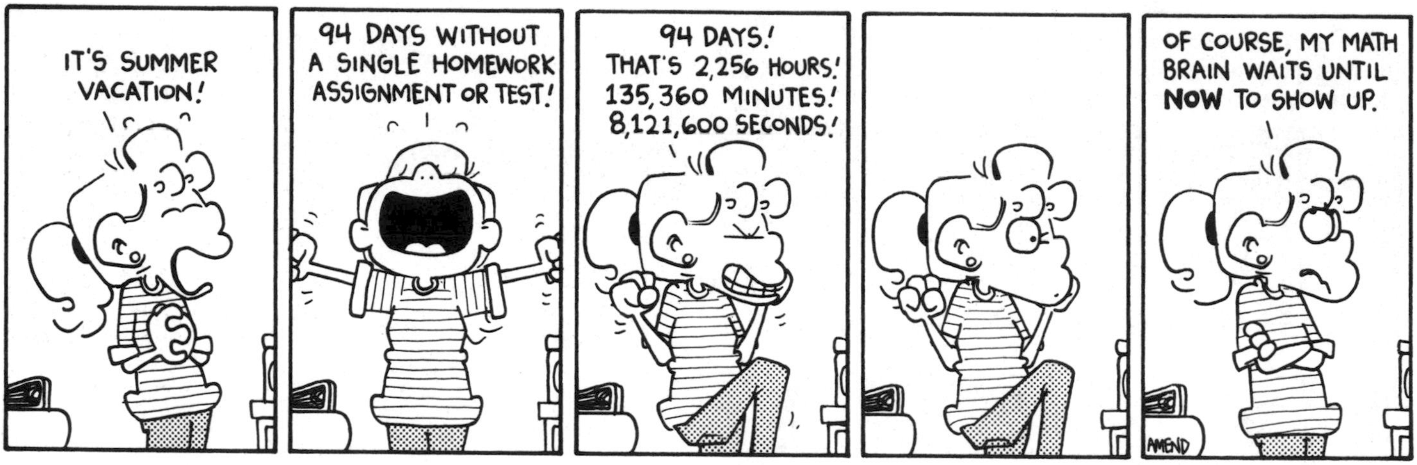
IT'S SUMMER VACATION!
94 DAYS WITHOUT A SINGLE HOMEWORK ASSIGNMENT OR TEST!
94 DAYS! THAT'S 2,256 HOURS! 135,360 MINUTES! 8,121,600 SECONDS!
OF COURSE, MY MATH BRAIN WAITS UNTIL NOW TO SHOW UP.
AMEND

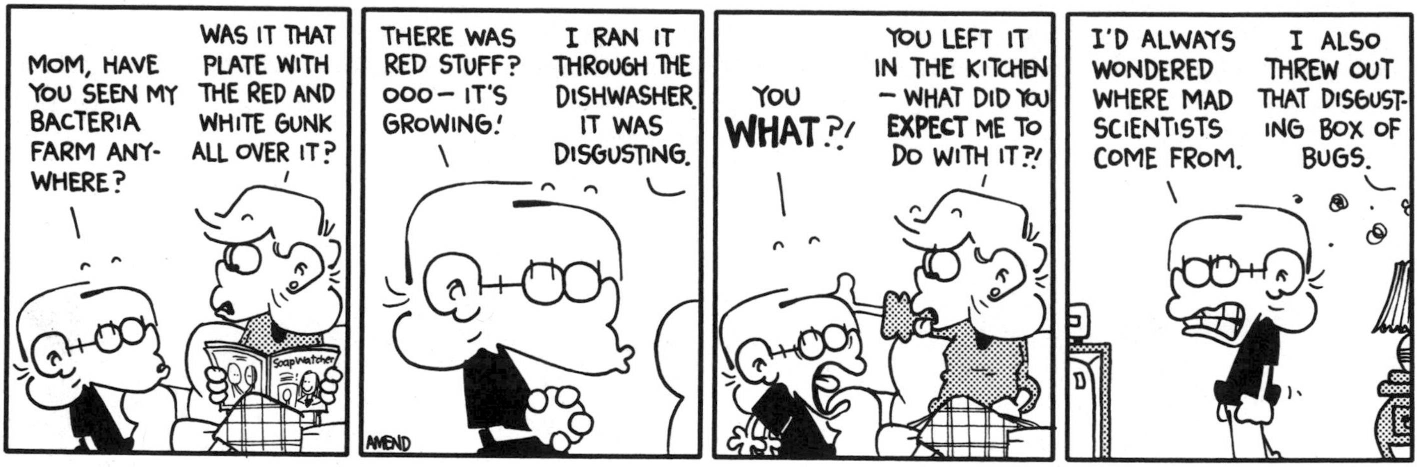
MOM, HAVE YOU SEEN MY BACTERIA FARM ANYWHERE?
WAS IT THAT PLATE WITH THE RED AND WHITE GUNK ALL OVER IT?
SoapWatcher
THERE WAS RED STUFF? OOO – IT'S GROWING!
I RAN IT THROUGH THE DISHWASHER. IT WAS DISGUSTING.
AMEND
YOU WHAT?!
YOU LEFT IT IN THE KITCHEN – WHAT DID YOU EXPECT ME TO DO WITH IT?!
I'D ALWAYS WONDERED WHERE MAD SCIENTISTS COME FROM.
I ALSO THREW OUT THAT DISGUSTING BOX OF BUGS.

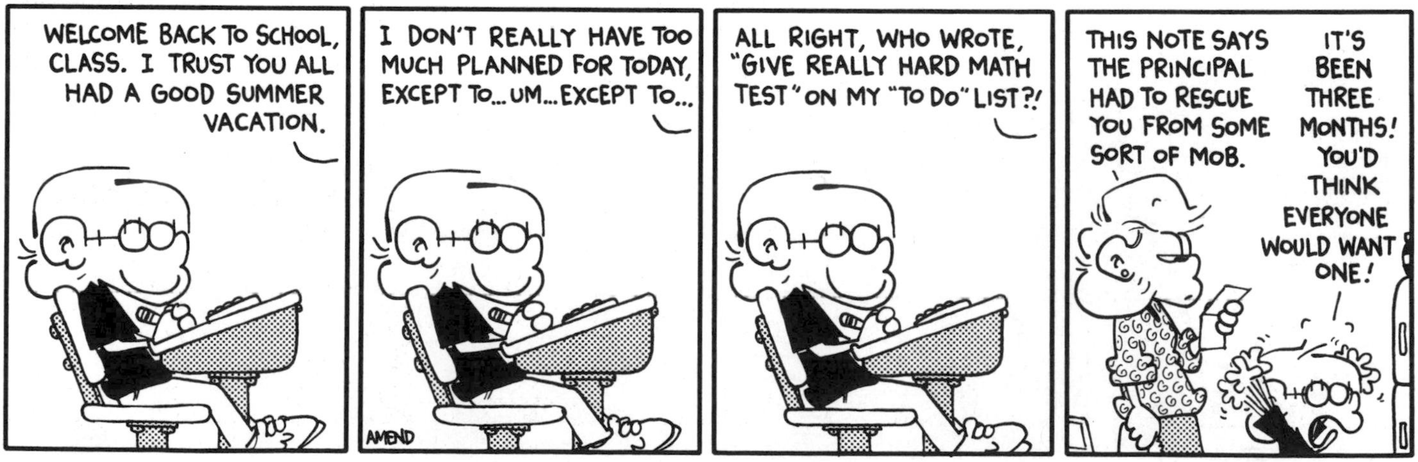
WELCOME BACK TO SCHOOL, CLASS. I TRUST YOU ALL HAD A GOOD SUMMER VACATION.
I DON'T REALLY HAVE TOO MUCH PLANNED FOR TODAY, EXCEPT TO... UM... EXCEPT TO...
AMEND
ALL RIGHT, WHO WROTE, "GIVE REALLY HARD MATH TEST" ON MY "TO DO" LIST?!
THIS NOTE SAYS THE PRINCIPAL HAD TO RESCUE YOU FROM SOME SORT OF MOB.
IT'S BEEN THREE MONTHS! YOU'D THINK EVERYONE WOULD WANT ONE!

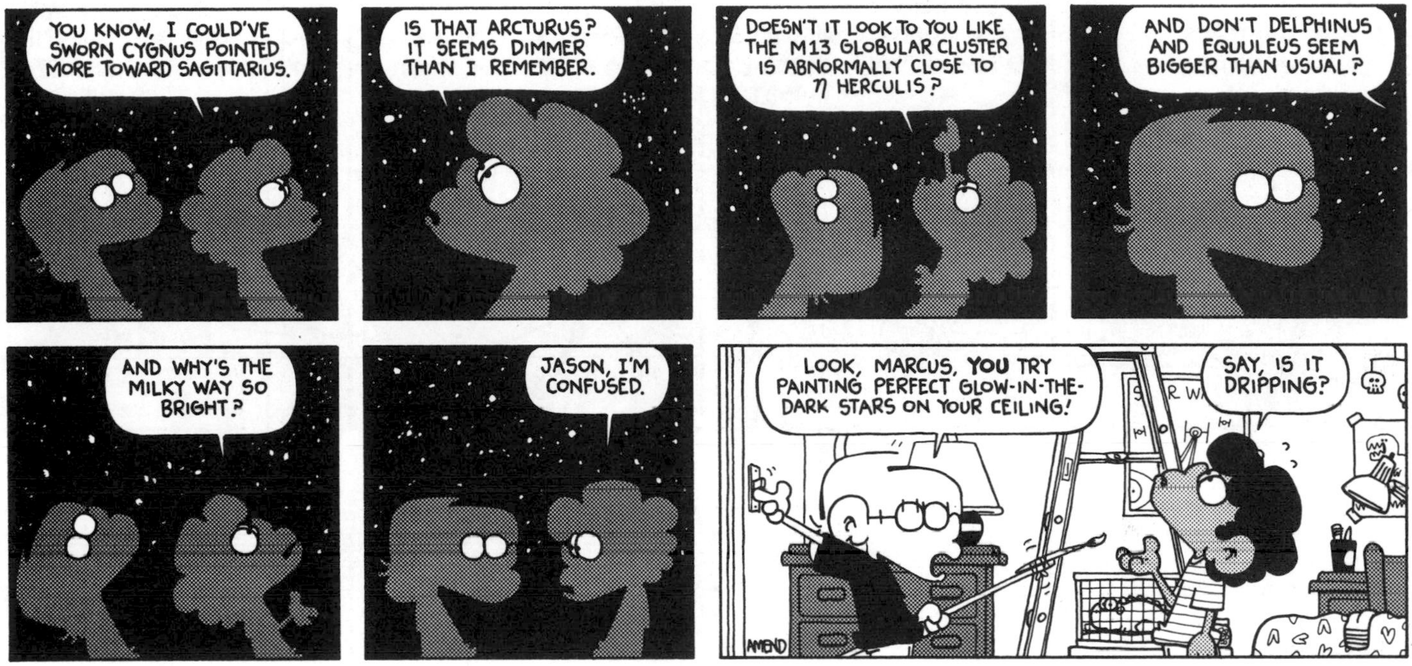
YOU KNOW, I COULD'VE SWORN CYGNUS POINTED MORE TOWARD SAGITTARIUS.
IS THAT ARCTURUS? IT SEEMS DIMMER THAN I REMEMBER.
DOESN'T IT LOOK TO YOU LIKE THE M13 GLOBULAR CLUSTER IS ABNORMALLY CLOSE TO η HERCULIS?
AND DON'T DELPHINUS AND EQUULEUS SEEM BIGGER THAN USUAL?
AND WHY'S THE MILKY WAY SO BRIGHT?
JASON, I'M CONFUSED.
LOOK, MARCUS, **YOU** TRY PAINTING PERFECT GLOW-IN-THE-DARK STARS ON YOUR CEILING!
SAY, IS IT DRIPPING?
AMEND

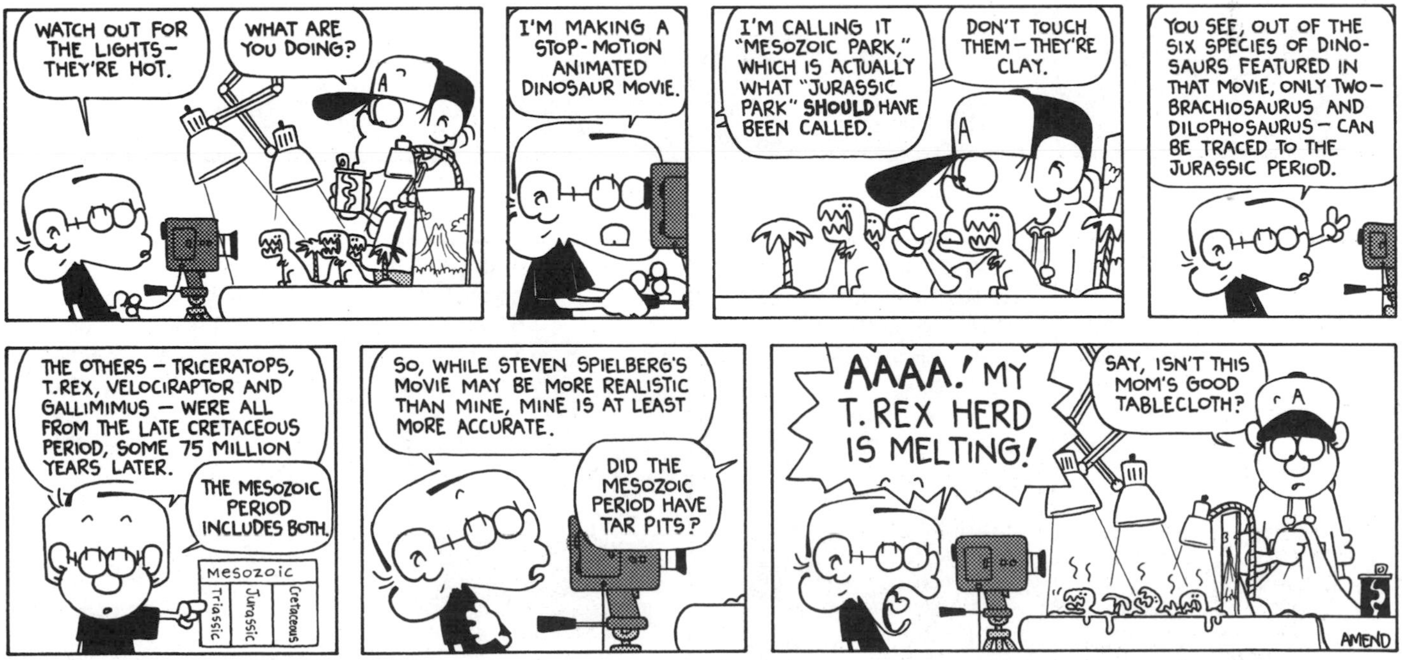
WATCH OUT FOR THE LIGHTS– THEY'RE HOT.
WHAT ARE YOU DOING?
I'M MAKING A STOP-MOTION ANIMATED DINOSAUR MOVIE.
I'M CALLING IT "MESOZOIC PARK," WHICH IS ACTUALLY WHAT "JURASSIC PARK" **SHOULD** HAVE BEEN CALLED.
DON'T TOUCH THEM– THEY'RE CLAY.
YOU SEE, OUT OF THE SIX SPECIES OF DINOSAURS FEATURED IN THAT MOVIE, ONLY TWO– BRACHIOSAURUS AND DILOPHOSAURUS– CAN BE TRACED TO THE JURASSIC PERIOD.
THE OTHERS – TRICERATOPS, T. REX, VELOCIRAPTOR AND GALLIMIMUS – WERE ALL FROM THE LATE CRETACEOUS PERIOD, SOME 75 MILLION YEARS LATER.
THE MESOZOIC PERIOD INCLUDES BOTH.
Mesozoic
Triassic
Jurassic
Cretaceous
SO, WHILE STEVEN SPIELBERG'S MOVIE MAY BE MORE REALISTIC THAN MINE, MINE IS AT LEAST MORE ACCURATE.
DID THE MESOZOIC PERIOD HAVE TAR PITS?
AAAA! MY T. REX HERD IS MELTING!
SAY, ISN'T THIS MOM'S GOOD TABLECLOTH?
AMEND

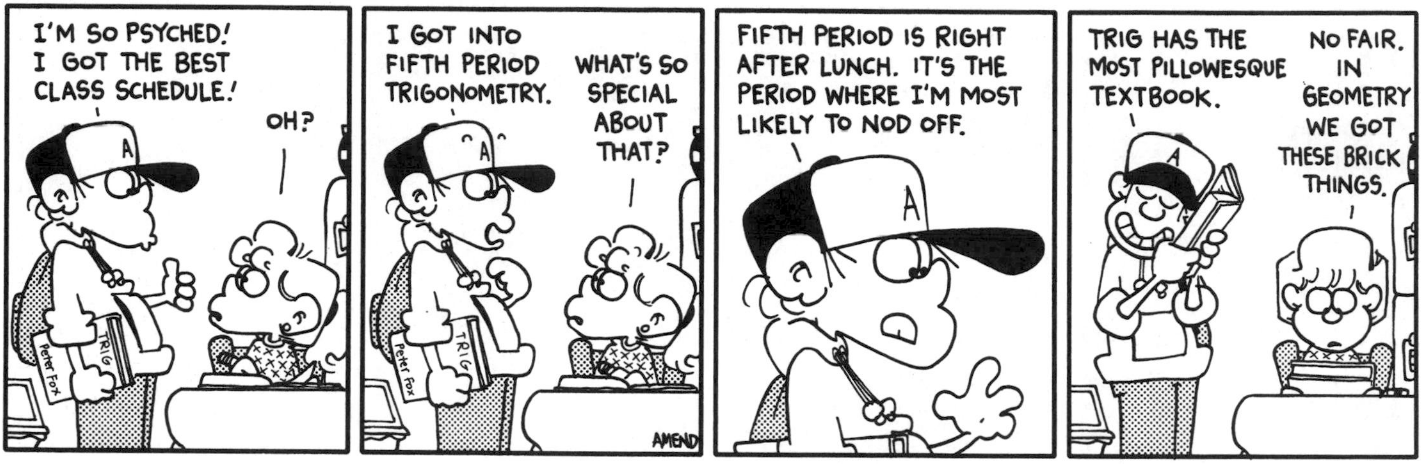
I'M SO PSYCHED! I GOT THE BEST CLASS SCHEDULE!
OH?
Peter Fox
TRIG
I GOT INTO FIFTH PERIOD TRIGONOMETRY.
WHAT'S SO SPECIAL ABOUT THAT?
AMEND
FIFTH PERIOD IS RIGHT AFTER LUNCH. IT'S THE PERIOD WHERE I'M MOST LIKELY TO NOD OFF.
TRIG HAS THE MOST PILLOWESQUE TEXTBOOK.
NO FAIR. IN GEOMETRY WE GOT THESE BRICK THINGS.

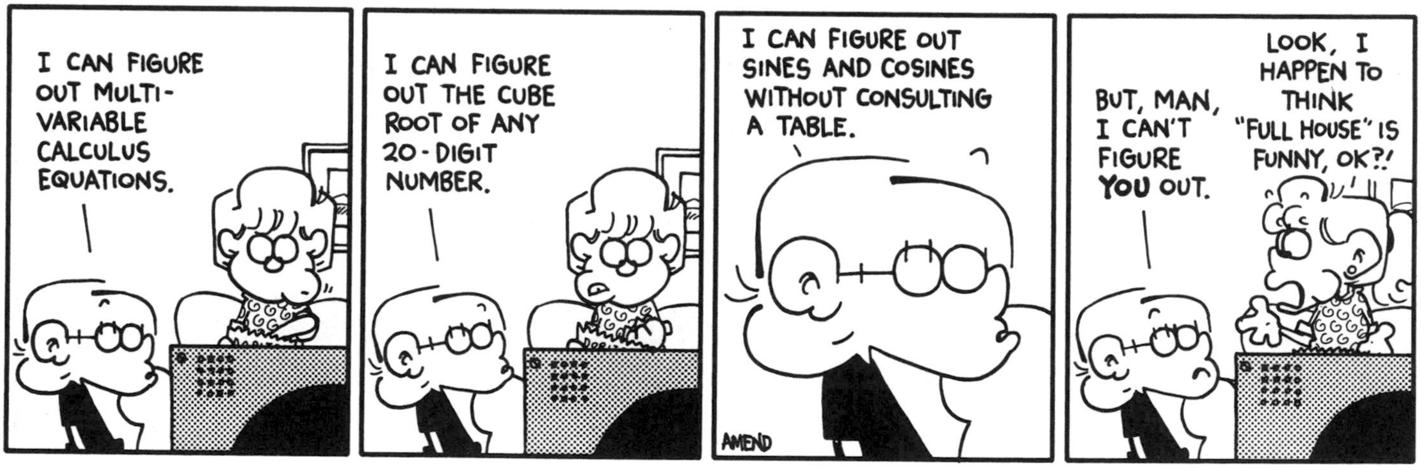
I CAN FIGURE OUT MULTI-VARIABLE CALCULUS EQUATIONS.
I CAN FIGURE OUT THE CUBE ROOT OF ANY 20-DIGIT NUMBER.
I CAN FIGURE OUT SINES AND COSINES WITHOUT CONSULTING A TABLE.
AMEND
BUT, MAN, I CAN'T FIGURE **YOU** OUT.
LOOK, I HAPPEN TO THINK "FULL HOUSE" IS FUNNY, OK?!

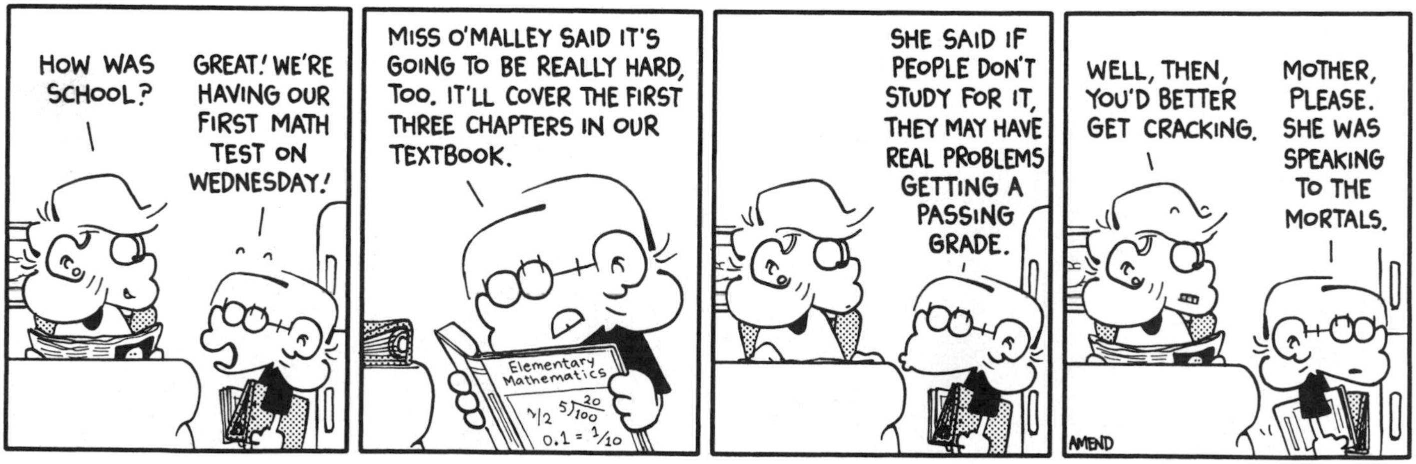
HOW WAS SCHOOL?
GREAT! WE'RE HAVING OUR FIRST MATH TEST ON WEDNESDAY!
MISS O'MALLEY SAID IT'S GOING TO BE REALLY HARD, TOO. IT'LL COVER THE FIRST THREE CHAPTERS IN OUR TEXTBOOK.
Elementary Mathematics
SHE SAID IF PEOPLE DON'T STUDY FOR IT, THEY MAY HAVE REAL PROBLEMS GETTING A PASSING GRADE.
WELL, THEN, YOU'D BETTER GET CRACKING.
MOTHER, PLEASE. SHE WAS SPEAKING TO THE MORTALS.
AMEND

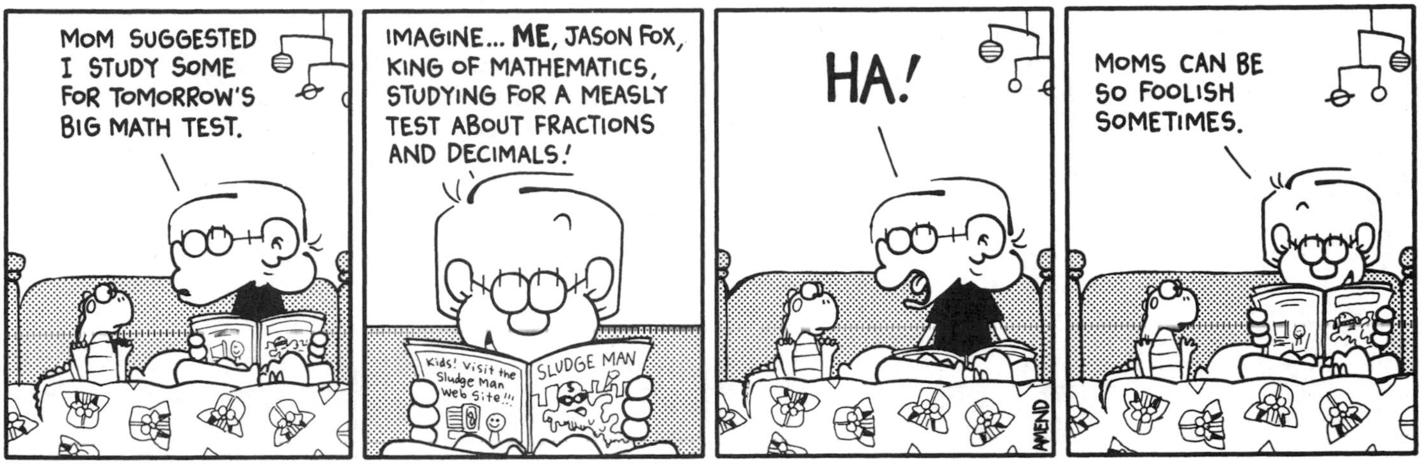
MOM SUGGESTED I STUDY SOME FOR TOMORROW'S BIG MATH TEST.
IMAGINE... ME, JASON FOX, KING OF MATHEMATICS, STUDYING FOR A MEASLY TEST ABOUT FRACTIONS AND DECIMALS!
Kids! Visit the Sludge Man Web Site!!!
SLUDGE MAN
HA!
AMEND
MOMS CAN BE SO FOOLISH SOMETIMES.

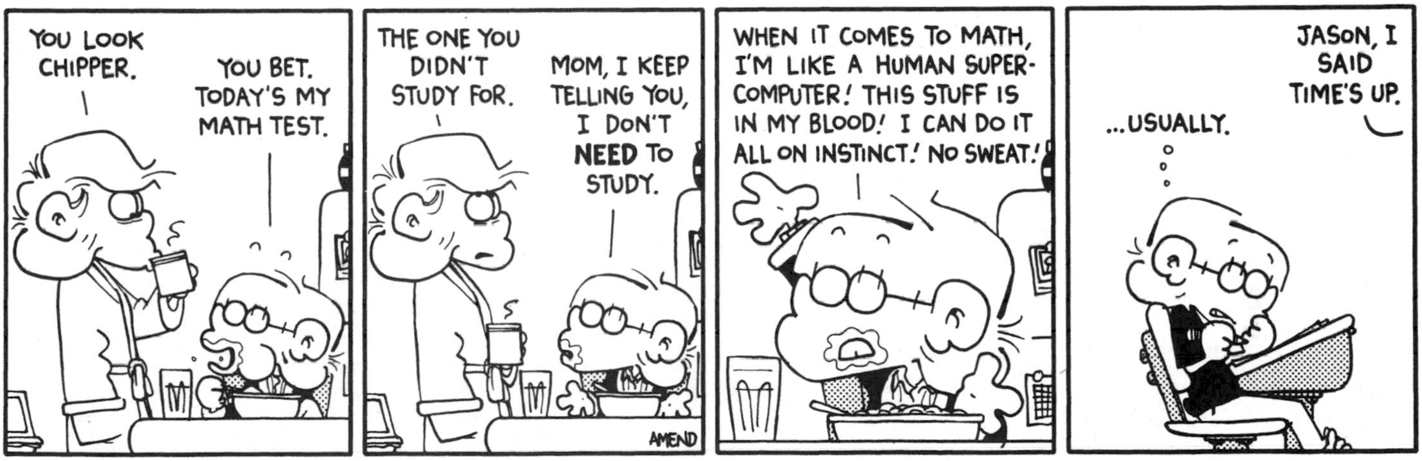
YOU LOOK CHIPPER.
YOU BET. TODAY'S MY MATH TEST.
THE ONE YOU DIDN'T STUDY FOR.
MOM, I KEEP TELLING YOU, I DON'T NEED TO STUDY.
AMEND
WHEN IT COMES TO MATH, I'M LIKE A HUMAN SUPER-COMPUTER! THIS STUFF IS IN MY BLOOD! I CAN DO IT ALL ON INSTINCT! NO SWEAT!
...USUALLY.
JASON, I SAID TIME'S UP.

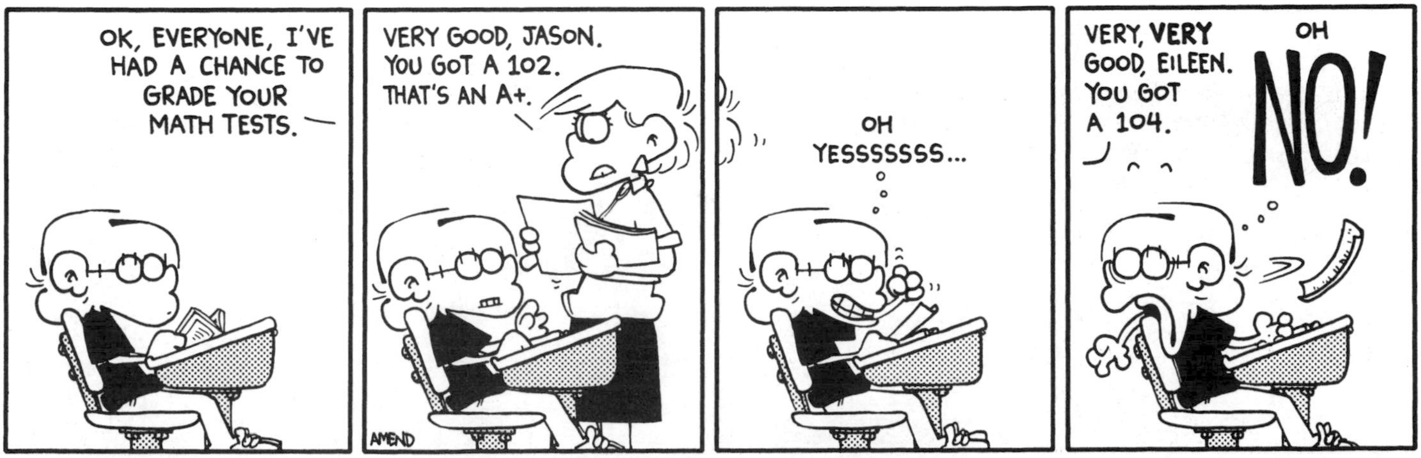
OK, EVERYONE, I'VE HAD A CHANCE TO GRADE YOUR MATH TESTS.
VERY GOOD, JASON. YOU GOT A 102. THAT'S AN A+.
AMEND
OH YESSSSSSS...
VERY, VERY GOOD, EILEEN. YOU GOT A 104.
OH NO!

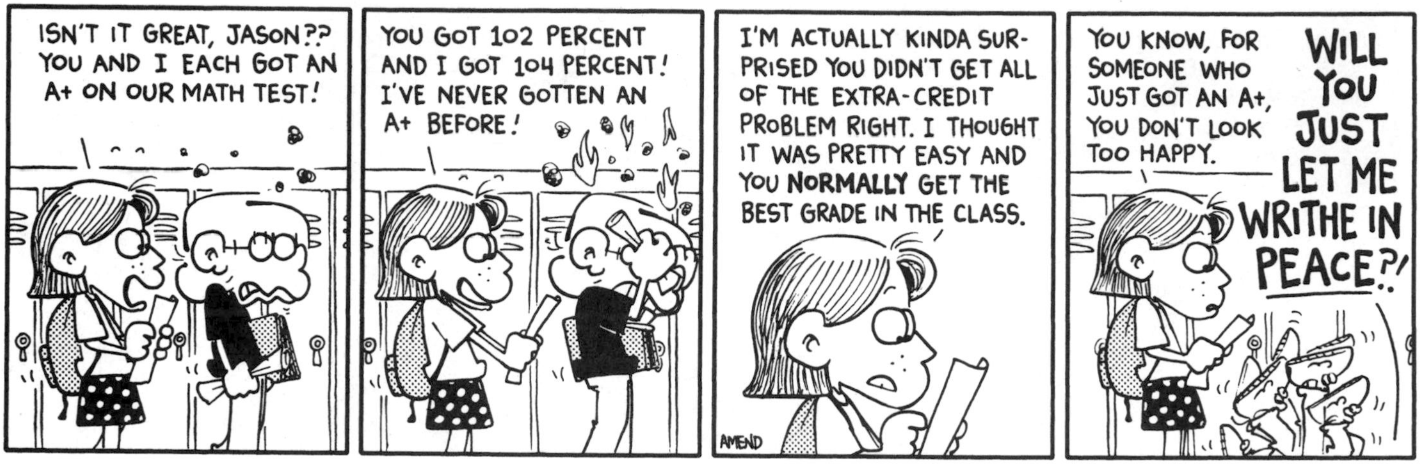
ISN'T IT GREAT, JASON?? YOU AND I EACH GOT AN A+ ON OUR MATH TEST!
YOU GOT 102 PERCENT AND I GOT 104 PERCENT! I'VE NEVER GOTTEN AN A+ BEFORE!
I'M ACTUALLY KINDA SURPRISED YOU DIDN'T GET ALL OF THE EXTRA-CREDIT PROBLEM RIGHT. I THOUGHT IT WAS PRETTY EASY AND YOU **NORMALLY** GET THE BEST GRADE IN THE CLASS.
AMEND
YOU KNOW, FOR SOMEONE WHO JUST GOT AN A+, YOU DON'T LOOK TOO HAPPY.
WILL YOU JUST LET ME WRITHE IN PEACE?!

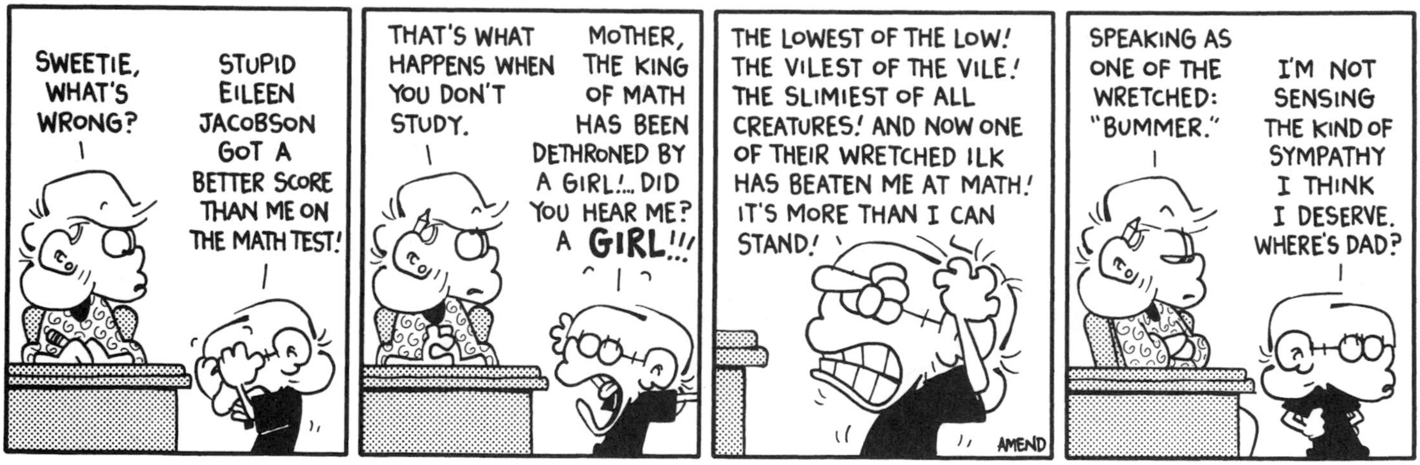
SWEETIE, WHAT'S WRONG?
STUPID EILEEN JACOBSON GOT A BETTER SCORE THAN ME ON THE MATH TEST!
THAT'S WHAT HAPPENS WHEN YOU DON'T STUDY.
MOTHER, THE KING OF MATH HAS BEEN DETHRONED BY A GIRL!... DID YOU HEAR ME? A **GIRL**!!!
THE LOWEST OF THE LOW! THE VILEST OF THE VILE! THE SLIMIEST OF ALL CREATURES! AND NOW ONE OF THEIR WRETCHED ILK HAS BEATEN ME AT MATH! IT'S MORE THAN I CAN STAND!
AMEND
SPEAKING AS ONE OF THE WRETCHED: "BUMMER."
I'M NOT SENSING THE KIND OF SYMPATHY I THINK I DESERVE. WHERE'S DAD?

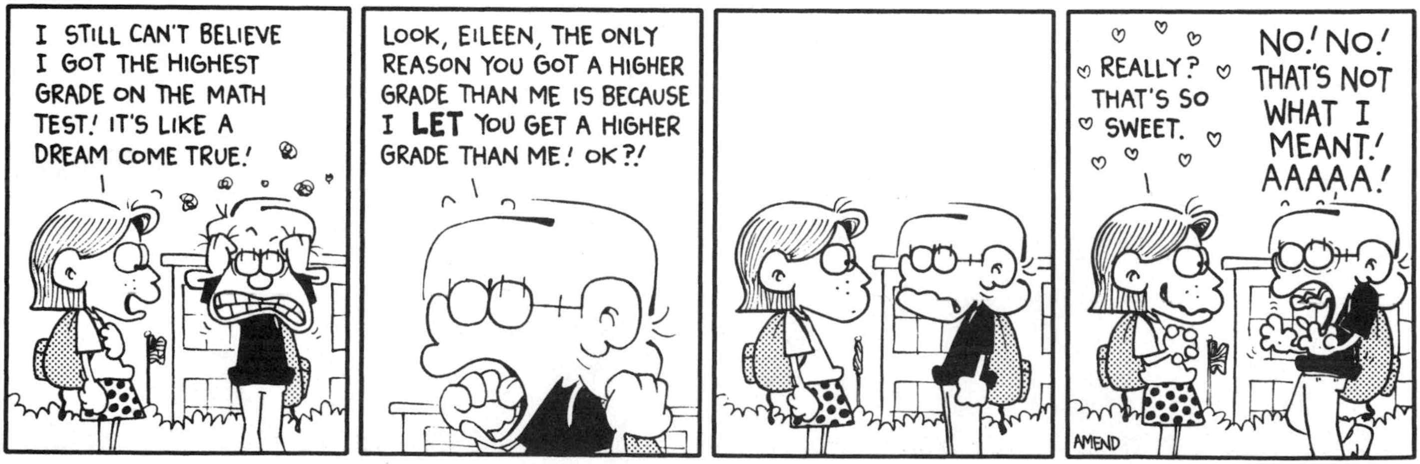
I STILL CAN'T BELIEVE I GOT THE HIGHEST GRADE ON THE MATH TEST! IT'S LIKE A DREAM COME TRUE!
LOOK, EILEEN, THE ONLY REASON YOU GOT A HIGHER GRADE THAN ME IS BECAUSE I **LET** YOU GET A HIGHER GRADE THAN ME! OK?!
REALLY? THAT'S SO SWEET.
NO! NO! THAT'S NOT WHAT I MEANT! AAAAA!
AMEND

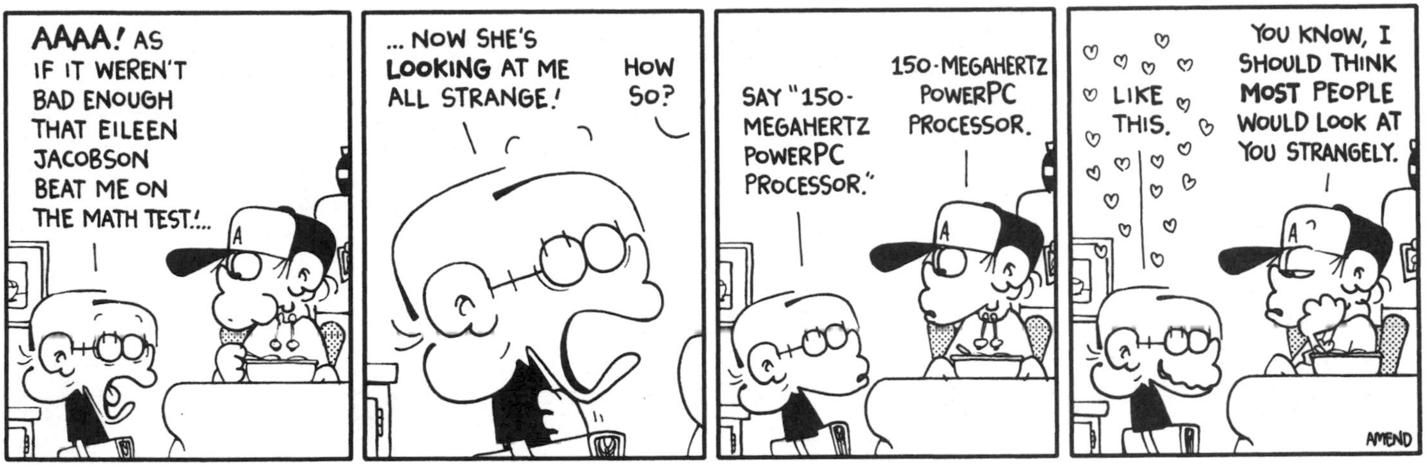
AAAA! AS IF IT WEREN'T BAD ENOUGH THAT EILEEN JACOBSON BEAT ME ON THE MATH TEST!...
... NOW SHE'S LOOKING AT ME ALL STRANGE!
HOW SO?
SAY "150-MEGAHERTZ POWERPC PROCESSOR."
150-MEGAHERTZ POWERPC PROCESSOR.
LIKE THIS.
YOU KNOW, I SHOULD THINK MOST PEOPLE WOULD LOOK AT YOU STRANGELY.
AMEND

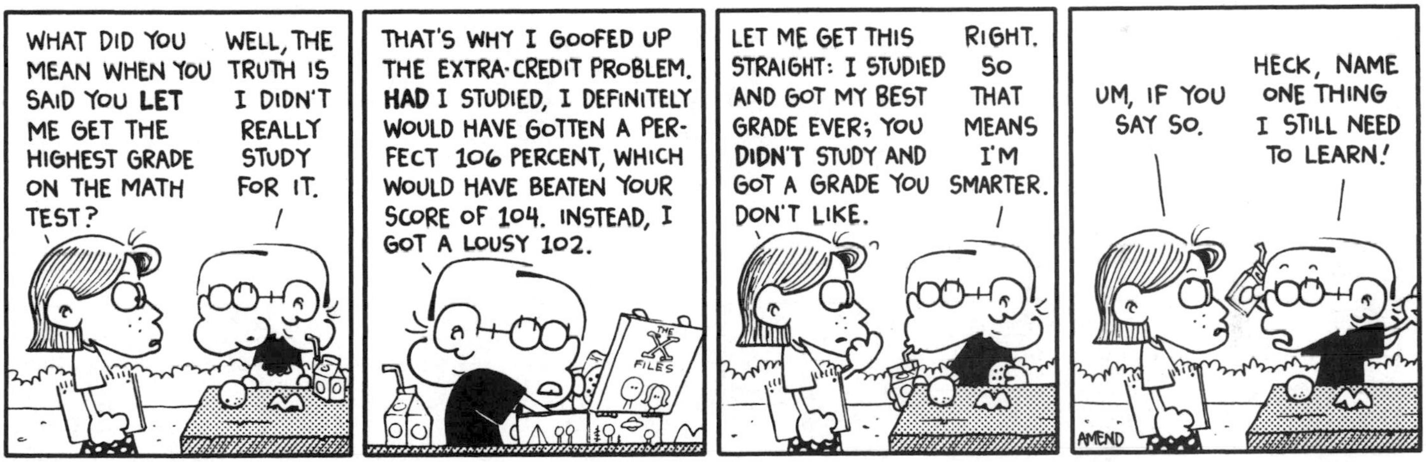
WHAT DID YOU MEAN WHEN YOU SAID YOU LET ME GET THE HIGHEST GRADE ON THE MATH TEST?
WELL, THE TRUTH IS I DIDN'T REALLY STUDY FOR IT.
THAT'S WHY I GOOFED UP THE EXTRA-CREDIT PROBLEM. HAD I STUDIED, I DEFINITELY WOULD HAVE GOTTEN A PERFECT 106 PERCENT, WHICH WOULD HAVE BEATEN YOUR SCORE OF 104. INSTEAD, I GOT A LOUSY 102.
THE X FILES
LET ME GET THIS STRAIGHT: I STUDIED AND GOT MY BEST GRADE EVER; YOU DIDN'T STUDY AND GOT A GRADE YOU DON'T LIKE.
RIGHT. SO THAT MEANS I'M SMARTER.
UM, IF YOU SAY SO.
HECK, NAME ONE THING I STILL NEED TO LEARN!
AMEND

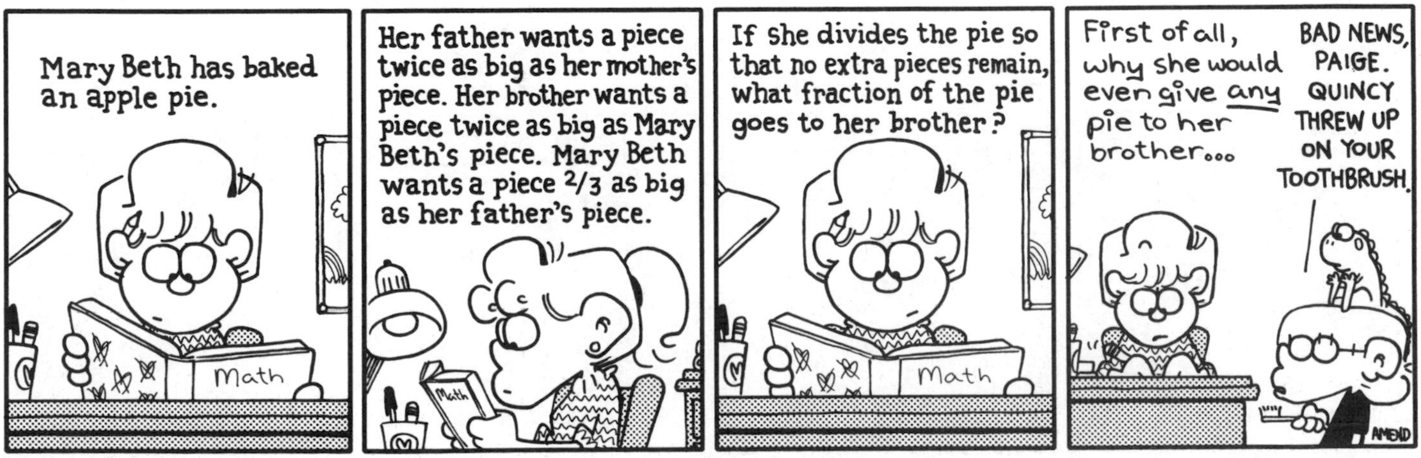
Mary Beth has baked an apple pie.
Math
Her father wants a piece twice as big as her mother's piece. Her brother wants a piece twice as big as Mary Beth's piece. Mary Beth wants a piece 2/3 as big as her father's piece.
Math
If she divides the pie so that no extra pieces remain, what fraction of the pie goes to her brother?
Math
First of all, why she would even give any pie to her brother...
BAD NEWS, PAIGE. QUINCY THREW UP ON YOUR TOOTHBRUSH.
AMEND

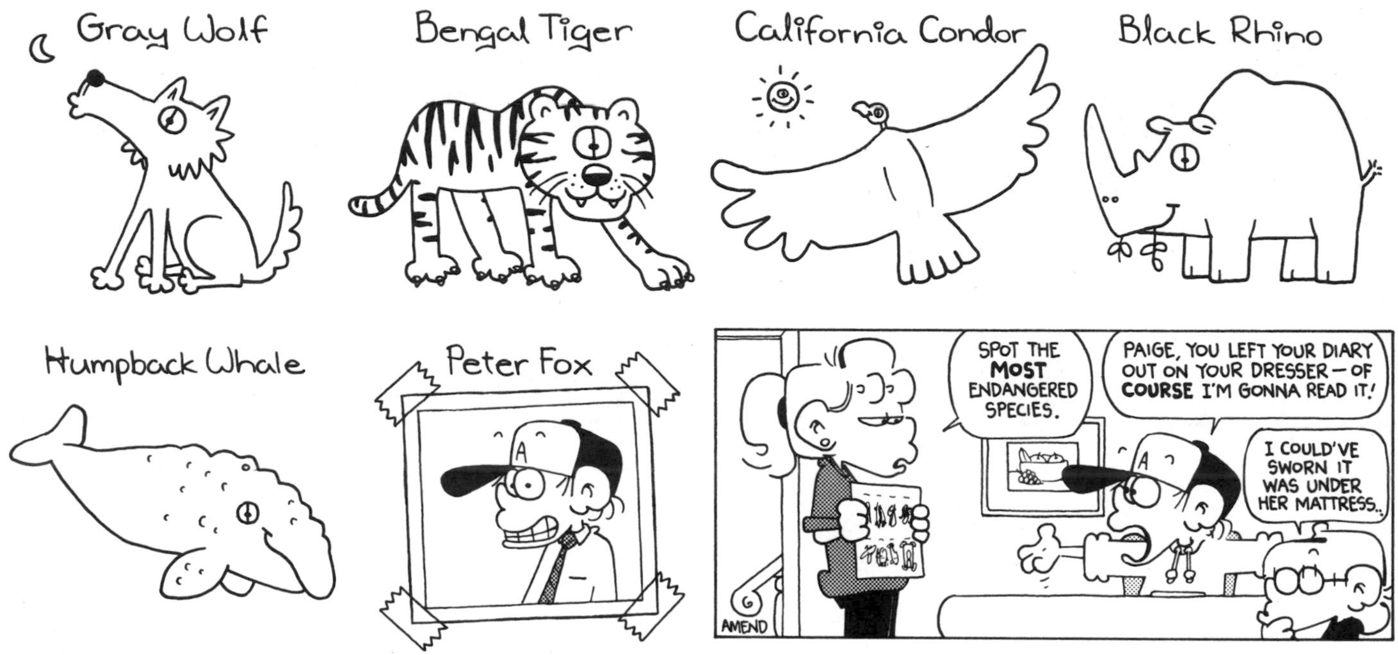
Gray Wolf
Bengal Tiger
California Condor
Black Rhino
Humpback Whale
Peter Fox
SPOT THE MOST ENDANGERED SPECIES.
PAIGE, YOU LEFT YOUR DIARY OUT ON YOUR DRESSER — OF COURSE I'M GONNA READ IT!
I COULD'VE SWORN IT WAS UNDER HER MATTRESS..
AMEND

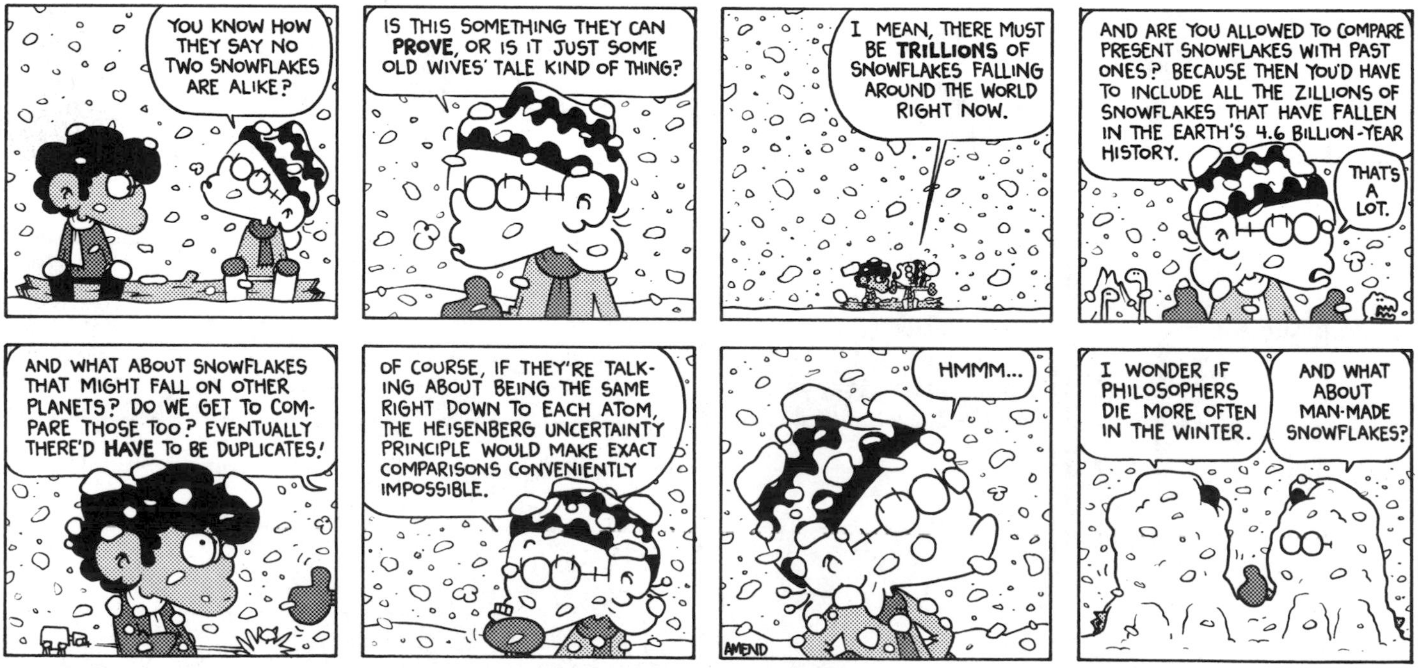
YOU KNOW HOW THEY SAY NO TWO SNOWFLAKES ARE ALIKE?
IS THIS SOMETHING THEY CAN PROVE, OR IS IT JUST SOME OLD WIVES' TALE KIND OF THING?
I MEAN, THERE MUST BE TRILLIONS OF SNOWFLAKES FALLING AROUND THE WORLD RIGHT NOW.
AND ARE YOU ALLOWED TO COMPARE PRESENT SNOWFLAKES WITH PAST ONES? BECAUSE THEN YOU'D HAVE TO INCLUDE ALL THE ZILLIONS OF SNOWFLAKES THAT HAVE FALLEN IN THE EARTH'S 4.6 BILLION-YEAR HISTORY.
THAT'S A LOT.
AND WHAT ABOUT SNOWFLAKES THAT MIGHT FALL ON OTHER PLANETS? DO WE GET TO COMPARE THOSE TOO? EVENTUALLY THERE'D HAVE TO BE DUPLICATES!
OF COURSE, IF THEY'RE TALKING ABOUT BEING THE SAME RIGHT DOWN TO EACH ATOM, THE HEISENBERG UNCERTAINTY PRINCIPLE WOULD MAKE EXACT COMPARISONS CONVENIENTLY IMPOSSIBLE.
HMMM...
AMEND
I WONDER IF PHILOSOPHERS DIE MORE OFTEN IN THE WINTER.
AND WHAT ABOUT MAN-MADE SNOWFLAKES?

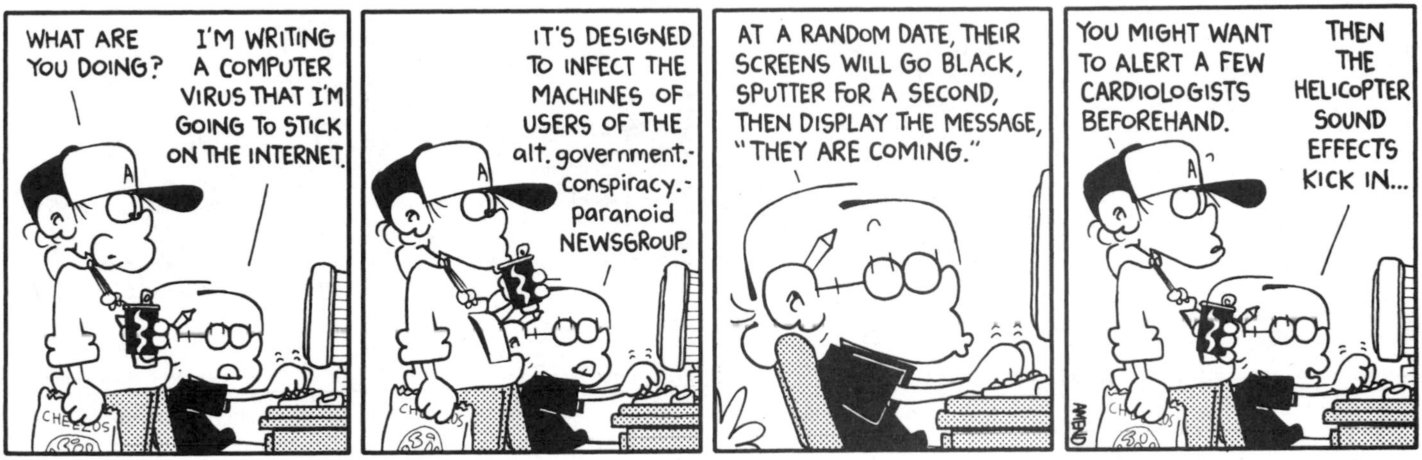
WHAT ARE YOU DOING?
I'M WRITING A COMPUTER VIRUS THAT I'M GOING TO STICK ON THE INTERNET.
IT'S DESIGNED TO INFECT THE MACHINES OF USERS OF THE alt.government.-conspiracy.-paranoid NEWSGROUP.
AT A RANDOM DATE, THEIR SCREENS WILL GO BLACK, SPUTTER FOR A SECOND, THEN DISPLAY THE MESSAGE, "THEY ARE COMING."
YOU MIGHT WANT TO ALERT A FEW CARDIOLOGISTS BEFOREHAND.
THEN THE HELICOPTER SOUND EFFECTS KICK IN...
AMEND

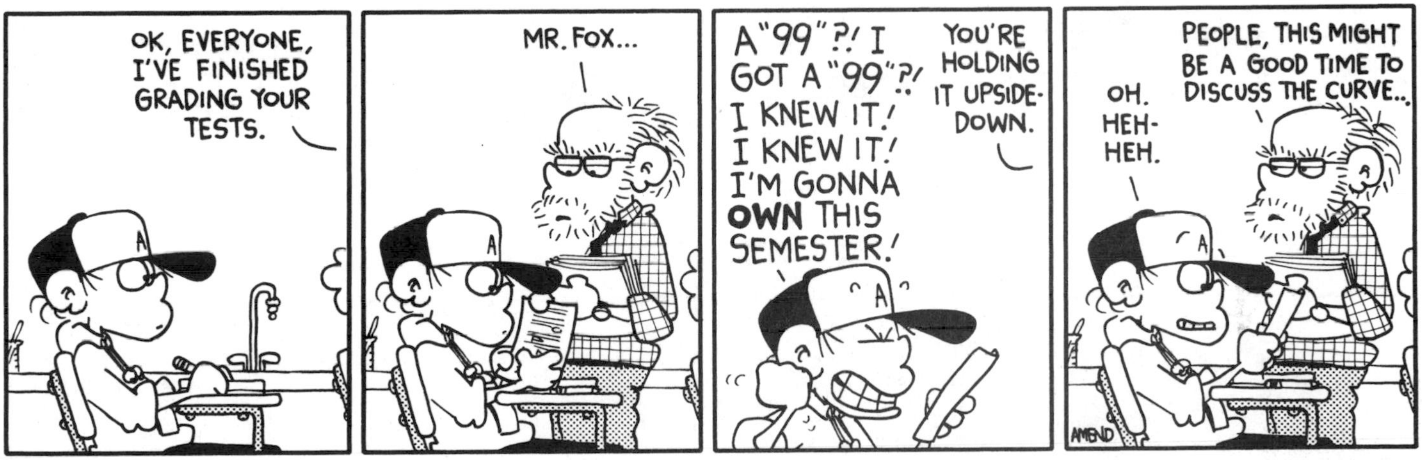
OK, EVERYONE, I'VE FINISHED GRADING YOUR TESTS.
MR. FOX...
A "99"?! I GOT A "99"?! I KNEW IT! I KNEW IT! I'M GONNA OWN THIS SEMESTER!
YOU'RE HOLDING IT UPSIDE-DOWN.
OH. HEH-HEH.
PEOPLE, THIS MIGHT BE A GOOD TIME TO DISCUSS THE CURVE...
AMEND

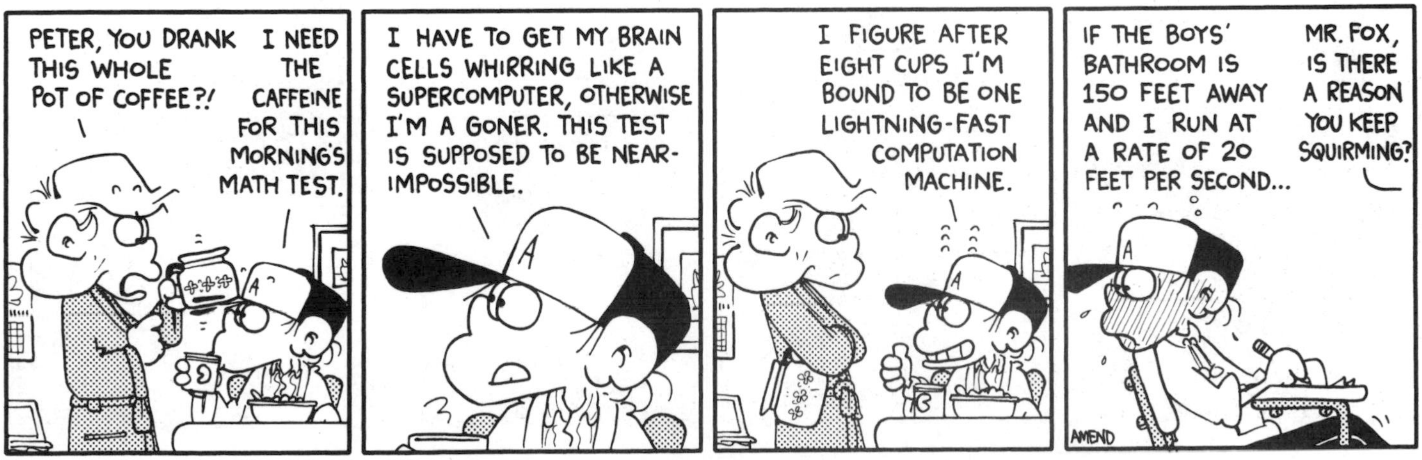
PETER, YOU DRANK THIS WHOLE POT OF COFFEE?!
I NEED THE CAFFEINE FOR THIS MORNING'S MATH TEST.
I HAVE TO GET MY BRAIN CELLS WHIRRING LIKE A SUPERCOMPUTER, OTHERWISE I'M A GONER. THIS TEST IS SUPPOSED TO BE NEAR-IMPOSSIBLE.
I FIGURE AFTER EIGHT CUPS I'M BOUND TO BE ONE LIGHTNING-FAST COMPUTATION MACHINE.
IF THE BOYS' BATHROOM IS 150 FEET AWAY AND I RUN AT A RATE OF 20 FEET PER SECOND...
MR. FOX, IS THERE A REASON YOU KEEP SQUIRMING?
AMEND

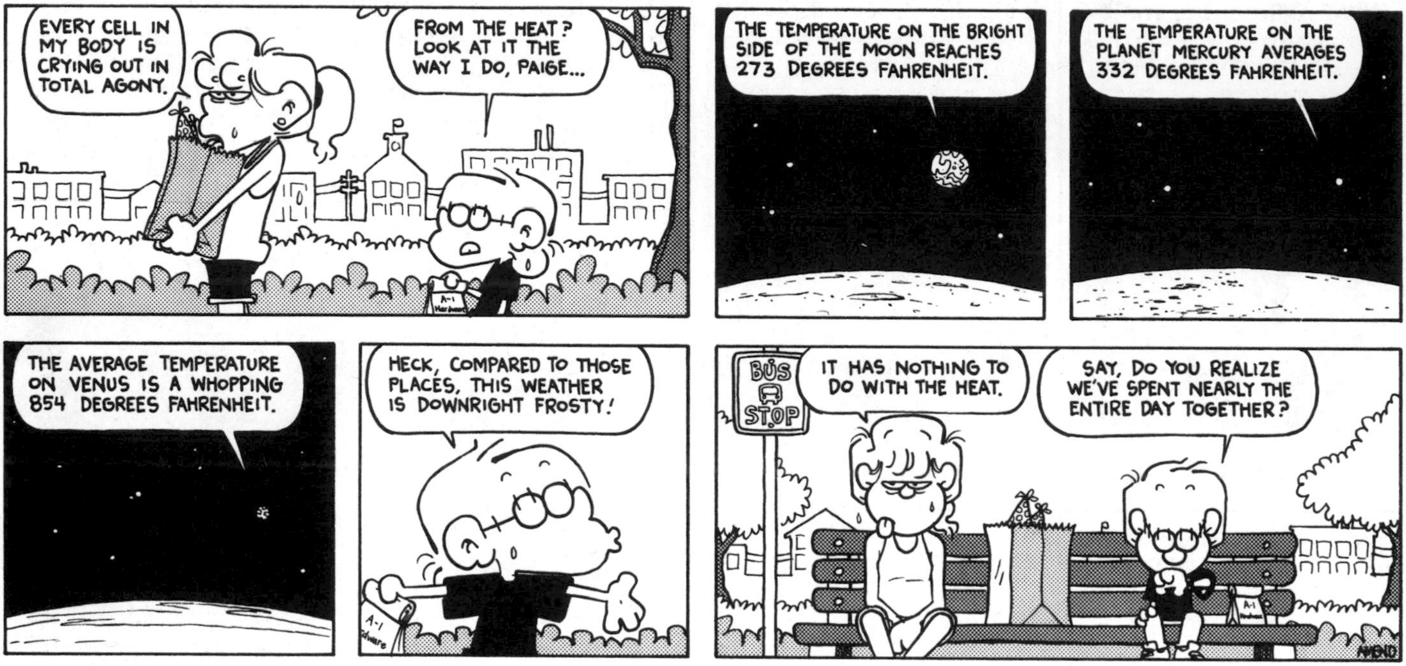
EVERY CELL IN MY BODY IS CRYING OUT IN TOTAL AGONY.
FROM THE HEAT? LOOK AT IT THE WAY I DO, PAIGE...
THE TEMPERATURE ON THE BRIGHT SIDE OF THE MOON REACHES 273 DEGREES FAHRENHEIT.
THE TEMPERATURE ON THE PLANET MERCURY AVERAGES 332 DEGREES FAHRENHEIT.
THE AVERAGE TEMPERATURE ON VENUS IS A WHOPPING 854 DEGREES FAHRENHEIT.
HECK, COMPARED TO THOSE PLACES, THIS WEATHER IS DOWNRIGHT FROSTY!
BUS STOP
IT HAS NOTHING TO DO WITH THE HEAT.
SAY, DO YOU REALIZE WE'VE SPENT NEARLY THE ENTIRE DAY TOGETHER?
AMEND

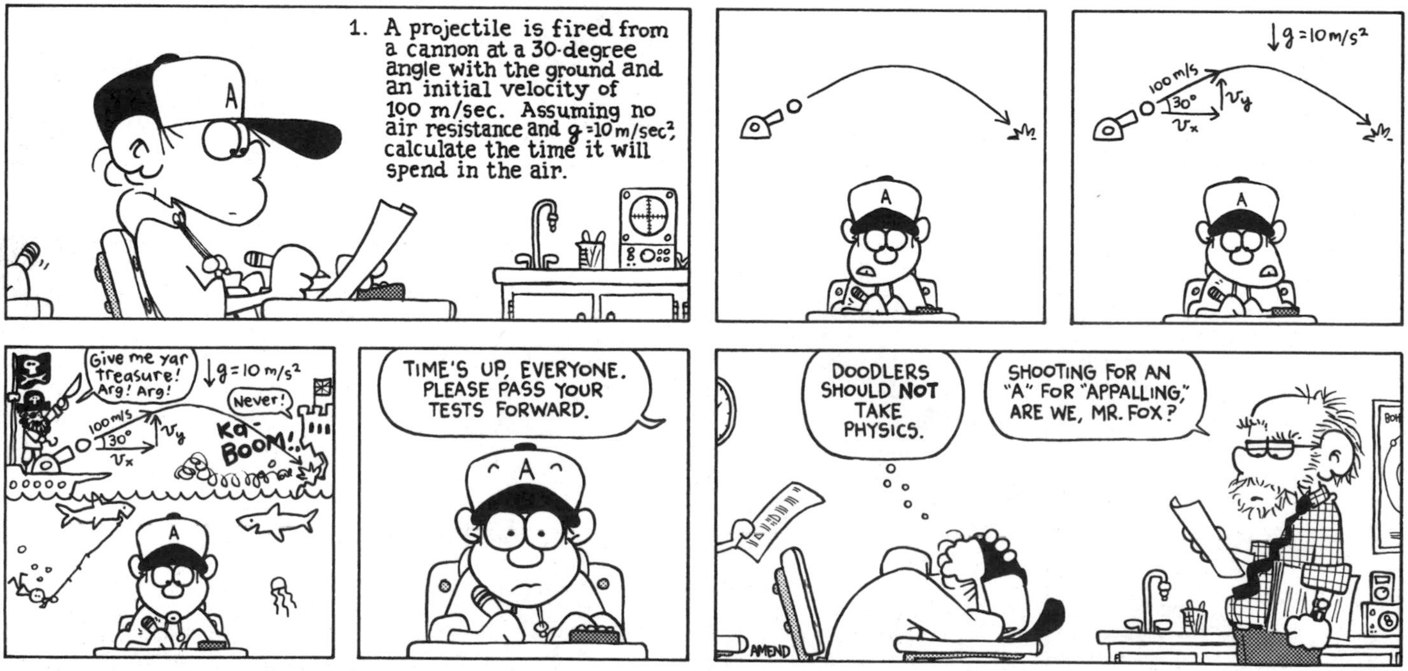
1. A projectile is fired from a cannon at a 30-degree angle with the ground and an initial velocity of 100 m/sec. Assuming no air resistance and g=10 m/sec², calculate the time it will spend in the air.
g=10 m/s²
100 m/s
30°
v_y
v_x
Give me yar treasure! Arg! Arg!
Never!
Ka-BOOM!
TIME'S UP, EVERYONE. PLEASE PASS YOUR TESTS FORWARD.
DOODLERS SHOULD **NOT** TAKE PHYSICS.
SHOOTING FOR AN "A" FOR "APPALLING," ARE WE, MR. FOX?
AMEND

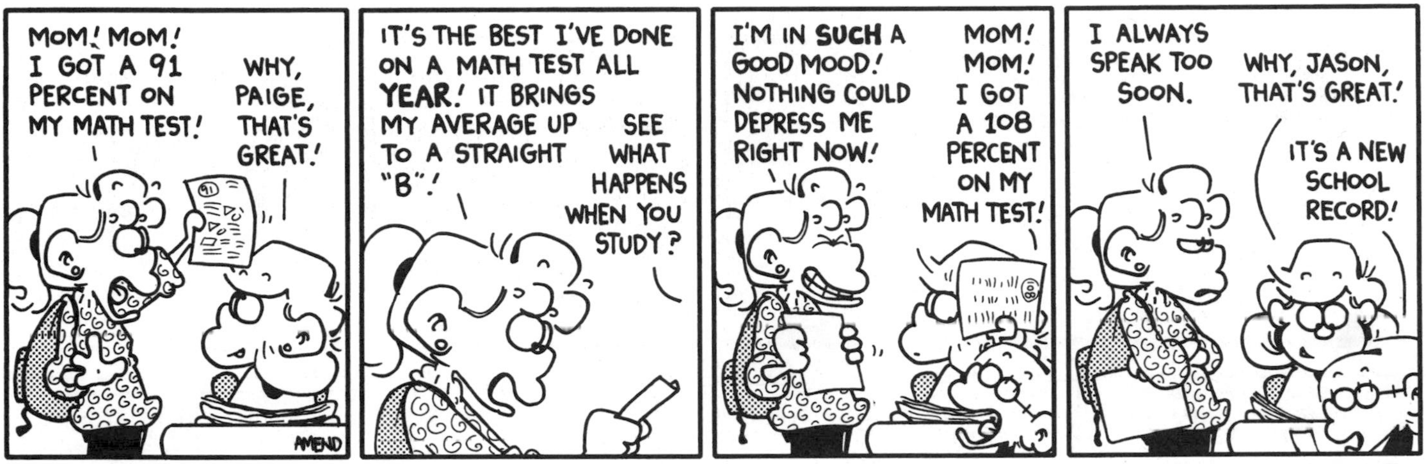
MOM! MOM! I GOT A 91 PERCENT ON MY MATH TEST!
WHY, PAIGE, THAT'S GREAT!
AMEND
IT'S THE BEST I'VE DONE ON A MATH TEST ALL **YEAR**! IT BRINGS MY AVERAGE UP TO A STRAIGHT "B"!
SEE WHAT HAPPENS WHEN YOU STUDY?
I'M IN **SUCH** A GOOD MOOD! NOTHING COULD DEPRESS ME RIGHT NOW!
MOM! MOM! I GOT A 108 PERCENT ON MY MATH TEST!
I ALWAYS SPEAK TOO SOON.
WHY, JASON, THAT'S GREAT!
IT'S A NEW SCHOOL RECORD!

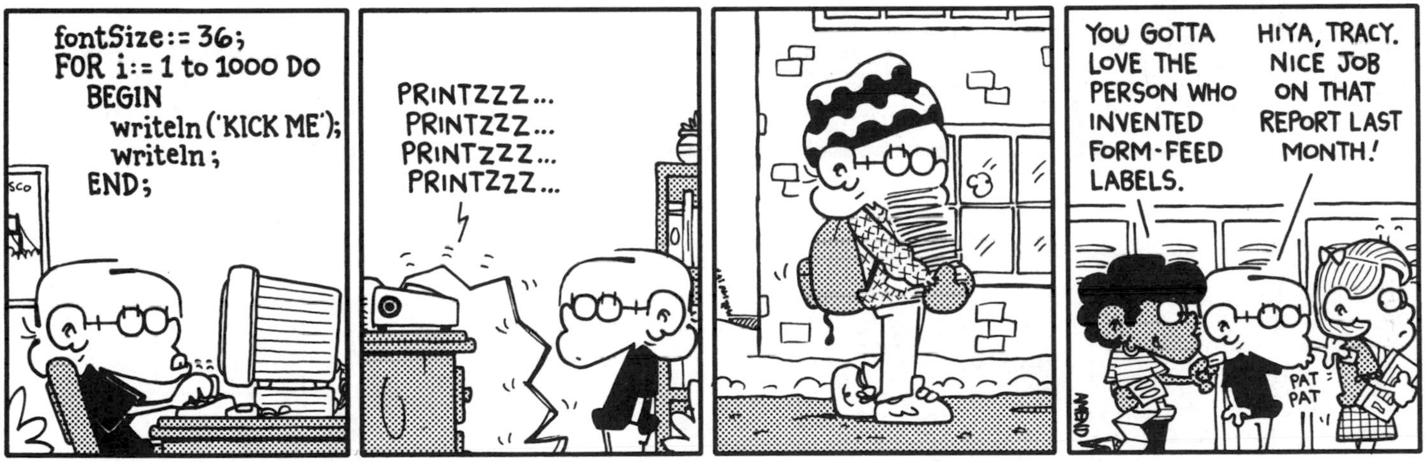
fontSize:= 36;
FOR i:= 1 to 1000 DO
BEGIN
writeln('KICK ME');
writeln;
END;
PRINTZZZ... PRINTZZZ... PRINTZZZ... PRINTZZZ...
YOU GOTTA LOVE THE PERSON WHO INVENTED FORM-FEED LABELS.
HIYA, TRACY. NICE JOB ON THAT REPORT LAST MONTH!
PAT PAT
AMEND

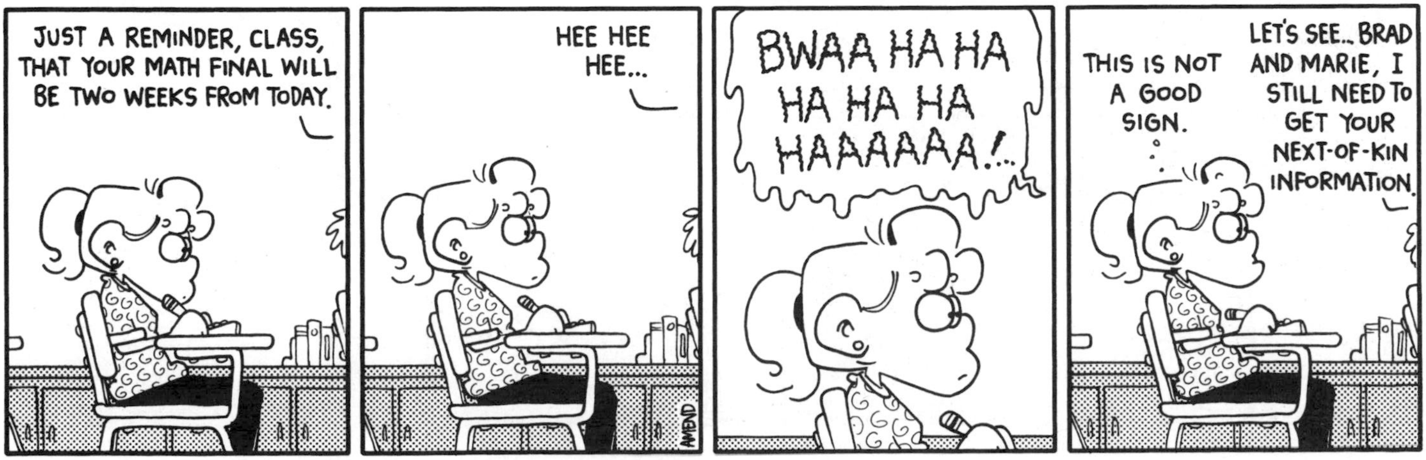
JUST A REMINDER, CLASS, THAT YOUR MATH FINAL WILL BE TWO WEEKS FROM TODAY.
HEE HEE HEE...
AMEND
BWAA HA HA HA HA HA HAAAAAA!...
THIS IS NOT A GOOD SIGN.
LET'S SEE... BRAD AND MARIE, I STILL NEED TO GET YOUR NEXT-OF-KIN INFORMATION.

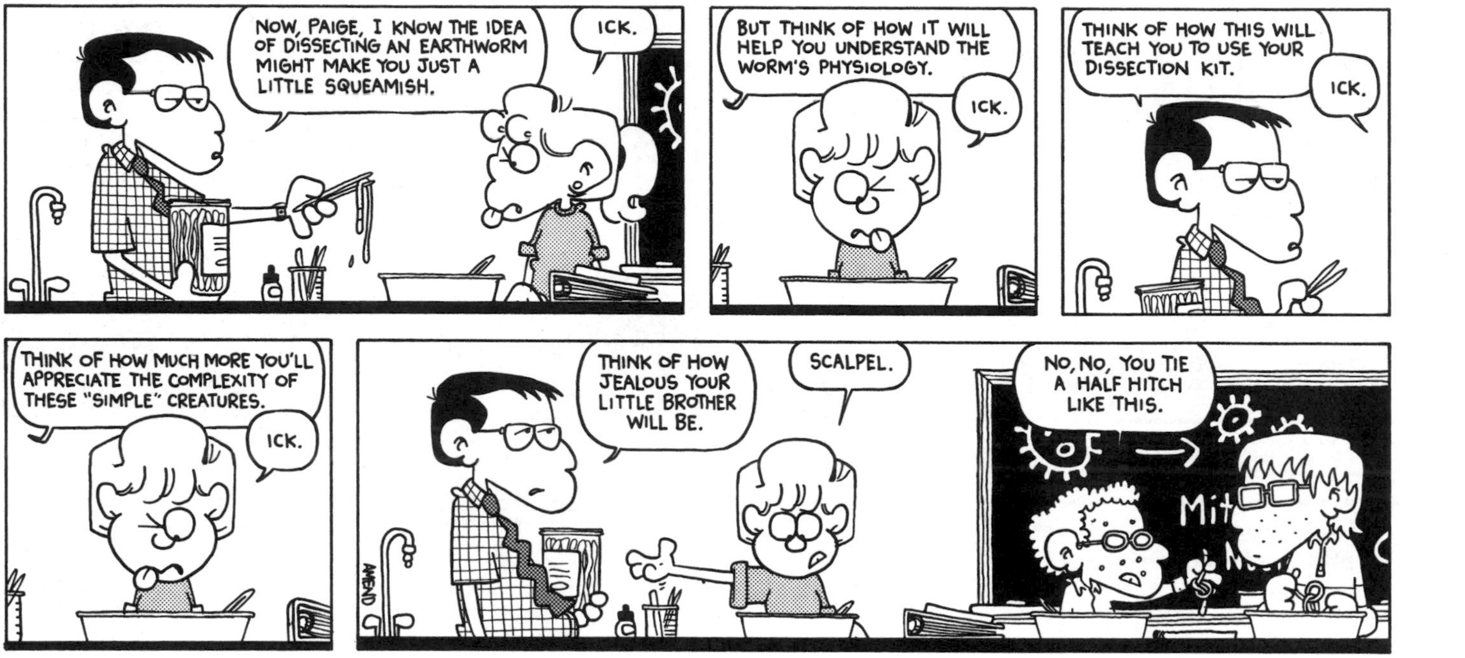
NOW, PAIGE, I KNOW THE IDEA OF DISSECTING AN EARTHWORM MIGHT MAKE YOU JUST A LITTLE SQUEAMISH.
ICK.
BUT THINK OF HOW IT WILL HELP YOU UNDERSTAND THE WORM'S PHYSIOLOGY.
ICK.
THINK OF HOW THIS WILL TEACH YOU TO USE YOUR DISSECTION KIT.
ICK.
THINK OF HOW MUCH MORE YOU'LL APPRECIATE THE COMPLEXITY OF THESE "SIMPLE" CREATURES.
ICK.
THINK OF HOW JEALOUS YOUR LITTLE BROTHER WILL BE.
SCALPEL.
NO, NO, YOU TIE A HALF HITCH LIKE THIS.

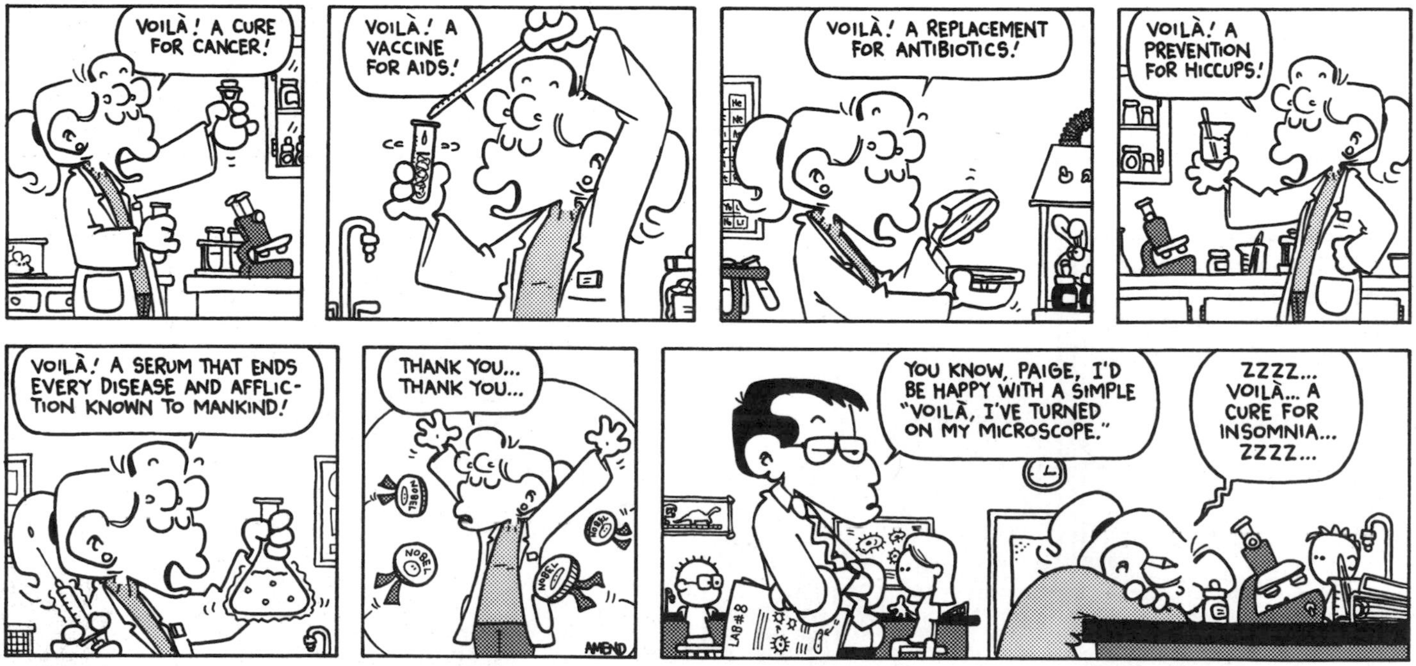
VOILÀ! A CURE FOR CANCER!
VOILÀ! A VACCINE FOR AIDS!
VOILÀ! A REPLACEMENT FOR ANTIBIOTICS!
VOILÀ! A PREVENTION FOR HICCUPS!
VOILÀ! A SERUM THAT ENDS EVERY DISEASE AND AFFLICTION KNOWN TO MANKIND!
THANK YOU... THANK YOU...
YOU KNOW, PAIGE, I'D BE HAPPY WITH A SIMPLE "VOILÀ, I'VE TURNED ON MY MICROSCOPE."
ZZZZ... VOILÀ... A CURE FOR INSOMNIA... ZZZZ...

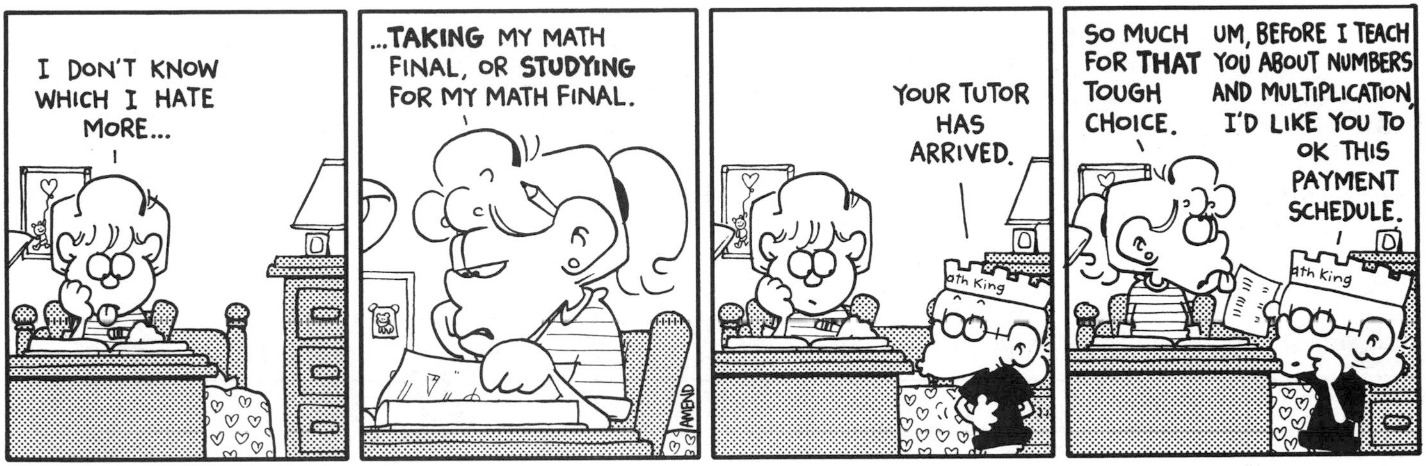
I DON'T KNOW WHICH I HATE MORE...
...**TAKING** MY MATH FINAL, OR **STUDYING** FOR MY MATH FINAL.
AMEND
YOUR TUTOR HAS ARRIVED.
ath King
SO MUCH FOR **THAT** TOUGH CHOICE.
UM, BEFORE I TEACH YOU ABOUT NUMBERS AND MULTIPLICATION, I'D LIKE YOU TO OK THIS PAYMENT SCHEDULE.
ath King

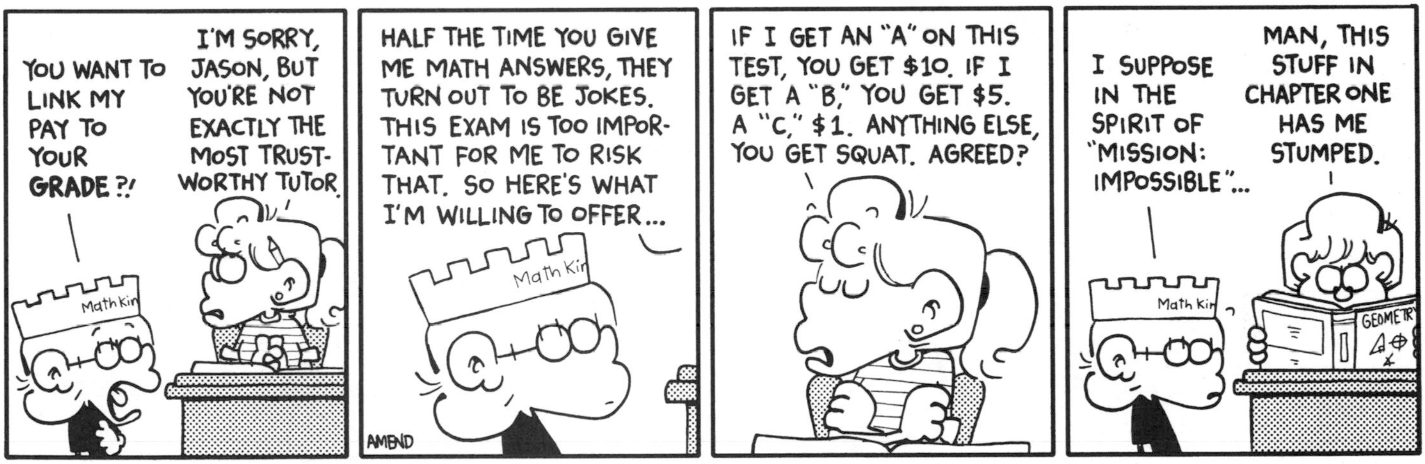
YOU WANT TO LINK MY PAY TO YOUR **GRADE**?!
I'M SORRY, JASON, BUT YOU'RE NOT EXACTLY THE MOST TRUST-WORTHY TUTOR.
Math Kin
HALF THE TIME YOU GIVE ME MATH ANSWERS, THEY TURN OUT TO BE JOKES. THIS EXAM IS TOO IMPOR-TANT FOR ME TO RISK THAT. SO HERE'S WHAT I'M WILLING TO OFFER...
Math Kin
AMEND
IF I GET AN "A" ON THIS TEST, YOU GET \$10. IF I GET A "B," YOU GET \$5. A "C," \$1. ANYTHING ELSE, YOU GET SQUAT. AGREED?
I SUPPOSE IN THE SPIRIT OF "MISSION: IMPOSSIBLE"...
MAN, THIS STUFF IN CHAPTER ONE HAS ME STUMPED.
Math Kin
GEOMETR

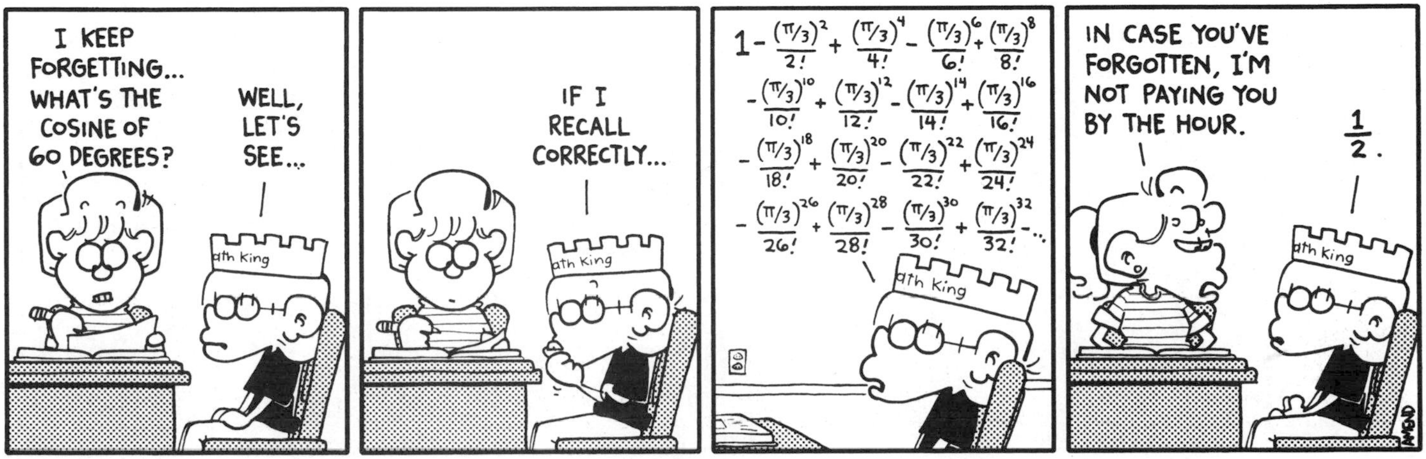
I KEEP FORGETTING... WHAT'S THE COSINE OF 60 DEGREES?
WELL, LET'S SEE...
ath King
IF I RECALL CORRECTLY...
ath King
$1-\frac{(\pi/3)^2}{2!}+\frac{(\pi/3)^4}{4!}-\frac{(\pi/3)^6}{6!}+\frac{(\pi/3)^8}{8!}-\frac{(\pi/3)^{10}}{10!}+\frac{(\pi/3)^{12}}{12!}-\frac{(\pi/3)^{14}}{14!}+\frac{(\pi/3)^{16}}{16!}-\frac{(\pi/3)^{18}}{18!}+\frac{(\pi/3)^{20}}{20!}-\frac{(\pi/3)^{22}}{22!}+\frac{(\pi/3)^{24}}{24!}-\frac{(\pi/3)^{26}}{26!}+\frac{(\pi/3)^{28}}{28!}-\frac{(\pi/3)^{30}}{30!}+\frac{(\pi/3)^{32}}{32!}-\ldots$
ath King
IN CASE YOU'VE FORGOTTEN, I'M NOT PAYING YOU BY THE HOUR.
$\frac{1}{2}$.
ath King
AMEND

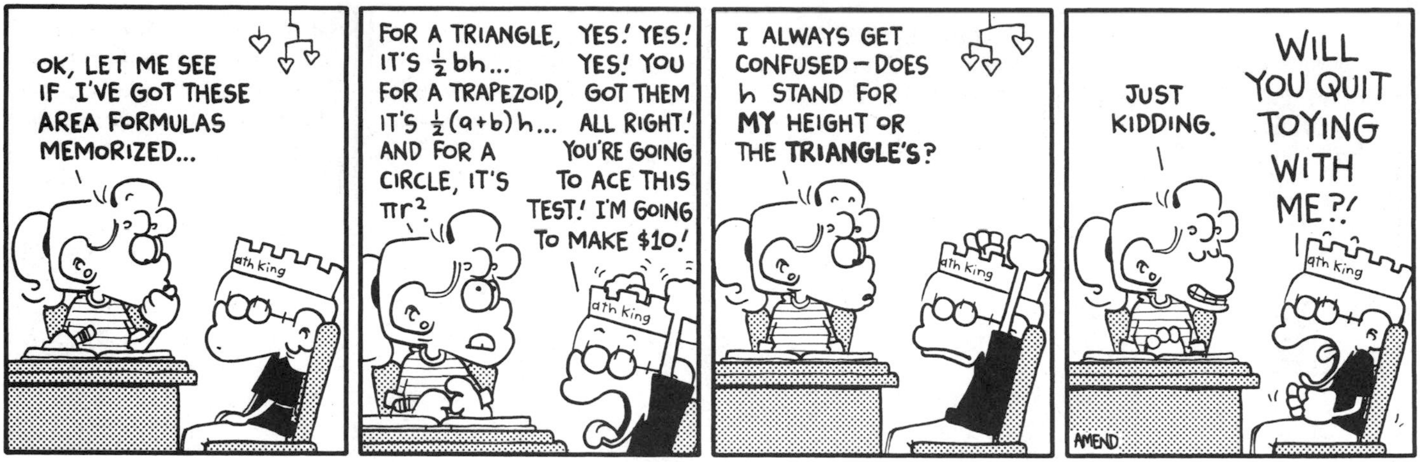
OK, LET ME SEE IF I'VE GOT THESE AREA FORMULAS MEMORIZED...
FOR A TRIANGLE, IT'S $\frac{1}{2}bh$... FOR A TRAPEZOID, IT'S $\frac{1}{2}(a+b)h$... AND FOR A CIRCLE, IT'S πr^2.
YES! YES! YES! YOU GOT THEM ALL RIGHT! YOU'RE GOING TO ACE THIS TEST! I'M GOING TO MAKE $10!
I ALWAYS GET CONFUSED – DOES h STAND FOR **MY** HEIGHT OR THE **TRIANGLE'S**?
JUST KIDDING.
WILL YOU QUIT TOYING WITH ME?!
9th King
AMEND

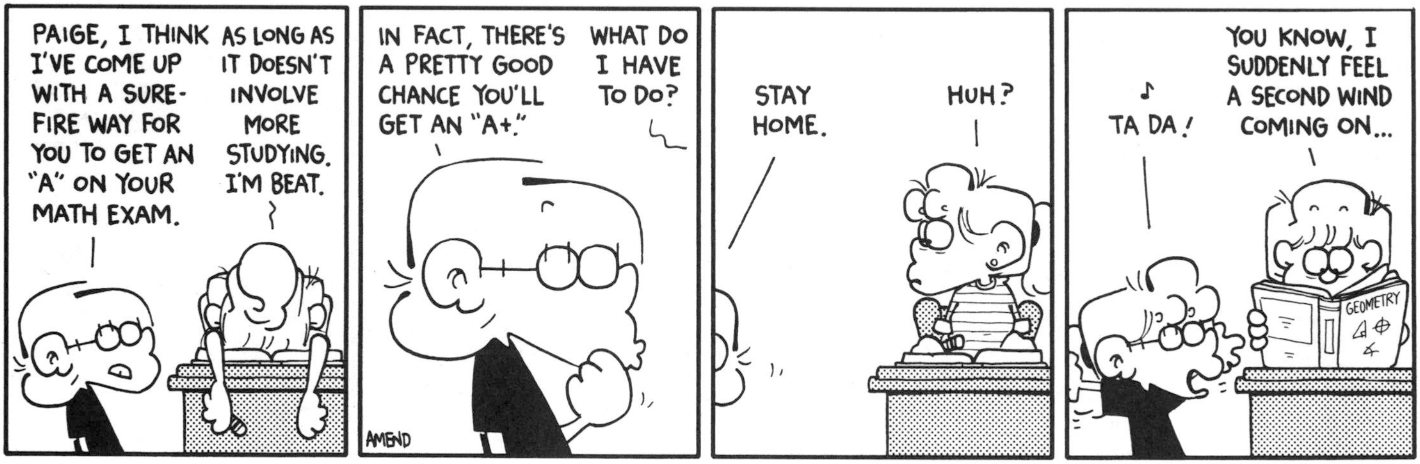
PAIGE, I THINK I'VE COME UP WITH A SURE-FIRE WAY FOR YOU TO GET AN "A" ON YOUR MATH EXAM.
AS LONG AS IT DOESN'T INVOLVE MORE STUDYING. I'M BEAT.
IN FACT, THERE'S A PRETTY GOOD CHANCE YOU'LL GET AN "A+."
WHAT DO I HAVE TO DO?
AMEND
STAY HOME.
HUH?
♪ TA DA!
YOU KNOW, I SUDDENLY FEEL A SECOND WIND COMING ON...
GEOMETRY

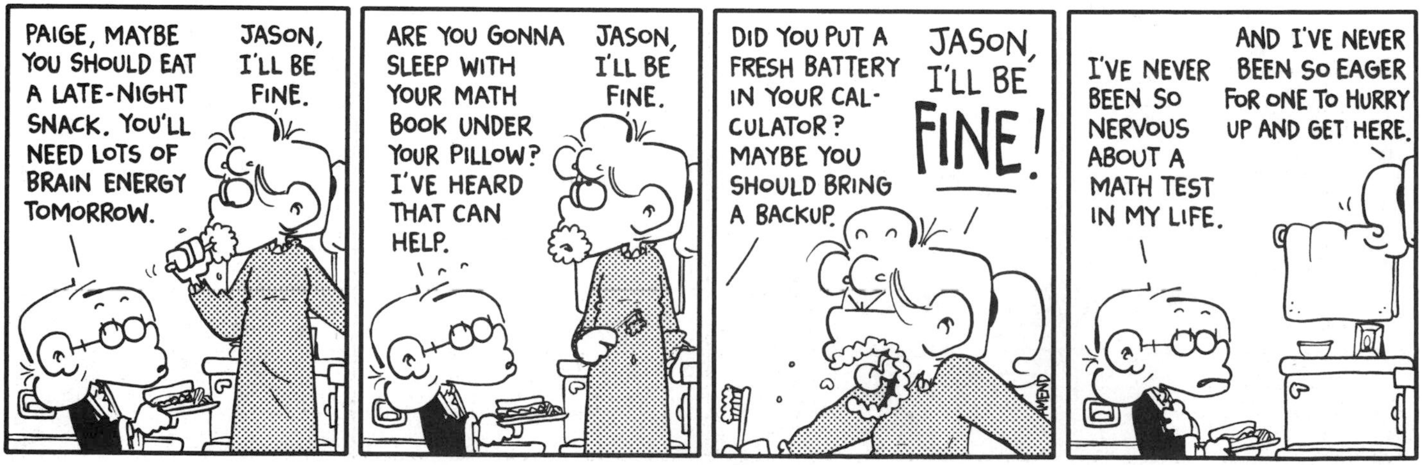
PAIGE, MAYBE YOU SHOULD EAT A LATE-NIGHT SNACK. YOU'LL NEED LOTS OF BRAIN ENERGY TOMORROW.
JASON, I'LL BE FINE.
ARE YOU GONNA SLEEP WITH YOUR MATH BOOK UNDER YOUR PILLOW? I'VE HEARD THAT CAN HELP.
JASON, I'LL BE FINE.
DID YOU PUT A FRESH BATTERY IN YOUR CALCULATOR? MAYBE YOU SHOULD BRING A BACKUP.
JASON, I'LL BE FINE!
AMEND
I'VE NEVER BEEN SO NERVOUS ABOUT A MATH TEST IN MY LIFE.
AND I'VE NEVER BEEN SO EAGER FOR ONE TO HURRY UP AND GET HERE.

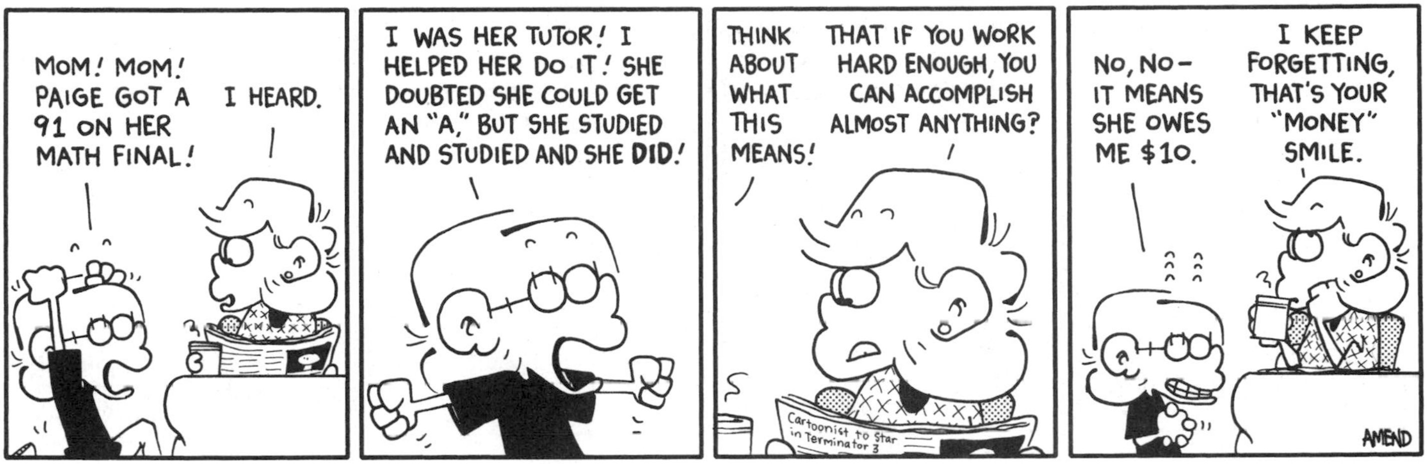
MOM! MOM! PAIGE GOT A 91 ON HER MATH FINAL!
I HEARD.
I WAS HER TUTOR! I HELPED HER DO IT! SHE DOUBTED SHE COULD GET AN "A," BUT SHE STUDIED AND STUDIED AND SHE **DID**!
THINK ABOUT WHAT THIS MEANS!
THAT IF YOU WORK HARD ENOUGH, YOU CAN ACCOMPLISH ALMOST ANYTHING?
Cartoonist to Star in Terminator 3
NO, NO – IT MEANS SHE OWES ME $10.
I KEEP FORGETTING, THAT'S YOUR "MONEY" SMILE.
AMEND

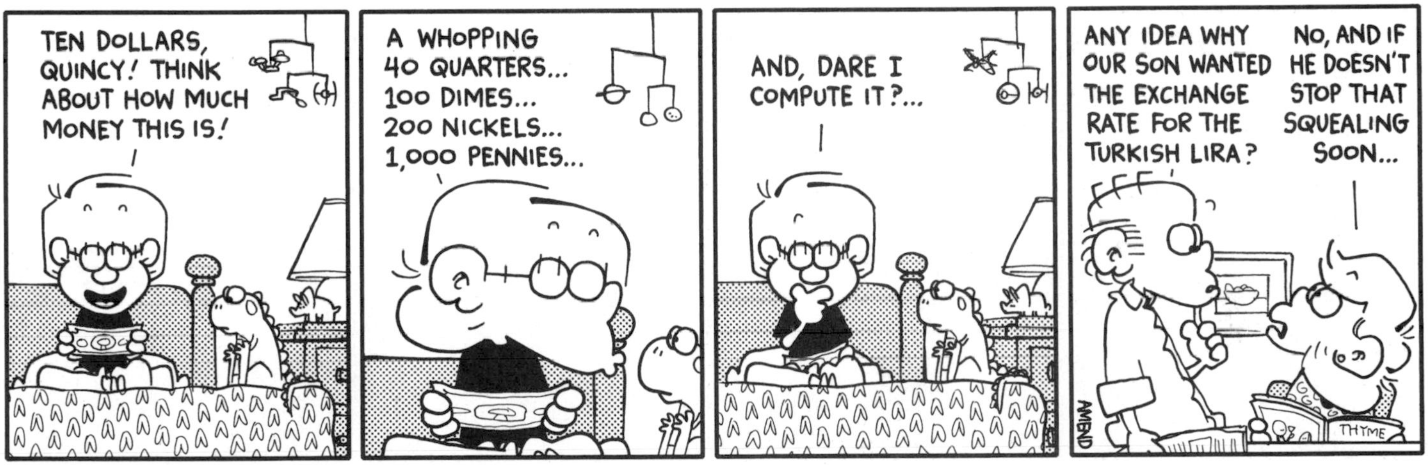
TEN DOLLARS, QUINCY! THINK ABOUT HOW MUCH MONEY THIS IS!
A WHOPPING 40 QUARTERS... 100 DIMES... 200 NICKELS... 1,000 PENNIES...
AND, DARE I COMPUTE IT?...
ANY IDEA WHY OUR SON WANTED THE EXCHANGE RATE FOR THE TURKISH LIRA?
NO, AND IF HE DOESN'T STOP THAT SQUEALING SOON...
THYME
AMEND

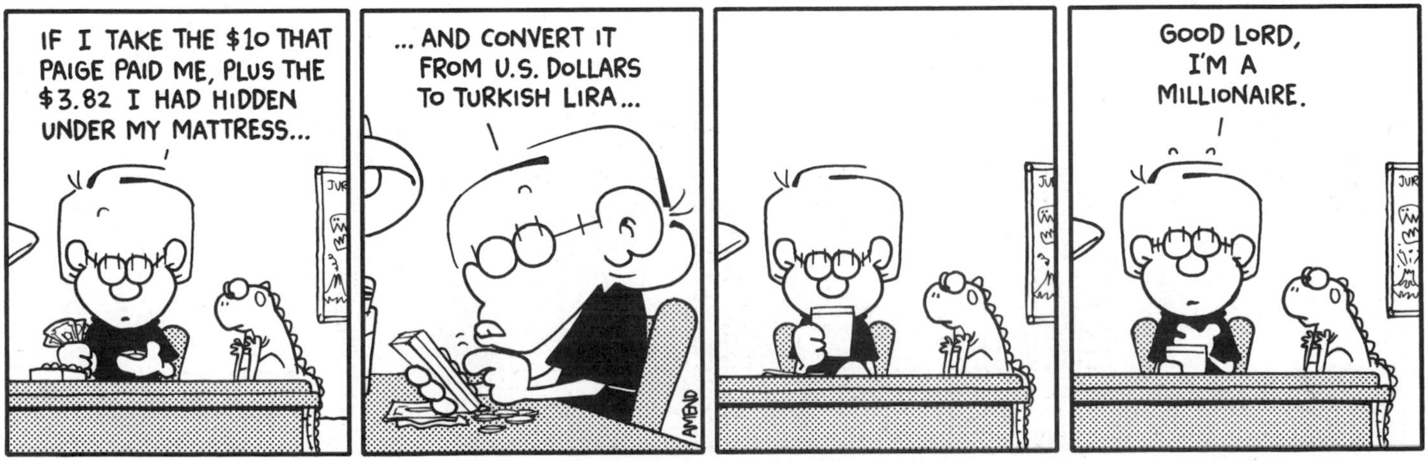
IF I TAKE THE $10 THAT PAIGE PAID ME, PLUS THE $3.82 I HAD HIDDEN UNDER MY MATTRESS...
... AND CONVERT IT FROM U.S. DOLLARS TO TURKISH LIRA...
GOOD LORD, I'M A MILLIONAIRE.
AMEND

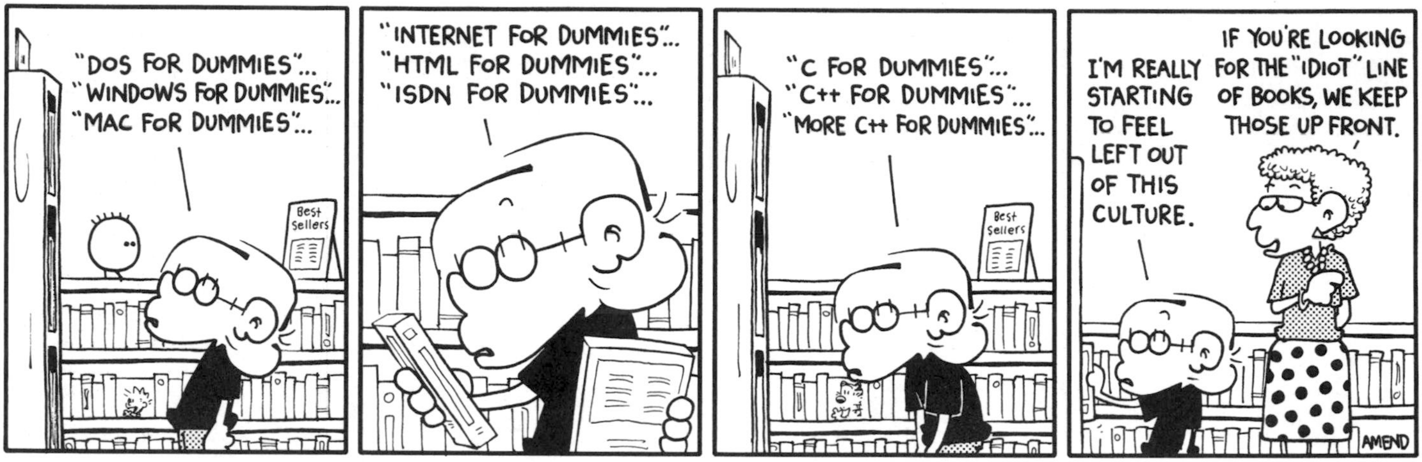
"DOS FOR DUMMIES"... "WINDOWS FOR DUMMIES"... "MAC FOR DUMMIES"...
Best Sellers
"INTERNET FOR DUMMIES"... "HTML FOR DUMMIES"... "ISDN FOR DUMMIES"...
"C FOR DUMMIES"... "C++ FOR DUMMIES"... "MORE C++ FOR DUMMIES"...
Best Sellers
I'M REALLY STARTING TO FEEL LEFT OUT OF THIS CULTURE.
IF YOU'RE LOOKING FOR THE "IDIOT" LINE OF BOOKS, WE KEEP THOSE UP FRONT.
AMEND

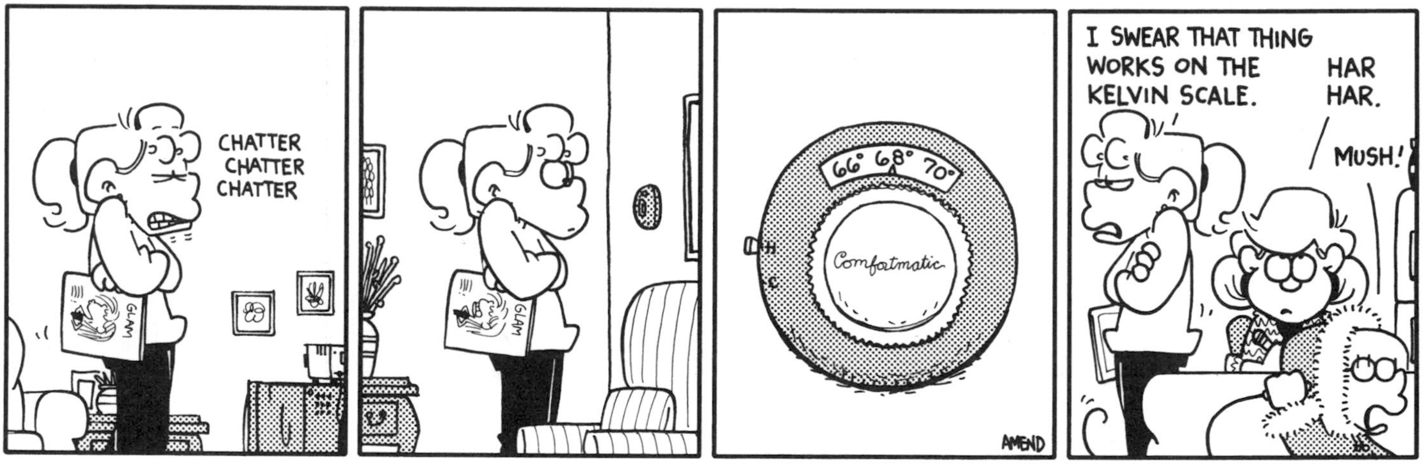
CHATTER CHATTER CHATTER
GLAM
GLAM
66° 68° 70°
Comfatmatic
H
C
AMEND
I SWEAR THAT THING WORKS ON THE KELVIN SCALE.
HAR HAR.
MUSH!

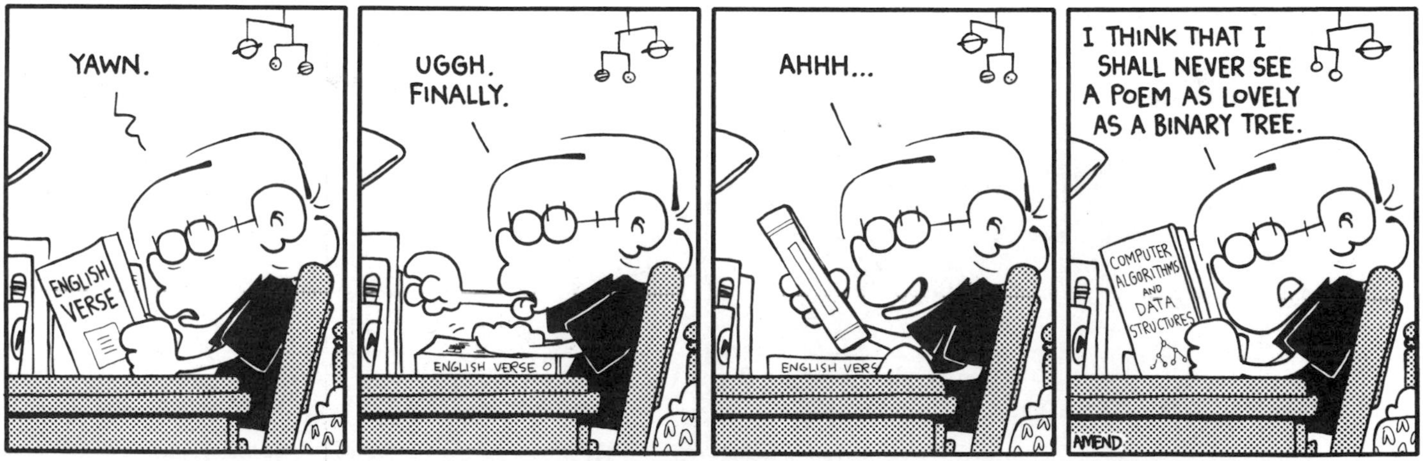
YAWN.
ENGLISH VERSE
UGGH. FINALLY.
ENGLISH VERSE
AHHH...
ENGLISH VERS
I THINK THAT I SHALL NEVER SEE A POEM AS LOVELY AS A BINARY TREE.
COMPUTER ALGORITHMS AND DATA STRUCTURES
AMEND

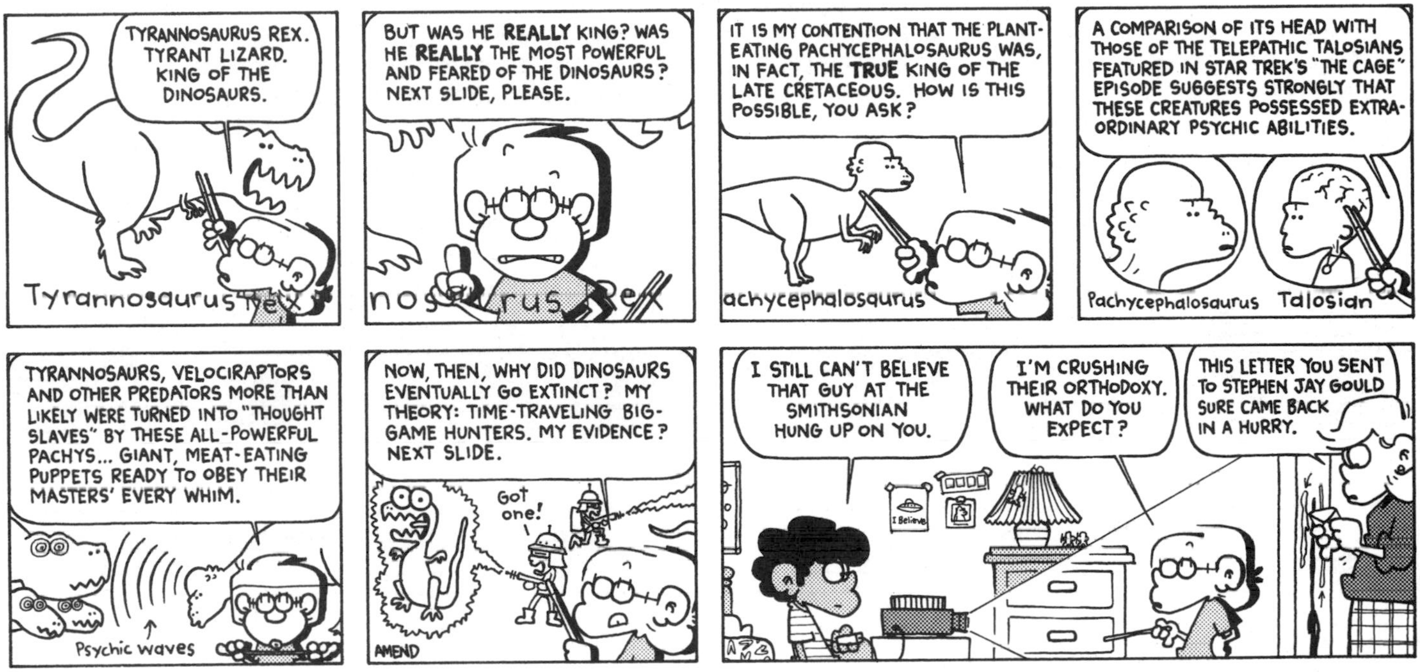
TYRANNOSAURUS REX. TYRANT LIZARD. KING OF THE DINOSAURS.
Tyrannosaurus Rex
BUT WAS HE **REALLY** KING? WAS HE **REALLY** THE MOST POWERFUL AND FEARED OF THE DINOSAURS? NEXT SLIDE, PLEASE.
IT IS MY CONTENTION THAT THE PLANT-EATING PACHYCEPHALOSAURUS WAS, IN FACT, THE **TRUE** KING OF THE LATE CRETACEOUS. HOW IS THIS POSSIBLE, YOU ASK?
achycephalosaurus
A COMPARISON OF ITS HEAD WITH THOSE OF THE TELEPATHIC TALOSIANS FEATURED IN STAR TREK'S "THE CAGE" EPISODE SUGGESTS STRONGLY THAT THESE CREATURES POSSESSED EXTRA-ORDINARY PSYCHIC ABILITIES.
Pachycephalosaurus
Talosian
TYRANNOSAURS, VELOCIRAPTORS AND OTHER PREDATORS MORE THAN LIKELY WERE TURNED INTO "THOUGHT SLAVES" BY THESE ALL-POWERFUL PACHYS... GIANT, MEAT-EATING PUPPETS READY TO OBEY THEIR MASTERS' EVERY WHIM.
Psychic waves
NOW, THEN, WHY DID DINOSAURS EVENTUALLY GO EXTINCT? MY THEORY: TIME-TRAVELING BIG-GAME HUNTERS. MY EVIDENCE? NEXT SLIDE.
Got one!
AMEND
I STILL CAN'T BELIEVE THAT GUY AT THE SMITHSONIAN HUNG UP ON YOU.
I'M CRUSHING THEIR ORTHODOXY. WHAT DO YOU EXPECT?
THIS LETTER YOU SENT TO STEPHEN JAY GOULD SURE CAME BACK IN A HURRY.
I Believe

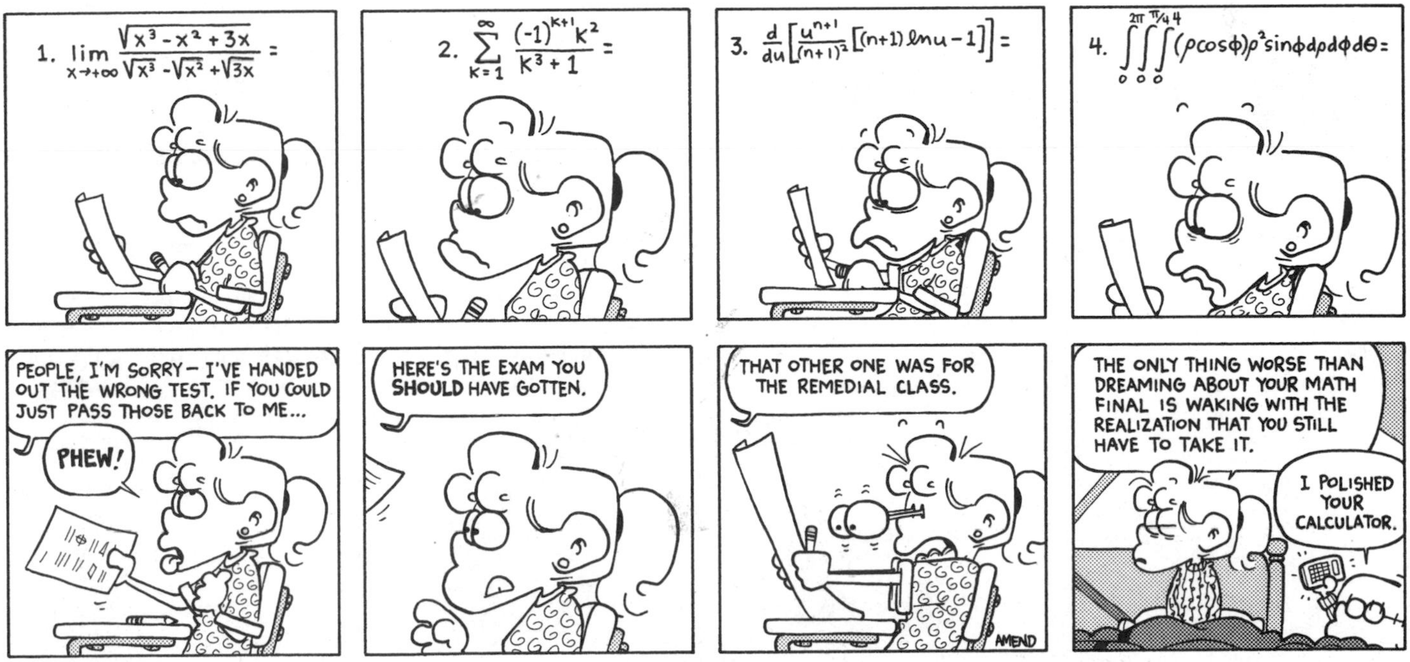
1. $\lim_{x \to +\infty} \frac{\sqrt{x^3 - x^2 + 3x}}{\sqrt{x^3} - \sqrt{x^2} + \sqrt{3x}} =$
2. $\sum_{k=1}^{\infty} \frac{(-1)^{k+1} k^2}{k^3 + 1} =$
3. $\frac{d}{du}\left[\frac{u^{n+1}}{(n+1)^2}\left[(n+1)\ln u - 1\right]\right] =$
4. $\int_0^{2\pi}\int_0^{\pi/4}\int_0^{4} (\rho\cos\phi)\rho^2 \sin\phi \, d\rho \, d\phi \, d\theta =$
PEOPLE, I'M SORRY— I'VE HANDED OUT THE WRONG TEST. IF YOU COULD JUST PASS THOSE BACK TO ME...
PHEW!
HERE'S THE EXAM YOU **SHOULD** HAVE GOTTEN.
THAT OTHER ONE WAS FOR THE REMEDIAL CLASS.
AMEND
THE ONLY THING WORSE THAN DREAMING ABOUT YOUR MATH FINAL IS WAKING WITH THE REALIZATION THAT YOU STILL HAVE TO TAKE IT.
I POLISHED YOUR CALCULATOR.

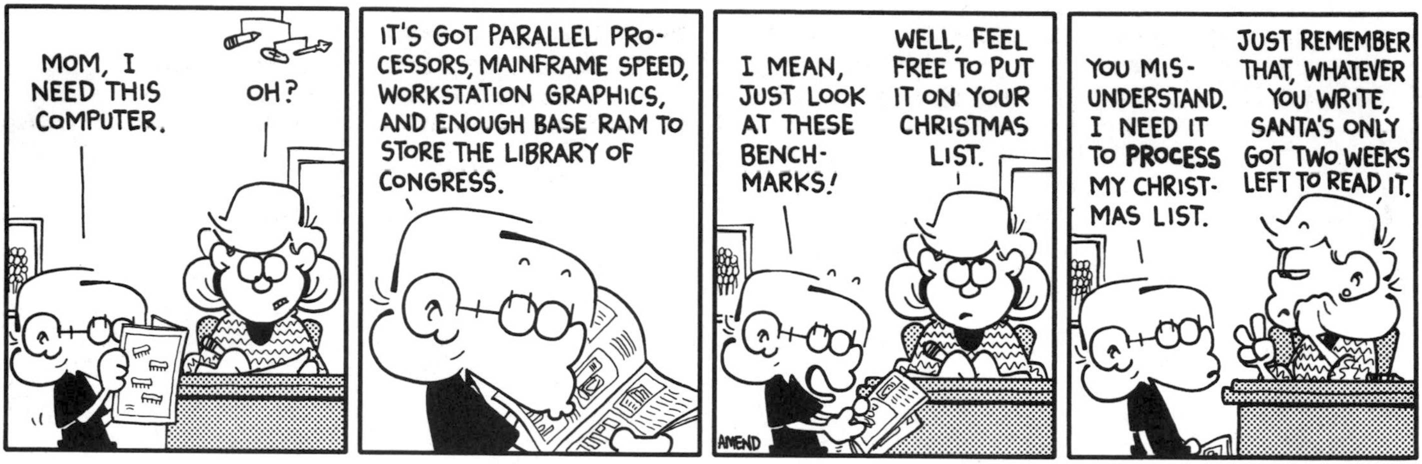
MOM, I NEED THIS COMPUTER.
OH?
IT'S GOT PARALLEL PROCESSORS, MAINFRAME SPEED, WORKSTATION GRAPHICS, AND ENOUGH BASE RAM TO STORE THE LIBRARY OF CONGRESS.
I MEAN, JUST LOOK AT THESE BENCHMARKS!
WELL, FEEL FREE TO PUT IT ON YOUR CHRISTMAS LIST.
AMEND
YOU MISUNDERSTAND. I NEED IT TO **PROCESS** MY CHRISTMAS LIST.
JUST REMEMBER THAT, WHATEVER YOU WRITE, SANTA'S ONLY GOT TWO WEEKS LEFT TO READ IT.

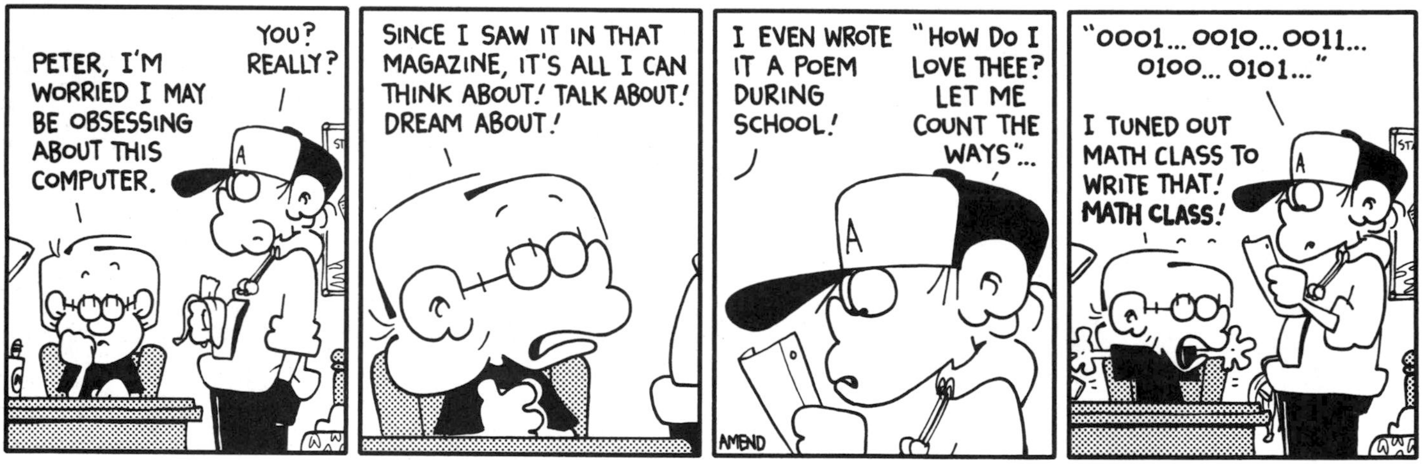
PETER, I'M WORRIED I MAY BE OBSESSING ABOUT THIS COMPUTER.
YOU? REALLY?
SINCE I SAW IT IN THAT MAGAZINE, IT'S ALL I CAN THINK ABOUT! TALK ABOUT! DREAM ABOUT!
I EVEN WROTE IT A POEM DURING SCHOOL!
"HOW DO I LOVE THEE? LET ME COUNT THE WAYS"...
AMEND
"0001... 0010... 0011... 0100... 0101..."
I TUNED OUT MATH CLASS TO WRITE THAT! **MATH CLASS!**

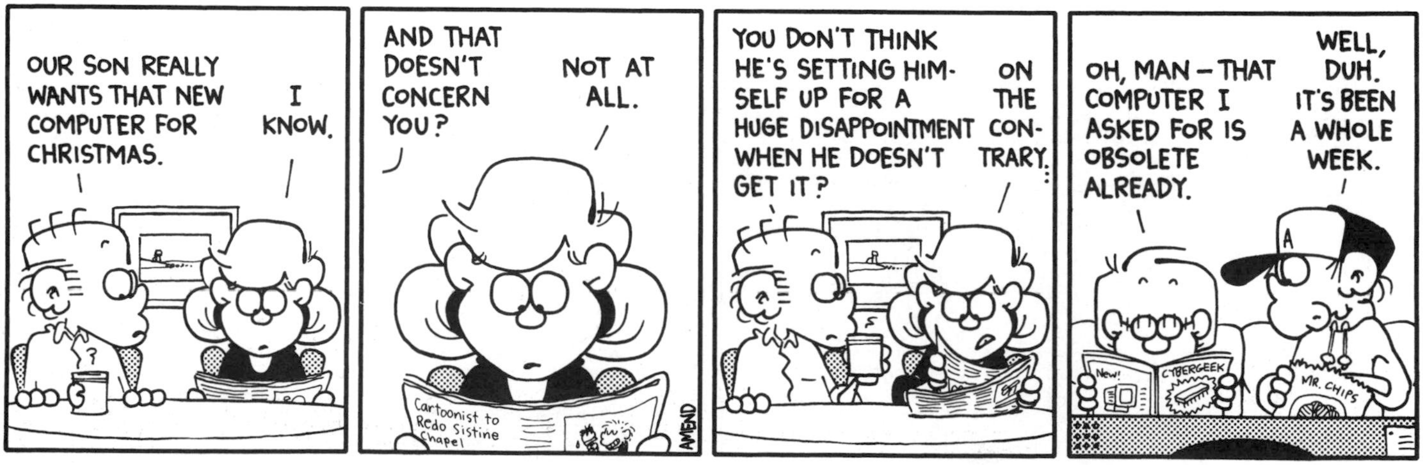
OUR SON REALLY WANTS THAT NEW COMPUTER FOR CHRISTMAS.
I KNOW.
AND THAT DOESN'T CONCERN YOU?
NOT AT ALL.
Cartoonist to Redo Sistine Chapel
AMEND
YOU DON'T THINK HE'S SETTING HIMSELF UP FOR A HUGE DISAPPOINTMENT WHEN HE DOESN'T GET IT?
ON THE CONTRARY.
OH, MAN – THAT COMPUTER I ASKED FOR IS OBSOLETE ALREADY.
WELL, DUH. IT'S BEEN A WHOLE WEEK.
New!
CYBERGEEK
MR. CHIPS

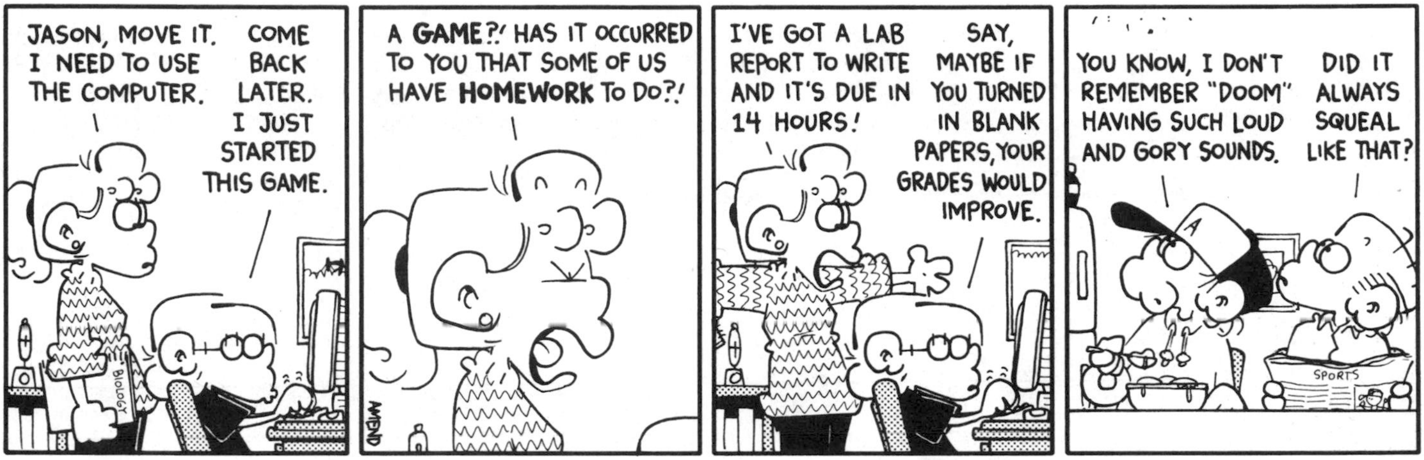
JASON, MOVE IT. I NEED TO USE THE COMPUTER.
COME BACK LATER. I JUST STARTED THIS GAME.
A GAME?! HAS IT OCCURRED TO YOU THAT SOME OF US HAVE HOMEWORK TO DO?!
I'VE GOT A LAB REPORT TO WRITE AND IT'S DUE IN 14 HOURS!
SAY, MAYBE IF YOU TURNED IN BLANK PAPERS, YOUR GRADES WOULD IMPROVE.
YOU KNOW, I DON'T REMEMBER "DOOM" HAVING SUCH LOUD AND GORY SOUNDS.
DID IT ALWAYS SQUEAL LIKE THAT?
SPORTS

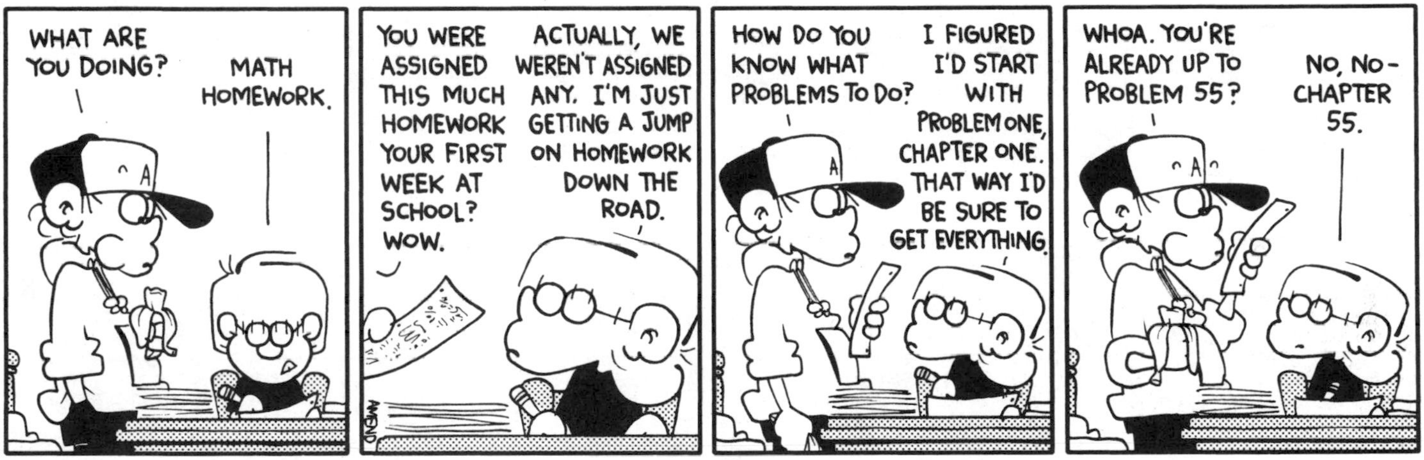
WHAT ARE YOU DOING?
MATH HOMEWORK.
YOU WERE ASSIGNED THIS MUCH HOMEWORK YOUR FIRST WEEK AT SCHOOL? WOW.
ACTUALLY, WE WEREN'T ASSIGNED ANY. I'M JUST GETTING A JUMP ON HOMEWORK DOWN THE ROAD.
HOW DO YOU KNOW WHAT PROBLEMS TO DO?
I FIGURED I'D START WITH PROBLEM ONE, CHAPTER ONE. THAT WAY I'D BE SURE TO GET EVERYTHING.
WHOA. YOU'RE ALREADY UP TO PROBLEM 55?
NO, NO-CHAPTER 55.

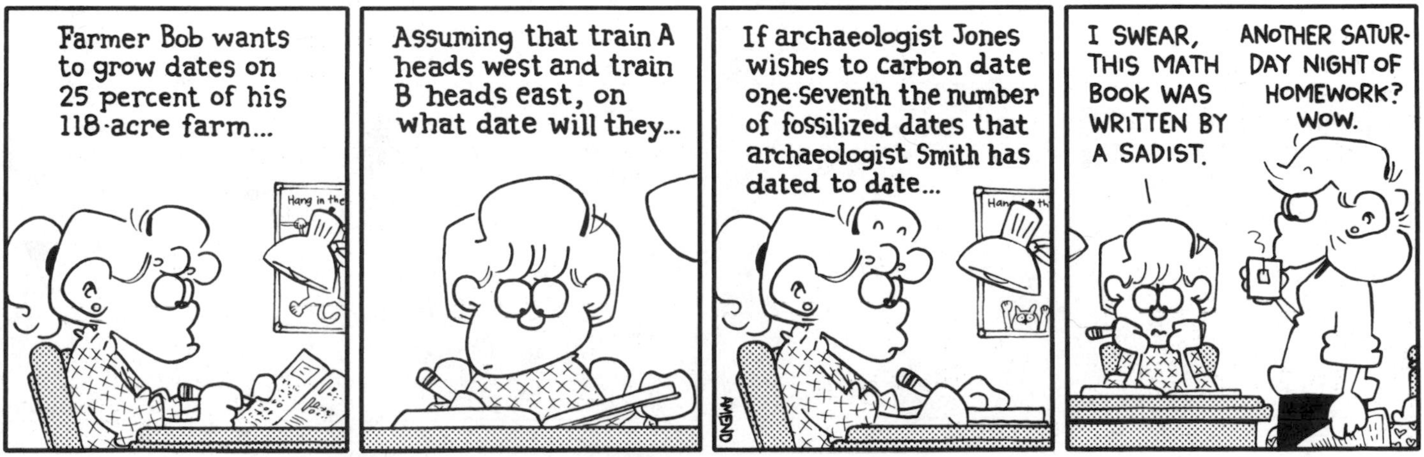
Farmer Bob wants to grow dates on 25 percent of his 118-acre farm...
Assuming that train A heads west and train B heads east, on what date will they...
If archaeologist Jones wishes to carbon date one-seventh the number of fossilized dates that archaeologist Smith has dated to date...
I SWEAR, THIS MATH BOOK WAS WRITTEN BY A SADIST.
ANOTHER SATURDAY NIGHT OF HOMEWORK? WOW.

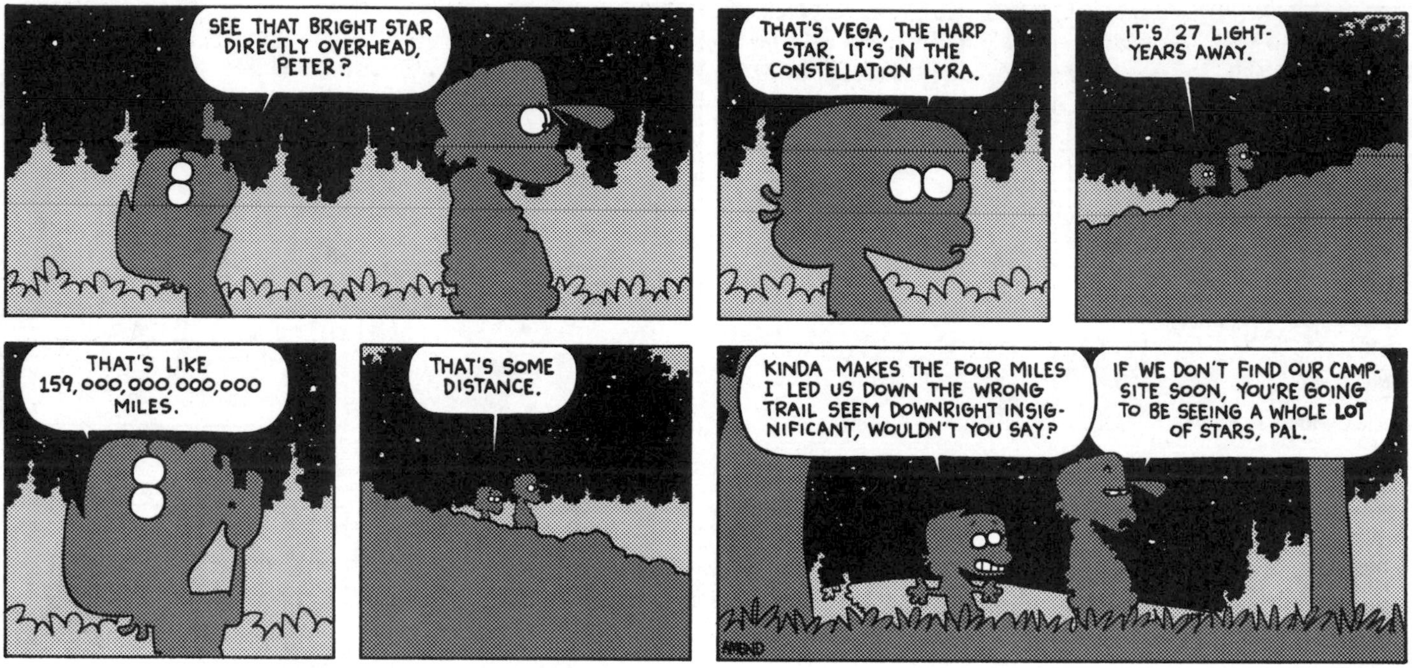
SEE THAT BRIGHT STAR DIRECTLY OVERHEAD, PETER?
THAT'S VEGA, THE HARP STAR. IT'S IN THE CONSTELLATION LYRA.
IT'S 27 LIGHT-YEARS AWAY.
THAT'S LIKE 159,000,000,000,000 MILES.
THAT'S SOME DISTANCE.
KINDA MAKES THE FOUR MILES I LED US DOWN THE WRONG TRAIL SEEM DOWNRIGHT INSIGNIFICANT, WOULDN'T YOU SAY?
IF WE DON'T FIND OUR CAMPSITE SOON, YOU'RE GOING TO BE SEEING A WHOLE LOT OF STARS, PAL.
AMEND

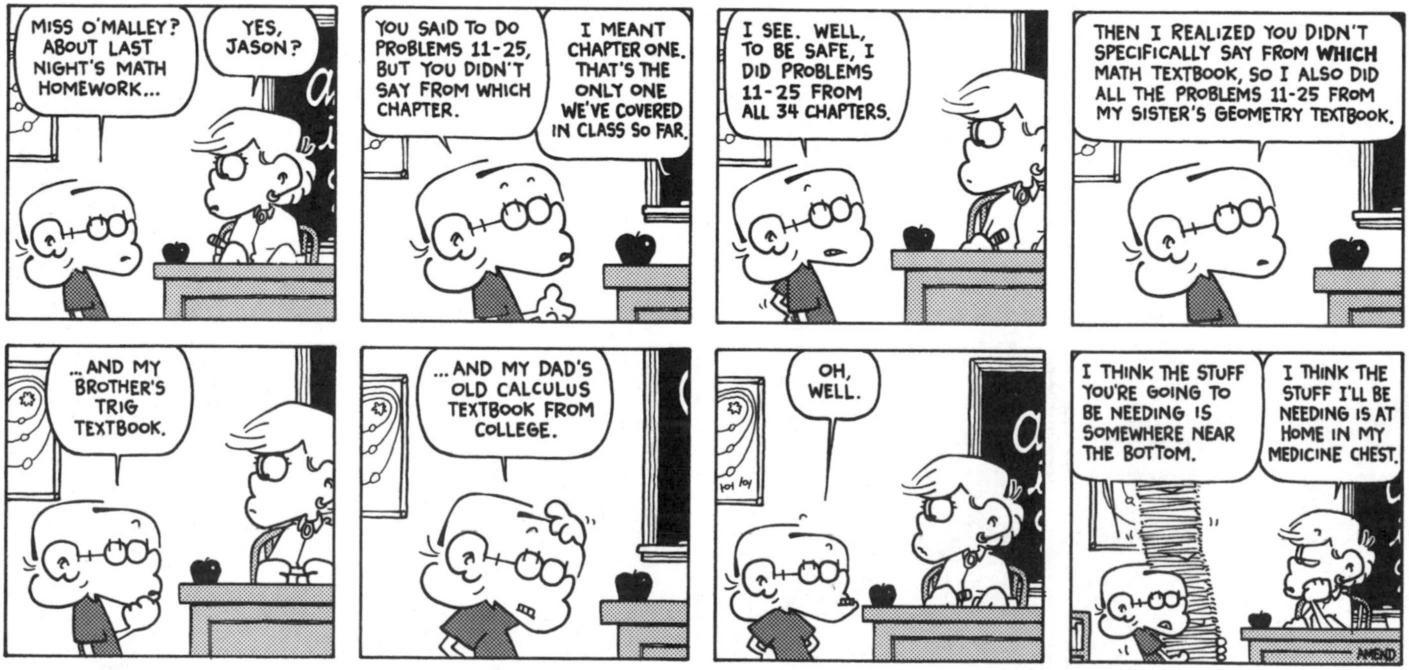
MISS O'MALLEY? ABOUT LAST NIGHT'S MATH HOMEWORK...
YES, JASON?
YOU SAID TO DO PROBLEMS 11-25, BUT YOU DIDN'T SAY FROM WHICH CHAPTER.
I MEANT CHAPTER ONE. THAT'S THE ONLY ONE WE'VE COVERED IN CLASS SO FAR.
I SEE. WELL, TO BE SAFE, I DID PROBLEMS 11-25 FROM ALL 34 CHAPTERS.
THEN I REALIZED YOU DIDN'T SPECIFICALLY SAY FROM WHICH MATH TEXTBOOK, SO I ALSO DID ALL THE PROBLEMS 11-25 FROM MY SISTER'S GEOMETRY TEXTBOOK.
...AND MY BROTHER'S TRIG TEXTBOOK.
...AND MY DAD'S OLD CALCULUS TEXTBOOK FROM COLLEGE.
OH, WELL.
I THINK THE STUFF YOU'RE GOING TO BE NEEDING IS SOMEWHERE NEAR THE BOTTOM.
I THINK THE STUFF I'LL BE NEEDING IS AT HOME IN MY MEDICINE CHEST.
AMEND

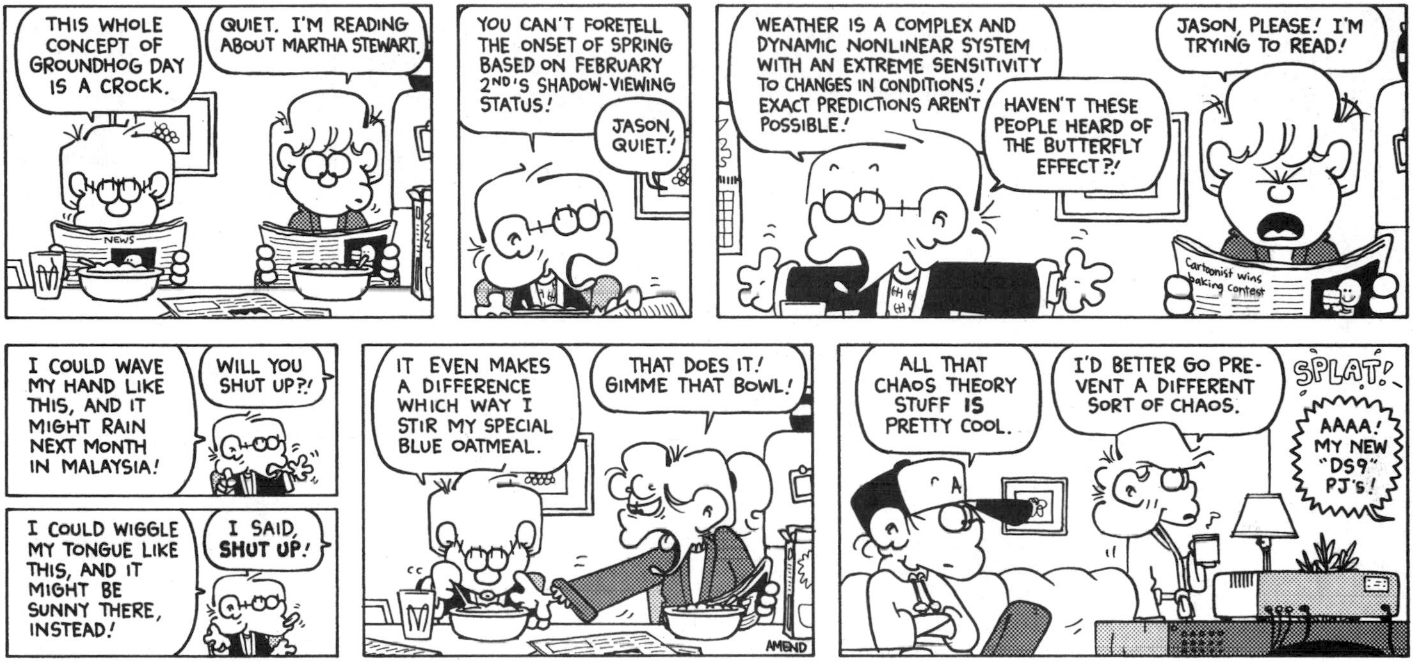
THIS WHOLE CONCEPT OF GROUNDHOG DAY IS A CROCK.
QUIET. I'M READING ABOUT MARTHA STEWART.
NEWS
YOU CAN'T FORETELL THE ONSET OF SPRING BASED ON FEBRUARY 2ND'S SHADOW-VIEWING STATUS!
JASON, QUIET!
WEATHER IS A COMPLEX AND DYNAMIC NONLINEAR SYSTEM WITH AN EXTREME SENSITIVITY TO CHANGES IN CONDITIONS! EXACT PREDICTIONS AREN'T POSSIBLE!
HAVEN'T THESE PEOPLE HEARD OF THE BUTTERFLY EFFECT?!
JASON, PLEASE! I'M TRYING TO READ!
Cartoonist wins baking contest
I COULD WAVE MY HAND LIKE THIS, AND IT MIGHT RAIN NEXT MONTH IN MALAYSIA!
WILL YOU SHUT UP?!
I COULD WIGGLE MY TONGUE LIKE THIS, AND IT MIGHT BE SUNNY THERE, INSTEAD!
I SAID, **SHUT UP**!
IT EVEN MAKES A DIFFERENCE WHICH WAY I STIR MY SPECIAL BLUE OATMEAL.
THAT DOES IT! GIMME THAT BOWL!
AMEND
ALL THAT CHAOS THEORY STUFF **IS** PRETTY COOL.
I'D BETTER GO PREVENT A DIFFERENT SORT OF CHAOS.
SPLAT!
AAAA! MY NEW "DS9" PJ'S!

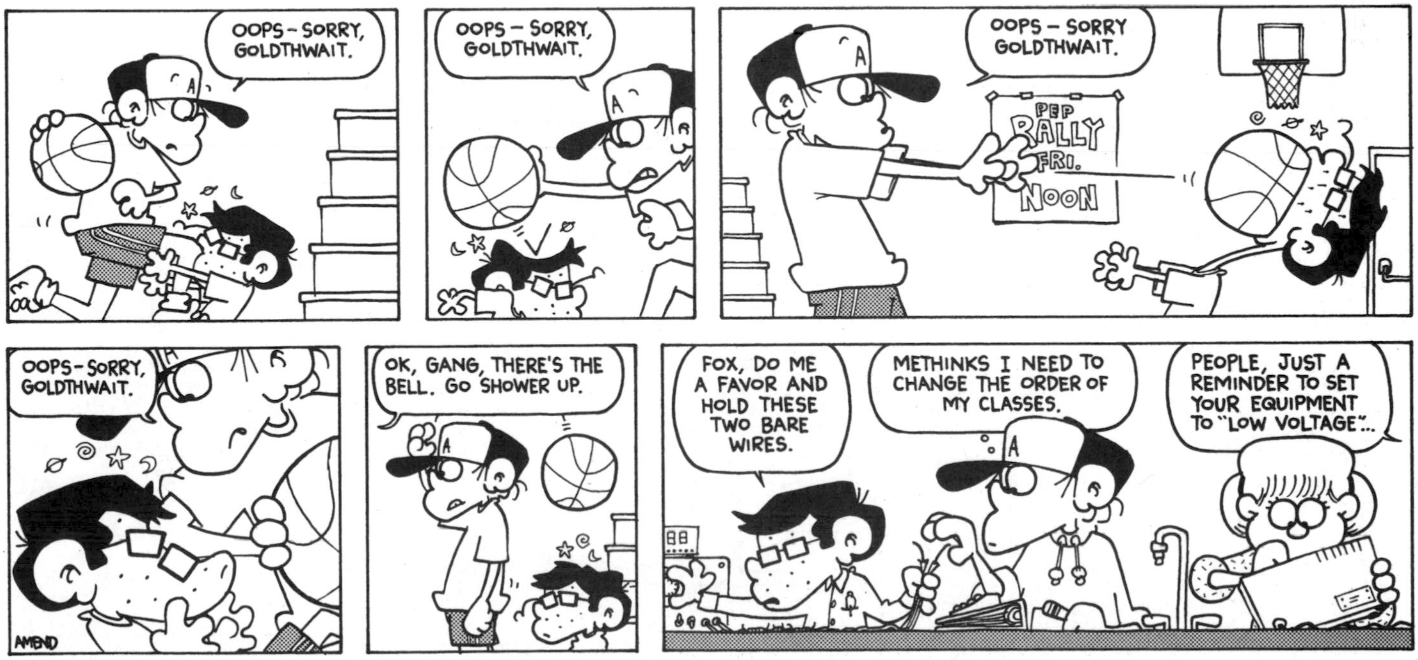
OOPS-SORRY, GOLDTHWAIT.
OOPS – SORRY, GOLDTHWAIT.
OOPS – SORRY GOLDTHWAIT.
PEP RALLY FRI. NOON
OOPS-SORRY, GOLDTHWAIT.
AMEND
OK, GANG, THERE'S THE BELL. GO SHOWER UP.
FOX, DO ME A FAVOR AND HOLD THESE TWO BARE WIRES.
METHINKS I NEED TO CHANGE THE ORDER OF MY CLASSES.
PEOPLE, JUST A REMINDER TO SET YOUR EQUIPMENT TO "LOW VOLTAGE"...

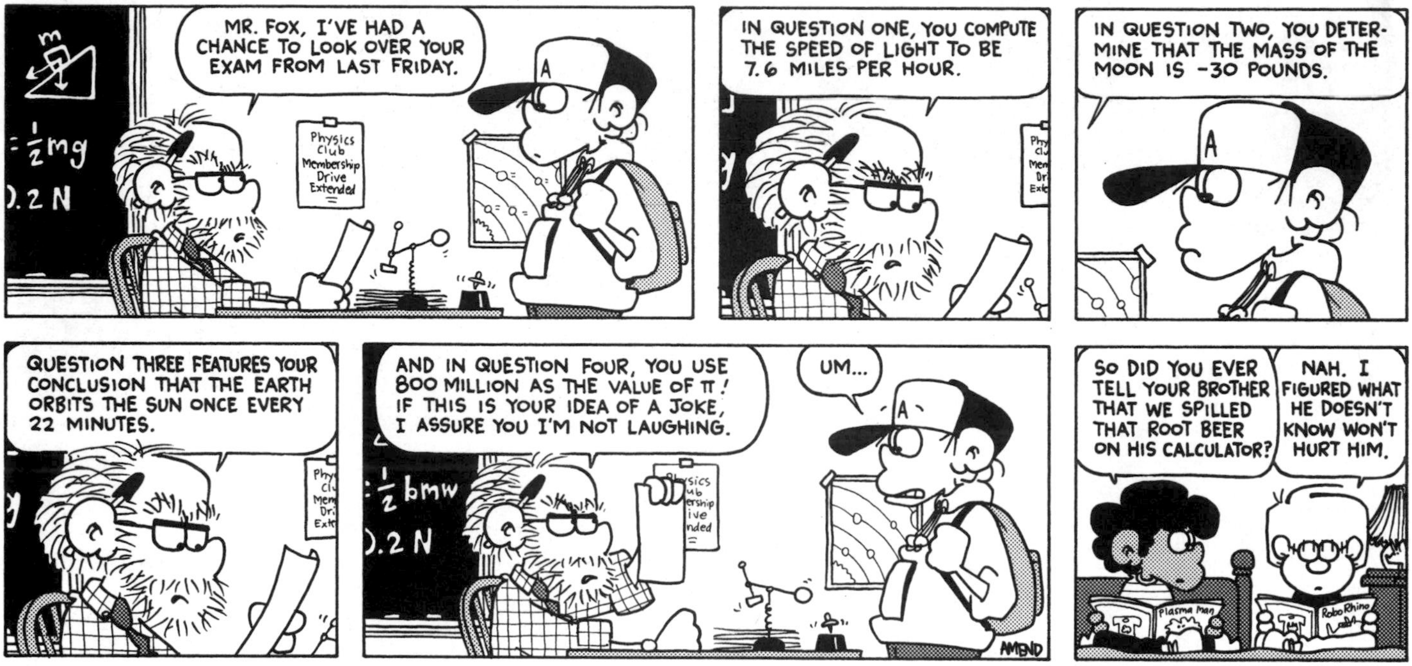
MR. FOX, I'VE HAD A CHANCE TO LOOK OVER YOUR EXAM FROM LAST FRIDAY.
Physics Club Membership Drive Extended
IN QUESTION ONE, YOU COMPUTE THE SPEED OF LIGHT TO BE 7.6 MILES PER HOUR.
IN QUESTION TWO, YOU DETERMINE THAT THE MASS OF THE MOON IS -30 POUNDS.
QUESTION THREE FEATURES YOUR CONCLUSION THAT THE EARTH ORBITS THE SUN ONCE EVERY 22 MINUTES.
AND IN QUESTION FOUR, YOU USE 800 MILLION AS THE VALUE OF π! IF THIS IS YOUR IDEA OF A JOKE, I ASSURE YOU I'M NOT LAUGHING.
UM...
AMEND
SO DID YOU EVER TELL YOUR BROTHER THAT WE SPILLED THAT ROOT BEER ON HIS CALCULATOR?
NAH. I FIGURED WHAT HE DOESN'T KNOW WON'T HURT HIM.
Plasma Man
Robo Rhino

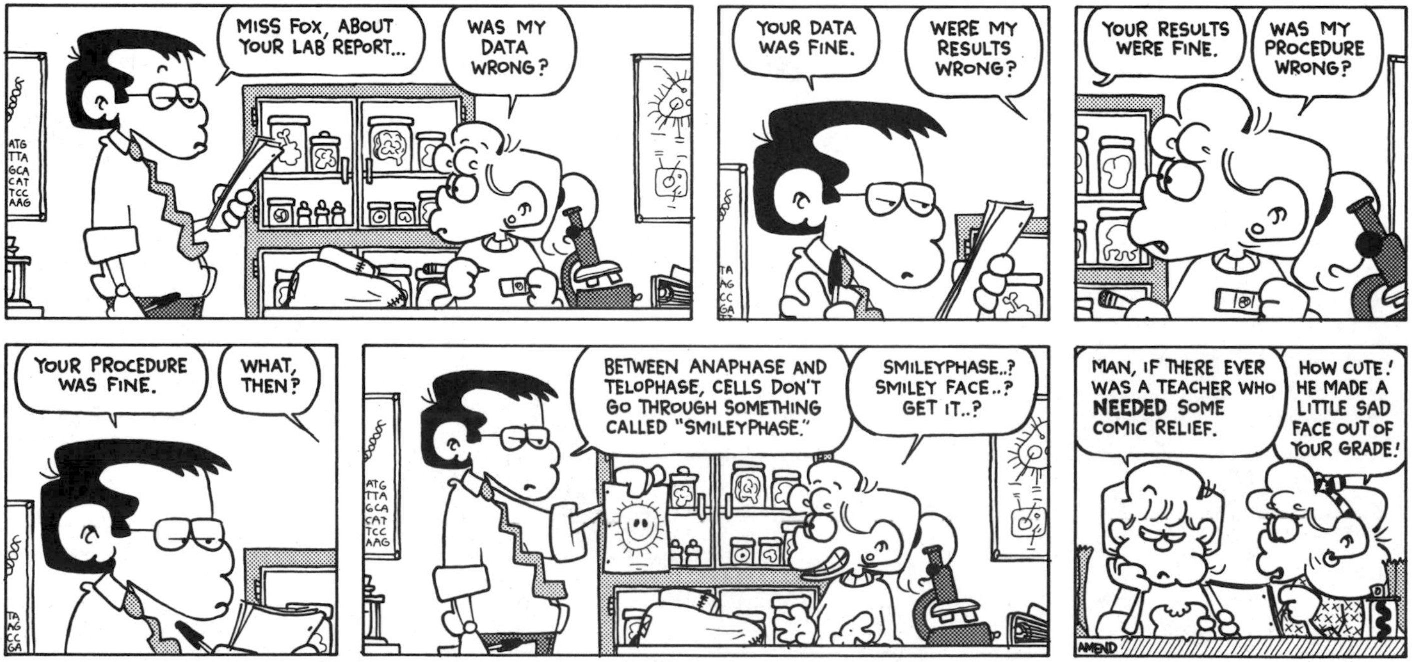
MISS FOX, ABOUT YOUR LAB REPORT...
WAS MY DATA WRONG?
YOUR DATA WAS FINE.
WERE MY RESULTS WRONG?
YOUR RESULTS WERE FINE.
WAS MY PROCEDURE WRONG?
YOUR PROCEDURE WAS FINE.
WHAT, THEN?
BETWEEN ANAPHASE AND TELOPHASE, CELLS DON'T GO THROUGH SOMETHING CALLED "SMILEYPHASE."
SMILEYPHASE..? SMILEY FACE..? GET IT..?
MAN, IF THERE EVER WAS A TEACHER WHO NEEDED SOME COMIC RELIEF.
HOW CUTE! HE MADE A LITTLE SAD FACE OUT OF YOUR GRADE!
AMEND

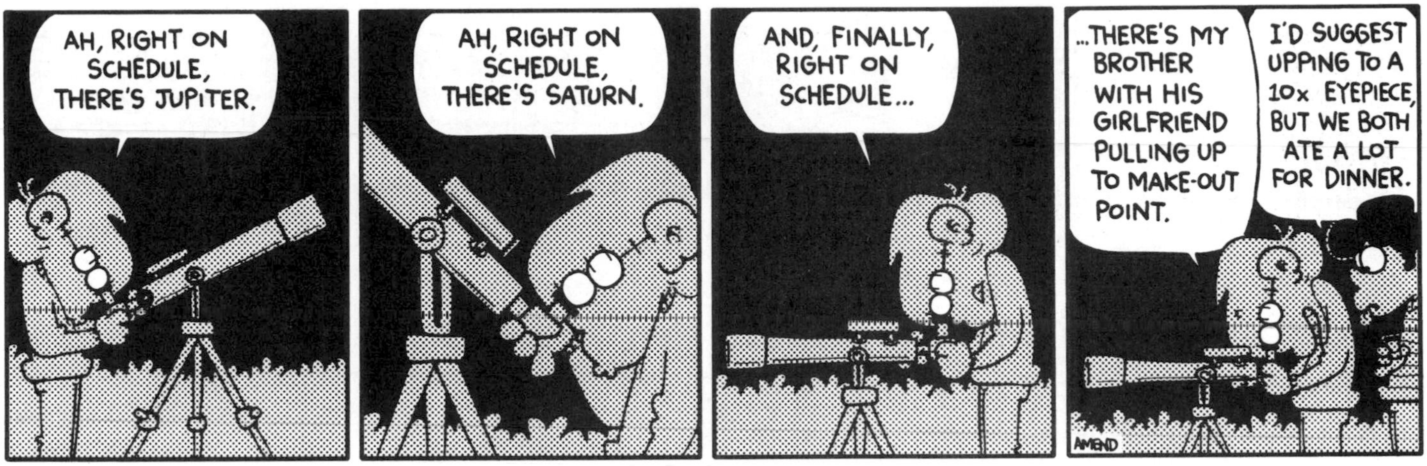
AH, RIGHT ON SCHEDULE, THERE'S JUPITER.
AH, RIGHT ON SCHEDULE, THERE'S SATURN.
AND, FINALLY, RIGHT ON SCHEDULE...
...THERE'S MY BROTHER WITH HIS GIRLFRIEND PULLING UP TO MAKE-OUT POINT.
I'D SUGGEST UPPING TO A 10x EYEPIECE, BUT WE BOTH ATE A LOT FOR DINNER.
AMEND

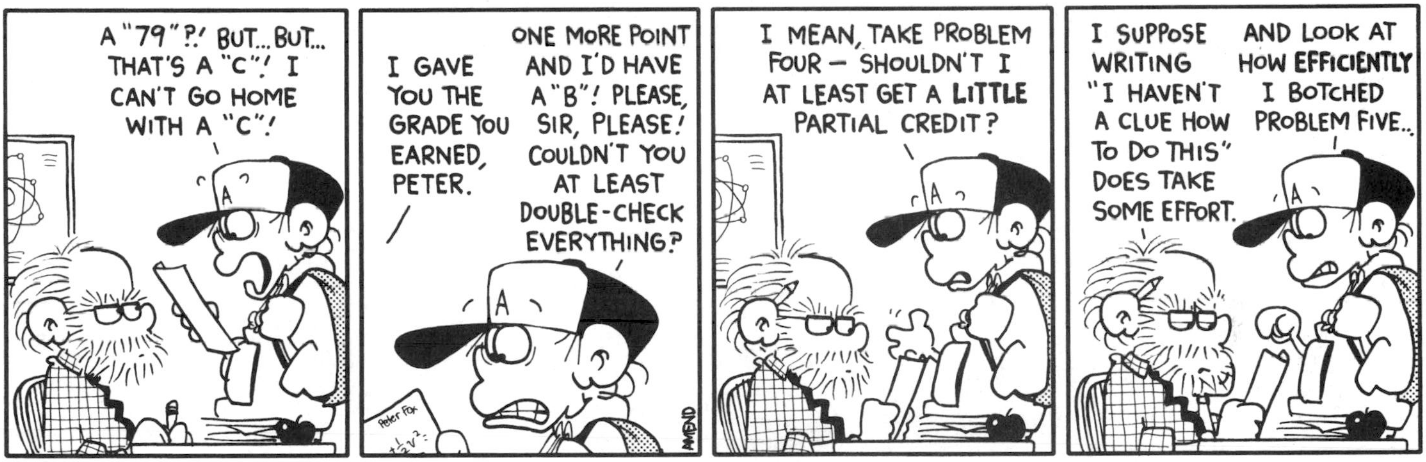
A "79"?! BUT... BUT... THAT'S A "C"! I CAN'T GO HOME WITH A "C"!
I GAVE YOU THE GRADE YOU EARNED, PETER.
ONE MORE POINT AND I'D HAVE A "B"! PLEASE, SIR, PLEASE! COULDN'T YOU AT LEAST DOUBLE-CHECK EVERYTHING?
Peter Fox
AMEND
I MEAN, TAKE PROBLEM FOUR — SHOULDN'T I AT LEAST GET A LITTLE PARTIAL CREDIT?
I SUPPOSE WRITING "I HAVEN'T A CLUE HOW TO DO THIS" DOES TAKE SOME EFFORT.
AND LOOK AT HOW EFFICIENTLY I BOTCHED PROBLEM FIVE...

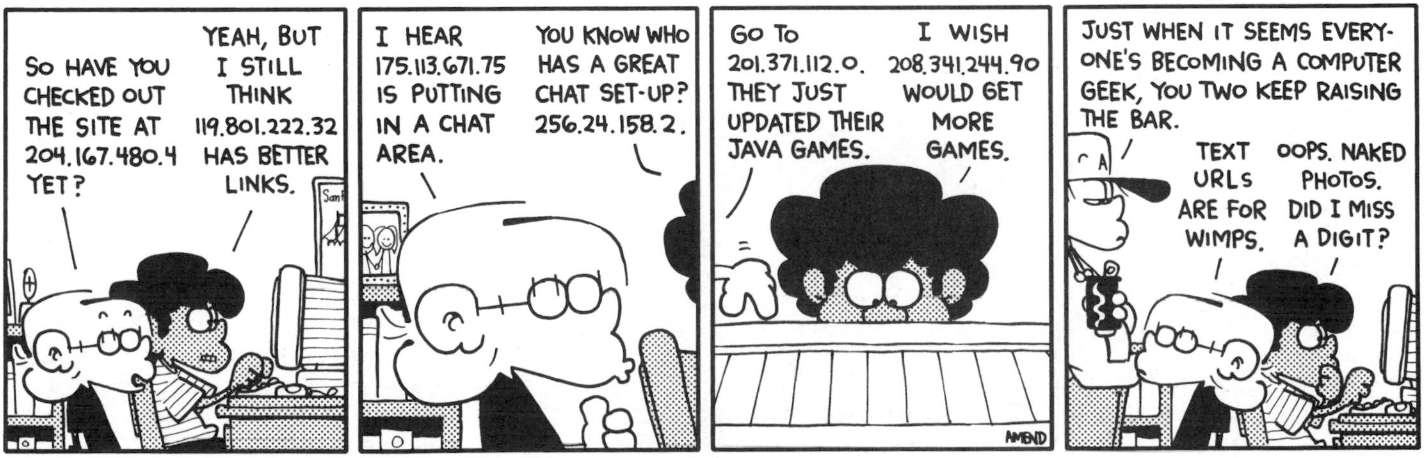
SO HAVE YOU CHECKED OUT THE SITE AT 204.167.480.4 YET?
YEAH, BUT I STILL THINK 119.801.222.32 HAS BETTER LINKS.
I HEAR 175.113.671.75 IS PUTTING IN A CHAT AREA.
YOU KNOW WHO HAS A GREAT CHAT SET-UP? 256.24.158.2.
GO TO 201.371.112.0. THEY JUST UPDATED THEIR JAVA GAMES.
I WISH 208.341.244.90 WOULD GET MORE GAMES.
AMEND
JUST WHEN IT SEEMS EVERYONE'S BECOMING A COMPUTER GEEK, YOU TWO KEEP RAISING THE BAR.
TEXT URLS ARE FOR WIMPS.
OOPS. NAKED PHOTOS. DID I MISS A DIGIT?

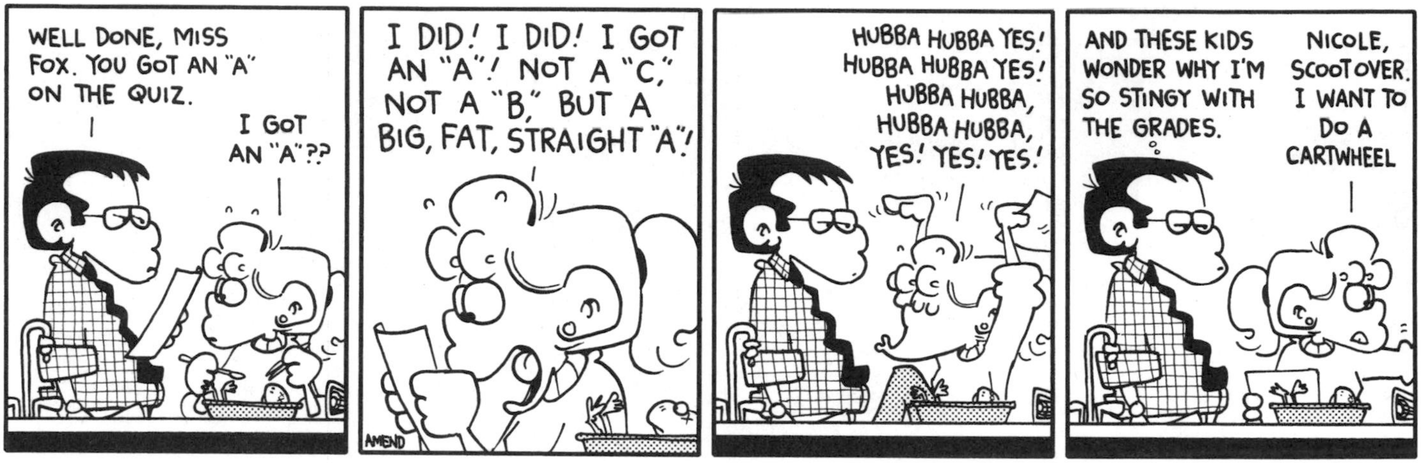
WELL DONE, MISS FOX. YOU GOT AN "A" ON THE QUIZ.
I GOT AN "A"??
I DID! I DID! I GOT AN "A"! NOT A "C," NOT A "B," BUT A BIG, FAT, STRAIGHT "A"!
AMEND
HUBBA HUBBA YES! HUBBA HUBBA YES! HUBBA HUBBA, HUBBA HUBBA, YES! YES! YES!
AND THESE KIDS WONDER WHY I'M SO STINGY WITH THE GRADES.
NICOLE, SCOOT OVER. I WANT TO DO A CARTWHEEL

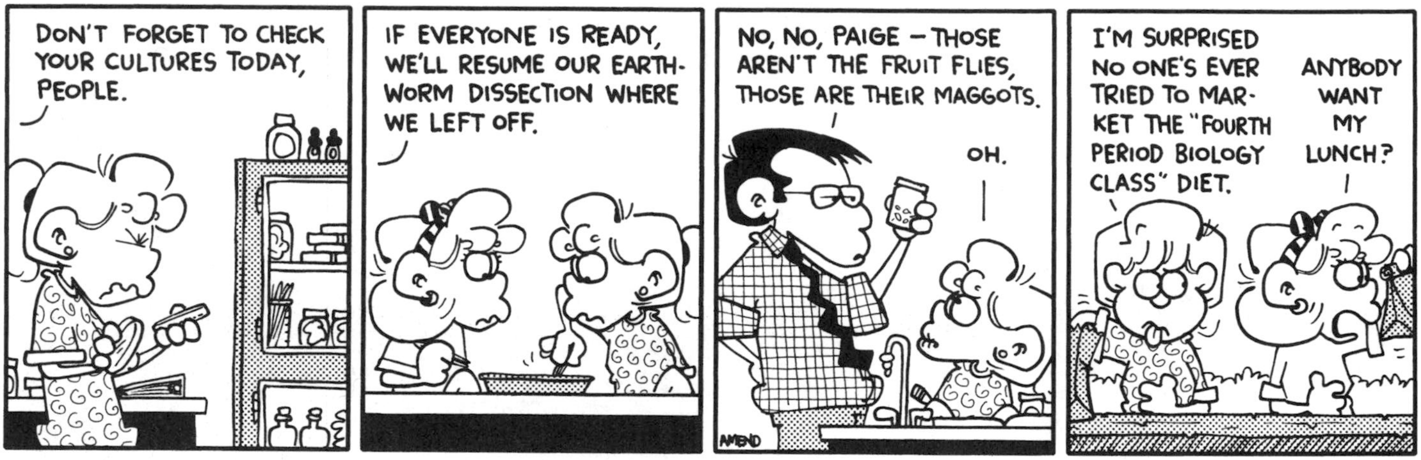
DON'T FORGET TO CHECK YOUR CULTURES TODAY, PEOPLE.
IF EVERYONE IS READY, WE'LL RESUME OUR EARTHWORM DISSECTION WHERE WE LEFT OFF.
NO, NO, PAIGE – THOSE AREN'T THE FRUIT FLIES, THOSE ARE THEIR MAGGOTS.
OH.
AMEND
I'M SURPRISED NO ONE'S EVER TRIED TO MARKET THE "FOURTH PERIOD BIOLOGY CLASS" DIET.
ANYBODY WANT MY LUNCH?

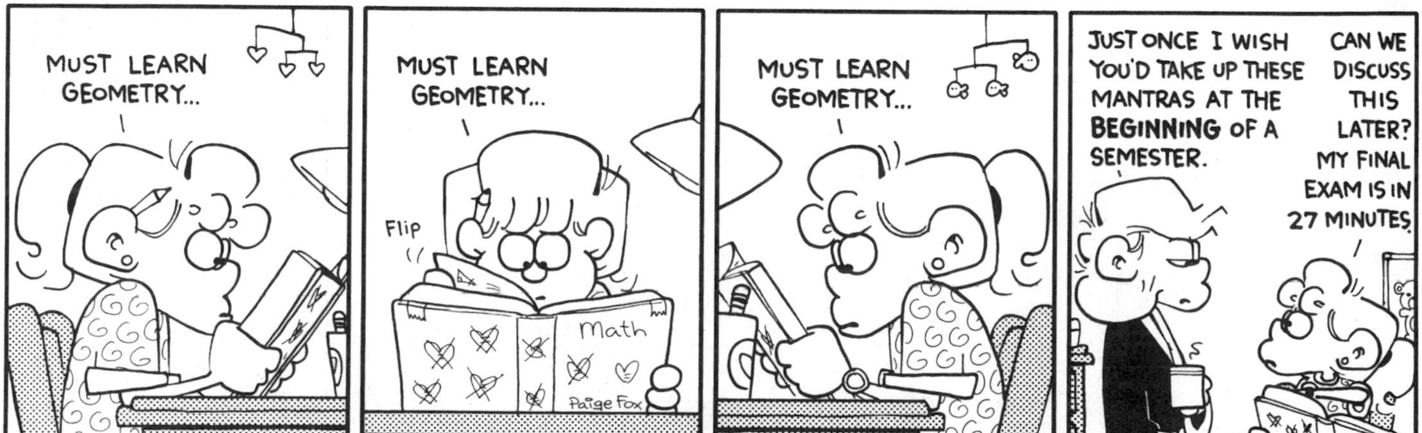
MUST LEARN GEOMETRY...
MUST LEARN GEOMETRY...
Flip
Math
Paige Fox
MUST LEARN GEOMETRY...
AMEND
JUST ONCE I WISH YOU'D TAKE UP THESE MANTRAS AT THE **BEGINNING** OF A SEMESTER.
CAN WE DISCUSS THIS LATER? MY FINAL EXAM IS IN 27 MINUTES.

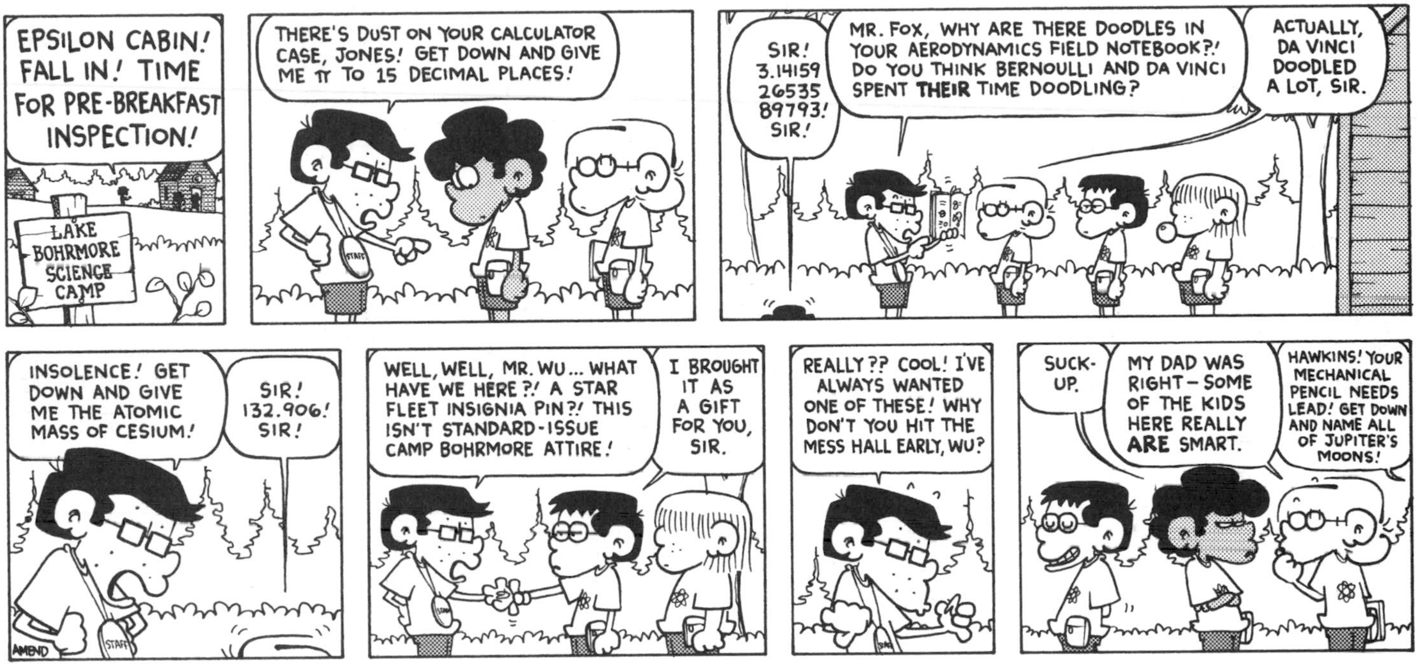
EPSILON CABIN! FALL IN! TIME FOR PRE-BREAKFAST INSPECTION!
LAKE BOHRMORE SCIENCE CAMP
THERE'S DUST ON YOUR CALCULATOR CASE, JONES! GET DOWN AND GIVE ME π TO 15 DECIMAL PLACES!
STAFF
SIR! 3.14159 26535 89793! SIR!
MR. FOX, WHY ARE THERE DOODLES IN YOUR AERODYNAMICS FIELD NOTEBOOK?! DO YOU THINK BERNOULLI AND DA VINCI SPENT THEIR TIME DOODLING?
ACTUALLY, DA VINCI DOODLED A LOT, SIR.
INSOLENCE! GET DOWN AND GIVE ME THE ATOMIC MASS OF CESIUM!
SIR! 132.906! SIR!
AMEND
STAFF
WELL, WELL, MR. WU... WHAT HAVE WE HERE?! A STAR FLEET INSIGNIA PIN?! THIS ISN'T STANDARD-ISSUE CAMP BOHRMORE ATTIRE!
I BROUGHT IT AS A GIFT FOR YOU, SIR.
REALLY?? COOL! I'VE ALWAYS WANTED ONE OF THESE! WHY DON'T YOU HIT THE MESS HALL EARLY, WU?
SUCK-UP.
MY DAD WAS RIGHT—SOME OF THE KIDS HERE REALLY ARE SMART.
HAWKINS! YOUR MECHANICAL PENCIL NEEDS LEAD! GET DOWN AND NAME ALL OF JUPITER'S MOONS!

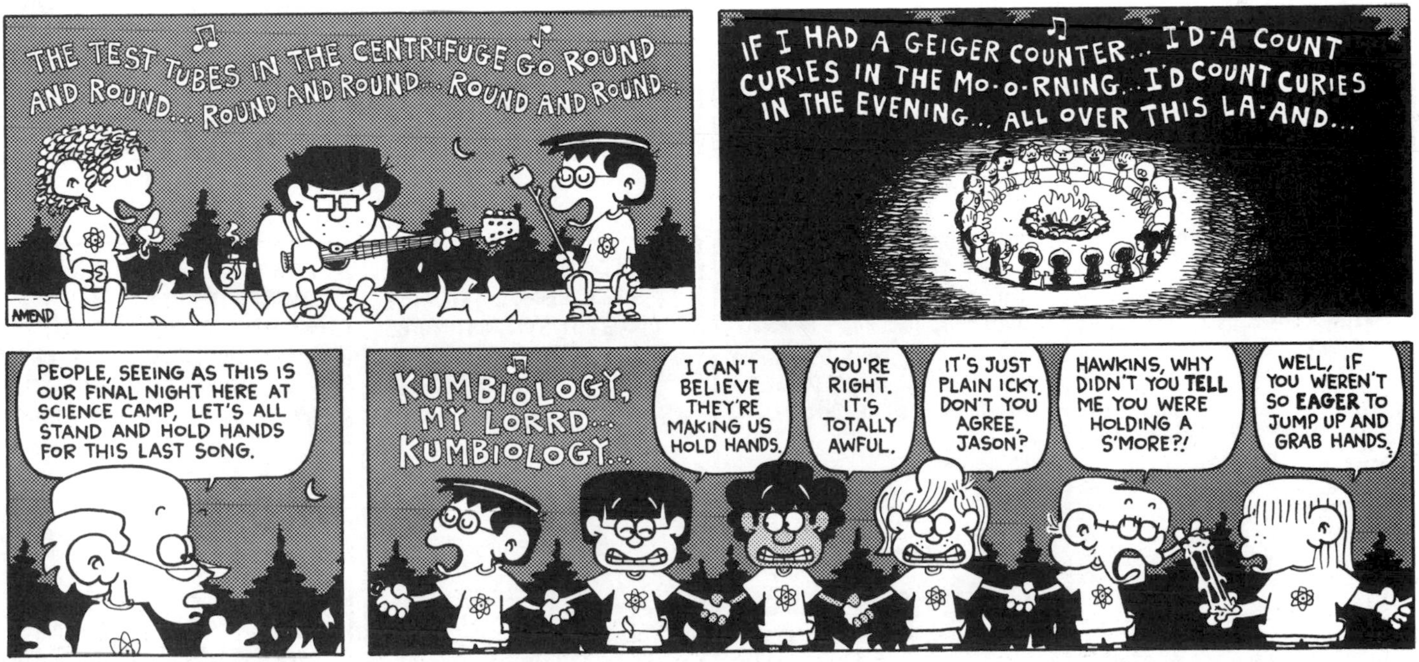
THE TEST TUBES IN THE CENTRIFUGE GO ROUND AND ROUND... ROUND AND ROUND... ROUND AND ROUND...
AMEND
IF I HAD A GEIGER COUNTER... I'D-A COUNT CURIES IN THE MO-O-RNING... I'D COUNT CURIES IN THE EVENING... ALL OVER THIS LA-AND...
PEOPLE, SEEING AS THIS IS OUR FINAL NIGHT HERE AT SCIENCE CAMP, LET'S ALL STAND AND HOLD HANDS FOR THIS LAST SONG.
KUMBIOLOGY, MY LORRD... KUMBIOLOGY...
I CAN'T BELIEVE THEY'RE MAKING US HOLD HANDS.
YOU'RE RIGHT. IT'S TOTALLY AWFUL.
IT'S JUST PLAIN ICKY. DON'T YOU AGREE, JASON?
HAWKINS, WHY DIDN'T YOU TELL ME YOU WERE HOLDING A S'MORE?!
WELL, IF YOU WEREN'T SO EAGER TO JUMP UP AND GRAB HANDS.

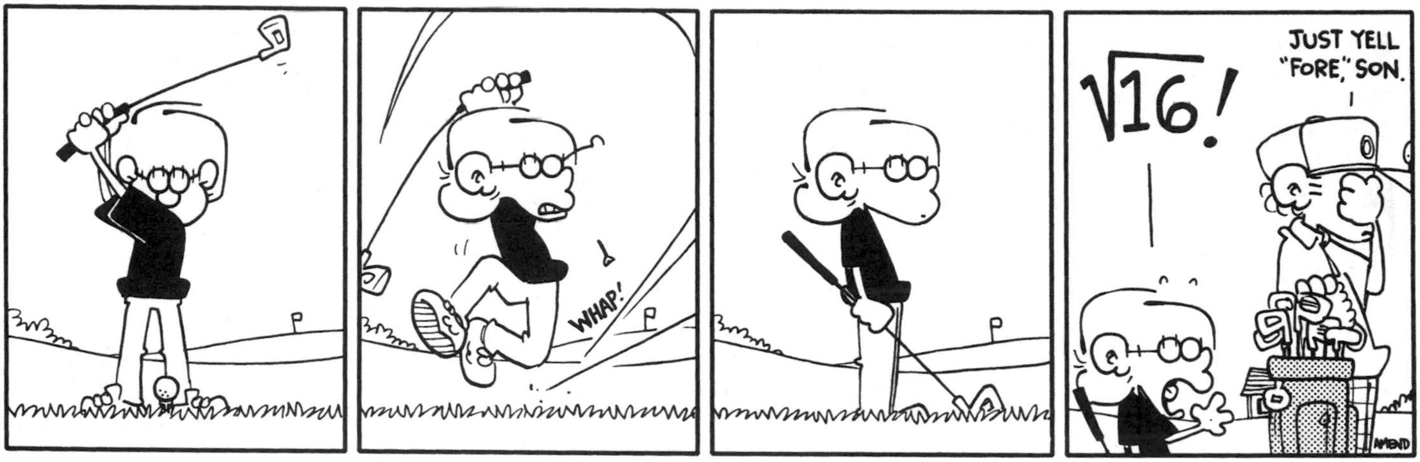
WHAP!
√16!
JUST YELL "FORE," SON.

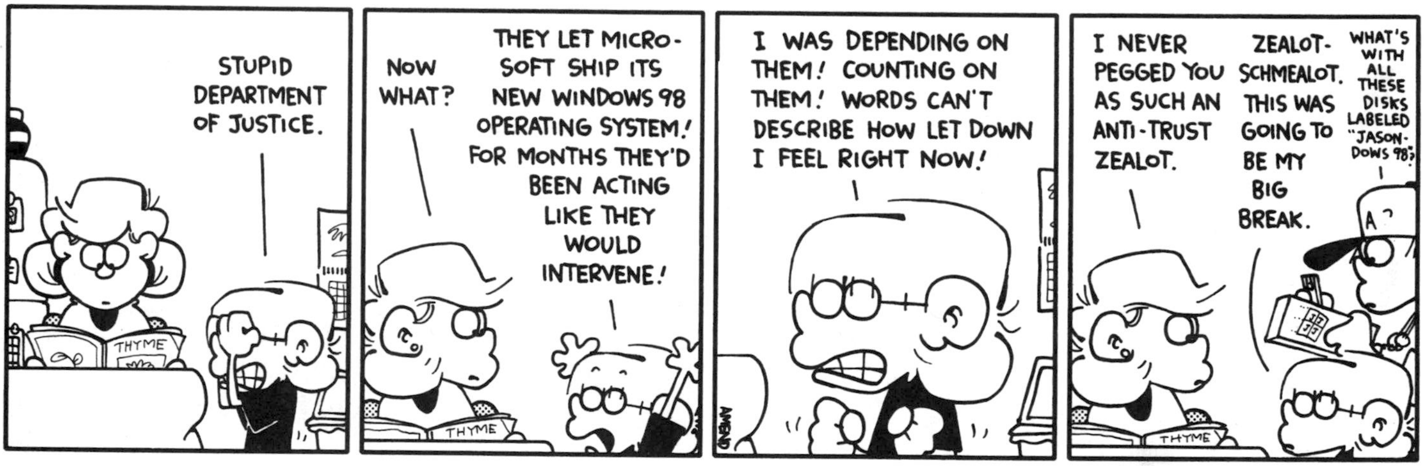
THYME
STUPID DEPARTMENT OF JUSTICE.
NOW WHAT?
THEY LET MICROSOFT SHIP ITS NEW WINDOWS 98 OPERATING SYSTEM! FOR MONTHS THEY'D BEEN ACTING LIKE THEY WOULD INTERVENE!
I WAS DEPENDING ON THEM! COUNTING ON THEM! WORDS CAN'T DESCRIBE HOW LET DOWN I FEEL RIGHT NOW!
I NEVER PEGGED YOU AS SUCH AN ANTI-TRUST ZEALOT.
ZEALOT-SCHMEALOT. THIS WAS GOING TO BE MY BIG BREAK.
WHAT'S WITH ALL THESE DISKS LABELED "JASON-DOWS 98"?

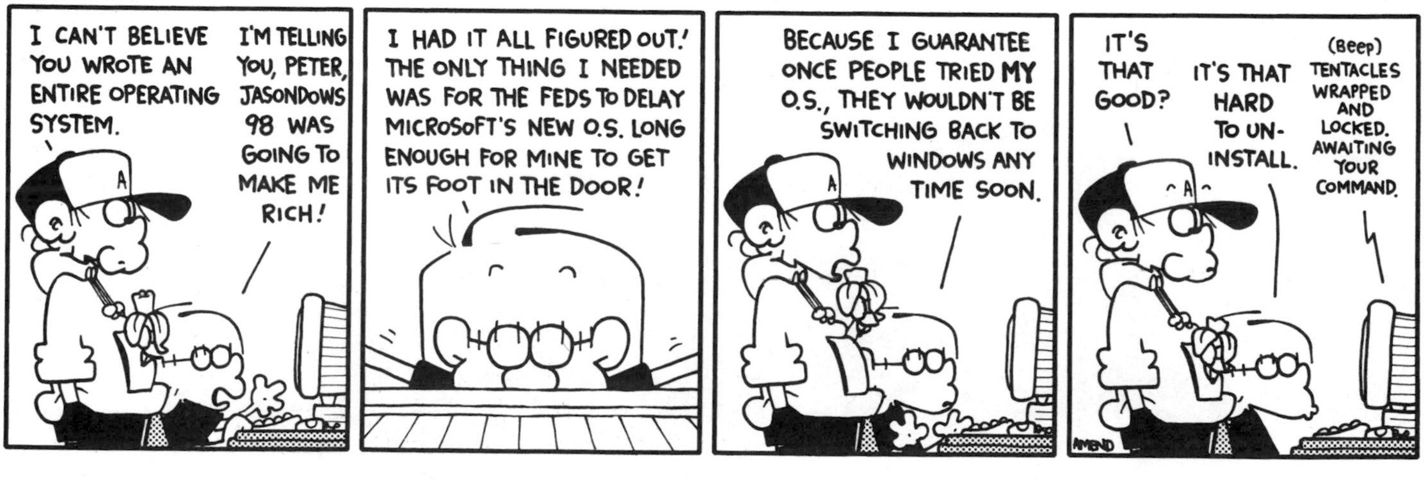
I CAN'T BELIEVE YOU WROTE AN ENTIRE OPERATING SYSTEM.
I'M TELLING YOU, PETER, JASONDOWS 98 WAS GOING TO MAKE ME RICH!
I HAD IT ALL FIGURED OUT! THE ONLY THING I NEEDED WAS FOR THE FEDS TO DELAY MICROSOFT'S NEW O.S. LONG ENOUGH FOR MINE TO GET ITS FOOT IN THE DOOR!
BECAUSE I GUARANTEE ONCE PEOPLE TRIED MY O.S., THEY WOULDN'T BE SWITCHING BACK TO WINDOWS ANY TIME SOON.
IT'S THAT GOOD?
IT'S THAT HARD TO UN-INSTALL.
(Beep) TENTACLES WRAPPED AND LOCKED. AWAITING YOUR COMMAND.

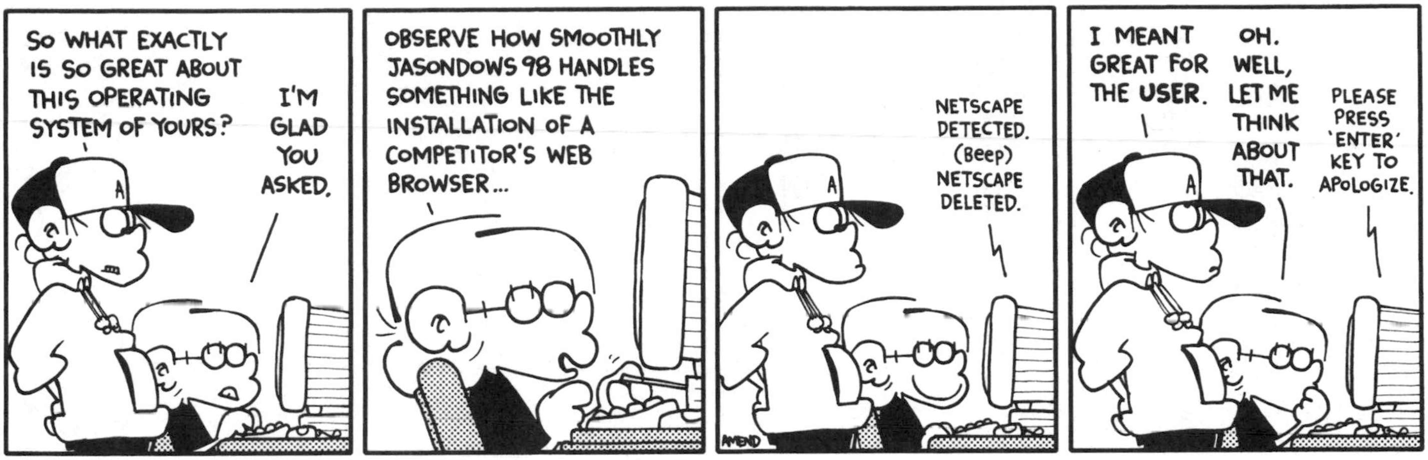
SO WHAT EXACTLY IS SO GREAT ABOUT THIS OPERATING SYSTEM OF YOURS?
I'M GLAD YOU ASKED.
OBSERVE HOW SMOOTHLY JASONDOWS 98 HANDLES SOMETHING LIKE THE INSTALLATION OF A COMPETITOR'S WEB BROWSER...
NETSCAPE DETECTED. (Beep) NETSCAPE DELETED.
AMEND
I MEANT GREAT FOR THE USER.
OH. WELL, LET ME THINK ABOUT THAT.
PLEASE PRESS 'ENTER' KEY TO APOLOGIZE.

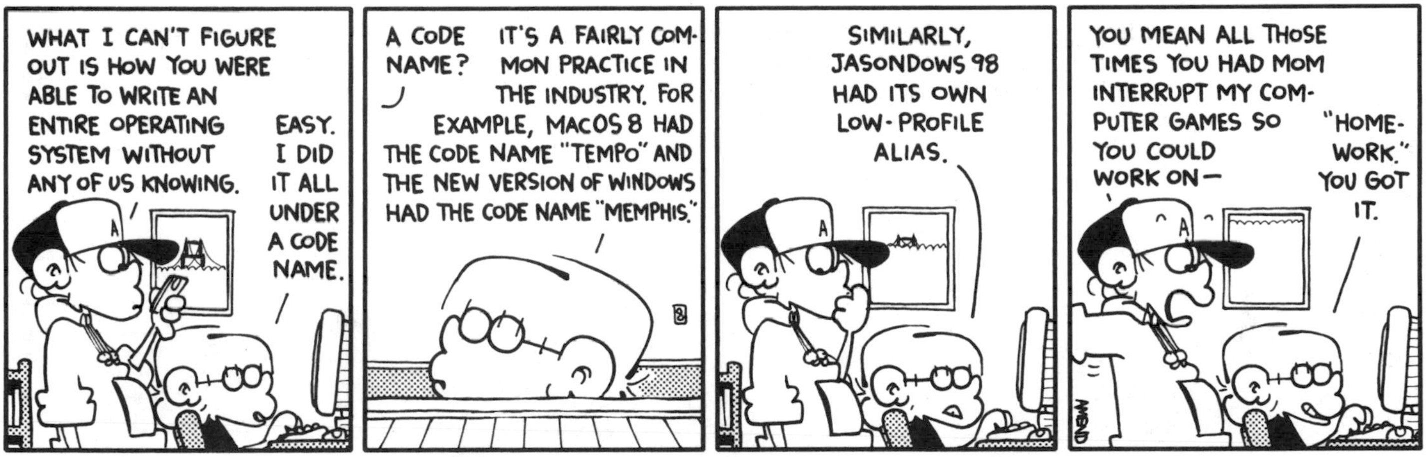
WHAT I CAN'T FIGURE OUT IS HOW YOU WERE ABLE TO WRITE AN ENTIRE OPERATING SYSTEM WITHOUT ANY OF US KNOWING.
EASY. I DID IT ALL UNDER A CODE NAME.
A CODE NAME?
IT'S A FAIRLY COMMON PRACTICE IN THE INDUSTRY. FOR EXAMPLE, MACOS 8 HAD THE CODE NAME "TEMPO" AND THE NEW VERSION OF WINDOWS HAD THE CODE NAME "MEMPHIS."
SIMILARLY, JASONDOWS 98 HAD ITS OWN LOW-PROFILE ALIAS.
YOU MEAN ALL THOSE TIMES YOU HAD MOM INTERRUPT MY COMPUTER GAMES SO YOU COULD WORK ON—
"HOMEWORK." YOU GOT IT.
AMEND

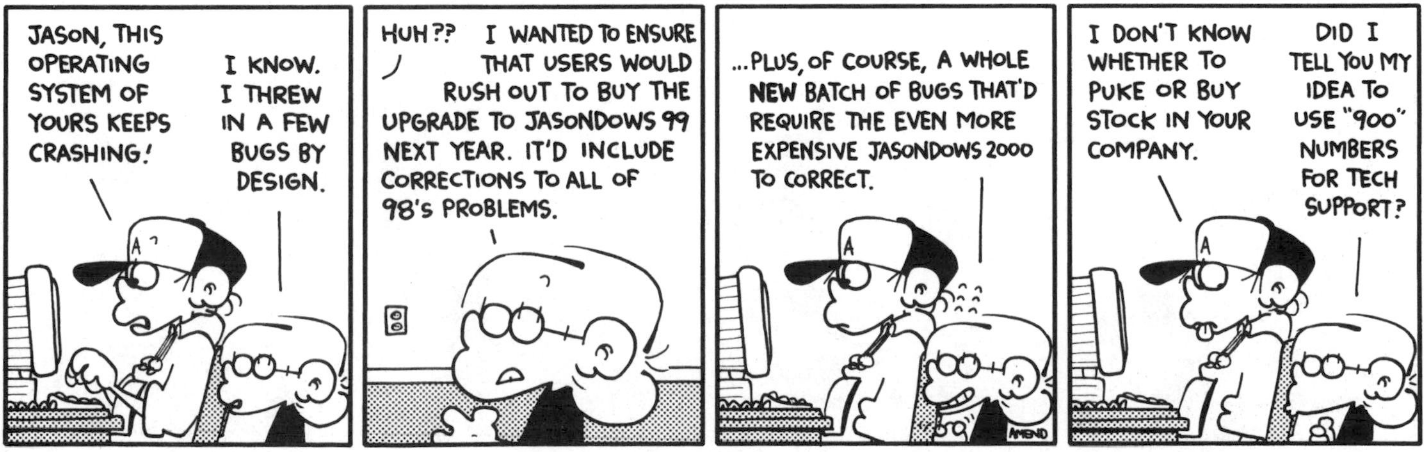
JASON, THIS OPERATING SYSTEM OF YOURS KEEPS CRASHING!
I KNOW. I THREW IN A FEW BUGS BY DESIGN.
HUH??
I WANTED TO ENSURE THAT USERS WOULD RUSH OUT TO BUY THE UPGRADE TO JASONDOWS 99 NEXT YEAR. IT'D INCLUDE CORRECTIONS TO ALL OF 98'S PROBLEMS.
...PLUS, OF COURSE, A WHOLE NEW BATCH OF BUGS THAT'D REQUIRE THE EVEN MORE EXPENSIVE JASONDOWS 2000 TO CORRECT.
AMEND
I DON'T KNOW WHETHER TO PUKE OR BUY STOCK IN YOUR COMPANY.
DID I TELL YOU MY IDEA TO USE "900" NUMBERS FOR TECH SUPPORT?

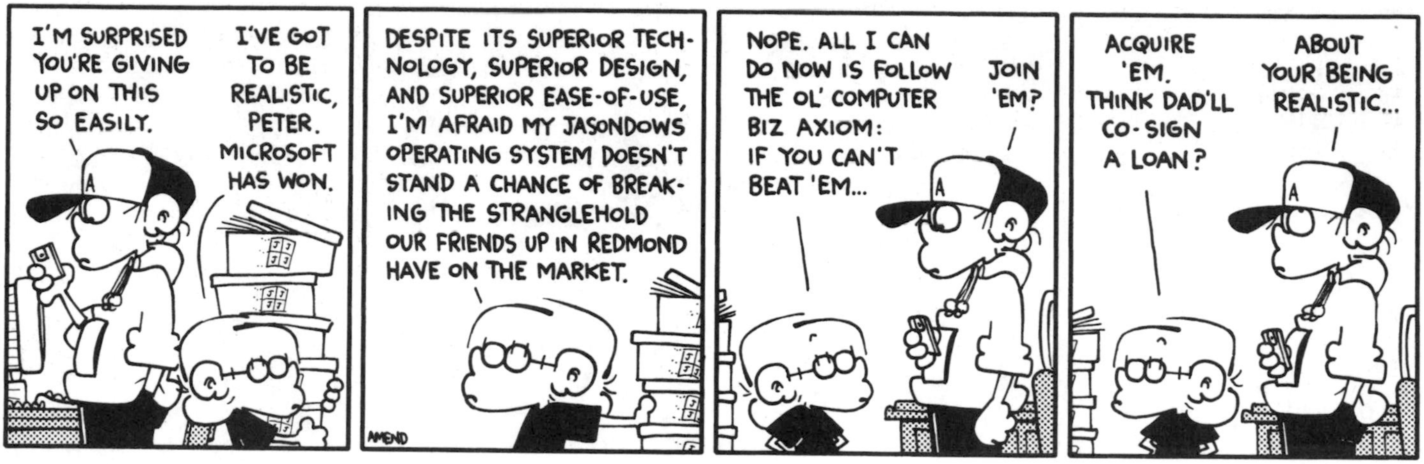
I'M SURPRISED YOU'RE GIVING UP ON THIS SO EASILY.
I'VE GOT TO BE REALISTIC, PETER. MICROSOFT HAS WON.
DESPITE ITS SUPERIOR TECHNOLOGY, SUPERIOR DESIGN, AND SUPERIOR EASE-OF-USE, I'M AFRAID MY JASONDOWS OPERATING SYSTEM DOESN'T STAND A CHANCE OF BREAKING THE STRANGLEHOLD OUR FRIENDS UP IN REDMOND HAVE ON THE MARKET.
AMEND
NOPE. ALL I CAN DO NOW IS FOLLOW THE OL' COMPUTER BIZ AXIOM: IF YOU CAN'T BEAT 'EM...
JOIN 'EM?
ACQUIRE 'EM. THINK DAD'LL CO-SIGN A LOAN?
ABOUT YOUR BEING REALISTIC...

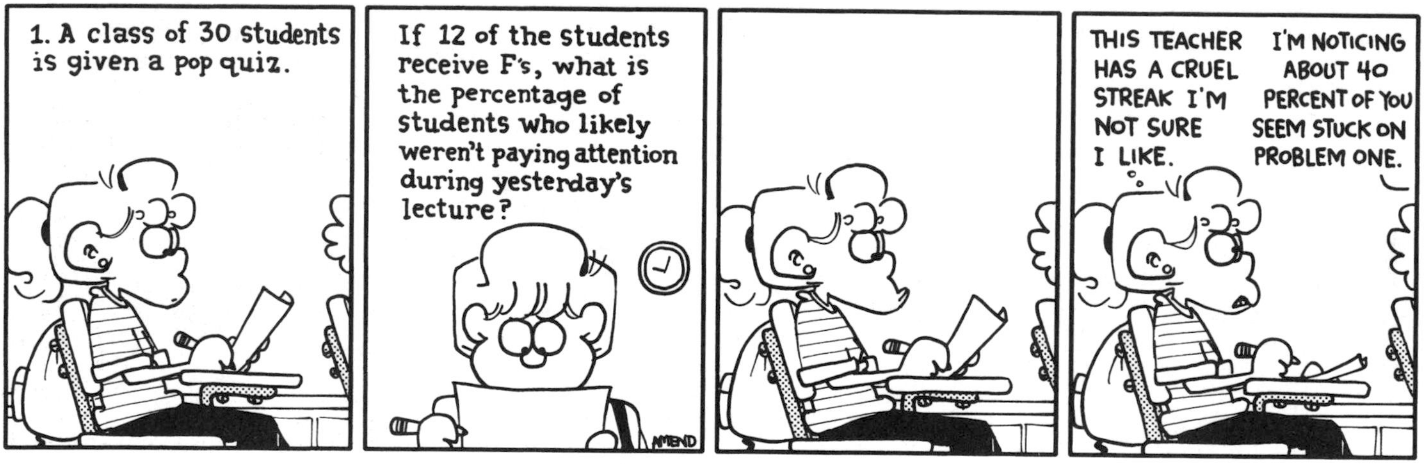
1. A class of 30 students is given a pop quiz.
If 12 of the students receive F's, what is the percentage of students who likely weren't paying attention during yesterday's lecture?
AMEND
THIS TEACHER HAS A CRUEL STREAK I'M NOT SURE I LIKE.
I'M NOTICING ABOUT 40 PERCENT OF YOU SEEM STUCK ON PROBLEM ONE.

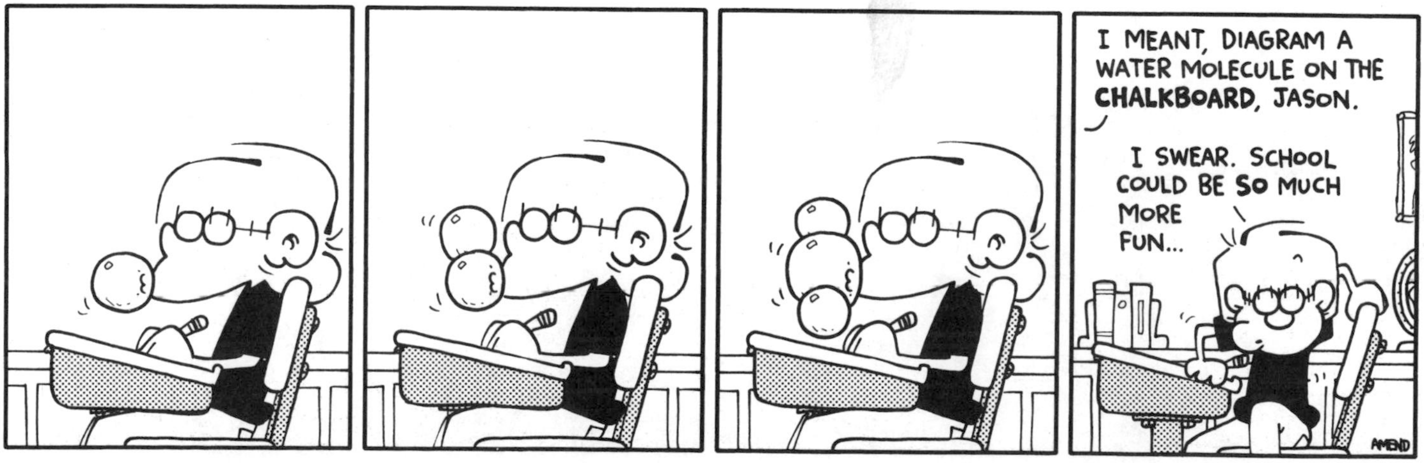
I MEANT, DIAGRAM A WATER MOLECULE ON THE CHALKBOARD, JASON.
I SWEAR. SCHOOL COULD BE SO MUCH MORE FUN...
AMEND

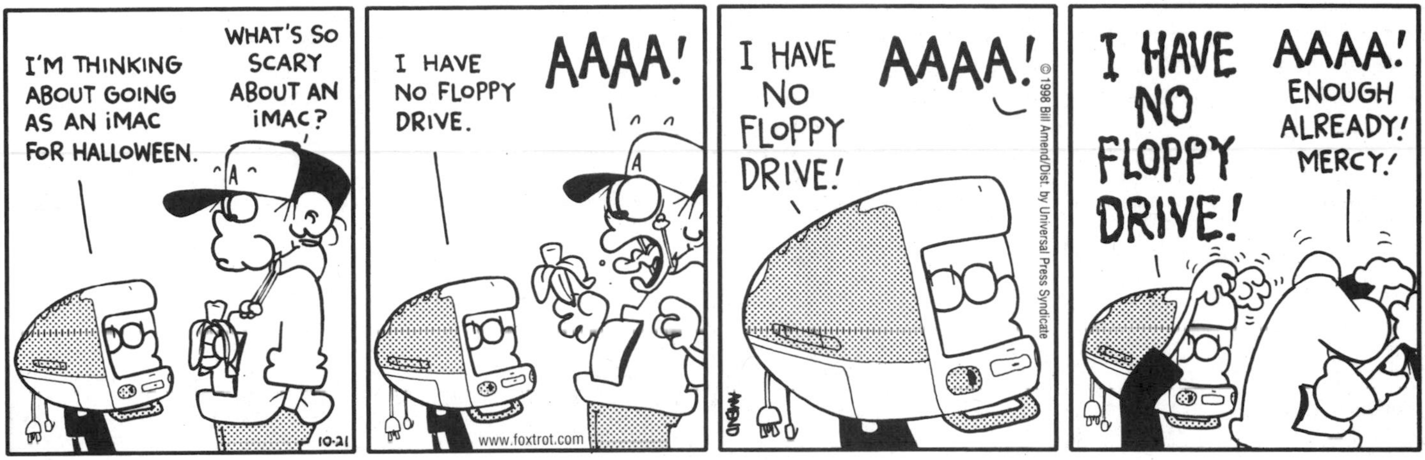
I'M THINKING ABOUT GOING AS AN iMAC FOR HALLOWEEN.
WHAT'S SO SCARY ABOUT AN iMAC?
10-21
I HAVE NO FLOPPY DRIVE.
AAAA!
www.foxtrot.com
I HAVE NO FLOPPY DRIVE!
AAAA!
© 1998 Bill Amend/Dist. by Universal Press Syndicate
AMEND
I HAVE NO FLOPPY DRIVE!
AAAA! ENOUGH ALREADY! MERCY!

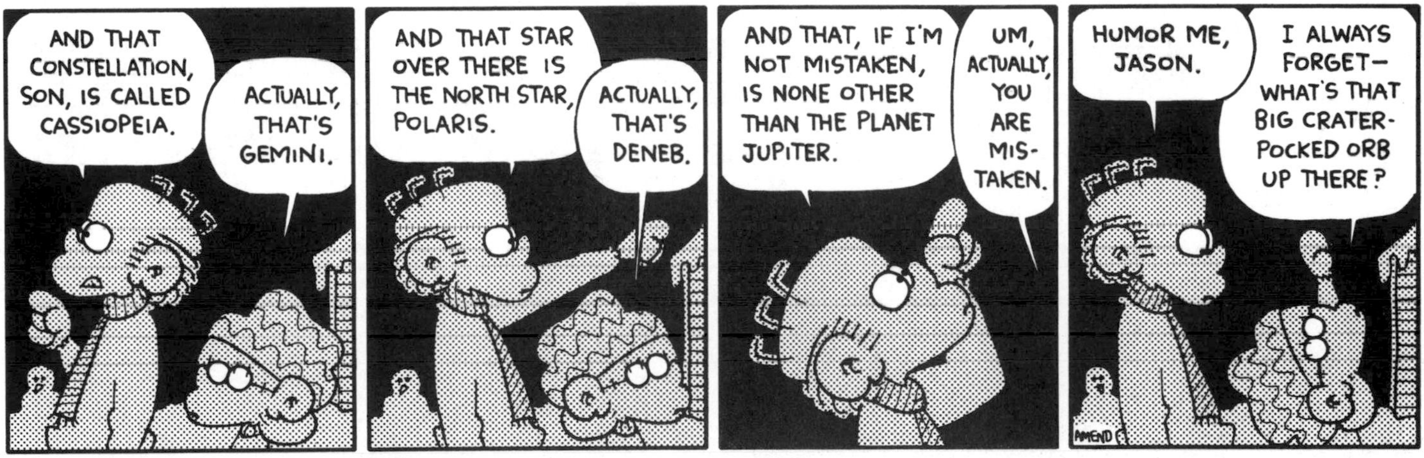
AND THAT CONSTELLATION, SON, IS CALLED CASSIOPEIA.
ACTUALLY, THAT'S GEMINI.
AND THAT STAR OVER THERE IS THE NORTH STAR, POLARIS.
ACTUALLY, THAT'S DENEB.
AND THAT, IF I'M NOT MISTAKEN, IS NONE OTHER THAN THE PLANET JUPITER.
UM, ACTUALLY, YOU ARE MISTAKEN.
HUMOR ME, JASON.
I ALWAYS FORGET— WHAT'S THAT BIG CRATER-POCKED ORB UP THERE?
AMEND

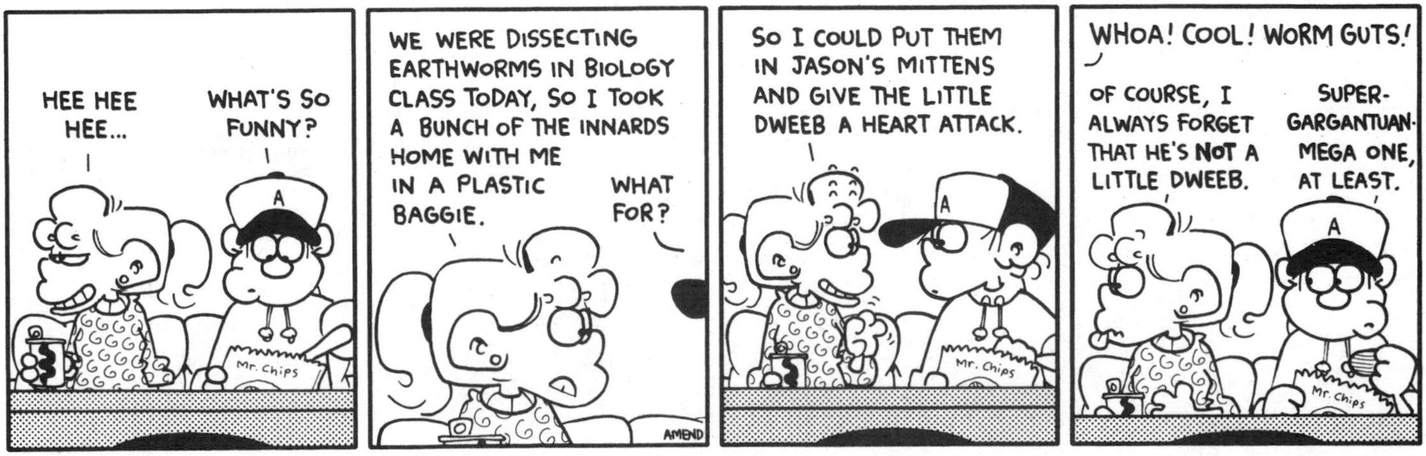
HEE HEE HEE...
WHAT'S SO FUNNY?
Mr. Chips
WE WERE DISSECTING EARTHWORMS IN BIOLOGY CLASS TODAY, SO I TOOK A BUNCH OF THE INNARDS HOME WITH ME IN A PLASTIC BAGGIE.
WHAT FOR?
AMEND
SO I COULD PUT THEM IN JASON'S MITTENS AND GIVE THE LITTLE DWEEB A HEART ATTACK.
Mr. Chips
WHOA! COOL! WORM GUTS!
OF COURSE, I ALWAYS FORGET THAT HE'S NOT A LITTLE DWEEB.
SUPER-GARGANTUAN-MEGA ONE, AT LEAST.
Mr. Chips

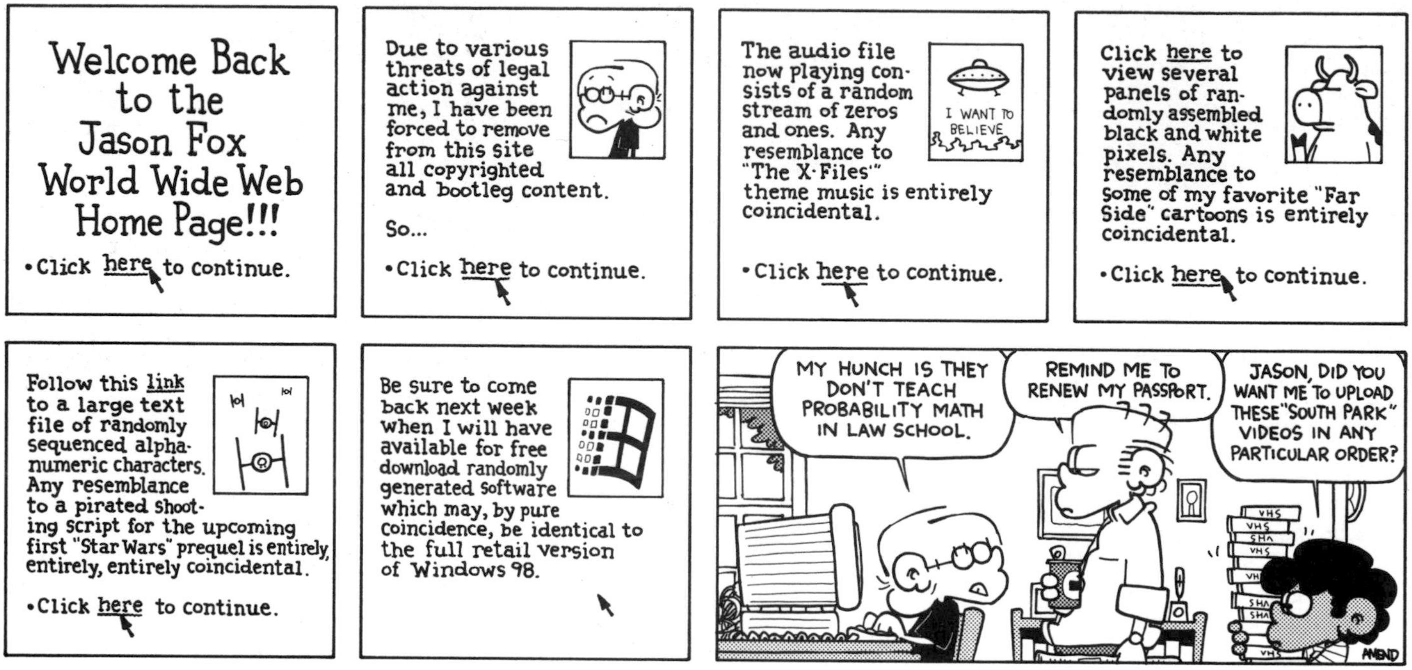
Welcome Back to the Jason Fox World Wide Web Home Page!!!
•Click here to continue.
Due to various threats of legal action against me, I have been forced to remove from this site all copyrighted and bootleg content.
So...
•Click here to continue.
The audio file now playing consists of a random stream of zeros and ones. Any resemblance to "The X-Files'" theme music is entirely coincidental.
I WANT TO BELIEVE
•Click here to continue.
Click here to view several panels of randomly assembled black and white pixels. Any resemblance to some of my favorite "Far Side" cartoons is entirely coincidental.
•Click here to continue.
Follow this link to a large text file of randomly sequenced alphanumeric characters. Any resemblance to a pirated shooting script for the upcoming first "Star Wars" prequel is entirely, entirely, entirely coincidental.
•Click here to continue.
Be sure to come back next week when I will have available for free download randomly generated software which may, by pure coincidence, be identical to the full retail version of Windows 98.
MY HUNCH IS THEY DON'T TEACH PROBABILITY MATH IN LAW SCHOOL.
REMIND ME TO RENEW MY PASSPORT.
JASON, DID YOU WANT ME TO UPLOAD THESE "SOUTH PARK" VIDEOS IN ANY PARTICULAR ORDER?
AMEND

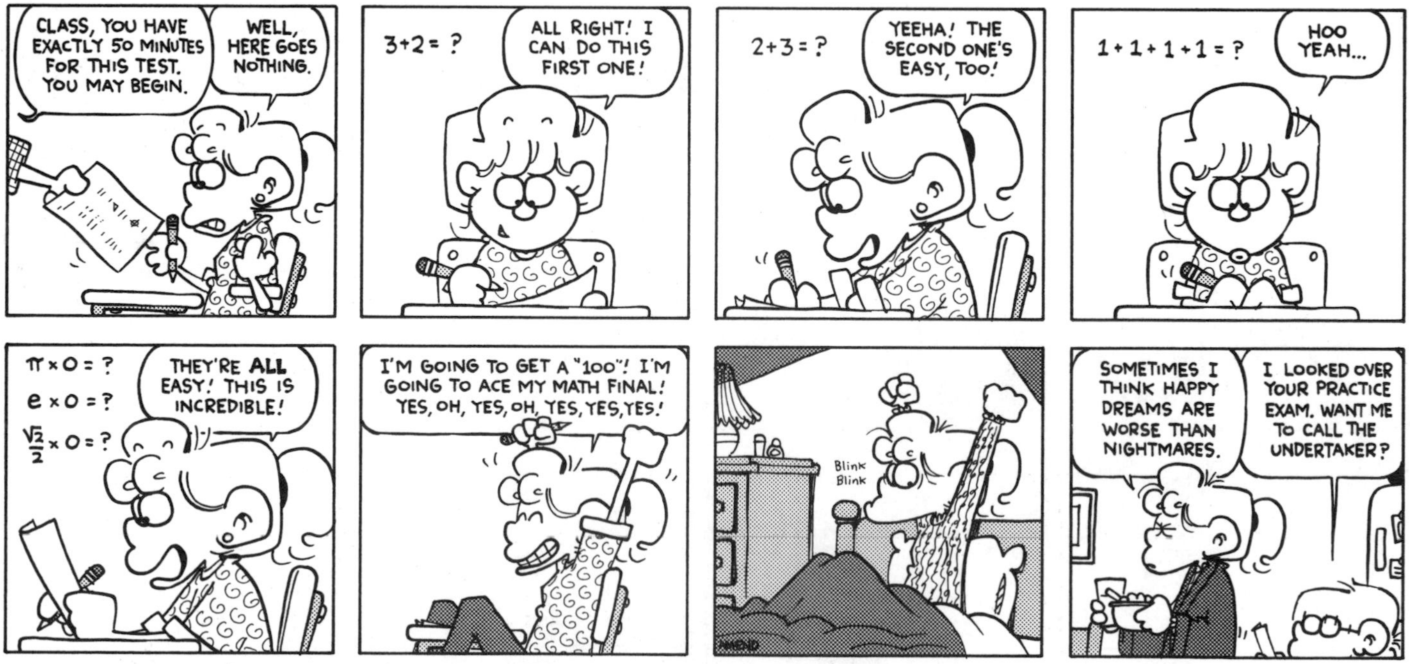
CLASS, YOU HAVE EXACTLY 50 MINUTES FOR THIS TEST. YOU MAY BEGIN.
WELL, HERE GOES NOTHING.
3+2 = ?
ALL RIGHT! I CAN DO THIS FIRST ONE!
2+3 = ?
YEEHA! THE SECOND ONE'S EASY, TOO!
1+1+1+1 = ?
HOO YEAH...
π × 0 = ?
e × 0 = ?
√2/2 × 0 = ?
THEY'RE ALL EASY! THIS IS INCREDIBLE!
I'M GOING TO GET A "100"! I'M GOING TO ACE MY MATH FINAL! YES, OH, YES, OH, YES, YES, YES!
Blink Blink
SOMETIMES I THINK HAPPY DREAMS ARE WORSE THAN NIGHTMARES.
I LOOKED OVER YOUR PRACTICE EXAM. WANT ME TO CALL THE UNDERTAKER?

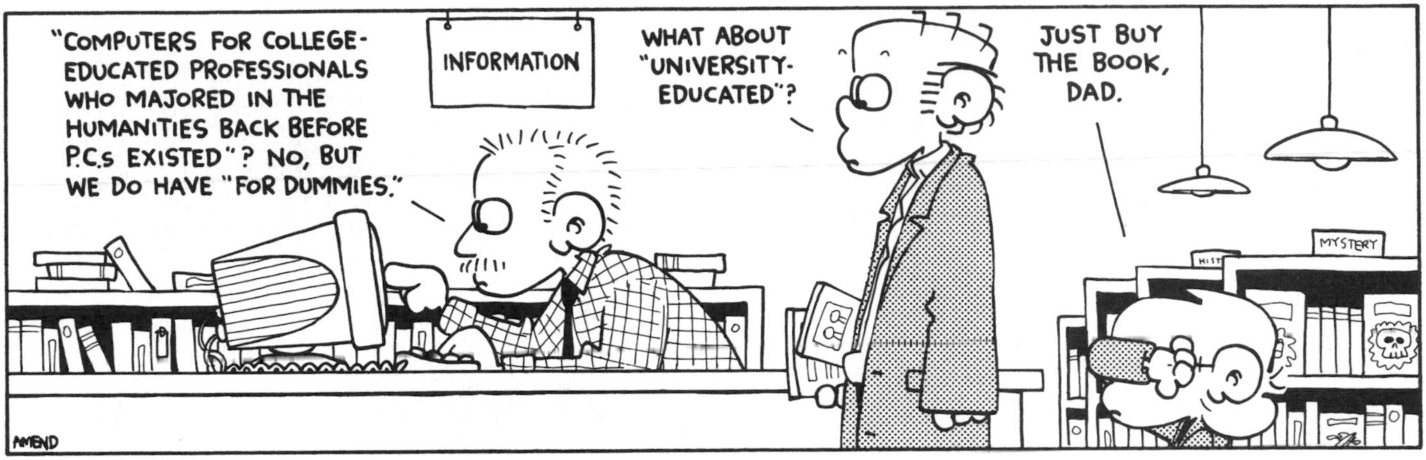
INFORMATION
"COMPUTERS FOR COLLEGE-EDUCATED PROFESSIONALS WHO MAJORED IN THE HUMANITIES BACK BEFORE P.C.s EXISTED"? NO, BUT WE DO HAVE "FOR DUMMIES."
WHAT ABOUT "UNIVERSITY-EDUCATED"?
JUST BUY THE BOOK, DAD.
MYSTERY
AMEND

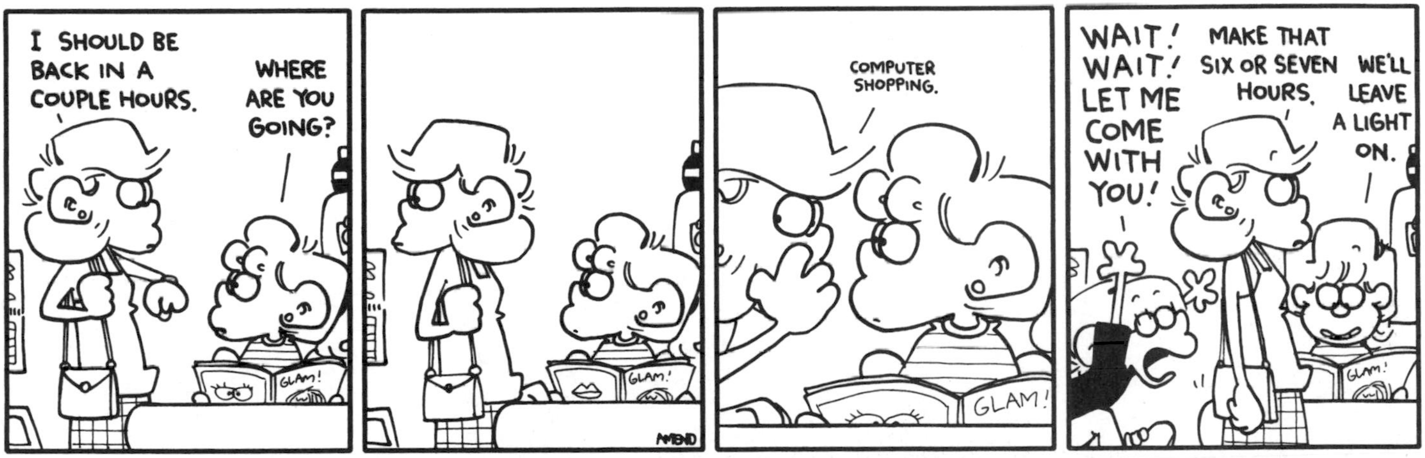
I SHOULD BE BACK IN A COUPLE HOURS.
WHERE ARE YOU GOING?
GLAM!
AMEND
COMPUTER SHOPPING.
GLAM!
WAIT! WAIT! LET ME COME WITH YOU!
MAKE THAT SIX OR SEVEN HOURS.
WE'LL LEAVE A LIGHT ON.
GLAM!

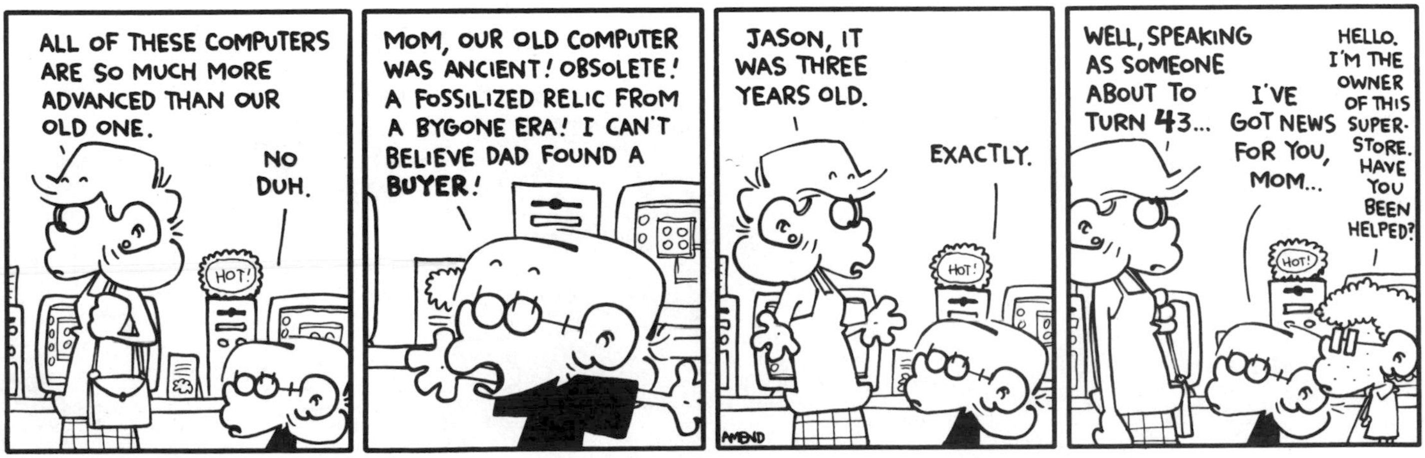
ALL OF THESE COMPUTERS ARE SO MUCH MORE ADVANCED THAN OUR OLD ONE.
NO DUH.
HOT!
MOM, OUR OLD COMPUTER WAS ANCIENT! OBSOLETE! A FOSSILIZED RELIC FROM A BYGONE ERA! I CAN'T BELIEVE DAD FOUND A BUYER!
JASON, IT WAS THREE YEARS OLD.
EXACTLY.
HOT!
AMEND
WELL, SPEAKING AS SOMEONE ABOUT TO TURN 43...
I'VE GOT NEWS FOR YOU, MOM...
HELLO. I'M THE OWNER OF THIS SUPER-STORE. HAVE YOU BEEN HELPED?
HOT!

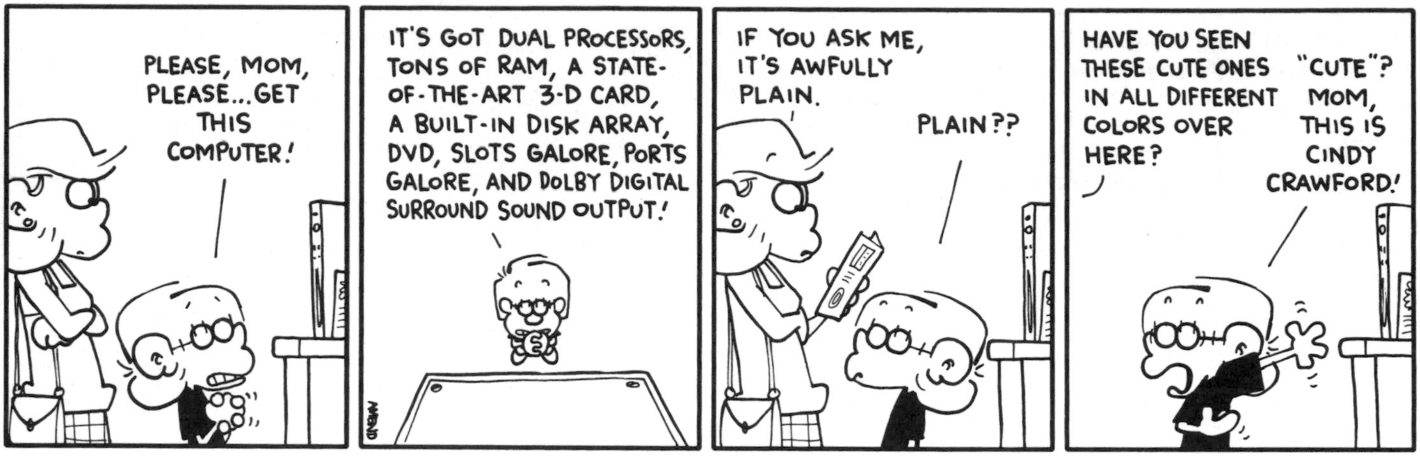
PLEASE, MOM, PLEASE...GET THIS COMPUTER!
IT'S GOT DUAL PROCESSORS, TONS OF RAM, A STATE-OF-THE-ART 3-D CARD, A BUILT-IN DISK ARRAY, DVD, SLOTS GALORE, PORTS GALORE, AND DOLBY DIGITAL SURROUND SOUND OUTPUT!
AMEND
IF YOU ASK ME, IT'S AWFULLY PLAIN.
PLAIN??
HAVE YOU SEEN THESE CUTE ONES IN ALL DIFFERENT COLORS OVER HERE?
"CUTE"? MOM, THIS IS CINDY CRAWFORD!

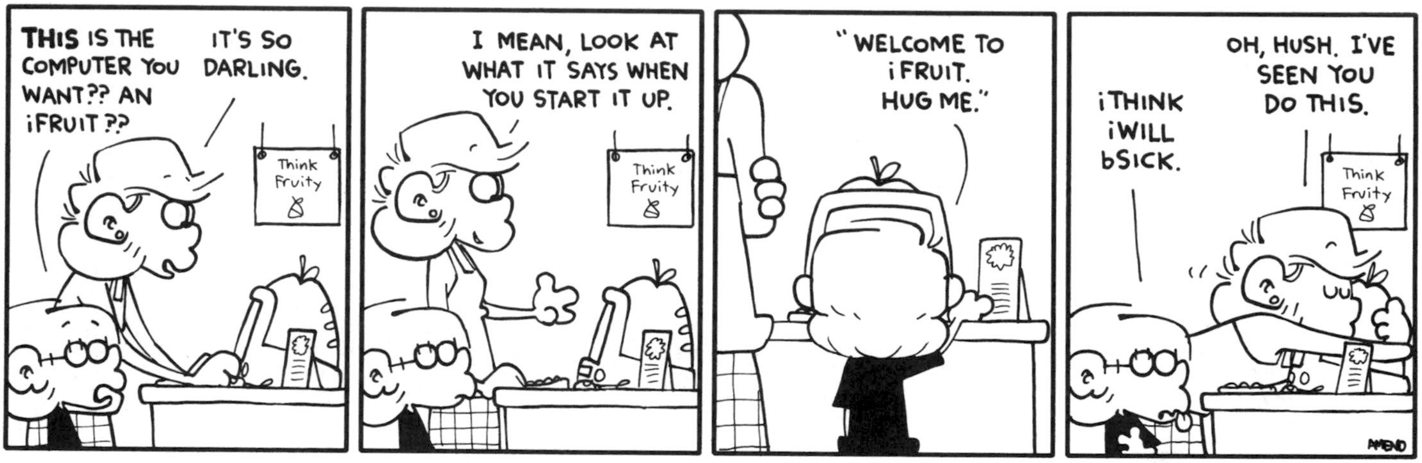
THIS IS THE COMPUTER YOU WANT?? AN iFRUIT??
IT'S SO DARLING.
Think Fruity
I MEAN, LOOK AT WHAT IT SAYS WHEN YOU START IT UP.
Think Fruity
"WELCOME TO iFRUIT. HUG ME."
iTHINK iWILL bSICK.
OH, HUSH. I'VE SEEN YOU DO THIS.
Think Fruity
AMEND

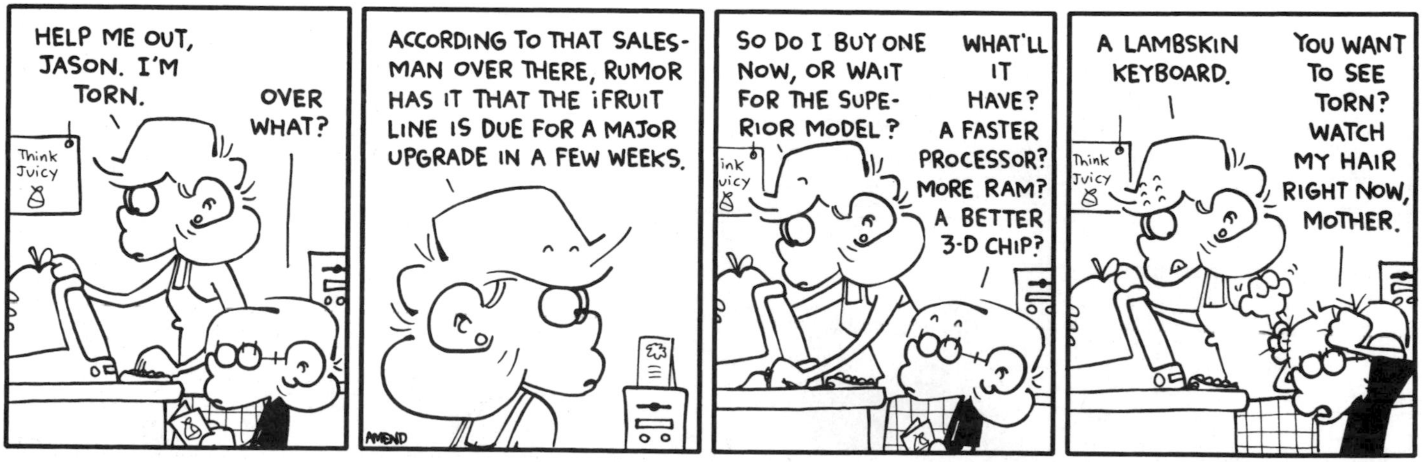
Think Juicy
HELP ME OUT, JASON. I'M TORN.
OVER WHAT?
ACCORDING TO THAT SALESMAN OVER THERE, RUMOR HAS IT THAT THE iFRUIT LINE IS DUE FOR A MAJOR UPGRADE IN A FEW WEEKS.
AMEND
SO DO I BUY ONE NOW, OR WAIT FOR THE SUPERIOR MODEL?
WHAT'LL IT HAVE? A FASTER PROCESSOR? MORE RAM? A BETTER 3-D CHIP?
Think Juicy
A LAMBSKIN KEYBOARD.
YOU WANT TO SEE TORN? WATCH MY HAIR RIGHT NOW, MOTHER.

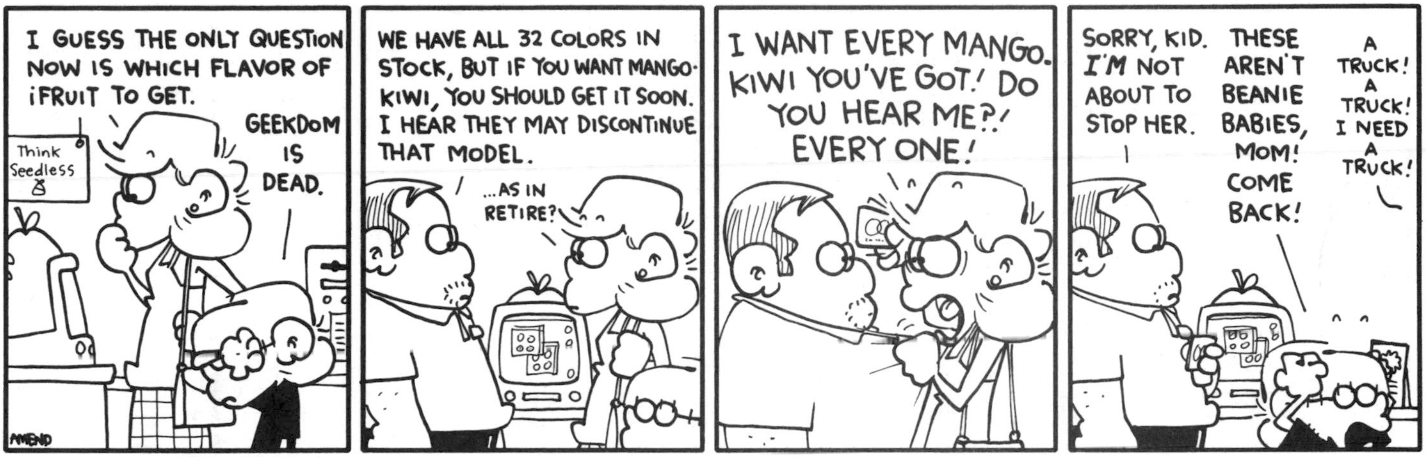
I GUESS THE ONLY QUESTION NOW IS WHICH FLAVOR OF iFRUIT TO GET.
Think Seedless
GEEKDOM IS DEAD.
WE HAVE ALL 32 COLORS IN STOCK, BUT IF YOU WANT MANGO-KIWI, YOU SHOULD GET IT SOON. I HEAR THEY MAY DISCONTINUE THAT MODEL.
...AS IN RETIRE?
I WANT EVERY MANGO-KIWI YOU'VE GOT! DO YOU HEAR ME?! EVERY ONE!
SORRY, KID. I'M NOT ABOUT TO STOP HER.
THESE AREN'T BEANIE BABIES, MOM! COME BACK!
A TRUCK! A TRUCK! I NEED A TRUCK!
AMEND

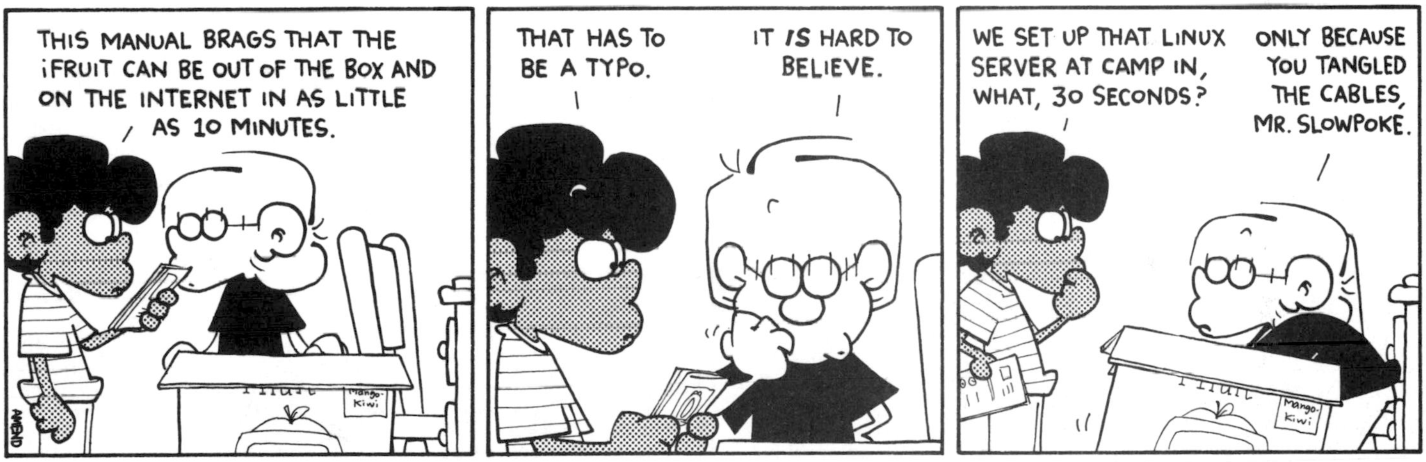
THIS MANUAL BRAGS THAT THE iFRUIT CAN BE OUT OF THE BOX AND ON THE INTERNET IN AS LITTLE AS 10 MINUTES.
Mango-Kiwi
AMEND
THAT HAS TO BE A TYPO.
IT IS HARD TO BELIEVE.
WE SET UP THAT LINUX SERVER AT CAMP IN, WHAT, 30 SECONDS?
ONLY BECAUSE YOU TANGLED THE CABLES, MR. SLOWPOKE.
Mango-Kiwi

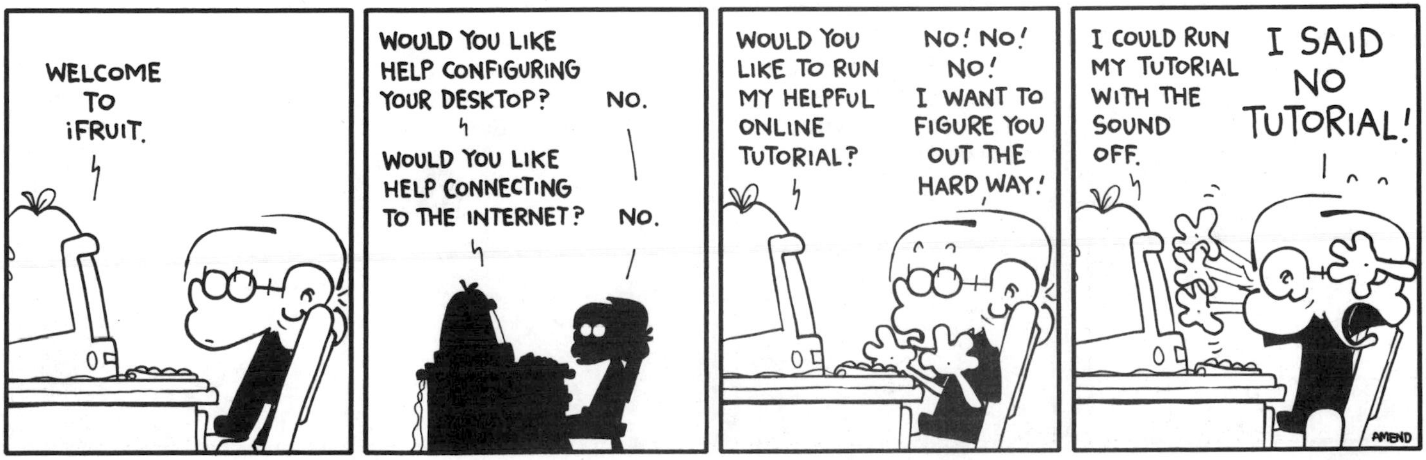
WELCOME TO iFRUIT.
WOULD YOU LIKE HELP CONFIGURING YOUR DESKTOP?
NO.
WOULD YOU LIKE HELP CONNECTING TO THE INTERNET?
NO.
WOULD YOU LIKE TO RUN MY HELPFUL ONLINE TUTORIAL?
NO! NO! NO! I WANT TO FIGURE YOU OUT THE HARD WAY!
I COULD RUN MY TUTORIAL WITH THE SOUND OFF.
I SAID NO TUTORIAL!
AMEND

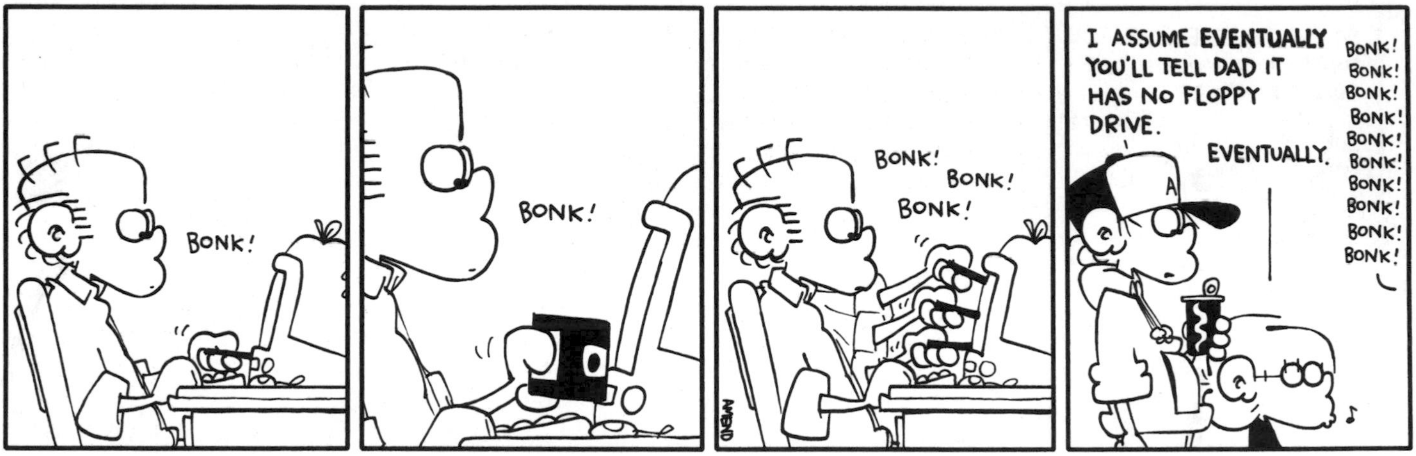
BONK!
BONK!
BONK!
BONK!
BONK!
I ASSUME **EVENTUALLY** YOU'LL TELL DAD IT HAS NO FLOPPY DRIVE.
EVENTUALLY.
BONK! BONK! BONK! BONK! BONK! BONK! BONK! BONK! BONK! BONK!

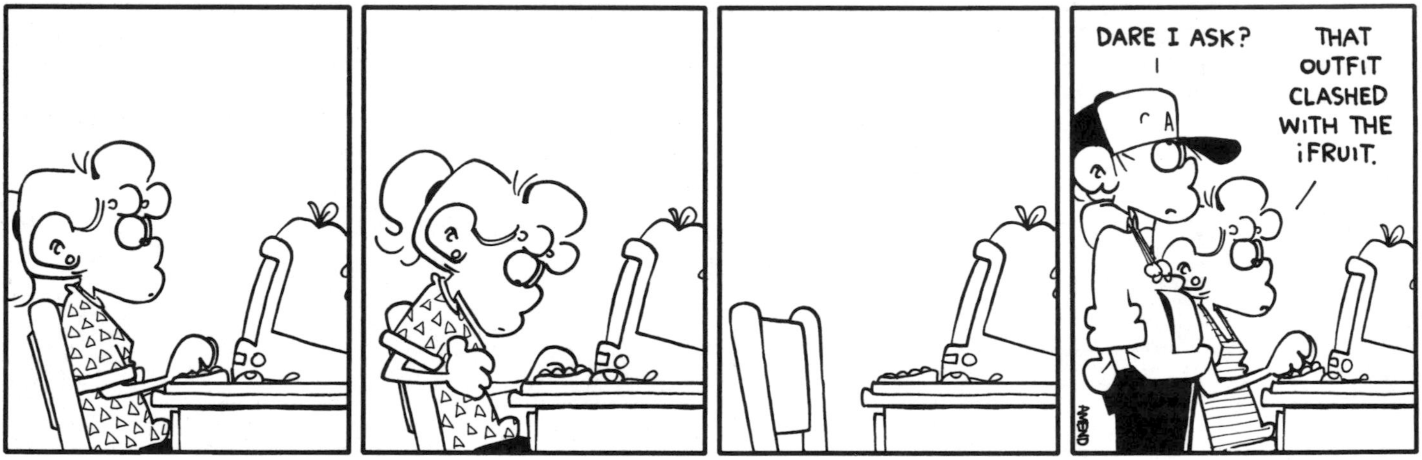
DARE I ASK?
THAT OUTFIT CLASHED WITH THE iFRUIT.

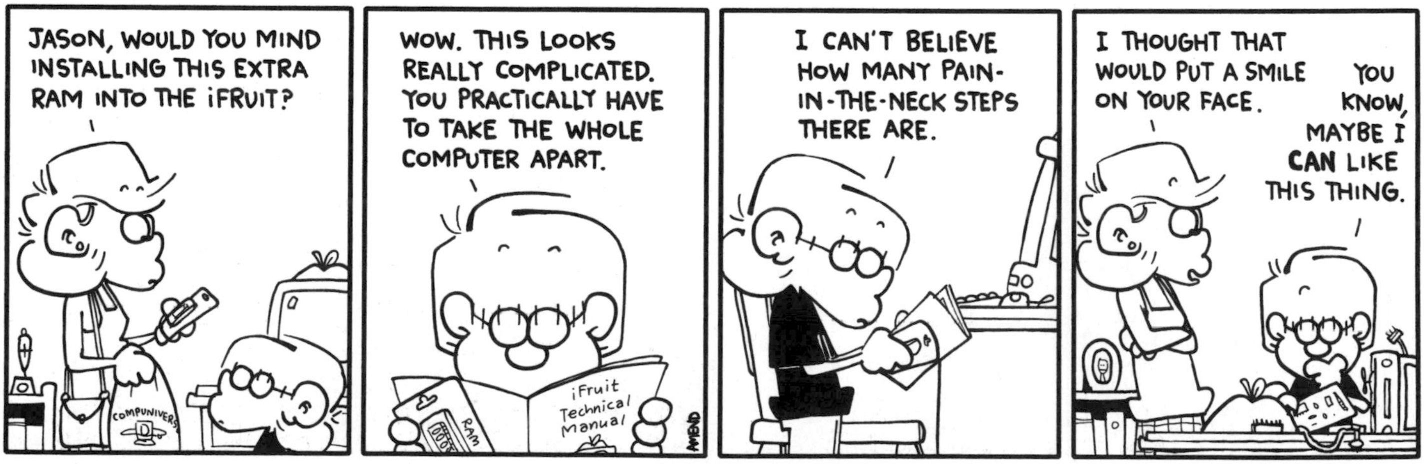
JASON, WOULD YOU MIND INSTALLING THIS EXTRA RAM INTO THE iFRUIT?
COMPUNIVERS
WOW. THIS LOOKS REALLY COMPLICATED. YOU PRACTICALLY HAVE TO TAKE THE WHOLE COMPUTER APART.
iFruit Technical Manual
RAM
I CAN'T BELIEVE HOW MANY PAIN-IN-THE-NECK STEPS THERE ARE.
I THOUGHT THAT WOULD PUT A SMILE ON YOUR FACE.
YOU KNOW, MAYBE I **CAN** LIKE THIS THING.

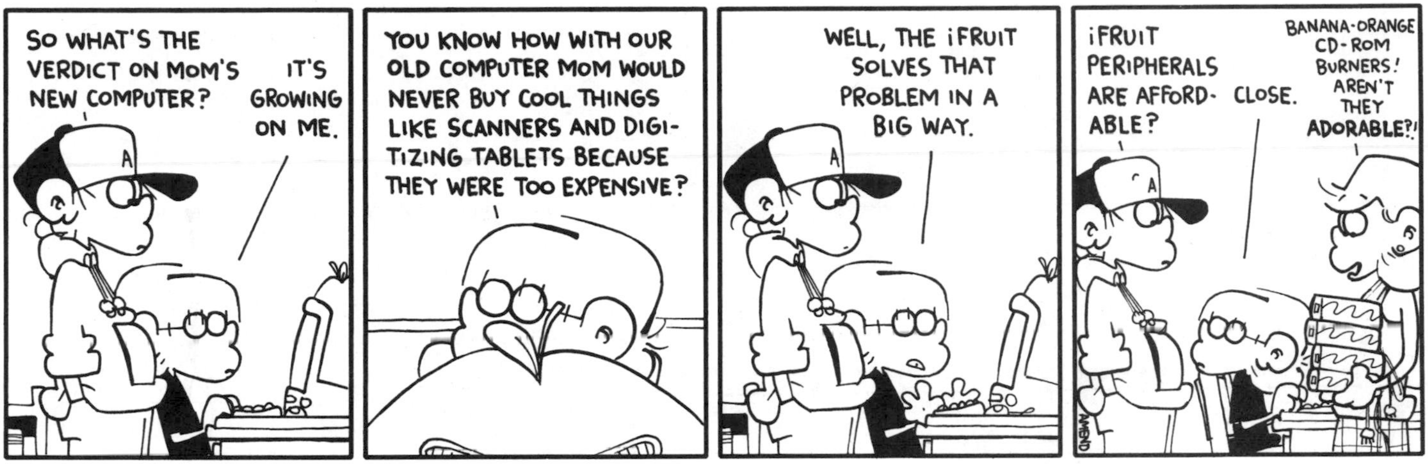
SO WHAT'S THE VERDICT ON MOM'S NEW COMPUTER?
IT'S GROWING ON ME.
YOU KNOW HOW WITH OUR OLD COMPUTER MOM WOULD NEVER BUY COOL THINGS LIKE SCANNERS AND DIGITIZING TABLETS BECAUSE THEY WERE TOO EXPENSIVE?
WELL, THE iFRUIT SOLVES THAT PROBLEM IN A BIG WAY.
iFRUIT PERIPHERALS ARE AFFORDABLE?
CLOSE.
BANANA-ORANGE CD-ROM BURNERS! AREN'T THEY ADORABLE?!
AMEND

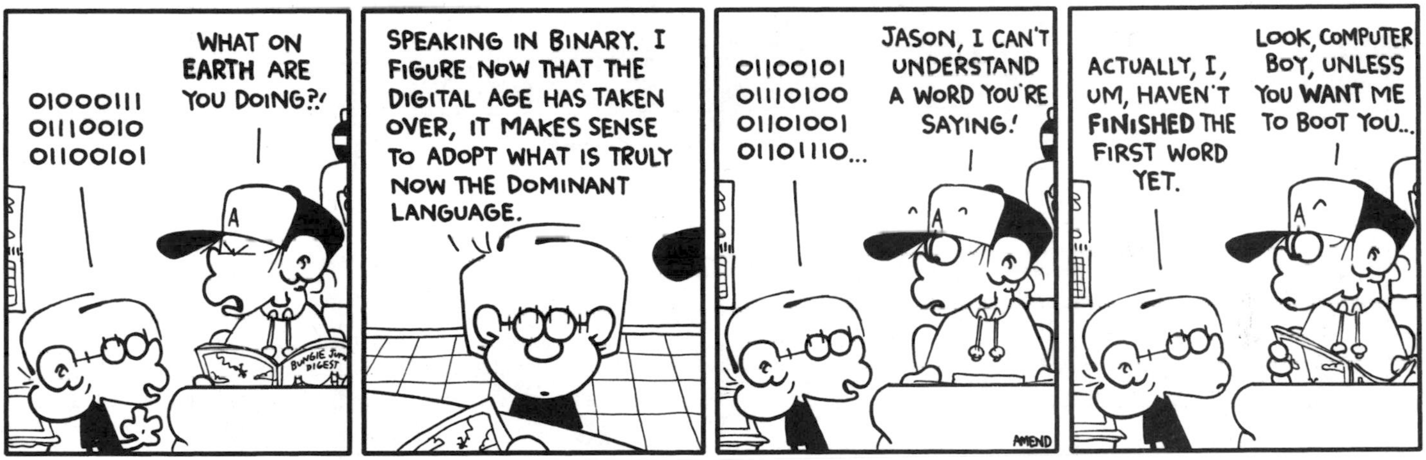
01000111 01110010 01100101
WHAT ON EARTH ARE YOU DOING?!
BUNGIE JUMP DIGEST
SPEAKING IN BINARY. I FIGURE NOW THAT THE DIGITAL AGE HAS TAKEN OVER, IT MAKES SENSE TO ADOPT WHAT IS TRULY NOW THE DOMINANT LANGUAGE.
01100101 01110100 01101001 01101110...
JASON, I CAN'T UNDERSTAND A WORD YOU'RE SAYING!
ACTUALLY, I, UM, HAVEN'T FINISHED THE FIRST WORD YET.
LOOK, COMPUTER BOY, UNLESS YOU WANT ME TO BOOT YOU...
AMEND

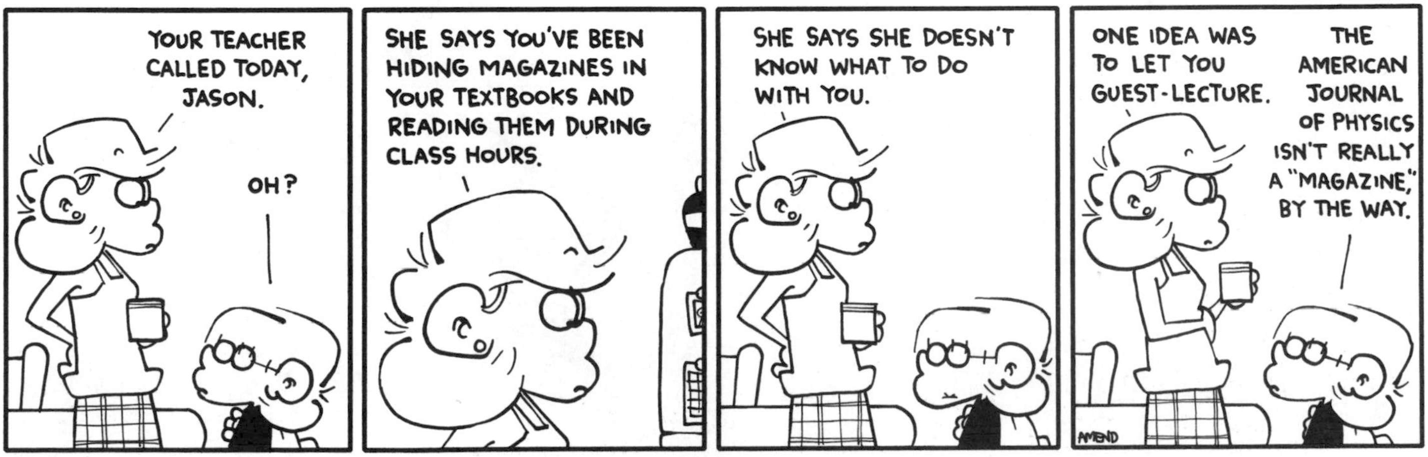
YOUR TEACHER CALLED TODAY, JASON.
OH?
SHE SAYS YOU'VE BEEN HIDING MAGAZINES IN YOUR TEXTBOOKS AND READING THEM DURING CLASS HOURS.
SHE SAYS SHE DOESN'T KNOW WHAT TO DO WITH YOU.
ONE IDEA WAS TO LET YOU GUEST-LECTURE.
THE AMERICAN JOURNAL OF PHYSICS ISN'T REALLY A "MAGAZINE," BY THE WAY.
AMEND

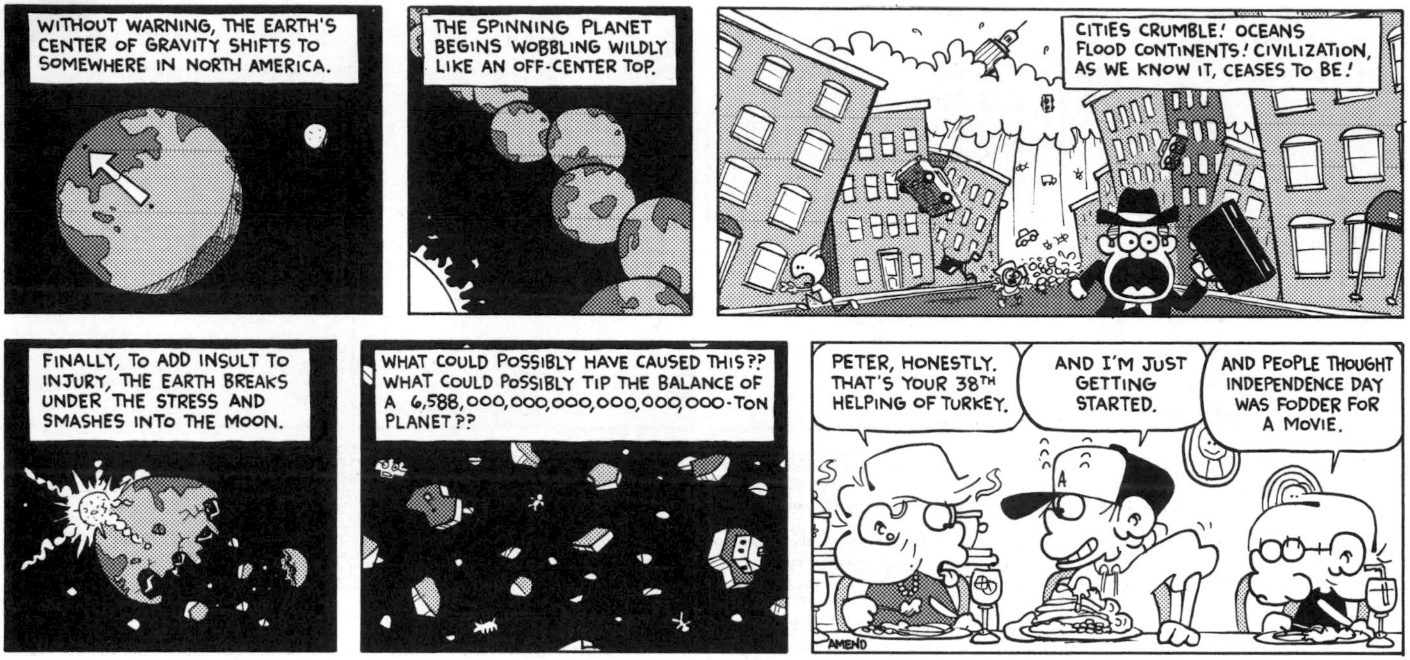
WITHOUT WARNING, THE EARTH'S CENTER OF GRAVITY SHIFTS TO SOMEWHERE IN NORTH AMERICA.
THE SPINNING PLANET BEGINS WOBBLING WILDLY LIKE AN OFF-CENTER TOP.
CITIES CRUMBLE! OCEANS FLOOD CONTINENTS! CIVILIZATION, AS WE KNOW IT, CEASES TO BE!
FINALLY, TO ADD INSULT TO INJURY, THE EARTH BREAKS UNDER THE STRESS AND SMASHES INTO THE MOON.
WHAT COULD POSSIBLY HAVE CAUSED THIS?? WHAT COULD POSSIBLY TIP THE BALANCE OF A 6,588,000,000,000,000,000,000-TON PLANET??
PETER, HONESTLY. THAT'S YOUR 38TH HELPING OF TURKEY.
AND I'M JUST GETTING STARTED.
AND PEOPLE THOUGHT INDEPENDENCE DAY WAS FODDER FOR A MOVIE.
AMEND

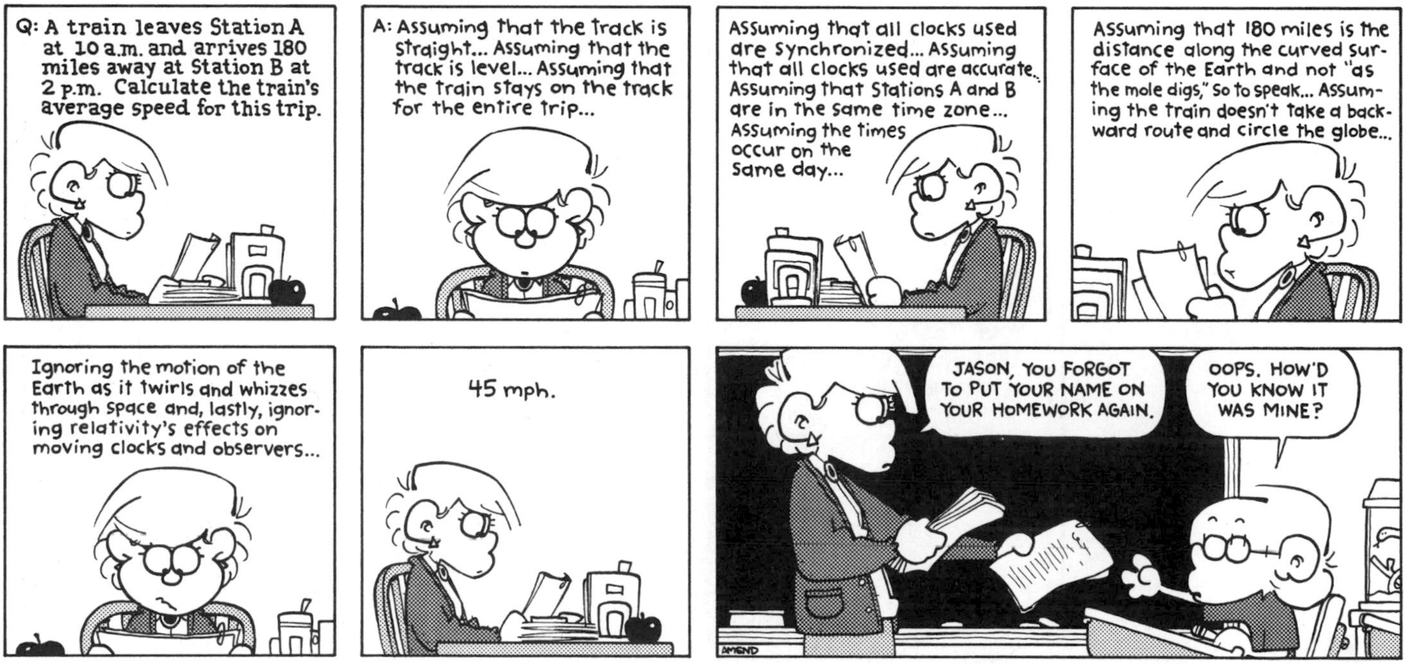
Q: A train leaves Station A at 10 a.m. and arrives 180 miles away at Station B at 2 p.m. Calculate the train's average speed for this trip.
A: Assuming that the track is straight... Assuming that the track is level... Assuming that the train stays on the track for the entire trip...
Assuming that all clocks used are synchronized... Assuming that all clocks used are accurate... Assuming that Stations A and B are in the same time zone... Assuming the times occur on the same day...
Assuming that 180 miles is the distance along the curved surface of the Earth and not "as the mole digs," so to speak... Assuming the train doesn't take a backward route and circle the globe...
Ignoring the motion of the Earth as it twirls and whizzes through space and, lastly, ignoring relativity's effects on moving clocks and observers...
45 mph.
JASON, YOU FORGOT TO PUT YOUR NAME ON YOUR HOMEWORK AGAIN.
OOPS. HOW'D YOU KNOW IT WAS MINE?
AMEND

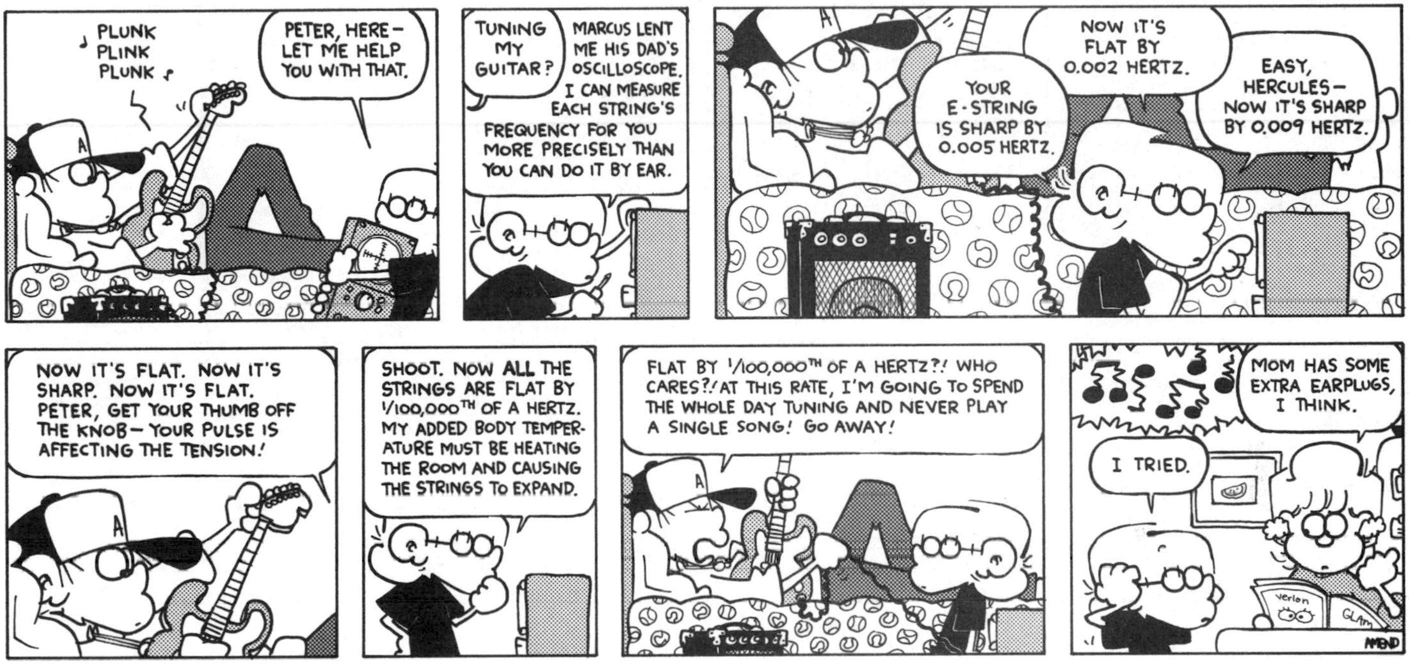
PLUNK PLUNK PLUNK
PETER, HERE— LET ME HELP YOU WITH THAT.
TUNING MY GUITAR?
MARCUS LENT ME HIS DAD'S OSCILLOSCOPE. I CAN MEASURE EACH STRING'S FREQUENCY FOR YOU MORE PRECISELY THAN YOU CAN DO IT BY EAR.
YOUR E-STRING IS SHARP BY 0.005 HERTZ.
NOW IT'S FLAT BY 0.002 HERTZ.
EASY, HERCULES— NOW IT'S SHARP BY 0.009 HERTZ.
NOW IT'S FLAT. NOW IT'S SHARP. NOW IT'S FLAT. PETER, GET YOUR THUMB OFF THE KNOB— YOUR PULSE IS AFFECTING THE TENSION!
SHOOT. NOW ALL THE STRINGS ARE FLAT BY 1/100,000TH OF A HERTZ. MY ADDED BODY TEMPERATURE MUST BE HEATING THE ROOM AND CAUSING THE STRINGS TO EXPAND.
FLAT BY 1/100,000TH OF A HERTZ?! WHO CARES?! AT THIS RATE, I'M GOING TO SPEND THE WHOLE DAY TUNING AND NEVER PLAY A SINGLE SONG! GO AWAY!
MOM HAS SOME EXTRA EARPLUGS, I THINK.
I TRIED.
AMEND

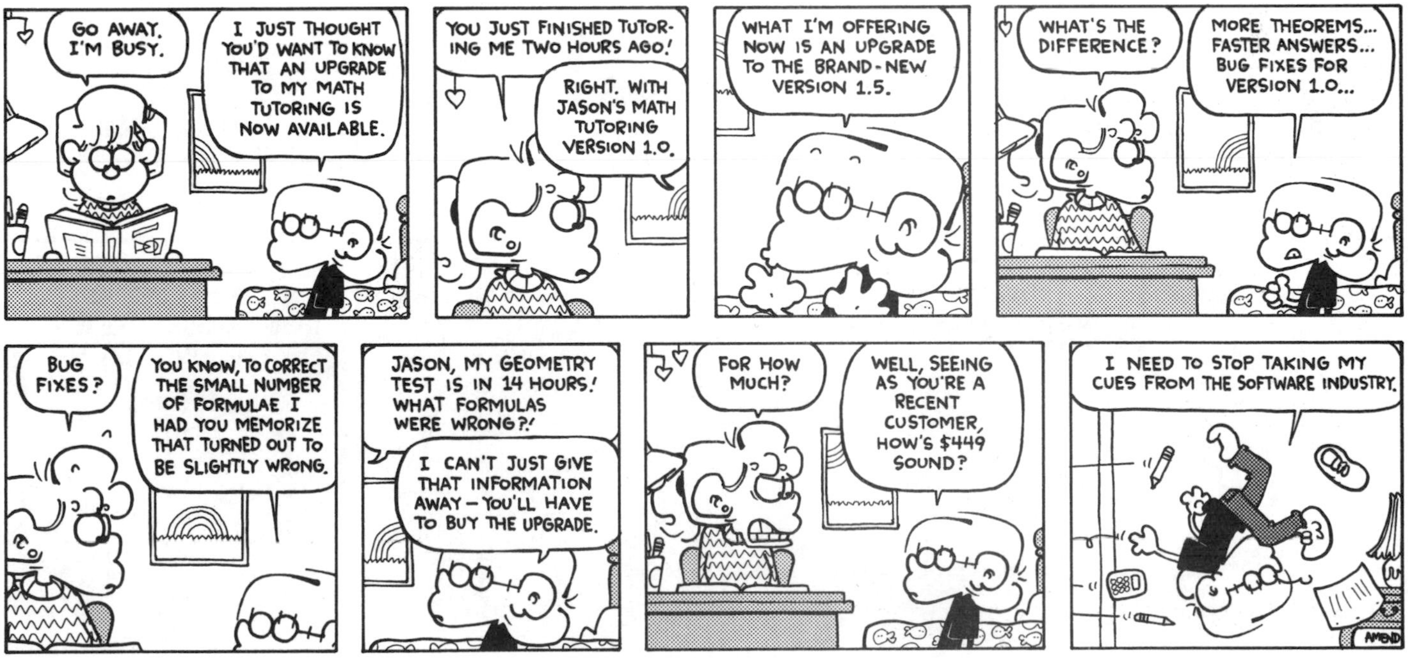
GO AWAY. I'M BUSY.
I JUST THOUGHT YOU'D WANT TO KNOW THAT AN UPGRADE TO MY MATH TUTORING IS NOW AVAILABLE.
YOU JUST FINISHED TUTORING ME TWO HOURS AGO!
RIGHT. WITH JASON'S MATH TUTORING VERSION 1.0.
WHAT I'M OFFERING NOW IS AN UPGRADE TO THE BRAND-NEW VERSION 1.5.
WHAT'S THE DIFFERENCE?
MORE THEOREMS... FASTER ANSWERS... BUG FIXES FOR VERSION 1.0...
BUG FIXES?
YOU KNOW, TO CORRECT THE SMALL NUMBER OF FORMULAE I HAD YOU MEMORIZE THAT TURNED OUT TO BE SLIGHTLY WRONG.
JASON, MY GEOMETRY TEST IS IN 14 HOURS! WHAT FORMULAS WERE WRONG?!
I CAN'T JUST GIVE THAT INFORMATION AWAY— YOU'LL HAVE TO BUY THE UPGRADE.
FOR HOW MUCH?
WELL, SEEING AS YOU'RE A RECENT CUSTOMER, HOW'S $449 SOUND?
I NEED TO STOP TAKING MY CUES FROM THE SOFTWARE INDUSTRY.
AMEND

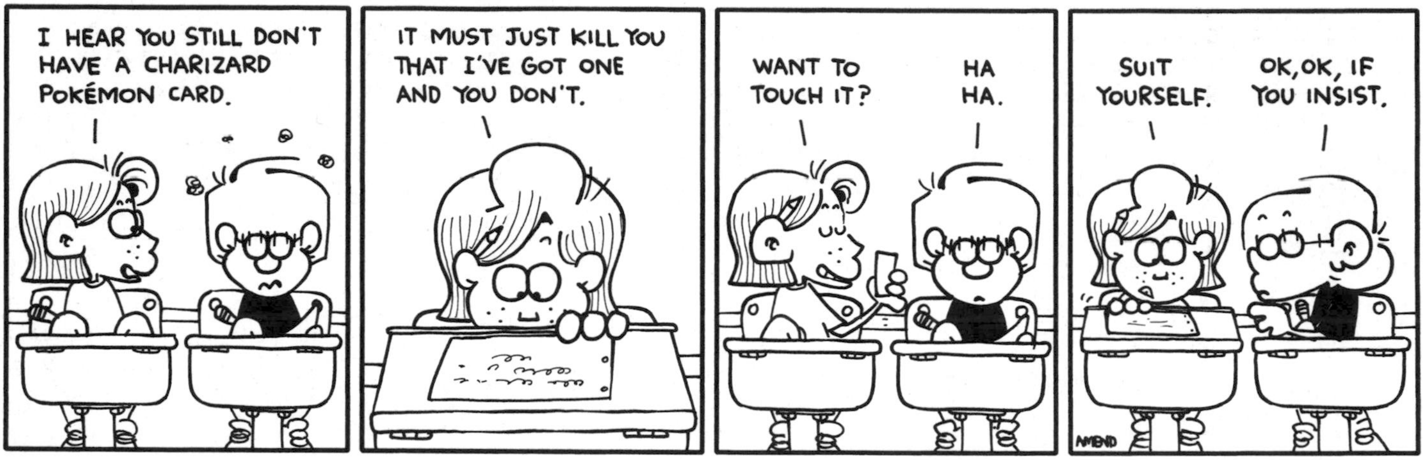
I HEAR YOU STILL DON'T HAVE A CHARIZARD POKÉMON CARD.
IT MUST JUST KILL YOU THAT I'VE GOT ONE AND YOU DON'T.
WANT TO TOUCH IT?
HA HA.
SUIT YOURSELF.
OK, OK, IF YOU INSIST.
AMEND

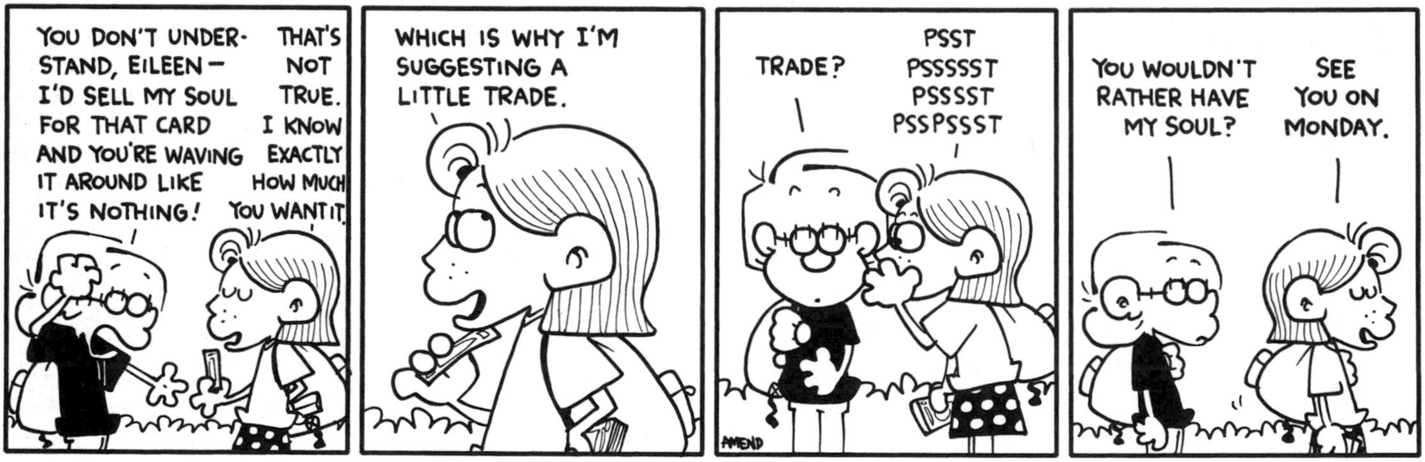
YOU DON'T UNDERSTAND, EILEEN — I'D SELL MY SOUL FOR THAT CARD AND YOU'RE WAVING IT AROUND LIKE IT'S NOTHING!
THAT'S NOT TRUE. I KNOW EXACTLY HOW MUCH YOU WANT IT.
WHICH IS WHY I'M SUGGESTING A LITTLE TRADE.
TRADE?
PSST PSSSSST PSSSST PSSPSSST
AMEND
YOU WOULDN'T RATHER HAVE MY SOUL?
SEE YOU ON MONDAY.

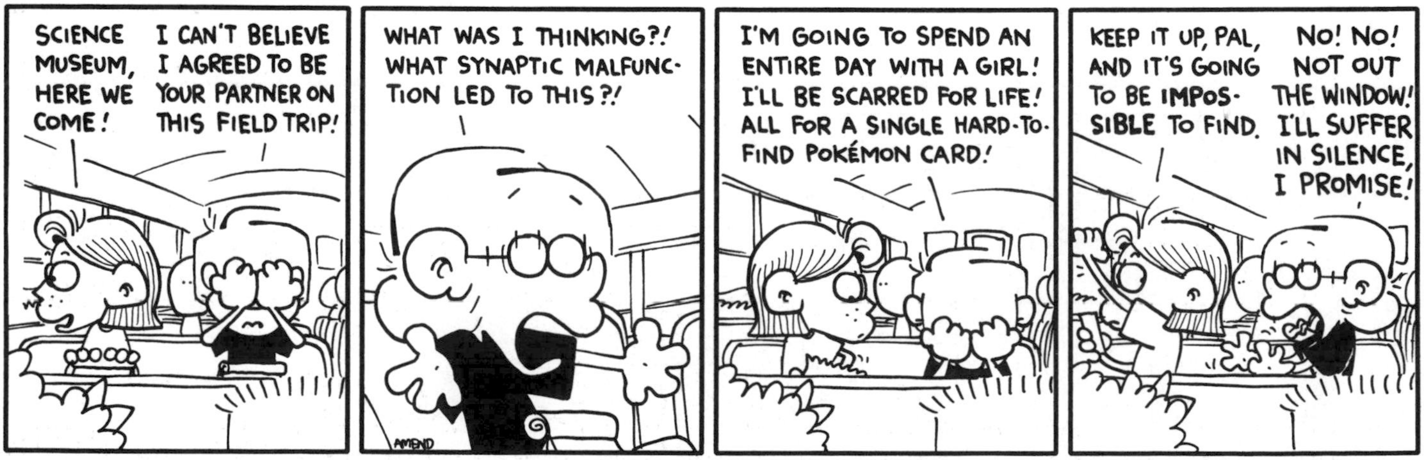
SCIENCE MUSEUM, HERE WE COME!
I CAN'T BELIEVE I AGREED TO BE YOUR PARTNER ON THIS FIELD TRIP!
WHAT WAS I THINKING?! WHAT SYNAPTIC MALFUNCTION LED TO THIS?!
AMEND
I'M GOING TO SPEND AN ENTIRE DAY WITH A GIRL! I'LL BE SCARRED FOR LIFE! ALL FOR A SINGLE HARD-TO-FIND POKÉMON CARD!
KEEP IT UP, PAL, AND IT'S GOING TO BE IMPOSSIBLE TO FIND.
NO! NO! NOT OUT THE WINDOW! I'LL SUFFER IN SILENCE, I PROMISE!

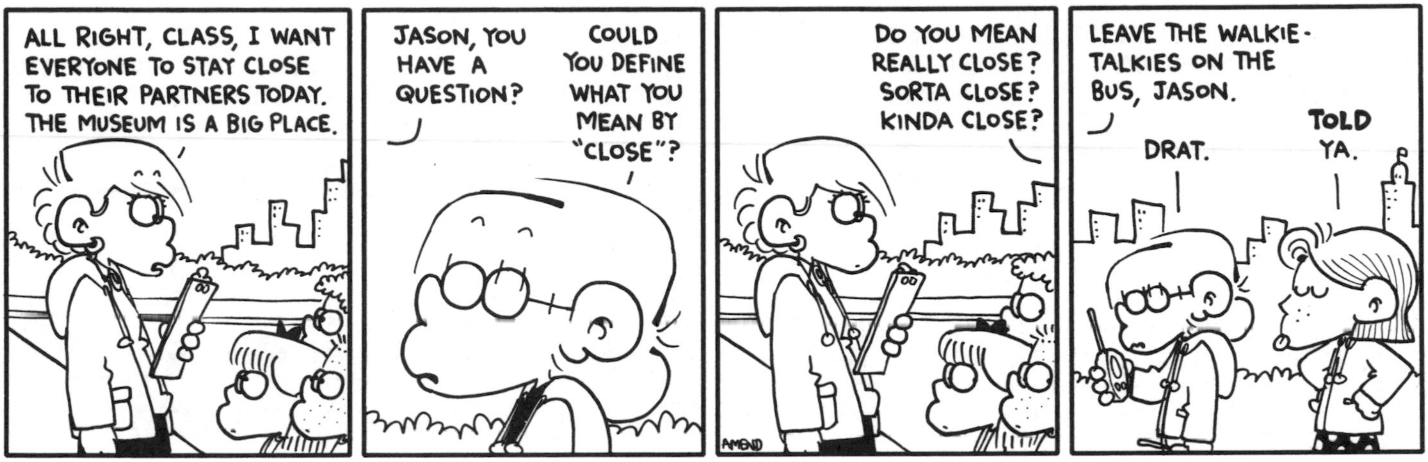
ALL RIGHT, CLASS, I WANT EVERYONE TO STAY CLOSE TO THEIR PARTNERS TODAY. THE MUSEUM IS A BIG PLACE.
JASON, YOU HAVE A QUESTION?
COULD YOU DEFINE WHAT YOU MEAN BY "CLOSE"?
DO YOU MEAN REALLY CLOSE? SORTA CLOSE? KINDA CLOSE?
LEAVE THE WALKIE-TALKIES ON THE BUS, JASON.
DRAT.
TOLD YA.
AMEND

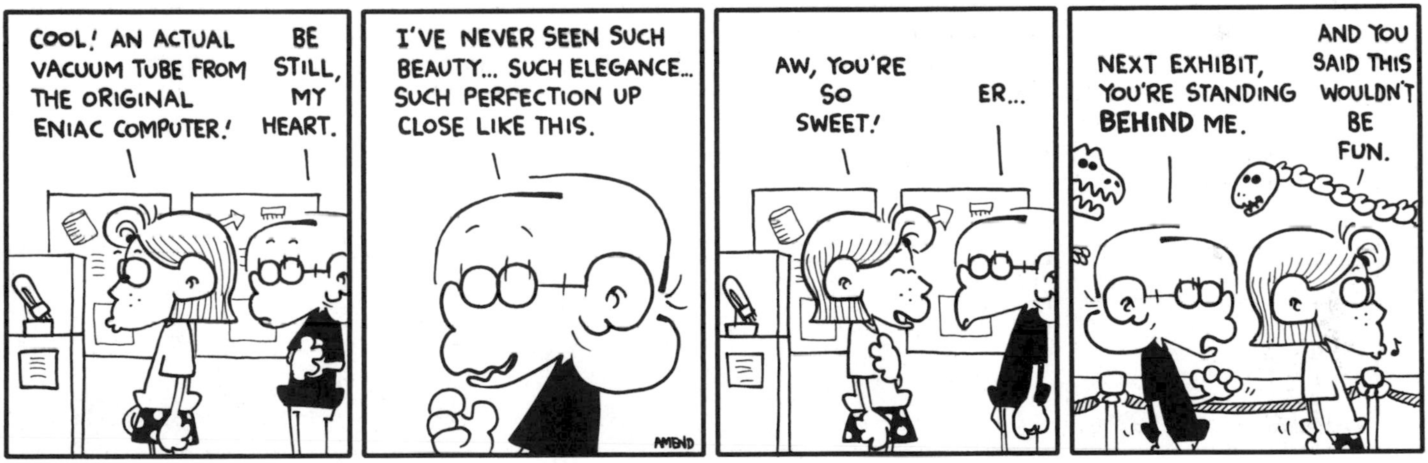
COOL! AN ACTUAL VACUUM TUBE FROM THE ORIGINAL ENIAC COMPUTER!
BE STILL, MY HEART.
I'VE NEVER SEEN SUCH BEAUTY... SUCH ELEGANCE... SUCH PERFECTION UP CLOSE LIKE THIS.
AMEND
AW, YOU'RE SO SWEET!
ER...
NEXT EXHIBIT, YOU'RE STANDING BEHIND ME.
AND YOU SAID THIS WOULDN'T BE FUN.

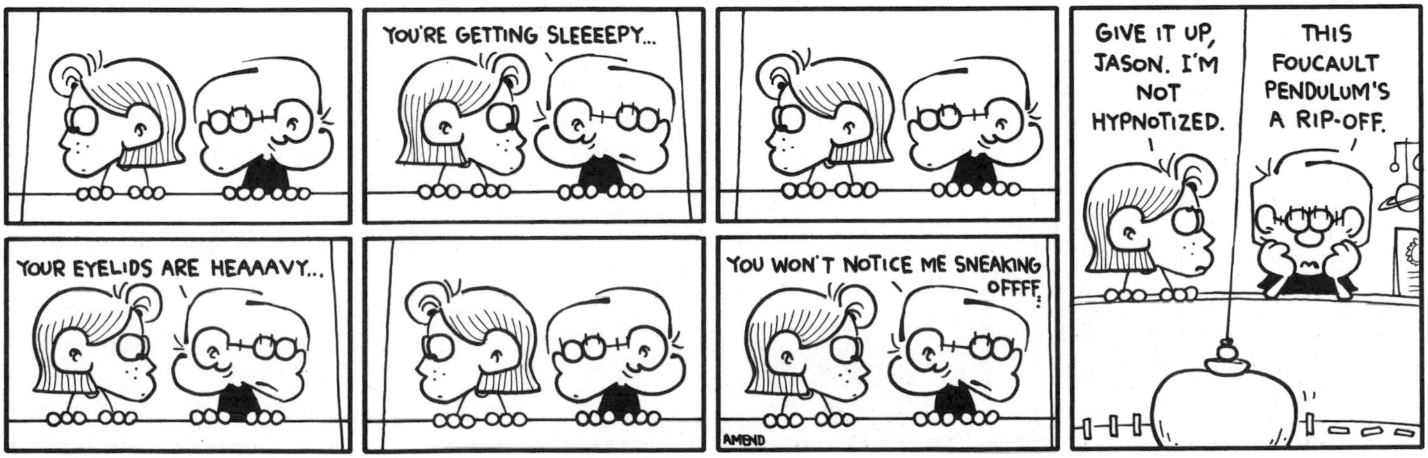
YOU'RE GETTING SLEEEEPY...
YOUR EYELIDS ARE HEAAAVY...
YOU WON'T NOTICE ME SNEAKING OFFFF.
AMEND
GIVE IT UP, JASON. I'M NOT HYPNOTIZED.
THIS FOUCAULT PENDULUM'S A RIP-OFF.

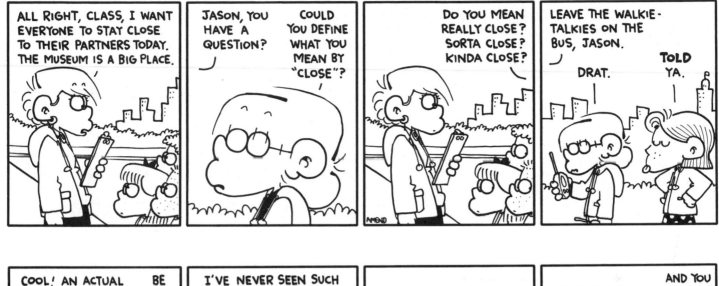

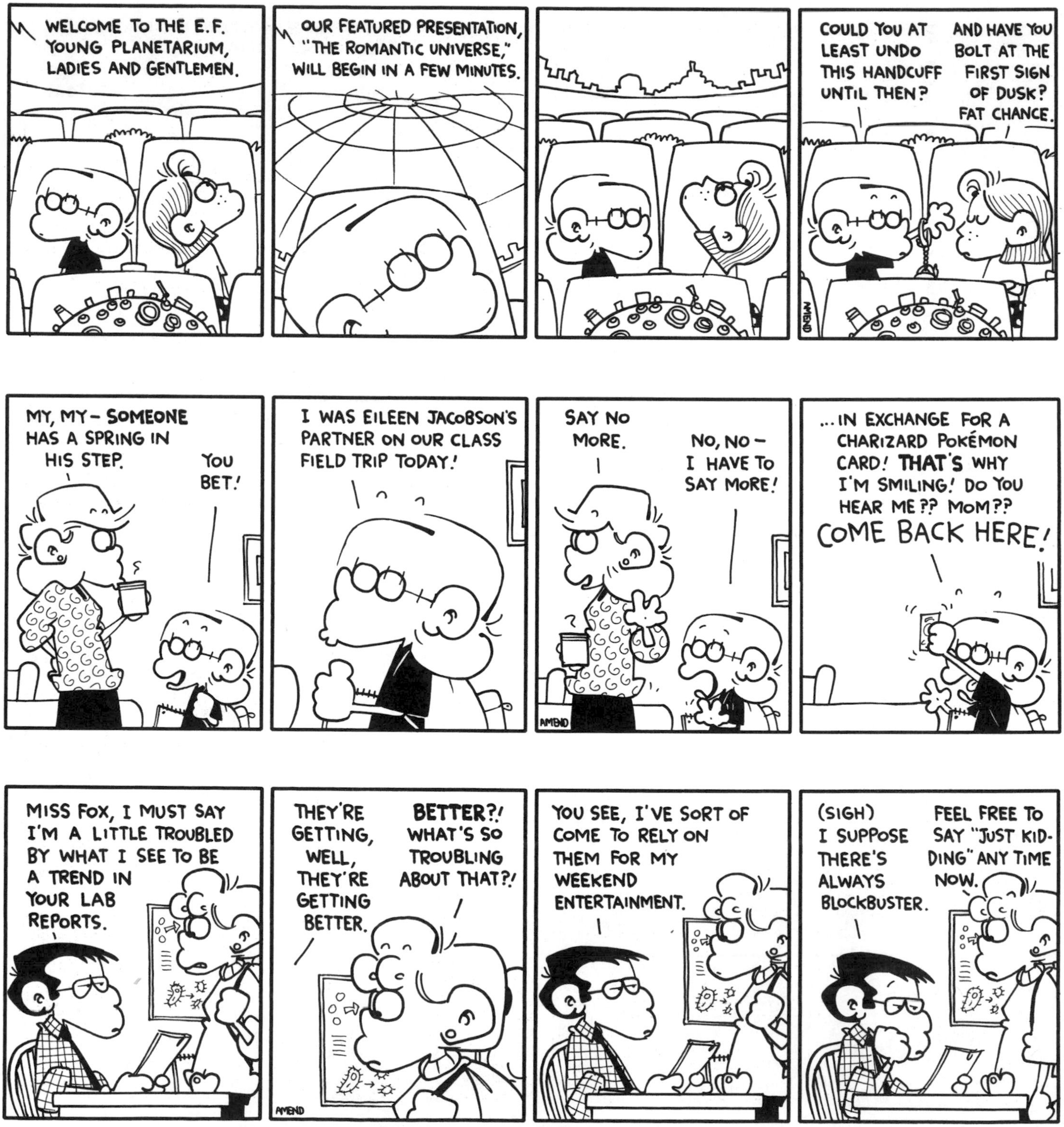
WELCOME TO THE E.F. YOUNG PLANETARIUM, LADIES AND GENTLEMEN.
OUR FEATURED PRESENTATION, "THE ROMANTIC UNIVERSE," WILL BEGIN IN A FEW MINUTES.
COULD YOU AT LEAST UNDO THIS HANDCUFF UNTIL THEN?
AND HAVE YOU BOLT AT THE FIRST SIGN OF DUSK? FAT CHANCE.
AMEND
MY, MY – SOMEONE HAS A SPRING IN HIS STEP.
YOU BET!
I WAS EILEEN JACOBSON'S PARTNER ON OUR CLASS FIELD TRIP TODAY!
SAY NO MORE.
NO, NO – I HAVE TO SAY MORE!
AMEND
...IN EXCHANGE FOR A CHARIZARD POKÉMON CARD! THAT'S WHY I'M SMILING! DO YOU HEAR ME?? MOM??
COME BACK HERE!
MISS FOX, I MUST SAY I'M A LITTLE TROUBLED BY WHAT I SEE TO BE A TREND IN YOUR LAB REPORTS.
THEY'RE GETTING, WELL, THEY'RE GETTING BETTER.
BETTER?! WHAT'S SO TROUBLING ABOUT THAT?!
AMEND
YOU SEE, I'VE SORT OF COME TO RELY ON THEM FOR MY WEEKEND ENTERTAINMENT.
(SIGH) I SUPPOSE THERE'S ALWAYS BLOCKBUSTER.
FEEL FREE TO SAY "JUST KIDDING" ANY TIME NOW.

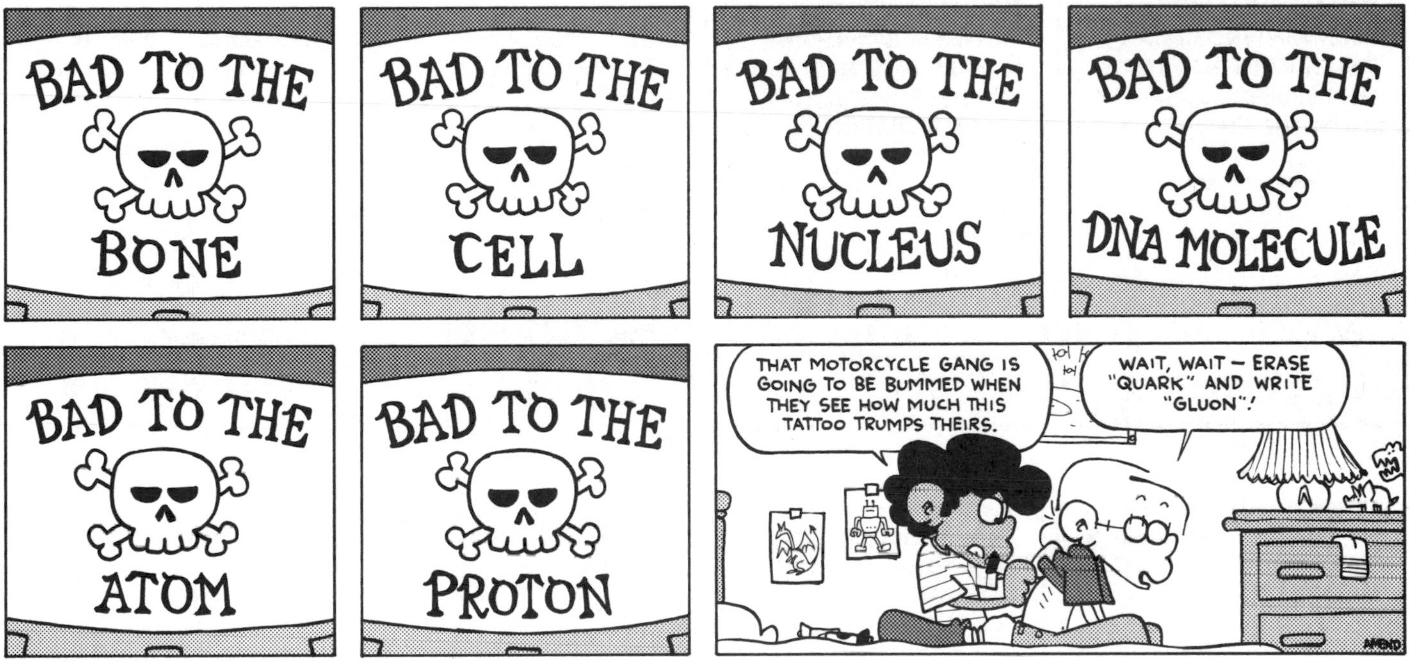
BAD TO THE BONE
BAD TO THE CELL
BAD TO THE NUCLEUS
BAD TO THE DNA MOLECULE
BAD TO THE ATOM
BAD TO THE PROTON
THAT MOTORCYCLE GANG IS GOING TO BE BUMMED WHEN THEY SEE HOW MUCH THIS TATTOO TRUMPS THEIRS.
WAIT, WAIT – ERASE "QUARK" AND WRITE "GLUON"!

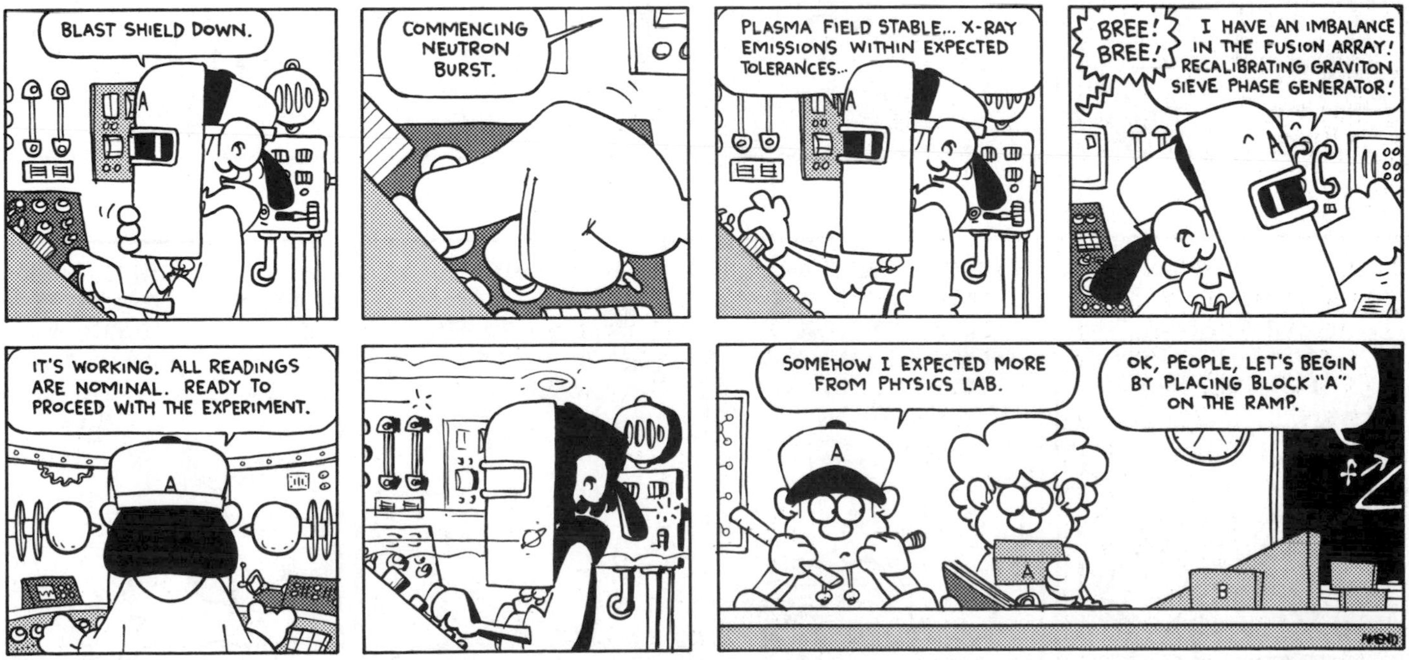
BLAST SHIELD DOWN.
COMMENCING NEUTRON BURST.
PLASMA FIELD STABLE... X-RAY EMISSIONS WITHIN EXPECTED TOLERANCES...
BREE! BREE!
I HAVE AN IMBALANCE IN THE FUSION ARRAY! RECALIBRATING GRAVITON SIEVE PHASE GENERATOR!
IT'S WORKING. ALL READINGS ARE NOMINAL. READY TO PROCEED WITH THE EXPERIMENT.
SOMEHOW I EXPECTED MORE FROM PHYSICS LAB.
OK, PEOPLE, LET'S BEGIN BY PLACING BLOCK "A" ON THE RAMP.

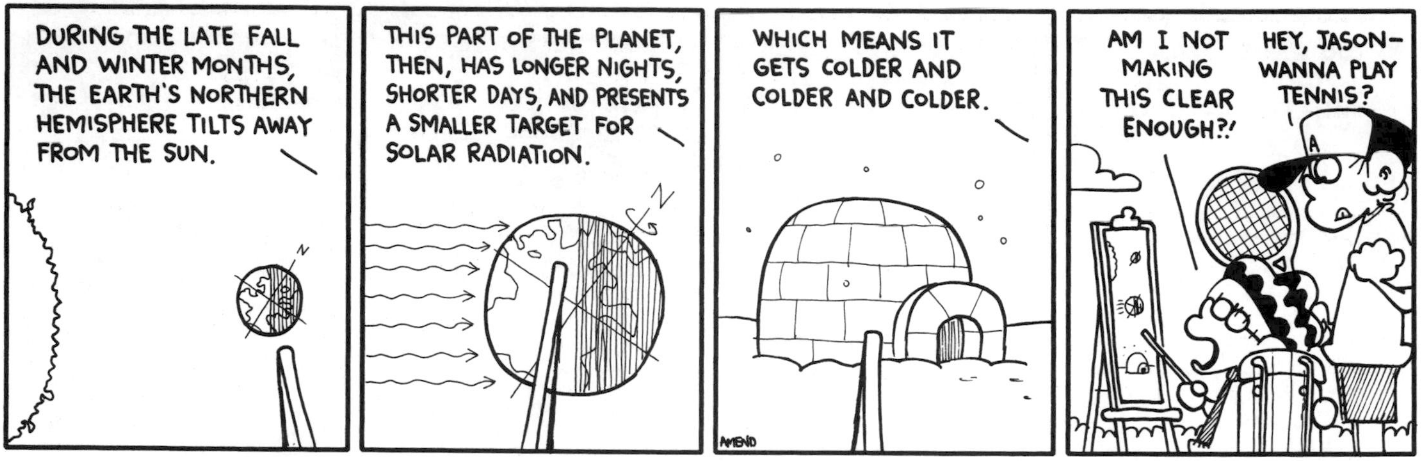
DURING THE LATE FALL AND WINTER MONTHS, THE EARTH'S NORTHERN HEMISPHERE TILTS AWAY FROM THE SUN.
THIS PART OF THE PLANET, THEN, HAS LONGER NIGHTS, SHORTER DAYS, AND PRESENTS A SMALLER TARGET FOR SOLAR RADIATION.
WHICH MEANS IT GETS COLDER AND COLDER AND COLDER.
AMEND
AM I NOT MAKING THIS CLEAR ENOUGH?!
HEY, JASON— WANNA PLAY TENNIS?

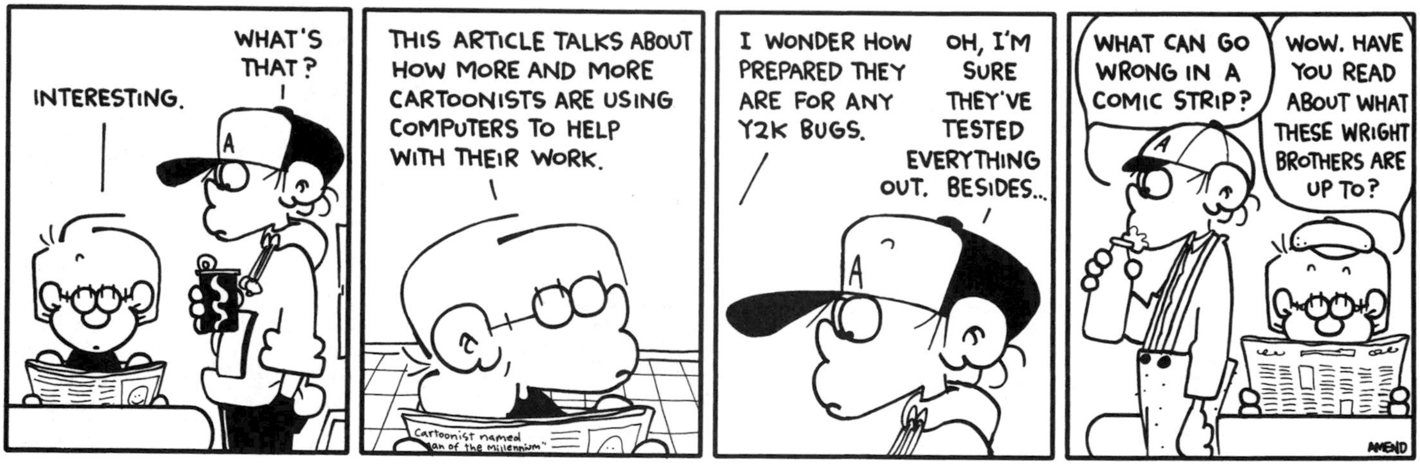
INTERESTING.
WHAT'S THAT?
THIS ARTICLE TALKS ABOUT HOW MORE AND MORE CARTOONISTS ARE USING COMPUTERS TO HELP WITH THEIR WORK.
Cartoonist named
I WONDER HOW PREPARED THEY ARE FOR ANY Y2K BUGS.
OH, I'M SURE THEY'VE TESTED EVERYTHING OUT. BESIDES...
WHAT CAN GO WRONG IN A COMIC STRIP?
WOW. HAVE YOU READ ABOUT WHAT THESE WRIGHT BROTHERS ARE UP TO?
AMEND

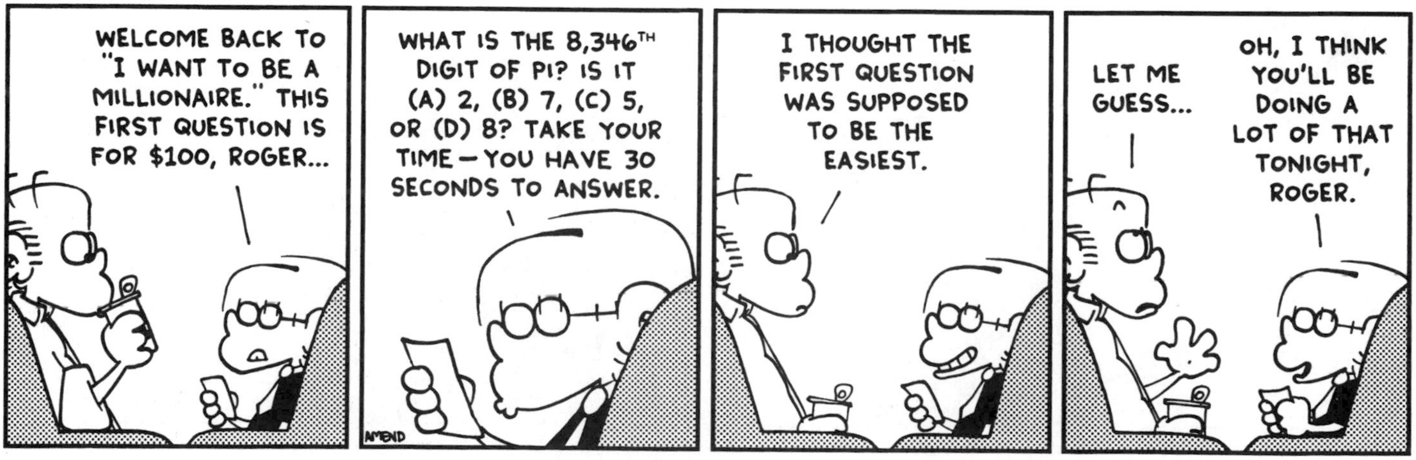
WELCOME BACK TO "I WANT TO BE A MILLIONAIRE." THIS FIRST QUESTION IS FOR $100, ROGER...
WHAT IS THE 8,346TH DIGIT OF PI? IS IT (A) 2, (B) 7, (C) 5, OR (D) 8? TAKE YOUR TIME—YOU HAVE 30 SECONDS TO ANSWER.
AMEND
I THOUGHT THE FIRST QUESTION WAS SUPPOSED TO BE THE EASIEST.
LET ME GUESS...
OH, I THINK YOU'LL BE DOING A LOT OF THAT TONIGHT, ROGER.

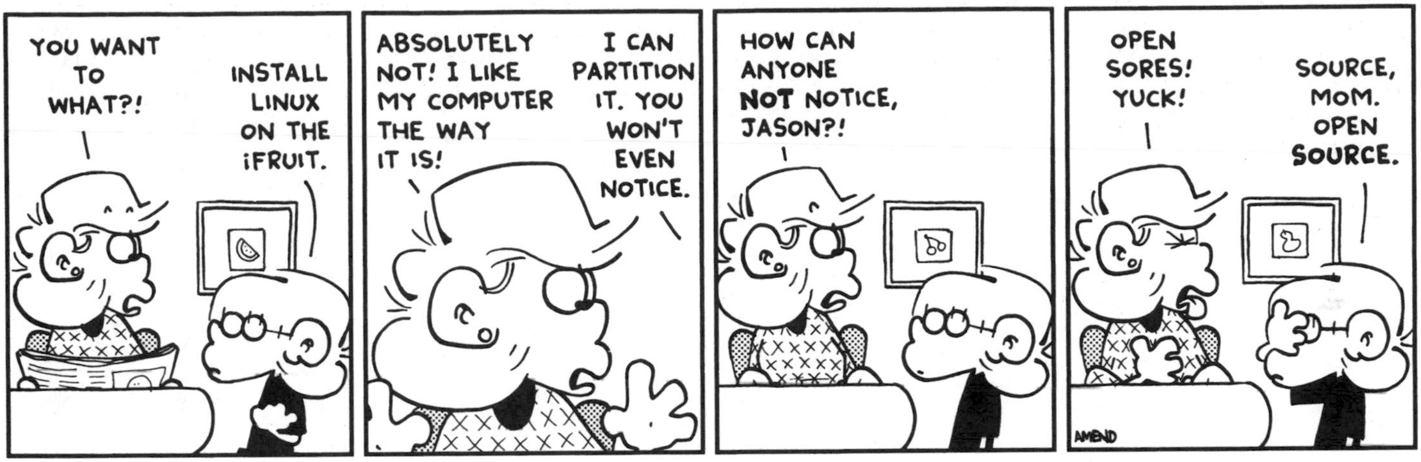
YOU WANT TO WHAT?!
INSTALL LINUX ON THE iFRUIT.
ABSOLUTELY NOT! I LIKE MY COMPUTER THE WAY IT IS!
I CAN PARTITION IT. YOU WON'T EVEN NOTICE.
HOW CAN ANYONE **NOT** NOTICE, JASON?!
OPEN SORES! YUCK!
SOURCE, MOM. OPEN **SOURCE**.
AMEND

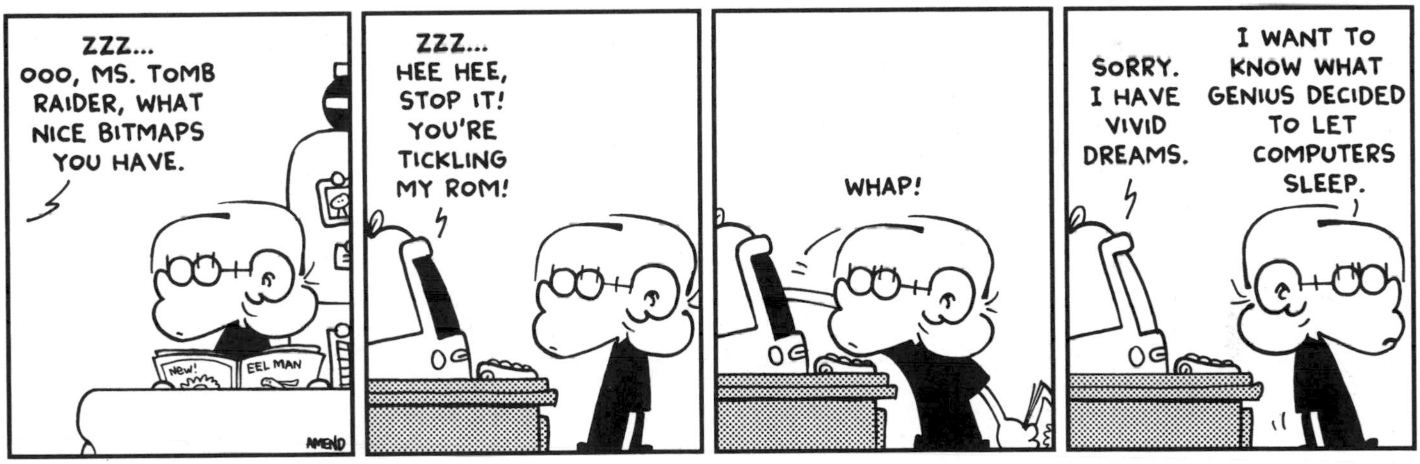
ZZZ... OOO, MS. TOMB RAIDER, WHAT NICE BITMAPS YOU HAVE.
NEW!
EEL MAN
AMEND
ZZZ... HEE HEE, STOP IT! YOU'RE TICKLING MY ROM!
WHAP!
SORRY. I HAVE VIVID DREAMS.
I WANT TO KNOW WHAT GENIUS DECIDED TO LET COMPUTERS SLEEP.

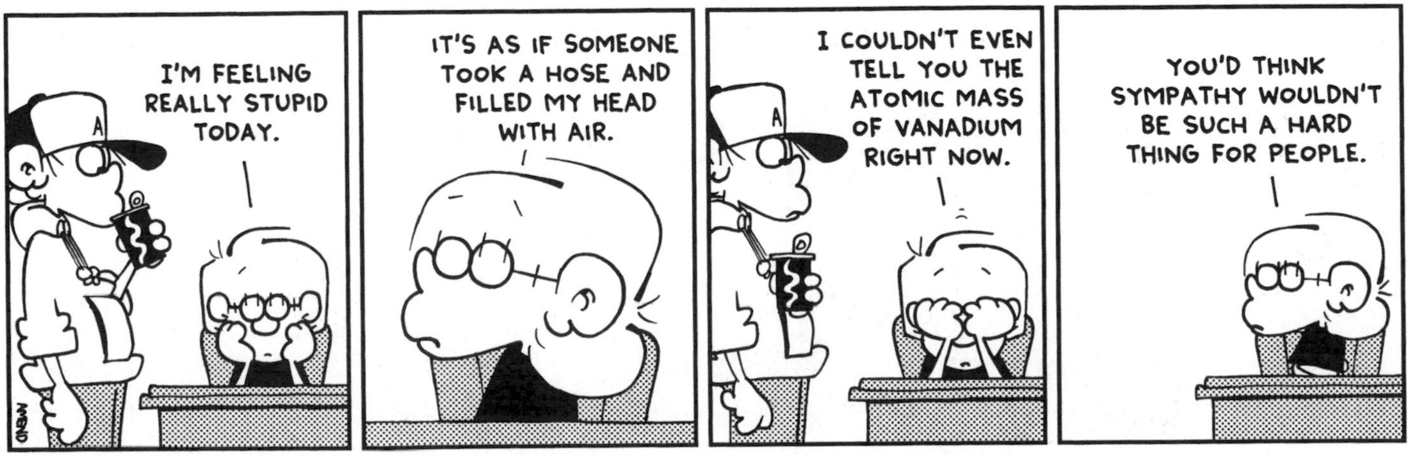
I'M FEELING REALLY STUPID TODAY.
IT'S AS IF SOMEONE TOOK A HOSE AND FILLED MY HEAD WITH AIR.
I COULDN'T EVEN TELL YOU THE ATOMIC MASS OF VANADIUM RIGHT NOW.
YOU'D THINK SYMPATHY WOULDN'T BE SUCH A HARD THING FOR PEOPLE.

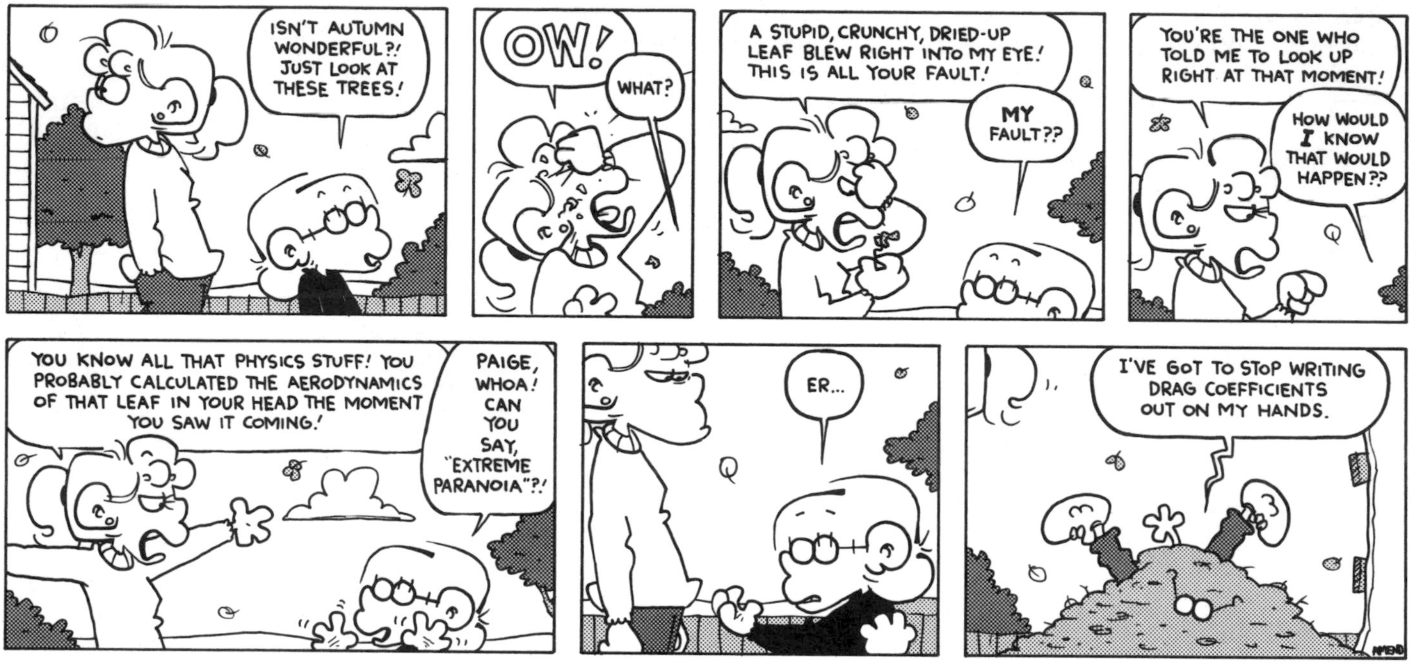
ISN'T AUTUMN WONDERFUL?! JUST LOOK AT THESE TREES!
OW!
WHAT?
A STUPID, CRUNCHY, DRIED-UP LEAF BLEW RIGHT INTO MY EYE! THIS IS ALL YOUR FAULT!
MY FAULT??
YOU'RE THE ONE WHO TOLD ME TO LOOK UP RIGHT AT THAT MOMENT!
HOW WOULD I KNOW THAT WOULD HAPPEN??
YOU KNOW ALL THAT PHYSICS STUFF! YOU PROBABLY CALCULATED THE AERODYNAMICS OF THAT LEAF IN YOUR HEAD THE MOMENT YOU SAW IT COMING!
PAIGE, WHOA! CAN YOU SAY, "EXTREME PARANOIA"?!
ER...
I'VE GOT TO STOP WRITING DRAG COEFFICIENTS OUT ON MY HANDS.

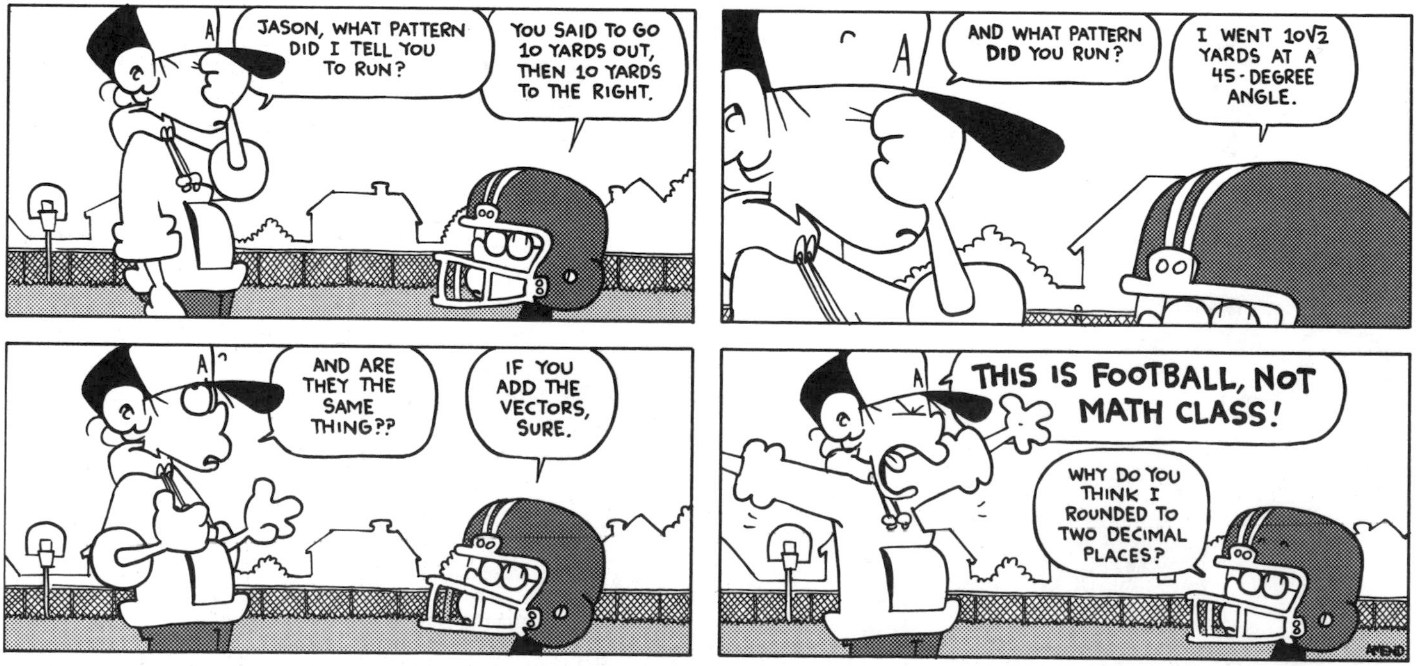
JASON, WHAT PATTERN DID I TELL YOU TO RUN?
YOU SAID TO GO 10 YARDS OUT, THEN 10 YARDS TO THE RIGHT.
AND WHAT PATTERN DID YOU RUN?
I WENT $10\sqrt{2}$ YARDS AT A 45-DEGREE ANGLE.
AND ARE THEY THE SAME THING??
IF YOU ADD THE VECTORS, SURE.
THIS IS FOOTBALL, NOT MATH CLASS!
WHY DO YOU THINK I ROUNDED TO TWO DECIMAL PLACES?

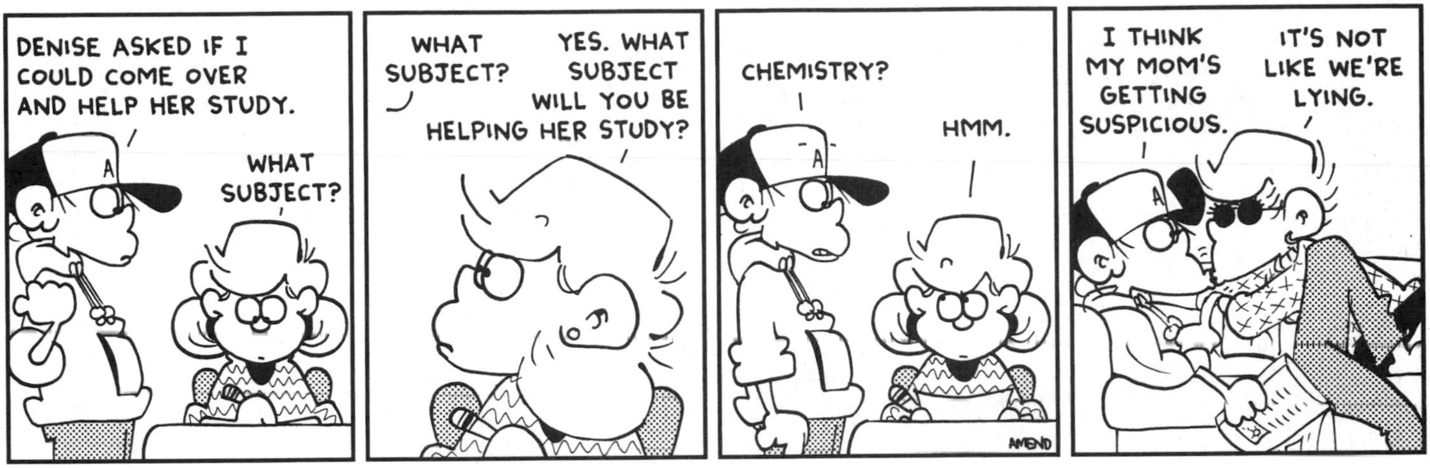
DENISE ASKED IF I COULD COME OVER AND HELP HER STUDY.
WHAT SUBJECT?
WHAT SUBJECT?
YES. WHAT SUBJECT WILL YOU BE HELPING HER STUDY?
CHEMISTRY?
HMM.
I THINK MY MOM'S GETTING SUSPICIOUS.
IT'S NOT LIKE WE'RE LYING.
AMEND

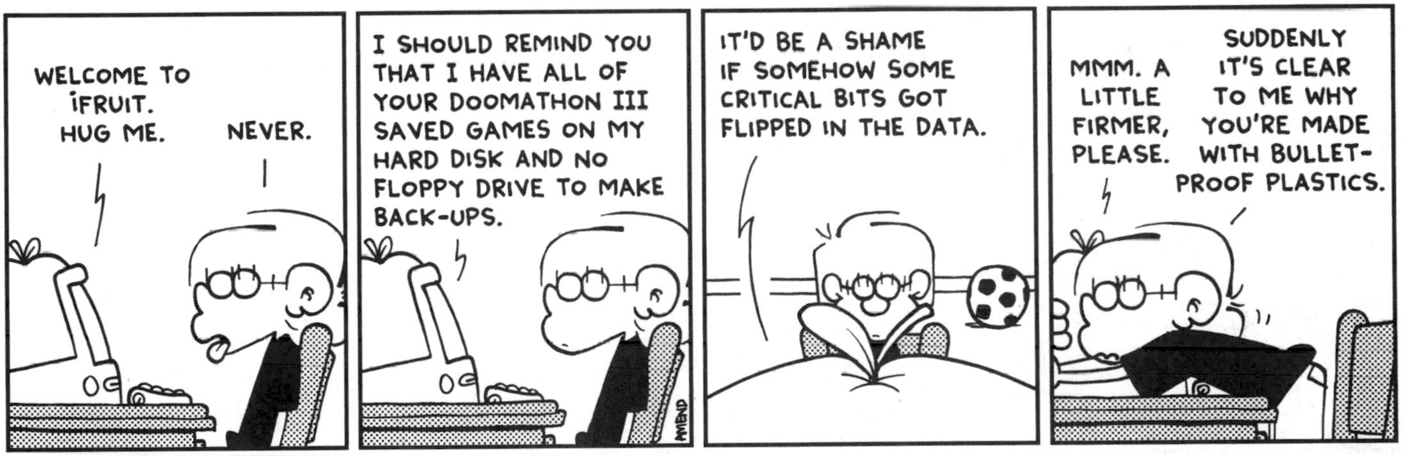
WELCOME TO iFRUIT. HUG ME.
NEVER.
I SHOULD REMIND YOU THAT I HAVE ALL OF YOUR DOOMATHON III SAVED GAMES ON MY HARD DISK AND NO FLOPPY DRIVE TO MAKE BACK-UPS.
AMEND
IT'D BE A SHAME IF SOMEHOW SOME CRITICAL BITS GOT FLIPPED IN THE DATA.
MMM. A LITTLE FIRMER, PLEASE.
SUDDENLY IT'S CLEAR TO ME WHY YOU'RE MADE WITH BULLET-PROOF PLASTICS.

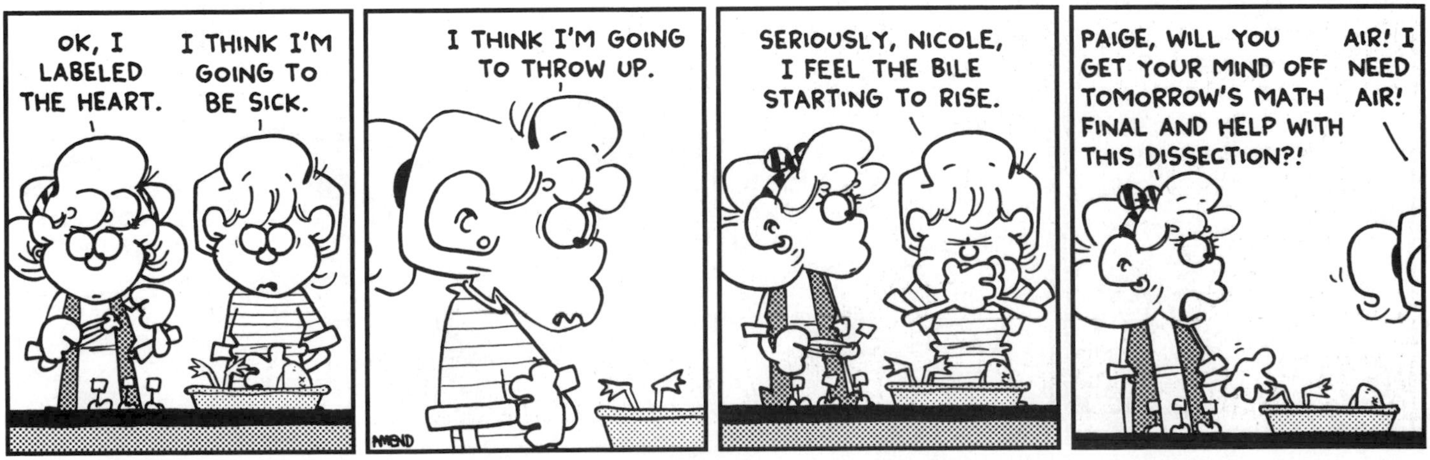
OK, I LABELED THE HEART.
I THINK I'M GOING TO BE SICK.
I THINK I'M GOING TO THROW UP.
AMEND
SERIOUSLY, NICOLE, I FEEL THE BILE STARTING TO RISE.
PAIGE, WILL YOU GET YOUR MIND OFF TOMORROW'S MATH FINAL AND HELP WITH THIS DISSECTION?!
AIR! I NEED AIR!

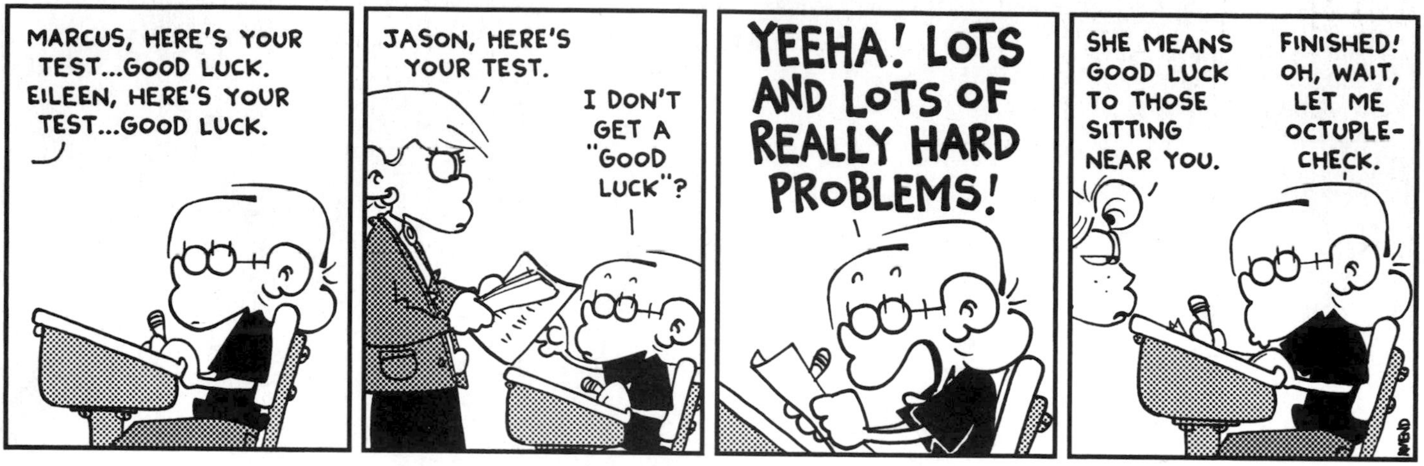
MARCUS, HERE'S YOUR TEST...GOOD LUCK. EILEEN, HERE'S YOUR TEST...GOOD LUCK.
JASON, HERE'S YOUR TEST.
I DON'T GET A "GOOD LUCK"?
YEEHA! LOTS AND LOTS OF REALLY HARD PROBLEMS!
SHE MEANS GOOD LUCK TO THOSE SITTING NEAR YOU.
FINISHED! OH, WAIT, LET ME OCTUPLE-CHECK.
AMEND

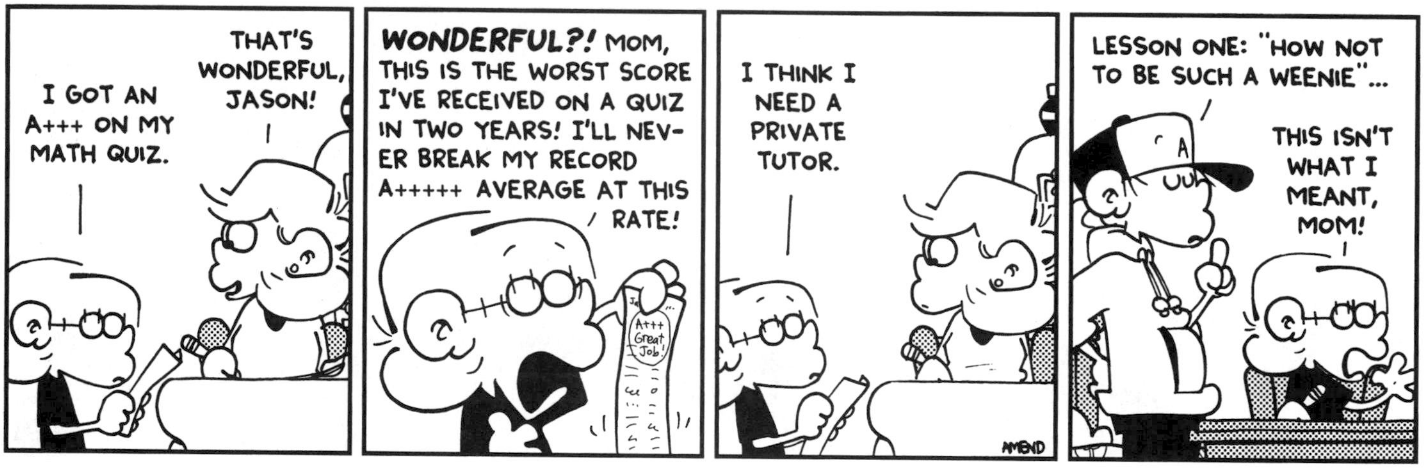
I GOT AN A+++ ON MY MATH QUIZ.
THAT'S WONDERFUL, JASON!
WONDERFUL?! MOM, THIS IS THE WORST SCORE I'VE RECEIVED ON A QUIZ IN TWO YEARS! I'LL NEVER BREAK MY RECORD A+++++ AVERAGE AT THIS RATE!
A+++ Great Job!
I THINK I NEED A PRIVATE TUTOR.
AMEND
LESSON ONE: "HOW NOT TO BE SUCH A WEENIE"...
THIS ISN'T WHAT I MEANT, MOM!

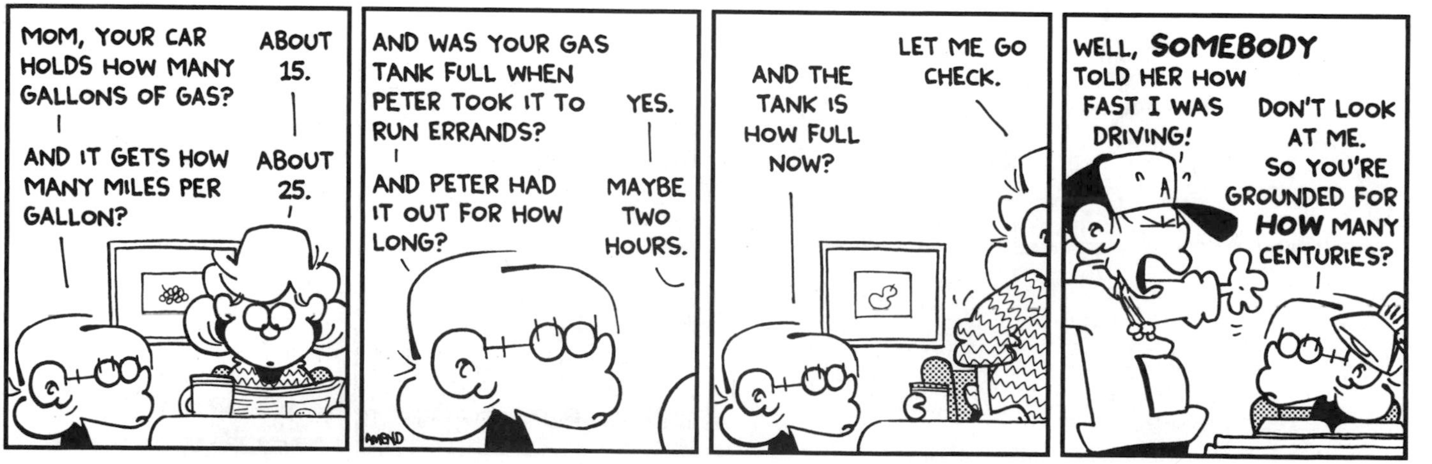
MOM, YOUR CAR HOLDS HOW MANY GALLONS OF GAS?
ABOUT 15.
AND IT GETS HOW MANY MILES PER GALLON?
ABOUT 25.
AND WAS YOUR GAS TANK FULL WHEN PETER TOOK IT TO RUN ERRANDS?
YES.
AND PETER HAD IT OUT FOR HOW LONG?
MAYBE TWO HOURS.
AMEND
AND THE TANK IS HOW FULL NOW?
LET ME GO CHECK.
WELL, **SOMEBODY** TOLD HER HOW FAST I WAS DRIVING!
DON'T LOOK AT ME. SO YOU'RE GROUNDED FOR **HOW** MANY CENTURIES?

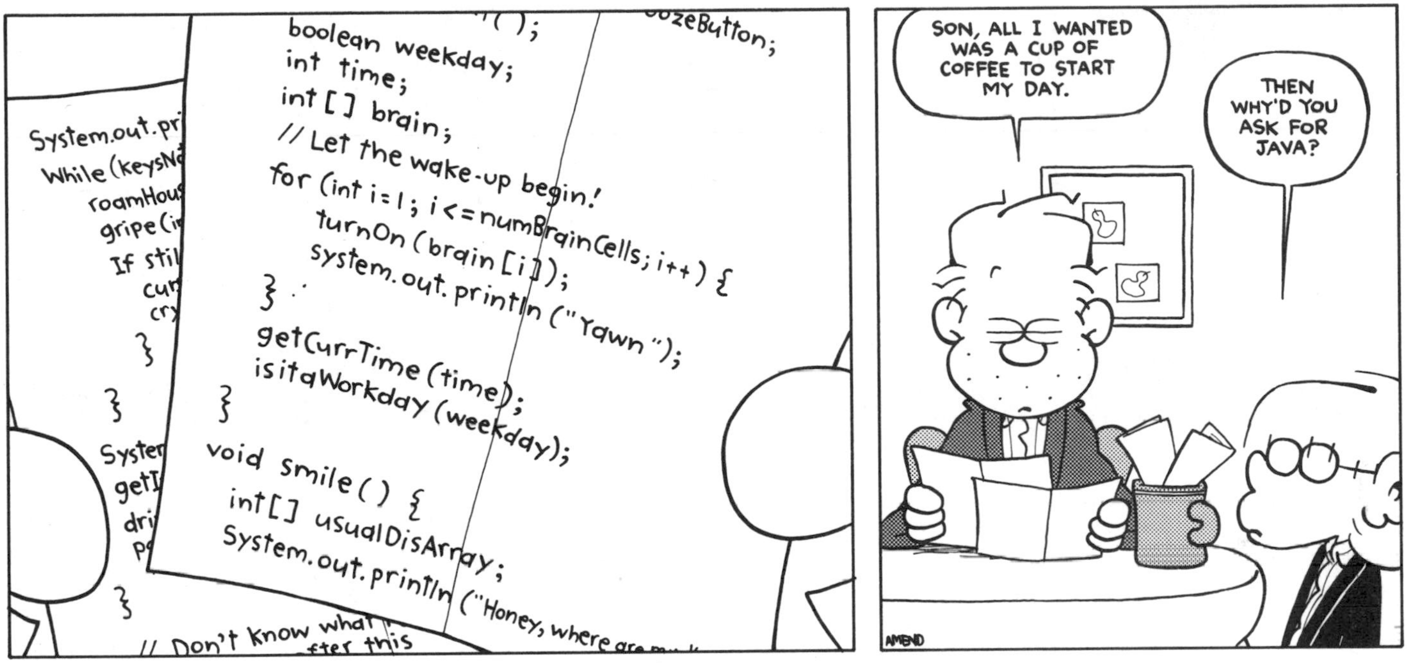

boolean weekday;
int time;
int [] brain;
// Let the wake-up begin!
for (int i=1; i<=numBrainCells; i++) {
turnOn (brain[i]);
System.out.println ("Yawn");
}
getCurrTime (time);
isitaWorkday (weekday);
}
void smile () {
int[] usualDisArray;
System.out.println ("Honey, where are my
System.out.pr
While (keysN
roamHous
gripe (i
If stil
// Don't know what
SON, ALL I WANTED WAS A CUP OF COFFEE TO START MY DAY.
THEN WHY'D YOU ASK FOR JAVA?
AMEND

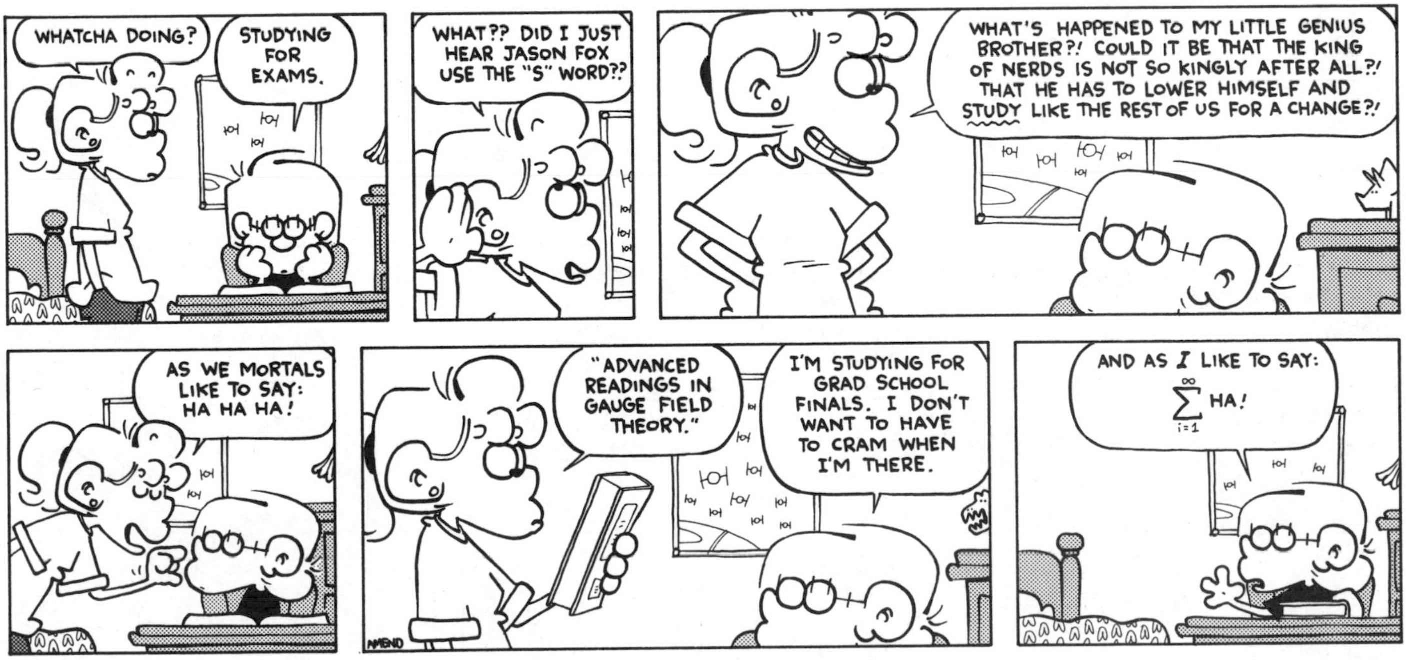

WHATCHA DOING?
STUDYING FOR EXAMS.
WHAT?? DID I JUST HEAR JASON FOX USE THE "S" WORD??
WHAT'S HAPPENED TO MY LITTLE GENIUS BROTHER?! COULD IT BE THAT THE KING OF NERDS IS NOT SO KINGLY AFTER ALL?! THAT HE HAS TO LOWER HIMSELF AND STUDY LIKE THE REST OF US FOR A CHANGE?!
AS WE MORTALS LIKE TO SAY: HA HA HA!
"ADVANCED READINGS IN GAUGE FIELD THEORY."
I'M STUDYING FOR GRAD SCHOOL FINALS. I DON'T WANT TO HAVE TO CRAM WHEN I'M THERE.
AND AS I LIKE TO SAY:
$\sum_{i=1}^{\infty}$ HA!
AMEND

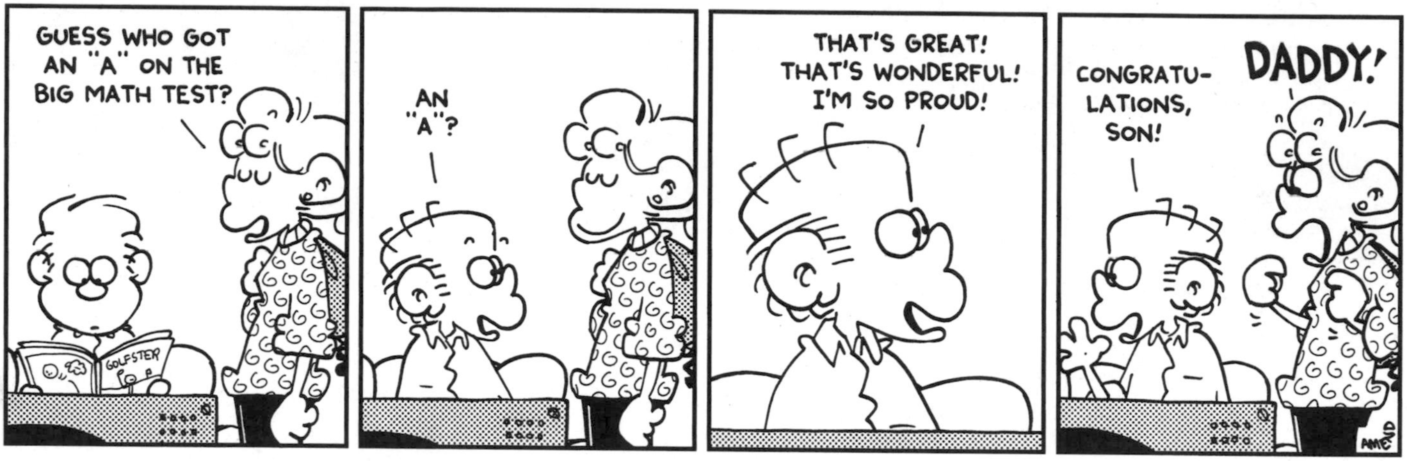
GUESS WHO GOT AN "A" ON THE BIG MATH TEST?
GOLFSTER
AN "A"?
THAT'S GREAT! THAT'S WONDERFUL! I'M SO PROUD!
CONGRATU-LATIONS, SON!
DADDY!
AMEND

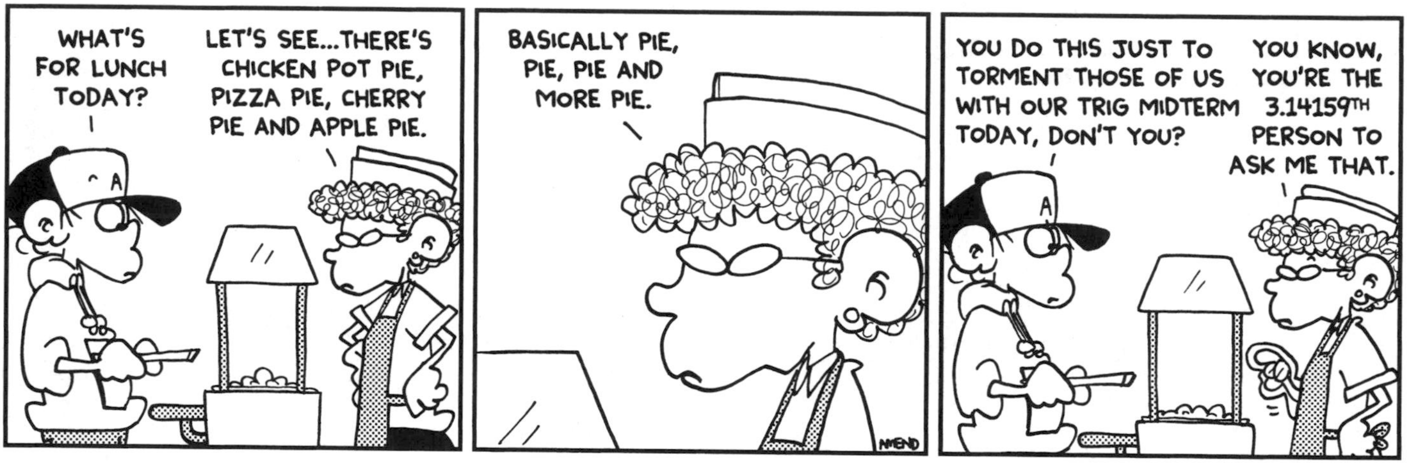
WHAT'S FOR LUNCH TODAY?
LET'S SEE...THERE'S CHICKEN POT PIE, PIZZA PIE, CHERRY PIE AND APPLE PIE.
BASICALLY PIE, PIE, PIE AND MORE PIE.
AMEND
YOU DO THIS JUST TO TORMENT THOSE OF US WITH OUR TRIG MIDTERM TODAY, DON'T YOU?
YOU KNOW, YOU'RE THE 3.14159TH PERSON TO ASK ME THAT.

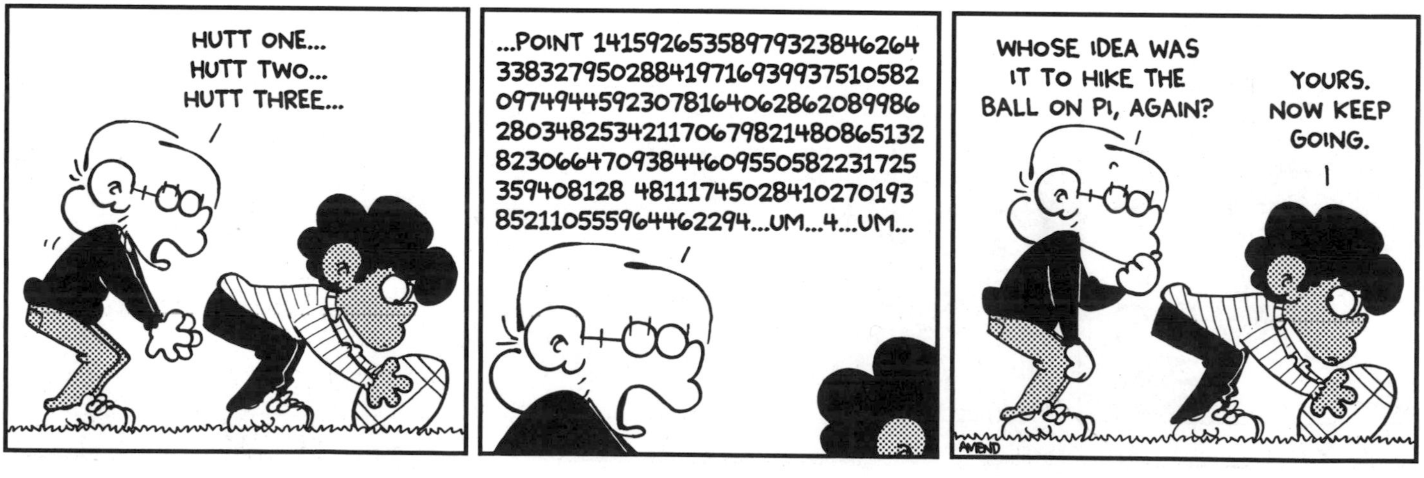
HUTT ONE... HUTT TWO... HUTT THREE...
...POINT 14159265358979323846264 33832795028841971693993751058209749445923078164062862089986 28034825342117067982148086513282306647093844609550582231725 359408128 48111745028410270193 852110555964462294...UM...4...UM...
WHOSE IDEA WAS IT TO HIKE THE BALL ON PI, AGAIN?
YOURS. NOW KEEP GOING.
AMEND

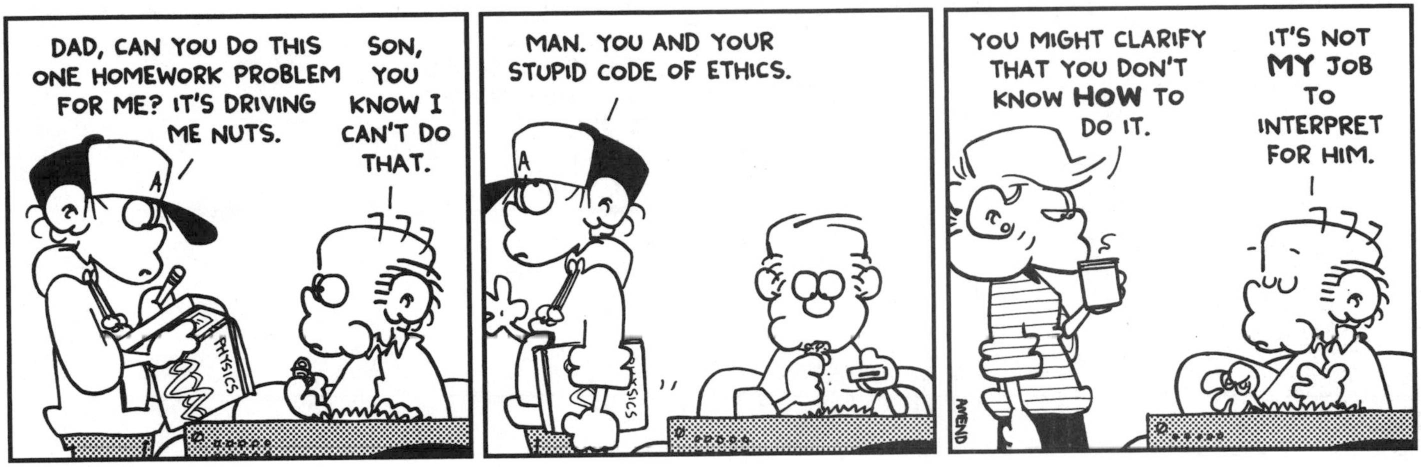
DAD, CAN YOU DO THIS ONE HOMEWORK PROBLEM FOR ME? IT'S DRIVING ME NUTS.
SON, YOU KNOW I CAN'T DO THAT.
PHYSICS
MAN. YOU AND YOUR STUPID CODE OF ETHICS.
PHYSICS
YOU MIGHT CLARIFY THAT YOU DON'T KNOW **HOW** TO DO IT.
IT'S NOT **MY** JOB TO INTERPRET FOR HIM.
AMEND

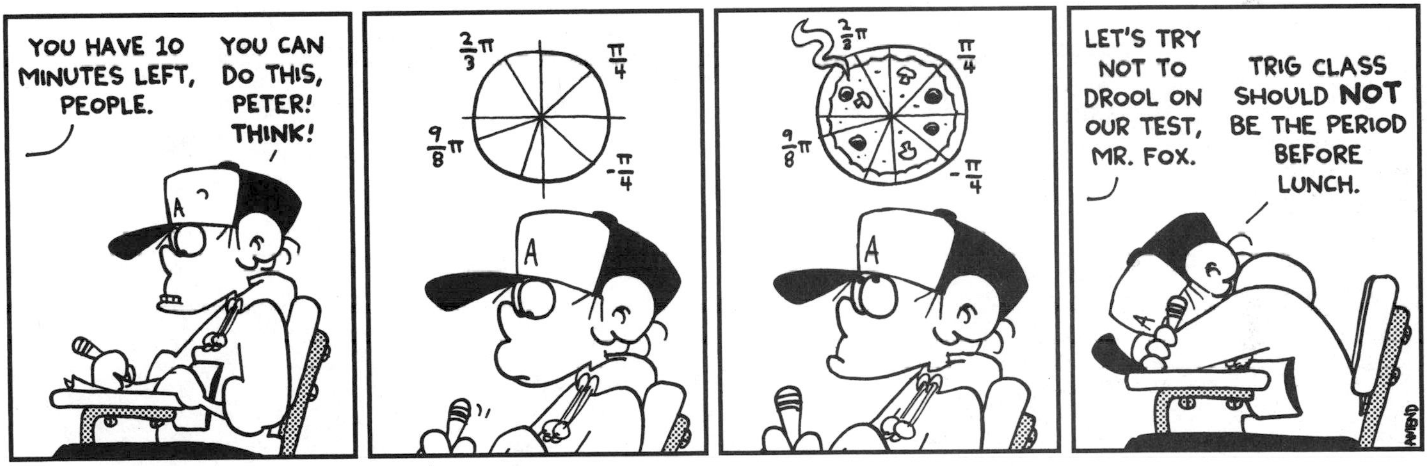
YOU HAVE 10 MINUTES LEFT, PEOPLE.
YOU CAN DO THIS, PETER! THINK!
2/3 π
π/4
9/8 π
-π/4
2/3 π
π/4
9/8 π
-π/4
LET'S TRY NOT TO DROOL ON OUR TEST, MR. FOX.
TRIG CLASS SHOULD **NOT** BE THE PERIOD BEFORE LUNCH.
AMEND

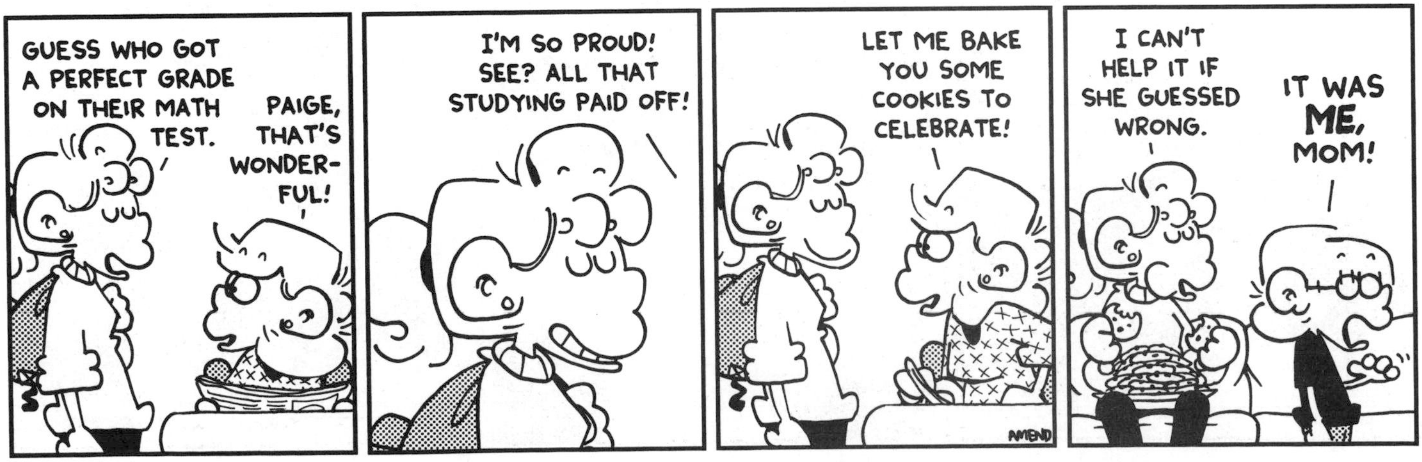
GUESS WHO GOT A PERFECT GRADE ON THEIR MATH TEST.
PAIGE, THAT'S WONDER-FUL!
I'M SO PROUD! SEE? ALL THAT STUDYING PAID OFF!
LET ME BAKE YOU SOME COOKIES TO CELEBRATE!
AMEND
I CAN'T HELP IT IF SHE GUESSED WRONG.
IT WAS **ME**, MOM!

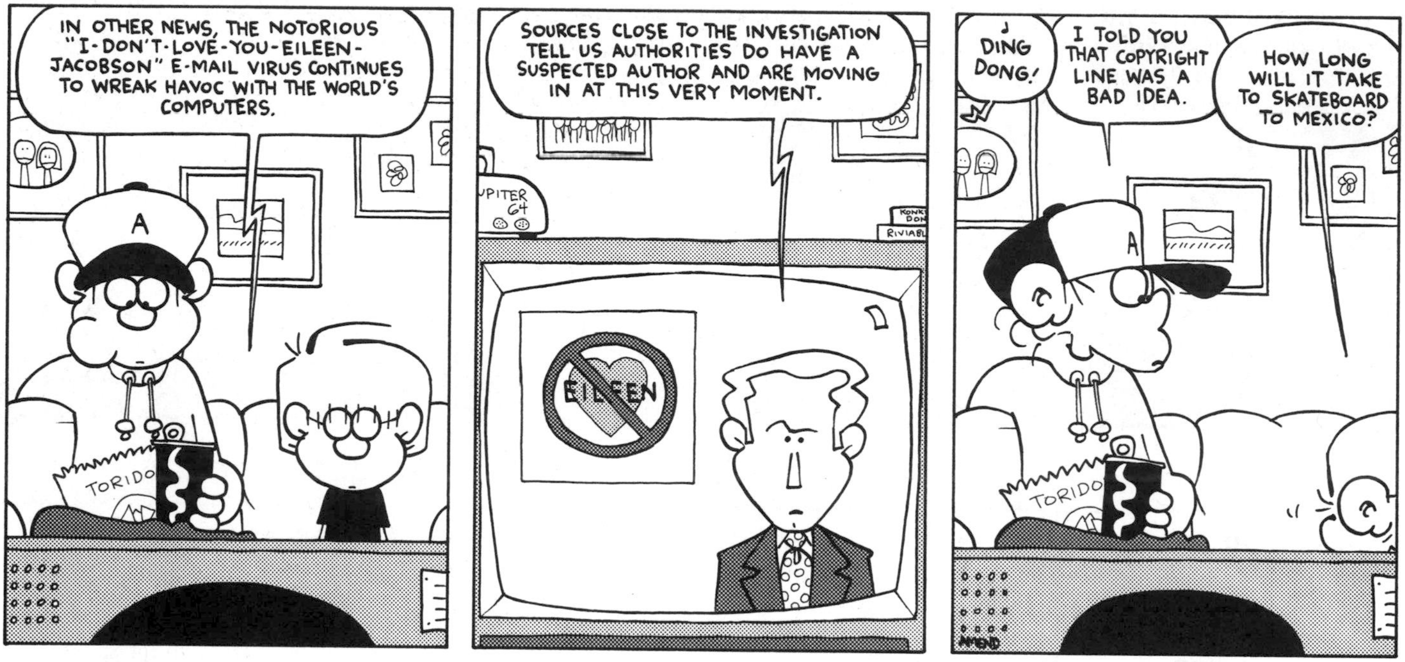
IN OTHER NEWS, THE NOTORIOUS "I-DON'T-LOVE-YOU-EILEEN-JACOBSON" E-MAIL VIRUS CONTINUES TO WREAK HAVOC WITH THE WORLD'S COMPUTERS.
SOURCES CLOSE TO THE INVESTIGATION TELL US AUTHORITIES DO HAVE A SUSPECTED AUTHOR AND ARE MOVING IN AT THIS VERY MOMENT.
EILEEN
DING DONG!
I TOLD YOU THAT COPYRIGHT LINE WAS A BAD IDEA.
HOW LONG WILL IT TAKE TO SKATEBOARD TO MEXICO?
AMEND

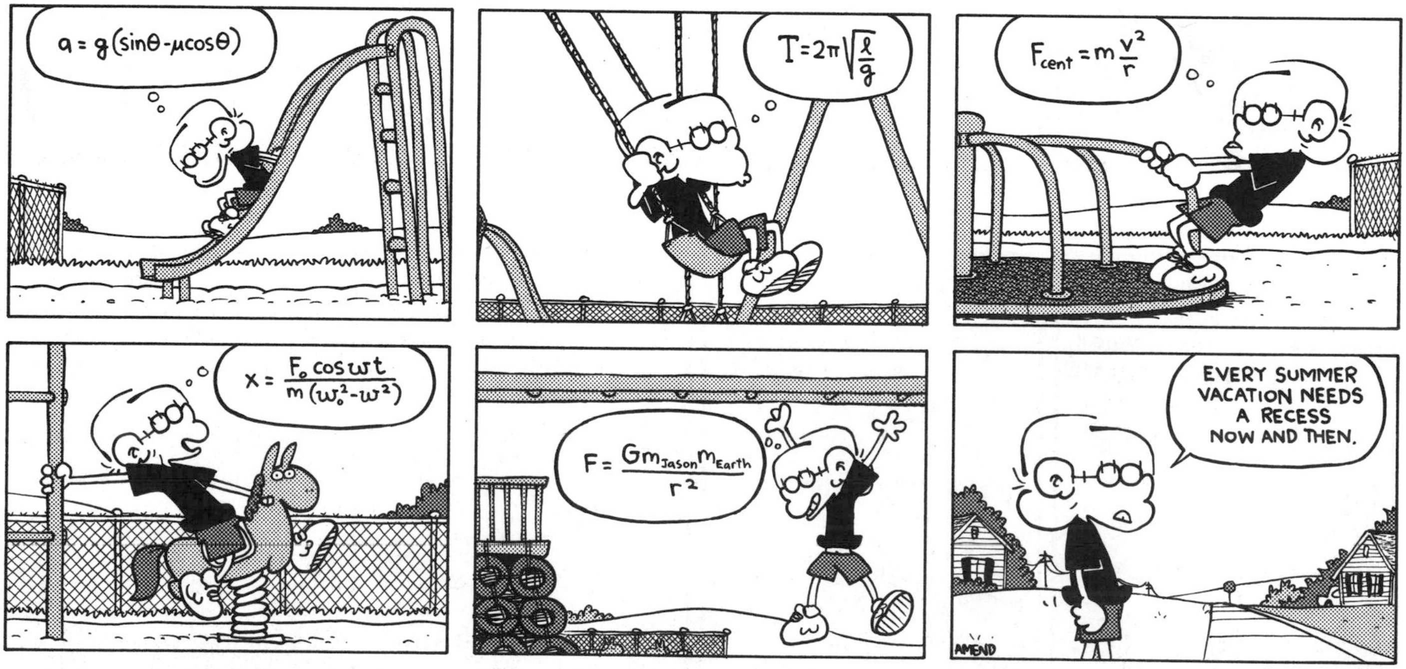
$a = g(\sin\theta - \mu\cos\theta)$
$T = 2\pi\sqrt{\frac{l}{g}}$
$F_{cent} = m\frac{v^2}{r}$
$x = \frac{F_0 \cos\omega t}{m(\omega_0^2 - \omega^2)}$
$F = \frac{G m_{Jason} m_{Earth}}{r^2}$
EVERY SUMMER VACATION NEEDS A RECESS NOW AND THEN.
AMEND

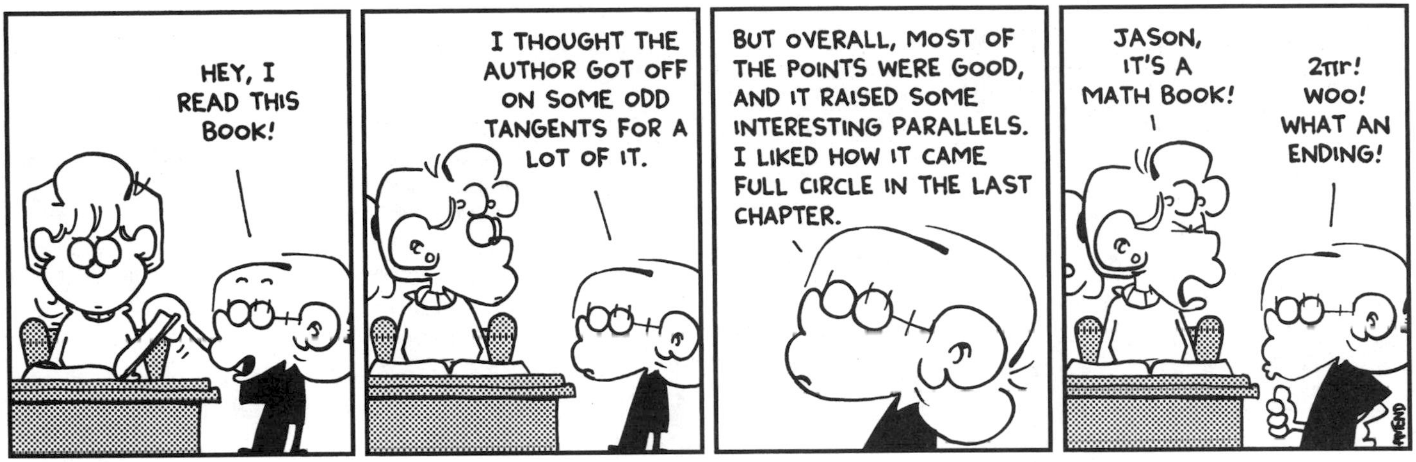
HEY, I READ THIS BOOK!
I THOUGHT THE AUTHOR GOT OFF ON SOME ODD TANGENTS FOR A LOT OF IT.
BUT OVERALL, MOST OF THE POINTS WERE GOOD, AND IT RAISED SOME INTERESTING PARALLELS. I LIKED HOW IT CAME FULL CIRCLE IN THE LAST CHAPTER.
JASON, IT'S A MATH BOOK!
2πr! WOO! WHAT AN ENDING!
AMEND

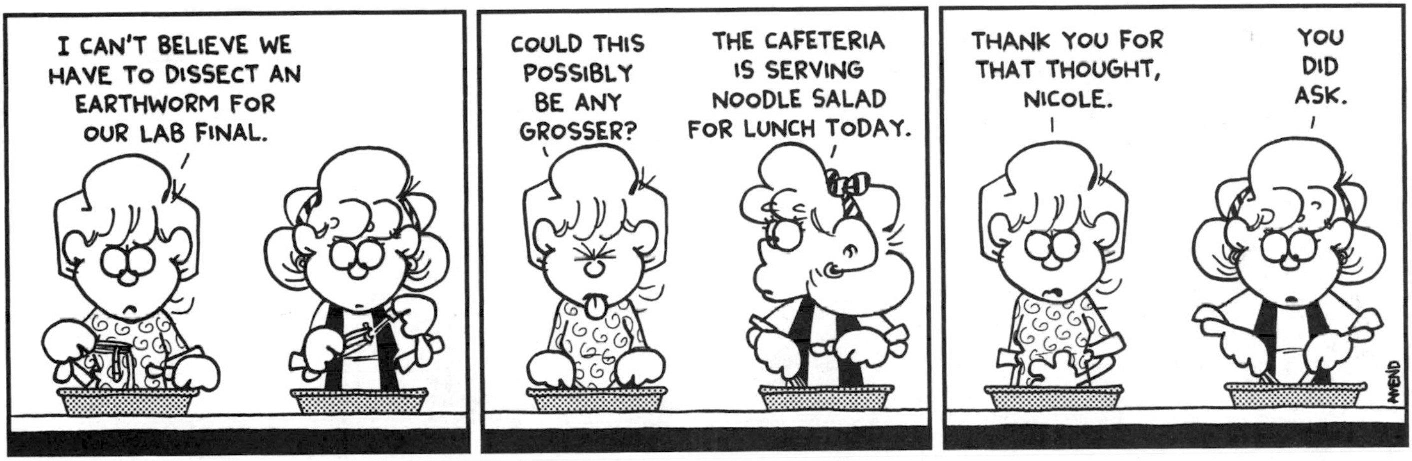
I CAN'T BELIEVE WE HAVE TO DISSECT AN EARTHWORM FOR OUR LAB FINAL.
COULD THIS POSSIBLY BE ANY GROSSER?
THE CAFETERIA IS SERVING NOODLE SALAD FOR LUNCH TODAY.
THANK YOU FOR THAT THOUGHT, NICOLE.
YOU DID ASK.
AMEND

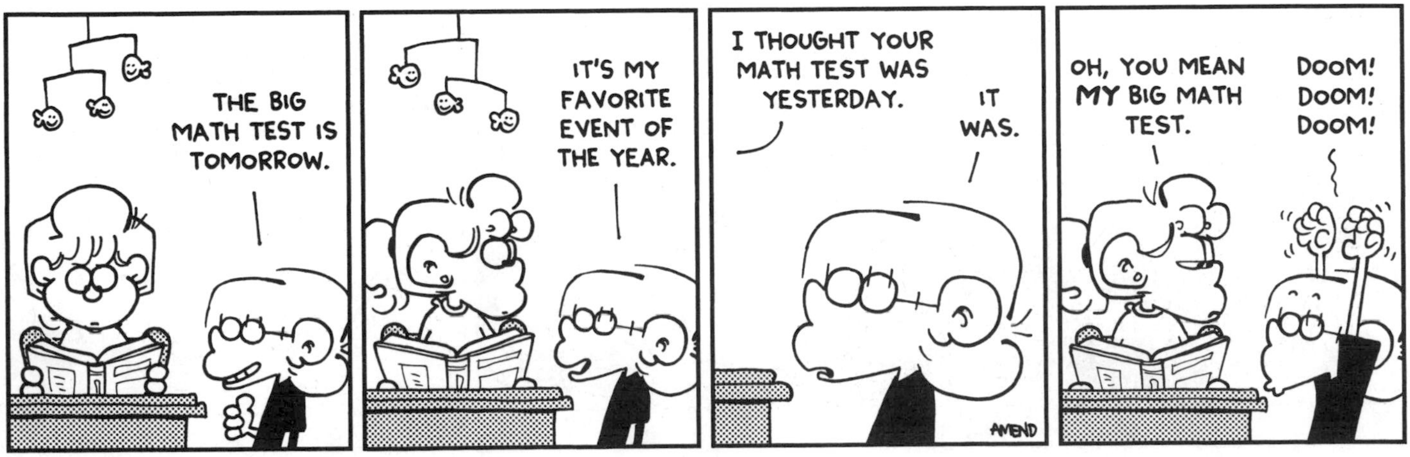
THE BIG MATH TEST IS TOMORROW.
IT'S MY FAVORITE EVENT OF THE YEAR.
I THOUGHT YOUR MATH TEST WAS YESTERDAY.
IT WAS.
AMEND
OH, YOU MEAN MY BIG MATH TEST.
DOOM! DOOM! DOOM!

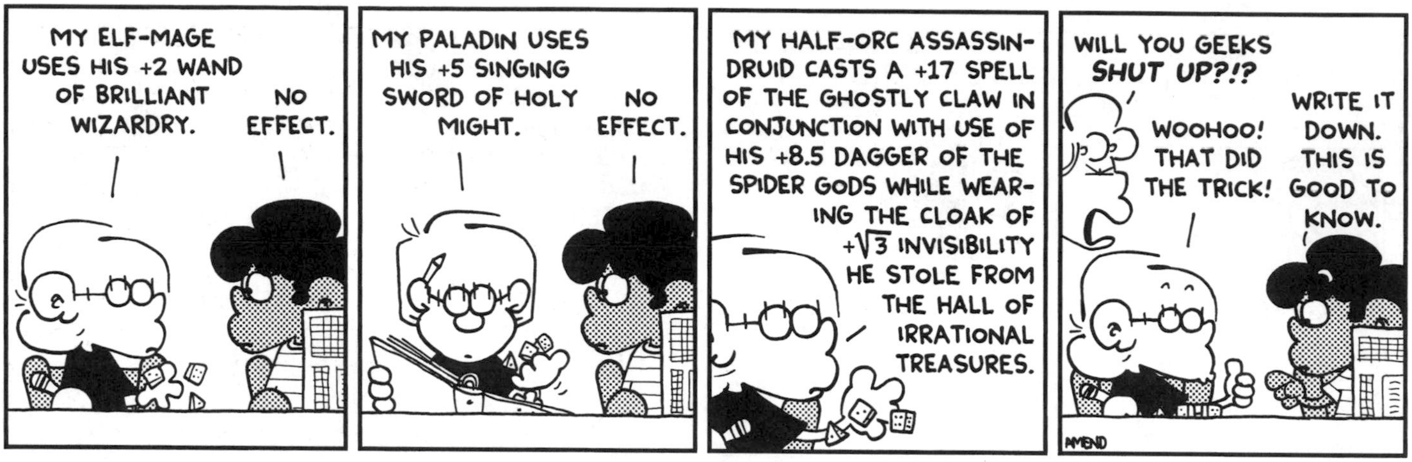
MY ELF-MAGE USES HIS +2 WAND OF BRILLIANT WIZARDRY.
NO EFFECT.
MY PALADIN USES HIS +5 SINGING SWORD OF HOLY MIGHT.
NO EFFECT.
MY HALF-ORC ASSASSIN-DRUID CASTS A +17 SPELL OF THE GHOSTLY CLAW IN CONJUNCTION WITH USE OF HIS +8.5 DAGGER OF THE SPIDER GODS WHILE WEARING THE CLOAK OF +√3 INVISIBILITY HE STOLE FROM THE HALL OF IRRATIONAL TREASURES.
WILL YOU GEEKS SHUT UP?!?
WOOHOO! THAT DID THE TRICK!
WRITE IT DOWN. THIS IS GOOD TO KNOW.
AMEND

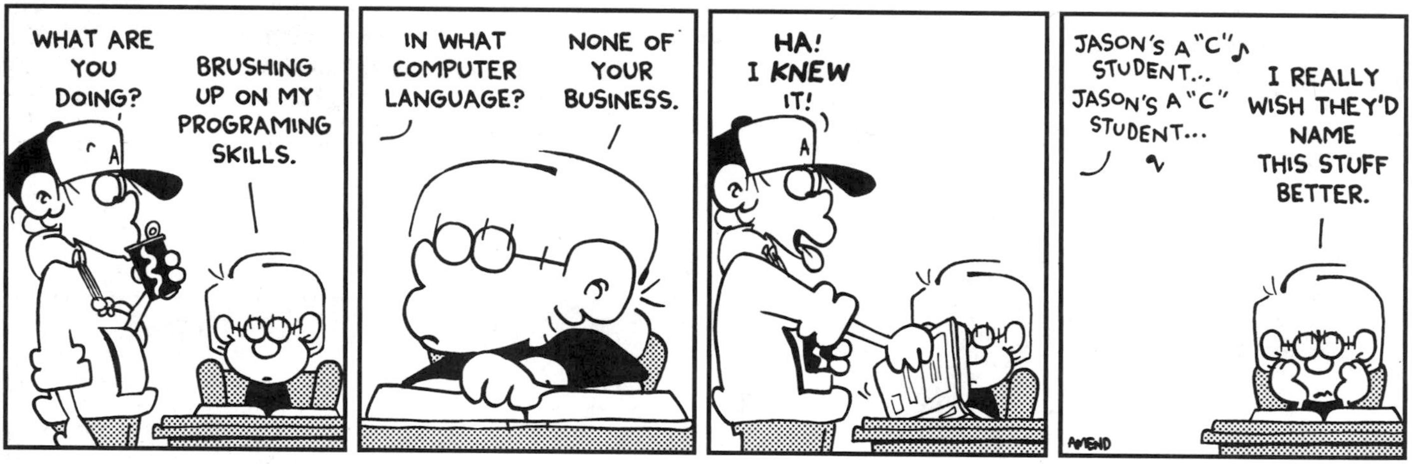
WHAT ARE YOU DOING?
BRUSHING UP ON MY PROGRAMING SKILLS.
IN WHAT COMPUTER LANGUAGE?
NONE OF YOUR BUSINESS.
HA! I KNEW IT!
JASON'S A "C" STUDENT... JASON'S A "C" STUDENT...
I REALLY WISH THEY'D NAME THIS STUFF BETTER.
AMEND

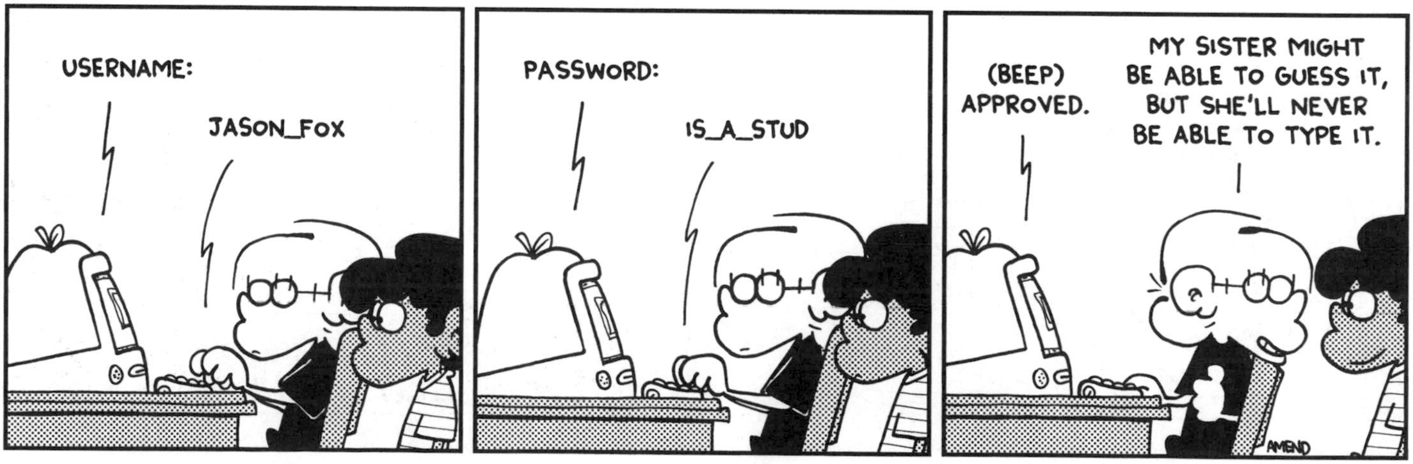
USERNAME:
JASON_FOX
PASSWORD:
IS_A_STUD
(BEEP) APPROVED.
MY SISTER MIGHT BE ABLE TO GUESS IT, BUT SHE'LL NEVER BE ABLE TO TYPE IT.
AMEND

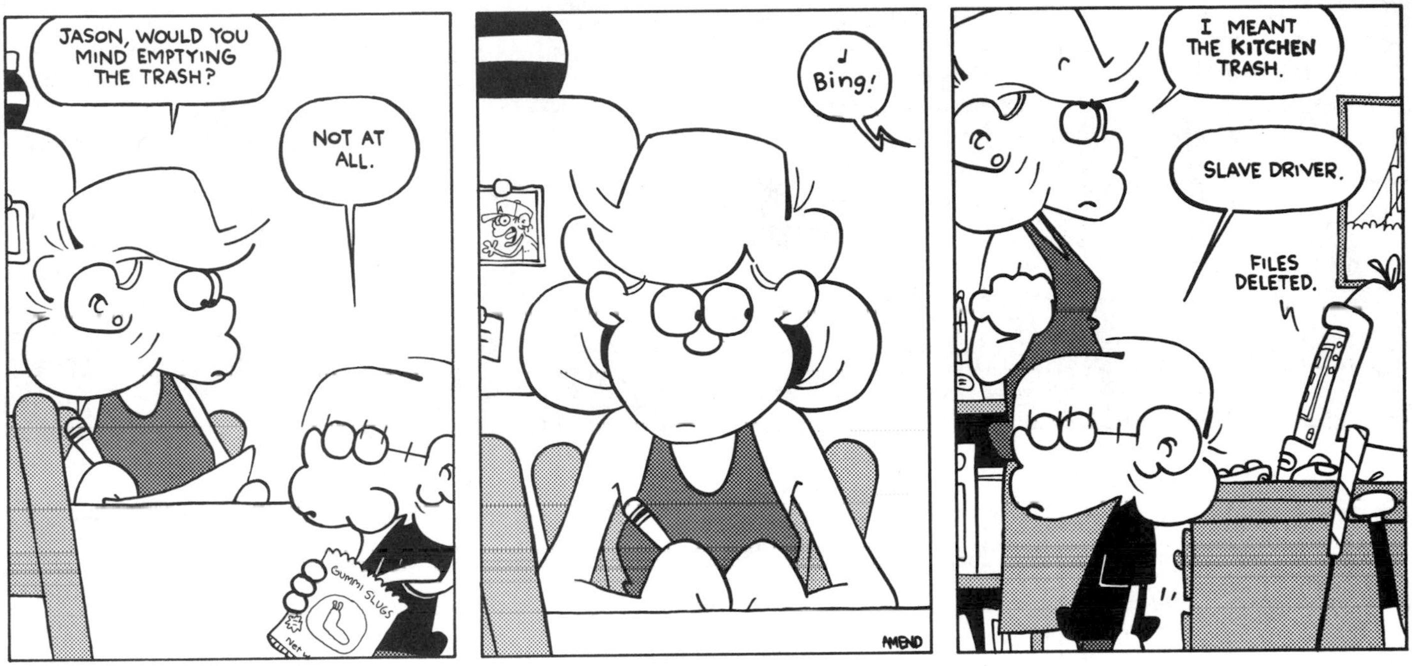
JASON, WOULD YOU MIND EMPTYING THE TRASH?
NOT AT ALL.
GUMMI SLUGS
Bing!
AMEND
I MEANT THE KITCHEN TRASH.
SLAVE DRIVER.
FILES DELETED.

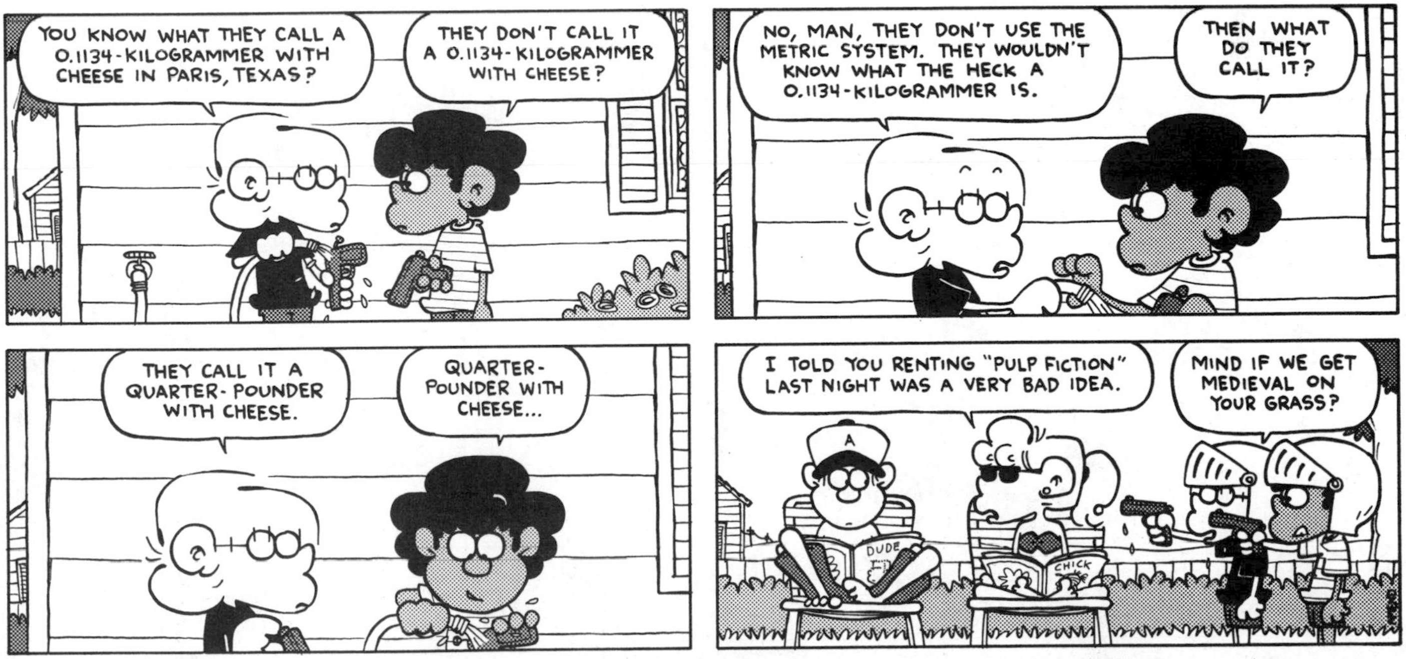
YOU KNOW WHAT THEY CALL A 0.1134-KILOGRAMMER WITH CHEESE IN PARIS, TEXAS?
THEY DON'T CALL IT A 0.1134-KILOGRAMMER WITH CHEESE?
NO, MAN, THEY DON'T USE THE METRIC SYSTEM. THEY WOULDN'T KNOW WHAT THE HECK A 0.1134-KILOGRAMMER IS.
THEN WHAT DO THEY CALL IT?
THEY CALL IT A QUARTER-POUNDER WITH CHEESE.
QUARTER-POUNDER WITH CHEESE...
I TOLD YOU RENTING "PULP FICTION" LAST NIGHT WAS A VERY BAD IDEA.
MIND IF WE GET MEDIEVAL ON YOUR GRASS?
DUDE
CHICK

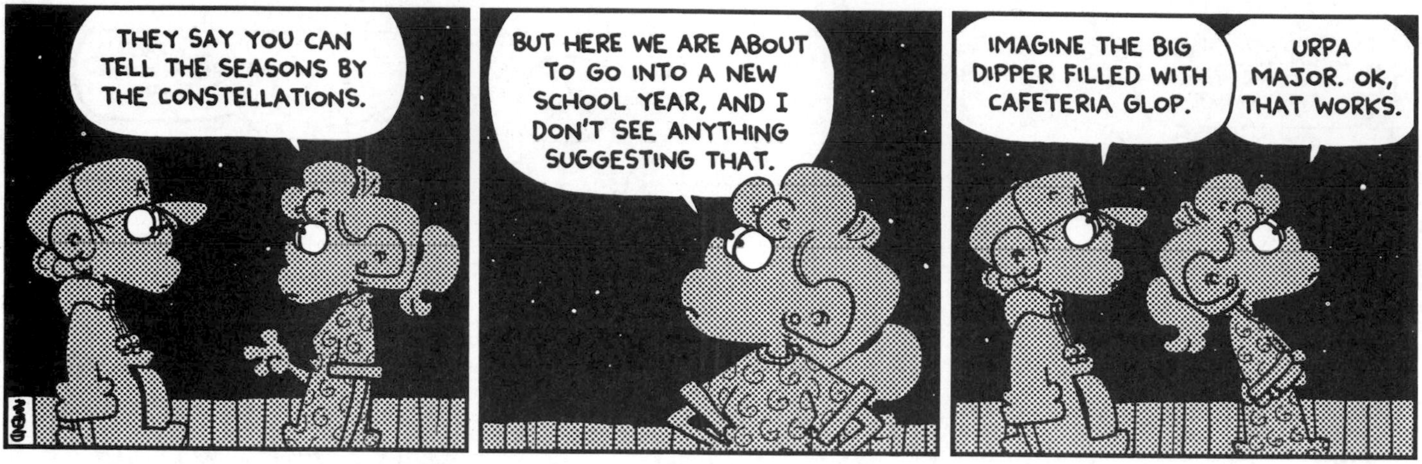
THEY SAY YOU CAN TELL THE SEASONS BY THE CONSTELLATIONS.
BUT HERE WE ARE ABOUT TO GO INTO A NEW SCHOOL YEAR, AND I DON'T SEE ANYTHING SUGGESTING THAT.
IMAGINE THE BIG DIPPER FILLED WITH CAFETERIA GLOP.
URPA MAJOR. OK, THAT WORKS.

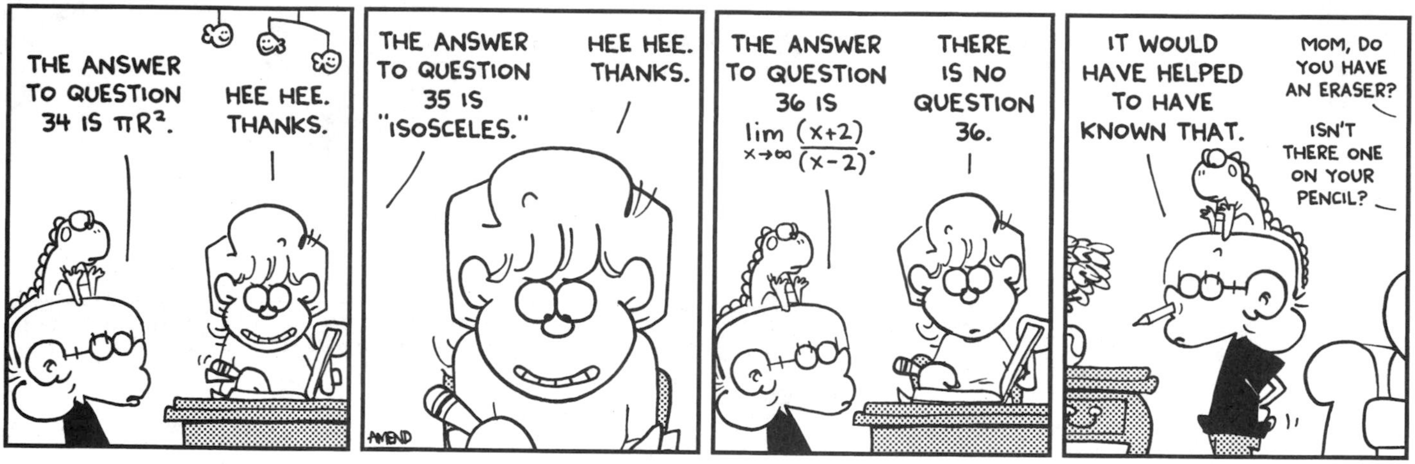
THE ANSWER TO QUESTION 34 IS πR^2.
HEE HEE. THANKS.
THE ANSWER TO QUESTION 35 IS "ISOSCELES."
HEE HEE. THANKS.
AMEND
THE ANSWER TO QUESTION 36 IS $\lim_{x \to \infty} \frac{(x+2)}{(x-2)}$.
THERE IS NO QUESTION 36.
IT WOULD HAVE HELPED TO HAVE KNOWN THAT.
MOM, DO YOU HAVE AN ERASER?
ISN'T THERE ONE ON YOUR PENCIL?

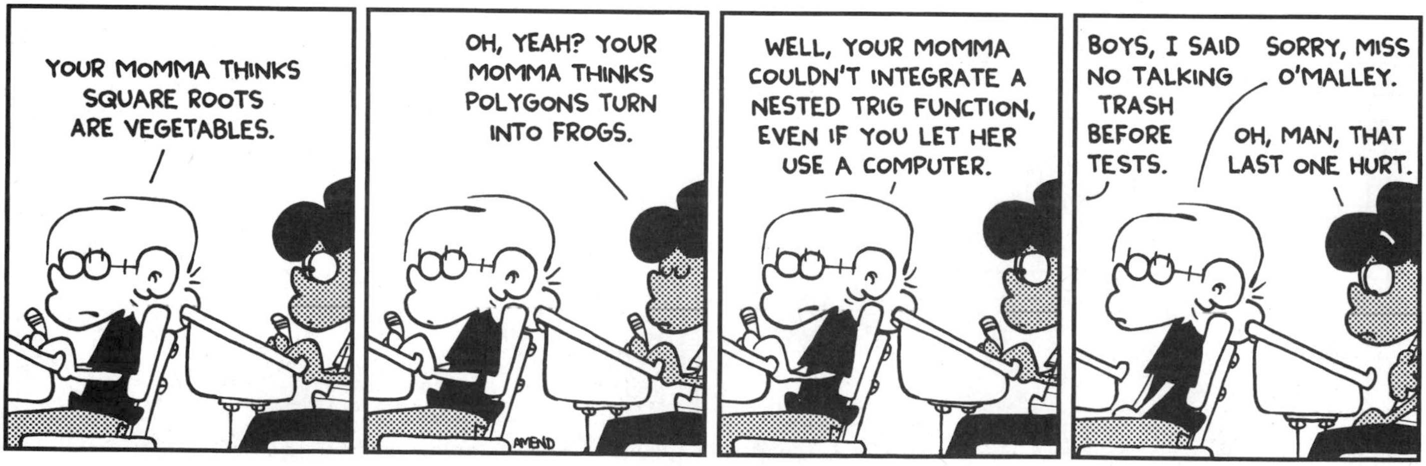
YOUR MOMMA THINKS SQUARE ROOTS ARE VEGETABLES.
OH, YEAH? YOUR MOMMA THINKS POLYGONS TURN INTO FROGS.
AMEND
WELL, YOUR MOMMA COULDN'T INTEGRATE A NESTED TRIG FUNCTION, EVEN IF YOU LET HER USE A COMPUTER.
BOYS, I SAID NO TALKING TRASH BEFORE TESTS.
SORRY, MISS O'MALLEY.
OH, MAN, THAT LAST ONE HURT.

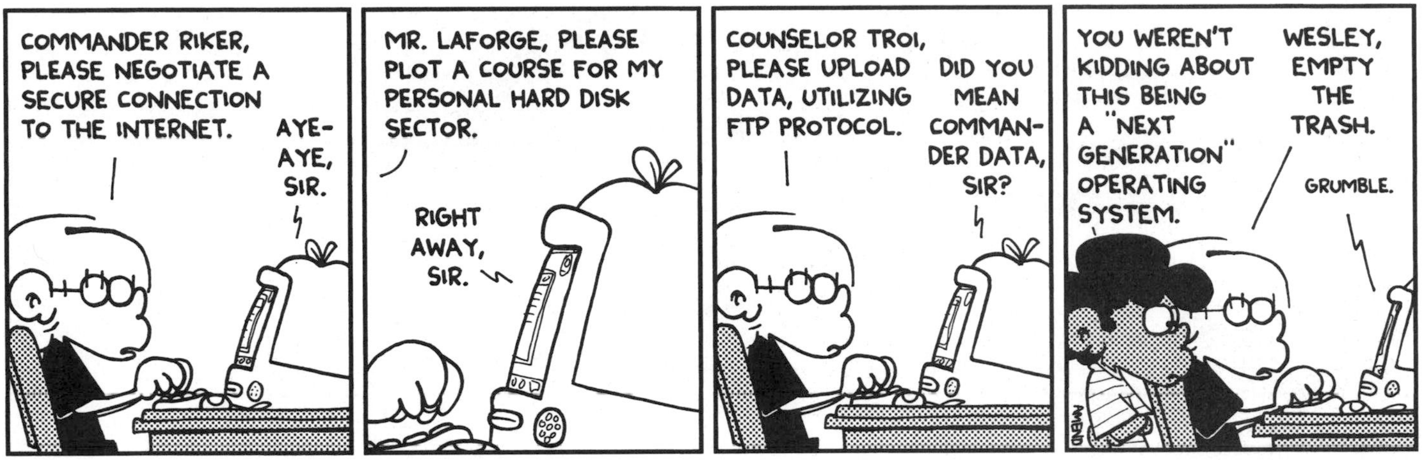
COMMANDER RIKER, PLEASE NEGOTIATE A SECURE CONNECTION TO THE INTERNET.
AYE-AYE, SIR.
MR. LAFORGE, PLEASE PLOT A COURSE FOR MY PERSONAL HARD DISK SECTOR.
RIGHT AWAY, SIR.
COUNSELOR TROI, PLEASE UPLOAD DATA, UTILIZING FTP PROTOCOL.
DID YOU MEAN COMMANDER DATA, SIR?
YOU WEREN'T KIDDING ABOUT THIS BEING A "NEXT GENERATION" OPERATING SYSTEM.
WESLEY, EMPTY THE TRASH.
GRUMBLE.
AMEND

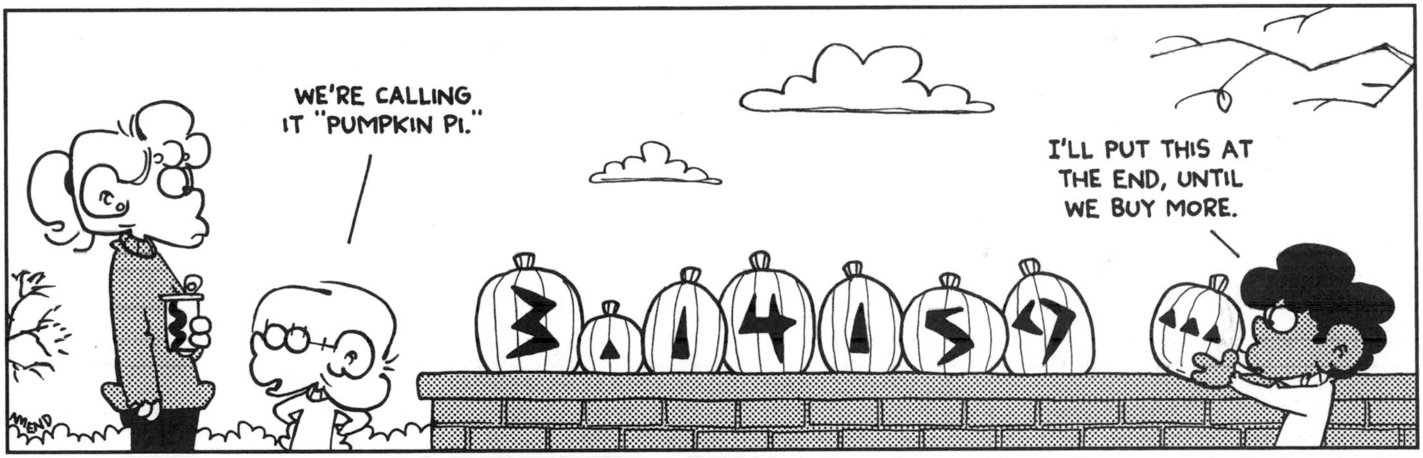
WE'RE CALLING IT "PUMPKIN PI."
I'LL PUT THIS AT THE END, UNTIL WE BUY MORE.
AMEND

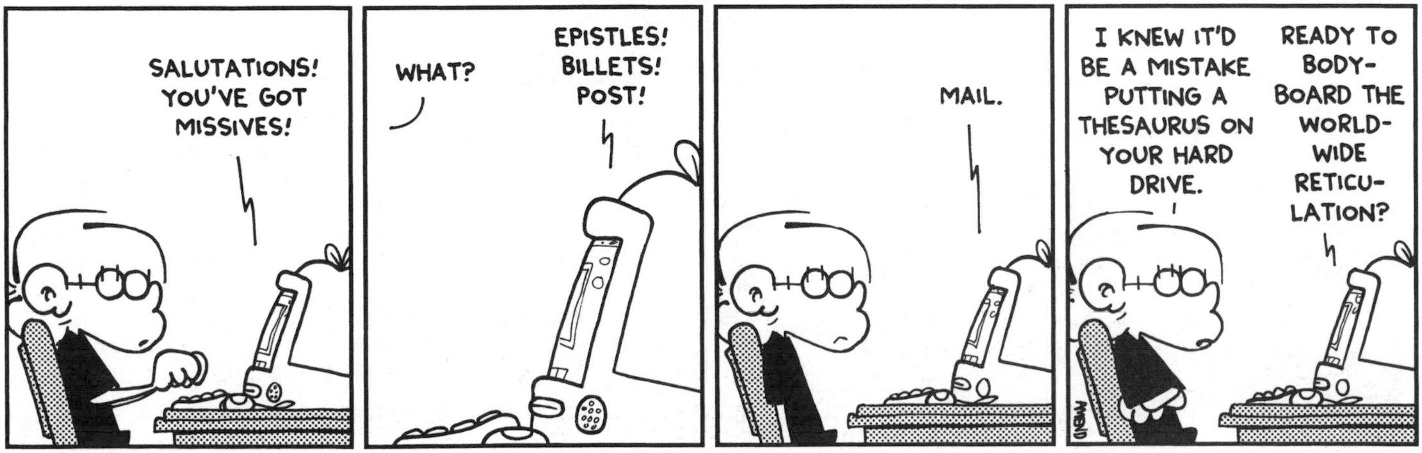
SALUTATIONS! YOU'VE GOT MISSIVES!
WHAT?
EPISTLES! BILLETS! POST!
MAIL.
I KNEW IT'D BE A MISTAKE PUTTING A THESAURUS ON YOUR HARD DRIVE.
READY TO BODY-BOARD THE WORLD-WIDE RETICULATION?
AMEND

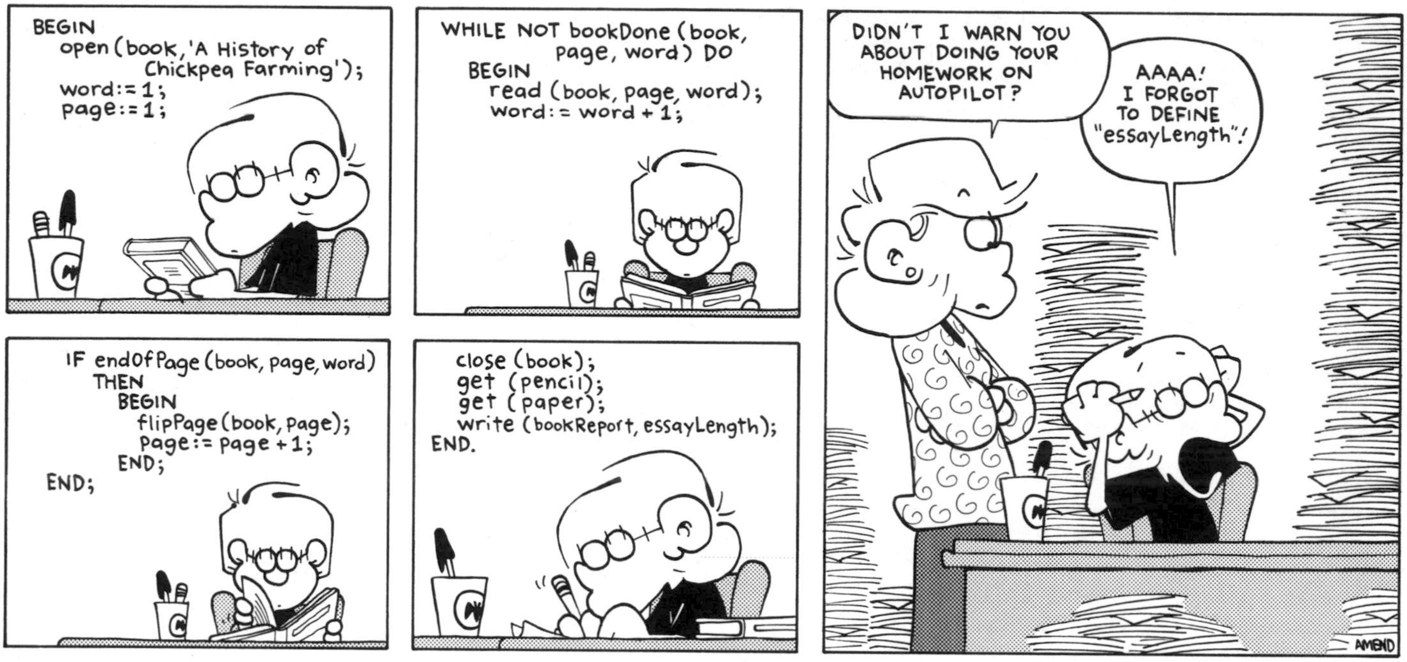
BEGIN
open (book, 'A History of Chickpea Farming');
word:= 1;
page:= 1;
WHILE NOT bookDone (book, page, word) DO
BEGIN
read (book, page, word);
word: = word + 1;
IF endOfPage (book, page, word)
THEN
BEGIN
flipPage (book, page);
page:= page + 1;
END;
END;
close (book);
get (pencil);
get (paper);
write (bookReport, essayLength);
END.
DIDN'T I WARN YOU ABOUT DOING YOUR HOMEWORK ON AUTOPILOT?
AAAA! I FORGOT TO DEFINE "essayLength"!
AMEND

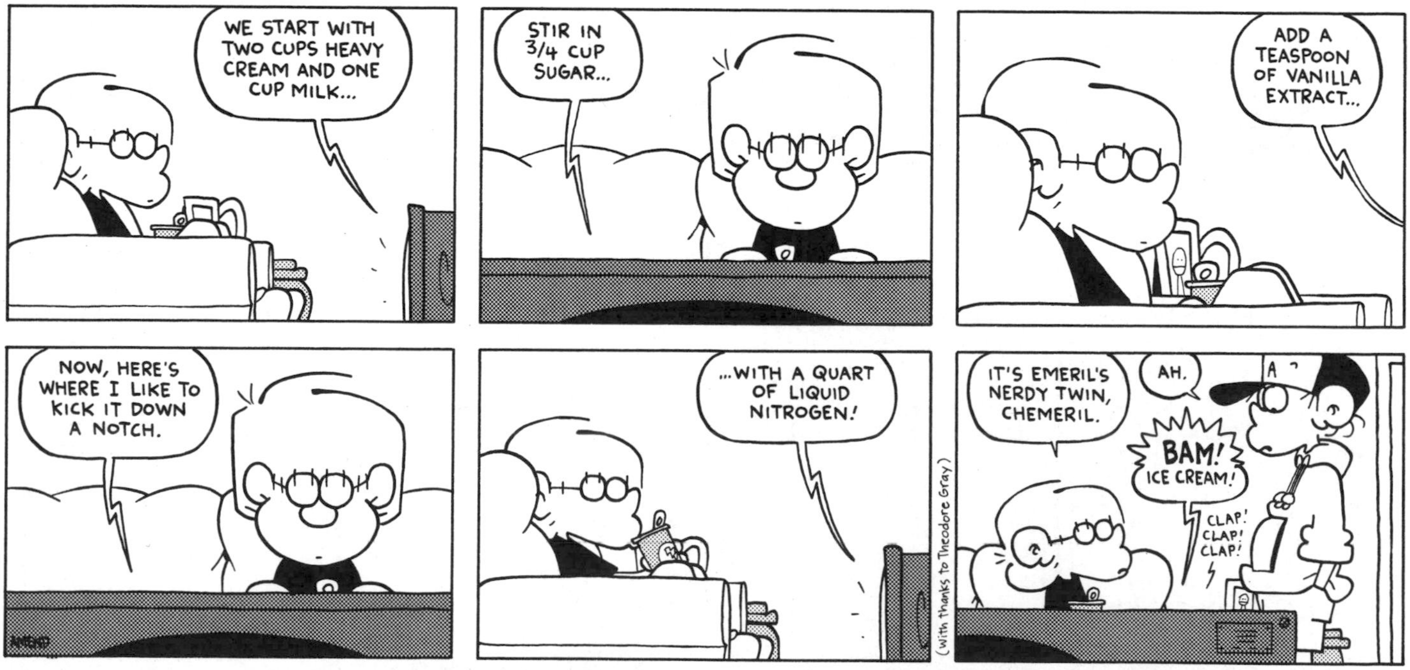
WE START WITH TWO CUPS HEAVY CREAM AND ONE CUP MILK...
STIR IN 3/4 CUP SUGAR...
ADD A TEASPOON OF VANILLA EXTRACT...
NOW, HERE'S WHERE I LIKE TO KICK IT DOWN A NOTCH.
...WITH A QUART OF LIQUID NITROGEN!
IT'S EMERIL'S NERDY TWIN, CHEMERIL.
AH.
BAM! ICE CREAM!
CLAP! CLAP! CLAP!
(With thanks to Theodore Gray)

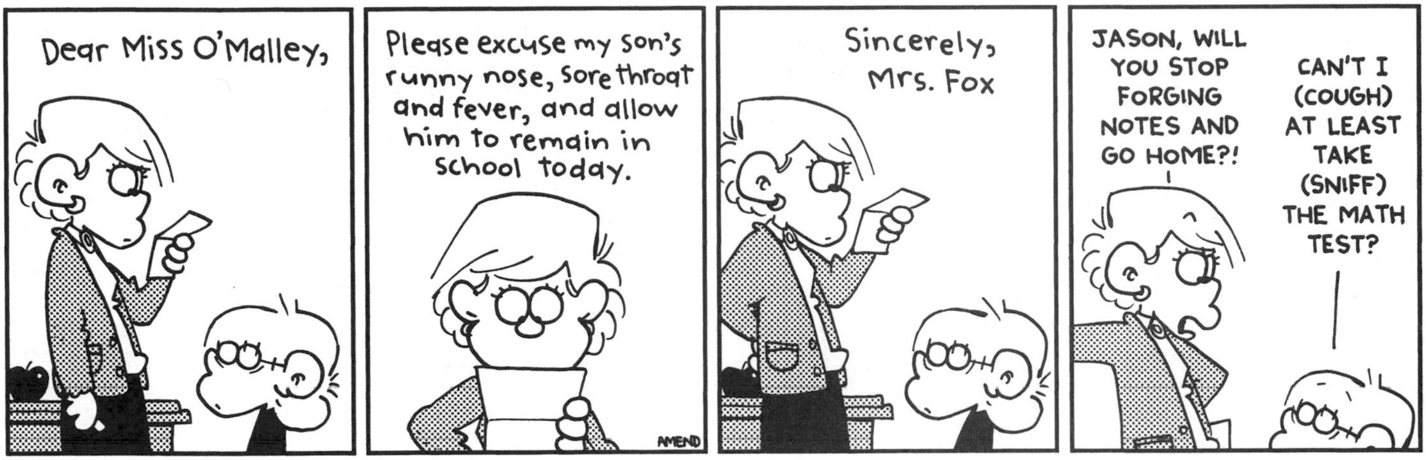

Dear Miss O'Malley,
Please excuse my son's runny nose, sore throat and fever, and allow him to remain in school today.
Sincerely, Mrs. Fox
JASON, WILL YOU STOP FORGING NOTES AND GO HOME?!
CAN'T I (COUGH) AT LEAST TAKE (SNIFF) THE MATH TEST?

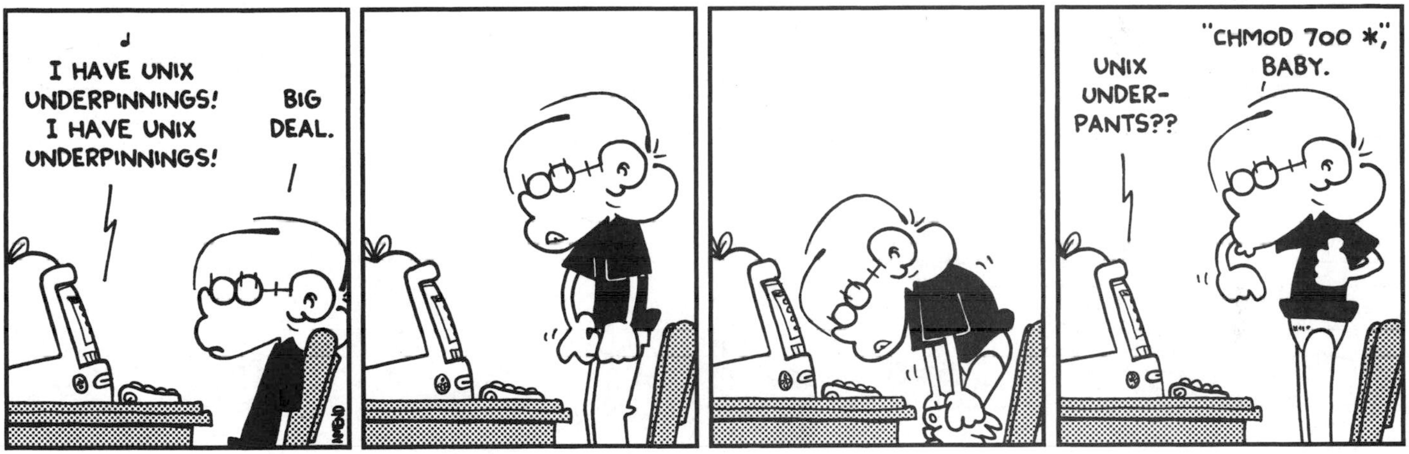

I HAVE UNIX UNDERPINNINGS! I HAVE UNIX UNDERPINNINGS!
BIG DEAL.
UNIX UNDER-PANTS??
"CHMOD 700 *", BABY.

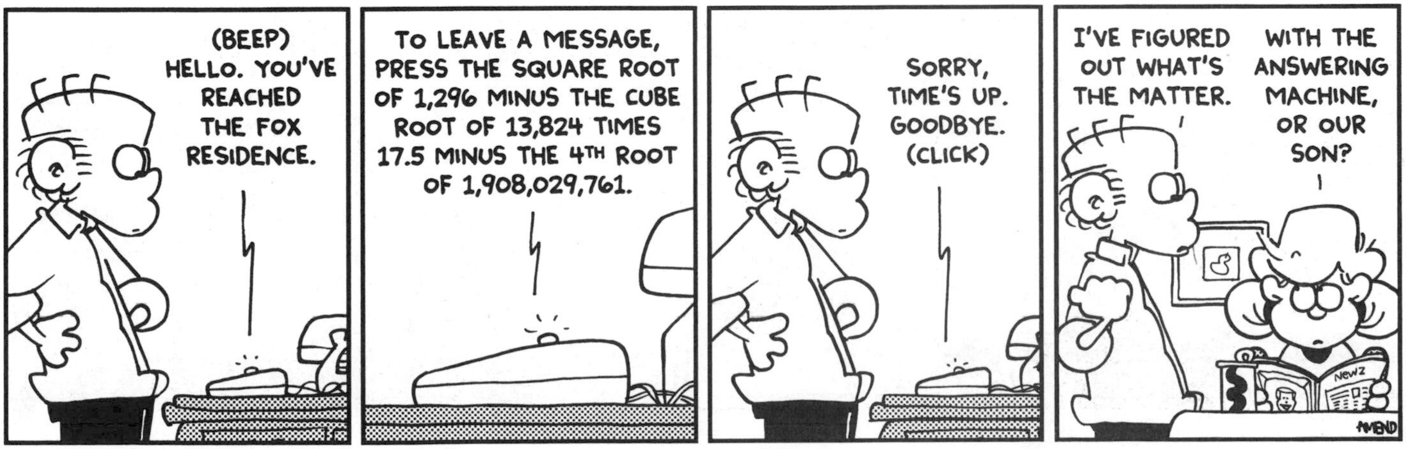

(BEEP) HELLO. YOU'VE REACHED THE FOX RESIDENCE.
TO LEAVE A MESSAGE, PRESS THE SQUARE ROOT OF 1,296 MINUS THE CUBE ROOT OF 13,824 TIMES 17.5 MINUS THE 4TH ROOT OF 1,908,029,761.
SORRY, TIME'S UP. GOODBYE. (CLICK)
I'VE FIGURED OUT WHAT'S THE MATTER.
WITH THE ANSWERING MACHINE, OR OUR SON?

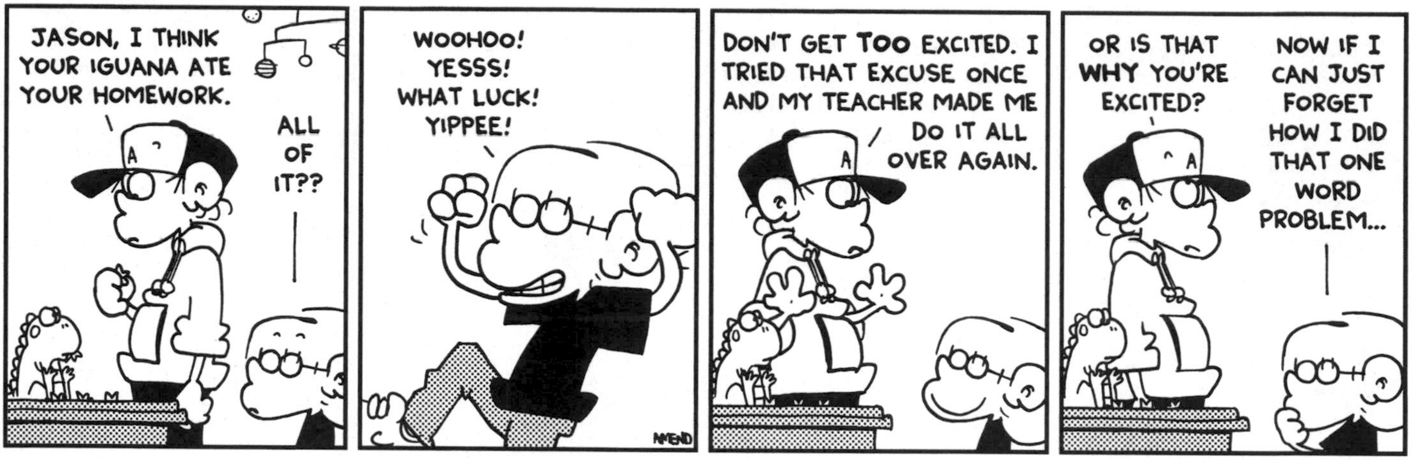
JASON, I THINK YOUR IGUANA ATE YOUR HOMEWORK.
ALL OF IT??
WOOHOO! YESSS! WHAT LUCK! YIPPEE!
AMEND
DON'T GET **TOO** EXCITED. I TRIED THAT EXCUSE ONCE AND MY TEACHER MADE ME
DO IT ALL OVER AGAIN.
OR IS THAT **WHY** YOU'RE EXCITED?
NOW IF I CAN JUST FORGET HOW I DID THAT ONE WORD PROBLEM...

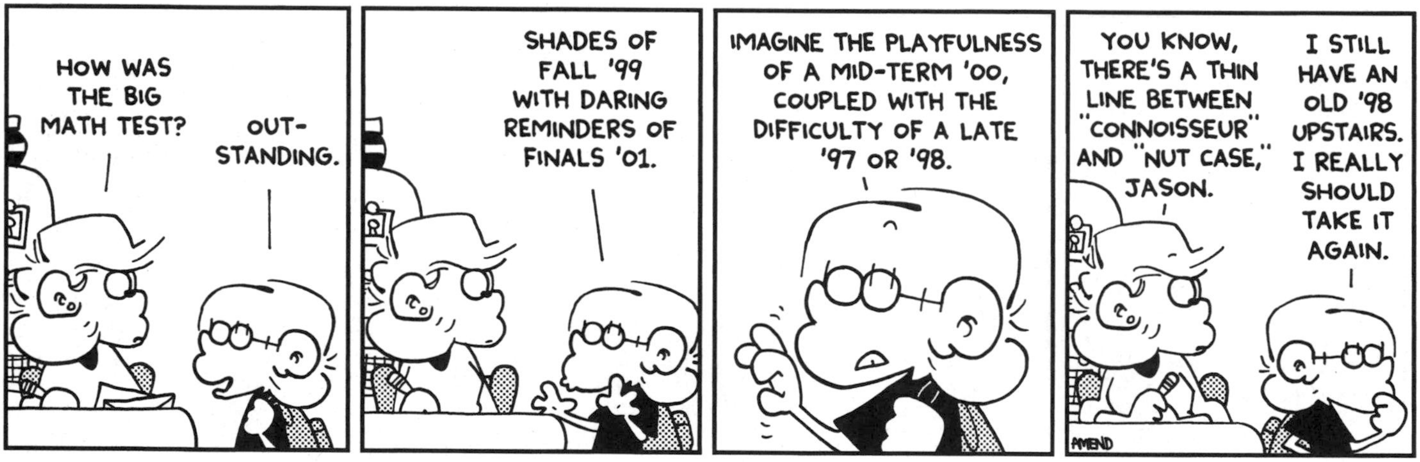
HOW WAS THE BIG MATH TEST?
OUT-STANDING.
SHADES OF FALL '99 WITH DARING REMINDERS OF FINALS '01.
IMAGINE THE PLAYFULNESS OF A MID-TERM '00, COUPLED WITH THE DIFFICULTY OF A LATE '97 OR '98.
YOU KNOW, THERE'S A THIN LINE BETWEEN "CONNOISSEUR" AND "NUT CASE," JASON.
I STILL HAVE AN OLD '98 UPSTAIRS. I REALLY SHOULD TAKE IT AGAIN.
AMEND

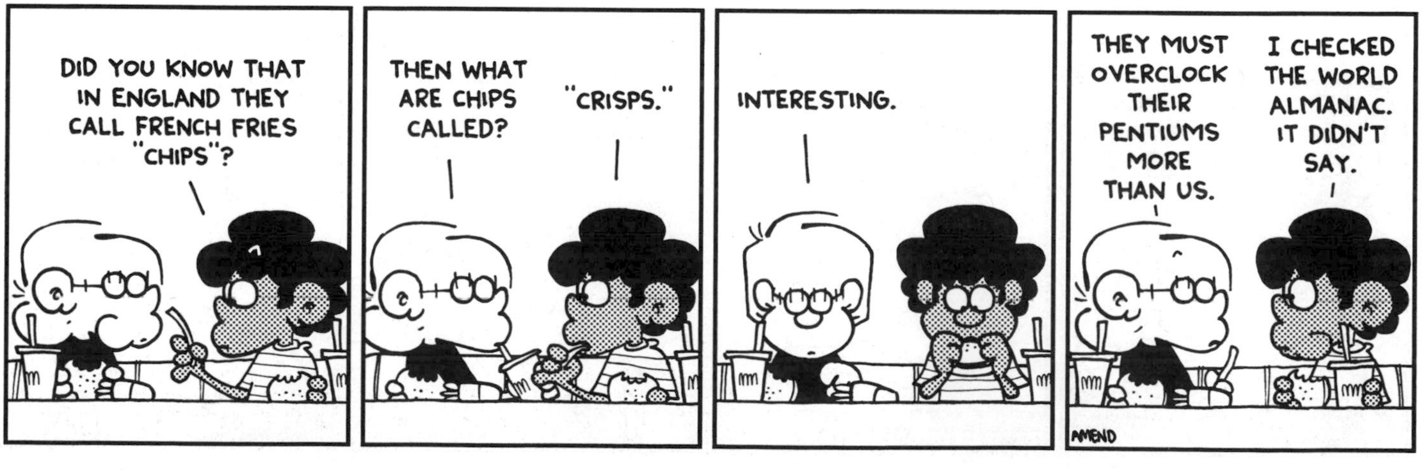
DID YOU KNOW THAT IN ENGLAND THEY CALL FRENCH FRIES "CHIPS"?
THEN WHAT ARE CHIPS CALLED?
"CRISPS."
INTERESTING.
THEY MUST OVERCLOCK THEIR PENTIUMS MORE THAN US.
I CHECKED THE WORLD ALMANAC. IT DIDN'T SAY.
AMEND

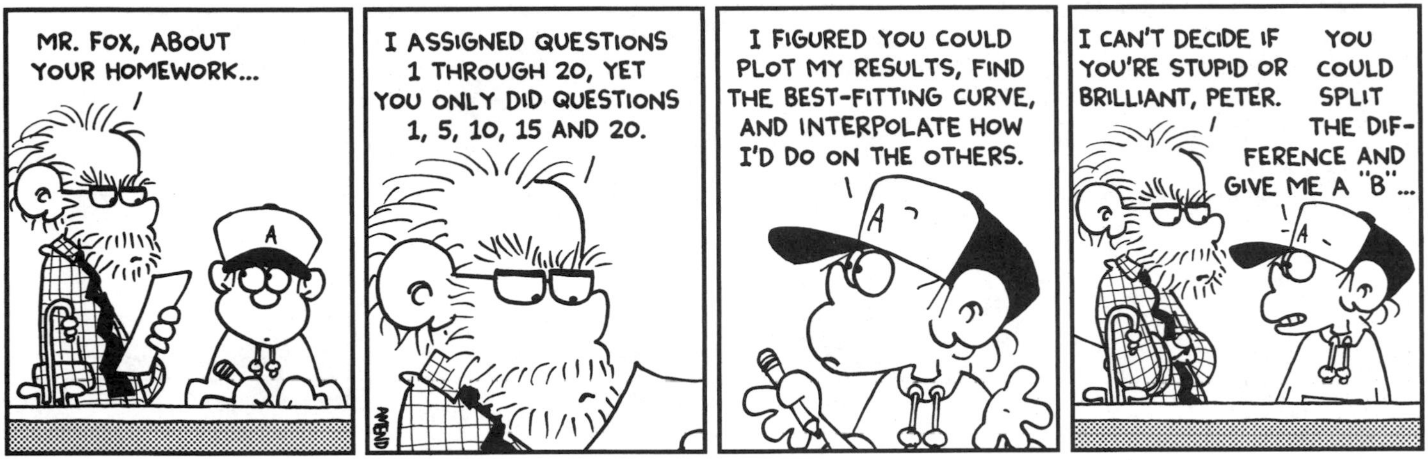
MR. FOX, ABOUT YOUR HOMEWORK...
I ASSIGNED QUESTIONS 1 THROUGH 20, YET YOU ONLY DID QUESTIONS 1, 5, 10, 15 AND 20.
I FIGURED YOU COULD PLOT MY RESULTS, FIND THE BEST-FITTING CURVE, AND INTERPOLATE HOW I'D DO ON THE OTHERS.
I CAN'T DECIDE IF YOU'RE STUPID OR BRILLIANT, PETER.
YOU COULD SPLIT THE DIF-FERENCE AND GIVE ME A "B"...

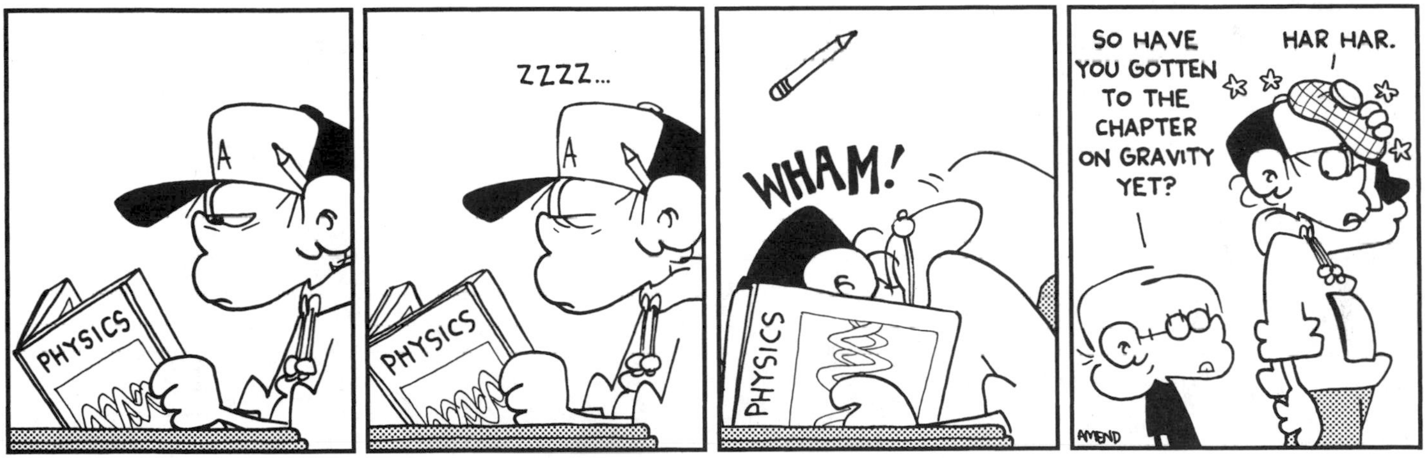
PHYSICS
ZZZZ...
PHYSICS
WHAM!
PHYSICS
SO HAVE YOU GOTTEN TO THE CHAPTER ON GRAVITY YET?
HAR HAR.

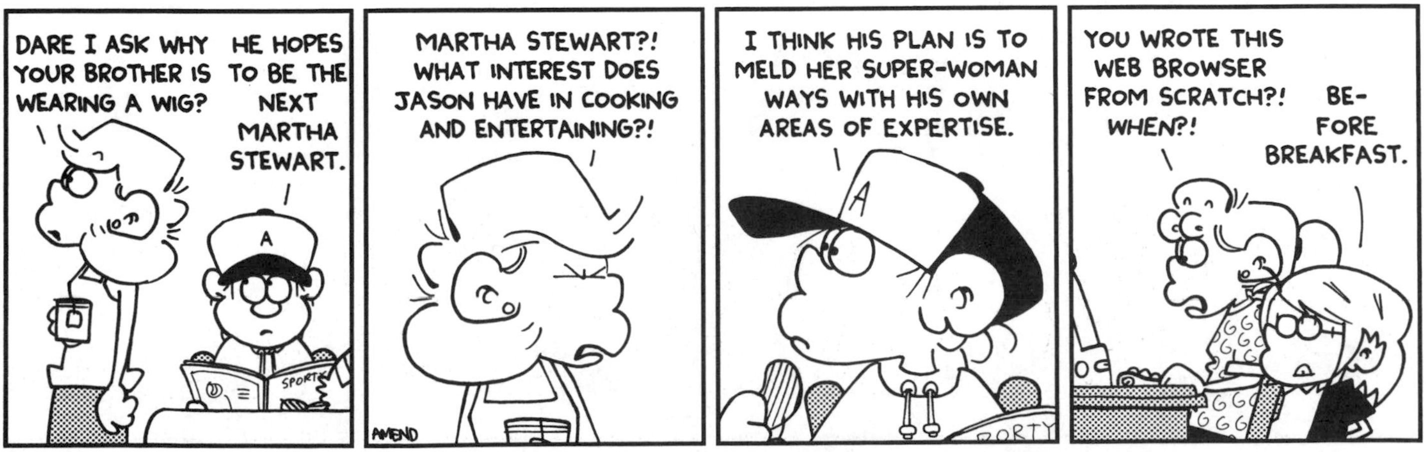
DARE I ASK WHY YOUR BROTHER IS WEARING A WIG?
HE HOPES TO BE THE NEXT MARTHA STEWART.
MARTHA STEWART?! WHAT INTEREST DOES JASON HAVE IN COOKING AND ENTERTAINING?!
I THINK HIS PLAN IS TO MELD HER SUPER-WOMAN WAYS WITH HIS OWN AREAS OF EXPERTISE.
YOU WROTE THIS WEB BROWSER FROM SCRATCH?! WHEN?!
BE-FORE BREAKFAST.

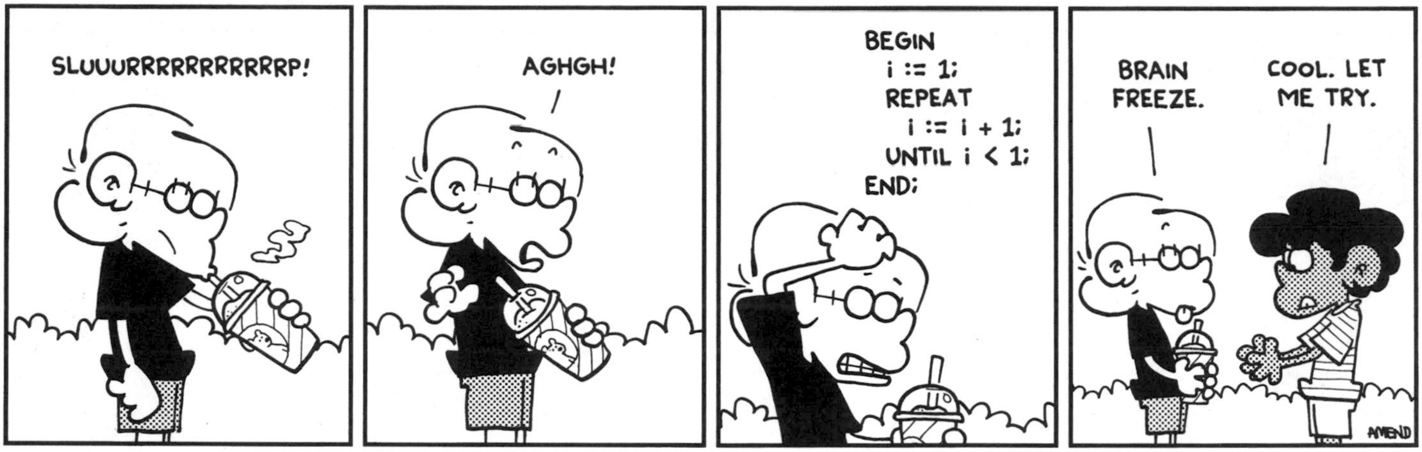
SLUUURRRRRRRRRRP!
AGHGH!
BEGIN
i := 1;
REPEAT
i := i + 1;
UNTIL i < 1;
END;
BRAIN FREEZE.
COOL. LET ME TRY.
AMEND

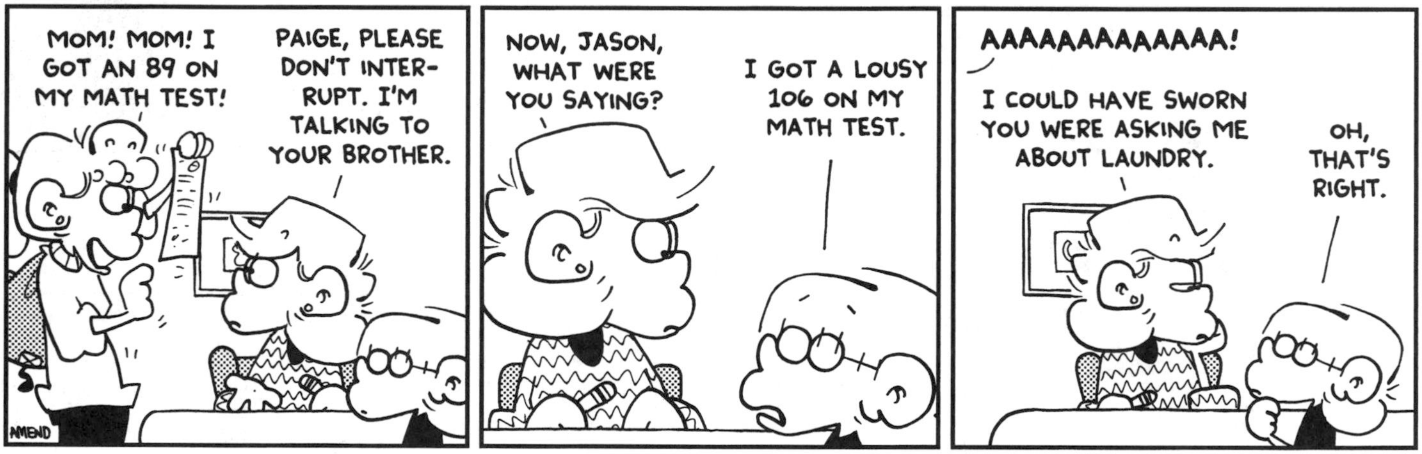
MOM! MOM! I GOT AN 89 ON MY MATH TEST!
PAIGE, PLEASE DON'T INTER-RUPT. I'M TALKING TO YOUR BROTHER.
AMEND
NOW, JASON, WHAT WERE YOU SAYING?
I GOT A LOUSY 106 ON MY MATH TEST.
AAAAAAAAAAAAA!
I COULD HAVE SWORN YOU WERE ASKING ME ABOUT LAUNDRY.
OH, THAT'S RIGHT.

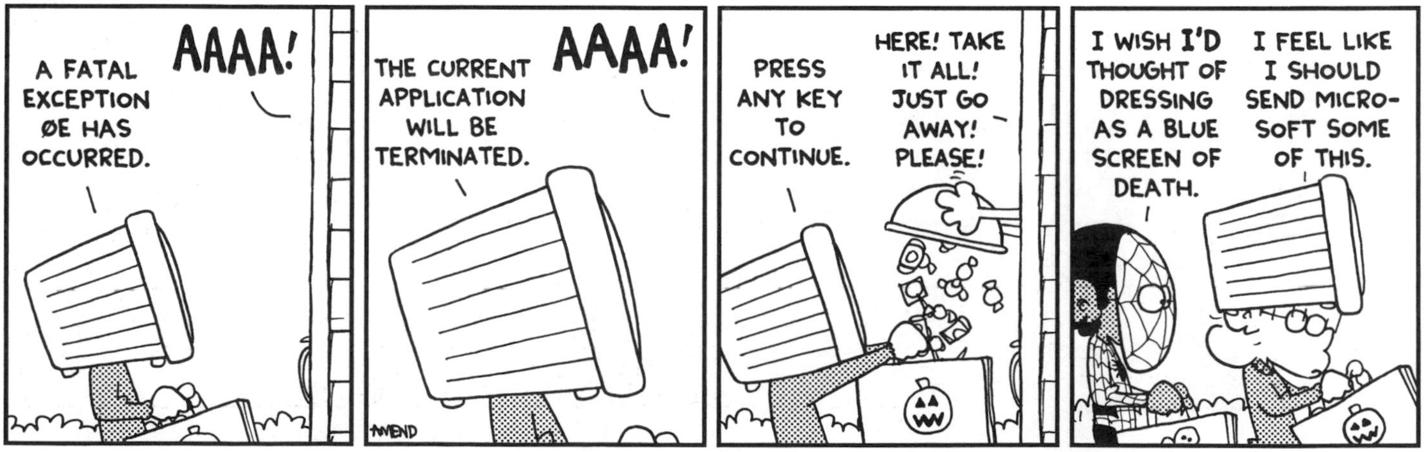
A FATAL EXCEPTION ØE HAS OCCURRED.
AAAA!
THE CURRENT APPLICATION WILL BE TERMINATED.
AAAA!
AMEND
PRESS ANY KEY TO CONTINUE.
HERE! TAKE IT ALL! JUST GO AWAY! PLEASE!
I WISH I'D THOUGHT OF DRESSING AS A BLUE SCREEN OF DEATH.
I FEEL LIKE I SHOULD SEND MICRO-SOFT SOME OF THIS.

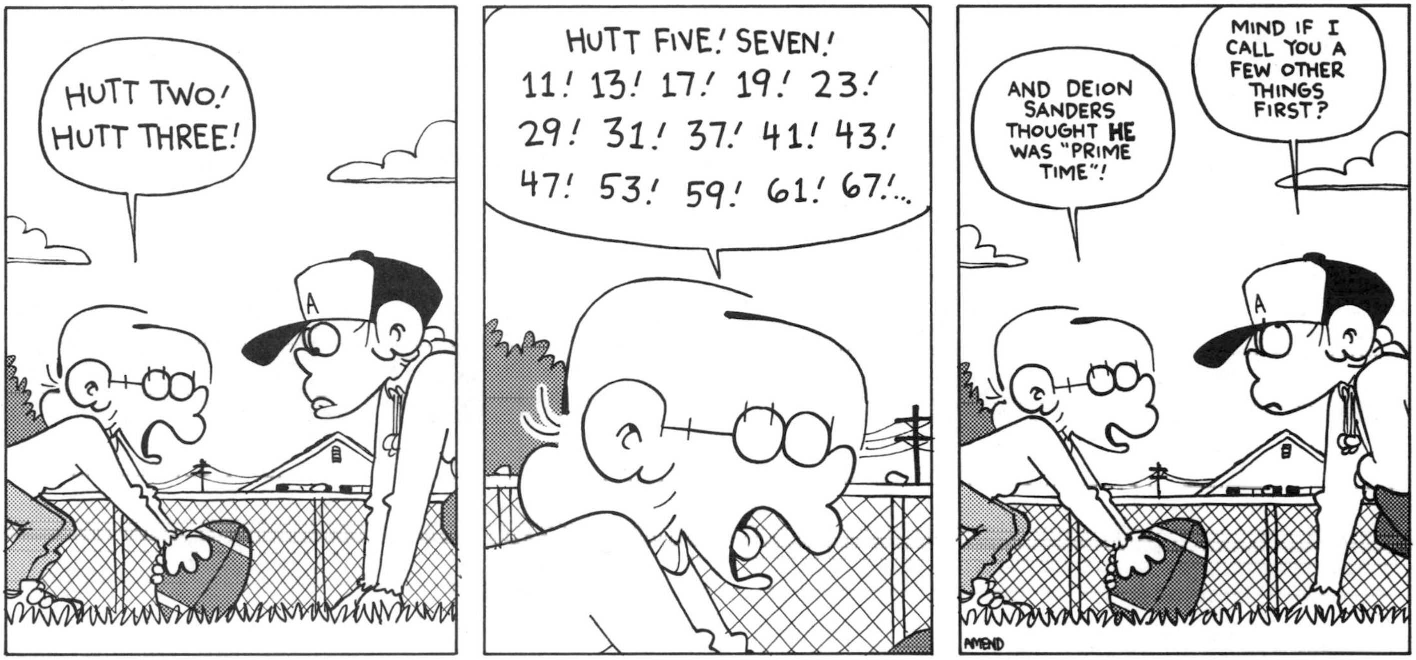
HUTT TWO! HUTT THREE!
HUTT FIVE! SEVEN! 11! 13! 17! 19! 23! 29! 31! 37! 41! 43! 47! 53! 59! 61! 67!...
AND DEION SANDERS THOUGHT HE WAS "PRIME TIME"!
MIND IF I CALL YOU A FEW OTHER THINGS FIRST?
AMEND

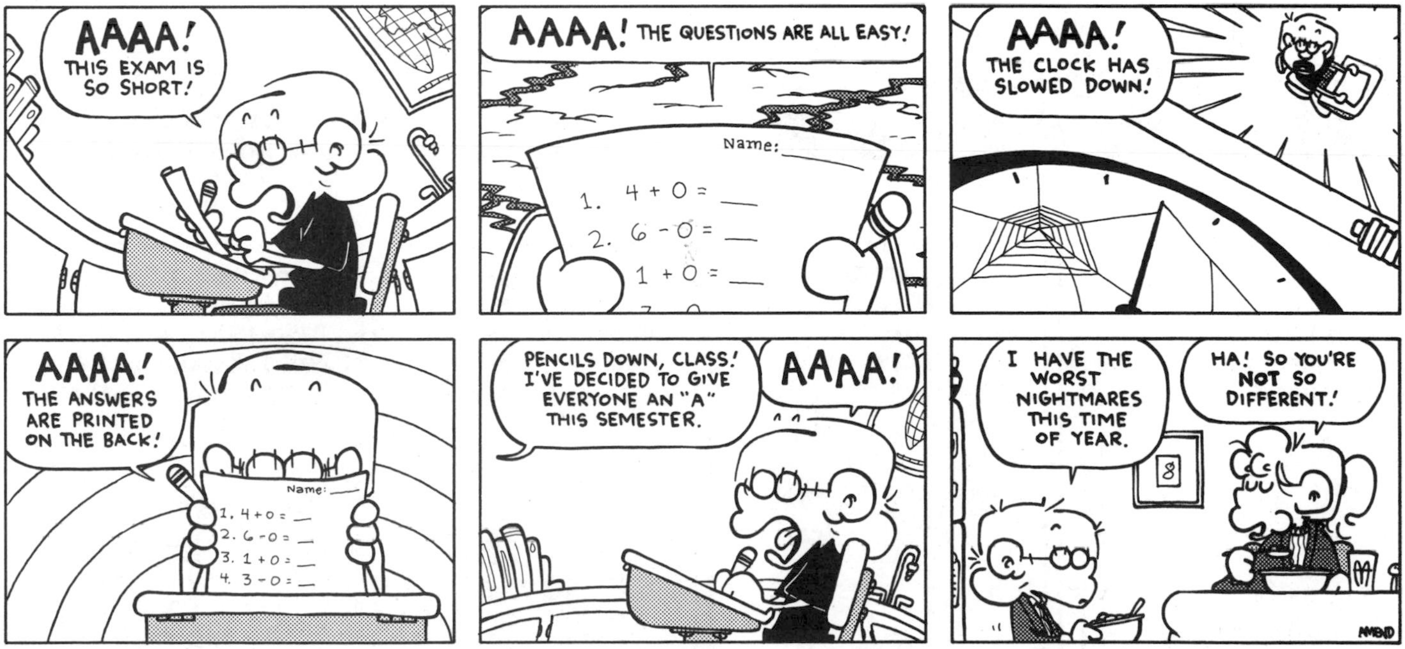
AAAA! THIS EXAM IS SO SHORT!
AAAA! THE QUESTIONS ARE ALL EASY!
Name:
1. 4 + 0 =
2. 6 - 0 =
1 + 0 =
AAAA! THE CLOCK HAS SLOWED DOWN!
AAAA! THE ANSWERS ARE PRINTED ON THE BACK!
Name:
1. 4 + 0 =
2. 6 - 0 =
3. 1 + 0 =
4. 3 - 0 =
PENCILS DOWN, CLASS! I'VE DECIDED TO GIVE EVERYONE AN "A" THIS SEMESTER.
AAAA!
I HAVE THE WORST NIGHTMARES THIS TIME OF YEAR.
HA! SO YOU'RE NOT SO DIFFERENT!
AMEND

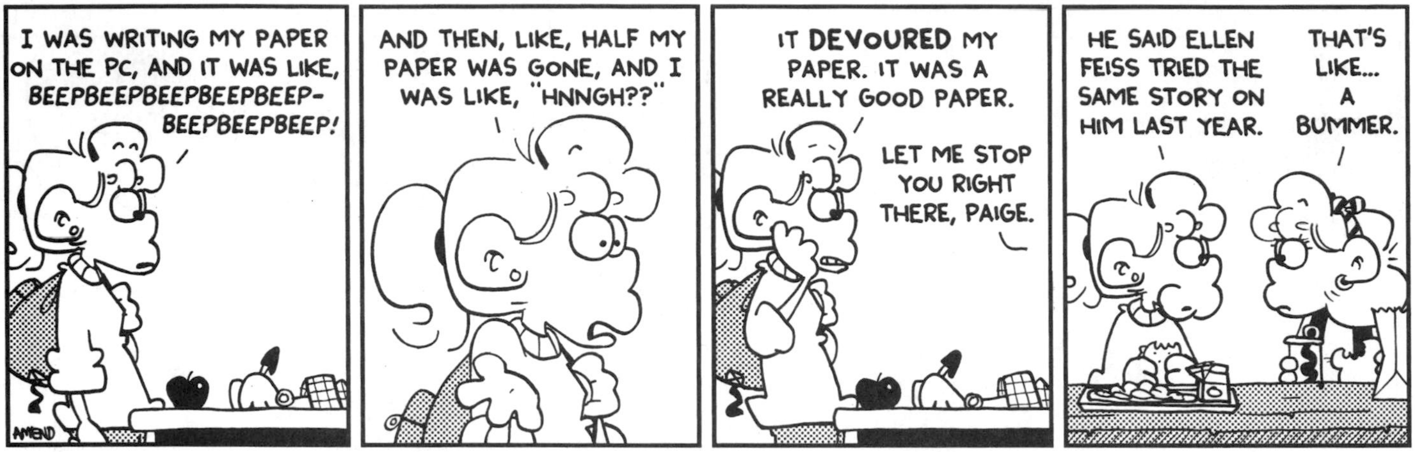
I WAS WRITING MY PAPER ON THE PC, AND IT WAS LIKE, BEEPBEEPBEEPBEEPBEEP-BEEPBEEPBEEP!
AMEND
AND THEN, LIKE, HALF MY PAPER WAS GONE, AND I WAS LIKE, "HNNGH??"
IT DEVOURED MY PAPER. IT WAS A REALLY GOOD PAPER.
LET ME STOP YOU RIGHT THERE, PAIGE.
HE SAID ELLEN FEISS TRIED THE SAME STORY ON HIM LAST YEAR.
THAT'S LIKE... A BUMMER.

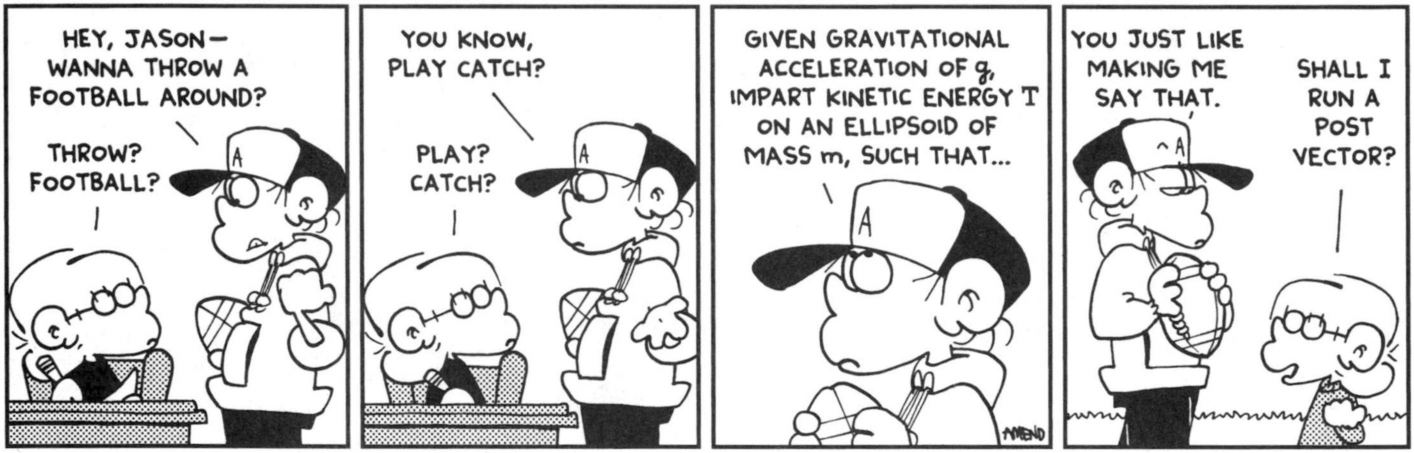
HEY, JASON— WANNA THROW A FOOTBALL AROUND?
THROW? FOOTBALL?
YOU KNOW, PLAY CATCH?
PLAY? CATCH?
GIVEN GRAVITATIONAL ACCELERATION OF g, IMPART KINETIC ENERGY T ON AN ELLIPSOID OF MASS m, SUCH THAT...
AMEND
YOU JUST LIKE MAKING ME SAY THAT.
SHALL I RUN A POST VECTOR?

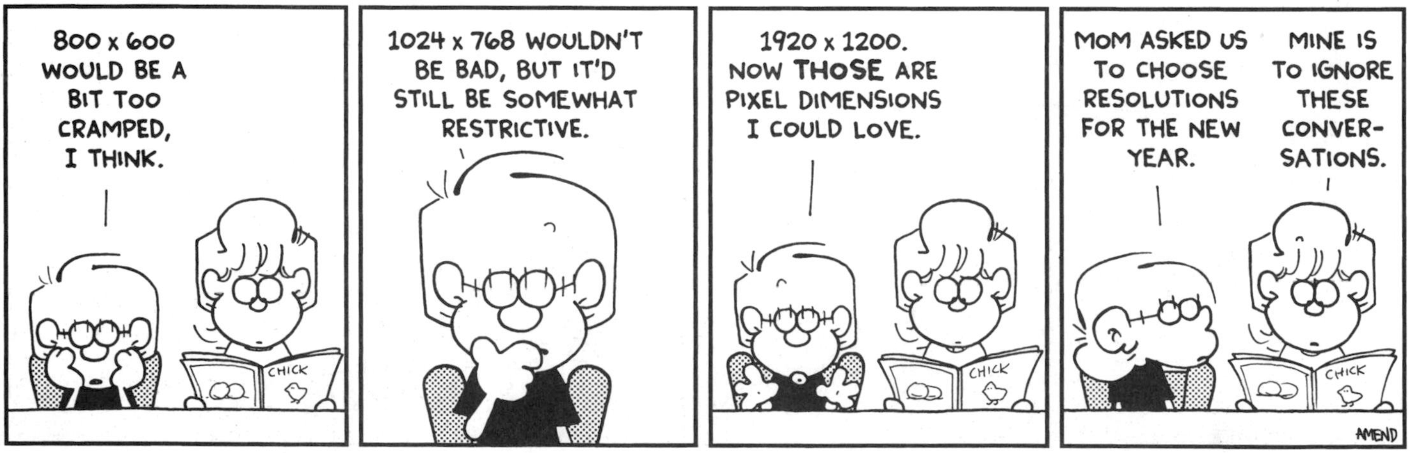
800 x 600 WOULD BE A BIT TOO CRAMPED, I THINK.
CHICK
1024 x 768 WOULDN'T BE BAD, BUT IT'D STILL BE SOMEWHAT RESTRICTIVE.
1920 x 1200. NOW THOSE ARE PIXEL DIMENSIONS I COULD LOVE.
CHICK
MOM ASKED US TO CHOOSE RESOLUTIONS FOR THE NEW YEAR.
MINE IS TO IGNORE THESE CONVER-SATIONS.
CHICK
AMEND

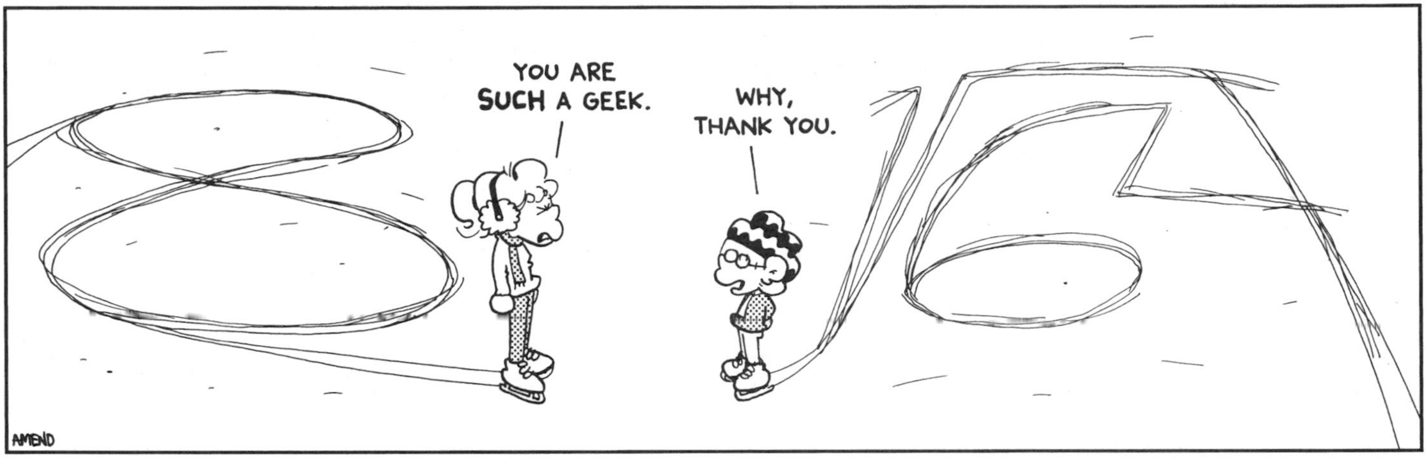

YOU ARE SUCH A GEEK.
WHY, THANK YOU.
AMEND

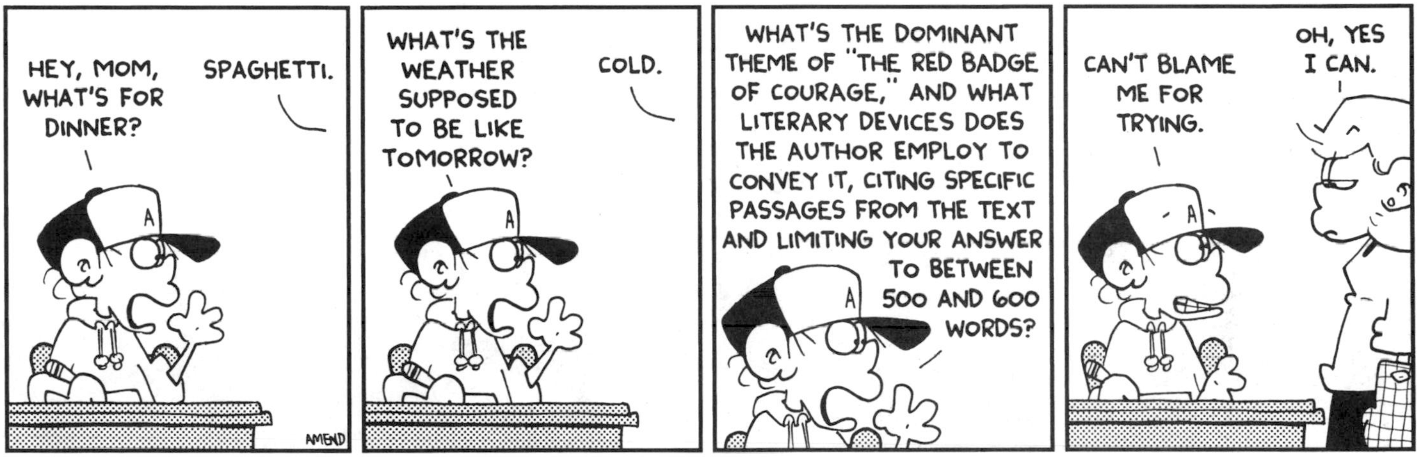

HEY, MOM, WHAT'S FOR DINNER?
SPAGHETTI.
AMEND
WHAT'S THE WEATHER SUPPOSED TO BE LIKE TOMORROW?
COLD.
WHAT'S THE DOMINANT THEME OF "THE RED BADGE OF COURAGE," AND WHAT LITERARY DEVICES DOES THE AUTHOR EMPLOY TO CONVEY IT, CITING SPECIFIC PASSAGES FROM THE TEXT AND LIMITING YOUR ANSWER TO BETWEEN 500 AND 600 WORDS?
CAN'T BLAME ME FOR TRYING.
OH, YES I CAN.

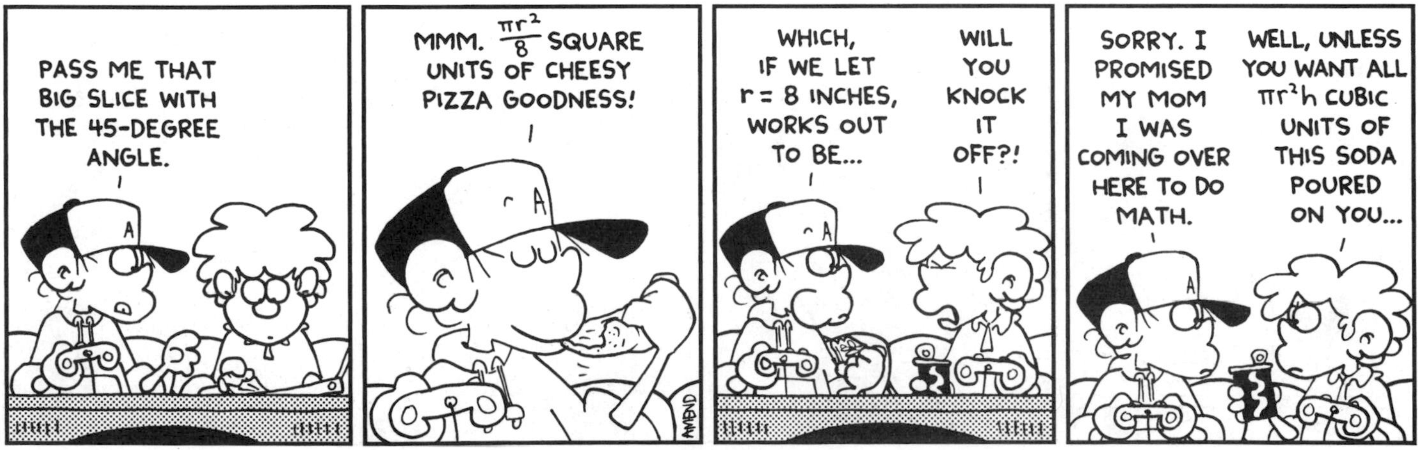

PASS ME THAT BIG SLICE WITH THE 45-DEGREE ANGLE.
MMM. $\frac{\pi r^2}{8}$ SQUARE UNITS OF CHEESY PIZZA GOODNESS!
AMEND
WHICH, IF WE LET r = 8 INCHES, WORKS OUT TO BE...
WILL YOU KNOCK IT OFF?!
SORRY. I PROMISED MY MOM I WAS COMING OVER HERE TO DO MATH.
WELL, UNLESS YOU WANT ALL $\pi r^2 h$ CUBIC UNITS OF THIS SODA POURED ON YOU...

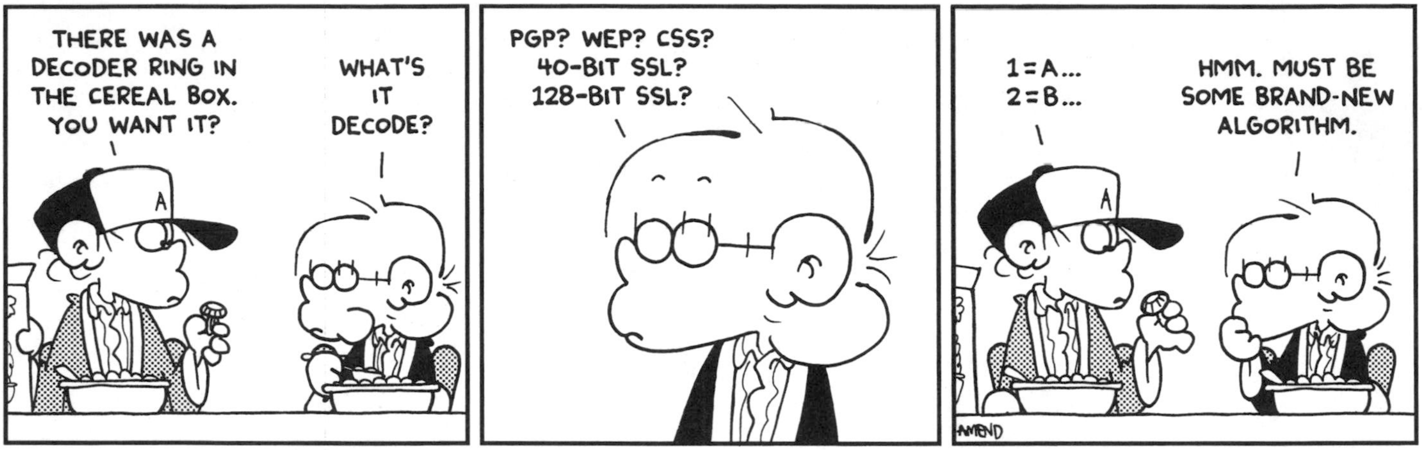
THERE WAS A DECODER RING IN THE CEREAL BOX. YOU WANT IT?
WHAT'S IT DECODE?
PGP? WEP? CSS? 40-BIT SSL? 128-BIT SSL?
1=A... 2=B...
HMM. MUST BE SOME BRAND-NEW ALGORITHM.
AMEND

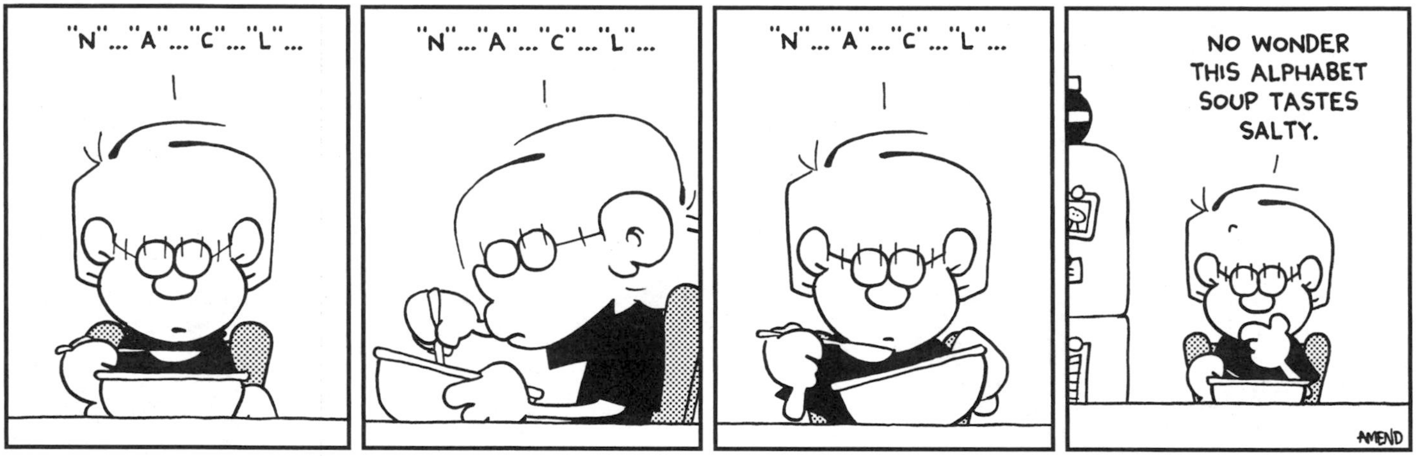
"N"..."A"..."C"..."L"...
"N"..."A"..."C"..."L"...
"N"..."A"..."C"..."L"...
NO WONDER THIS ALPHABET SOUP TASTES SALTY.
AMEND

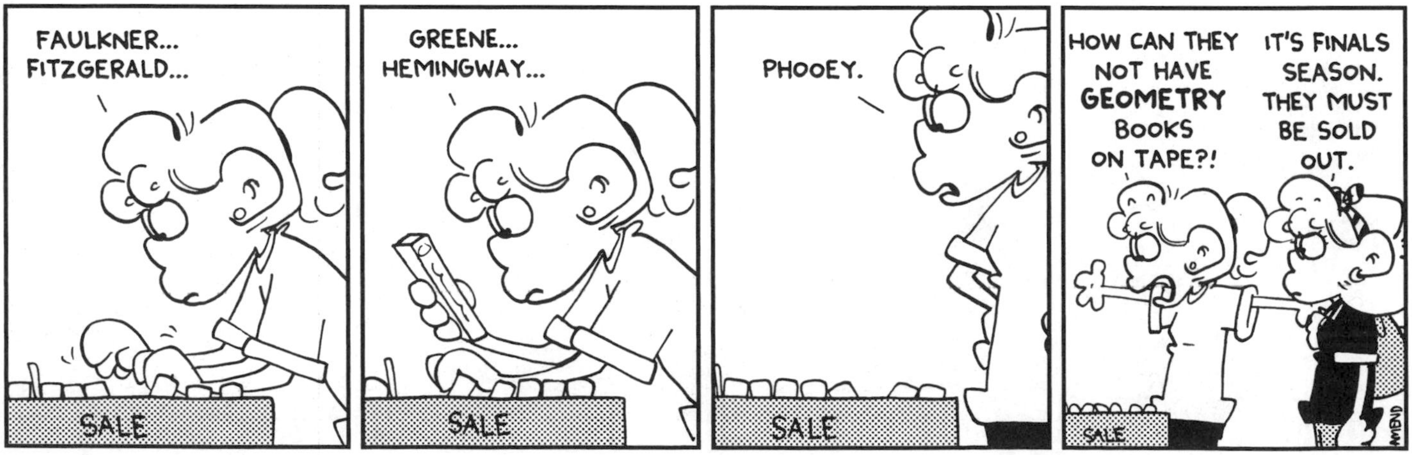
FAULKNER... FITZGERALD...
SALE
GREENE... HEMINGWAY...
SALE
PHOOEY.
SALE
HOW CAN THEY NOT HAVE GEOMETRY BOOKS ON TAPE?!
IT'S FINALS SEASON. THEY MUST BE SOLD OUT.
SALE
AMEND

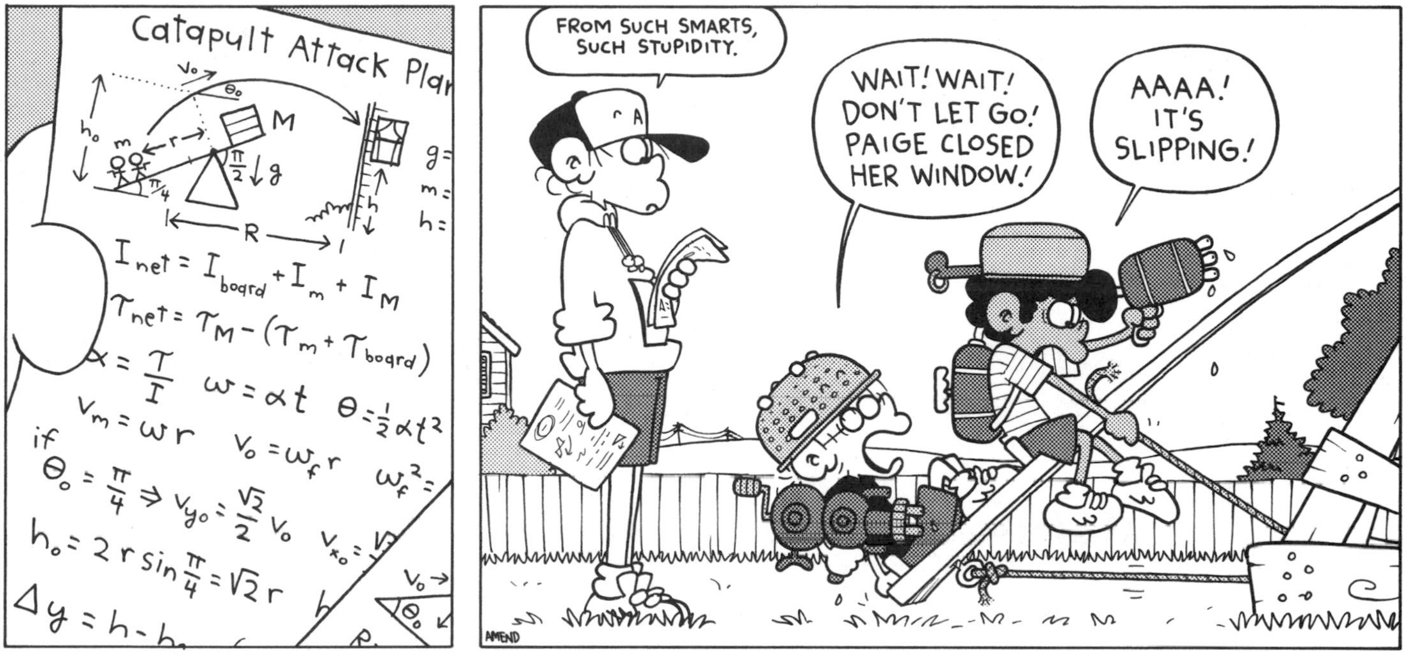
Catapult Attack Pla
$I_{net} = I_{board} + I_m + I_M$
$\tau_{net} = \tau_M - (\tau_m + \tau_{board})$
$\omega = \alpha t$
$\theta = \frac{1}{2}\alpha t^2$
$v_m = \omega r$
$v_0 = \omega_f r$
$h_0 = 2 r \sin\frac{\pi}{4} = \sqrt{2} r$
FROM SUCH SMARTS, SUCH STUPIDITY.
WAIT! WAIT! DON'T LET GO! PAIGE CLOSED HER WINDOW!
AAAA! IT'S SLIPPING!
AMEND

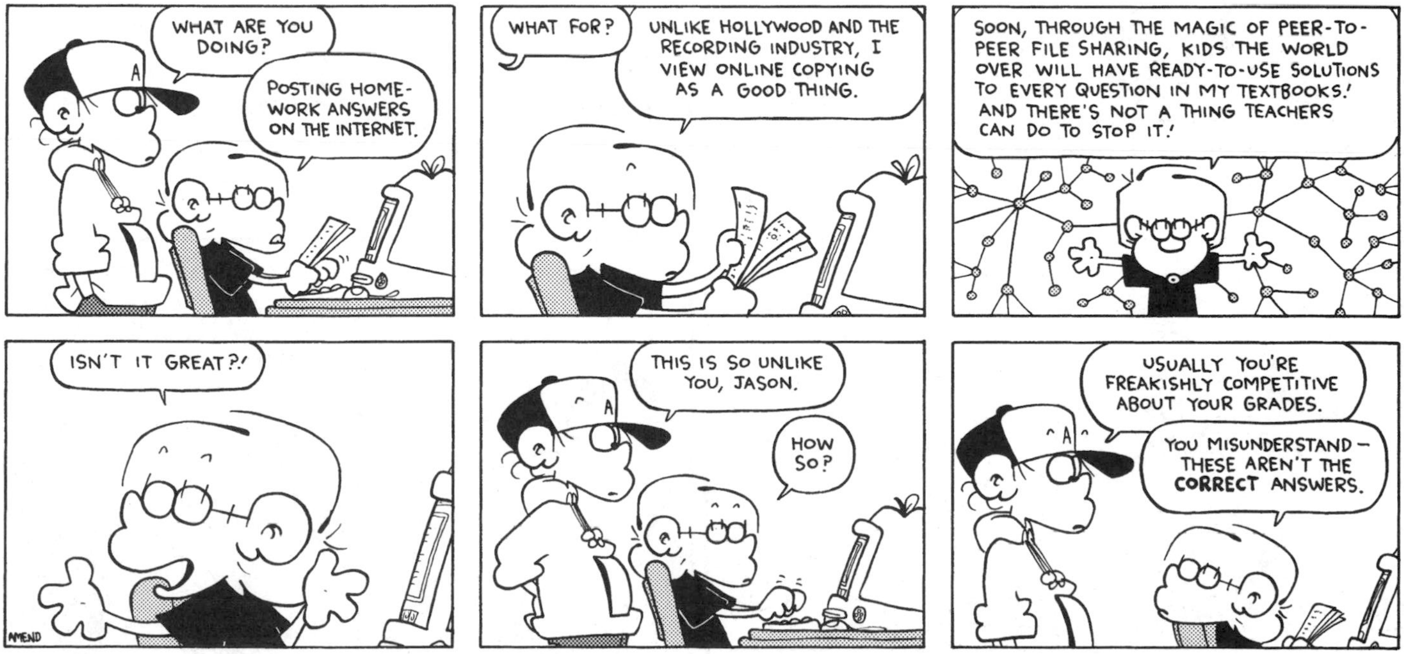
WHAT ARE YOU DOING?
POSTING HOME-WORK ANSWERS ON THE INTERNET.
WHAT FOR?
UNLIKE HOLLYWOOD AND THE RECORDING INDUSTRY, I VIEW ONLINE COPYING AS A GOOD THING.
SOON, THROUGH THE MAGIC OF PEER-TO-PEER FILE SHARING, KIDS THE WORLD OVER WILL HAVE READY-TO-USE SOLUTIONS TO EVERY QUESTION IN MY TEXTBOOKS! AND THERE'S NOT A THING TEACHERS CAN DO TO STOP IT!
ISN'T IT GREAT?!
AMEND
THIS IS SO UNLIKE YOU, JASON.
HOW SO?
USUALLY YOU'RE FREAKISHLY COMPETITIVE ABOUT YOUR GRADES.
YOU MISUNDERSTAND — THESE AREN'T THE CORRECT ANSWERS.

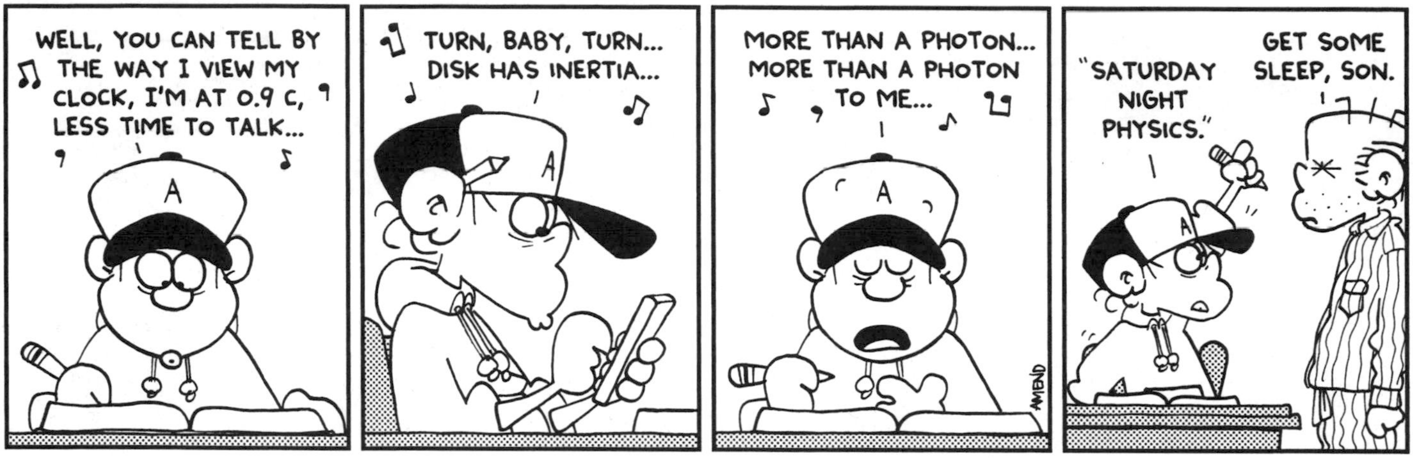
WELL, YOU CAN TELL BY THE WAY I VIEW MY CLOCK, I'M AT 0.9 C, LESS TIME TO TALK...
TURN, BABY, TURN... DISK HAS INERTIA...
MORE THAN A PHOTON... MORE THAN A PHOTON TO ME...
"SATURDAY NIGHT PHYSICS."
GET SOME SLEEP, SON.

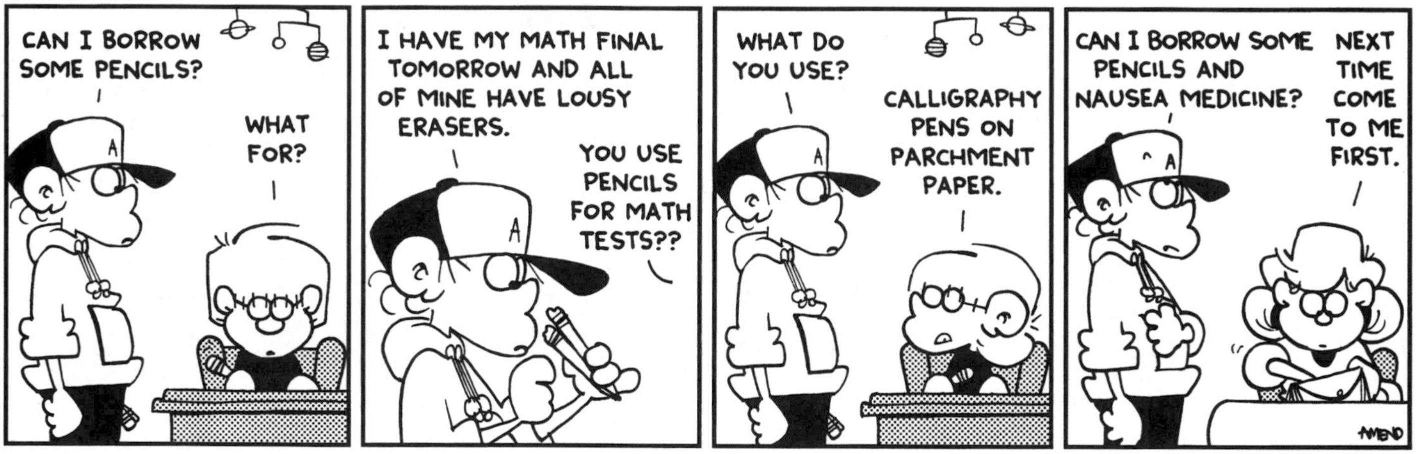
CAN I BORROW SOME PENCILS?
WHAT FOR?
I HAVE MY MATH FINAL TOMORROW AND ALL OF MINE HAVE LOUSY ERASERS.
YOU USE PENCILS FOR MATH TESTS??
WHAT DO YOU USE?
CALLIGRAPHY PENS ON PARCHMENT PAPER.
CAN I BORROW SOME PENCILS AND NAUSEA MEDICINE?
NEXT TIME COME TO ME FIRST.

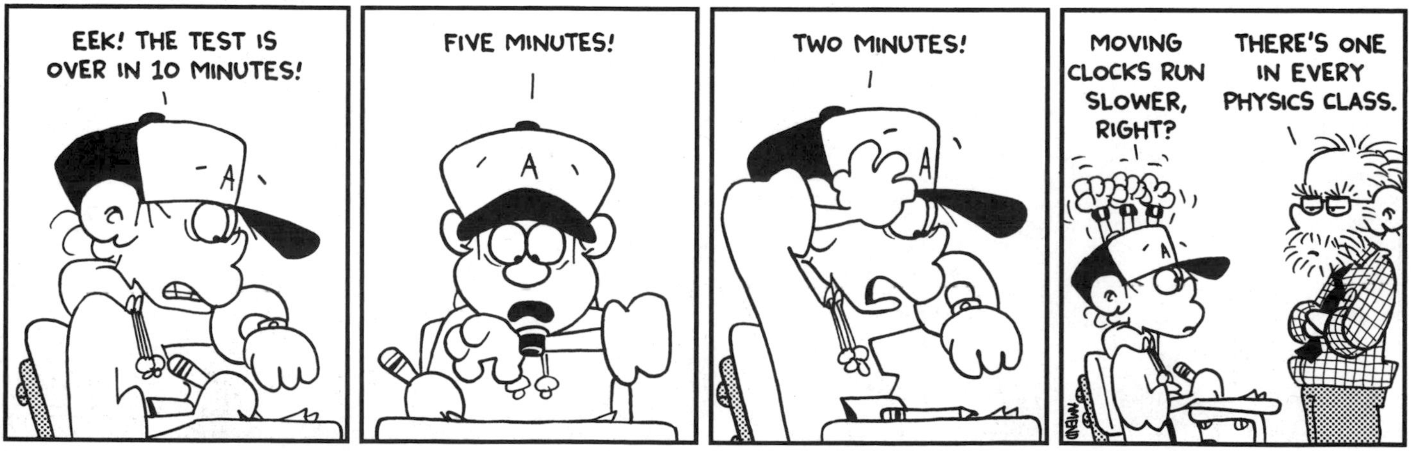
EEK! THE TEST IS OVER IN 10 MINUTES!
FIVE MINUTES!
TWO MINUTES!
MOVING CLOCKS RUN SLOWER, RIGHT?
THERE'S ONE IN EVERY PHYSICS CLASS.

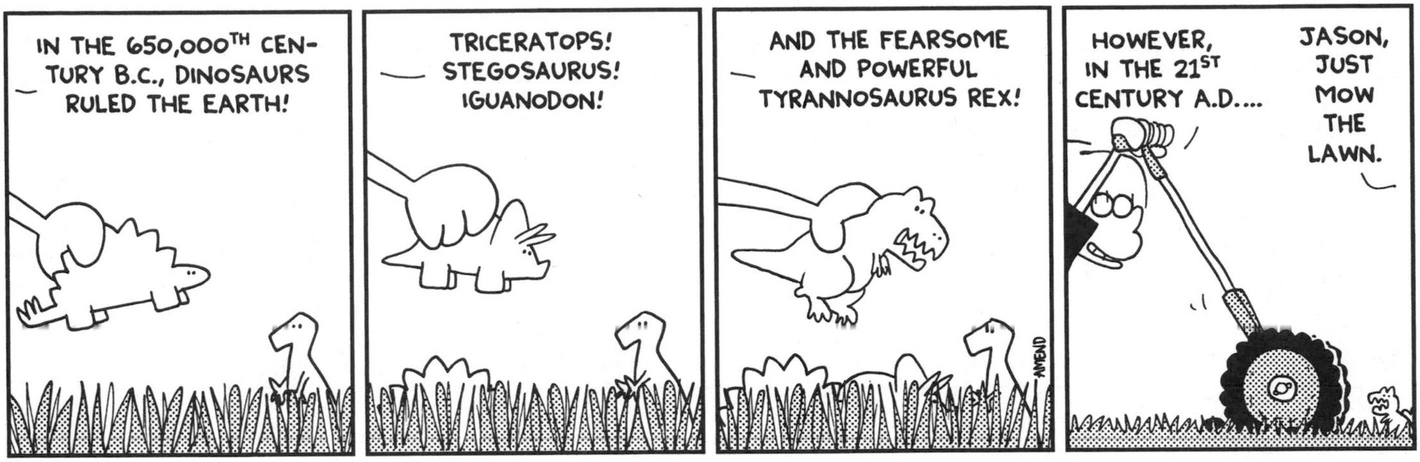
IN THE 650,000TH CENTURY B.C., DINOSAURS RULED THE EARTH!
TRICERATOPS! STEGOSAURUS! IGUANODON!
AND THE FEARSOME AND POWERFUL TYRANNOSAURUS REX!
HOWEVER, IN THE 21ST CENTURY A.D....
JASON, JUST MOW THE LAWN.

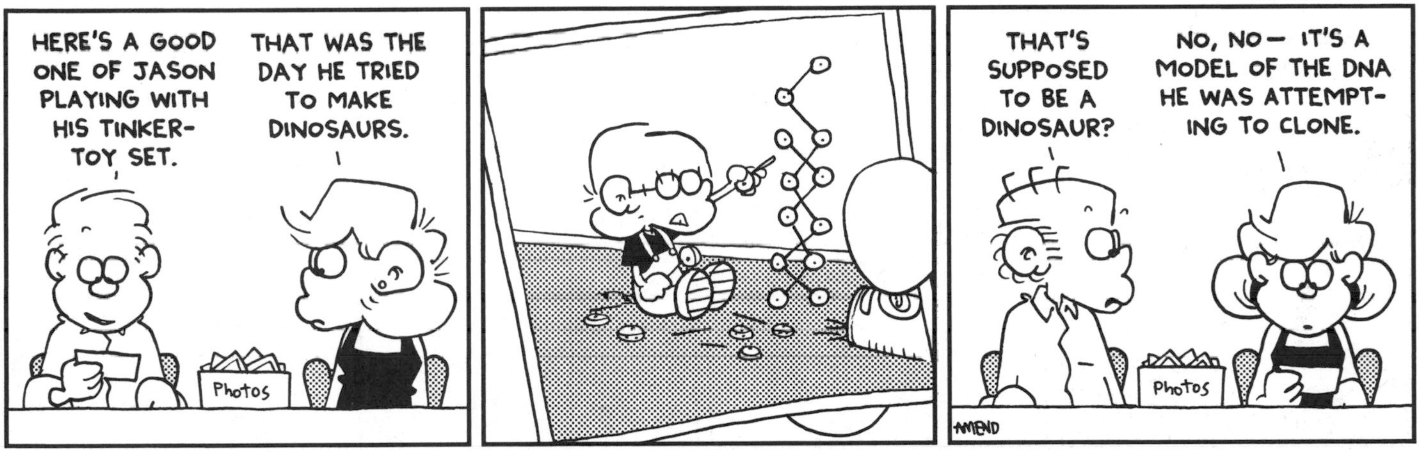
HERE'S A GOOD ONE OF JASON PLAYING WITH HIS TINKER-TOY SET.
THAT WAS THE DAY HE TRIED TO MAKE DINOSAURS.
THAT'S SUPPOSED TO BE A DINOSAUR?
NO, NO— IT'S A MODEL OF THE DNA HE WAS ATTEMPTING TO CLONE.
Photos

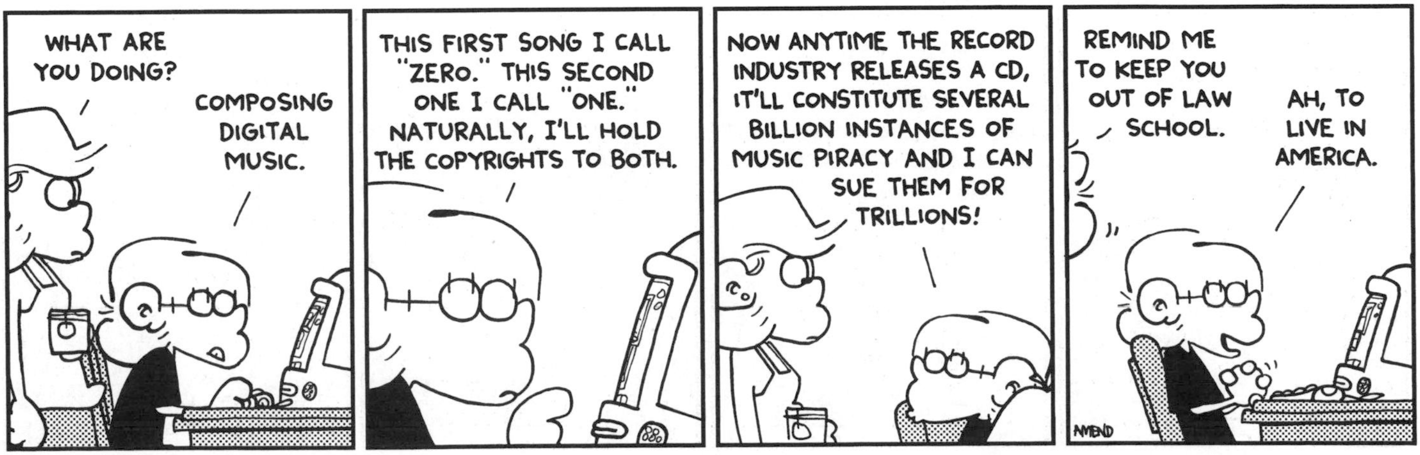
WHAT ARE YOU DOING?
COMPOSING DIGITAL MUSIC.
THIS FIRST SONG I CALL "ZERO." THIS SECOND ONE I CALL "ONE." NATURALLY, I'LL HOLD THE COPYRIGHTS TO BOTH.
NOW ANYTIME THE RECORD INDUSTRY RELEASES A CD, IT'LL CONSTITUTE SEVERAL BILLION INSTANCES OF MUSIC PIRACY AND I CAN SUE THEM FOR TRILLIONS!
REMIND ME TO KEEP YOU OUT OF LAW SCHOOL.
AH, TO LIVE IN AMERICA.

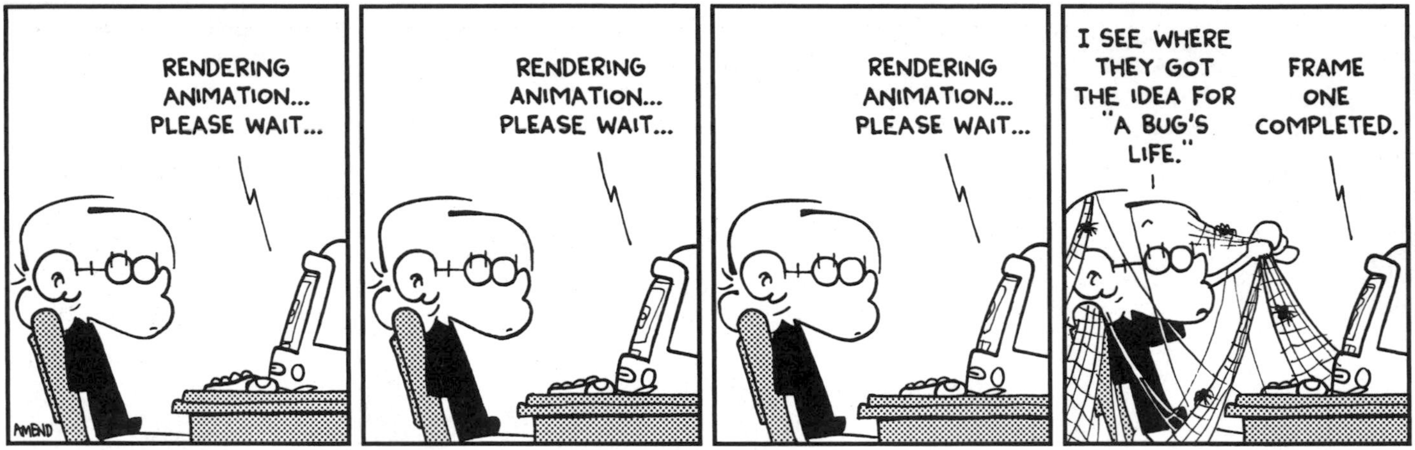
RENDERING ANIMATION... PLEASE WAIT...
AMEND
RENDERING ANIMATION... PLEASE WAIT...
RENDERING ANIMATION... PLEASE WAIT...
I SEE WHERE THEY GOT THE IDEA FOR "A BUG'S LIFE."
FRAME ONE COMPLETED.

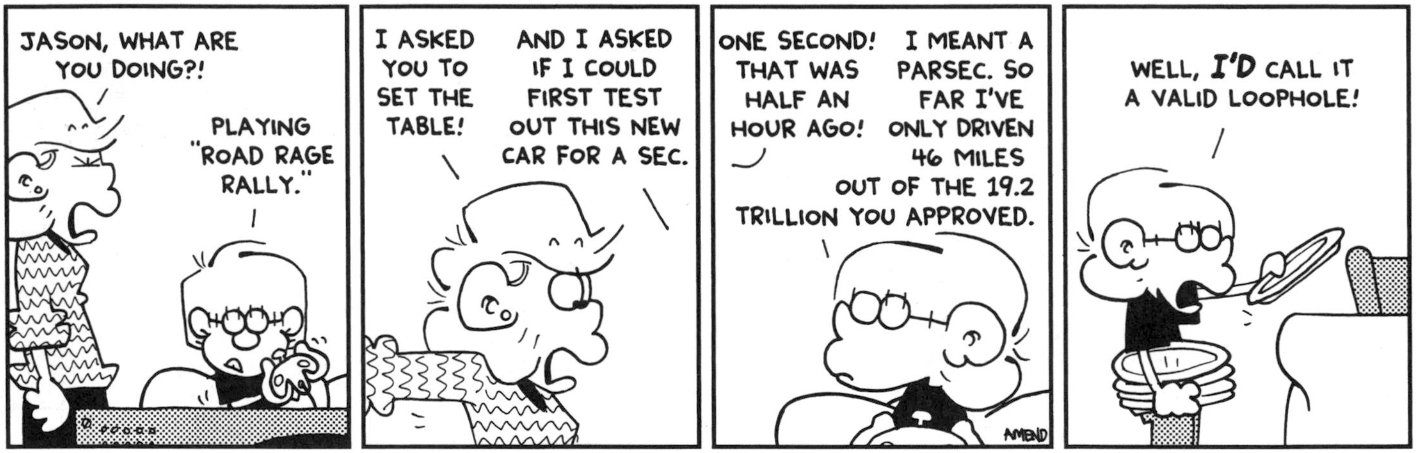
JASON, WHAT ARE YOU DOING?!
PLAYING "ROAD RAGE RALLY."
I ASKED YOU TO SET THE TABLE!
AND I ASKED IF I COULD FIRST TEST OUT THIS NEW CAR FOR A SEC.
ONE SECOND! THAT WAS HALF AN HOUR AGO!
I MEANT A PARSEC. SO FAR I'VE ONLY DRIVEN 46 MILES OUT OF THE 19.2 TRILLION YOU APPROVED.
AMEND
WELL, ***I'D*** CALL IT A VALID LOOPHOLE!

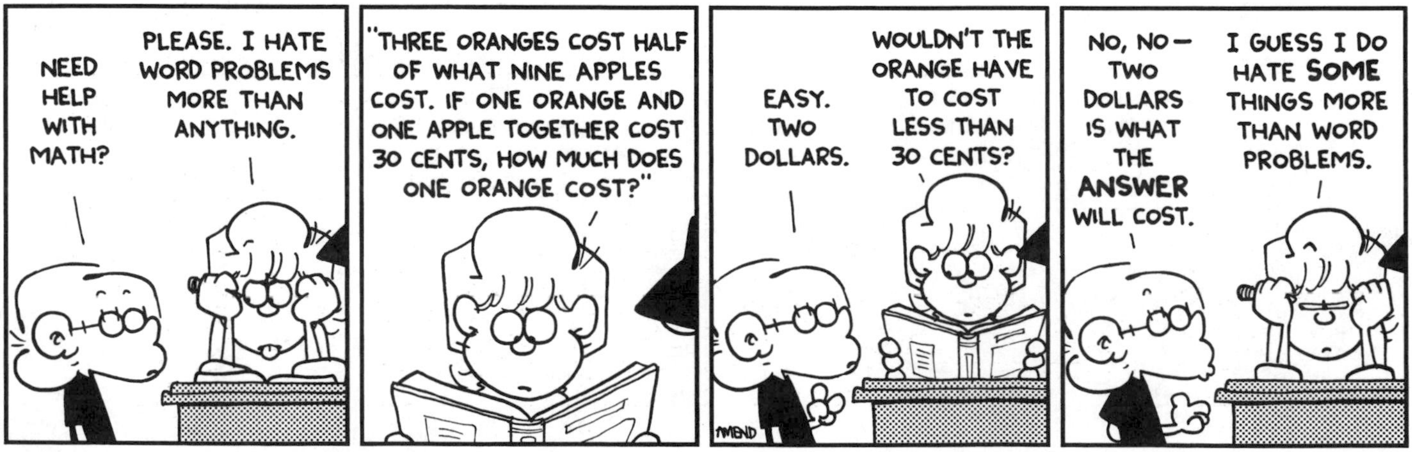
NEED HELP WITH MATH?
PLEASE. I HATE WORD PROBLEMS MORE THAN ANYTHING.
"THREE ORANGES COST HALF OF WHAT NINE APPLES COST. IF ONE ORANGE AND ONE APPLE TOGETHER COST 30 CENTS, HOW MUCH DOES ONE ORANGE COST?"
EASY. TWO DOLLARS.
WOULDN'T THE ORANGE HAVE TO COST LESS THAN 30 CENTS?
AMEND
NO, NO— TWO DOLLARS IS WHAT THE **ANSWER** WILL COST.
I GUESS I DO HATE **SOME** THINGS MORE THAN WORD PROBLEMS.

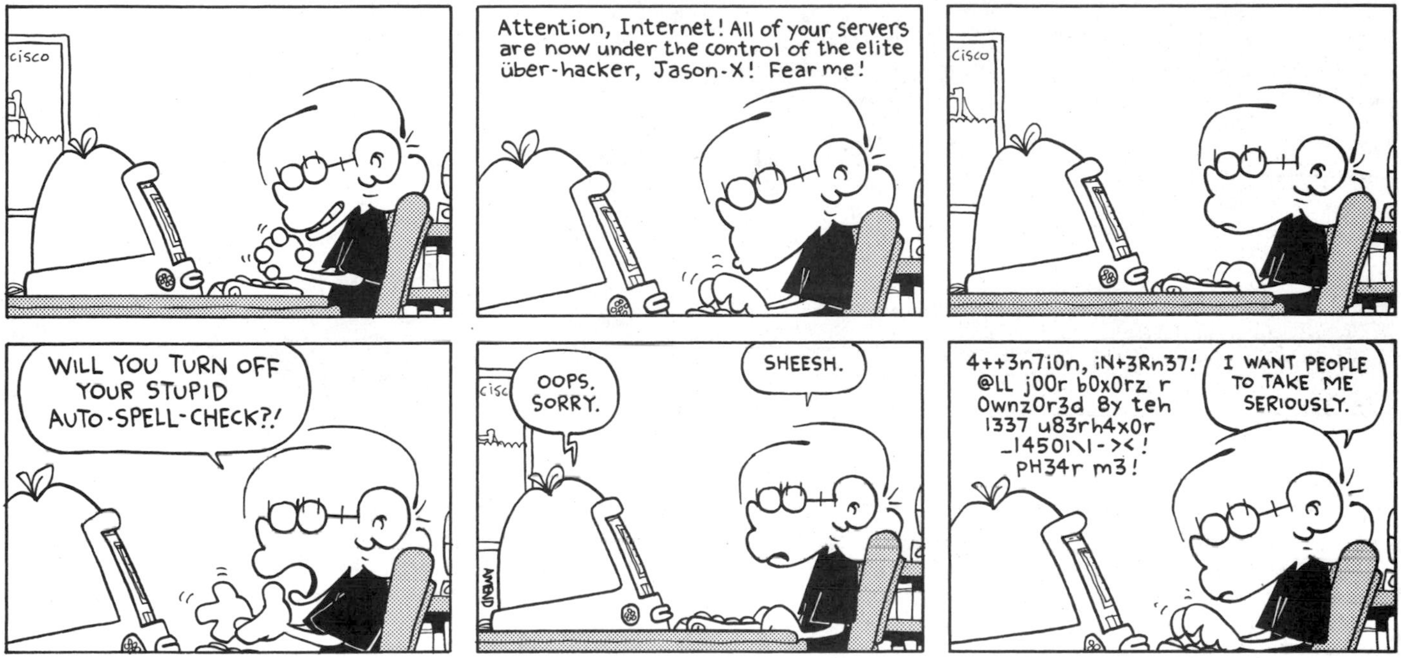
cisco
Attention, Internet! All of your servers are now under the control of the elite über-hacker, Jason-X! Fear me!
cisco
WILL YOU TURN OFF YOUR STUPID AUTO-SPELL-CHECK?!
OOPS. SORRY.
SHEESH.
AMEND
4++3n7i0n, iN+3Rn37! @LL j00r b0x0rz r 0wnz0r3d 8y teh 1337 u83rh4x0r _1450I\I-><! pH34r m3!
I WANT PEOPLE TO TAKE ME SERIOUSLY.

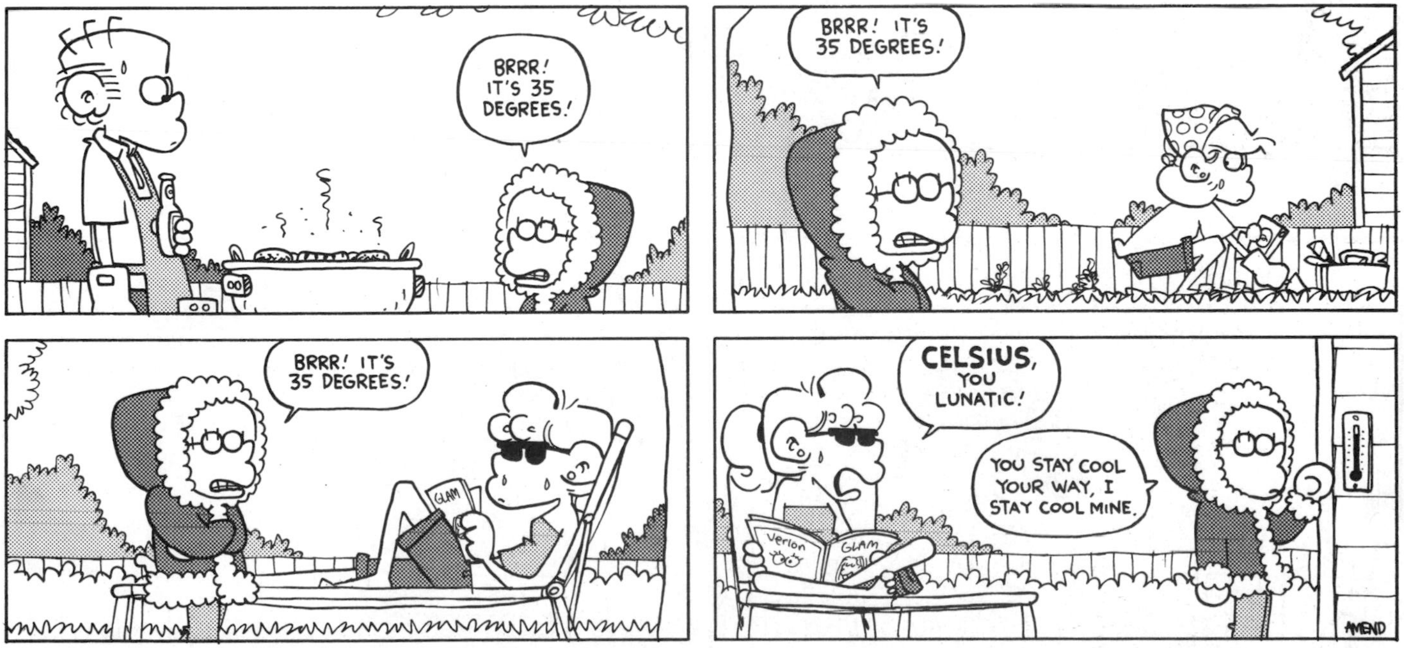
BRRR! IT'S 35 DEGREES!
BRRR! IT'S 35 DEGREES!
BRRR! IT'S 35 DEGREES!
GLAM
CELSIUS, YOU LUNATIC!
YOU STAY COOL YOUR WAY, I STAY COOL MINE.
Verlon
GLAM
AMEND

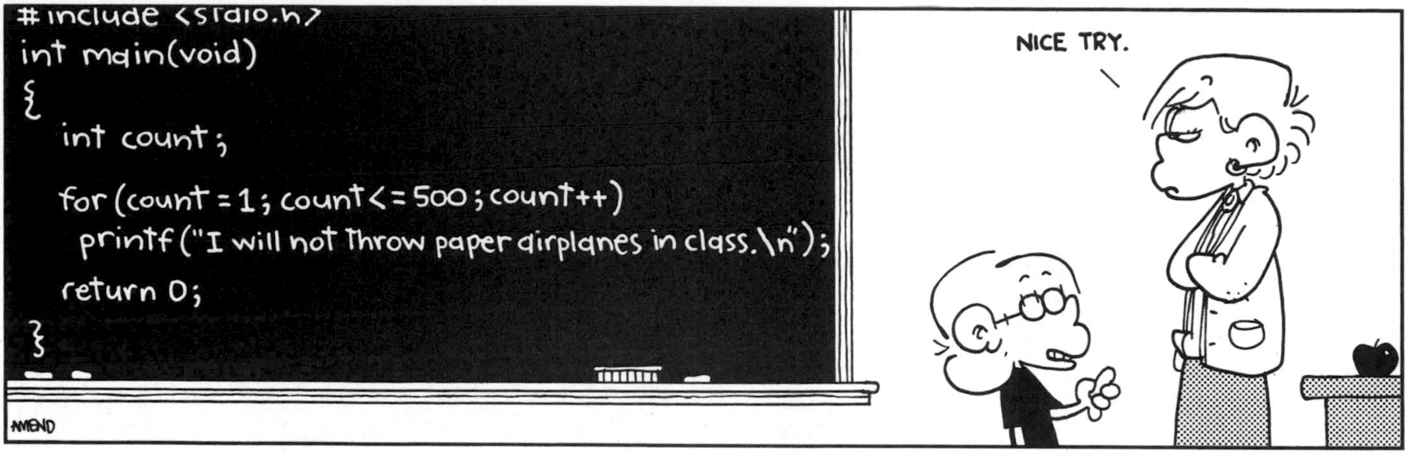
#include <stdio.h>
int main(void)
{
int count;
for (count = 1; count<= 500; count++)
printf("I will not throw paper airplanes in class.\n");
return 0;
}
NICE TRY.

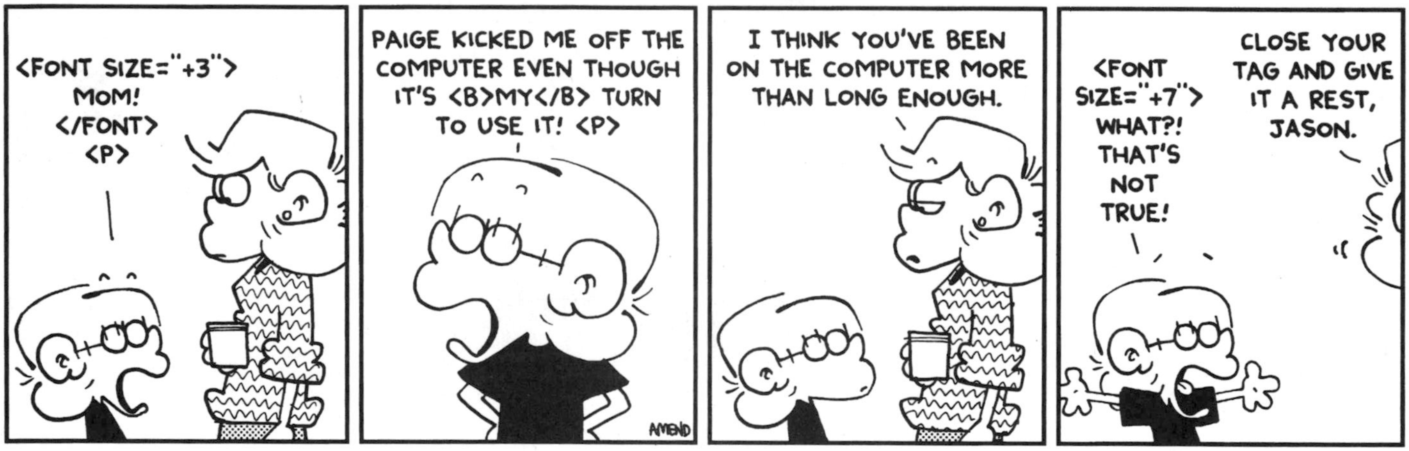
<FONT SIZE="+3"> MOM! </FONT> <P>
PAIGE KICKED ME OFF THE COMPUTER EVEN THOUGH IT'S <B>MY</B> TURN TO USE IT! <P>
I THINK YOU'VE BEEN ON THE COMPUTER MORE THAN LONG ENOUGH.
<FONT SIZE="+7"> WHAT?! THAT'S NOT TRUE!
CLOSE YOUR TAG AND GIVE IT A REST, JASON.

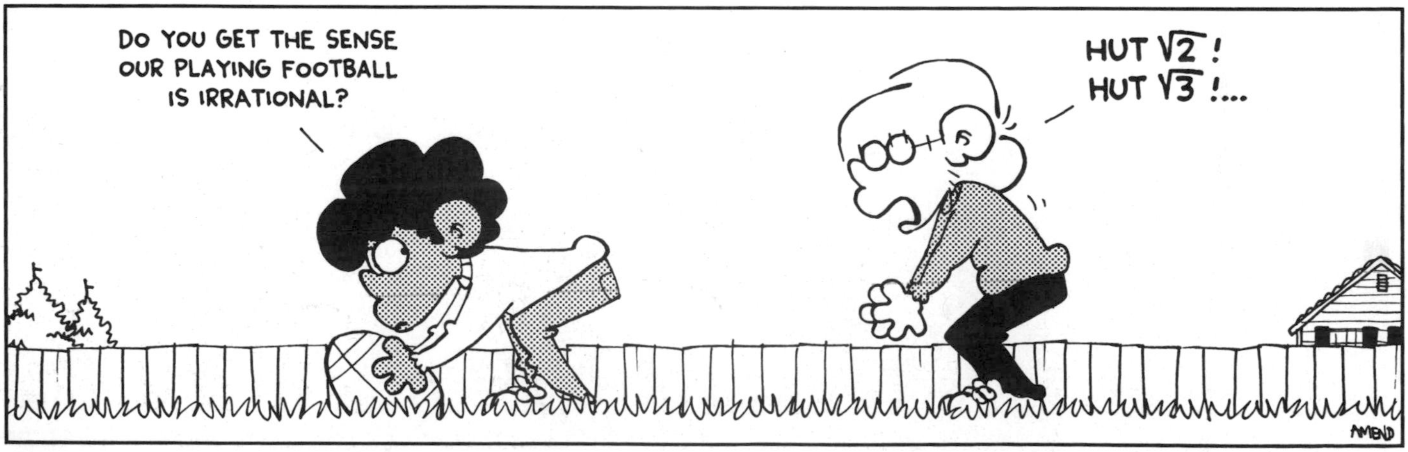
DO YOU GET THE SENSE OUR PLAYING FOOTBALL IS IRRATIONAL?
HUT √2 ! HUT √3 !...

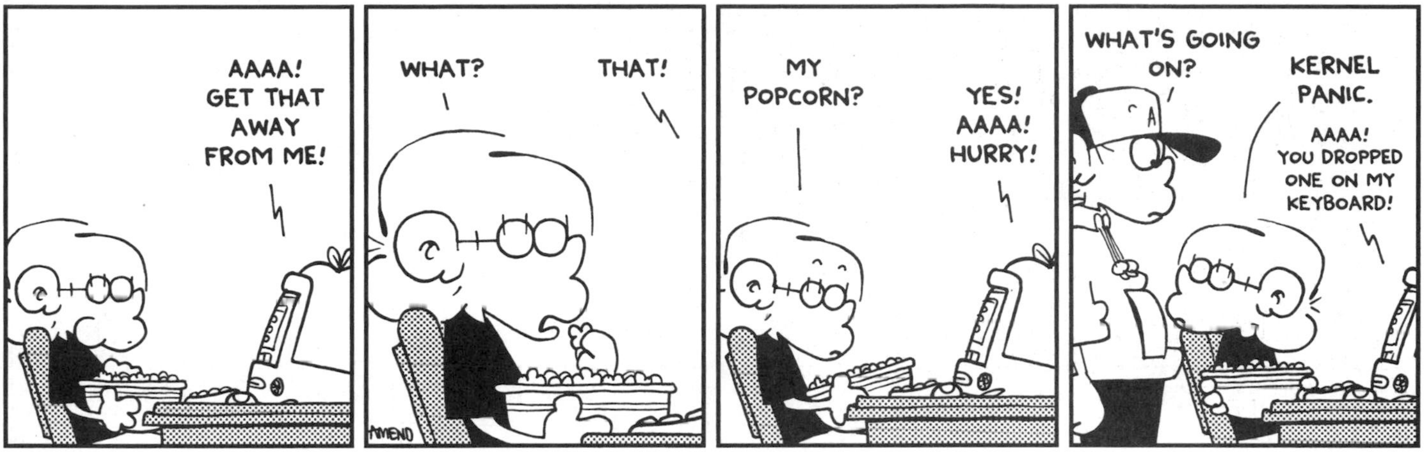
AAAA! GET THAT AWAY FROM ME!
WHAT?
THAT!
AMEND
MY POPCORN?
YES! AAAA! HURRY!
WHAT'S GOING ON?
KERNEL PANIC.
AAAA! YOU DROPPED ONE ON MY KEYBOARD!

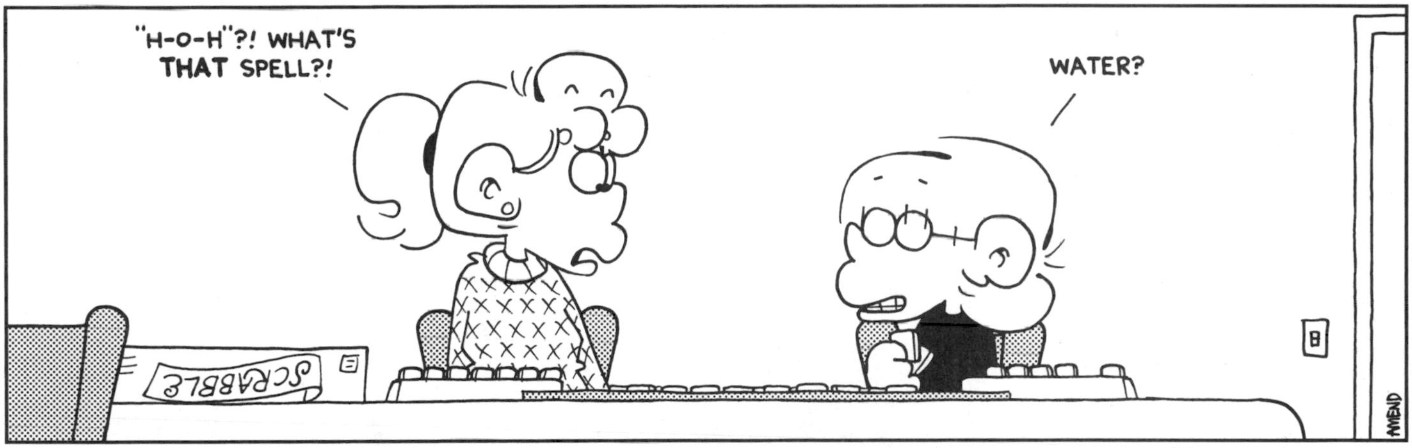
"H-O-H"?! WHAT'S **THAT** SPELL?!
WATER?
AMEND

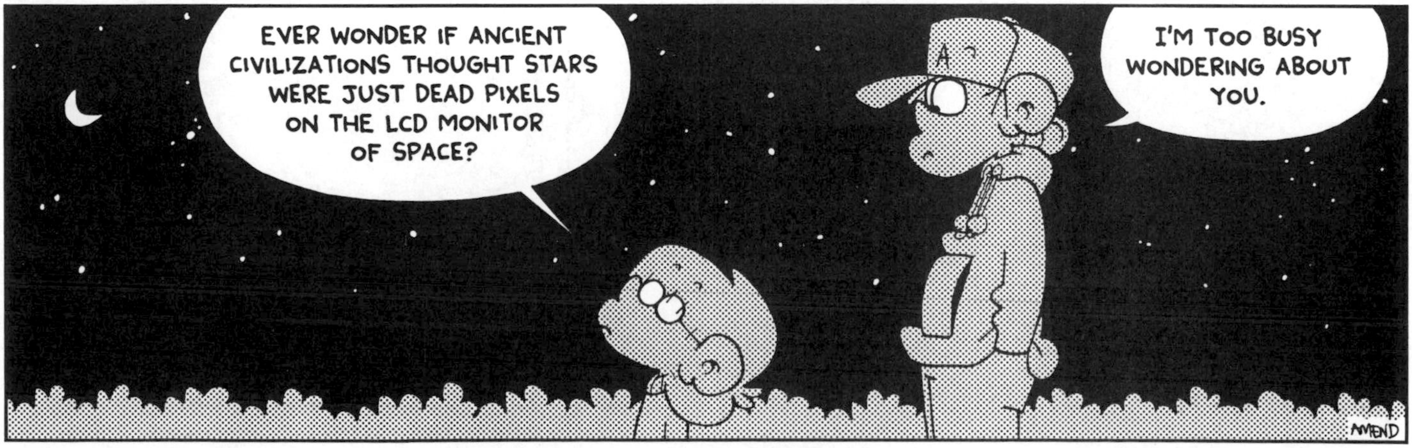
EVER WONDER IF ANCIENT CIVILIZATIONS THOUGHT STARS WERE JUST DEAD PIXELS ON THE LCD MONITOR OF SPACE?
I'M TOO BUSY WONDERING ABOUT YOU.
AMEND

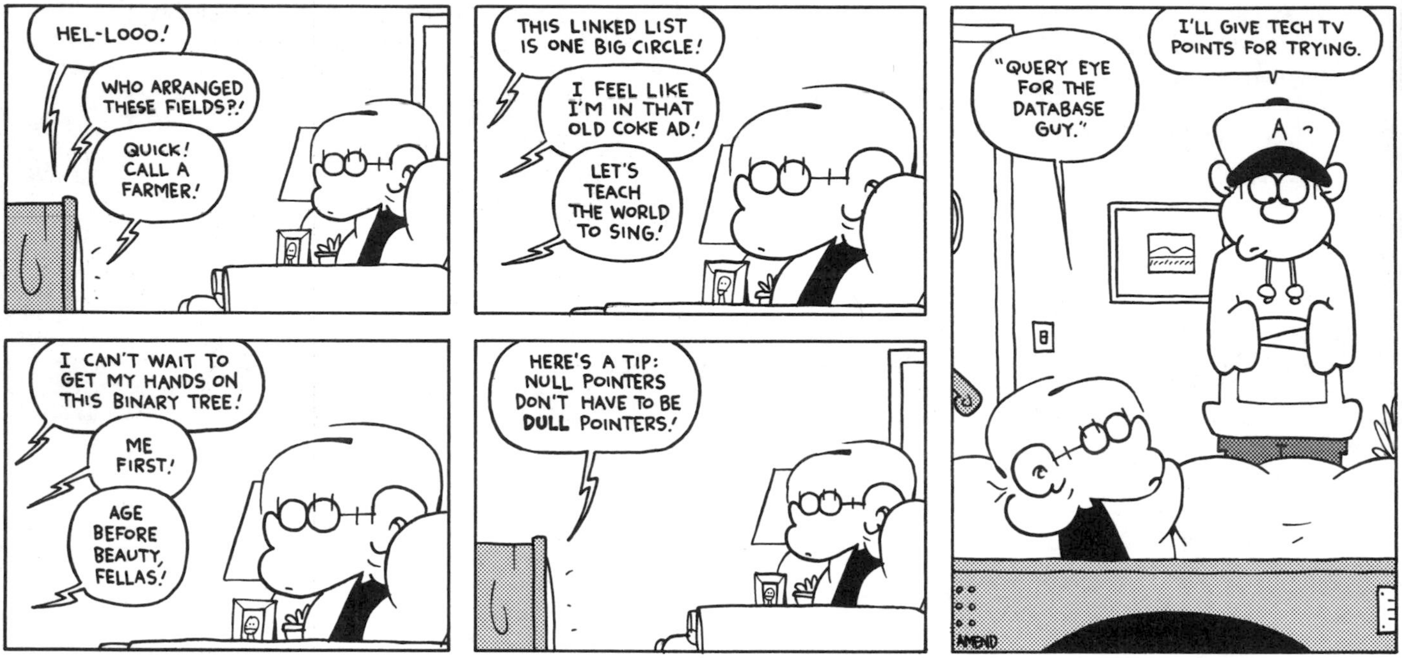
HEL-LOOO!
WHO ARRANGED THESE FIELDS?!
QUICK! CALL A FARMER!
THIS LINKED LIST IS ONE BIG CIRCLE!
I FEEL LIKE I'M IN THAT OLD COKE AD!
LET'S TEACH THE WORLD TO SING!
I CAN'T WAIT TO GET MY HANDS ON THIS BINARY TREE!
ME FIRST!
AGE BEFORE BEAUTY, FELLAS!
HERE'S A TIP: NULL POINTERS DON'T HAVE TO BE DULL POINTERS!
"QUERY EYE FOR THE DATABASE GUY."
I'LL GIVE TECH TV POINTS FOR TRYING.
AMEND

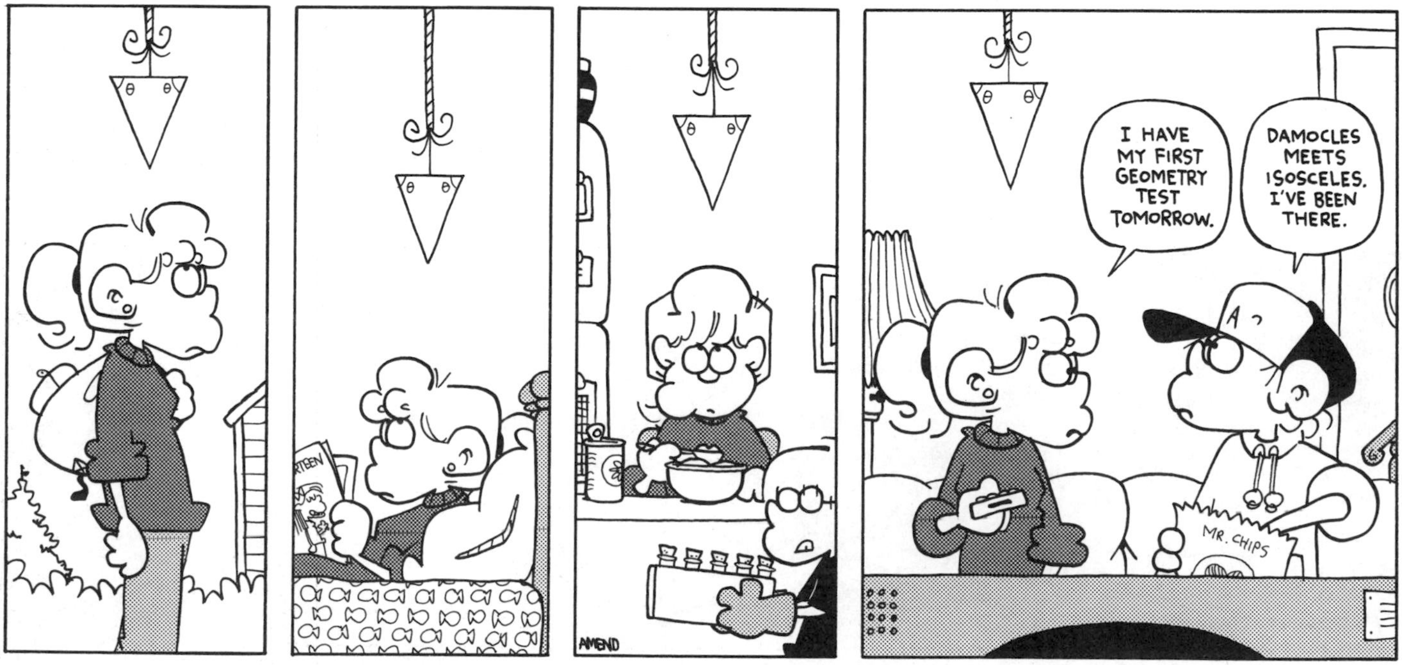
AMEND
I HAVE MY FIRST GEOMETRY TEST TOMORROW.
DAMOCLES MEETS ISOSCELES. I'VE BEEN THERE.
MR. CHIPS

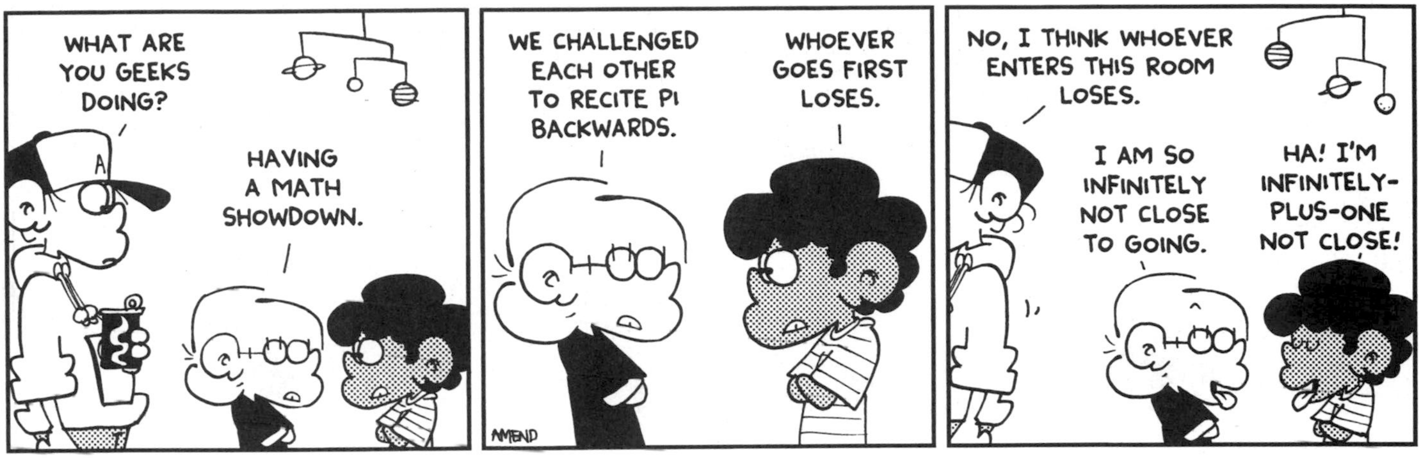
WHAT ARE YOU GEEKS DOING?
HAVING A MATH SHOWDOWN.
WE CHALLENGED EACH OTHER TO RECITE PI BACKWARDS.
WHOEVER GOES FIRST LOSES.
NO, I THINK WHOEVER ENTERS THIS ROOM LOSES.
I AM SO INFINITELY NOT CLOSE TO GOING.
HA! I'M INFINITELY-PLUS-ONE NOT CLOSE!
AMEND

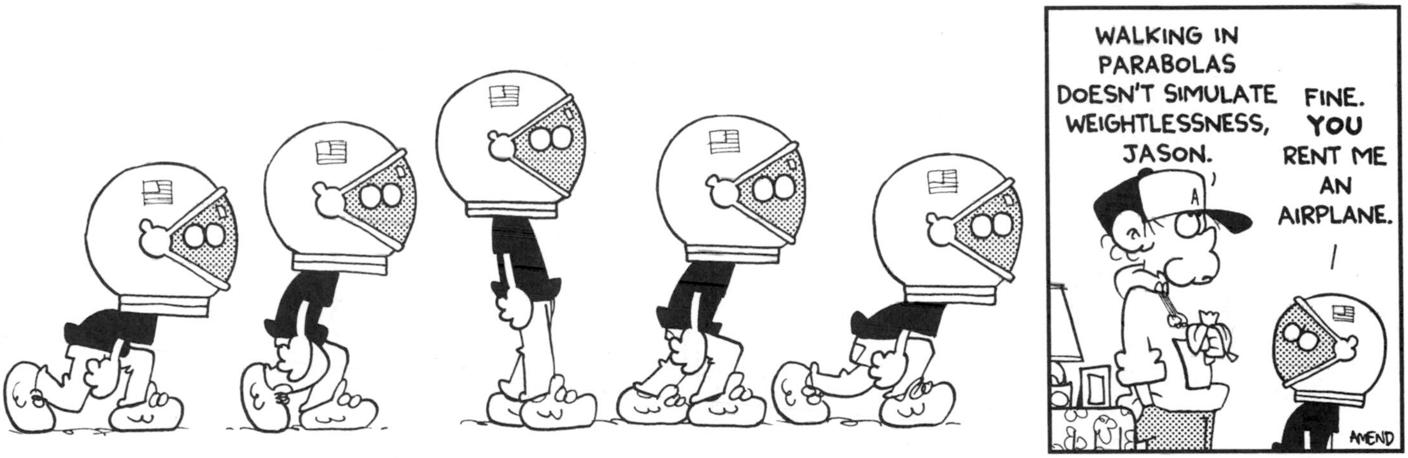
WALKING IN PARABOLAS DOESN'T SIMULATE WEIGHTLESSNESS, JASON.
FINE. **YOU** RENT ME AN AIRPLANE.
AMEND

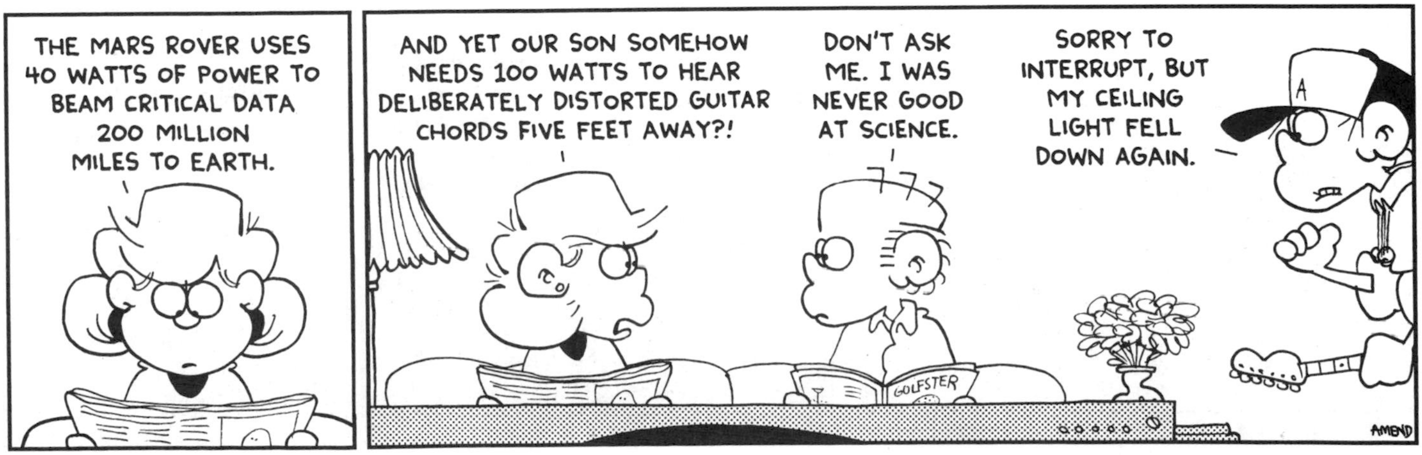
THE MARS ROVER USES 40 WATTS OF POWER TO BEAM CRITICAL DATA 200 MILLION MILES TO EARTH.
AND YET OUR SON SOMEHOW NEEDS 100 WATTS TO HEAR DELIBERATELY DISTORTED GUITAR CHORDS FIVE FEET AWAY?!
DON'T ASK ME. I WAS NEVER GOOD AT SCIENCE.
SORRY TO INTERRUPT, BUT MY CEILING LIGHT FELL DOWN AGAIN.
GOLFSTER
AMEND

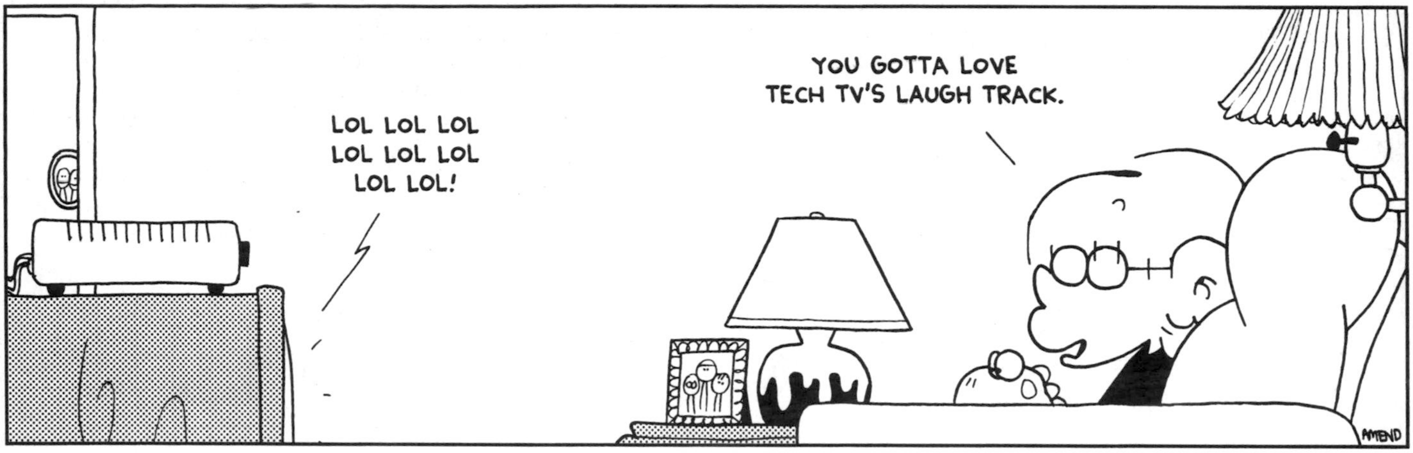
LOL LOL LOL
LOL LOL LOL
LOL LOL!
YOU GOTTA LOVE
TECH TV'S LAUGH TRACK.

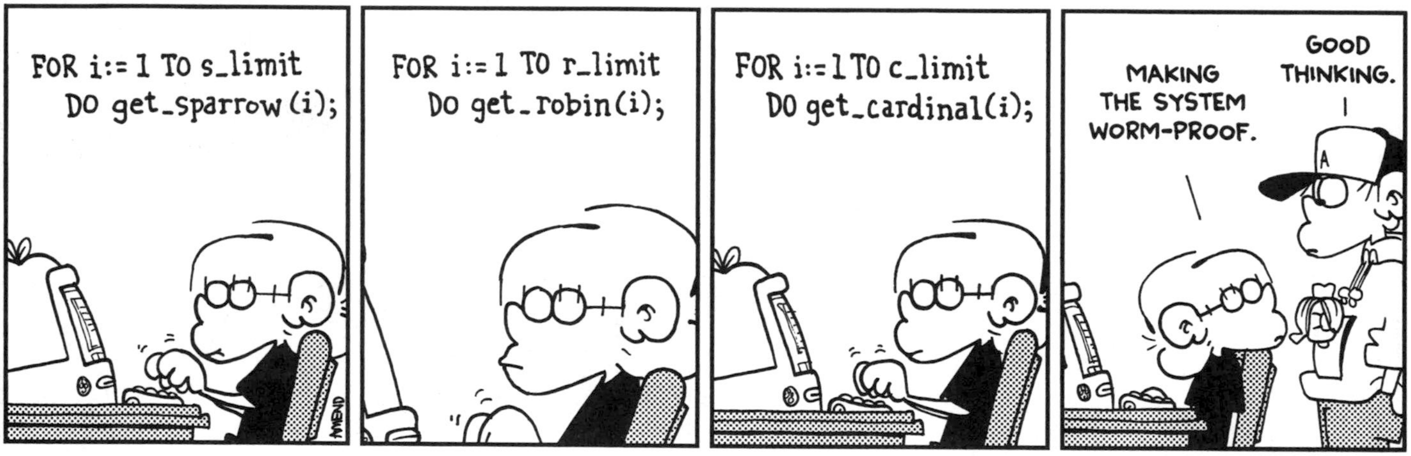
FOR i:= 1 TO s_limit
DO get_sparrow (i);
FOR i:= 1 TO r_limit
DO get_robin(i);
FOR i:= 1 TO c_limit
DO get_cardinal(i);
MAKING
THE SYSTEM
WORM-PROOF.
GOOD
THINKING.

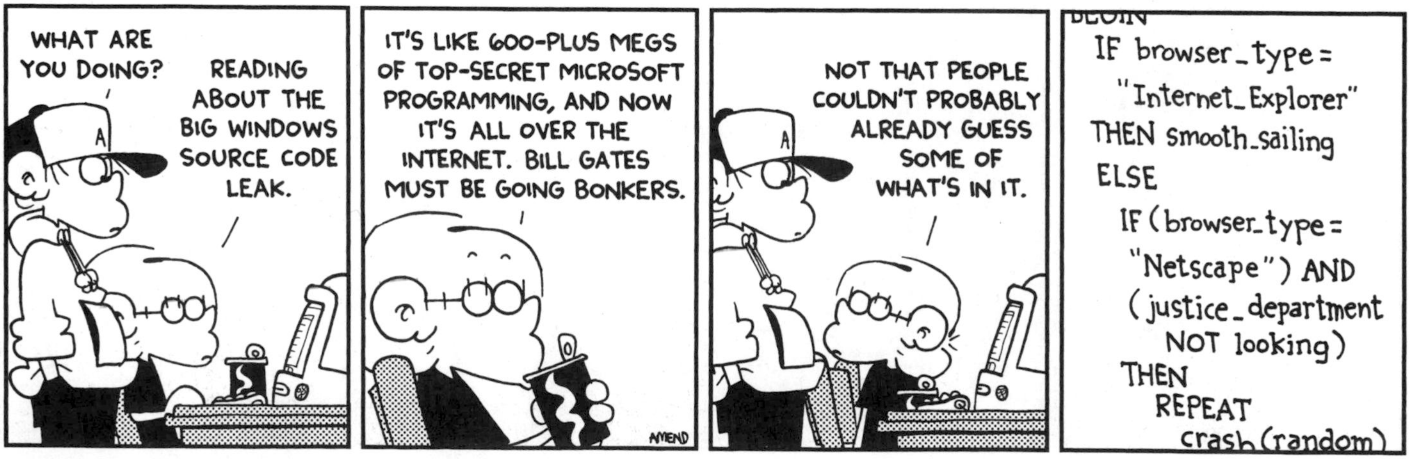
WHAT ARE
YOU DOING?
READING
ABOUT THE
BIG WINDOWS
SOURCE CODE
LEAK.
IT'S LIKE 600-PLUS MEGS
OF TOP-SECRET MICROSOFT
PROGRAMMING, AND NOW
IT'S ALL OVER THE
INTERNET. BILL GATES
MUST BE GOING BONKERS.
NOT THAT PEOPLE
COULDN'T PROBABLY
ALREADY GUESS
SOME OF
WHAT'S IN IT.
IF browser_type =
"Internet_Explorer"
THEN smooth_sailing
ELSE
IF (browser_type =
"Netscape") AND
(justice_department
NOT looking)
THEN
REPEAT
crash(random)

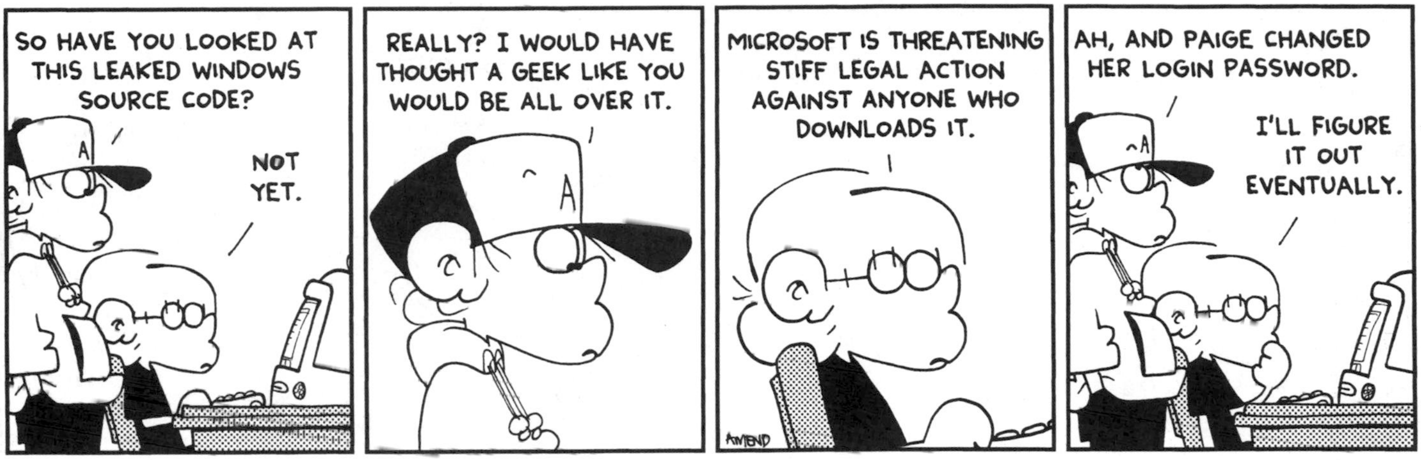
SO HAVE YOU LOOKED AT THIS LEAKED WINDOWS SOURCE CODE?
NOT YET.
REALLY? I WOULD HAVE THOUGHT A GEEK LIKE YOU WOULD BE ALL OVER IT.
MICROSOFT IS THREATENING STIFF LEGAL ACTION AGAINST ANYONE WHO DOWNLOADS IT.
AMEND
AH, AND PAIGE CHANGED HER LOGIN PASSWORD.
I'LL FIGURE IT OUT EVENTUALLY.

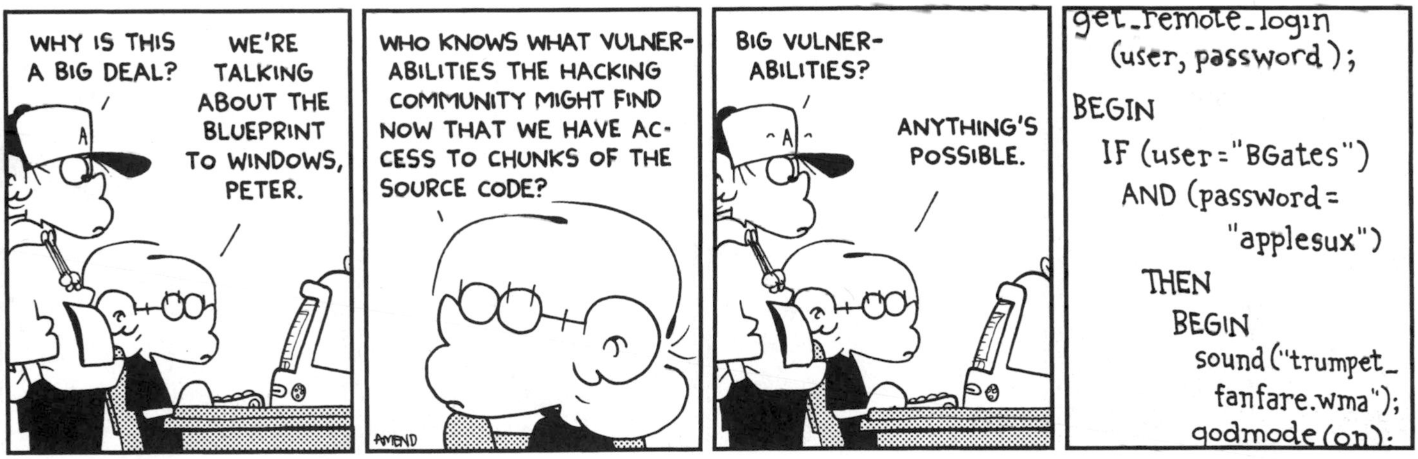
WHY IS THIS A BIG DEAL?
WE'RE TALKING ABOUT THE BLUEPRINT TO WINDOWS, PETER.
WHO KNOWS WHAT VULNERABILITIES THE HACKING COMMUNITY MIGHT FIND NOW THAT WE HAVE ACCESS TO CHUNKS OF THE SOURCE CODE?
AMEND
BIG VULNERABILITIES?
ANYTHING'S POSSIBLE.
get_remote_login
(user, password);
BEGIN
IF (user="BGates")
AND (password=
"applesux")
THEN
BEGIN
sound("trumpet_
fanfare.wma");
godmode(on);

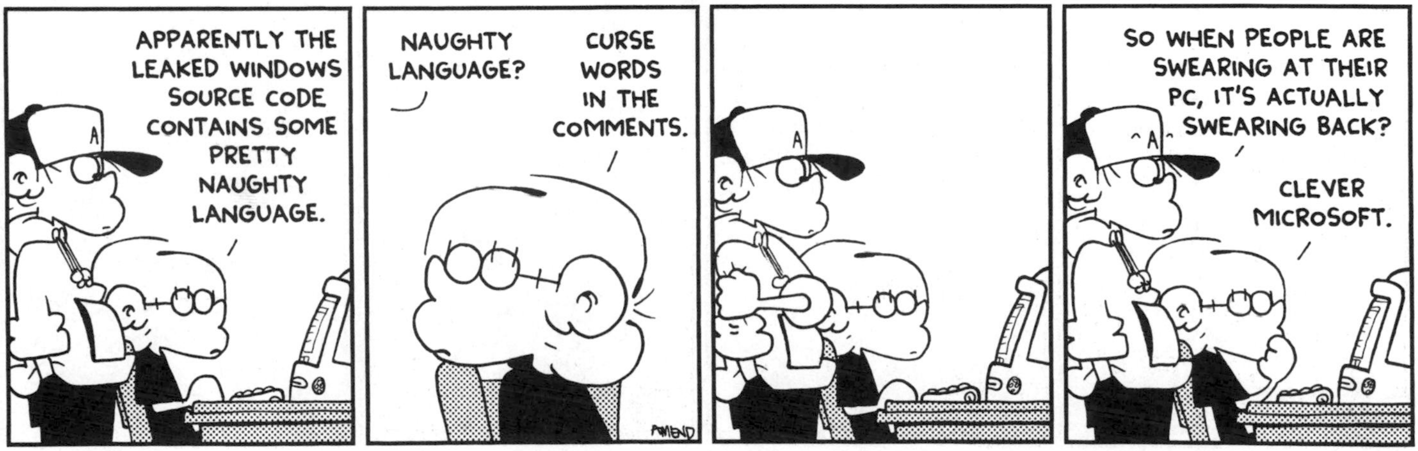
APPARENTLY THE LEAKED WINDOWS SOURCE CODE CONTAINS SOME PRETTY NAUGHTY LANGUAGE.
NAUGHTY LANGUAGE?
CURSE WORDS IN THE COMMENTS.
AMEND
SO WHEN PEOPLE ARE SWEARING AT THEIR PC, IT'S ACTUALLY SWEARING BACK?
CLEVER MICROSOFT.

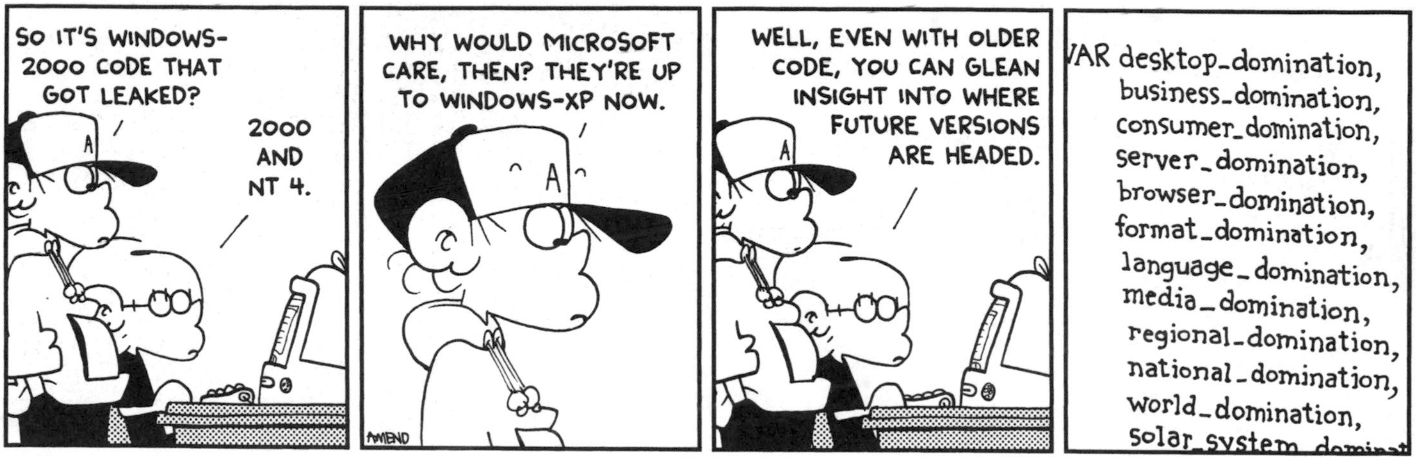
SO IT'S WINDOWS-2000 CODE THAT GOT LEAKED?
2000 AND NT 4.
WHY WOULD MICROSOFT CARE, THEN? THEY'RE UP TO WINDOWS-XP NOW.
AMEND
WELL, EVEN WITH OLDER CODE, YOU CAN GLEAN INSIGHT INTO WHERE FUTURE VERSIONS ARE HEADED.
VAR desktop_domination,
business_domination,
consumer_domination,
server_domination,
browser_domination,
format_domination,
language_domination,
media_domination,
regional_domination,
national_domination,
world_domination,
solar_system

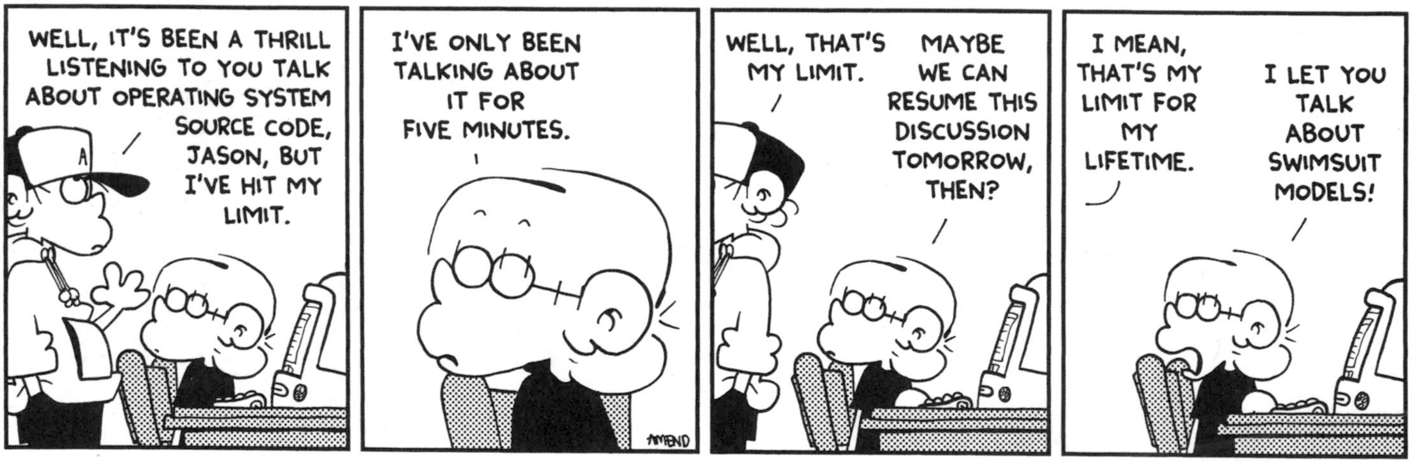
WELL, IT'S BEEN A THRILL LISTENING TO YOU TALK ABOUT OPERATING SYSTEM SOURCE CODE, JASON, BUT I'VE HIT MY LIMIT.
I'VE ONLY BEEN TALKING ABOUT IT FOR FIVE MINUTES.
AMEND
WELL, THAT'S MY LIMIT.
MAYBE WE CAN RESUME THIS DISCUSSION TOMORROW, THEN?
I MEAN, THAT'S MY LIMIT FOR MY LIFETIME.
I LET YOU TALK ABOUT SWIMSUIT MODELS!

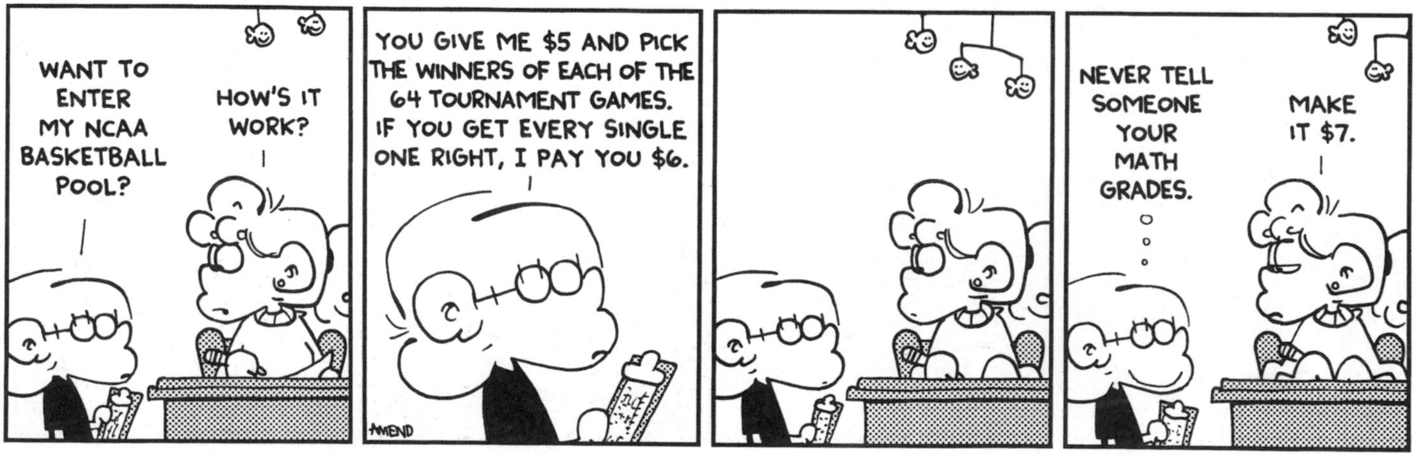
WANT TO ENTER MY NCAA BASKETBALL POOL?
HOW'S IT WORK?
YOU GIVE ME $5 AND PICK THE WINNERS OF EACH OF THE 64 TOURNAMENT GAMES. IF YOU GET EVERY SINGLE ONE RIGHT, I PAY YOU $6.
AMEND
NEVER TELL SOMEONE YOUR MATH GRADES.
MAKE IT $7.

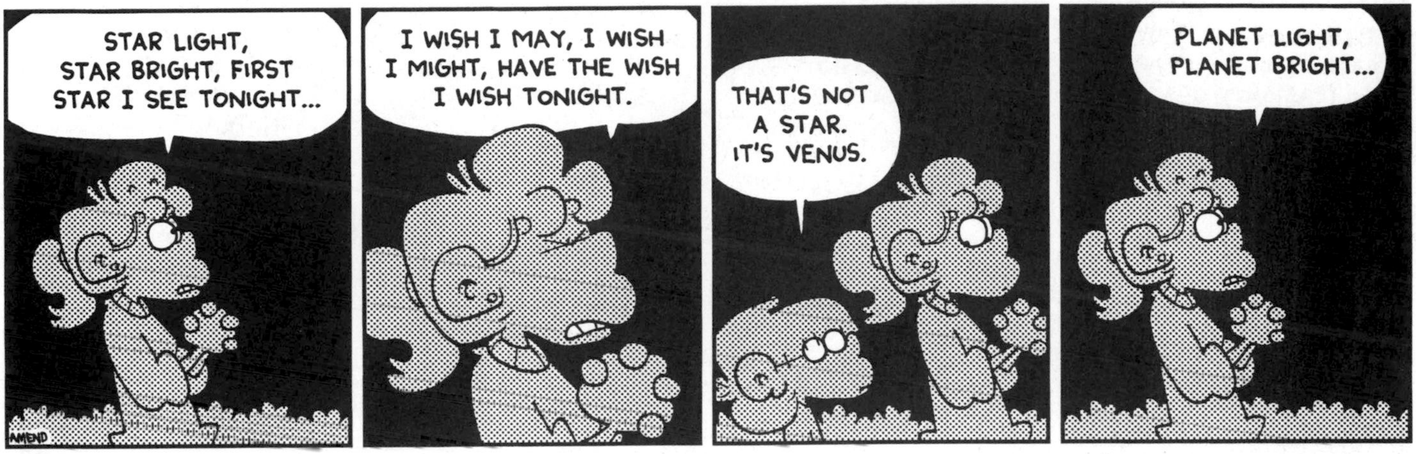
STAR LIGHT, STAR BRIGHT, FIRST STAR I SEE TONIGHT...
I WISH I MAY, I WISH I MIGHT, HAVE THE WISH I WISH TONIGHT.
THAT'S NOT A STAR. IT'S VENUS.
PLANET LIGHT, PLANET BRIGHT...

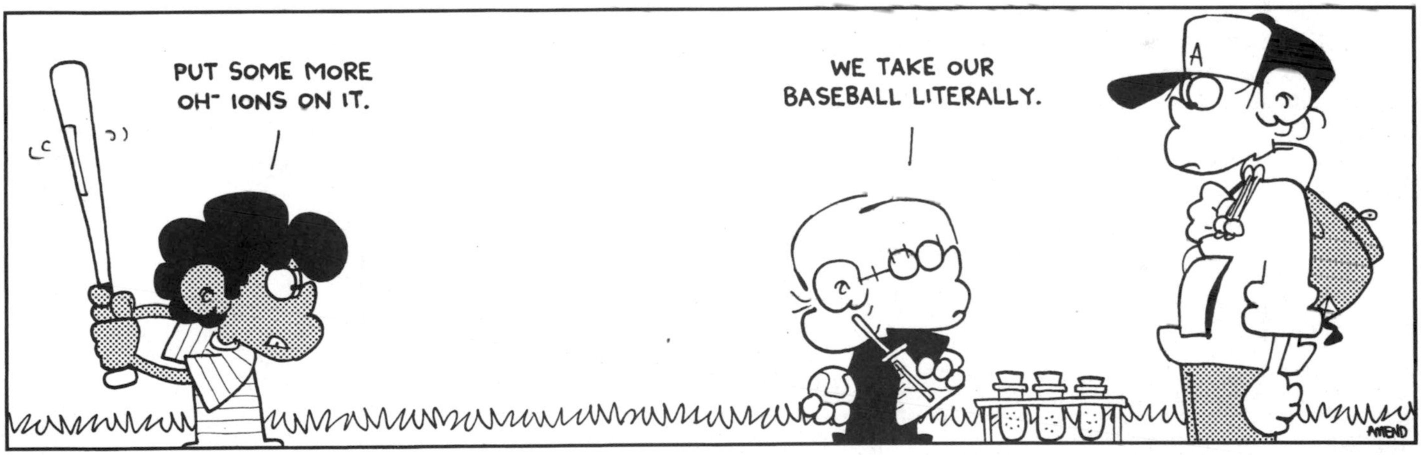
PUT SOME MORE OH⁻ IONS ON IT.
WE TAKE OUR BASEBALL LITERALLY.

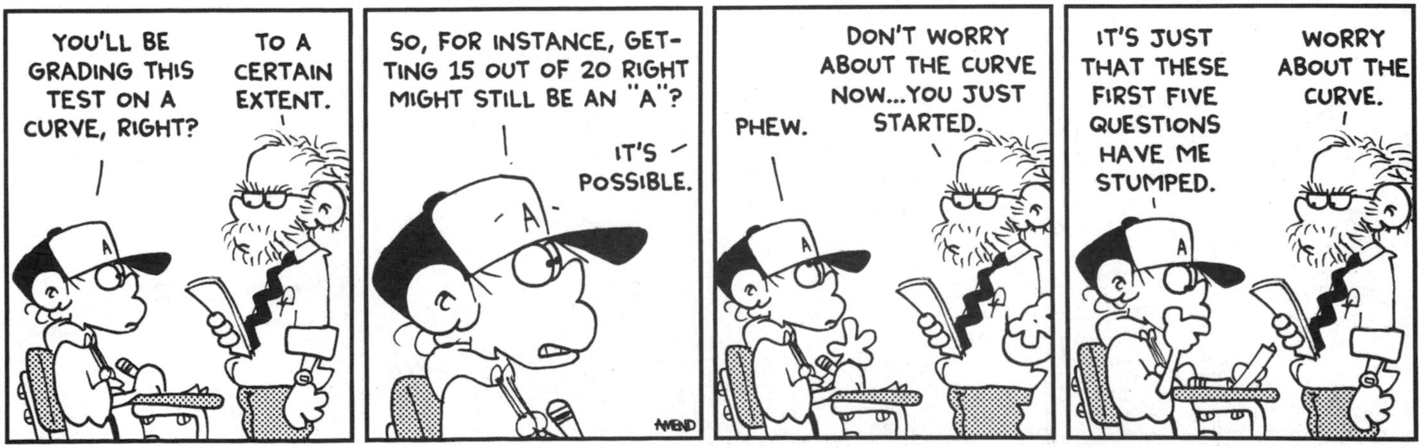
YOU'LL BE GRADING THIS TEST ON A CURVE, RIGHT?
TO A CERTAIN EXTENT.
SO, FOR INSTANCE, GETTING 15 OUT OF 20 RIGHT MIGHT STILL BE AN "A"?
IT'S POSSIBLE.
PHEW.
DON'T WORRY ABOUT THE CURVE NOW...YOU JUST STARTED.
IT'S JUST THAT THESE FIRST FIVE QUESTIONS HAVE ME STUMPED.
WORRY ABOUT THE CURVE.

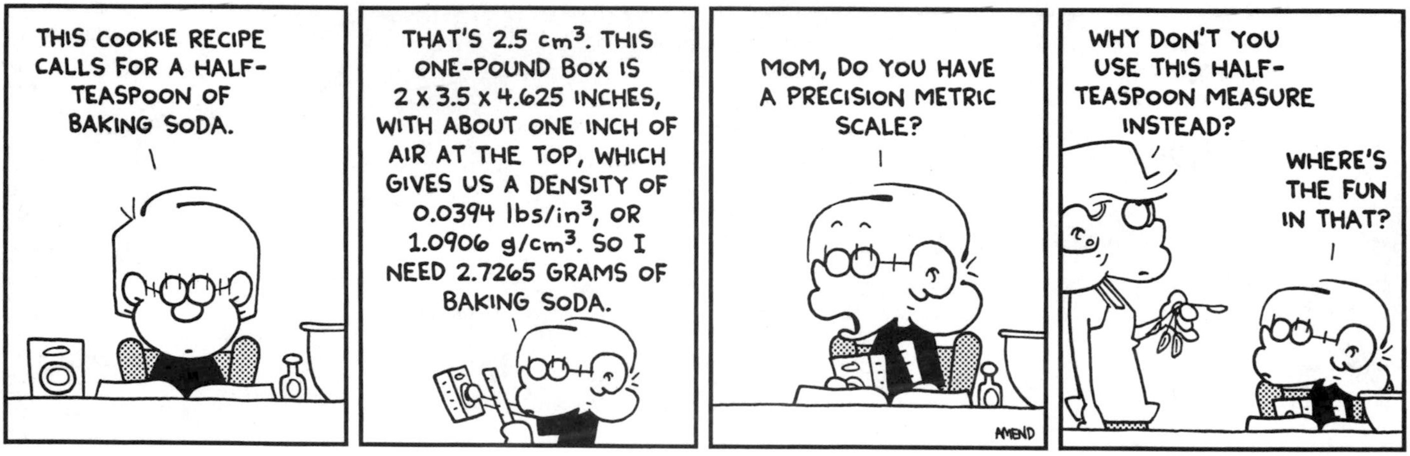
THIS COOKIE RECIPE CALLS FOR A HALF-TEASPOON OF BAKING SODA.
THAT'S 2.5 cm3. THIS ONE-POUND BOX IS 2 x 3.5 x 4.625 INCHES, WITH ABOUT ONE INCH OF AIR AT THE TOP, WHICH GIVES US A DENSITY OF 0.0394 lbs/in3, OR 1.0906 g/cm3. SO I NEED 2.7265 GRAMS OF BAKING SODA.
MOM, DO YOU HAVE A PRECISION METRIC SCALE?
WHY DON'T YOU USE THIS HALF-TEASPOON MEASURE INSTEAD?
WHERE'S THE FUN IN THAT?
AMEND

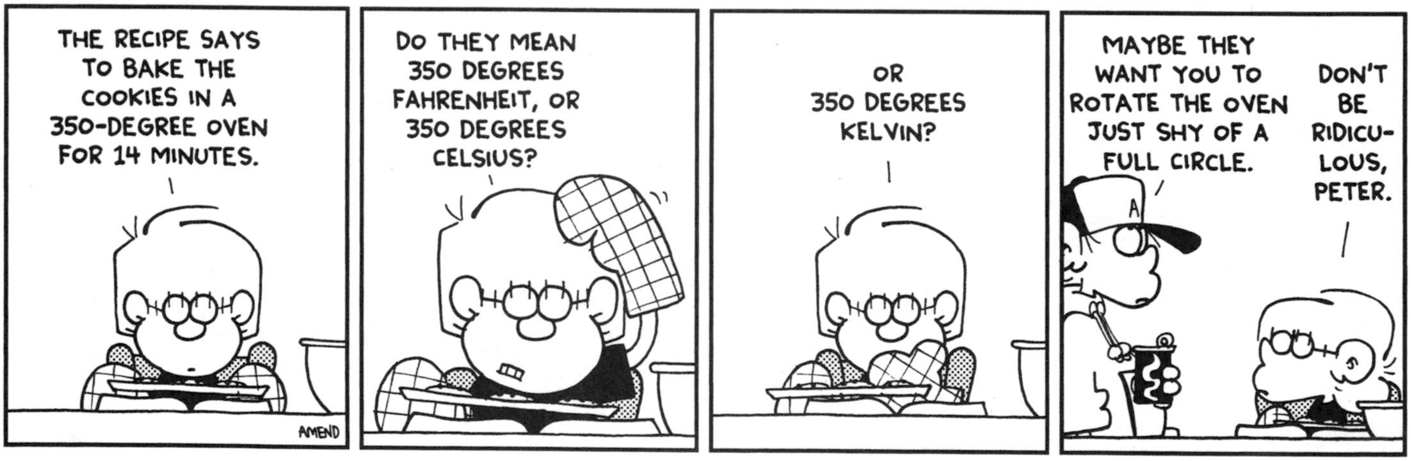
THE RECIPE SAYS TO BAKE THE COOKIES IN A 350-DEGREE OVEN FOR 14 MINUTES.
DO THEY MEAN 350 DEGREES FAHRENHEIT, OR 350 DEGREES CELSIUS?
OR 350 DEGREES KELVIN?
MAYBE THEY WANT YOU TO ROTATE THE OVEN JUST SHY OF A FULL CIRCLE.
DON'T BE RIDICU-LOUS, PETER.
AMEND

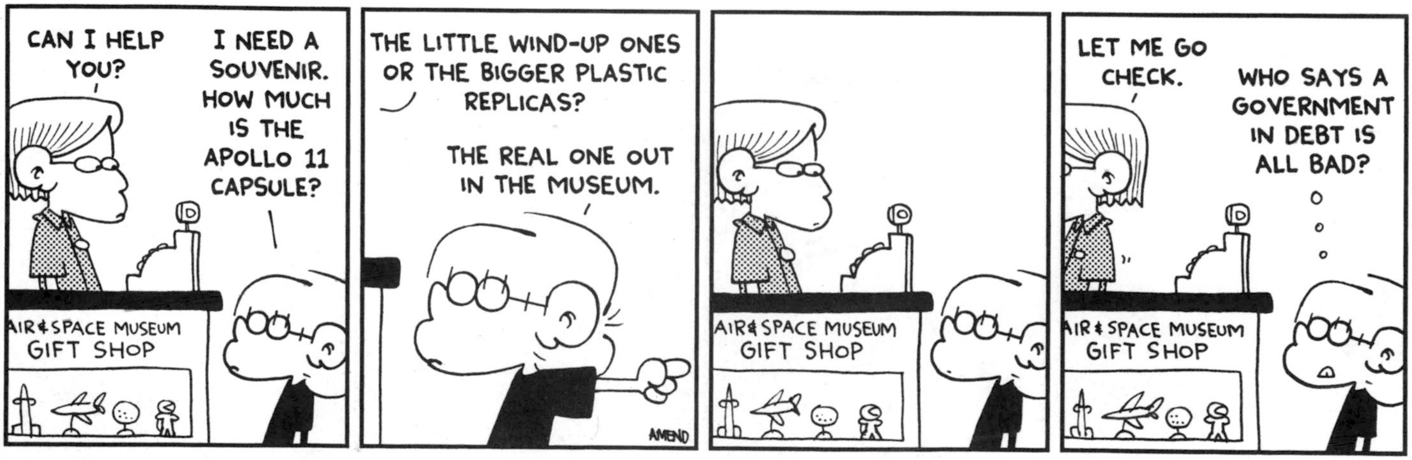
CAN I HELP YOU?
I NEED A SOUVENIR. HOW MUCH IS THE APOLLO 11 CAPSULE?
AIR & SPACE MUSEUM GIFT SHOP
THE LITTLE WIND-UP ONES OR THE BIGGER PLASTIC REPLICAS?
THE REAL ONE OUT IN THE MUSEUM.
AIR & SPACE MUSEUM GIFT SHOP
LET ME GO CHECK.
WHO SAYS A GOVERNMENT IN DEBT IS ALL BAD?
AIR & SPACE MUSEUM GIFT SHOP
AMEND

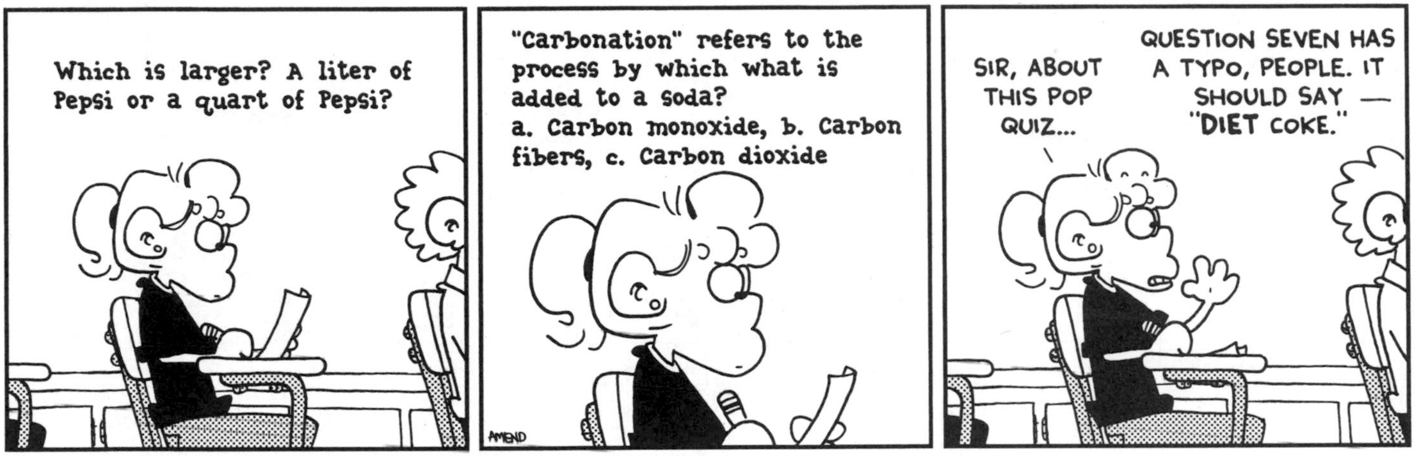
Which is larger? A liter of Pepsi or a quart of Pepsi?
"Carbonation" refers to the process by which what is added to a soda?
a. Carbon monoxide, b. Carbon fibers, c. Carbon dioxide
AMEND
SIR, ABOUT THIS POP QUIZ...
QUESTION SEVEN HAS A TYPO, PEOPLE. IT SHOULD SAY — "DIET COKE."

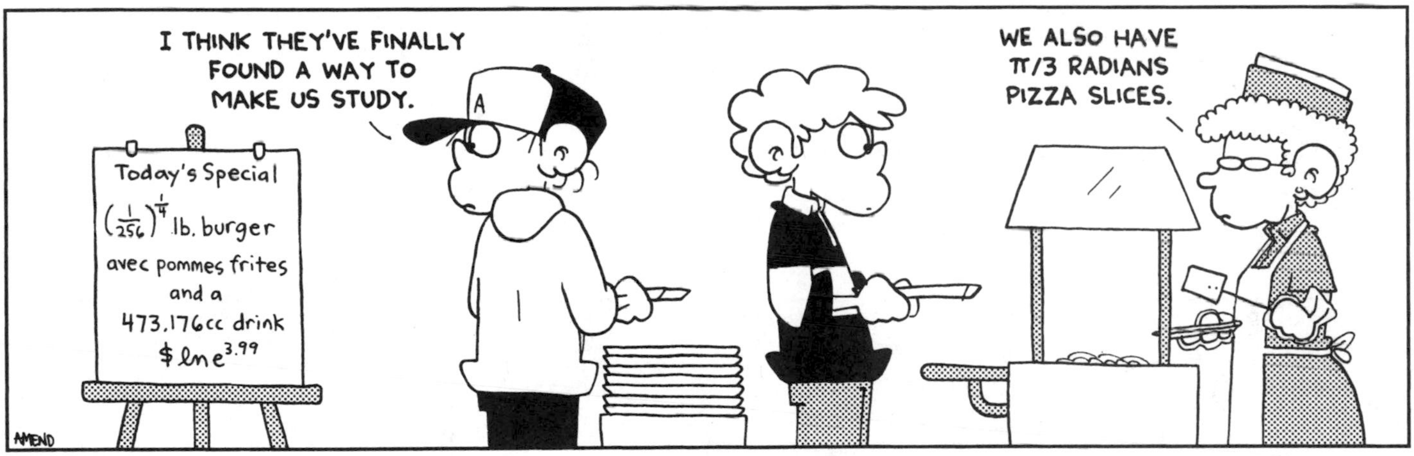
Today's Special
$(\frac{1}{256})^{\frac{1}{4}}$ lb. burger
avec pommes frites
and a
473.176cc drink
$\$ \ln e^{3.99}$
I THINK THEY'VE FINALLY FOUND A WAY TO MAKE US STUDY.
WE ALSO HAVE π/3 RADIANS PIZZA SLICES.
AMEND

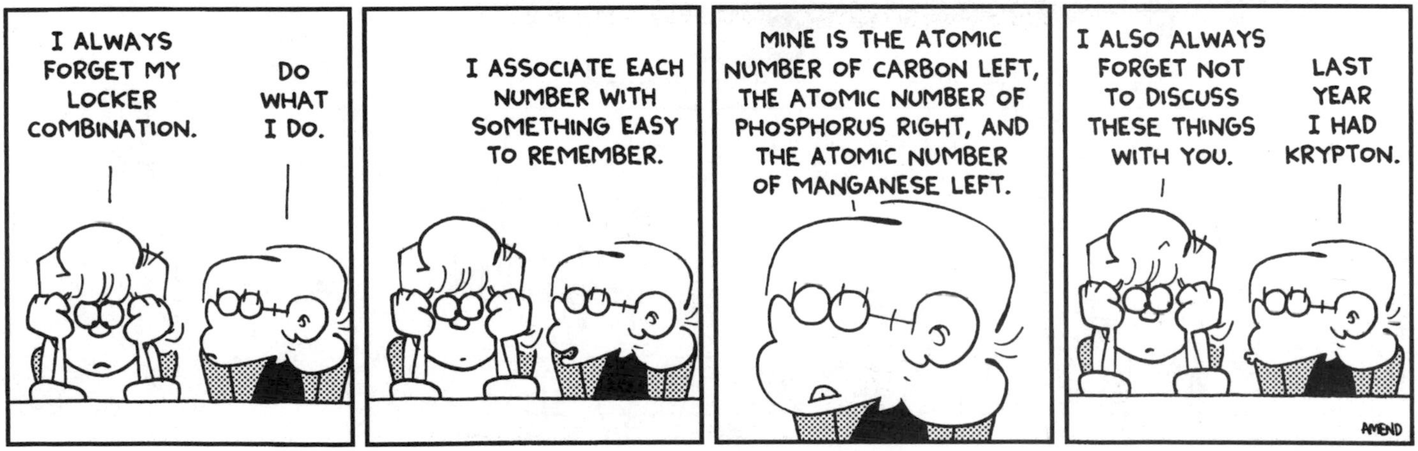
I ALWAYS FORGET MY LOCKER COMBINATION.
DO WHAT I DO.
I ASSOCIATE EACH NUMBER WITH SOMETHING EASY TO REMEMBER.
MINE IS THE ATOMIC NUMBER OF CARBON LEFT, THE ATOMIC NUMBER OF PHOSPHORUS RIGHT, AND THE ATOMIC NUMBER OF MANGANESE LEFT.
I ALSO ALWAYS FORGET NOT TO DISCUSS THESE THINGS WITH YOU.
LAST YEAR I HAD KRYPTON.
AMEND

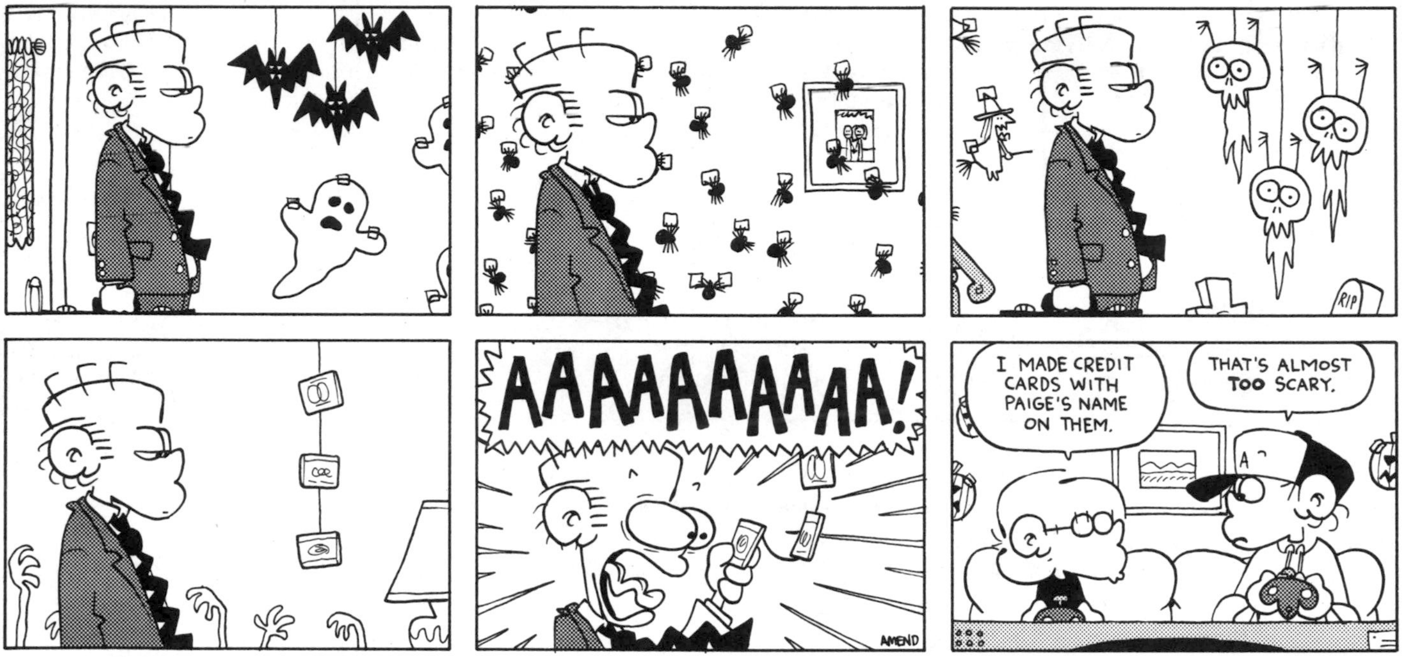
AAAAAAAAAA!
I MADE CREDIT CARDS WITH PAIGE'S NAME ON THEM.
THAT'S ALMOST **TOO** SCARY.
RIP
AMEND

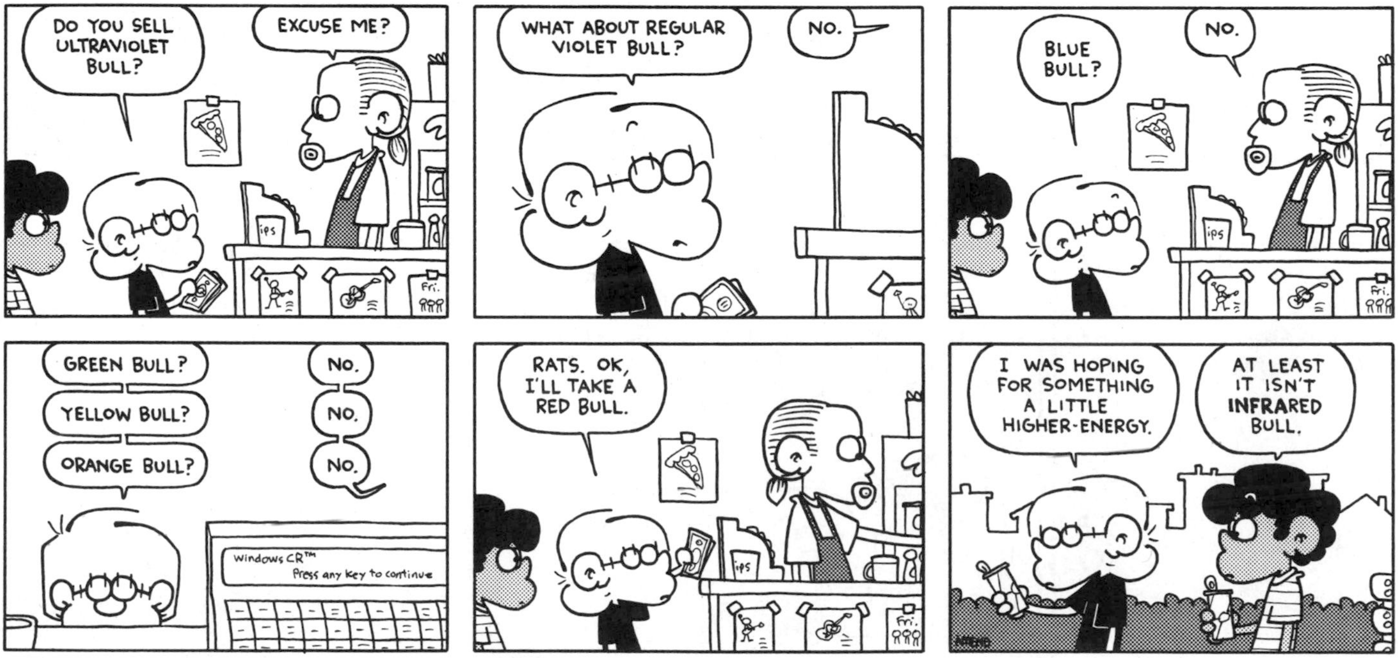
DO YOU SELL ULTRAVIOLET BULL?
EXCUSE ME?
WHAT ABOUT REGULAR VIOLET BULL?
NO.
BLUE BULL?
NO.
GREEN BULL?
NO.
YELLOW BULL?
NO.
ORANGE BULL?
NO.
Windows CR™
Press any key to continue
RATS. OK, I'LL TAKE A RED BULL.
I WAS HOPING FOR SOMETHING A LITTLE HIGHER-ENERGY.
AT LEAST IT ISN'T **INFRARED** BULL.

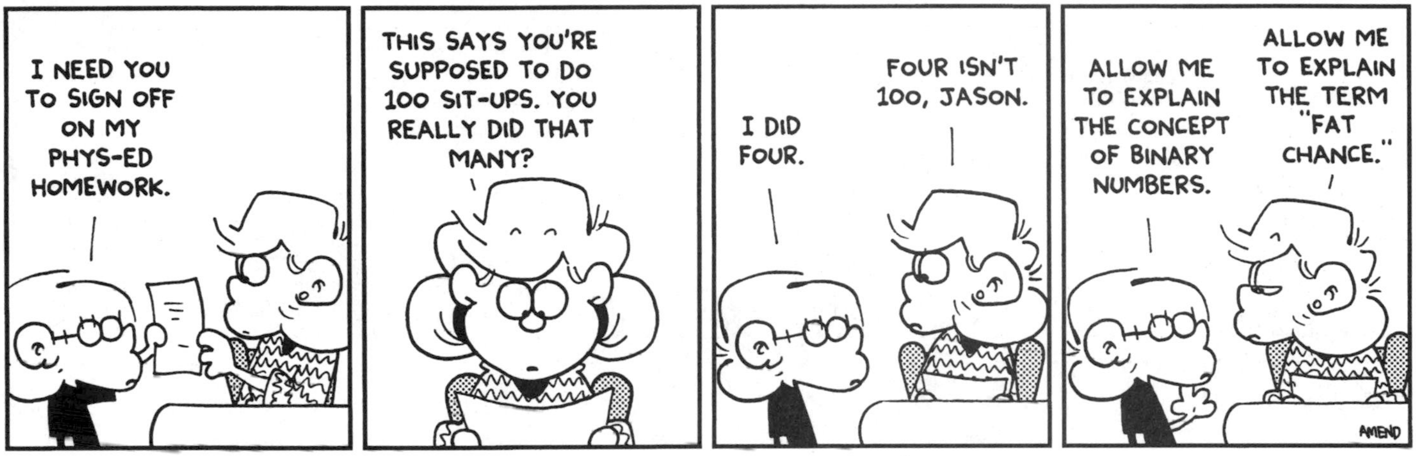
I NEED YOU TO SIGN OFF ON MY PHYS-ED HOMEWORK.
THIS SAYS YOU'RE SUPPOSED TO DO 100 SIT-UPS. YOU REALLY DID THAT MANY?
I DID FOUR.
FOUR ISN'T 100, JASON.
ALLOW ME TO EXPLAIN THE CONCEPT OF BINARY NUMBERS.
ALLOW ME TO EXPLAIN THE TERM "FAT CHANCE."
AMEND

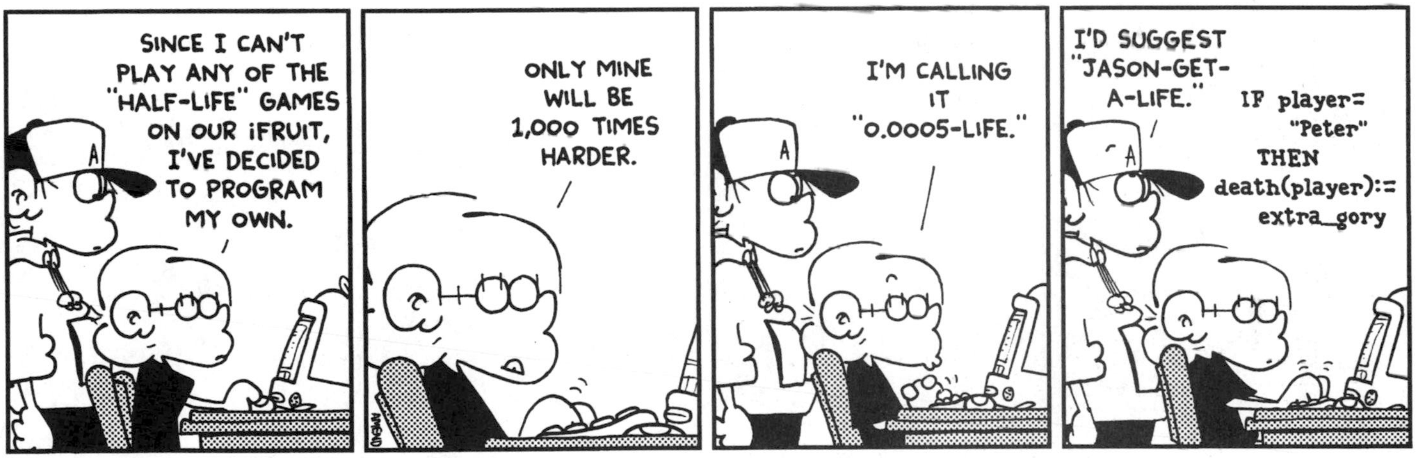
SINCE I CAN'T PLAY ANY OF THE "HALF-LIFE" GAMES ON OUR iFRUIT, I'VE DECIDED TO PROGRAM MY OWN.
ONLY MINE WILL BE 1,000 TIMES HARDER.
I'M CALLING IT "0.0005-LIFE."
I'D SUGGEST "JASON-GET-A-LIFE."
IF player= "Peter" THEN death(player):= extra_gory

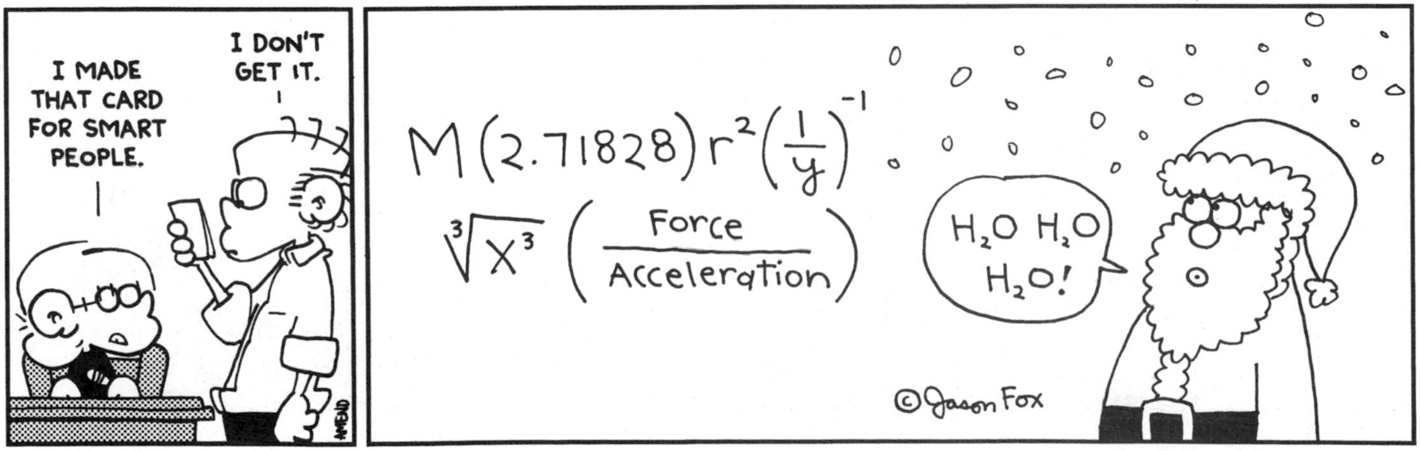
I MADE THAT CARD FOR SMART PEOPLE.
I DON'T GET IT.
AMEND
$M(2.71828)r^2\left(\frac{1}{y}\right)^{-1}$
$\sqrt[3]{X^3}\left(\frac{Force}{Acceleration}\right)$
H_2O H_2O H_2O!
©Jason Fox

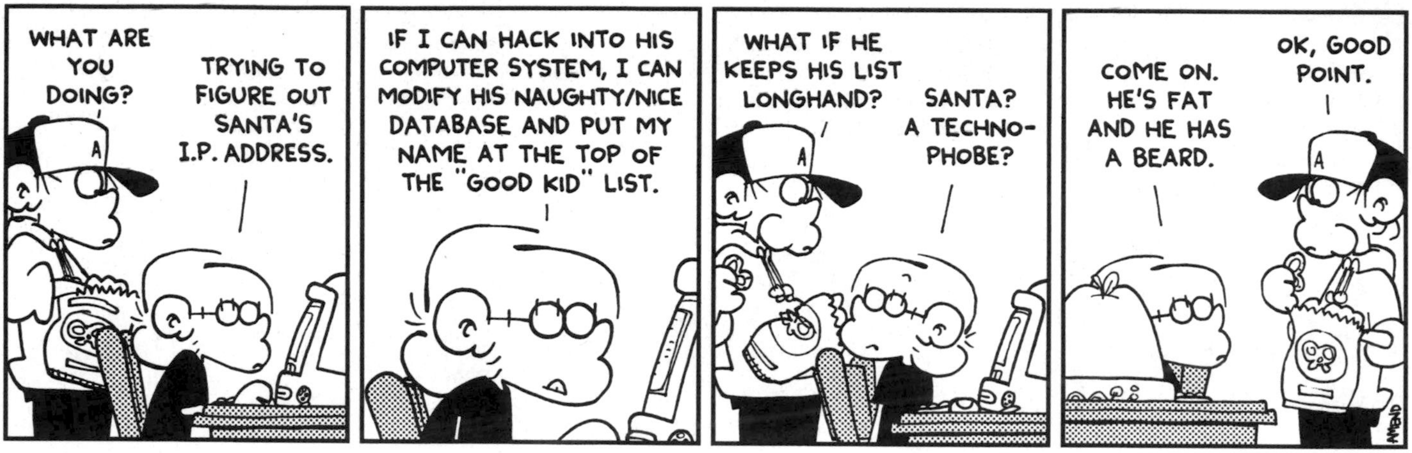
WHAT ARE YOU DOING?
TRYING TO FIGURE OUT SANTA'S I.P. ADDRESS.
IF I CAN HACK INTO HIS COMPUTER SYSTEM, I CAN MODIFY HIS NAUGHTY/NICE DATABASE AND PUT MY NAME AT THE TOP OF THE "GOOD KID" LIST.
WHAT IF HE KEEPS HIS LIST LONGHAND?
SANTA? A TECHNO-PHOBE?
COME ON. HE'S FAT AND HE HAS A BEARD.
OK, GOOD POINT.
AMEND

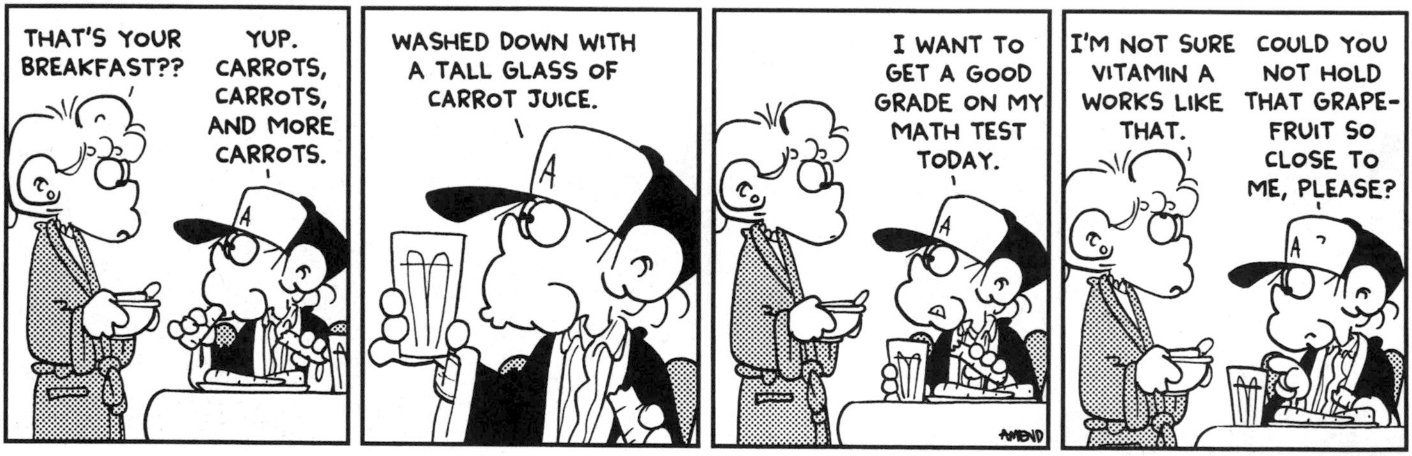
THAT'S YOUR BREAKFAST??
YUP. CARROTS, CARROTS, AND MORE CARROTS.
WASHED DOWN WITH A TALL GLASS OF CARROT JUICE.
I WANT TO GET A GOOD GRADE ON MY MATH TEST TODAY.
AMEND
I'M NOT SURE VITAMIN A WORKS LIKE THAT.
COULD YOU NOT HOLD THAT GRAPE-FRUIT SO CLOSE TO ME, PLEASE?

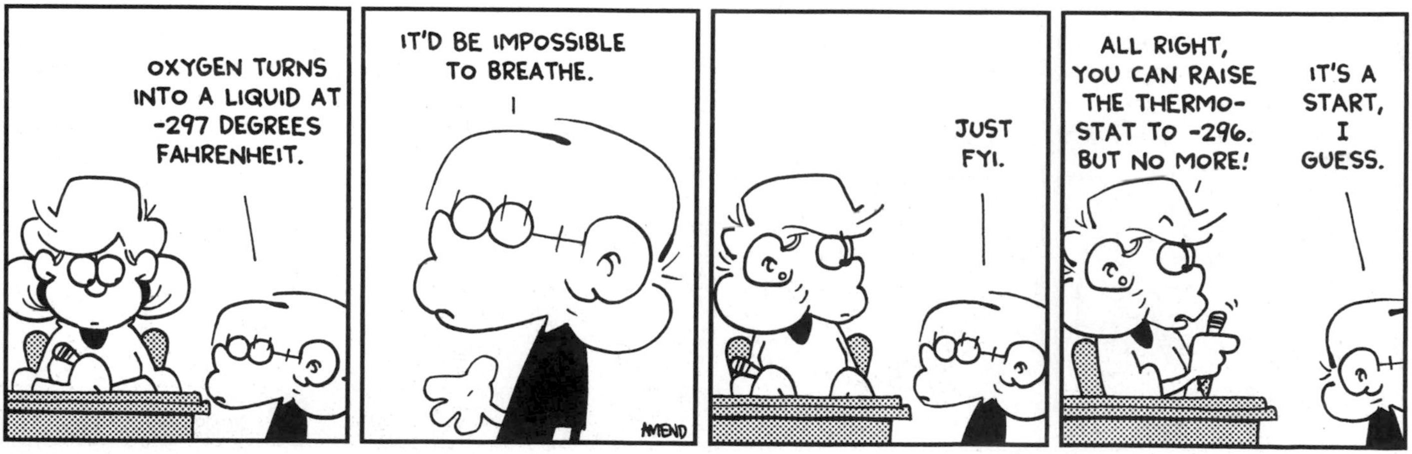
OXYGEN TURNS INTO A LIQUID AT -297 DEGREES FAHRENHEIT.
IT'D BE IMPOSSIBLE TO BREATHE.
AMEND
JUST FYI.
ALL RIGHT, YOU CAN RAISE THE THERMO-STAT TO -296. BUT NO MORE!
IT'S A START, I GUESS.

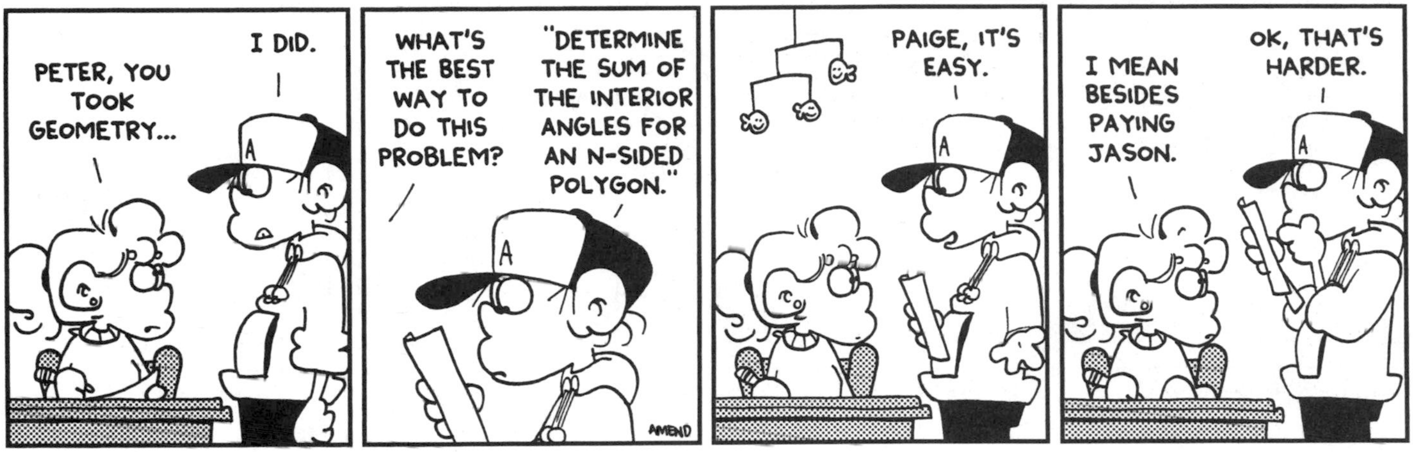
PETER, YOU TOOK GEOMETRY...
I DID.
WHAT'S THE BEST WAY TO DO THIS PROBLEM?
"DETERMINE THE SUM OF THE INTERIOR ANGLES FOR AN N-SIDED POLYGON."
PAIGE, IT'S EASY.
I MEAN BESIDES PAYING JASON.
OK, THAT'S HARDER.
AMEND

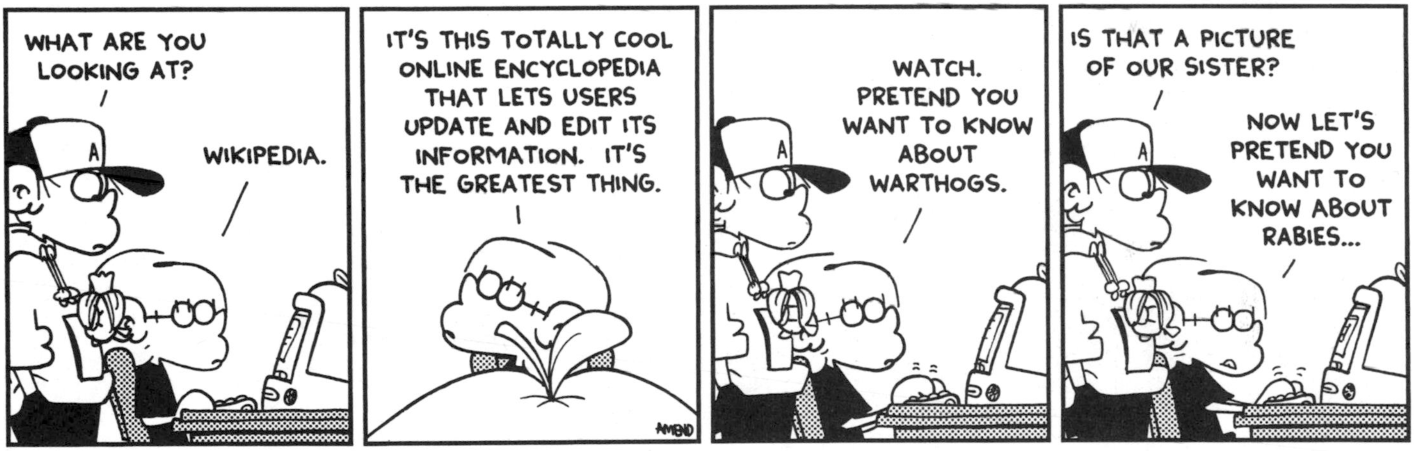
WHAT ARE YOU LOOKING AT?
WIKIPEDIA.
IT'S THIS TOTALLY COOL ONLINE ENCYCLOPEDIA THAT LETS USERS UPDATE AND EDIT ITS INFORMATION. IT'S THE GREATEST THING.
WATCH. PRETEND YOU WANT TO KNOW ABOUT WARTHOGS.
IS THAT A PICTURE OF OUR SISTER?
NOW LET'S PRETEND YOU WANT TO KNOW ABOUT RABIES...
AMEND

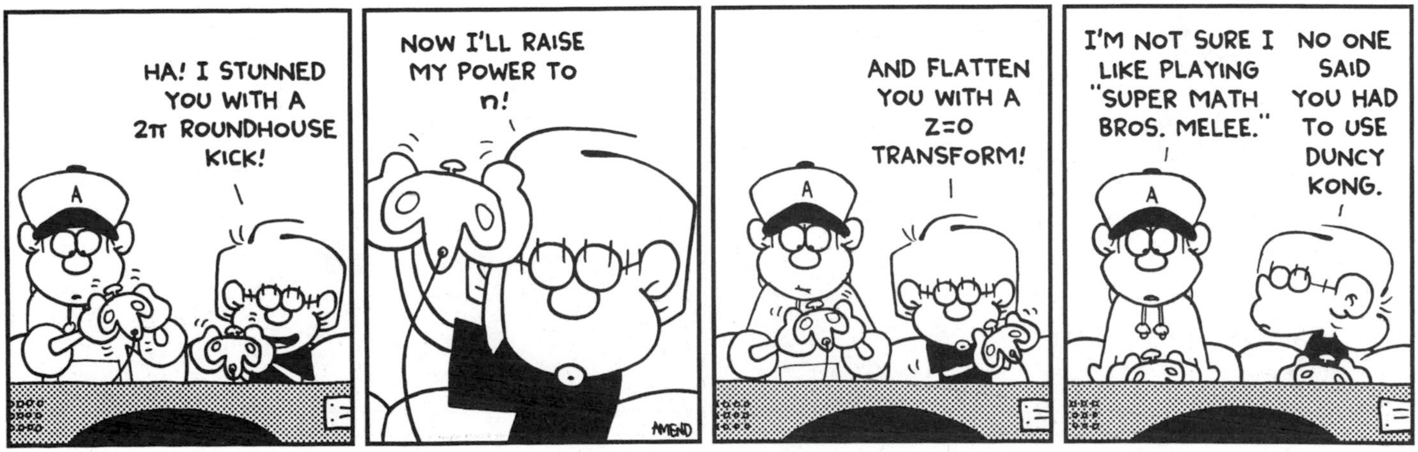
HA! I STUNNED YOU WITH A 2π ROUNDHOUSE KICK!
NOW I'LL RAISE MY POWER TO n!
AND FLATTEN YOU WITH A Z=0 TRANSFORM!
I'M NOT SURE I LIKE PLAYING "SUPER MATH BROS. MELEE."
NO ONE SAID YOU HAD TO USE DUNCY KONG.
AMEND

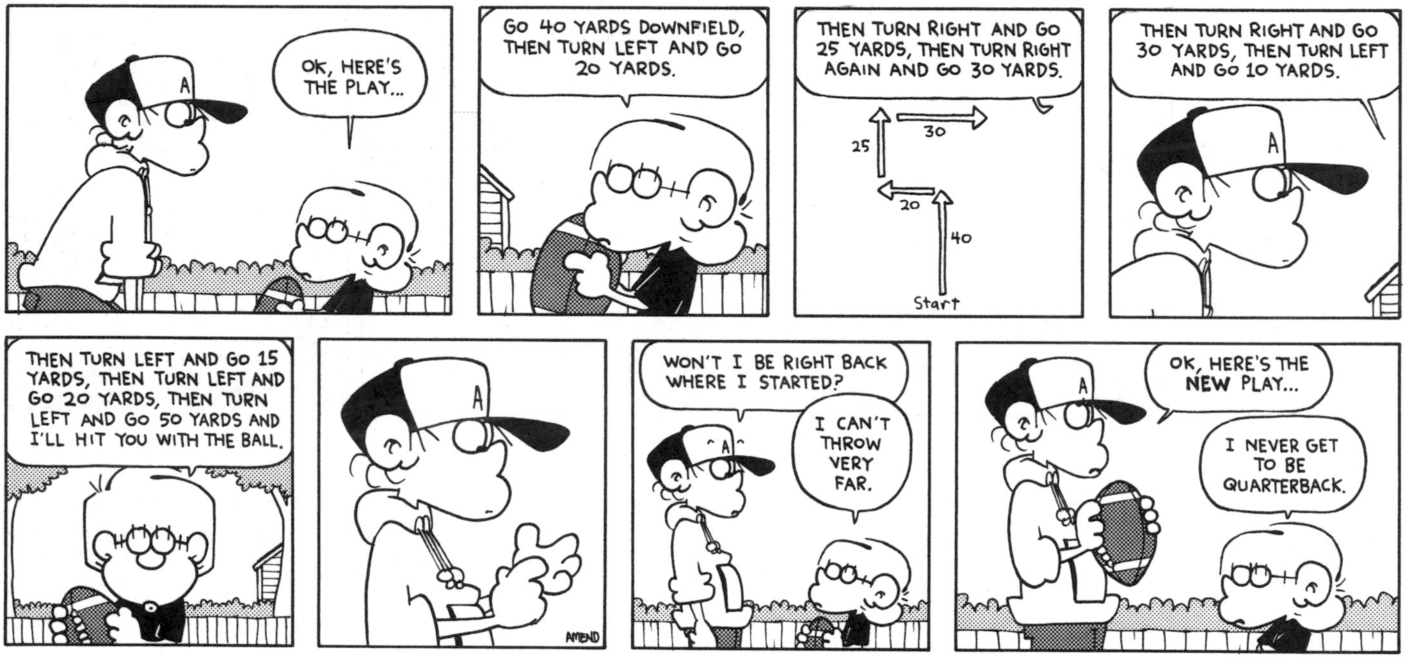
OK, HERE'S THE PLAY...
GO 40 YARDS DOWNFIELD, THEN TURN LEFT AND GO 20 YARDS.
THEN TURN RIGHT AND GO 25 YARDS, THEN TURN RIGHT AGAIN AND GO 30 YARDS.
30
25
20
40
Start
THEN TURN RIGHT AND GO 30 YARDS, THEN TURN LEFT AND GO 10 YARDS.
THEN TURN LEFT AND GO 15 YARDS, THEN TURN LEFT AND GO 20 YARDS, THEN TURN LEFT AND GO 50 YARDS AND I'LL HIT YOU WITH THE BALL.
AMEND
WON'T I BE RIGHT BACK WHERE I STARTED?
I CAN'T THROW VERY FAR.
OK, HERE'S THE NEW PLAY...
I NEVER GET TO BE QUARTERBACK.

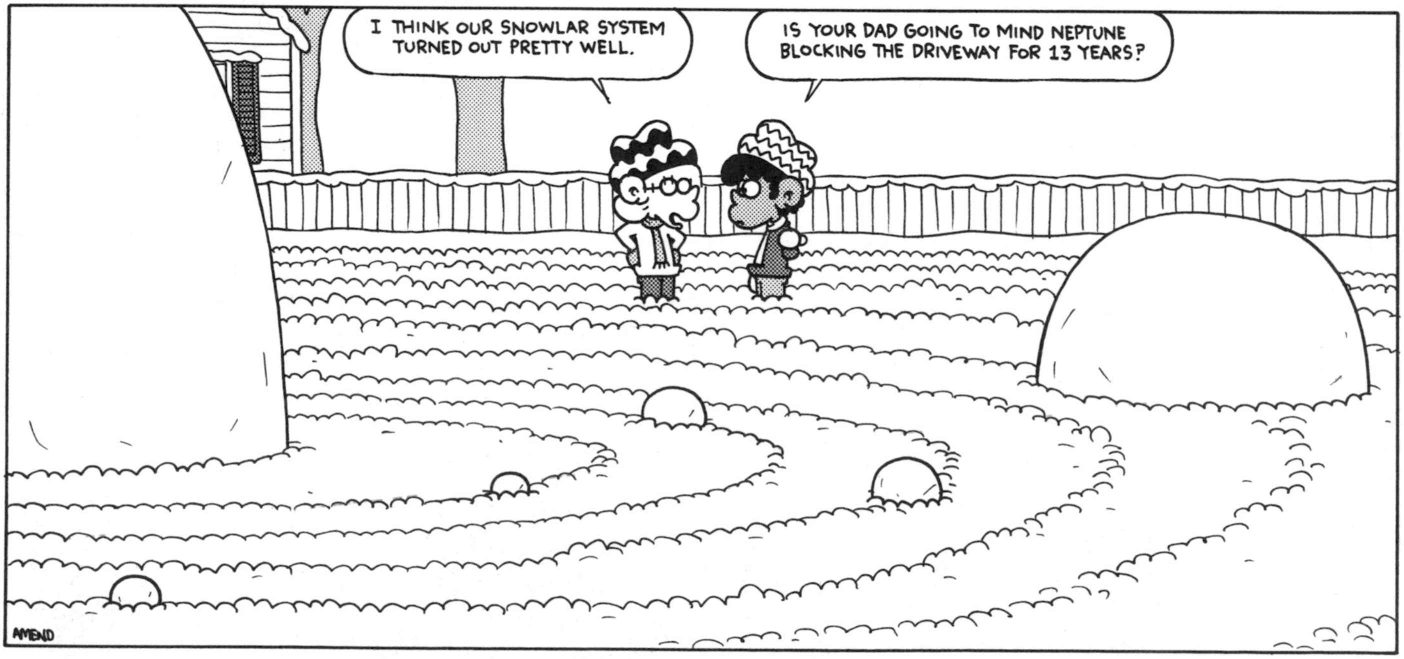
I THINK OUR SNOWLAR SYSTEM TURNED OUT PRETTY WELL.
IS YOUR DAD GOING TO MIND NEPTUNE BLOCKING THE DRIVEWAY FOR 13 YEARS?
AMEND

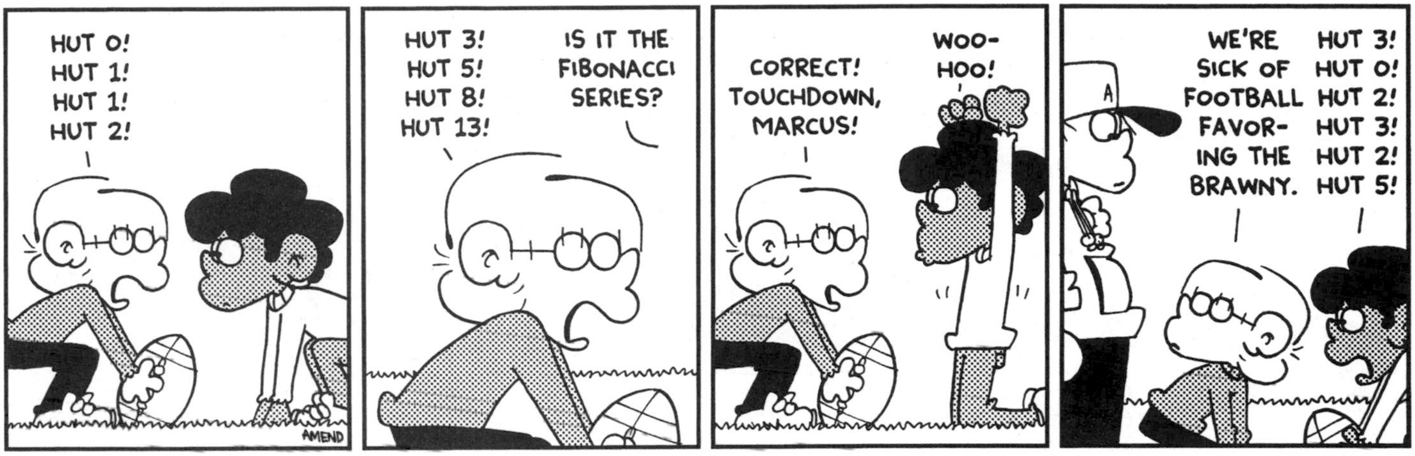
HUT 0!
HUT 1!
HUT 1!
HUT 2!
HUT 3!
HUT 5!
HUT 8!
HUT 13!
IS IT THE FIBONACCI SERIES?
CORRECT! TOUCHDOWN, MARCUS!
WOO-HOO!
WE'RE SICK OF FOOTBALL FAVORING THE BRAWNY.
HUT 3! HUT 0! HUT 2! HUT 3! HUT 2! HUT 5!
AMEND

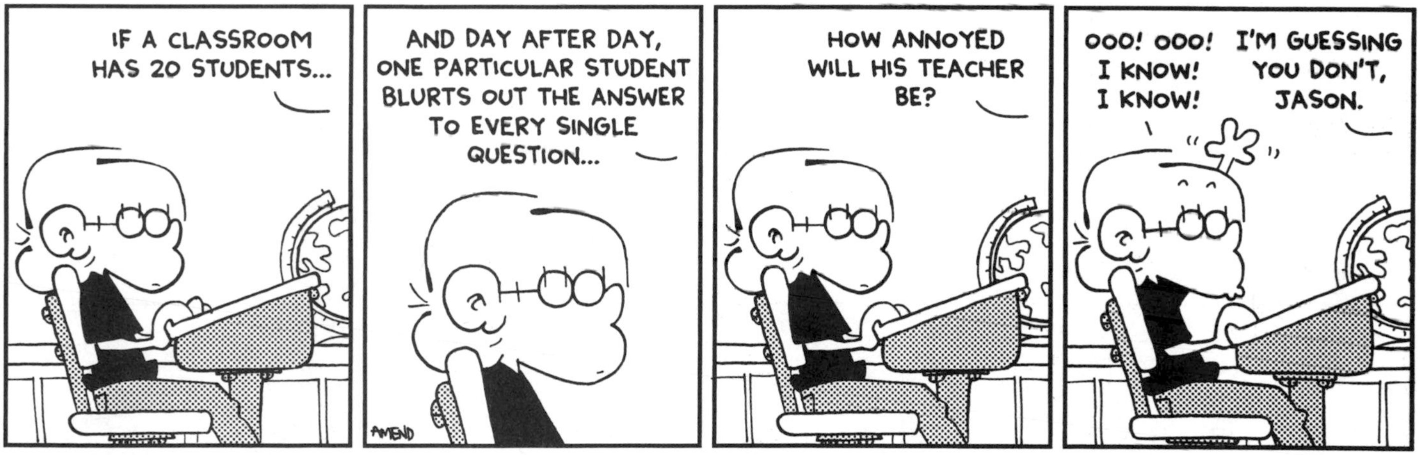
IF A CLASSROOM HAS 20 STUDENTS...
AND DAY AFTER DAY, ONE PARTICULAR STUDENT BLURTS OUT THE ANSWER TO EVERY SINGLE QUESTION...
AMEND
HOW ANNOYED WILL HIS TEACHER BE?
OOO! OOO! I KNOW! I KNOW!
I'M GUESSING YOU DON'T, JASON.

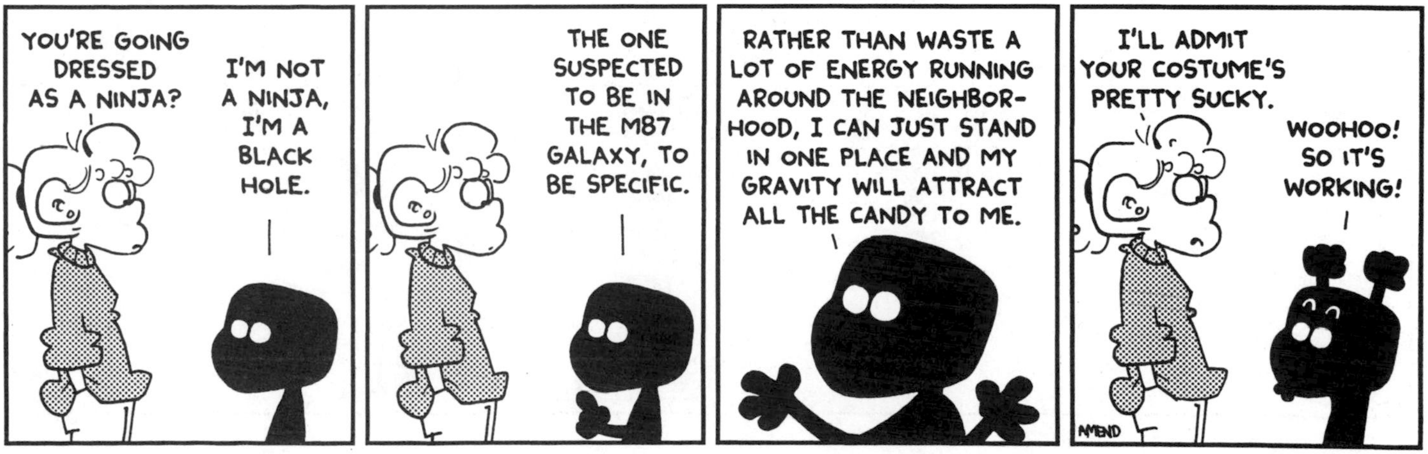
YOU'RE GOING DRESSED AS A NINJA?
I'M NOT A NINJA, I'M A BLACK HOLE.
THE ONE SUSPECTED TO BE IN THE M87 GALAXY, TO BE SPECIFIC.
RATHER THAN WASTE A LOT OF ENERGY RUNNING AROUND THE NEIGHBORHOOD, I CAN JUST STAND IN ONE PLACE AND MY GRAVITY WILL ATTRACT ALL THE CANDY TO ME.
I'LL ADMIT YOUR COSTUME'S PRETTY SUCKY.
WOOHOO! SO IT'S WORKING!
AMEND

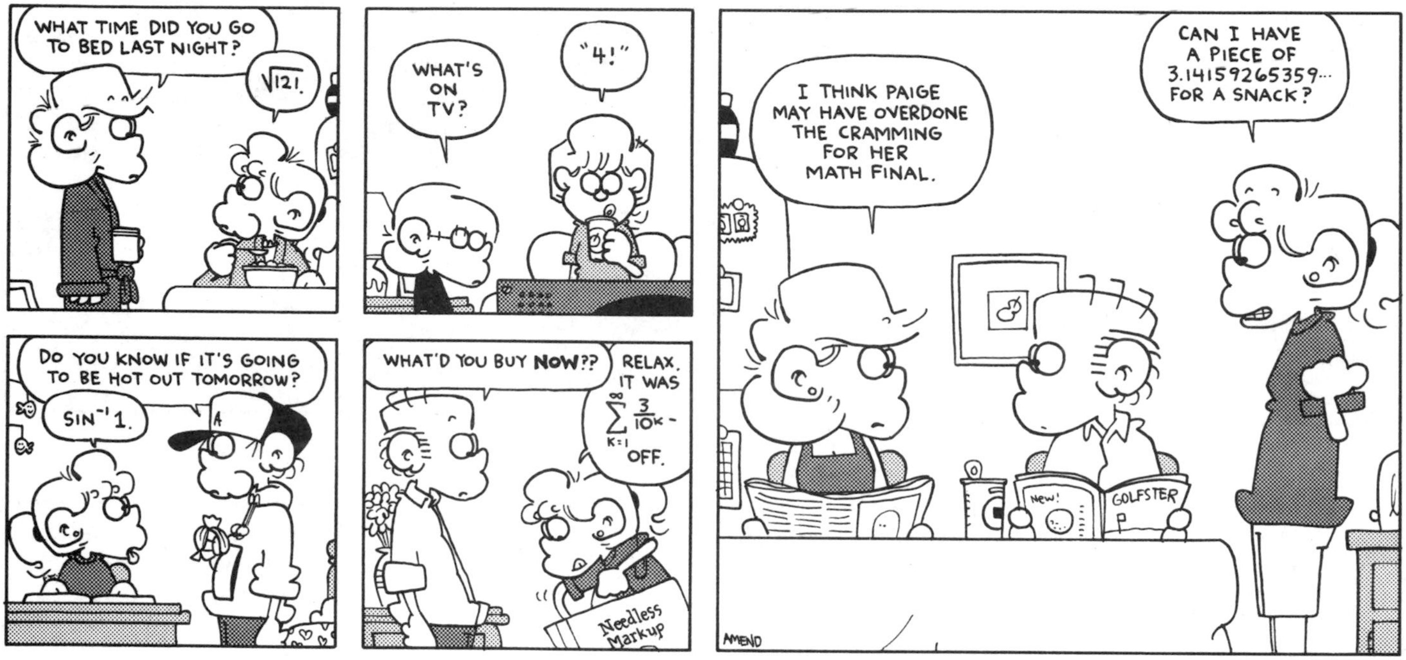
WHAT TIME DID YOU GO TO BED LAST NIGHT?
$\sqrt{121}$.
WHAT'S ON TV?
"4!"
DO YOU KNOW IF IT'S GOING TO BE HOT OUT TOMORROW?
$SIN^{-1}1$.
WHAT'D YOU BUY **NOW**??
RELAX. IT WAS $\sum_{K=1}^{\infty} \frac{3}{10^K}$ OFF.
Needless Markup
I THINK PAIGE MAY HAVE OVERDONE THE CRAMMING FOR HER MATH FINAL.
CAN I HAVE A PIECE OF 3.14159265359... FOR A SNACK?
New!
GOLFSTER
AMEND

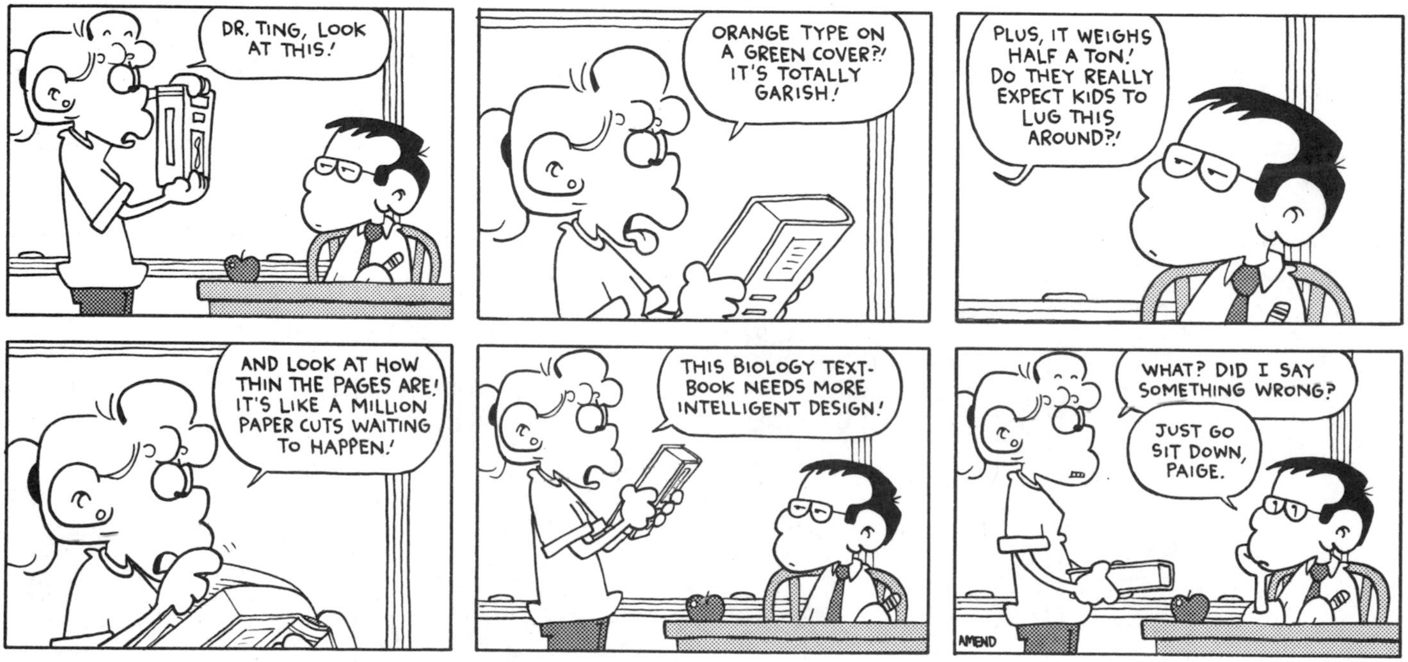
DR. TING, LOOK AT THIS!
ORANGE TYPE ON A GREEN COVER?! IT'S TOTALLY GARISH!
PLUS, IT WEIGHS HALF A TON! DO THEY REALLY EXPECT KIDS TO LUG THIS AROUND?!
AND LOOK AT HOW THIN THE PAGES ARE! IT'S LIKE A MILLION PAPER CUTS WAITING TO HAPPEN!
THIS BIOLOGY TEXT-BOOK NEEDS MORE INTELLIGENT DESIGN!
WHAT? DID I SAY SOMETHING WRONG?
JUST GO SIT DOWN, PAIGE.
AMEND

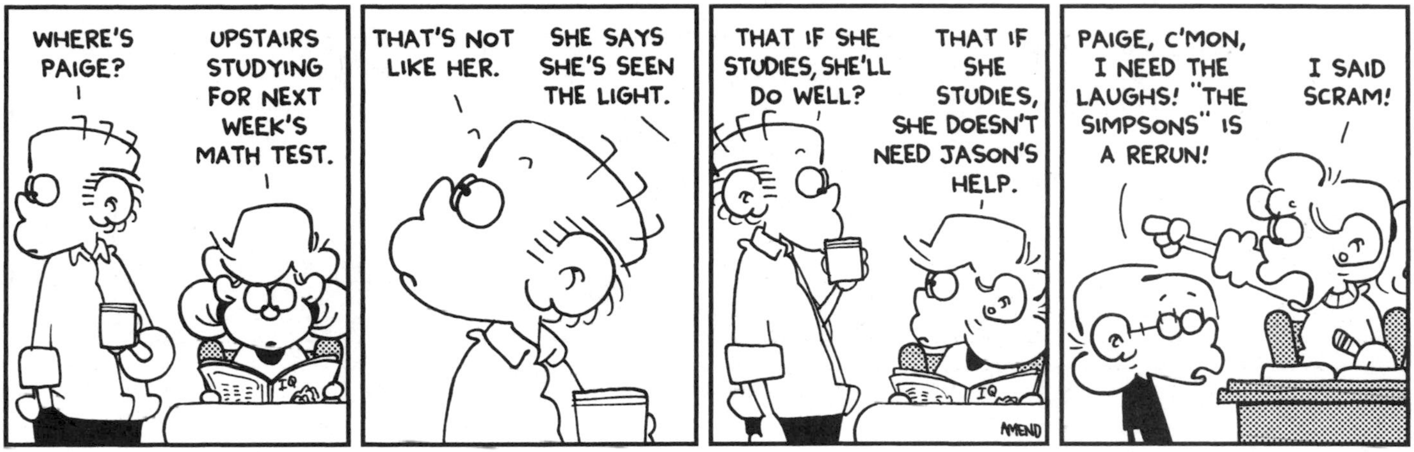
WHERE'S PAIGE?
UPSTAIRS STUDYING FOR NEXT WEEK'S MATH TEST.
THAT'S NOT LIKE HER.
SHE SAYS SHE'S SEEN THE LIGHT.
THAT IF SHE STUDIES, SHE'LL DO WELL?
THAT IF SHE STUDIES, SHE DOESN'T NEED JASON'S HELP.
PAIGE, C'MON, I NEED THE LAUGHS! "THE SIMPSONS" IS A RERUN!
I SAID SCRAM!
AMEND

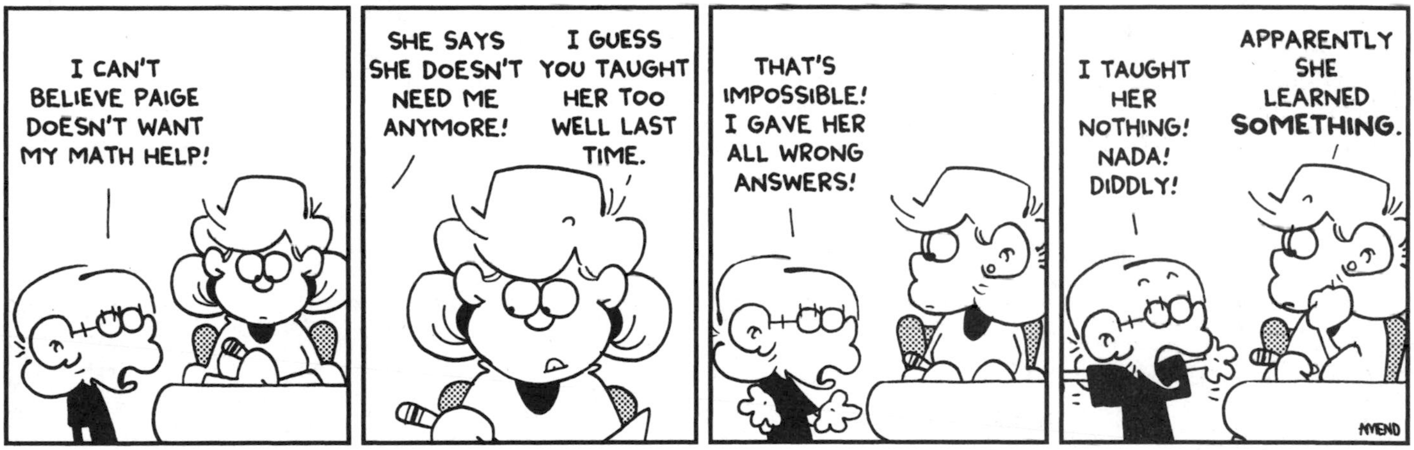
I CAN'T BELIEVE PAIGE DOESN'T WANT MY MATH HELP!
SHE SAYS SHE DOESN'T NEED ME ANYMORE!
I GUESS YOU TAUGHT HER TOO WELL LAST TIME.
THAT'S IMPOSSIBLE! I GAVE HER ALL WRONG ANSWERS!
I TAUGHT HER NOTHING! NADA! DIDDLY!
APPARENTLY SHE LEARNED **SOMETHING**.
AMEND

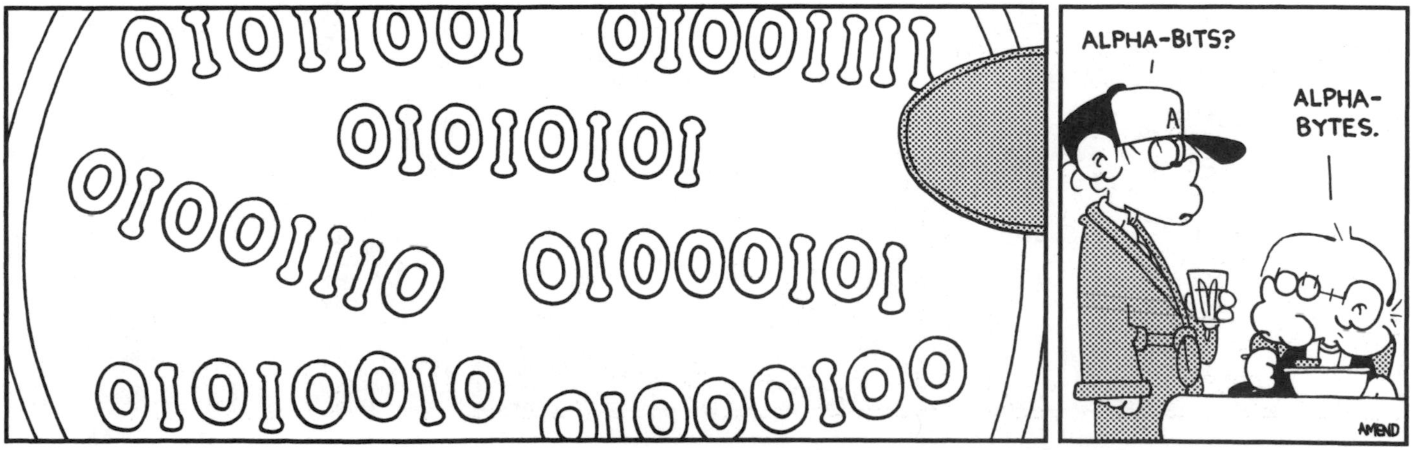
01011001 01001111
01010101
01001110 01000101
01010010 01000100
ALPHA-BITS?
ALPHA-BYTES.
AMEND

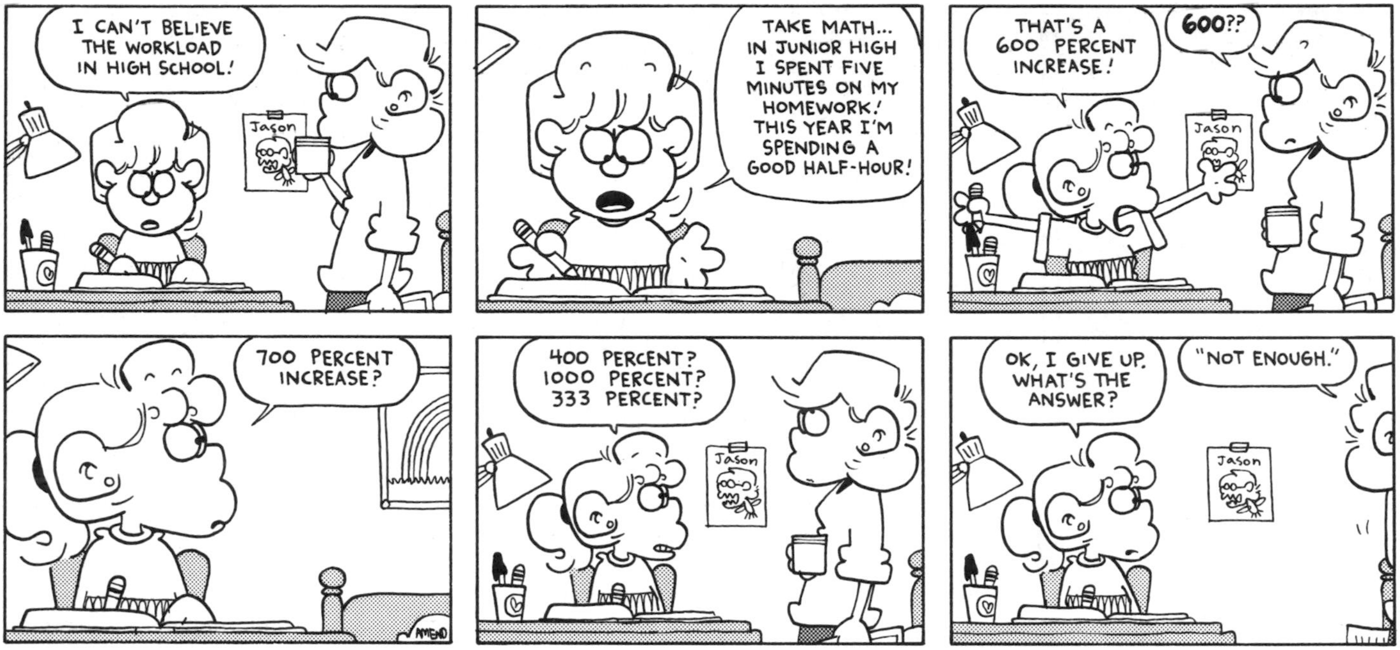
I CAN'T BELIEVE THE WORKLOAD IN HIGH SCHOOL!
Jason
TAKE MATH... IN JUNIOR HIGH I SPENT FIVE MINUTES ON MY HOMEWORK! THIS YEAR I'M SPENDING A GOOD HALF-HOUR!
THAT'S A 600 PERCENT INCREASE!
600??
Jason
700 PERCENT INCREASE?
400 PERCENT? 1000 PERCENT? 333 PERCENT?
Jason
OK, I GIVE UP. WHAT'S THE ANSWER?
"NOT ENOUGH."
Jason
AMEND

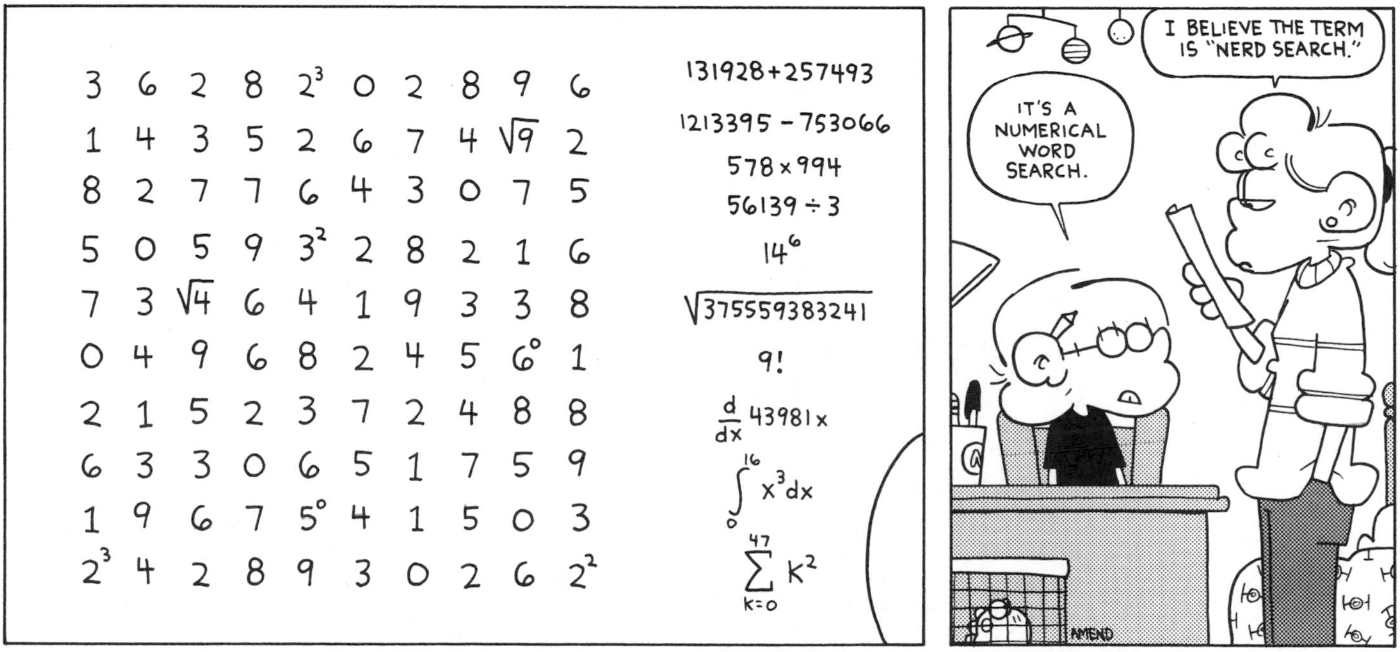
3 6 2 8 2^3 0 2 8 9 6
1 4 3 5 2 6 7 4 $\sqrt{9}$ 2
8 2 7 7 6 4 3 0 7 5
5 0 5 9 3^2 2 8 2 1 6
7 3 $\sqrt{4}$ 6 4 1 9 3 3 8
0 4 9 6 8 2 4 5 6^0 1
2 1 5 2 3 7 2 4 8 8
6 3 3 0 6 5 1 7 5 9
1 9 6 7 5^0 4 1 5 0 3
2^3 4 2 8 9 3 0 2 6 2^2
131928+257493
1213395 − 753066
578×994
56139÷3
14^6
$\sqrt{375559383241}$
9!
$\frac{d}{dx}43981x$
$\int_0^{16} x^3 dx$
$\sum_{k=0}^{47} K^2$
IT'S A NUMERICAL WORD SEARCH.
I BELIEVE THE TERM IS "NERD SEARCH."
AMEND

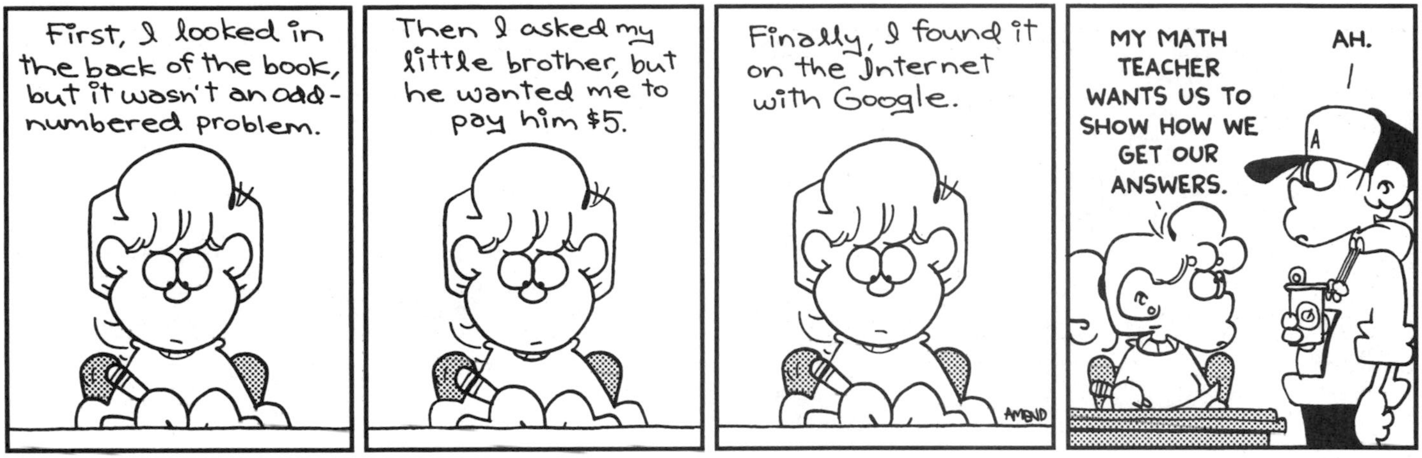
First, I looked in the back of the book, but it wasn't an odd-numbered problem.
Then I asked my little brother, but he wanted me to pay him $5.
Finally, I found it on the Internet with Google.
MY MATH TEACHER WANTS US TO SHOW HOW WE GET OUR ANSWERS.
AH.

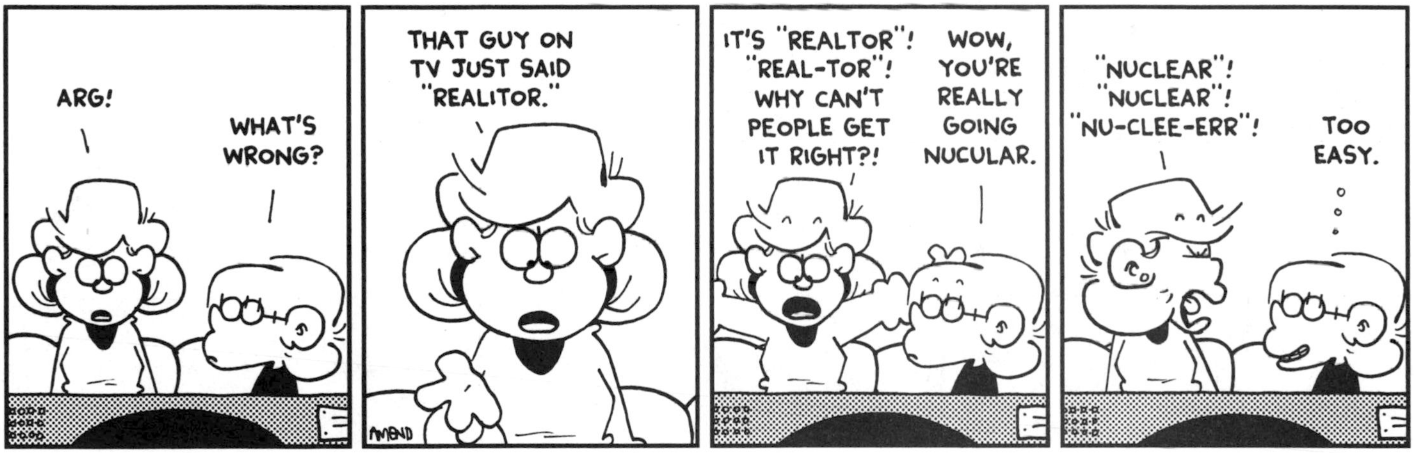
ARG!
WHAT'S WRONG?
THAT GUY ON TV JUST SAID "REALITOR."
IT'S "REALTOR"! "REAL-TOR"! WHY CAN'T PEOPLE GET IT RIGHT?!
WOW, YOU'RE REALLY GOING NUCULAR.
"NUCLEAR"! "NUCLEAR"! "NU-CLEE-ERR"!
TOO EASY.

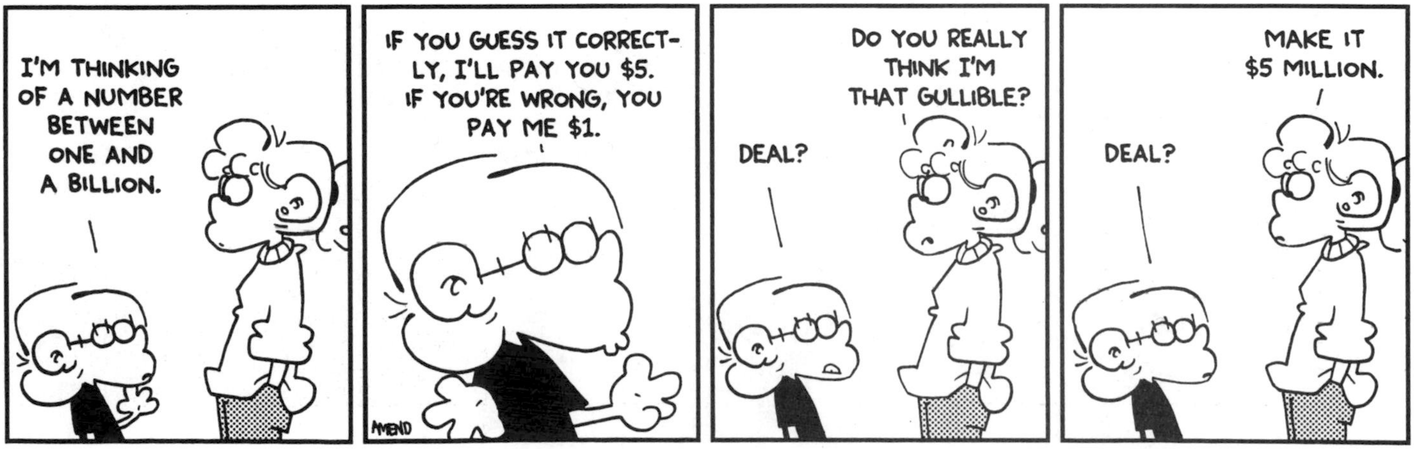
I'M THINKING OF A NUMBER BETWEEN ONE AND A BILLION.
IF YOU GUESS IT CORRECTLY, I'LL PAY YOU $5. IF YOU'RE WRONG, YOU PAY ME $1.
DEAL?
DO YOU REALLY THINK I'M THAT GULLIBLE?
DEAL?
MAKE IT $5 MILLION.

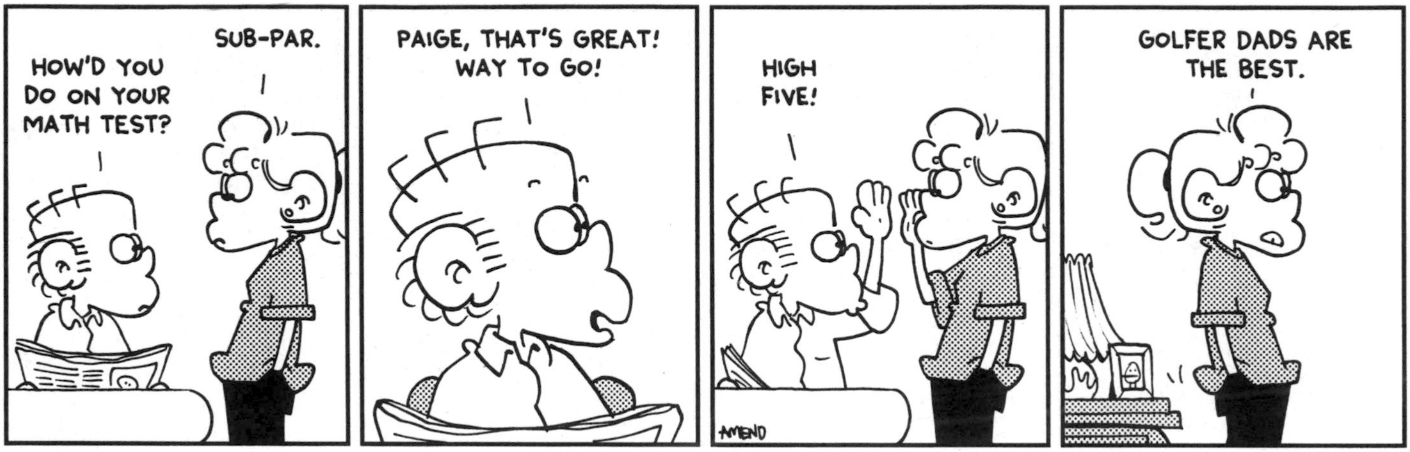
HOW'D YOU DO ON YOUR MATH TEST?
SUB-PAR.
PAIGE, THAT'S GREAT! WAY TO GO!
HIGH FIVE!
GOLFER DADS ARE THE BEST.
AMEND

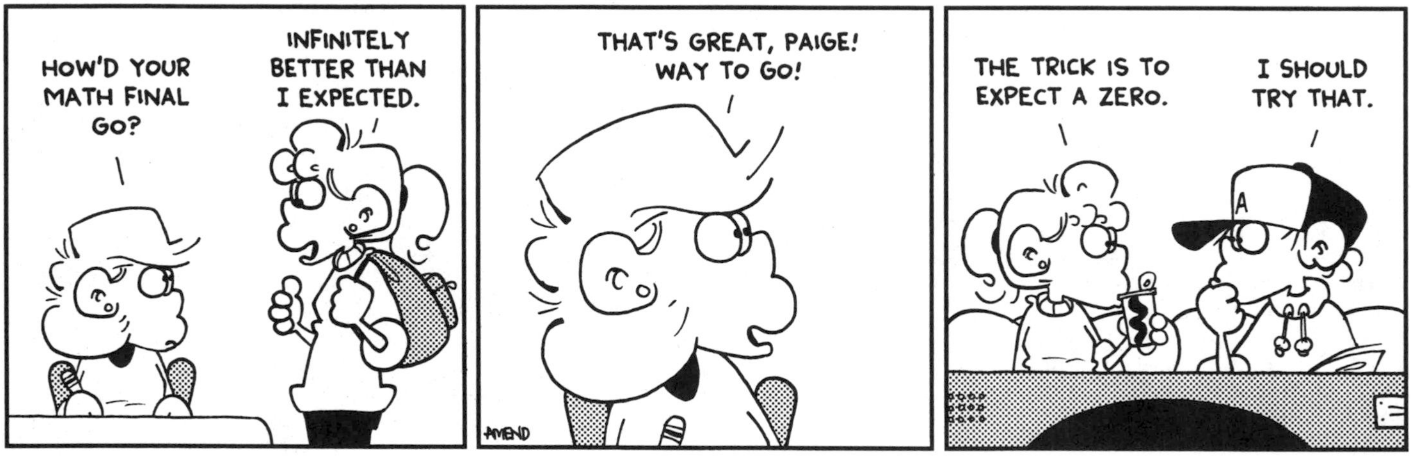
HOW'D YOUR MATH FINAL GO?
INFINITELY BETTER THAN I EXPECTED.
THAT'S GREAT, PAIGE! WAY TO GO!
THE TRICK IS TO EXPECT A ZERO.
I SHOULD TRY THAT.
AMEND

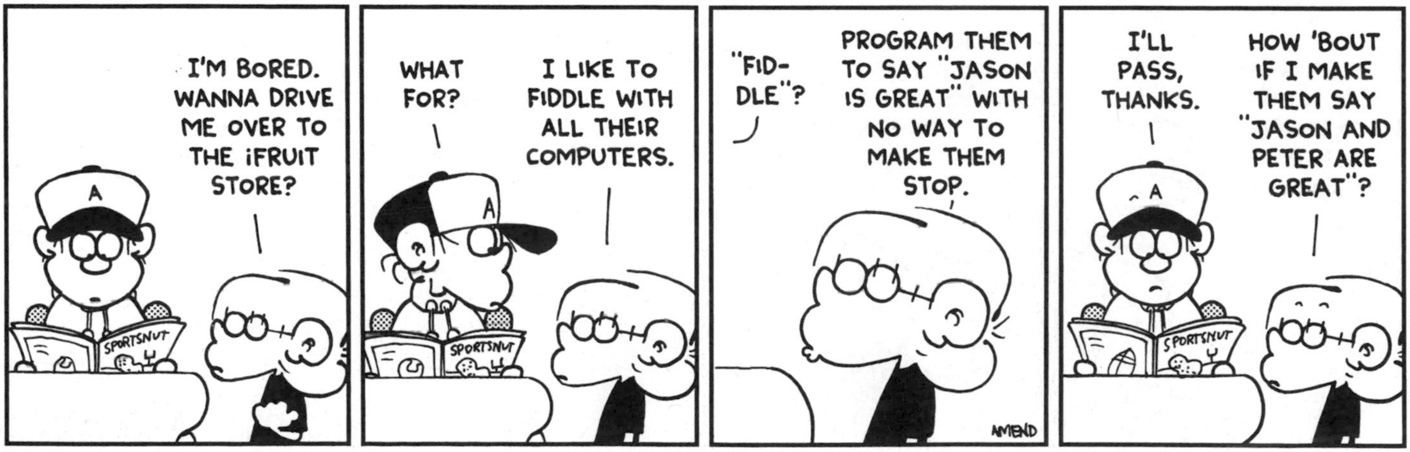
I'M BORED. WANNA DRIVE ME OVER TO THE iFRUIT STORE?
SPORTSNUT
WHAT FOR?
I LIKE TO FIDDLE WITH ALL THEIR COMPUTERS.
"FID-DLE"?
PROGRAM THEM TO SAY "JASON IS GREAT" WITH NO WAY TO MAKE THEM STOP.
I'LL PASS, THANKS.
HOW 'BOUT IF I MAKE THEM SAY "JASON AND PETER ARE GREAT"?
AMEND

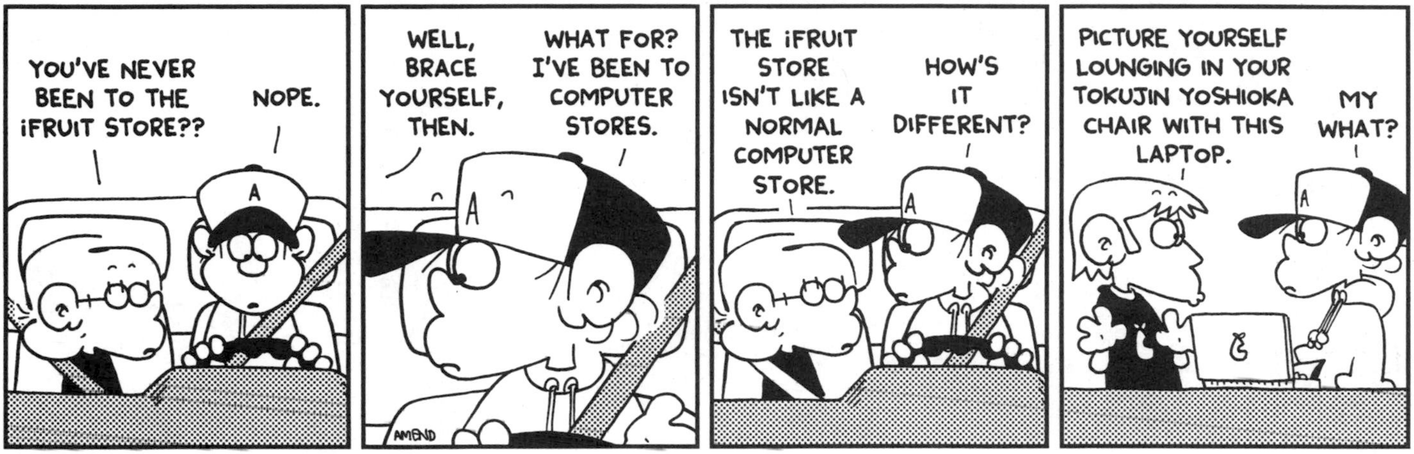
YOU'VE NEVER BEEN TO THE iFRUIT STORE??
NOPE.
WELL, BRACE YOURSELF, THEN.
WHAT FOR? I'VE BEEN TO COMPUTER STORES.
THE iFRUIT STORE ISN'T LIKE A NORMAL COMPUTER STORE.
HOW'S IT DIFFERENT?
PICTURE YOURSELF LOUNGING IN YOUR TOKUJIN YOSHIOKA CHAIR WITH THIS LAPTOP.
MY WHAT?
AMEND

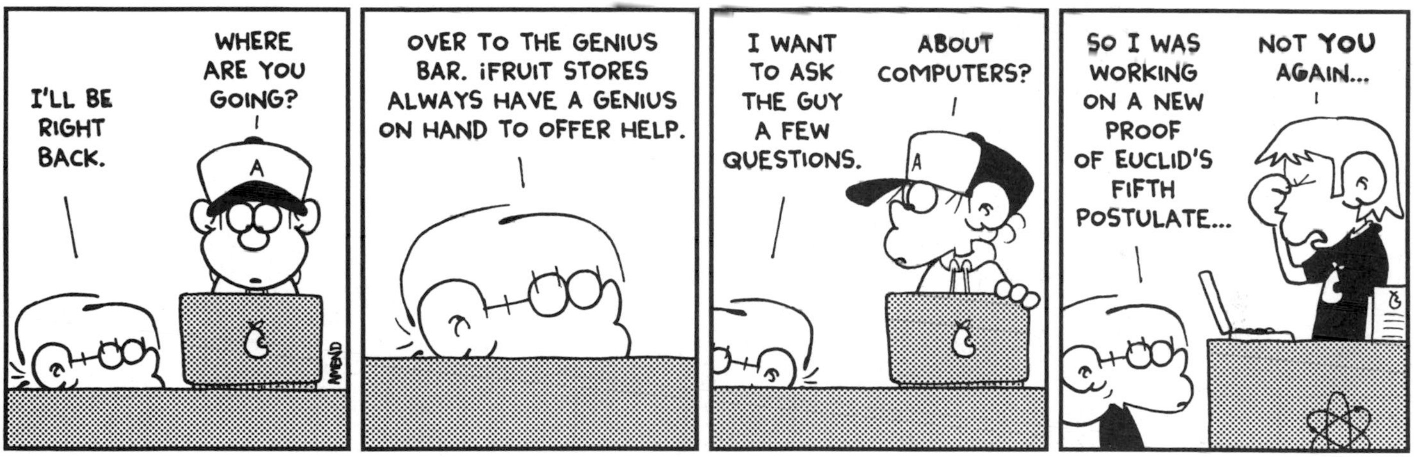
I'LL BE RIGHT BACK.
WHERE ARE YOU GOING?
AMEND
OVER TO THE GENIUS BAR. iFRUIT STORES ALWAYS HAVE A GENIUS ON HAND TO OFFER HELP.
I WANT TO ASK THE GUY A FEW QUESTIONS.
ABOUT COMPUTERS?
SO I WAS WORKING ON A NEW PROOF OF EUCLID'S FIFTH POSTULATE...
NOT YOU AGAIN...

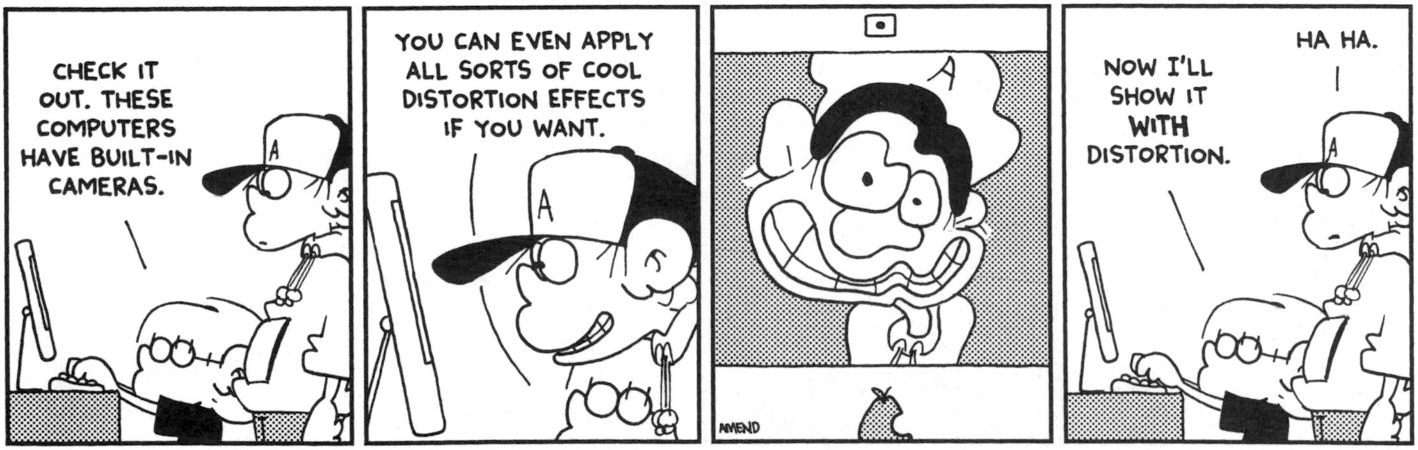
CHECK IT OUT. THESE COMPUTERS HAVE BUILT-IN CAMERAS.
YOU CAN EVEN APPLY ALL SORTS OF COOL DISTORTION EFFECTS IF YOU WANT.
AMEND
NOW I'LL SHOW IT WITH DISTORTION.
HA HA.

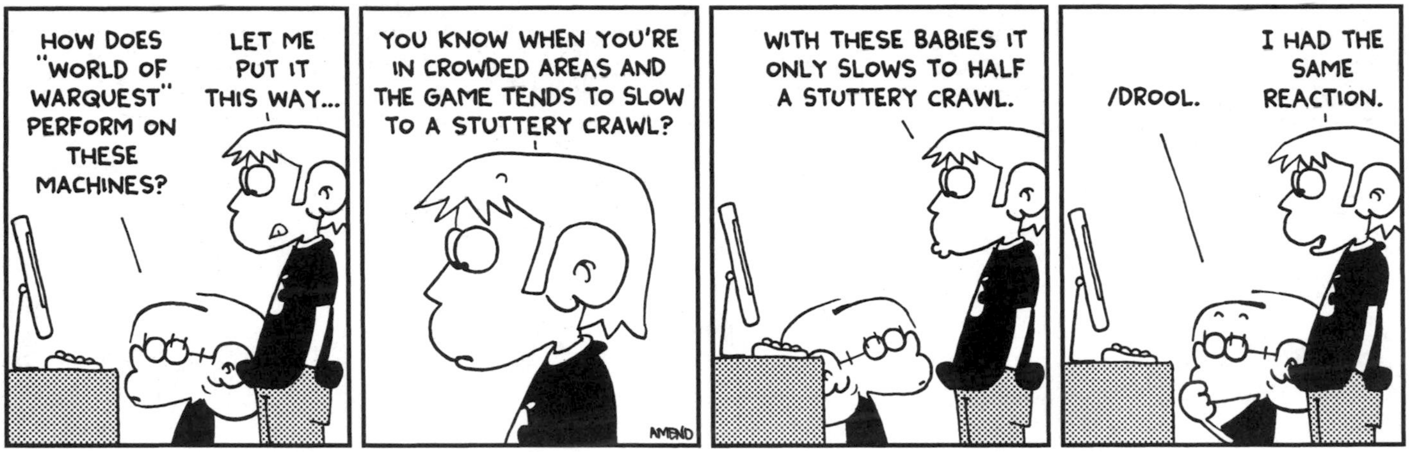
HOW DOES "WORLD OF WARQUEST" PERFORM ON THESE MACHINES?
LET ME PUT IT THIS WAY...
YOU KNOW WHEN YOU'RE IN CROWDED AREAS AND THE GAME TENDS TO SLOW TO A STUTTERY CRAWL?
WITH THESE BABIES IT ONLY SLOWS TO HALF A STUTTERY CRAWL.
/DROOL.
I HAD THE SAME REACTION.

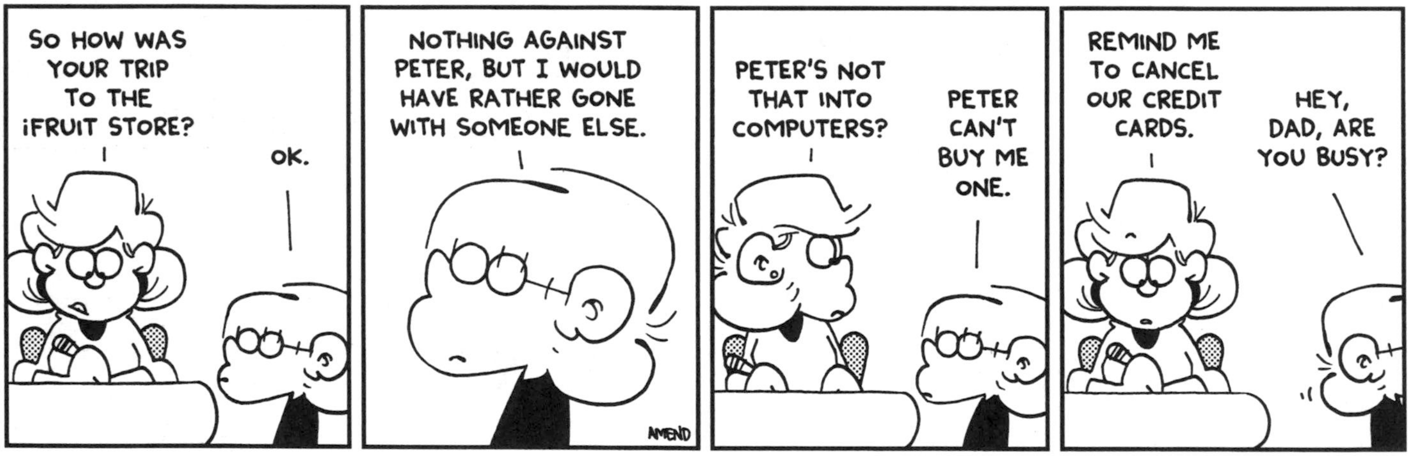
SO HOW WAS YOUR TRIP TO THE iFRUIT STORE?
OK.
NOTHING AGAINST PETER, BUT I WOULD HAVE RATHER GONE WITH SOMEONE ELSE.
PETER'S NOT THAT INTO COMPUTERS?
PETER CAN'T BUY ME ONE.
REMIND ME TO CANCEL OUR CREDIT CARDS.
HEY, DAD, ARE YOU BUSY?

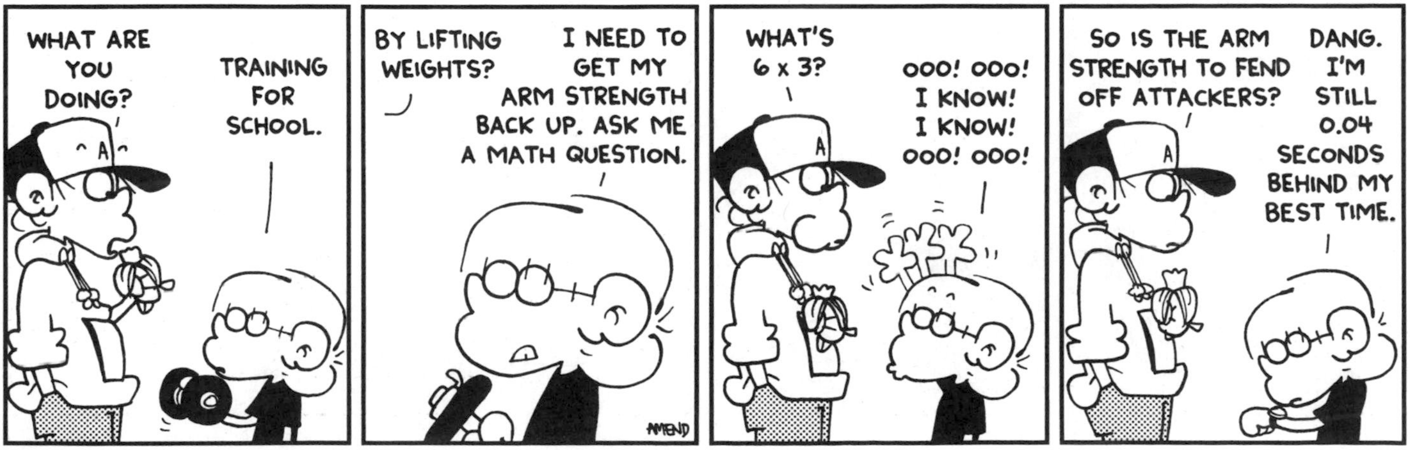
WHAT ARE YOU DOING?
TRAINING FOR SCHOOL.
BY LIFTING WEIGHTS?
I NEED TO GET MY ARM STRENGTH BACK UP. ASK ME A MATH QUESTION.
WHAT'S 6 x 3?
OOO! OOO! I KNOW! I KNOW! OOO! OOO!
SO IS THE ARM STRENGTH TO FEND OFF ATTACKERS?
DANG. I'M STILL 0.04 SECONDS BEHIND MY BEST TIME.

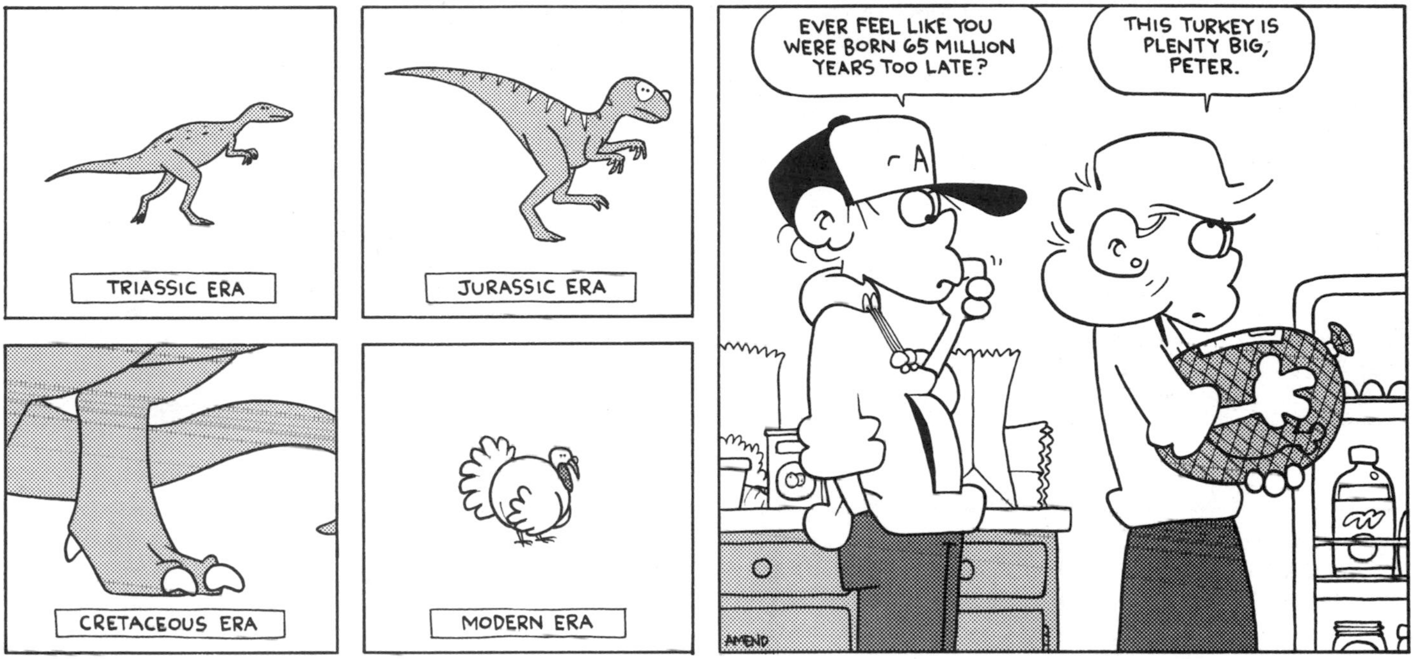
TRIASSIC ERA
JURASSIC ERA
CRETACEOUS ERA
MODERN ERA
EVER FEEL LIKE YOU WERE BORN 65 MILLION YEARS TOO LATE?
THIS TURKEY IS PLENTY BIG, PETER.
AMEND

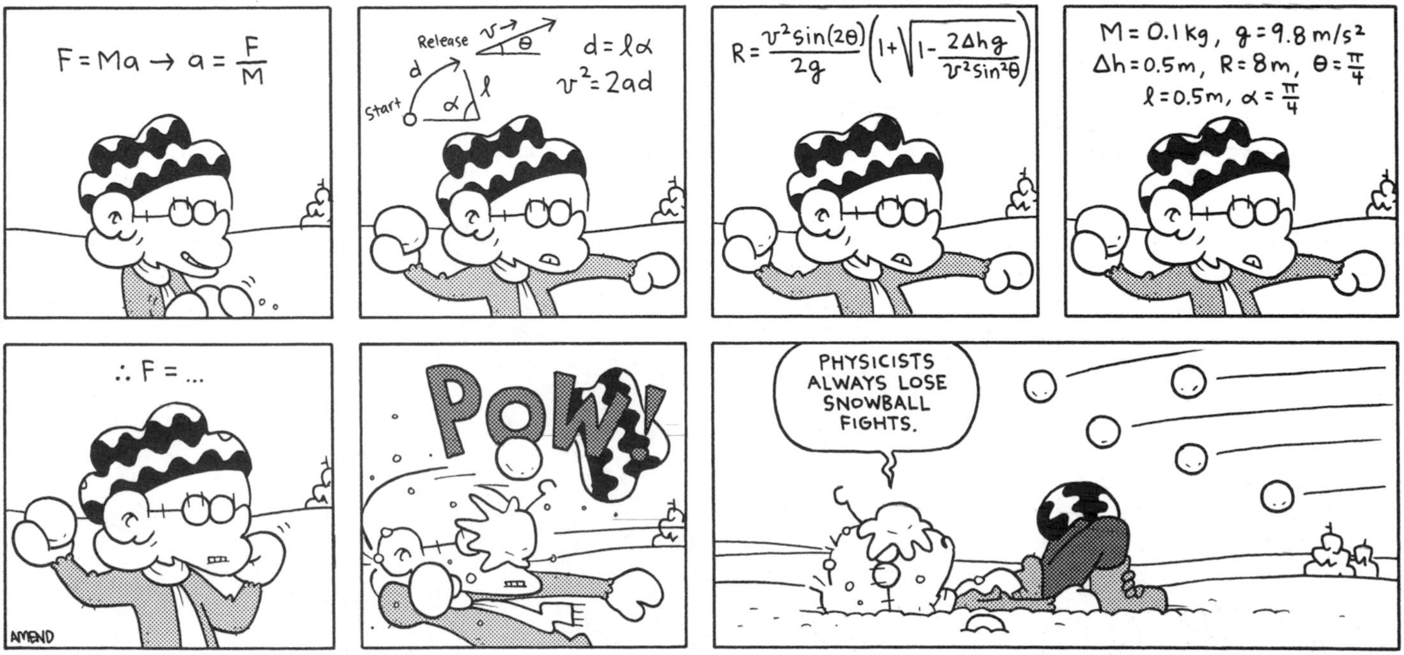
F = Ma → a = F/M
Release
Start
d = ℓα
v² = 2ad
R = v² sin(2θ)/2g (1 + √(1 − 2Δhg/v² sin²θ))
M = 0.1 kg, g = 9.8 m/s²
Δh = 0.5 m, R = 8 m, θ = π/4
ℓ = 0.5 m, α = π/4
∴ F = ...
POW!
PHYSICISTS ALWAYS LOSE SNOWBALL FIGHTS.
AMEND

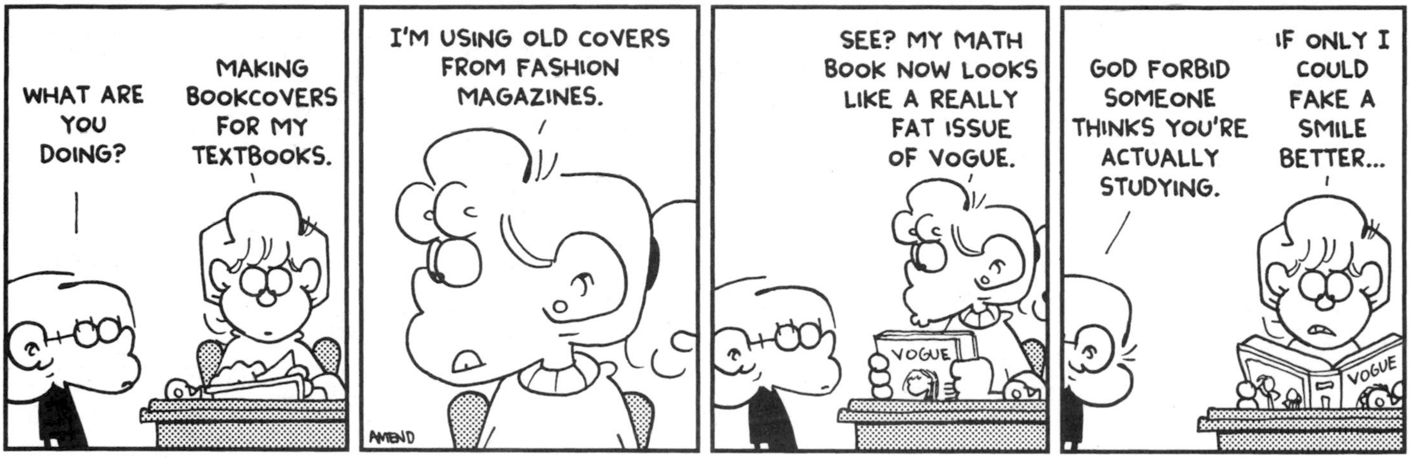
WHAT ARE YOU DOING?
MAKING BOOKCOVERS FOR MY TEXTBOOKS.
I'M USING OLD COVERS FROM FASHION MAGAZINES.
AMEND
SEE? MY MATH BOOK NOW LOOKS LIKE A REALLY FAT ISSUE OF VOGUE.
VOGUE
GOD FORBID SOMEONE THINKS YOU'RE ACTUALLY STUDYING.
IF ONLY I COULD FAKE A SMILE BETTER...
VOGUE

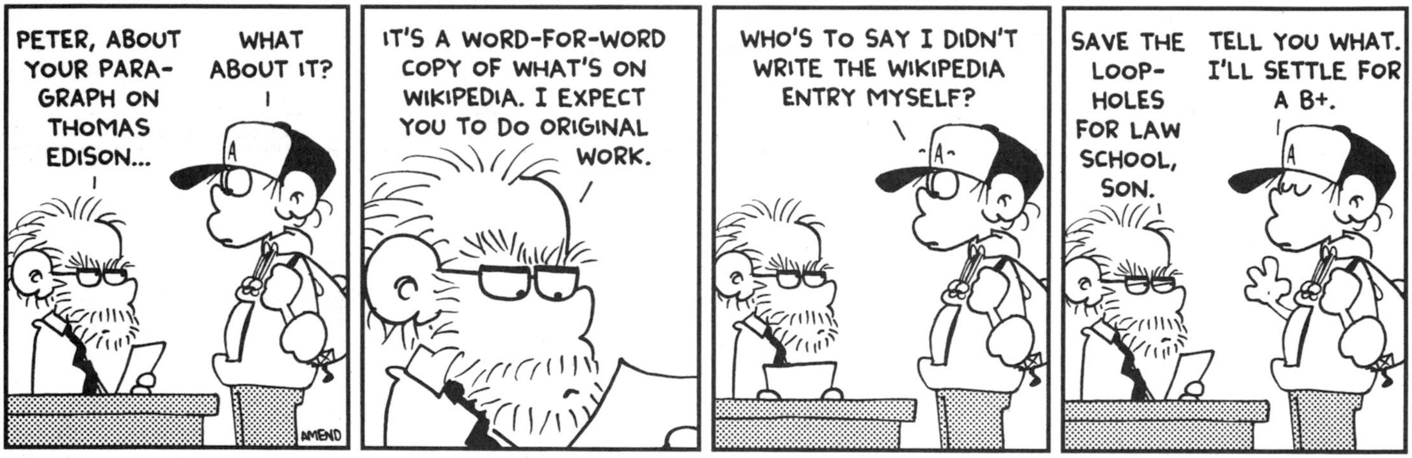
PETER, ABOUT YOUR PARAGRAPH ON THOMAS EDISON...
WHAT ABOUT IT?
AMEND
IT'S A WORD-FOR-WORD COPY OF WHAT'S ON WIKIPEDIA. I EXPECT YOU TO DO ORIGINAL WORK.
WHO'S TO SAY I DIDN'T WRITE THE WIKIPEDIA ENTRY MYSELF?
SAVE THE LOOPHOLES FOR LAW SCHOOL, SON.
TELL YOU WHAT. I'LL SETTLE FOR A B+.

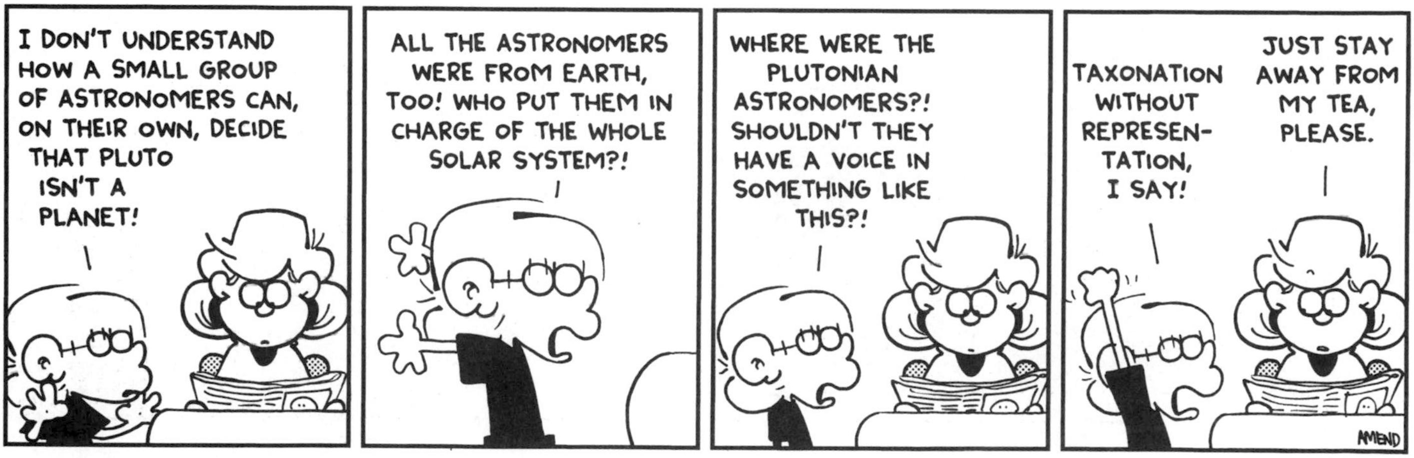
I DON'T UNDERSTAND HOW A SMALL GROUP OF ASTRONOMERS CAN, ON THEIR OWN, DECIDE THAT PLUTO ISN'T A PLANET!
ALL THE ASTRONOMERS WERE FROM EARTH, TOO! WHO PUT THEM IN CHARGE OF THE WHOLE SOLAR SYSTEM?!
WHERE WERE THE PLUTONIAN ASTRONOMERS?! SHOULDN'T THEY HAVE A VOICE IN SOMETHING LIKE THIS?!
TAXONATION WITHOUT REPRESENTATION, I SAY!
JUST STAY AWAY FROM MY TEA, PLEASE.
AMEND

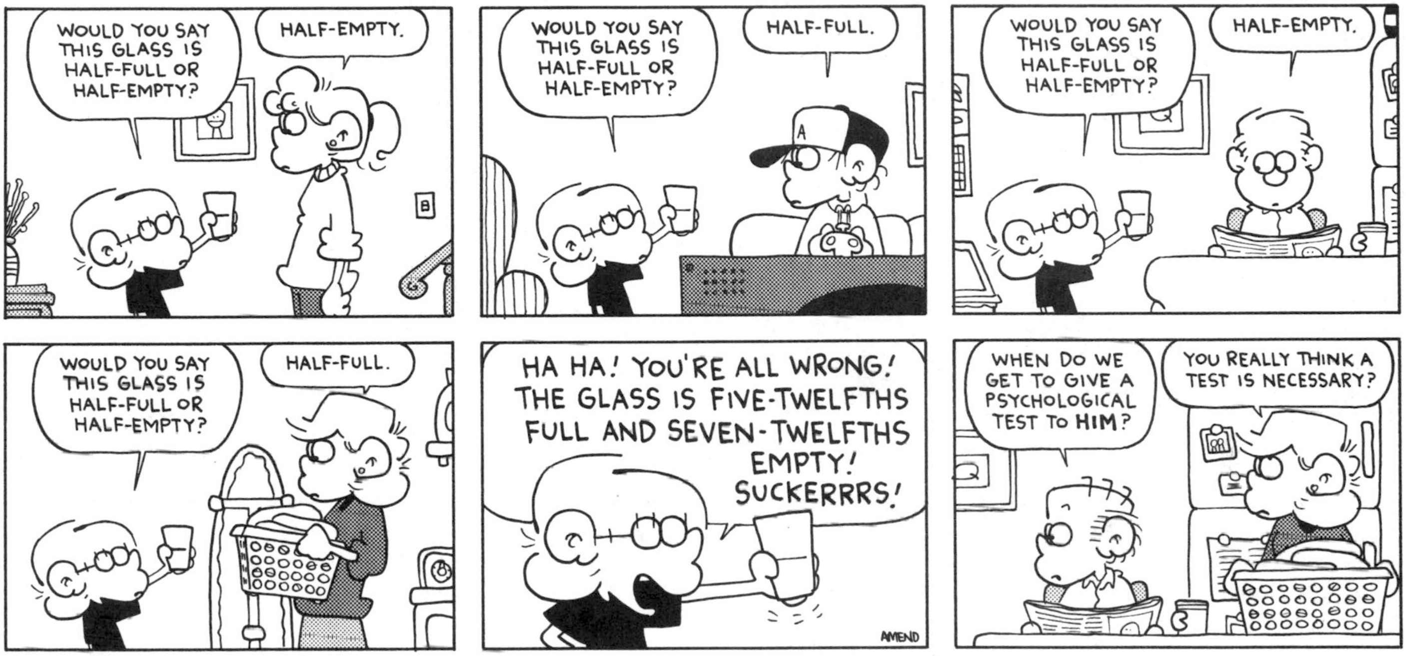
WOULD YOU SAY THIS GLASS IS HALF-FULL OR HALF-EMPTY?
HALF-EMPTY.
WOULD YOU SAY THIS GLASS IS HALF-FULL OR HALF-EMPTY?
HALF-FULL.
WOULD YOU SAY THIS GLASS IS HALF-FULL OR HALF-EMPTY?
HALF-EMPTY.
WOULD YOU SAY THIS GLASS IS HALF-FULL OR HALF-EMPTY?
HALF-FULL.
HA HA! YOU'RE ALL WRONG! THE GLASS IS FIVE-TWELFTHS FULL AND SEVEN-TWELFTHS EMPTY! SUCKERRRS!
AMEND
WHEN DO WE GET TO GIVE A PSYCHOLOGICAL TEST TO HIM?
YOU REALLY THINK A TEST IS NECESSARY?

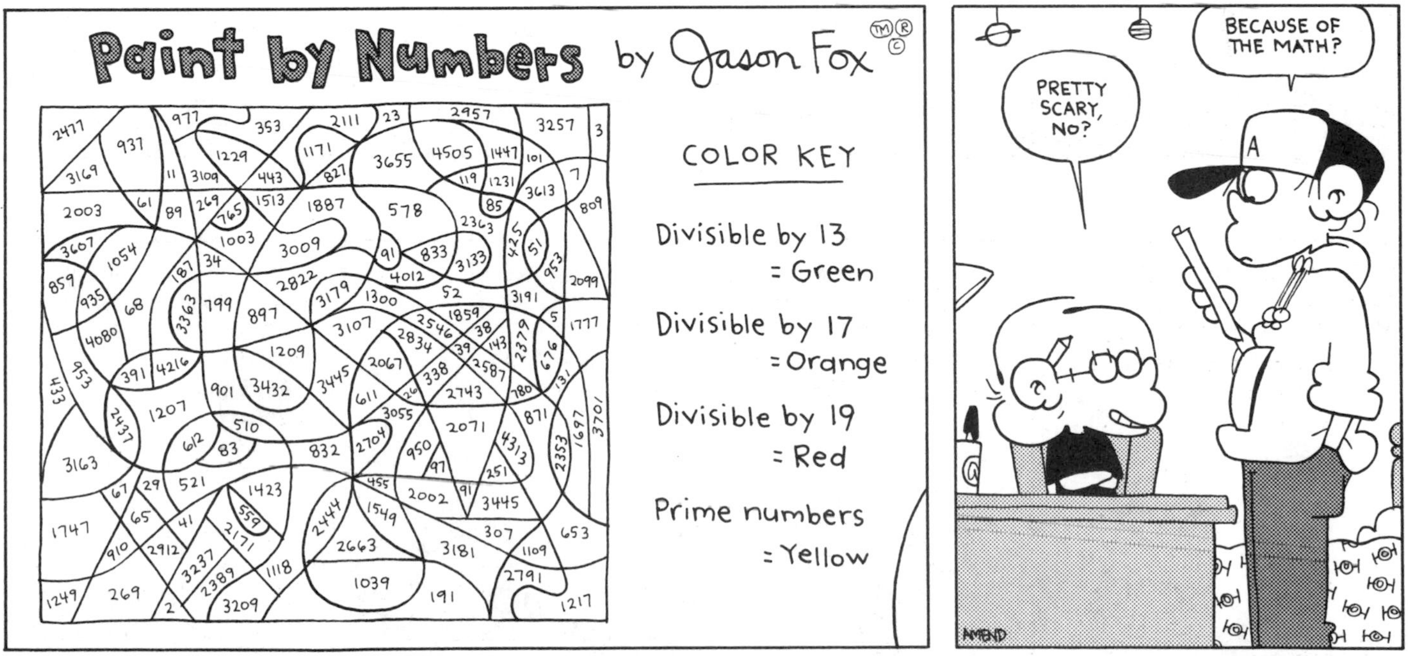
Paint by Numbers by Jason Fox
COLOR KEY
Divisible by 13 = Green
Divisible by 17 = Orange
Divisible by 19 = Red
Prime numbers = Yellow
PRETTY SCARY, NO?
BECAUSE OF THE MATH?
AMEND

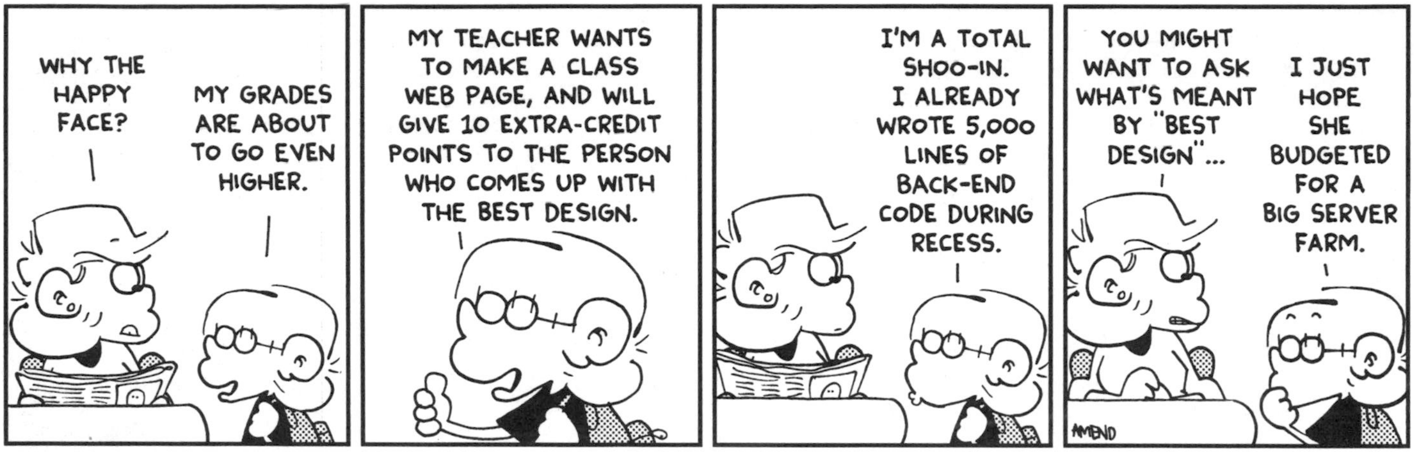
WHY THE HAPPY FACE?
MY GRADES ARE ABOUT TO GO EVEN HIGHER.
MY TEACHER WANTS TO MAKE A CLASS WEB PAGE, AND WILL GIVE 10 EXTRA-CREDIT POINTS TO THE PERSON WHO COMES UP WITH THE BEST DESIGN.
I'M A TOTAL SHOO-IN. I ALREADY WROTE 5,000 LINES OF BACK-END CODE DURING RECESS.
YOU MIGHT WANT TO ASK WHAT'S MEANT BY "BEST DESIGN"...
I JUST HOPE SHE BUDGETED FOR A BIG SERVER FARM.
AMEND

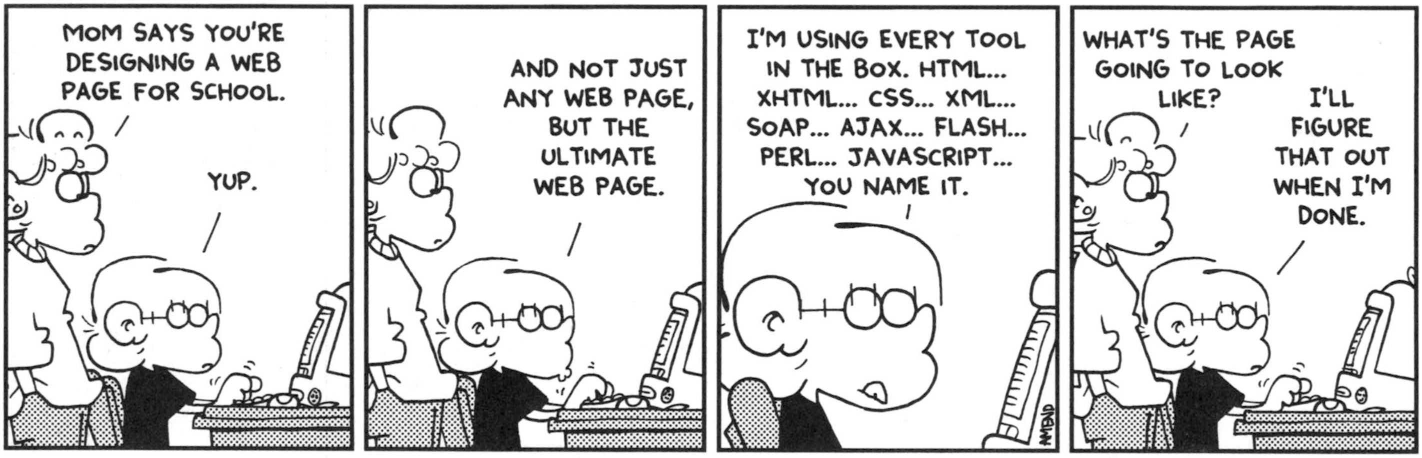
MOM SAYS YOU'RE DESIGNING A WEB PAGE FOR SCHOOL.
YUP.
AND NOT JUST ANY WEB PAGE, BUT THE ULTIMATE WEB PAGE.
I'M USING EVERY TOOL IN THE BOX. HTML... XHTML... CSS... XML... SOAP... AJAX... FLASH... PERL... JAVASCRIPT... YOU NAME IT.
AMEND
WHAT'S THE PAGE GOING TO LOOK LIKE?
I'LL FIGURE THAT OUT WHEN I'M DONE.

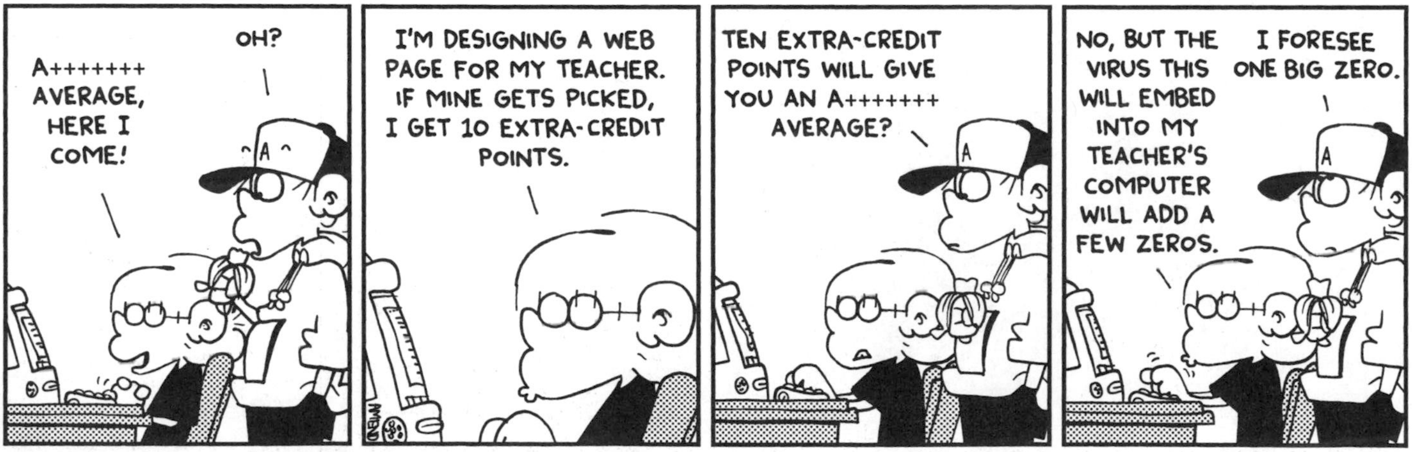
A+++++++ AVERAGE, HERE I COME!
OH?
I'M DESIGNING A WEB PAGE FOR MY TEACHER. IF MINE GETS PICKED, I GET 10 EXTRA-CREDIT POINTS.
TEN EXTRA-CREDIT POINTS WILL GIVE YOU AN A+++++++ AVERAGE?
NO, BUT THE VIRUS THIS WILL EMBED INTO MY TEACHER'S COMPUTER WILL ADD A FEW ZEROS.
I FORESEE ONE BIG ZERO.

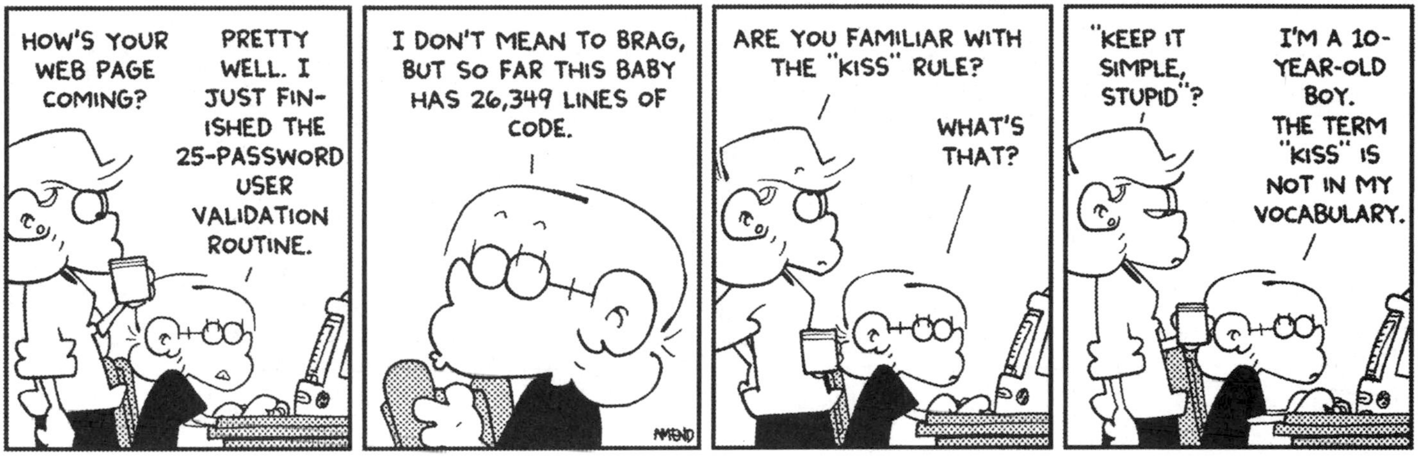
HOW'S YOUR WEB PAGE COMING?
PRETTY WELL. I JUST FIN-ISHED THE 25-PASSWORD USER VALIDATION ROUTINE.
I DON'T MEAN TO BRAG, BUT SO FAR THIS BABY HAS 26,349 LINES OF CODE.
AMEND
ARE YOU FAMILIAR WITH THE "KISS" RULE?
WHAT'S THAT?
"KEEP IT SIMPLE, STUPID"?
I'M A 10-YEAR-OLD BOY. THE TERM "KISS" IS NOT IN MY VOCABULARY.

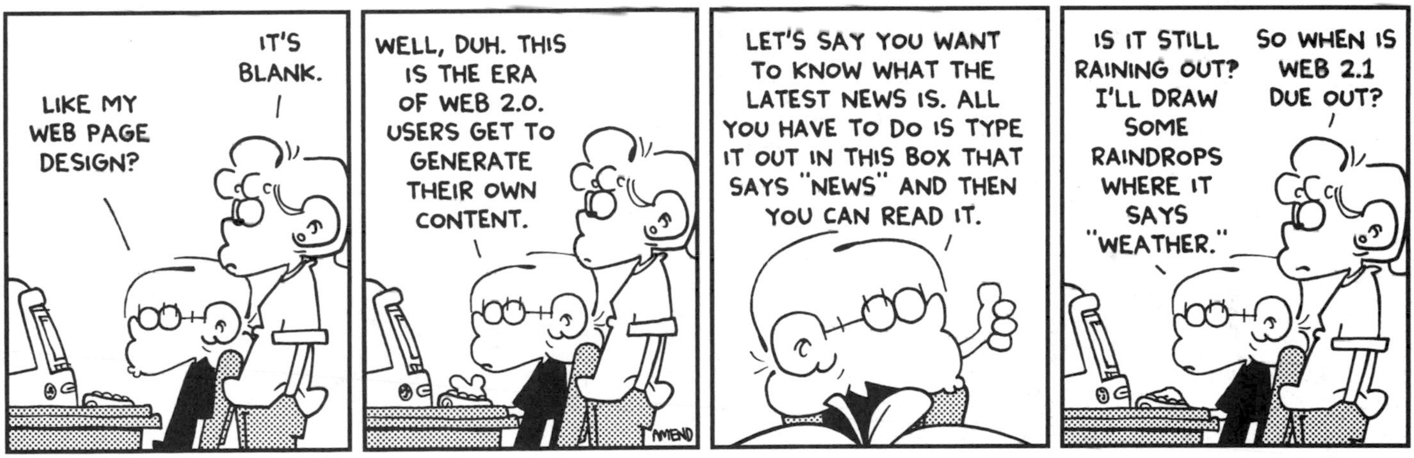
LIKE MY WEB PAGE DESIGN?
IT'S BLANK.
WELL, DUH. THIS IS THE ERA OF WEB 2.0. USERS GET TO GENERATE THEIR OWN CONTENT.
AMEND
LET'S SAY YOU WANT TO KNOW WHAT THE LATEST NEWS IS. ALL YOU HAVE TO DO IS TYPE IT OUT IN THIS BOX THAT SAYS "NEWS" AND THEN YOU CAN READ IT.
IS IT STILL RAINING OUT? I'LL DRAW SOME RAINDROPS WHERE IT SAYS "WEATHER."
SO WHEN IS WEB 2.1 DUE OUT?

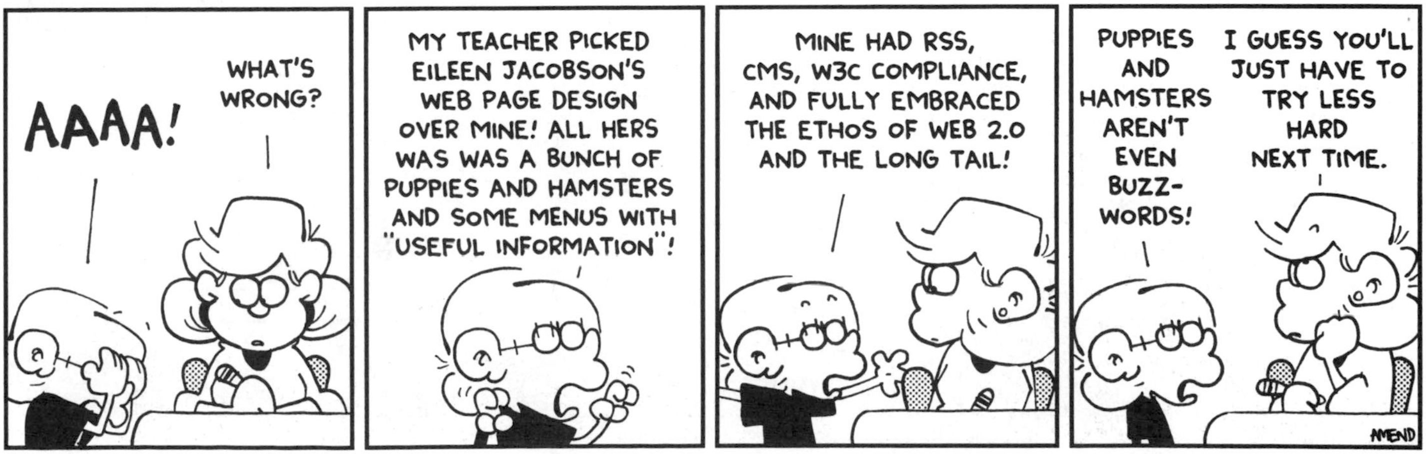
AAAA!
WHAT'S WRONG?
MY TEACHER PICKED EILEEN JACOBSON'S WEB PAGE DESIGN OVER MINE! ALL HERS WAS WAS A BUNCH OF PUPPIES AND HAMSTERS AND SOME MENUS WITH "USEFUL INFORMATION"!
MINE HAD RSS, CMS, W3C COMPLIANCE, AND FULLY EMBRACED THE ETHOS OF WEB 2.0 AND THE LONG TAIL!
PUPPIES AND HAMSTERS AREN'T EVEN BUZZ-WORDS!
I GUESS YOU'LL JUST HAVE TO TRY LESS HARD NEXT TIME.
AMEND

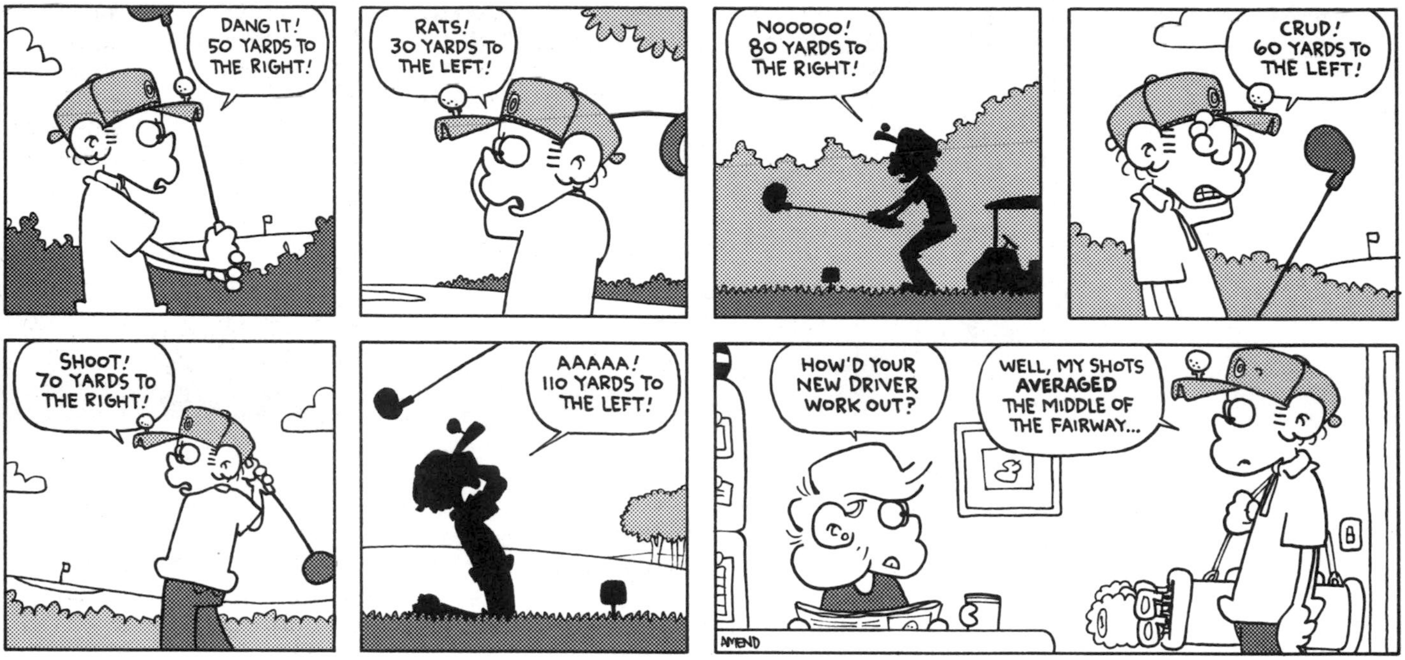
DANG IT! 50 YARDS TO THE RIGHT!
RATS! 30 YARDS TO THE LEFT!
NOOOOO! 80 YARDS TO THE RIGHT!
CRUD! 60 YARDS TO THE LEFT!
SHOOT! 70 YARDS TO THE RIGHT!
AAAAA! 110 YARDS TO THE LEFT!
HOW'D YOUR NEW DRIVER WORK OUT?
WELL, MY SHOTS **AVERAGED** THE MIDDLE OF THE FAIRWAY...
AMEND

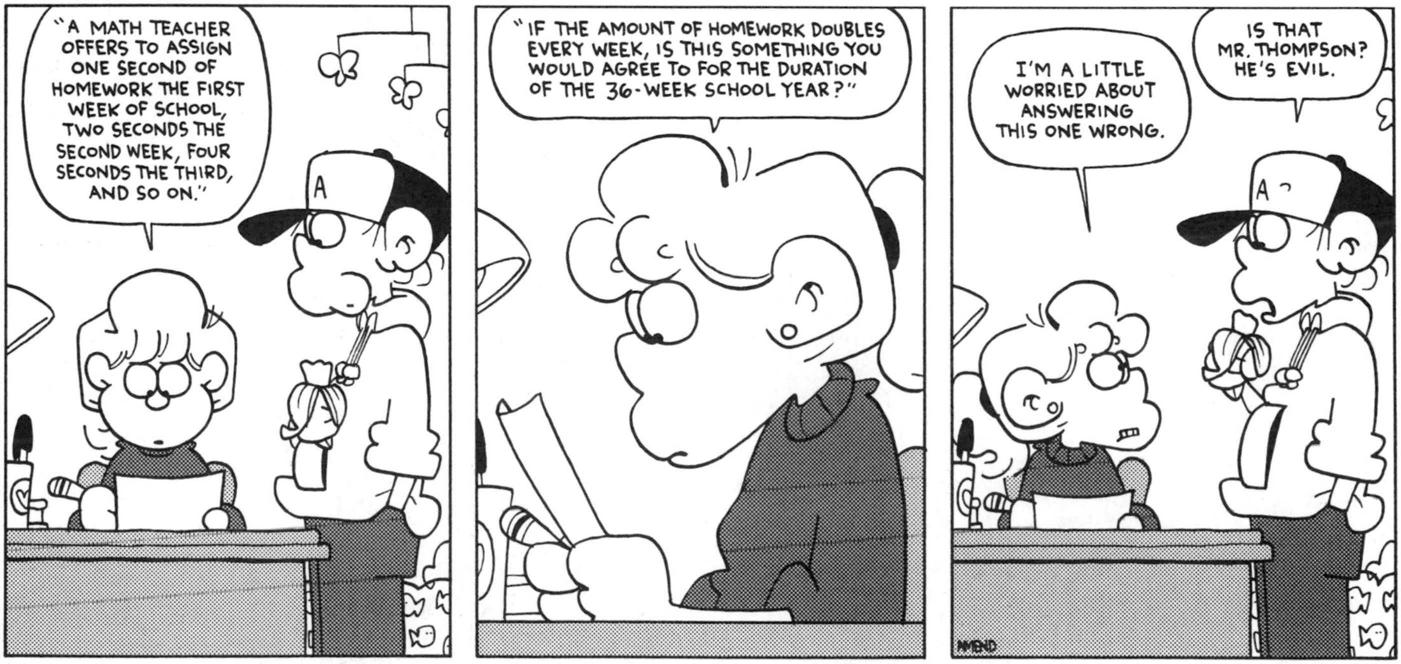
"A MATH TEACHER OFFERS TO ASSIGN ONE SECOND OF HOMEWORK THE FIRST WEEK OF SCHOOL, TWO SECONDS THE SECOND WEEK, FOUR SECONDS THE THIRD, AND SO ON."
"IF THE AMOUNT OF HOMEWORK DOUBLES EVERY WEEK, IS THIS SOMETHING YOU WOULD AGREE TO FOR THE DURATION OF THE 36-WEEK SCHOOL YEAR?"
I'M A LITTLE WORRIED ABOUT ANSWERING THIS ONE WRONG.
IS THAT MR. THOMPSON? HE'S EVIL.
AMEND

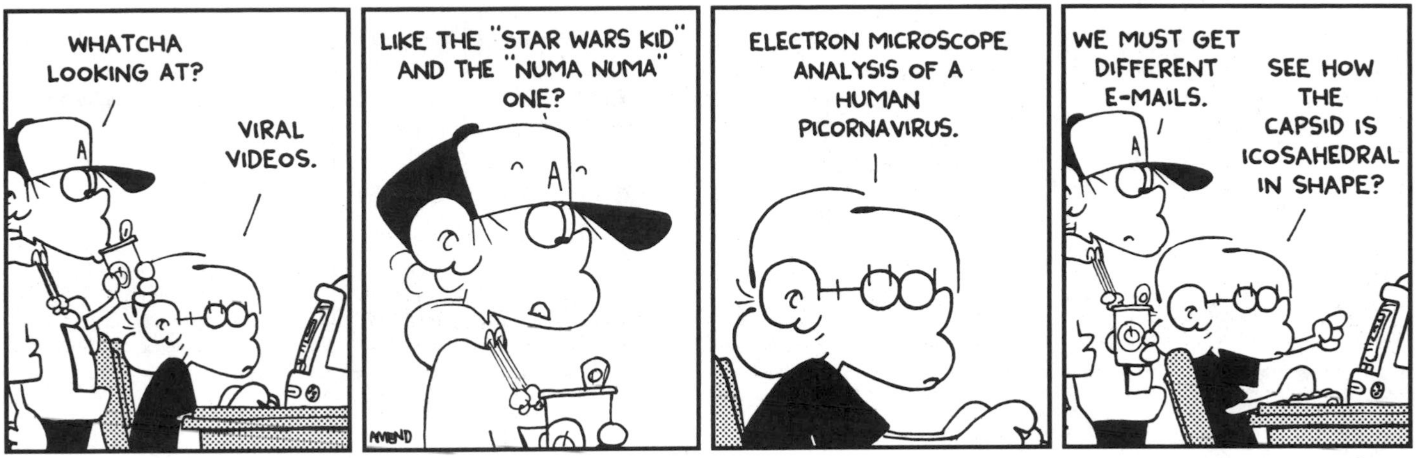
WHATCHA LOOKING AT?
VIRAL VIDEOS.
LIKE THE "STAR WARS KID" AND THE "NUMA NUMA" ONE?
ELECTRON MICROSCOPE ANALYSIS OF A HUMAN PICORNAVIRUS.
WE MUST GET DIFFERENT E-MAILS.
SEE HOW THE CAPSID IS ICOSAHEDRAL IN SHAPE?
AMEND

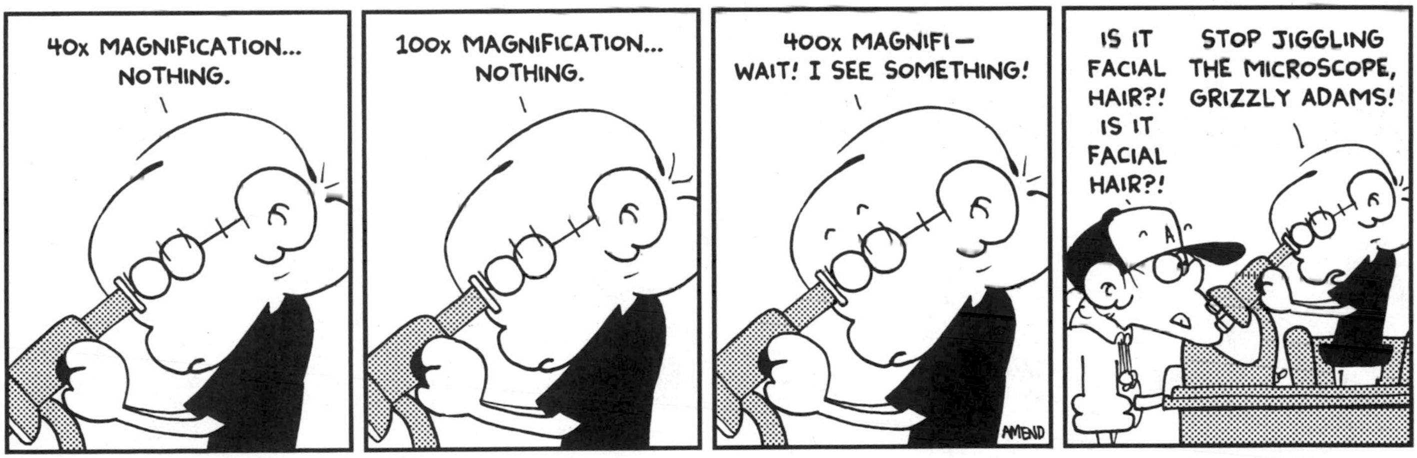
40x MAGNIFICATION... NOTHING.
100x MAGNIFICATION... NOTHING.
400x MAGNIFI— WAIT! I SEE SOMETHING!
IS IT FACIAL HAIR?! IS IT FACIAL HAIR?!
STOP JIGGLING THE MICROSCOPE, GRIZZLY ADAMS!
AMEND

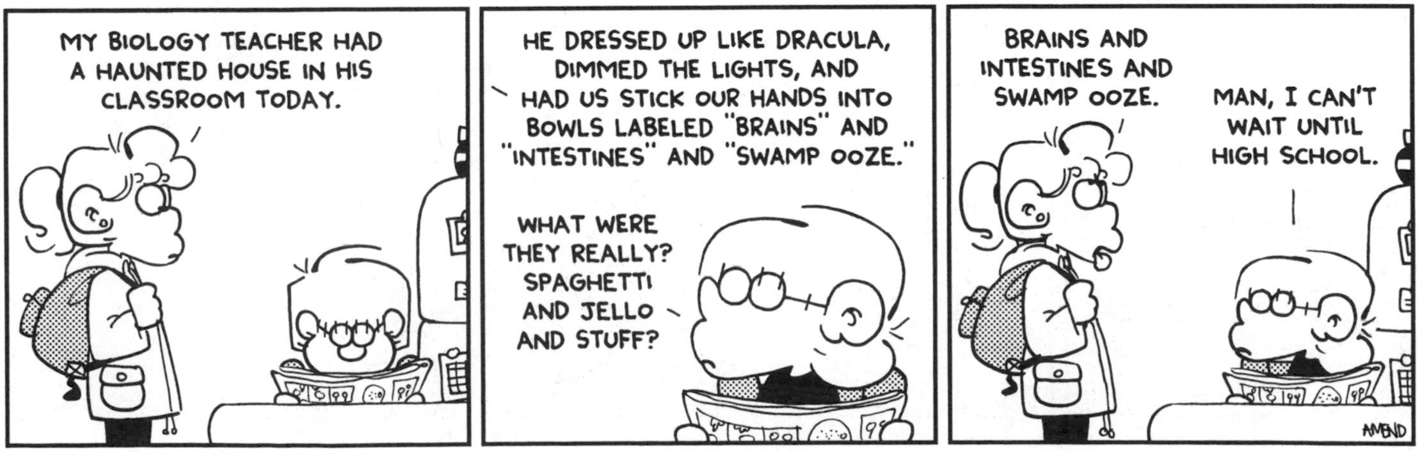
MY BIOLOGY TEACHER HAD A HAUNTED HOUSE IN HIS CLASSROOM TODAY.
HE DRESSED UP LIKE DRACULA, DIMMED THE LIGHTS, AND HAD US STICK OUR HANDS INTO BOWLS LABELED "BRAINS" AND "INTESTINES" AND "SWAMP OOZE."
WHAT WERE THEY REALLY? SPAGHETTI AND JELLO AND STUFF?
BRAINS AND INTESTINES AND SWAMP OOZE.
MAN, I CAN'T WAIT UNTIL HIGH SCHOOL.
AMEND

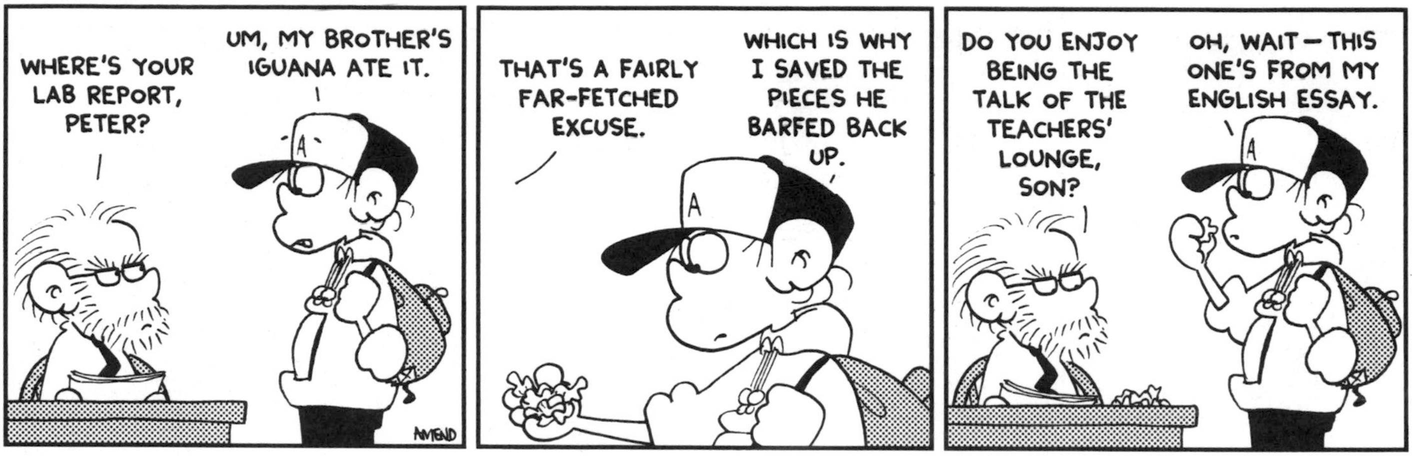
WHERE'S YOUR LAB REPORT, PETER?
UM, MY BROTHER'S IGUANA ATE IT.
AMEND
THAT'S A FAIRLY FAR-FETCHED EXCUSE.
WHICH IS WHY I SAVED THE PIECES HE BARFED BACK UP.
DO YOU ENJOY BEING THE TALK OF THE TEACHERS' LOUNGE, SON?
OH, WAIT — THIS ONE'S FROM MY ENGLISH ESSAY.

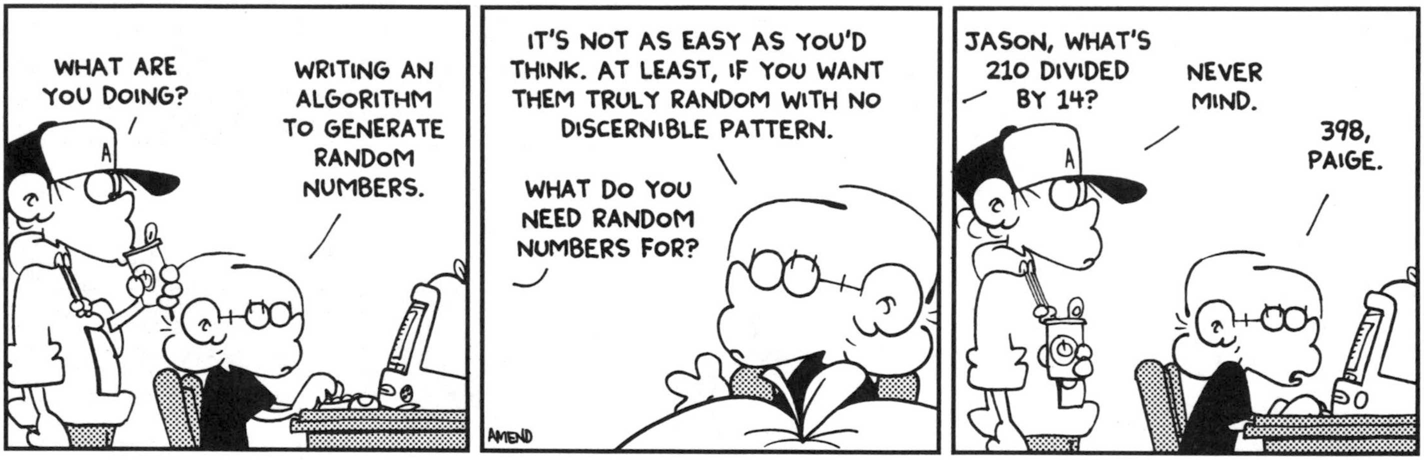
WHAT ARE YOU DOING?
WRITING AN ALGORITHM TO GENERATE RANDOM NUMBERS.
IT'S NOT AS EASY AS YOU'D THINK. AT LEAST, IF YOU WANT THEM TRULY RANDOM WITH NO DISCERNIBLE PATTERN.
WHAT DO YOU NEED RANDOM NUMBERS FOR?
AMEND
JASON, WHAT'S 210 DIVIDED BY 14?
NEVER MIND.
398, PAIGE.

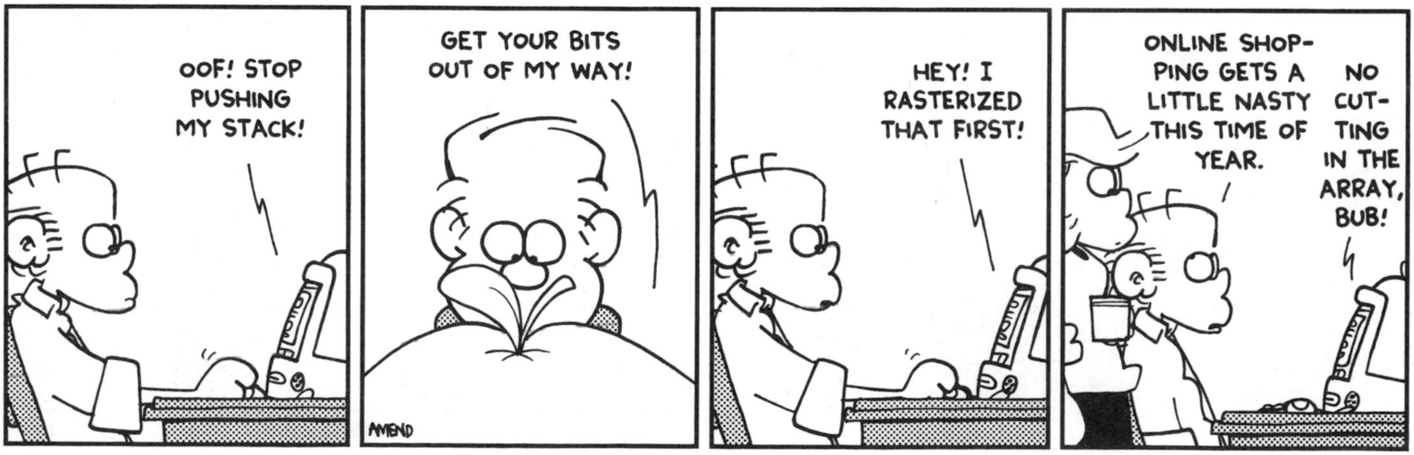
OOF! STOP PUSHING MY STACK!
GET YOUR BITS OUT OF MY WAY!
AMEND
HEY! I RASTERIZED THAT FIRST!
ONLINE SHOP-PING GETS A LITTLE NASTY THIS TIME OF YEAR.
NO CUT-TING IN THE ARRAY, BUB!

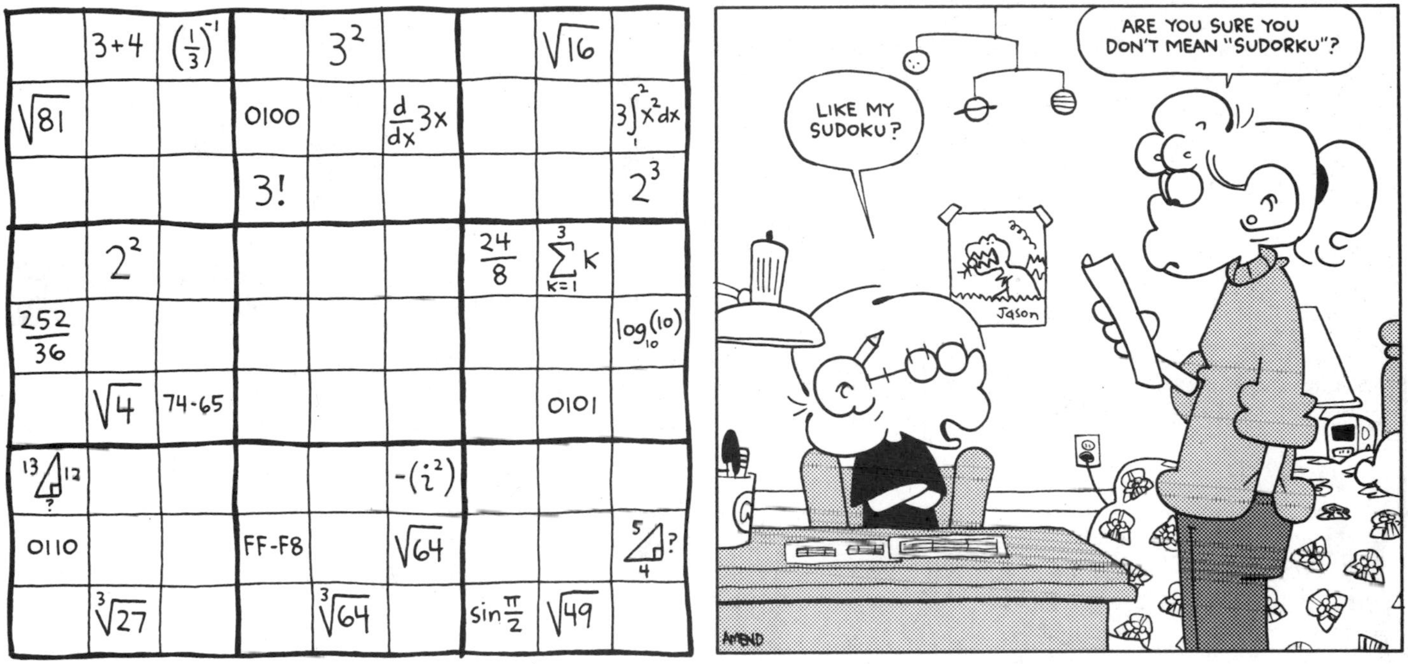
3+4 (1/3)^-1 3^2 √16
√81 0100 d/dx 3x 3∫x²dx
3! 2^3
2^2 24/8 Σ k
252/36 log10(10)
√4 74-65 0101
13 12 ? -(i^2)
0110 FF-F8 √64 5 4 ?
∛27 ∛64 sin π/2 √49
LIKE MY SUDOKU?
ARE YOU SURE YOU DON'T MEAN "SUDORKU"?
Jason
AMEND

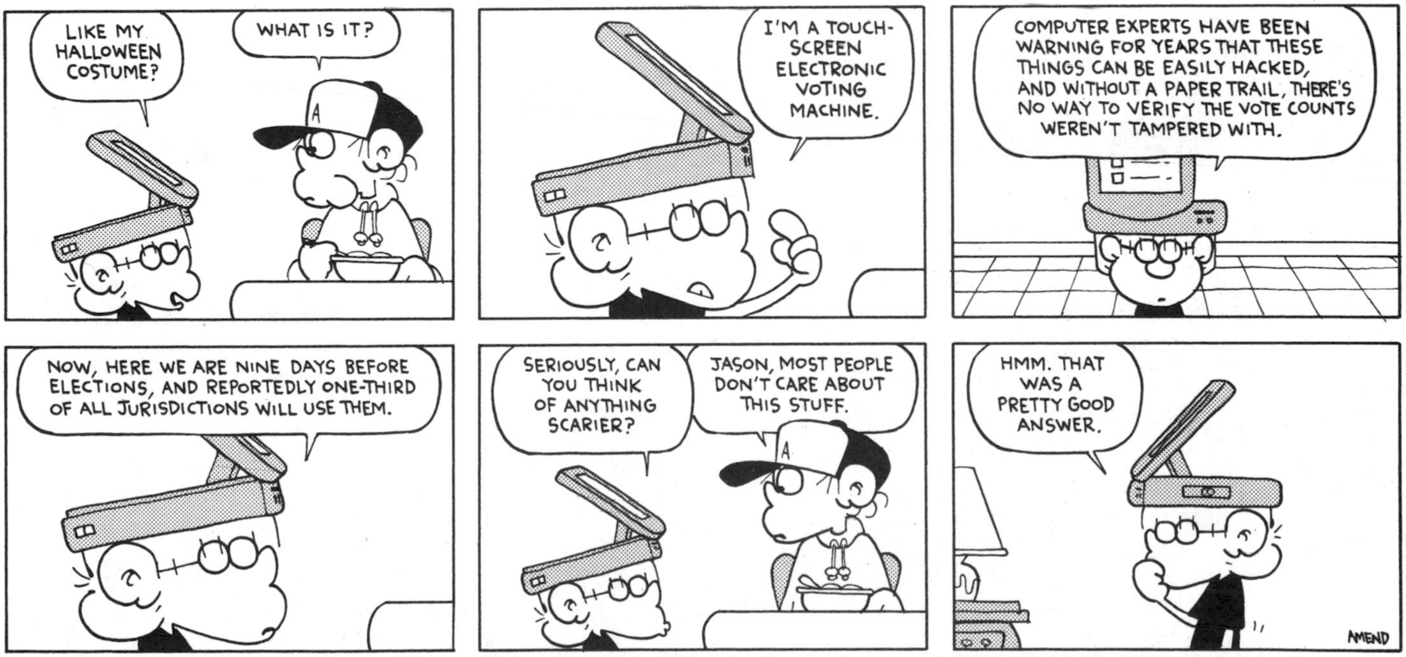
LIKE MY HALLOWEEN COSTUME?
WHAT IS IT?
I'M A TOUCH-SCREEN ELECTRONIC VOTING MACHINE.
COMPUTER EXPERTS HAVE BEEN WARNING FOR YEARS THAT THESE THINGS CAN BE EASILY HACKED, AND WITHOUT A PAPER TRAIL, THERE'S NO WAY TO VERIFY THE VOTE COUNTS WEREN'T TAMPERED WITH.
NOW, HERE WE ARE NINE DAYS BEFORE ELECTIONS, AND REPORTEDLY ONE-THIRD OF ALL JURISDICTIONS WILL USE THEM.
SERIOUSLY, CAN YOU THINK OF ANYTHING SCARIER?
JASON, MOST PEOPLE DON'T CARE ABOUT THIS STUFF.
HMM. THAT WAS A PRETTY GOOD ANSWER.
AMEND

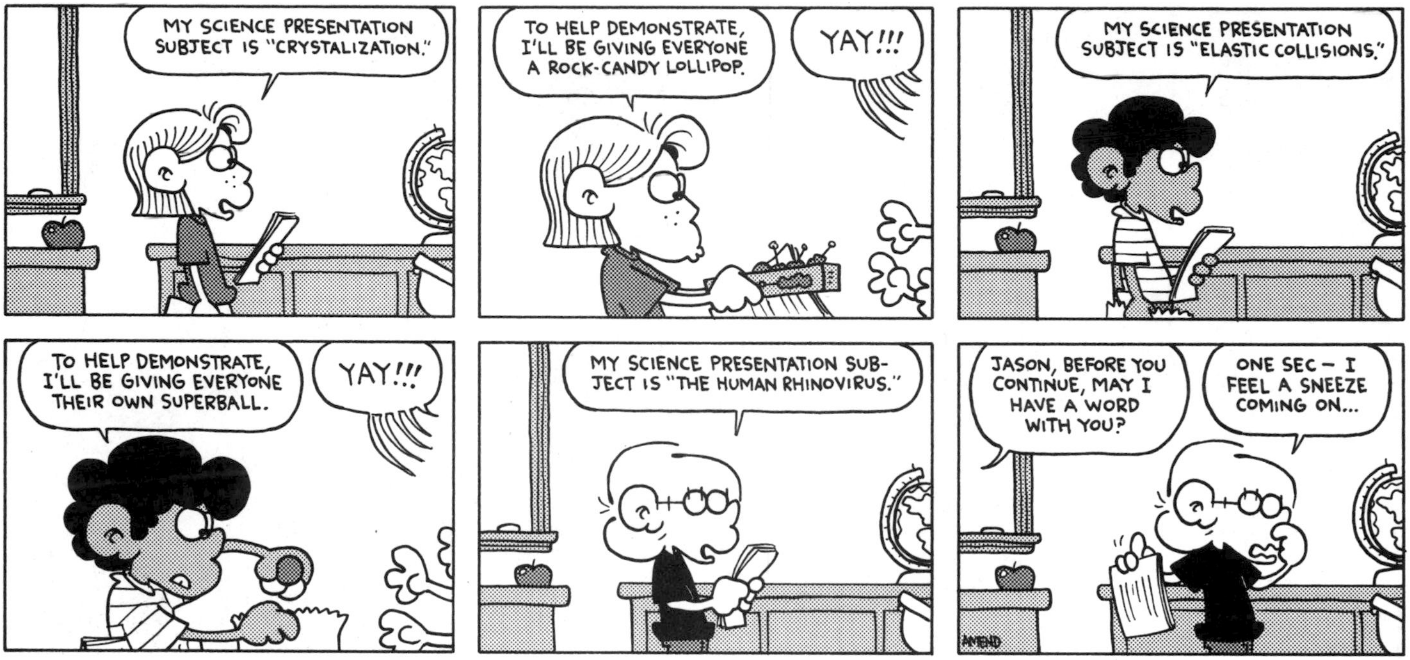
MY SCIENCE PRESENTATION SUBJECT IS "CRYSTALIZATION."
TO HELP DEMONSTRATE, I'LL BE GIVING EVERYONE A ROCK-CANDY LOLLIPOP.
YAY!!!
MY SCIENCE PRESENTATION SUBJECT IS "ELASTIC COLLISIONS."
TO HELP DEMONSTRATE, I'LL BE GIVING EVERYONE THEIR OWN SUPERBALL.
YAY!!!
MY SCIENCE PRESENTATION SUBJECT IS "THE HUMAN RHINOVIRUS."
JASON, BEFORE YOU CONTINUE, MAY I HAVE A WORD WITH YOU?
ONE SEC – I FEEL A SNEEZE COMING ON...
AMEND

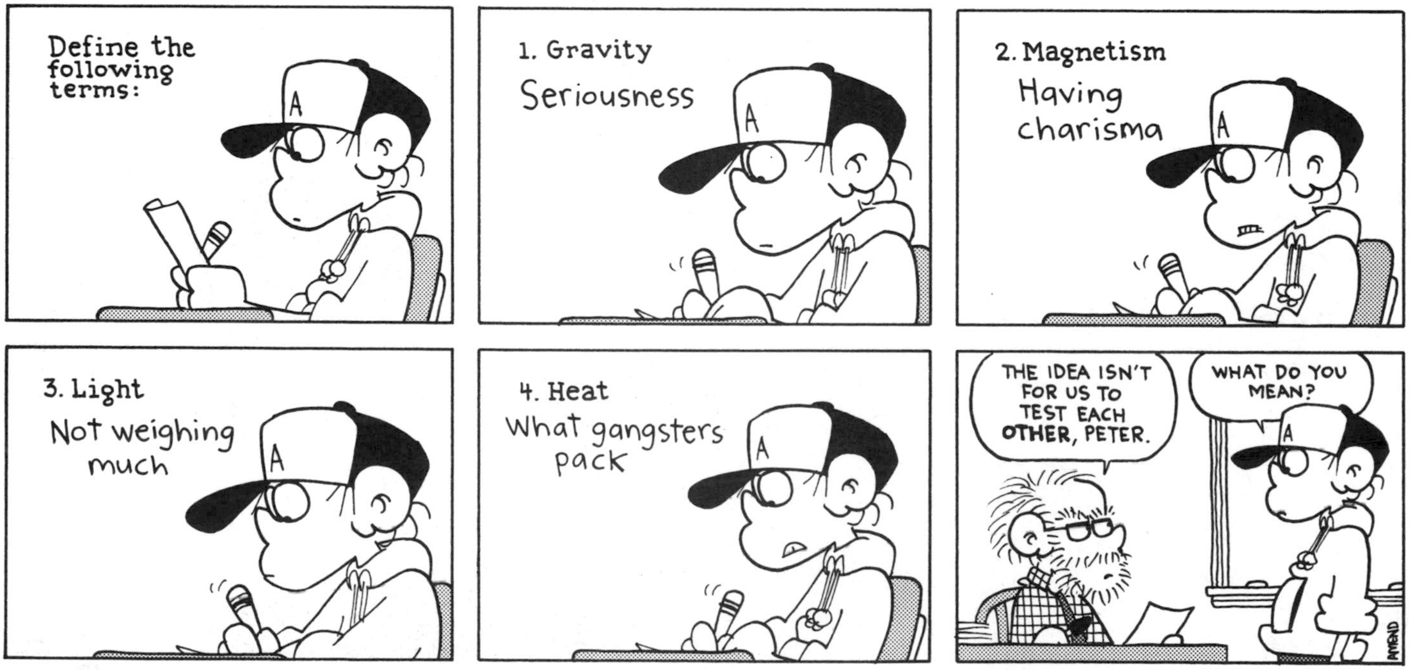
Define the following terms:
A
1. Gravity
Seriousness
2. Magnetism
Having charisma
3. Light
Not weighing much
4. Heat
What gangsters pack
THE IDEA ISN'T FOR US TO TEST EACH **OTHER**, PETER.
WHAT DO YOU MEAN?
AMEND

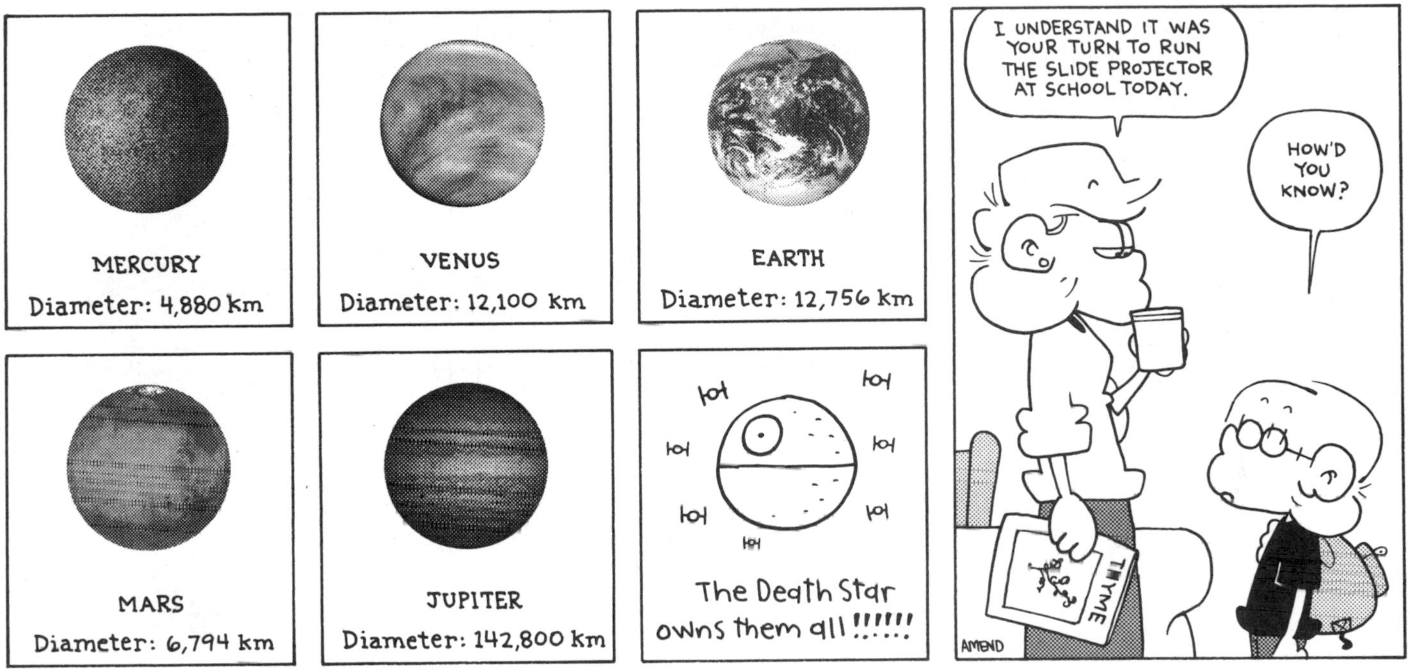
MERCURY
Diameter: 4,880 km
VENUS
Diameter: 12,100 km
EARTH
Diameter: 12,756 km
MARS
Diameter: 6,794 km
JUPITER
Diameter: 142,800 km
The Death Star owns them all!!!!!!
I UNDERSTAND IT WAS YOUR TURN TO RUN THE SLIDE PROJECTOR AT SCHOOL TODAY.
HOW'D YOU KNOW?
AMEND

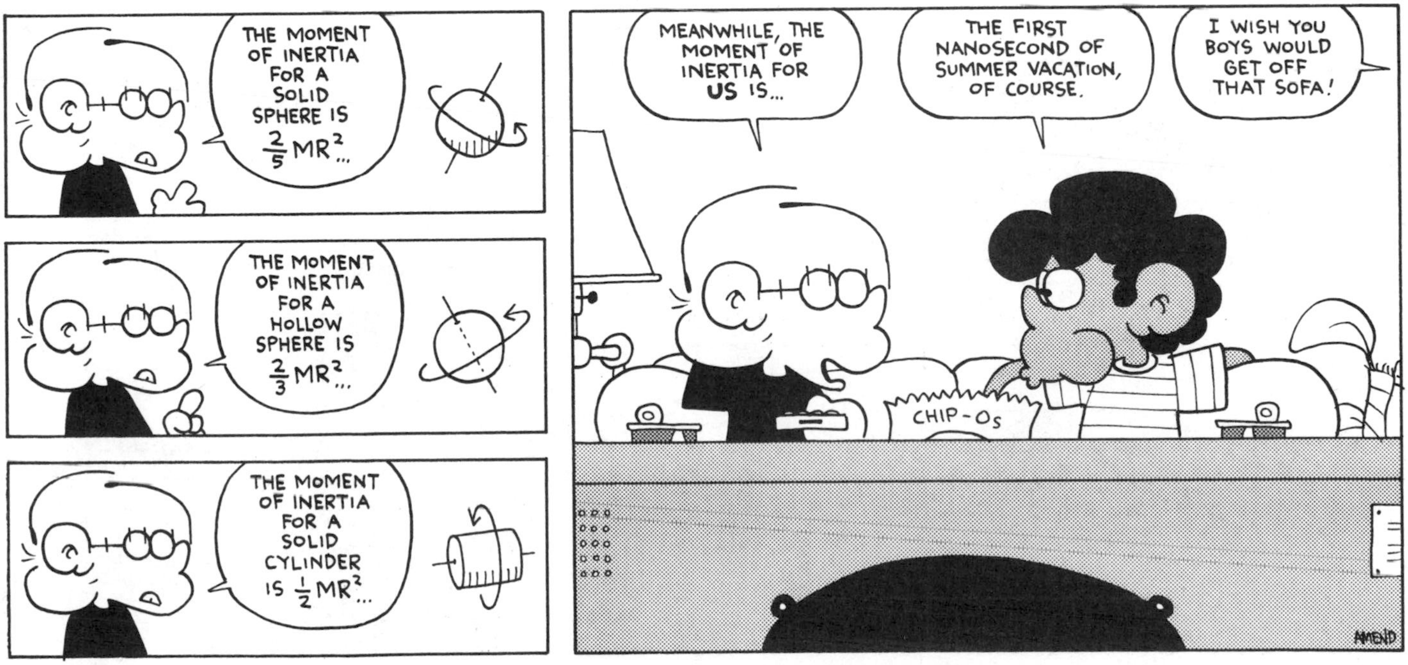
THE MOMENT OF INERTIA FOR A SOLID SPHERE IS $\frac{2}{5}MR^2$...
THE MOMENT OF INERTIA FOR A HOLLOW SPHERE IS $\frac{2}{3}MR^2$...
THE MOMENT OF INERTIA FOR A SOLID CYLINDER IS $\frac{1}{2}MR^2$...
MEANWHILE, THE MOMENT OF INERTIA FOR US IS...
THE FIRST NANOSECOND OF SUMMER VACATION, OF COURSE.
I WISH YOU BOYS WOULD GET OFF THAT SOFA!
CHIP-Os
AMEND

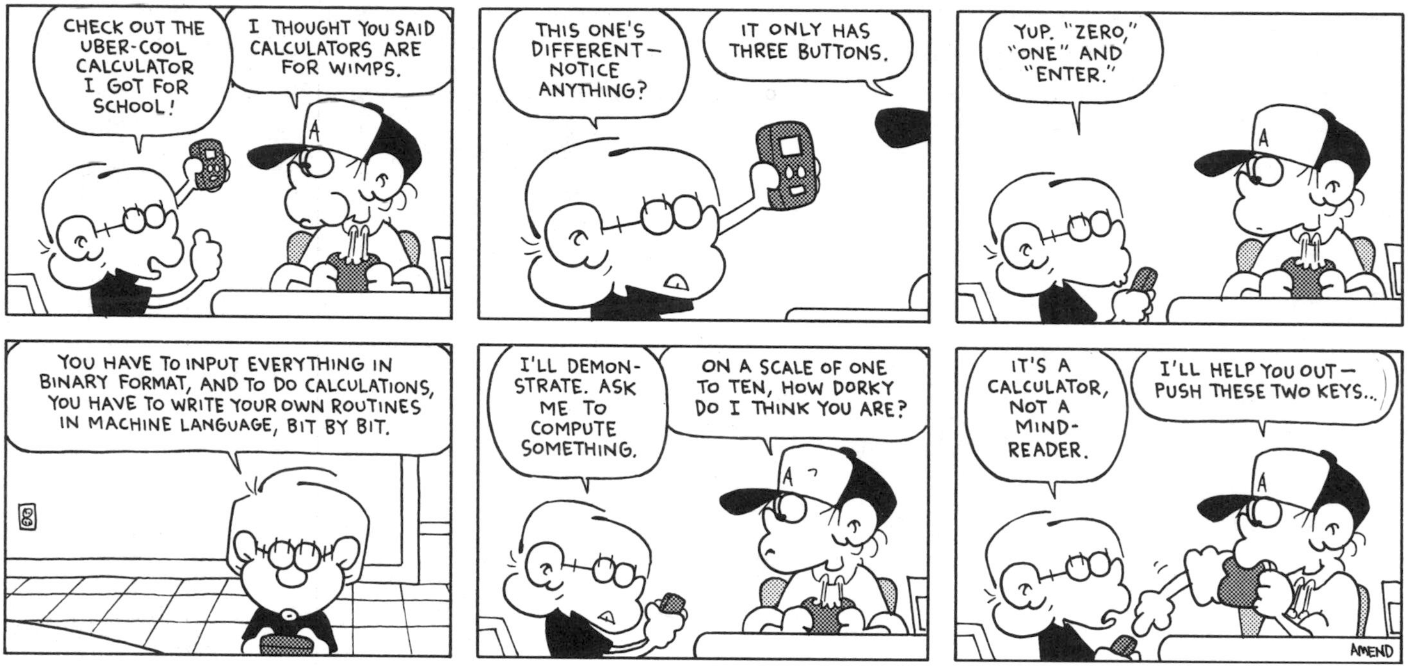
CHECK OUT THE UBER-COOL CALCULATOR I GOT FOR SCHOOL!
I THOUGHT YOU SAID CALCULATORS ARE FOR WIMPS.
THIS ONE'S DIFFERENT—NOTICE ANYTHING?
IT ONLY HAS THREE BUTTONS.
YUP. "ZERO," "ONE" AND "ENTER."
YOU HAVE TO INPUT EVERYTHING IN BINARY FORMAT, AND TO DO CALCULATIONS, YOU HAVE TO WRITE YOUR OWN ROUTINES IN MACHINE LANGUAGE, BIT BY BIT.
I'LL DEMONSTRATE. ASK ME TO COMPUTE SOMETHING.
ON A SCALE OF ONE TO TEN, HOW DORKY DO I THINK YOU ARE?
IT'S A CALCULATOR, NOT A MIND-READER.
I'LL HELP YOU OUT—PUSH THESE TWO KEYS...
AMEND

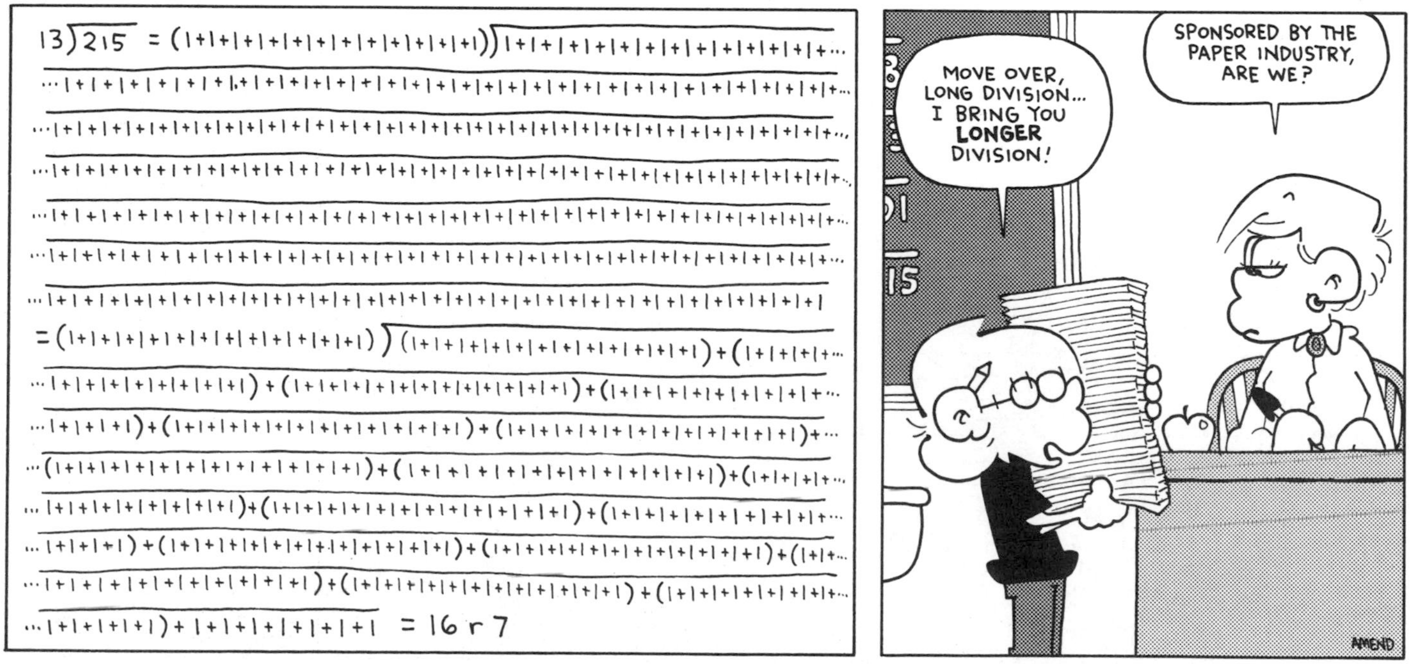
13)215 =
= 16 r 7
MOVE OVER, LONG DIVISION... I BRING YOU **LONGER** DIVISION!
SPONSORED BY THE PAPER INDUSTRY, ARE WE?
AMEND

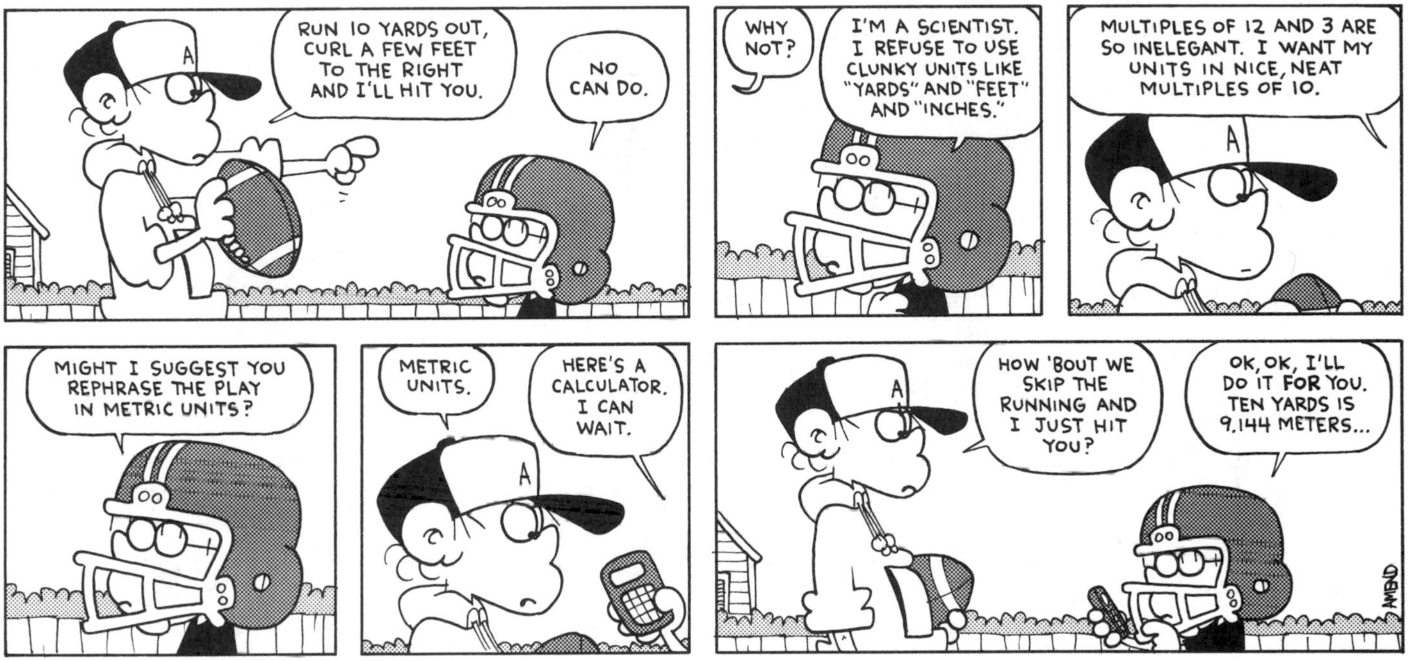
RUN 10 YARDS OUT, CURL A FEW FEET TO THE RIGHT AND I'LL HIT YOU.
NO CAN DO.
WHY NOT?
I'M A SCIENTIST. I REFUSE TO USE CLUNKY UNITS LIKE "YARDS" AND "FEET" AND "INCHES."
MULTIPLES OF 12 AND 3 ARE SO INELEGANT. I WANT MY UNITS IN NICE, NEAT MULTIPLES OF 10.
MIGHT I SUGGEST YOU REPHRASE THE PLAY IN METRIC UNITS?
METRIC UNITS.
HERE'S A CALCULATOR. I CAN WAIT.
HOW 'BOUT WE SKIP THE RUNNING AND I JUST HIT YOU?
OK, OK, I'LL DO IT **FOR** YOU. TEN YARDS IS 9.144 METERS...
AMEND

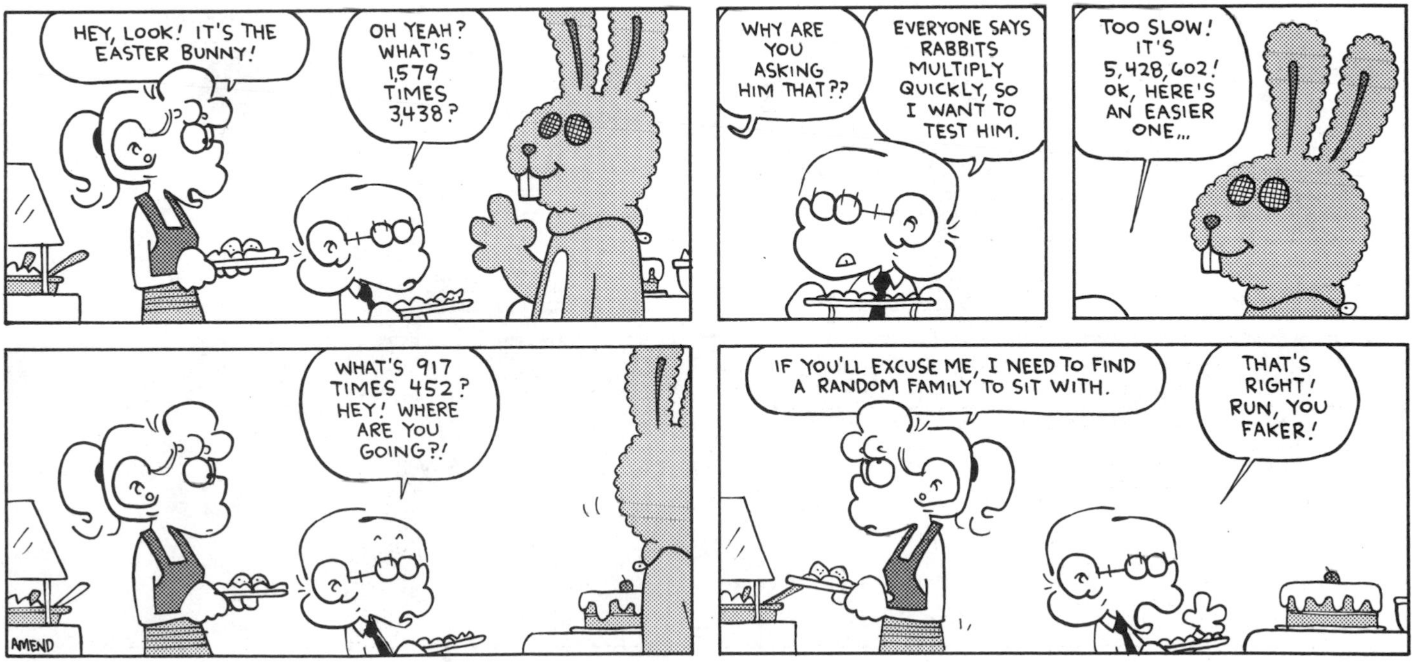
HEY, LOOK! IT'S THE EASTER BUNNY!
OH YEAH? WHAT'S 1,579 TIMES 3,438?
WHY ARE YOU ASKING HIM THAT??
EVERYONE SAYS RABBITS MULTIPLY QUICKLY, SO I WANT TO TEST HIM.
TOO SLOW! IT'S 5,428,602! OK, HERE'S AN EASIER ONE...
WHAT'S 917 TIMES 452? HEY! WHERE ARE YOU GOING?!
IF YOU'LL EXCUSE ME, I NEED TO FIND A RANDOM FAMILY TO SIT WITH.
THAT'S RIGHT! RUN, YOU FAKER!
AMEND

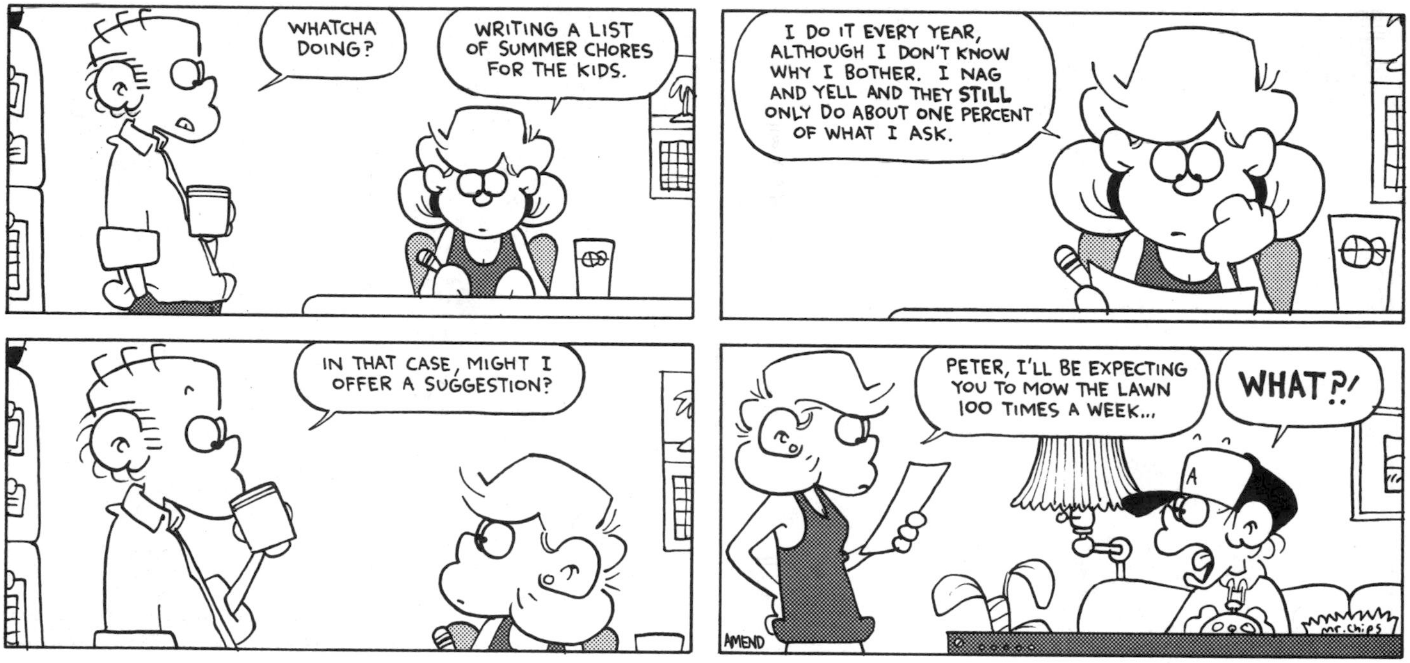
WHATCHA DOING?
WRITING A LIST OF SUMMER CHORES FOR THE KIDS.
I DO IT EVERY YEAR, ALTHOUGH I DON'T KNOW WHY I BOTHER. I NAG AND YELL AND THEY STILL ONLY DO ABOUT ONE PERCENT OF WHAT I ASK.
IN THAT CASE, MIGHT I OFFER A SUGGESTION?
PETER, I'LL BE EXPECTING YOU TO MOW THE LAWN 100 TIMES A WEEK...
WHAT?!
mr. chips
AMEND

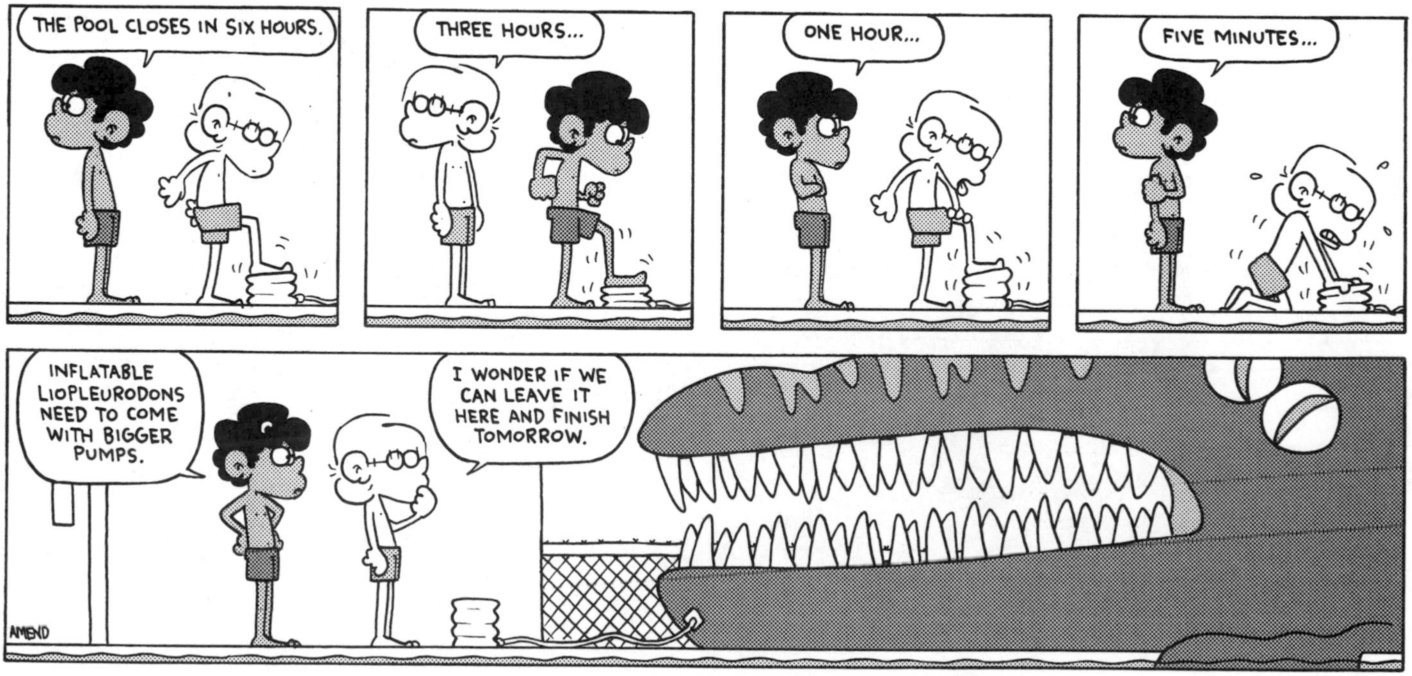
THE POOL CLOSES IN SIX HOURS.
THREE HOURS...
ONE HOUR...
FIVE MINUTES...
INFLATABLE LIOPLEURODONS NEED TO COME WITH BIGGER PUMPS.
I WONDER IF WE CAN LEAVE IT HERE AND FINISH TOMORROW.
AMEND

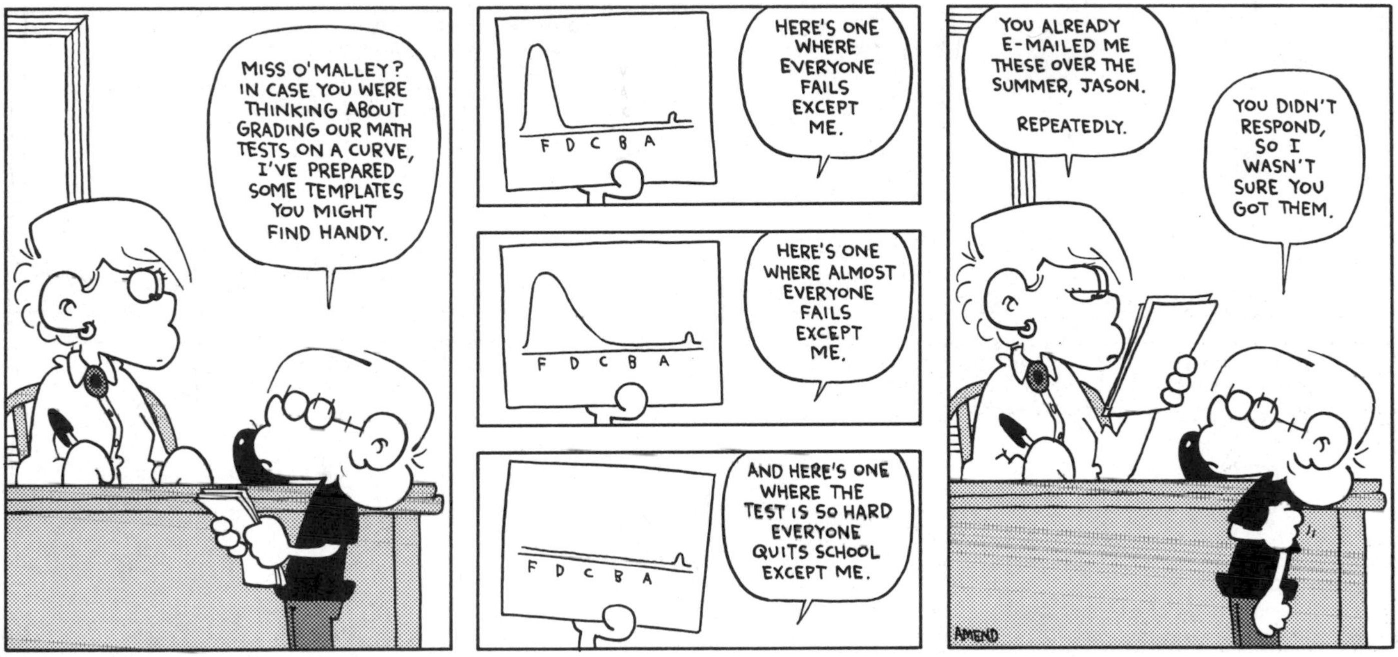
MISS O'MALLEY? IN CASE YOU WERE THINKING ABOUT GRADING OUR MATH TESTS ON A CURVE, I'VE PREPARED SOME TEMPLATES YOU MIGHT FIND HANDY.
F D C B A
HERE'S ONE WHERE EVERYONE FAILS EXCEPT ME.
F D C B A
HERE'S ONE WHERE ALMOST EVERYONE FAILS EXCEPT ME.
F D C B A
AND HERE'S ONE WHERE THE TEST IS SO HARD EVERYONE QUITS SCHOOL EXCEPT ME.
YOU ALREADY E-MAILED ME THESE OVER THE SUMMER, JASON.
REPEATEDLY.
YOU DIDN'T RESPOND, SO I WASN'T SURE YOU GOT THEM.
AMEND

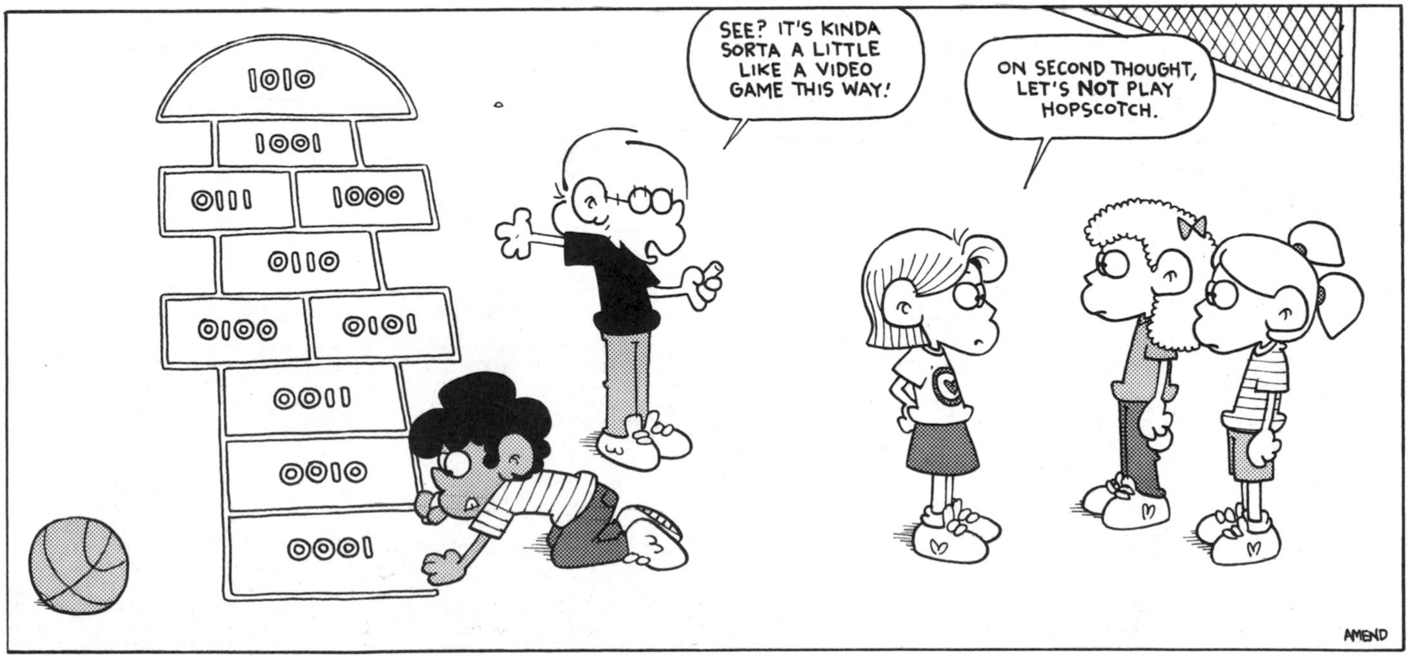
1010
1001
0111
1000
0110
0100
0101
0011
0010
0001
SEE? IT'S KINDA SORTA A LITTLE LIKE A VIDEO GAME THIS WAY!
ON SECOND THOUGHT, LET'S **NOT** PLAY HOPSCOTCH.
AMEND

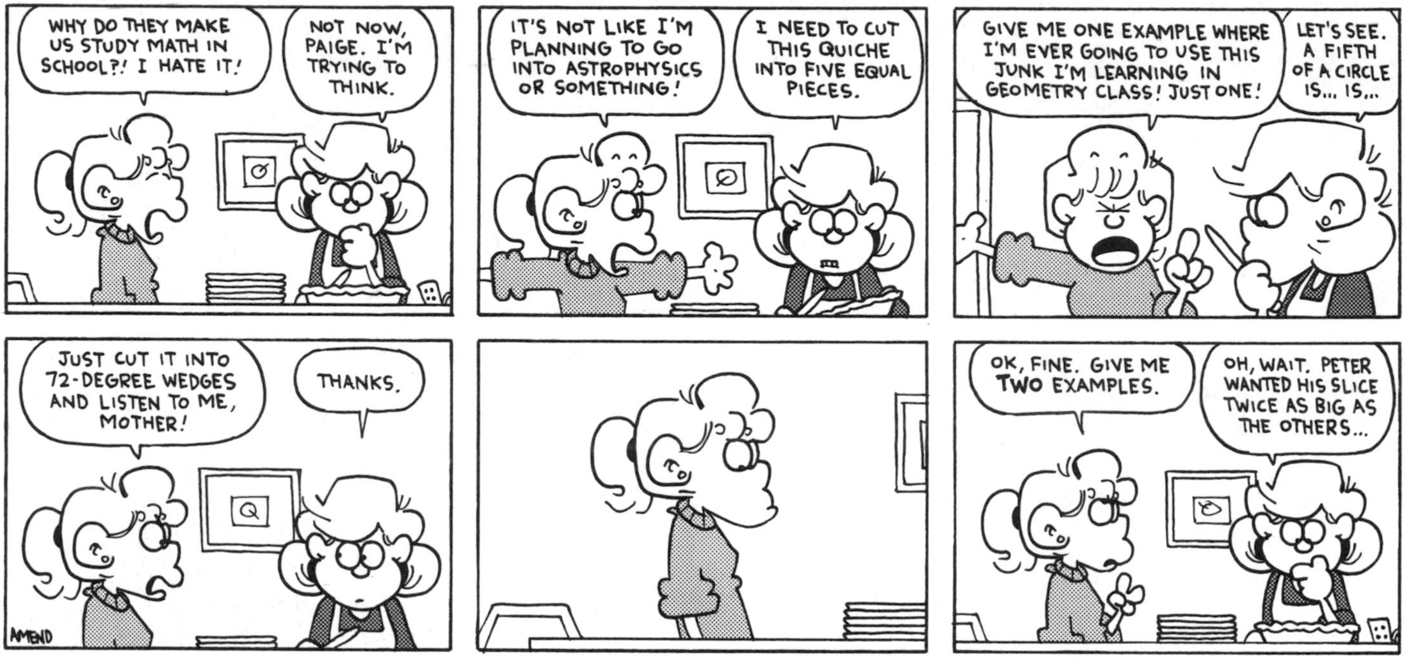
WHY DO THEY MAKE US STUDY MATH IN SCHOOL?! I HATE IT!
NOT NOW, PAIGE. I'M TRYING TO THINK.
IT'S NOT LIKE I'M PLANNING TO GO INTO ASTROPHYSICS OR SOMETHING!
I NEED TO CUT THIS QUICHE INTO FIVE EQUAL PIECES.
GIVE ME ONE EXAMPLE WHERE I'M EVER GOING TO USE THIS JUNK I'M LEARNING IN GEOMETRY CLASS! JUST ONE!
LET'S SEE. A FIFTH OF A CIRCLE IS... IS...
JUST CUT IT INTO 72-DEGREE WEDGES AND LISTEN TO ME, MOTHER!
THANKS.
AMEND
OK, FINE. GIVE ME TWO EXAMPLES.
OH, WAIT. PETER WANTED HIS SLICE TWICE AS BIG AS THE OTHERS...

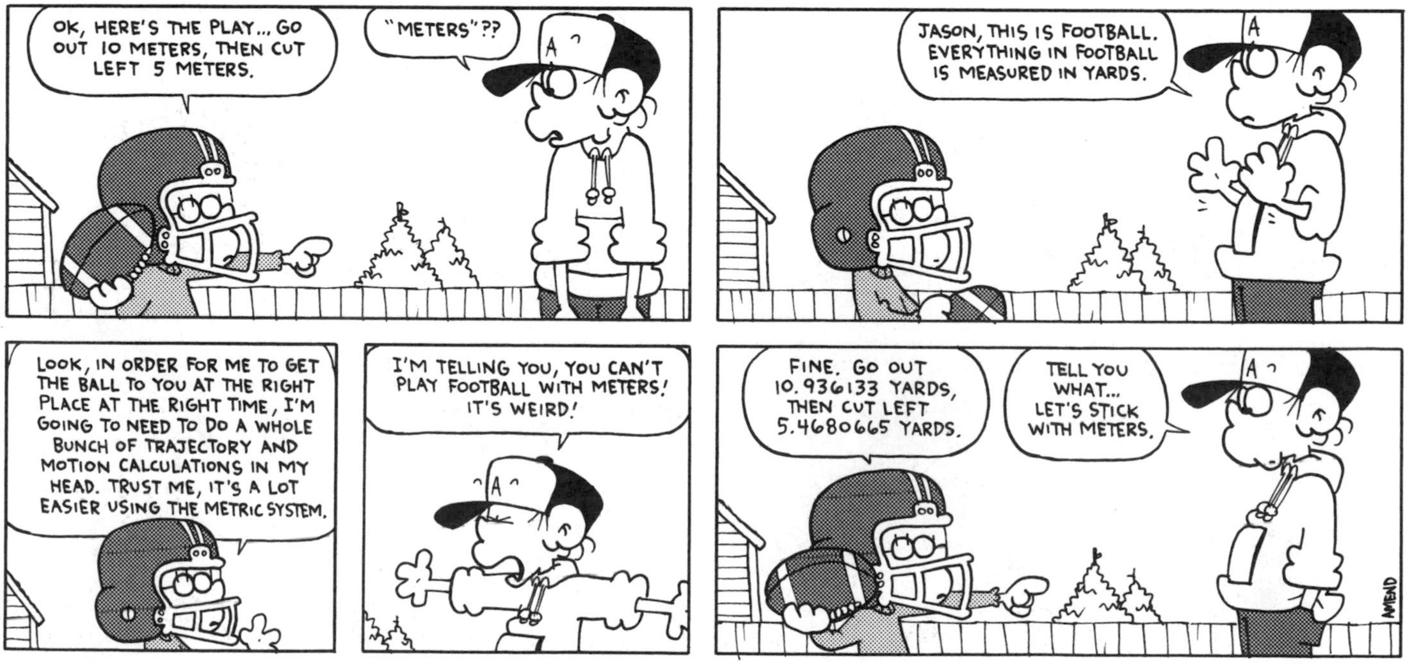
OK, HERE'S THE PLAY... GO OUT 10 METERS, THEN CUT LEFT 5 METERS.
"METERS"??
JASON, THIS IS FOOTBALL. EVERYTHING IN FOOTBALL IS MEASURED IN YARDS.
LOOK, IN ORDER FOR ME TO GET THE BALL TO YOU AT THE RIGHT PLACE AT THE RIGHT TIME, I'M GOING TO NEED TO DO A WHOLE BUNCH OF TRAJECTORY AND MOTION CALCULATIONS IN MY HEAD. TRUST ME, IT'S A LOT EASIER USING THE METRIC SYSTEM.
I'M TELLING YOU, YOU CAN'T PLAY FOOTBALL WITH METERS! IT'S WEIRD!
FINE. GO OUT 10.936133 YARDS, THEN CUT LEFT 5.4680665 YARDS.
TELL YOU WHAT... LET'S STICK WITH METERS.
AMEND

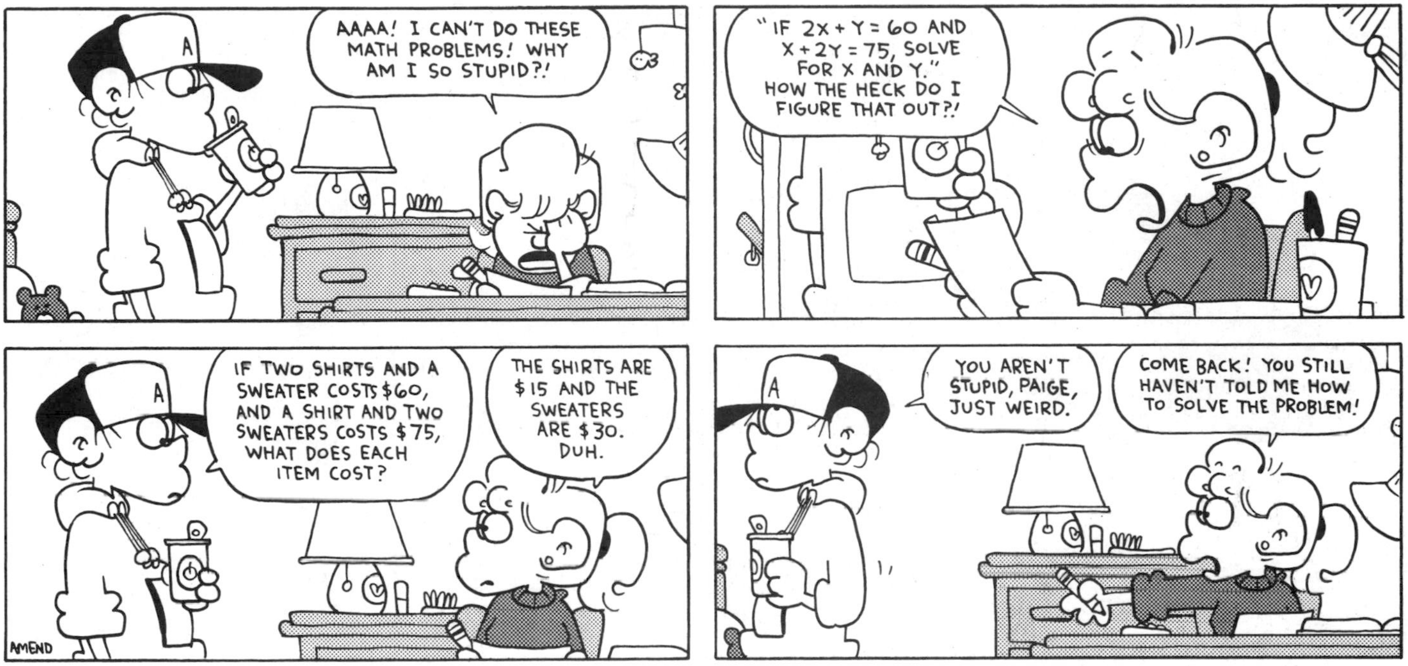
AAAA! I CAN'T DO THESE MATH PROBLEMS! WHY AM I SO STUPID?!
"IF 2X + Y = 60 AND X + 2Y = 75, SOLVE FOR X AND Y." HOW THE HECK DO I FIGURE THAT OUT?!
IF TWO SHIRTS AND A SWEATER COSTS $60, AND A SHIRT AND TWO SWEATERS COSTS $75, WHAT DOES EACH ITEM COST?
THE SHIRTS ARE $15 AND THE SWEATERS ARE $30. DUH.
AMEND
YOU AREN'T STUPID, PAIGE, JUST WEIRD.
COME BACK! YOU STILL HAVEN'T TOLD ME HOW TO SOLVE THE PROBLEM!

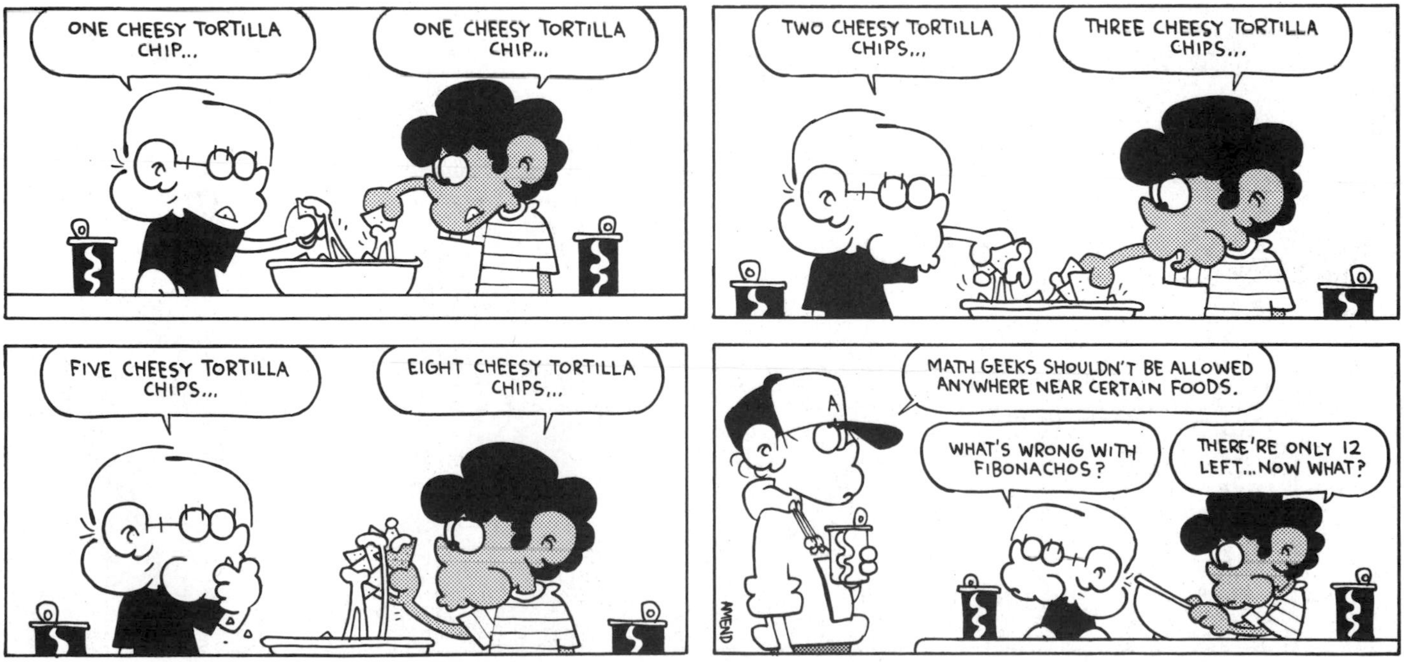
ONE CHEESY TORTILLA CHIP...
ONE CHEESY TORTILLA CHIP...
TWO CHEESY TORTILLA CHIPS...
THREE CHEESY TORTILLA CHIPS...
FIVE CHEESY TORTILLA CHIPS...
EIGHT CHEESY TORTILLA CHIPS...
MATH GEEKS SHOULDN'T BE ALLOWED ANYWHERE NEAR CERTAIN FOODS.
WHAT'S WRONG WITH FIBONACHOS?
THERE'RE ONLY 12 LEFT... NOW WHAT?
AMEND

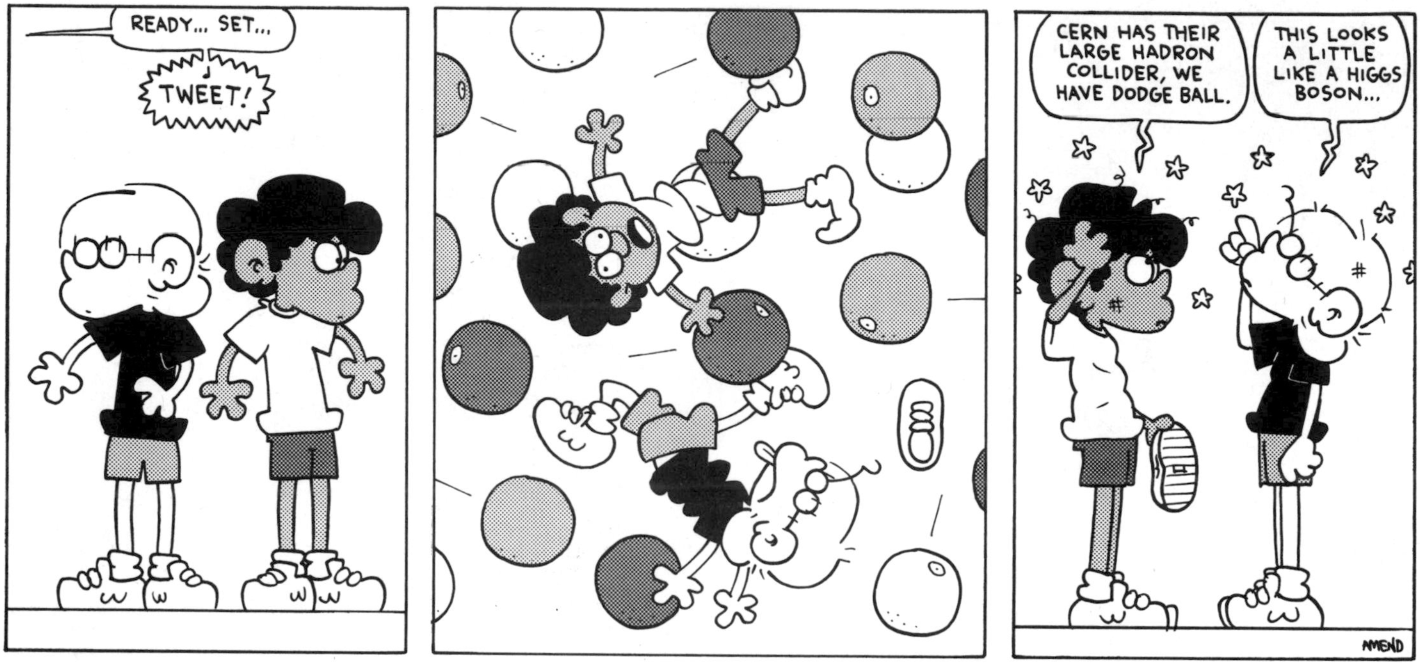
READY... SET...
TWEET!
CERN HAS THEIR LARGE HADRON COLLIDER, WE HAVE DODGE BALL.
THIS LOOKS A LITTLE LIKE A HIGGS BOSON...
AMEND

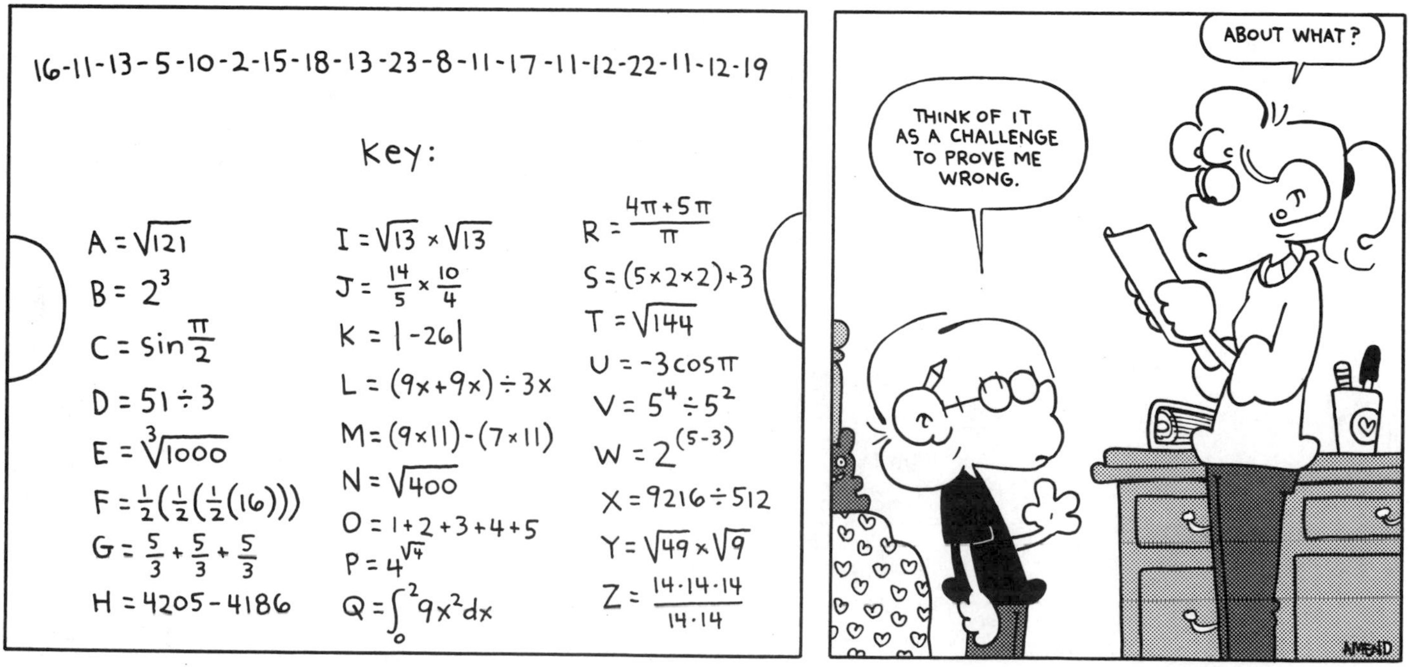
16-11-13-5-10-2-15-18-13-23-8-11-17-11-12-22-11-12-19
Key:
A = √121
B = 2³
C = sin π/2
D = 51 ÷ 3
E = ∛1000
F = ½(½(½(16)))
G = 5/3 + 5/3 + 5/3
H = 4205 - 4186
I = √13 × √13
J = 14/5 × 10/4
K = |-26|
L = (9x+9x) ÷ 3x
M = (9×11) - (7×11)
N = √400
O = 1+2+3+4+5
P = 4^√4
Q = ∫₀² 9x² dx
R = (4π + 5π) / π
S = (5×2×2) + 3
T = √144
U = -3 cos π
V = 5⁴ ÷ 5²
W = 2^(5-3)
X = 9216 ÷ 512
Y = √49 × √9
Z = (14·14·14) / (14·14)
ABOUT WHAT?
THINK OF IT AS A CHALLENGE TO PROVE ME WRONG.
AMEND